HUMAN LANGUAGE TECHNOLOGY

Proceedings of a workshop held at Plainsboro, New Jersey March 21-24, 1993

Sponsored by:
Advanced Research Projects Agency

This document contains copies of reports prepared for the ARPA Human Language Technology Workshop. Included are reports from ARPA sponsored programs and other materials prepared for use at the workshop.

Distributed by:
Morgan Kaufmann Publishers, Inc.
340 Pine Street, 6th Floor
San Francisco, CA 94104
ISBN 1-55860-324-7
Printed in the United States of America

Page

Page

Page

AUTHOR INDEX

SESSION PAPERS

Overview of the ARPA Human Language Technology Workshop

Madeleine Bates, Chair, Editor

BBN Systems & Technologies
70 Fawcett Street
Cambridge, MA 02138

1. PREVIOUS DARPA WORKSHOPS

For five years, 1988-1992, the Defense Advanced Projects Agency sponsored a series of meetings called the DARPA Speech and Natural Language Workshops. These workshops provided a forum where researchers in speech and natural language, particularly as relating to the DARPA programs in spoken and written language understanding, could exchange information about recent research and technical progress.

Participants included researchers funded under the DARPA programs, other researchers who voluntarily participated in these programs or in related evaluations, government researchers and consumers of these research results, and invited attendees from inside and outside the US.

Proceedings of these workshops were published by Morgan Kaufmann.

2. THE 1993 WORKSHOP: EXPANDED SCOPE

In 1993, the "D" was dropped from DARPA, reflecting a change in the organizational purposes and goals. Well before this change, however, the committee responsible for the annual workshop was directed to significantly broaden its focus, and the name of the meeting became The ARPA Human Language Technology (HLT) Workshop.

The HLT workshop provides a forum where researchers can exchange information about very recent technical progress in an informal, highly interactive setting. The scope includes not just speech recognition, speech understanding, text understanding, and machine translation, but also all spoken and written language work (broadly interpreted to include ARPA's TIPSTER, MT, MUC, and TREC programs) with an emphasis on topics of mutual interest, such as statistical language modeling. This workshop no longer focuses on spoken language systems evaluation, as another workshop fills that need.

The prime purpose of the newly constituted workshop was to facilitate productive technical discussions among key researchers on topics relating to human language technology and of interest to ARPA. This expanded workshop, in particular, was designed to facilitate cross-fertilization among diverse disciplines, and to introduce researchers to the state-of-the-art in areas outside their own. For this reason, the papers presented in this proceedings are both more wide-reaching and more accessible to non-experts in the field than has previously been the case.

The majority of the workshop participants received funding under ARPA's Human Language program. Other participants included researchers not funded by ARPA who voluntarily participate in these programs; government researchers and consumers of these research results; and, on a rotating basis, selected visitors from both inside and outside the United States. It is still the intention that the participants form a tightly-coupled research community in which results and research breakthroughs are evaluated, disseminated, and exploited with very short latency.

Aspects of this meeting included:

- technical presentations of both new research results and the ongoing development of large software systems, often months before this research is reported elsewhere;
- the presentation of summaries of standardized system evaluations;
- discussion of the future direction of the various DARPA programs in light of recent progress; and
- much discussion of ongoing work among individual researchers.

The format of the meeting was to mix 12-15 minute technical presentations (both reviewed and invited) in sessions organized around focused topics, with time for informal discussion and interaction. In most sessions, the chair presented a 15 minute introduction intended to provide a summary of the key points in each set of papers, and also a perspective of the research context in which the work was done, for those not in the primary area addressed by the papers in the session. The written version of those introductions will serve the same functions in this proceedings.

Participants selected by the program committee were invited to submit abstracts in a variety of areas. The committee received 131 abstracts (114 for regular presentations; 17 for demonstrations), 58 presentation and 13 demonstrations were accepted.

The final program sessions were: Spoken Language Systems, Invited Overviews of ARPA Program Areas, Continuous Speech Recognition, Natural Language, Discourse, Machine Translation, Demonstrations, Statistical Natural Language, Government Panel, Lexicon, Prosody, Information Retrieval, and New Directions.

Technical highlights included:

- Machine Translation session, chaired by Alex Waibel of CMU. This session featured invited tutorials by Peter Brown and Ed Hovy.
- A demonstration session (chaired by Hy Murveit of SRI and organized by Victor Abrash of SRI) showcased recent work in a variety of areas, and demonstrations were available almost continuously throughout the workshop for "hands-on" experience.
- A lexicon session, chaired by Ralph Grishman (NYU).
- Invited overviews of each of the areas of interest to ARPA in spoken and written language technology: MUC (Beth Sundheim), TREC (Donna Harmon), SLS (George Doddington), and Tipster (Tom Crystal).
- A government panel on Government Human Language Technology Needs, Funding, In-House Research, and Technology Transfer organized by Carol Van Ess-Dykema. The panelists were Helen Gigley (NRL), Joseph Kielman (FBI), Susan Chipman (ONR), Jesse Fussell (DoD), and Y.T. Chien (NSF).

The workshop attracted 207 attendees, approximately 2/3 from ARPA sites. The remainder were government representatives (30 individuals from 10 different organizations), foreign guests (11 individuals, from 11 organizations), non-ARPA attendees from the USA (31 individuals from 27 organizations) and young researchers (7 individuals, from 5 schools).

3. ACKNOWLEDGEMENTS

This meeting involved the work of a great many people. The Standing Workshop Committee (whose membership rotates slowly except for one government member) is responsible for the overall series of workshops. It was chaired this year by Patti Price (SRI); other members included Mitch Marcus (U. Penn), Madeleine Bates (BBN), Carol Van Ess-Dykema (DoD), Cliff Weinstein (Lincoln Lab), and Ralph Grishman (NYU). The standing committee, and Patti Price in particular, provided invaluable direction for the workshop.

The Program Committee, which is constituted each year by adding to the standing committee additional researchers selected for their expertise in specific areas, was chaired by me, and included (in addition to the standing committee members) Stephen Della Pietra, David Lewis, Kathy McKeown, Mary Ellen Okurowski, Stephanie Seneff, Beth Sundheim, and Alex Waibel. The program committee was responsible for reviewing abstracts to select papers and demonstrations for presentation, discussing various policy issues, and organizing the overall program.

Particular thanks are due to Hy Murveit and Victor Abrash, who took complete charge of the demonstration sessions and handled the myriad of technical problems inherent in arranging for a large number of live demos; to Alex Waibel, who organized the Machine Translation session (the keystone session of the entire workshop) while commuting from his office in Germany to his office in the US, and to Ralph Grishman, who organized the Lexicon session apparently effortlessly (which is to say, with extreme competence). Carol Van Ess-Dykema, assisted by Mary Ellen Okurowski, planned and chaired the government panel.

Denise Payne served as the workshop administrator, which means everything from email archivist to registrar. She handled all the interactions with the conference center, kept track of invitations, abstracts, and attendees. She kept one eye on the budget and one hand on the telephone. She prepared the notebooks of preliminary papers that were given to attendees at the workshop, and collected final versions of the papers for this proceedings.

From his new position as Program Manager at ARPA, George Doddington provided overall direction and encouragement to the workshop planners. His enthusiasm for his new role and his desire to continue the high technical standards of previous workshops helped to make this workshop, which was the first in a new series, a resounding success.

SESSION 1: SPOKEN LANGUAGE SYSTEMS

Alexander I. Rudnicky

School of Computer Science
Carnegie Mellon University
Pittsburgh PA 15213 USA

By themselves, speech recognition and natural language processing have limited applications. the reason is that each only accomplishes a part of what humans are capable of when they use language. Spoken language systems represent the merger of these two technologies and provide an integrated functionality that more closely approximates humans capabilities in speech communication.

The addition of natural language processing enhances speech recognition by allowing people to speak naturally without the need to remember specific command words or to keep within a specific grammar. In principle, as long as we are able to describe something verbally, a spoken language system should be able to understand us.

Without the ability to interpret natural language, speech recognition is suited only for a subset of tasks (though certainly not trivial ones), such as data entry, simple commands or dictation. Similarly, without speech recognition natural language is restricted to the interpretation of written language, a stylized form of human communication. Spoken language systems thus represent an attempt to automate speech communication. While limited in terms of the target behavior, they still represents an advance over the capabilities of the individual technologies.

The development of spoken language systems has many facets. Certainly it pushes the development of the basic technologies, speech recognition and natural language processing, since successful understanding ultimately depends on high quality processing at these levels. At the same time, spoken language generates the need for advances in other domains.

The requirements of fluent communication require engineering of algorithms to produce real-time understanding of speech; since human speech is a highly interactive medium real-time response is necessary for fluency. It also raises the need for incorporating additional aspects of analysis into the process. Prosody is a case in point. The development of spoken language systems also requires the implementation of running systems that can be used to perform non-trivial tasks. This in turn creates the need for studying the usability of spoken language systems, since some issues critical to performance reveal themselves only in the course of actual use. In turn these issues impact the development of processing strategies at the level of the individual technologies. The use of spoken language systems under more realistic conditions also serves as a stimulus for the study of robustness, a system's ability to handle variations in environment, microphone characteristics as well as the vagaries of human speech.

The development of spoken language systems requires support activities, such as the development of training and test corpora and the development of evaluation techniques. The spoken language community has developed a large corpus of speech data that attempts to approximate the speech that would occur under real conditions. t the same time, elaborate evaluation techniques have been developed that allow us to compare and diagnose the characteristics of spoken language systems.

The papers in this session at first glance appear to fall into two groups. One group concerns itself with evaluation and data collection while the other concerns itself with language processing techniques. In fact the two sets of papers share an important theme in common, that of *real data*. In reading these papers one is struck by the extent to which the use of real data has shaped what we do and how we do it.

The paper by Pallett *et al* describes the evaluation procedures currently in use in the spoken language technology program. In comparing the current evaluation procedures with those in use a few years ago, one is struck by the extent to which the program has progressed from the use of carefully controlled data to the use of more natural (and more difficult) speech. While the continuous speech recognition evaluation uses read speech for its main evaluations, a new "stress test" has been introduced which exposes systems to a variety of unpredictable material, a condition that begins to approximate what recognition system might actually be exposed to under realistic conditions. The spoken language evaluations have seen a similar progression from single sentences to edited scenarios to an attempt to use complete scenarios for evaluation.

Data collection, as described in the paper by Hirshman and the MADCOW committee has seen a similar progression, from read sentences generated from an artificial grammar, to collection through the use of wizard systems, to the use of real systems to collect data fro both training and testing. The paper by Thompson and Bard represents perhaps the logical conclusion of this process, the collection of speech from natural human-human interactions. While the Edinburgh corpus is meant for analysis rather than for speech system development, it nevertheless represents the kind of data that spoken language systems will ultimately be asked to process. In the discussion of this paper it was pointed out that human-computer communication might turn out to be quite different from human-human communication and that things learned from this corpus might not be transferrable to that situation. Some interest was also expressed in the phenomenon of overlap and its role in communication.

The three following papers, from Paramax, BBN and SRI describe current improvements to the natural language components of spoken language systems. All three papers attempt to deal with the problem of how to adapt a syntactic-based parser to the realities of language as spoken by humans and further transcribed (perhaps erroneously) by speech recognition systems. The paper by Linebarger *et al* describes a robustness heuristic (based on the ability to skip non-keywords) that allows the Paramax parser to interpret otherwise unprocessed inputs. The paper by Stallard and Bobrow also addresses the problem of salvaging otherwise unparsable inputs by the use of semantic structure when the use of syntactic structure fails to produce an interpretation. It was pointed out in the discussion that the semantic post-processing might not be portable. The paper by Dowding et al presents a parsing strategy that uses the mutual constraints of syntax an semantics to generate parses, together with heuristics that allow the system to produce an interpretation even if no satisfactory initial parse is found. Interestingly, for the ATIS task, none of the syntax based parsers can currently outperform a frame-based parser.

One of the key arguments that have been made in favor of syntax-based parsing is that the knowledge gained in one domain will transfer to other domains and will save the work of having to build a parser for the new domain. The paper by Linebarger *et al* describes how the Paramax robustness heuristics can be easily ported between domains. Portability can refer not only to transfer between domains but also to transfer between languages, a potentially more difficult task. The paper by Glass *et al* describes experiences in porting the MIT Voyager system from English to Japanese. While this paper is a good example of how a syntactic parser can be successfully ported to a new domain, it is nevertheless significant that the parsing strategy had to be altered in order to accommodate the structure of the Japanese language. In the discussion, it was pointed out that discourse-level processing might not, in principle, be portable, though the elementary processing need for the Voyager domain turned out to be portable.

BENCHMARK TESTS FOR THE DARPA SPOKEN LANGUAGE PROGRAM

David S. Pallett, Johathan G. Fiscus,
William M. Fisher, and John S. Garofolo

National Institute of Standards and Technology
Room A216, Building 225 (Technology)
Gaithersburg, MD 20899

1. INTRODUCTION

This paper documents benchmark tests implemented within the DARPA Spoken Language Program during the period November, 1992 - January, 1993. Tests were conducted using the Wall Street Journal-based Continuous Speech Recognition (WSJ-CSR) corpus and the Air Travel Information System (ATIS) corpus collected by the Multi-site ATIS Data COllection Working (MADCOW) Group. The WSJ-CSR tests consist of tests of large vocabulary (lexicons of 5,000 to more than 20,000 words) continuous speech recognition systems. The ATIS tests consist of tests of (1) ATIS-domain spontaneous speech (lexicons typically less than 2,000 words), (2) natural language understanding, and (3) spoken language understanding. These tests were reported on and discussed in detail at the Spoken Language Systems Technology Workshop held at the Massachusetts Institute of Technology, January 20-22, 1993.

Tests implemented during this period also included experimental or "dry run" implementation of two new tests. In the WSJ-CSR domain, a "stress test" was implemented, using test material that was drawn from unidentified sub-corpora. In the ATIS domain, an experimental "end-to-end" evaluation was conducted that included examination of the subject-session "logfile". Following precedents established previously, the results of these dry-run tests are not included as part of the "official" NIST test results and are not discussed at length in this paper.

Prior benchmark tests conducted within the DARPA Spoken Language Program are described in papers by Pallett, et al. in the several proceedings of the DARPA Speech and Natural Language Workshops from 1989 to 1992. Papers in the Proceedings of the February 1992 Speech and Natural Language Workshop describe the development of the WSJ-CSR corpus, collection procedures and initial experience in building systems for this domain. Initial use of the Pilot Corpus for a "dry run" of benchmark test procedures prior to the February 1992 Speech and Natural Language Workshop is reported in [1]. ATIS-domain tests that were reported at the February 1992 meeting are documented in [2].

System descriptions were submitted to NIST by the benchmark test participants and distributed at the Spoken Language Systems Technology Workshop. Additional information describing these systems can be found references 5-23. Detailed information is not available (in published papers) for some systems.

2. WSJ-CSR TESTS: NEW CONDITIONS

2.1. Stress Test

The established benchmark test protocols for speech recognition systems are such that system developers have prior knowledge of the nature of the test material, based on access to similar development test sets. Some developers have consistently declined to report results for material of particular interest to DARPA program management (e.g., for secondary microphone data). Concern has been expressed that the sensitivity or "robustness" of some DARPA-sponsored recognition algorithms has not been adequately probed or the systems "stressed".

DARPA program management requested that NIST implement, in early December, 1992, a "dry run" of a "stress test" in which the nature of the test material was unspecified. Participating DARPA contractors were required to document and freeze the system configuration used to process the test material prior to implementing the test, and to provide data for a baseline test of this system using the 20K NVP test subset of the Nov.'92 test material, as well as for the stress test set. Test hypotheses were scored by NIST using "conditional scoring" -- partitioning and reporting test results for individual test subsets.

The stress test material consisted of a set of 320 utterance files, chosen from three components: (1) read 20K sentences, for 4 female speakers, (2) read 5K sentences, for 4 female speakers, and (3) spontaneously dictated news articles, for 2 male and 2 female speakers. The read speech included both primary and secondary microphones, so that there were 5 test subsets in all, each consisting of either 60 or 80 utterances.

Reactions to the stress test, as well as to the test results, were mixed. In general, as would be expected, systems with trigram language models did better than those with bigrams. Degradations in performance for the secondary microphone data were relatively smaller for some systems than others -- particularly for those sites that had devoted special effort to the issue of "noise robustness". However, because the individual test subsets and the number of speakers were small, the results of many of the paired comparison significance tests were inconclusive, suggesting that future applications of such a test procedure must involve larger test subsets.

2.2. New Significance Tests

For several years, NIST has implemented two tests of statistical significance for the results of benchmark tests of speech recognition systems: the McNemar sentence error test (MN) and a Matched-Pair-Sentence-Segment-Word-Error (MAPSSWE) test, on the word error rate found in sentence segments. In more recent tests, NIST has also implemented two additional tests: a Signed-pair (SI) test, and the WIlcoxon signed rank (WI) test. These additional tests are relevant to the word error rates found for individual speakers, and as such are particularly sensitive to the number of speakers in the test set. References to these tests can be found in the literature on nonparametric or distribution-free statistics.

2.3. Uncertainty of Performance Measurement Results

Increasing attention is being paid, at NIST, to evaluating and expressing the uncertainty of measurement results. This attention is motivated, in part, by the realization that "in general, it is not possible to know in detail all of the uses to which a particular NIST measurement result will be put."[3] Current NIST policy is that "all NIST measurement results are to be accompanied by quantitative measurements of uncertainty". In substance, the recommended approach to expressing measurement uncertainty is that recommended by the International Committee for Weights and Measures (CIPM).

The CIPM-recommended approach includes: (1) determining and reporting the "standard uncertainty" or positive square root of the estimated variance for each component of uncertainty that contributes to the uncertainty of the measurement result, (2) combining the individual standard uncertainties into a determination of the "combined standard uncertainty", (3) multiplying the combined standard uncertainty by a factor of 2 (a "coverage factor", that for normally distributed data corresponds to the 95% confidence interval), and specifying this quantity as the "expanded uncertainty". The expanded uncertainty, along with the coverage factor, or else the combined standard uncertainty, is to be reported.

The paired-comparison significance tests outlined in the previous section represent specific instantiations of tests that evaluate the validity of null hypotheses regarding differences (in measured performance) between systems. In many cases, however, sufficiently detailed data is not available to implement these tests. In these cases it is important to refer to explicit estimates of uncertainties.

The case of evaluating the uncertainties associated with performance measurements for spoken language technology is particularly complex because of the number of known complicating factors. These factors include properties of the speaker population (e.g., gender, dialect region, speaking rate, vocal effort, etc.), properties of the training and test sets (e.g., vocabulary size, syntactic and semantic properties, microphone/channel, etc.) and other factors [4].

Performance measures used to date within the DARPA spoken language research community (and included in this paper) do not conform to the recommended approach, since the scoring software, in general, generates a single measurement for the ensemble of test data (e.g., one datum indicating word or utterance error rate for the entire multi-speaker, multi-utterance, test subset, rather than the mean error rate for the ensemble of speakers). These single-measurement performance evaluation procedures do not yield estimates of the variances "for each component of uncertainty that contributes to the uncertainty of the measurement result" that are required in order to implement the CIPM-recommended practice.

In future tests, revisions to the scoring software that would permit estimates of the variance across the speaker population (at the least) are in order. However, it would seem to be the case that identifying and obtaining quantitative estimates of "each component of uncertainty that contributes to the uncertainty of the measurement" will be difficult.

3. WSJ-CSR NOVEMBER 1992 TEST MATERIAL

The test material, as distributed, included a total of 16 identified test subsets. In general, these can be sub-categorized five ways: speaker dependent/independent (SD/SI), 5K/20K reference vocabularies, the use of verbalized/non-verbalized punctuation (VP/NVP), read/spontaneous speech, and primary (Sennheiser, close-talking)/secondary microphone. No one participant reported results on all subsets -- most reported results on only one or two, corresponding to conditions of particular local interest and/or algorithmic strength.

All of the test material was drawn from the WSJ-CSR Pilot Corpus that was collected at MIT/LCS, SRI International, and TI. The "spontaneous dictation" data was collected only at SRI.

Individual test set sizes varied from 72 utterances to (more typically) approximately 320 utterances. The number of speakers in each subset varied from 3 to 12 speakers. The actual number of sentence utterances per speaker varied somewhat, because the material was selected in paragraph blocks. A total of 8 secondary microphones was included in the various test subsets, including one speakerphone, a telephone handset, 3 boundary effect microphones (Crown PCC-160, PZM-6FS, and Shure SM91), two lavalier microphones, and a desk-stand mounted microphone.

4. WSJ-CSR TEST PROTOCOLS

Test protocols were similar to prior speech recognition benchmark tests. Test material was shipped to the participating sites on October 20th, results were reported on Nov. 23rd, and NIST reported scored results via ftp to the participants on Dec. 2nd. The stress test was conducted between Nov. 30th and Dec. 15th.

A "required baseline" test was defined for all participants. It consisted of processing the 5K word speaker independent, non-verbalized punctuation test set using a (common) bigram grammar. Six sites reported 5K baseline test results.

5. WSJ-CSR TEST SCORING

As for the test protocols, much of the scoring was routine, except for one new additional factor. Since previous "official" CSR benchmark tests had not included spontaneous speech, the community had not reviewed the adequacy of the transcription convention used for spontaneous speech, and several inconsistencies in the transcriptions were noted following release of the preliminary results. Some of these inconsistencies were resolved prior to releasing "official" results.

6. WSJ-CSR TEST PARTICIPANTS

Participants in these WSJ-CSR tests included the following DARPA contractors: BBN, CMU, Dragon Systems, MIT Lincoln Laboratory, and SRI International. A "volunteer" participant was the French CNRS LIMSI. LIMSI declined to participate in the "stress test".

7. WSJ-CSR BENCHMARK TEST RESULTS AND DISCUSSION

7.1. Test Results: Word and Utterance (Sentence) Error Rates

Table 1 presents the results for the several test sets on which results were reported. Section I of that table includes results reported by Paul at MIT Lincoln Laboratory [5] for Longitudinal Speaker Dependent (LSD) technology. Section II includes results reported by BBN for Speaker Dependent (SD) technology. Section III includes the results of Speaker Independent (SI) technology, for a number of sites for (a) the 20K NVP test set for both baseline and non-baseline SI systems, (b) the 5K NVP test set for both baseline and non-baseline SI systems, (c) the 5K NVP test set "other microphone" test set data, and (d) the 5K VP test set (on which only LIMSI reported results [6]). Section IV of Table 1 includes the results reported by BBN for the Spontaneous Dictation test set.

For the test set on which the largest number of results were reported -- the 5K NVP set, using the close-talking microphone -- the lowest word error rates were reported by CMU [7-9]: 6.9% for the baseline, bigram language model, and 5.3% using a trigram language model. The range of word error rates for the baseline condition for all systems tested was 6.9% to 15.0%, while for non-baseline conditions, the range was from 5.3% to 16.8%.

For the 5K NVP test set's secondary microphone data, as reported by CMU [8] and SRI [10,11], word error rates ranged from 17.7% to 38.9%.

For the 20K NVP test set, on which other baseline data were reported, the word error rates range from 15.2% to 27.8%.

The lowest error rate, reported by CMU, can be shown to be significantly different for all 4 significance tests when compared with the Dragon [13] and MIT Lincoln systems, but shown to be significantly different only for the MAPSSWE test when compared with the BBN system [14]. Thus the performance differences between the CMU and BBN systems for this baseline condition test are very small.

7.2. Significance Test Results

Table 2 presents the results, in a matrix form, of 4 paired-comparison significance tests for the baseline tests for the 5K NVP test set. The convention in this form of results tabulation is that if the result of a null-hypothesis test is valid, the word "same" is printed in the appropriate matrix element. If the null hypothesis is not valid, the identifier for the system with the lower (and significantly different) error rate is printed.

For this test set, recall that the CMU system (here identified as cmu1-a) had a word error rate of 6.9%. By comparing the results for the CMU system with the other 5 systems reporting baseline results, note that the significance test results all indicate that the null hypothesis is not valid. In other words, the error rates for the CMU system are significantly different (lower) than those for the other 5 systems for this test set and baseline conditions.

In general, for this test set, with 12 speakers and 310 utterances, the Wilcoxon signed rank test (WI) is more sensitive than the (ordinary) sign test (SI). As noted in previous tests, the McNemar test (MN), operating on the sentence error rate, is in general less sensitive than the matched-pair-sentence segment word error rate test (MAPSSWE).

8. ATIS TESTS: NEW CONDITIONS

Within the community of ATIS system developers, there is a continuing search for evaluation methodologies to complement the current evaluation methodology. In particular there is a recognized need for evaluation methodologies that can be shown to correlate well with expected performance of the technology in applications. Toward the end of 1992, several sites participated in an experimental "end-to-end" evaluation to assess systems in an interactive form. The end-to-end evaluation included (1) objective measures such as timing information and time to task completion, (2) human-derived judgements on correctness of system answers and user solutions, and (3) a user satisfaction questionnaire. The results of this "dry run" complementary evaluation experiment are reported by Hirschman et al. in [15].

9. ATIS TEST MATERIAL

Test material for the ATIS benchmark tests consisted of 1002 queries, for 118 subject-scenarios, involving 37 subjects. It was selected by NIST from set-aside material drawn from data previously collected within the MADCOW community at AT&T, BBN, CMU, MIT/LCS, and SRI. The selection and composition of this test material is described in more detail in [15].

As in previous years, queries were categorized into two categories of "answerable" queries, Class A, which are context-independent, and Class D, which are context-dependent; and "unanswerable", or Class X queries. In the final adjudicated test set, there were a total of 427 Class A queries, 247 Class D queries, and 328 Class X queries.

10. ATIS TEST PROTOCOLS

As was the case for the speech recognition benchmark tests, ATIS test protocols were similar to prior ATIS benchmark tests. The test material was shipped to the participating sites on October 20th, results were reported on Nov. 16th, and NIST reported preliminary scored results via ftp to the participants on Nov. 20th. After the process of formal "adjudication" had taken place, official results were reported on Dec. 20th.

11. ATIS SCORING AND ADJUDICATION

After the preliminary scoring results were distributed, the participating sites were invited to send requests for adjudication ("bug reports") to NIST, asking for changes in the scoring of specific queries. A total of 146 of these bug reports were adjudicated by NIST and SRI jointly. Since many of these requests for adjudication were duplicates, the number of distinct problems reported was less than 100. A decision was made on each request for adjudication and the corrected reference material or procedure was used in a final adjudicated re-run of the evaluation. The judgment was in favor of the plaintiff in approximately 2/3 of the cases.

A number of problems uncovered by this procedure were systematic, in that the same root problem affected several different queries. Most of these were simply human error, which can be made less likely in the future by working less hectically and making software to double-check the test material.

The major problem that cannot be attributed to just human error is that of transcribing and scoring correctly speech that is difficult to hear and understand. Some of this speech was "sotto voce"; some was mispronounced; some was truncated; and in some cases the phonetic transcription would have been unproblematical but division into lexical words was unclear, as in some contractions and compound words. The short-term solution adopted was just to make our best judgement on orthographic transcription, considering both acoustics and higher-level language modeling. But a better long-term cure is to make and use transcriptions that can indicate alternatives when the word spoken is uncertain; proposals to this effect are being considered by relevant committees.

12. ATIS TEST PARTICIPANTS

Participants in these ATIS tests included the following DARPA contractors: BBN, CMU, MIT Laboratory for Computer Science (MIT/LCS), and SRI. There were several "volunteers": AT&T Bell Laboratories [16], who have participated in previous years; Paramax [17], not a DARPA contractor at the time of these tests, but who have also participated in prior years' tests; and two participants from Canada, CRIM and INRS. A total of 8 system developers participated in some of the tests (i.e., the NL tests).

13. ATIS BENCHMARK TEST RESULTS

13.1. ATIS SPontaneous speech RECognition Tests (SPREC)

Table 3 presents the results for the SPREC tests for all systems and all subsets of the data. For the interesting case of the subset of all answerable queries, Class A+D, the word error rate ranged from 4.3% to 100%. The lowest value was reported by BBN [18,19], and the value of 100% was reported by INRS, for an incomplete ATIS system that (in effect) rejected every utterance, resulting in a scored word deletion error of 100%.

Table 4 presents a matrix tabulation of ATIS SPREC results for the set of answerable queries, Class A+D. This form of matrix tabulation is discussed in [2] for the February 1992 test results. Considerable variability can be noted for the performance of some systems on "local data", and there are indications of varying degree of difficulty for the subsets collected at different sites. As in the Feb.'92 test set, participants noted the presence of more disfluencies in the AT&T data than for other originating sites.

Word error rates for the "volunteers" in these tests (AT&T, CRIM and INRS) are in general higher than for DARPA contractors, perhaps reflecting a reduced level-of-effort, relative to "funded" efforts.

Table 5 presents the results, in a matrix form, of 4 paired-comparison significance tests for the 7 SPREC systems for the Class A+D subset.

For this test set, recall that the BBN system (here identified as bbn2a_d) had a word error rate of 4.3%. By comparing the results for this BBN system with the other 6 ATIS SPREC systems, note that the null hypothesis is not valid for all 4 significance tests for the comparisons with the AT&T, CRIM, INRS, MIT/LCS and SRI systems. In other words, the differences in performance are significant. However, when comparing the BBN and CMU SPREC systems, the null hypothesis is valid for 3 of the 4 tests. Thus, as was the case for the WSJ-CSR data, the performance differences, in this case for ATIS spontaneous speech, between the CMU and BBN speech recognition systems are very small.

13.2. Natural Language Understanding Tests (NL)

Table 6 presents a tabulation of the results for the NL tests for all systems and the "answerable" ATIS queries, Class A+D, as well as the subsets, Class A and Class D.

For the set of answerable queries, Class A+D, the weighted error ranges from 101.5% to 12.3%. For the Class A queries, the range is from 79.9% to 12.2%. And for the Class D queries, the range is from 138.9% to 12.6%. In each case, the lowest weighted error rate was reported by the CMU system [20].

Note that in general performance is considerably worse for Class D than for Class A. However, for the CMU and MIT/LCS [21] systems, performance for the Class D test material is comparable to that for Class A. These systems would appear to have superior procedures for handling context.

Table 7 presents a matrix tabulation of the NL results for the several subsets of test material. Note, however, that since the differences in performance between DARPA-contractor-developed systems and those of "volunteers", in general, are significant, the column averages presented in this table are not very informative.

Of the 3 CRIM systems, the best performing one (crim3) is one using neural networks to classify each query into 1 of 10 classes based on relation names in the underlying ATIS relational database, with subsequent use of specific parsers built for each class and another parser that determines the constraints [22].

There are two SRI NL systems [23]. The SRI NL-TM system, here designated sri1, uses template matching to generate database queries. The other SRI system, termed the "Gemini+TM ATIS System" by SRI, and here designated sri2, is an integration of SRI's unification-based natural-language processing system and the Template Matcher. Differences in performance do not appear to be pronounced.

As in previous ATIS NL tests, it is important to note that appropriate tests of statistical significance have not yet been developed for ATIS NL tests. Small differences in weighted error rate are probably of no significance. However, large, systematic, differences are noteworthy, even if of unknown statistical significance. The weighted error rates for the CMU NL system, which are in many cases approximately one-half those of the next best systems, are certainly noteworthy.

13.3. Spoken Language System Understanding (SLS)

Table 8 presents a tabulation of the results for the SLS tests for all systems and the "answerable" ATIS queries, Class A+D, as well as the subsets, Class A and Class D.

For the set of answerable queries, Class A+D, the weighted error ranges from 100% to 21.6%. For the Class A queries, the range is from 100% to 19.7%. And for the Class D queries, the range is from 140.1% to 23.9%. As in the case of the NL test results, and in each case, the lowest weighted error rate was reported for the CMU system.

The INRS data signify 100% usage of the No_Answer option, since the INRS SPREC system provided null hypothesis strings, causing the NL component to return the No_Answer response.

Note again that the CMU and MIT/LCS systems both handle context sensitivity well.

Table 9 presents a matrix tabulation of the SLS results for the several subsets of test material.

For the ATIS SLS with lowest overall weighted error rate (21.6%), the cmu1 system, there is an almost ten-fold range in error rate over the several test subsets: from 37.1%, for the AT&T subset, to 3.9% for the SRI subset. The CMU SLS weighted error rates for Class A+D are approximately two-thirds those of the next-best-performing systems, although for the Class A subset, differences in performance between the CMU system and the BBN and SRI systems are less pro-nounced.

14. ACKNOWLEDGEMENT

At NIST, our colleague Nancy Dahlgren contributed significantly to the DARPA ATIS community and had a major role in annotating data and implementing "bug fixes" in collaboration with the SRI annotation group and others. Nancy was severely injured in an automobile accident in November, 1992, and is undergoing rehabilitation therapy for treatment of head trauma. It is an understatement to say that we miss her very much.

Brett Tjaden also assisted us at NIST in preparing test material and other ways.

The cooperation of the many participants in the DARPA data and test infrastructure -- typically several individuals at each site -- is gratefully acknowledged.

References

1. Pallett, D.S., "DARPA February 1992 Pilot Corpus CSR 'Dry Run' Benchmark Test Results", in Proceedings of Speech and Natural Language Workshop, February 1992 (M. Marcus, ed.) ISBN 1-55860-272-0, Morgan Kaufmann Publishers, Inc., pp. 382-386.

2. Pallett, D.S., et al., "DARPA February 1992 ATIS Bench-mark Test Results", in Proceedings of Speech and Natural Language Workshop, February 1992 (M. Marcus, ed.) ISBN 1-55860-272-0, Morgan Kaufmann Publishers, Inc., pp. 15-27.

3. Taylor, B.N. and Kuyatt, C.E., "Guidelines for Evaluating and Expressing the Uncertainty of NIST Measurement Results", NIST Technical Note 1297, January 1993.

4. Pallett, D.S. "Performance Assessment of Automatic Speech Recognizers", J. Res. National Bureau of Standards, Volume 90, #5, Sept.-Oct. 1985, pp. 371-387.

5. Paul, D.B. and Necioglu, B.F., "The Lincoln Large-Vocabulary Stack-Decoder HMM CSR", Proceedings of ICASSP'93.

6. Gauvain, J.L., et al., "LIMSI Nov92 Evaluation", Oral Presentation at the Spoken Language Systems Technology Workshop, January 20-22, 1993, Cambridge, MA.

7. Huang, X., et al., "The SPHINX-II Speech Recognition System: An Overview", Computer Speech and Language, in press (1993).

8. Alleva, F., et al., "An Improved Search Algorithm for Continuous Speech Recognition", Proceedings of ICASSP'93.

9. Hwang, M.Y., et al., "Predicting Unseen Triphones with Senones", Proceedings of ICASSP'93.

10. Liu, F.-H., et al., "Efficient Cepstral Normalization for Robust Speech Recognition", in Proceedings of the Human Language Technology Workshop, March 1993 (M. Bates, ed.) Morgan Kaufmann Publishers, Inc.

11. Murveit, H., et al., "Large-Vocabulary Dictation using SRI's DECIPHER (tm) Speech Recognition System: Progressive Search Techniques", Proceedings of ICASSP'93.

12. Murveit, H., et al., "Progressive-search Algorithms for Large Vocabulary Speech Recognition", in Proceedings of the Human Language Technology Workshop, March 1993 (M. Bates, ed.) Morgan Kaufmann Publishers, Inc.

13. Roth, R., et al., "Large Vocabulary Continuous Speech Recognition of Wall Street Journal Data", Proceedings of ICASSP'93.

14. Schwartz, R., et al., "Comparative Experiments on Large Vocabulary Speech Recognition", in Proceedings of the Human Language Technology Workshop, March 1993 (M. Bates, ed.) Morgan Kaufmann Publishers, Inc.

15. Hirschman, L., et al., "Multi-Site Data Collection and Evaluation in Spoken Language Understanding", in Proceedings of the Human Language Technology Workshop, March 1993 (M. Bates, ed.) Morgan Kaufmann Publishers, Inc.

16. Tzoukermann, E., (Untitled) Oral Presentation at the Spoken Language Systems Technology Workshop, January 20-22, 1993, Cambridge, MA.

17. Linebarger, M.C., Norton, L.M. and Dahl, D.A., "A portable approach to last resort parsing and interpretation", in Proceedings of the Human Language Technology Workshop, March 1993 (M. Bates, ed.) Morgan Kaufmann Publishers, Inc.

18. Bates, M., et al., "Design and Performance of HARC, the BBN Spoken Language Understanding System", Proceedings of ICSLP-92, Banff, Alberta, Canada, October, 1992.

19. Bates, M., et al., "The BBN/HARC Spoken Language Understanding System", Proceedings of ICASSP'93.

20. Ward, W. and Issar, S., "CMU ATIS Benchmark Evaluation", Oral Presentation at the Spoken Language Systems Technology Workshop, January 20-22, 1993, Cambridge, MA.

21. Glass, et al., "The MIT ATIS System: January 1993 Progress Report", Oral Presentation at the Spoken Language Systems Technology Workshop, January 20-22, 1993, Cambridge, MA.

22. Cardin, R., et al., "CRIM's Speech Understanding System for the ATIS Task", Oral Presentation at the Spoken Language Systems Technology Workshop, January 20-22, 1993, Cambridge, MA.

23. Dowding, J., et al., "Gemini: A Natural Language System for Spoken-Language Understanding", in Proceedings of the Human Language Technology Workshop, March 1993 (M. Bates, ed.) Morgan Kaufmann Publishers, Inc.

I. Longitudinal Speaker Dependent Tests

a. LSD EVL 20K NVP Test Set

Systems	W.Err	U.Err	IDENTIFIER
mit_114-h	14.6	78.2	LL NOV92 CSR LSD 20K CLOSED NVP BIGRAM
mit_115-h	11.2	71.8	LL NOV92 CSR LSD 20K CLOSED NVP TRIGRAM

b. LSD EVL 20K VP Test Set

Systems	W.Err	U.Err	IDENTIFIER
mit_114-i	11.6	70.7	LL NOV92 CSR LSD 20K CLOSED VP BIGRAM
mit_115-i	7.6	56.0	LL NOV92 CSR LSD 20K CLOSED VP TRIGRAM

c. LSD EVL 5K NVP Test Set

Systems	W.Err	U.Err	IDENTIFIER
mit_114-f	8.3	62.5	LL NOV92 CSR LSD 5K CLOSED NVP BIGRAM
mit_115-f	5.6	48.8	LL NOV92 CSR LSD 5K CLOSED NVP TRIGRAM

d. LSD EVL 5K VP Test Set

Systems	W.Err	U.Err	IDENTIFIER
mit_114-g	6.7	68.1	LL NOV92 CSR LSD 5K CLOSED VP BIGRAM
mit_115-g	4.5	44.4	LL NOV92 CSR LSD 5K CLOSED VP TRIGRAM

II. Speaker Dependent Tests

a. SD EVL 5K NVP Test Set

Systems	W.Err	U.Err	IDENTIFIER
bbn2-e	8.2	54.5	BBN NOV92 CSR BYBLOS SD-600 5K BIGRAM
bbn3-e	6.1	44.5	BBN NOV92 CSR BYBLOS SD-600 5K TRIGRAM

III. Speaker Independent Tests: Read Speech

a. SI EVL 20K NVP Test Set (Baseline Tests)

Systems	W.Err	U.Err	IDENTIFIER
bbn1-d	16.7	81.1	BBN NOV92 CSR BYBLOS SI-12 20K BIGRAM BASELINE
cmu1-d	15.2	79.0	CMU NOV92 CSR SPHINX-II SI-84 20K BASELINE
dragon3-d	25.0	86.8	DRAGON NOV92 CSR MULTIPLE SI-12 20K NVP BASELINE
mit_111-d	25.2	88.0	LL NOV92 CSR SI-84 20K OPEN NVP BIGRAM BASELINE

SI EVL 20K NVP Test Set (Non-Baseline Tests)

Systems	W.Err	U.Err	IDENTIFIER
bbn3-d	14.8	75.7	BBN NOV92 CSR BYBLOS SI-12 20K TRIGRAM
cmu2-d	12.8	71.8	CMU NOV92 CSR SPHINX-II SI-84 20K TRIGRAM
dragon1-d	24.8	87.4	DRAGON NOV92 CSR GD SI-12 20K NVP
dragon2-d	27.8	87.4	DRAGON NOV92 CSR GI SI-12 20K NVP
mit_113-d	19.4	84.1	LL NOV92 CSR SI-84 20K OPEN NVP TRIGRAM ADAPTIVE

b. SI EVL 5K NVP Test Set (Baseline Tests)

Systems	W.Err	U.Err	IDENTIFIER
bbn1-a	8.7	63.6	BBN NOV92 CSR BYBLOS SI-12 5K BIGRAM BASELINE
cmu1-a	6.9	57.6	CMU NOV92 CSR SPHINX-II SI-84 5K BASELINE
dragon3-a	14.1	78.2	DRAGON NOV92 CSR MULTIPLE SI-12 5K NVP BASELINE
limsi1-a	9.7	64.5	LIMSI NOV92 CSR SI-84 5K-NVP BASELINE
mit_111-a	15.0	78.2	LL NOV92 CSR SI-84 5K CLOSED NVP BIGRAM BASELINE
sri1-a	13.0	73.9	SRI NOV92 CSR DECIPHER(TM) SI-84 BIGRAM BASELINE

SI EVL 5K NVP Test Set (Non-Baseline Tests)

Systems	W.Err	U.Err	IDENTIFIER
bbn3-a	7.3	53.0	BBN NOV92 CSR BYBLOS SI-12 5K TRIGRAM
cmu2-a	5.3	45.2	CMU NOV92 CSR SPHINX-II SI-84 5K TRIGRAM
cmu3-a	8.1	63.0	CMU NOV92 SPHINX-IIA MFCDCN W/O COMP CSR SI-84 5K NVP
cmu4-a	9.4	67.9	CMU NOV92 SPHINX-IIA MFCDCN W/ COMP CSR SI-84 5K NVP
cmu5-a	8.4	63.0	CMU NOV92 SPHINX-IIA CDCN W/O COMP CSR SI-84 5K NVP
cmu6-a	8.1	65.2	CMU NOV92 SPHINX-IIA CDCN W COMP CSR SI-84 5K NVP
dragon1-a	13.6	76.7	DRAGON NOV92 CSR GD SI-12 5K NVP
dragon2-a	16.8	76.4	DRAGON NOV92 CSR GI SI-12 5K NVP
mit_112-a	10.5	61.2	LL NOV92 CSR SI-84 5K CLOSED NVP TRIGRAM
mit_113-a	9.1	56.7	LL NOV92 CSR SI-84 5K CLOSED NVP TRIGRAM ADAPTIVE

c. SI EVL 5K NVP OTHER MICROPHONE Test Set

Systems	W.Err	U.Err	IDENTIFIER
cmu3-c	38.5	88.2	CMU NOV92 SPHINX-IIA MFCDCN W/O COMP CSR SI-84 5K NVP
cmu4-c	17.7	75.8	CMU NOV92 SPHINX-IIA MFCDCN W/ COMP CSR SI-84 5K NVP
cmu5-c	38.9	87.3	CMU NOV92 SPHINX-IIA CDCN W/O COMP CSR SI-84 5K NVP
cmu6-c	19.3	77.9	CMU NOV92 SPHINX-IIA CDCN W COMP CSR SI-84 5K NVP
sri1-c	27.3	87.6	SRI NOV92 CSR DECIPHER(TM) SI-84 BIGRAM BASELINE

d. SI EVL 5K VP Test Set

Systems	W.Err	U.Err	IDENTIFIER
limsi1-b	7.8	58.9	LIMSI NOV92 CSR SI-84 5K-VP

IV. Speaker Independent Test: Spontaneous Speech

a. SI SPONTANEOUS DICTATION NVP Test Set

Systems	W.Err	U.Err	IDENTIFIER
bbn2-j	26.5	94.1	BBN NOV92 CSR BYBLOS SI-12 SPON BIGRAM
bbn3-j	24.9	93.4	BBN NOV92 CSR BYBLOS SI-12 SPON TRIGRAM

Table 1: WSJ-CSR Benchmark Test Results

Composite Report of All Significance Tests
For the WSJ-CSR Nov 92 SI 5K NVP Baseline (Bigram) Test

Test Name	Abbrev.
Matched Pair Sentence Segment (Word Error) Test	MP
Signed Paired Comparison (Speaker Word Accuracy) Test	SI
Wilcoxon Signed Rank (Speaker Word Accuracy) Test	WI
McNemar (Sentence Error) Test	MN

	bbnl-a	cmul-a	dragon3-a	limsil-a	mit_111-a	sril-a
bbnl-a		MP cmul-a SI cmul-a WI cmul-a MN cmul-a	MP bbnl-a SI bbnl-a WI bbnl-a MN bbnl-a	MP same SI same WI same MN same	MP bbnl-a SI bbnl-a WI bbnl-a MN bbnl-a	MP bbnl-a SI bbnl-a WI bbnl-a MN bbnl-a
cmul-a			MP cmul-a SI cmul-a WI cmul-a MN cmul-a	MP cmul-a SI cmul-a WI cmul-a MN cmul-a	MP cmul-a SI cmul-a WI cmul-a MN cmul-a	MP cmul-a SI cmul-a WI cmul-a MN cmul-a
dragon3-a				MP limsil-a SI limsil-a WI limsil-a MN limsil-a	MP same SI same WI same MN same	MP same SI same WI same MN same
limsil-a					MP limsil-a SI limsil-a WI limsil-a MN limsil-a	MP limsil-a SI same WI limsil-a MN limsil-a
mit_111-a						MP sril-a SI same WI sril-a MN same
sril-a						

Table 2: Signficance Test Results: Baseline Tests Using the 5K NVP Test Set
(See text for explanation of format)

Nov92 ATIS SPREC Test Results

Class A+D+X Subset

	W. Err	Corr	Sub	Del	Ins	U. Err	# Utt.	Description
att2-adx	11.7	90.8	6.8	2.4	2.5	52.4	967	ATT Nov 92 SPREC Results
bbn2-adx	7.6	94.2	4.2	1.6	1.8	35.6	967	BBN Nov 92 SPREC Results
cmu2-adx	8.3	92.9	4.2	2.9	1.2	38.3	967	CMU Nov 92 SPREC Results
crim4-adx	19.3	84.1	12.1	3.8	3.4	64.1	967	CRIM Nov 92 SPREC Results
inrs2-adx	100.0	0.0	0.0	100.0	0.0	100.0	967	INRS Late Nov 92 SPREC Results
mit_lcs2-adx	12.6	89.8	7.3	2.9	2.4	47.8	967	MIT-LCS Nov 92 SPREC Results
sri3-adx	9.1	93.2	5.4	1.4	2.3	43.3	967	SRI Nov 92 SPREC Results

Class A+D Subset

	W. Err	Corr	Sub	Del	Ins	U. Err	# Utt.	Description
att2-a_d	8.4	93.6	4.6	1.8	2.0	44.7	674	ATT Nov 92 SPREC Results Class A+D
bbn2-a_d	4.3	96.7	2.5	0.9	0.9	25.2	674	BBN Nov 92 SPREC Results Class A+D
cmu2-a_d	4.7	96.0	2.8	1.2	0.7	28.9	674	CMU Nov 92 SPREC Results Class A+D
crim4-a_d	14.1	88.7	8.4	2.9	2.8	56.4	674	CRIM Nov 92 SPREC Results Class A+D
inrs2-a_d	100.0	0.0	0.0	100.0	0.0	100.0	674	INRS Late Nov 92 SPREC Results Class A+D
mit_lcs2-a_d	8.1	93.3	4.5	2.2	1.4	37.8	674	MIT-LCS Nov 92 SPREC Results Class A+D
sri3-a_d	5.7	95.7	3.5	0.9	1.4	33.8	674	SRI Nov 92 SPREC Results Class A+D

Class A Subset

	W. Err	Corr	Sub	Del	Ins	U. Err	# Utt.	Description
att2-a	8.0	93.8	4.4	1.8	1.8	45.4	427	ATT Nov 92 SPREC Results Class A
bbn2-a	4.0	96.7	2.3	1.0	0.8	25.3	427	BBN Nov 92 SPREC Results Class A
cmu2-a	4.4	96.1	2.7	1.2	0.5	30.7	427	CMU Nov 92 SPREC Results Class A
crim4-a	13.5	88.9	8.0	3.1	2.4	57.8	427	CRIM Nov 92 SPREC Results Class A
inrs2-a	100.0	0.0	0.0	100.0	0.0	100.0	427	INRS Late Nov 92 SPREC Results Class A
mit_lcs2-a	7.8	93.5	4.4	2.2	1.3	38.2	427	MIT-LCS Nov 92 SPREC Results Class A
sri3-a	5.2	96.0	3.2	0.9	1.1	34.2	427	SRI Nov 92 SPREC Results Class A

Class D Subset

	W. Err	Corr	Sub	Del	Ins	U. Err	# Utt.	Description
att2-d	9.2	93.2	5.0	1.7	2.4	43.3	247	ATT Nov 92 SPREC Results Class D
bbn2-d	4.8	96.5	2.8	0.7	1.3	25.1	247	BBN Nov 92 SPREC Results Class D
cmu2-d	5.4	95.7	3.2	1.1	1.1	25.9	247	CMU Nov 92 SPREC Results Class D
crim4-d	15.4	88.2	9.4	2.4	3.6	53.8	247	CRIM Nov 92 SPREC Results Class D
inrs2-d	100.0	0.0	0.0	100.0	0.0	100.0	247	INRS Late Nov 92 SPREC Results Class D
mit_lcs2-d	8.9	92.9	5.0	2.1	1.8	37.2	247	MIT-LCS Nov 92 SPREC Results Class D
sri3-d	7.1	95.0	4.1	0.8	2.1	33.2	247	SRI Nov 92 SPREC Results Class D

Class X Subset

	W. Err	Corr	Sub	Del	Ins	U. Err	# Utt.	Description
att2-x	18.5	85.1	11.3	3.6	3.5	70.3	293	ATT Nov 92 SPREC Results Class X
bbn2-x	14.5	89.2	7.8	3.0	3.7	59.0	293	BBN Nov 92 SPREC Results Class X
cmu2-x	15.6	86.6	7.0	6.5	2.2	59.7	293	CMU Nov 92 SPREC Results Class X
crim4-x	30.1	74.7	19.7	5.6	4.8	81.6	293	CRIM Nov 92 SPREC Results Class X
inrs2-x	100.0	0.0	0.0	100.0	0.0	100.0	293	INRS Late Nov 92 SPREC Results Class X
mit_lcs2-x	21.7	82.6	12.9	4.6	4.2	70.6	293	MIT-LCS Nov 92 SPREC Results Class X
sri3-x	15.8	88.1	9.4	2.4	4.0	64.8	293	SRI Nov 92 SPREC Results Class X

Table 3: ATIS SPREC Benchmark Test Results

Nov92 ATIS SPREC Test Results

	ATT (89 Utt.)	BBN (124 Utt.)	CMU (142 Utt.)	MIT (167 Utt.)	SRI (152 Utt.)	Overall Totals 674	Foreign Coll. Site Totals
	Class A+D Subset Originating Site of Test Data						
att2	8.7 3.4 3.0 15.1 74.2	7.7 1.9 2.1 11.7 58.1	1.8 2.2 3.0 7.0 44.4	3.9 1.1 0.9 5.9 34.1	1.8 0.8 1.2 3.8 28.3	4.6 1.8 2.0 8.4 44.7	3.9 1.5 1.8 7.1 40.2
bbn2	4.7 1.7 1.9 8.4 50.6	4.2 1.4 0.7 6.3 34.7	1.5 0.8 1.2 3.5 22.5	1.8 0.3 0.6 2.8 21.6	0.5 0.4 0.4 1.3 9.2	2.5 0.9 0.9 4.3 25.2	2.0 0.7 1.0 3.7 23.1
SYSTEMS cmu2	5.8 2.6 1.3 9.7 57.3	4.1 1.4 0.6 6.1 39.5	1.4 1.4 0.9 3.7 21.8	1.6 0.6 0.3 2.5 19.2	2.0 0.4 0.6 3.0 21.1	2.8 1.2 0.7 4.7 28.9	3.2 1.1 0.6 5.0 30.8
crim4	14.1 4.4 5.5 24.0 86.5	12.9 5.1 3.1 21.1 74.2	4.7 1.5 2.1 8.4 38.7	6.8 2.2 1.5 10.5 55.1	4.9 1.4 2.5 8.8 42.1	8.4 2.9 2.8 14.1 56.4	8.4 2.9 2.8 14.1 56.4
inrs2	0.0 100.0 0.0 100.0 100.0	0.0 100.0 0.0 100.0 100.0	0.0 100.0 0.0 100.0 100.0	0.0 100.0 0.0 100.0 100.0	0.0 100.0 0.0 100.0 100.0	0.0 100.0 0.0 100.0 100.0	0.0 100.0 0.0 100.0 100.0
mit_lcs2	8.9 3.5 3.5 15.9 57.3	6.8 2.8 1.8 11.4 54.0	4.4 2.3 1.5 8.2 43.0	1.7 1.3 0.3 3.3 19.2	2.3 1.2 0.8 4.2 28.9	4.5 2.2 1.4 8.1 37.8	5.4 2.4 1.8 9.7 44.0
sri3	4.9 1.5 3.4 9.8 61.8	5.8 1.4 1.2 8.4 50.0	3.2 1.0 1.7 5.9 33.8	2.3 0.3 0.8 3.4 25.1	1.4 0.3 0.7 2.4 13.8	3.5 0.9 1.4 5.7 33.8	3.9 1.0 1.6 6.5 39.7
Overall Totals	6.7 16.7 2.7 26.1 69.7	5.9 16.3 1.4 23.6 58.6	2.4 15.6 1.5 19.5 43.5	2.6 15.1 0.6 18.3 39.2	1.8 14.9 0.9 17.6 34.8		
Foreign System	6.4 18.9 2.6 27.9 68.9	6.2 18.8 1.5 26.4 62.6	2.6 18.0 1.6 22.2 47.1	2.7 17.4 0.7 20.8 42.5	1.9 17.4 0.9 20.2 38.3		%Sub %Del %Ins %W.Err %Utt.Err

Matrix tabulation of results for the Nov92 ATIS SPREC Test Results, for the Class A+D Subset.

Matrix columns present results for Test Data Subsets collected at several sites, and matrix rows present results for different systems.

Numbers printed at the top of the matrix columns indicate the number of utterances in the Test Data (sub)set from the corresponding site.

"Overall Totals" (column) present results for the entire Class A+D Subset for the system corresponding to that matrix row. "Foreign Coll. Site Totals" present results for "foreign site" data (i.e., excluding locally collected data) for the Class A+D Subset.

"Overall Totals" (row) present results accumulated over all systems corresponding to the Test Data (sub)set corresponding to that matrix column. "Foreign System Totals" present results accumulated over "foreign systems" (i.e., excluding results for the system(s) developed at the site responsible for collection of that Test Data subset.)

Table 4: ATIS SPREC Results: Class (A+D) by Collection Site

Composite Report of All Significance Tests
For the Nov92 ATIS SPREC Class A+D Test Results Test

Test Name	Abbrev.
Matched Pair Sentence Segment (Word Error) Test	MP
Signed Paired Comparison (Speaker Word Accuracy) Test	SI
Wilcoxon Signed Rank (Speaker Word Accuracy) Test	WI
McNemar (Sentence Error) Test	MN

	att2-a_d	bbn2-a_d	cmu2-a_d	crim4-a_d	inrs2-a_d	mit_lcs2-a_d	sri3-a_d
att2-a_d		MP bbn2-a_d SI bbn2-a_d WI bbn2-a_d MN bbn2-a_d	MP cmu2-a_d SI cmu2-a_d WI cmu2-a_d MN cmu2-a_d	MP att2-a_d SI att2-a_d WI att2-a_d MN att2-a_d	MP att2-a_d SI att2-a_d WI att2-a_d MN att2-a_d	MP same SI same WI same MN mit_lcs2-a_d	MP sri3-a_d SI sri3-a_d WI sri3-a_d MN sri3-a_d
bbn2-a_d			MP same SI same WI same MN bbn2-a_d	MP bbn2-a_d SI bbn2-a_d WI bbn2-a_d MN bbn2-a_d	MP bbn2-a_d SI bbn2-a_d WI bbn2-a_d MN bbn2-a_d	MP bbn2-a_d SI bbn2-a_d WI bbn2-a_d MN bbn2-a_d	MP bbn2-a_d SI bbn2-a_d WI bbn2-a_d MN bbn2-a_d
cmu2-a_d				MP cmu2-a_d SI cmu2-a_d WI cmu2-a_d MN cmu2-a_d	MP cmu2-a_d SI cmu2-a_d WI cmu2-a_d MN cmu2-a_d	MP cmu2-a_d SI cmu2-a_d WI cmu2-a_d MN cmu2-a_d	MP cmu2-a_d SI same WI same MN cmu2-a_d
crim4-a_d					MP crim4-a_d SI crim4-a_d WI crim4-a_d MN crim4-a_d	MP mit_lcs2-a_d SI mit_lcs2-a_d WI mit_lcs2-a_d MN mit_lcs2-a_d	MP sri3-a_d SI sri3-a_d WI sri3-a_d MN sri3-a_d
inrs2-a_d						MP mit_lcs2-a_d SI mit_lcs2-a_d WI mit_lcs2-a_d MN mit_lcs2-a_d	MP sri3-a_d SI sri3-a_d WI sri3-a_d MN sri3-a_d
mit_lcs2-a_d							MP sri3-a_d SI sri3-a_d WI sri3-a_d MN sri3-a_d
sri3-a_d							

Table 5: Signficance Test Results: ATIS SPREC Systems

system	Class A+D 674 Utt. W. Err(%)	Class A 427 Utt. W. Err(%)	Class D 247 Utt. W. Err(%)	Description
att1	42.4	34.7	55.9	ATT1 Nov 92 ATIS NL Results
bbn1	22.0	15.7	32.8	BBN1 Nov 92 ATIS NL Results
cmu1	12.3	12.2	12.6	CMU1 Nov 92 ATIS NL Results
crim1	71.2	40.5	124.3	CRIM1 CHANEL Nov 92 ATIS NL Results
crim2	69.4	50.1	102.8	CRIM2 CHANEL CD Nov 92 ATIS NL Results
crim3	49.7	31.1	81.8	CRIM3 NEURON Nov 92 ATIS NL Results
inrs1	101.5	79.9	138.9	INRS Late Nov 92 ATIS NL Results
mit_lcs1	18.4	18.3	18.6	MIT_LCS1 Nov 92 ATIS NL Results
paramax	55.6	44.0	75.7	PARAMAX Nov 92 ATIS NL Results
sri1	27.6	22.2	36.8	SRI1 TM Nov 92 ATIS NL Results
sri2	23.6	14.8	38.9	SRI2 GEMINI+TM Nov 92 ATIS NL Results

Table 6: ATIS NL Test Results

SYSTEMS	Class (A+D) Set, Originating Site of Test Data: ATT 89	BBN 124	CMU 142	MIT 167	SRI 152	Overall Totals 674	Foreign Coll. Site Totals
att1	71 14 4 80 16 4 36.0	79 29 16 64 23 13 59.7	93 45 4 65 32 3 66.2	137 25 5 82 15 3 32.9	135 14 3 89 9 2 20.4	515 127 32 76 19 5 42.4	444 113 28 76 19 5 43.4
bbn1	76 3 10 85 3 11 18.0	95 15 14 77 12 11 35.5	116 15 11 82 11 8 28.9	150 5 12 90 3 7 13.2	136 9 7 89 6 5 16.4	573 47 54 85 7 8 22.0	478 32 40 87 6 7 18.9
cmu1	84 5 0 94 6 0 11.2	100 20 4 81 16 3 35.5	138 4 0 97 3 0 5.6	158 8 1 95 5 1 10.2	150 2 0 99 1 0 2.6	630 39 5 93 6 1 12.3	492 35 5 92 7 1 14.1
crim1	36 17 36 40 19 40 78.7	67 24 33 54 19 27 65.3	65 41 36 46 29 25 83.1	77 28 62 46 17 37 70.7	91 32 29 60 21 19 61.2	336 142 196 50 21 29 71.2	336 142 196 50 21 29 71.2
crim2	43 27 19 48 30 21 82.0	67 39 18 54 31 15 77.4	69 54 19 49 38 13 89.4	95 23 49 57 14 29 56.9	106 31 15 70 20 10 50.7	380 174 120 56 26 18 69.4	380 174 120 56 26 18 69.4
crim3	63 21 5 71 24 6 52.8	88 32 4 71 26 3 54.8	101 39 2 71 27 1 56.3	119 40 8 71 24 5 52.7	126 26 0 83 17 0 34.2	497 158 19 74 23 3 49.7	497 158 19 74 23 3 49.7
inrs1	38 47 4 43 53 4 110.1	51 65 8 41 52 6 111.3	56 83 3 39 58 2 119.0	74 79 14 44 47 8 103.0	98 53 1 64 35 1 70.4	317 327 30 47 49 4 101.5	317 327 30 47 49 4 101.5
mit_lcs1	78 7 4 88 8 4 20.2	93 21 10 75 17 8 41.9	132 8 2 93 6 1 12.7	154 9 4 92 5 2 13.2	143 5 4 94 3 3 9.2	600 50 24 89 7 4 18.4	446 41 20 88 8 4 20.1
paramax	33 10 46 37 11 52 74.2	59 17 48 48 14 39 66.1	65 37 40 46 26 28 80.3	110 11 46 66 7 28 40.7	121 14 17 80 9 11 29.6	388 89 197 58 13 29 55.6	388 89 197 58 13 29 55.6
sri1	69 12 8 78 13 9 36.0	91 19 14 73 15 11 41.9	109 17 16 77 12 11 35.2	144 7 16 86 4 10 18.0	137 7 8 90 5 5 14.5	550 62 62 82 9 9 27.6	413 55 54 79 11 10 31.4
sri2	74 11 4 83 12 4 29.2	93 16 15 75 13 12 37.9	108 19 15 76 13 11 37.3	150 5 12 90 3 7 13.2	146 5 1 96 3 1 7.2	571 56 47 85 8 7 23.6	425 51 46 81 10 9 28.4
Overall Totals	665 174 140 68 18 14 49.8	883 297 184 65 22 13 57.0	1052 362 148 67 23 9 55.8	1368 240 229 74 13 12 38.6	1389 198 85 83 12 5 28.8		
Foreign System Totals	594 160 136 67 18 15 51.2	788 282 170 64 23 14 59.2	914 358 148 64 25 10 60.8	1214 231 225 73 14 13 41.1	1106 186 76 81 14 6 32.7		

Legend:

#T	#F	#NA
%T	%F	%NA
% Weighted Error		

Table 7: ATIS NL Results: Class (A+D) by Collection Site

system	Class A+D 674 Utt. W. Err(%)	Class A 427 Utt. W. Err(%)	Class D 247 Utt. W. Err(%)	Description
att1	82.8	49.6	140.1	ATT1 Nov 92 ATIS SLS Results
bbn1	30.6	23.7	42.5	BBN1 Nov 92 ATIS SLS Results
cmu1	21.2	19.7	23.9	CMU1 Nov 92 ATIS SLS Results
crim1	82.3	56.9	126.3	CRIM1 CHANEL Nov 92 ATIS SLS Results
crim2	82.9	66.3	111.7	CRIM2 CHANEL CD Nov 92 ATIS SLS Results
crim3	75.2	57.1	106.5	CRIM3 NEURON Nov 92 ATIS SLS Results
inrs1	100.0	100.0	100.0	INRS1 LATE Nov 92 ATIS SLS Results
mit_lcs1	29.7	30.4	28.3	MIT_LCS1 Nov 92 ATIS SLS Results
sri1	37.4	31.9	47.0	SRI1 TM Nov 92 ATIS SLS Results
sri2	33.2	26.5	44.9	SRI2 GEMINI+TM Nov 92 ATIS SLS Results

Table 8: ATIS SLS Test Results

	Class (A+D) Set Originating Site of Test Data ATT 89	BBN 124	CMU 142	MIT 167	SRI 152	Overall Totals 674	Foreign Coll. Site Totals
SYSTEMS: att1	35 41 13 39 46 , 15 106.7	62 42 20 50 34 16 83.9	61 76 5 43 54 4 110.6	98 56 13 59 34 8 74.9	110 35 7 72 23 5 50.7	366 250 58 54 37 9 82.8	331 209 45 57 36 8 79.1
bbn1	60 14 15 67 16 17 48.3	88 17 19 71 14 15 42.7	112 22 8 79 15 6 36.6	147 14 6 88 8 4 20.4	139 11 2 91 7 1 15.8	546 78 50 81 12 7 30.6	458 61 31 83 11 6 27.8
cmu1	72 16 1 81 18 1 37.1	92 27 5 74 22 4 47.6	129 13 0 91 9 0 18.3	157 9 1 94 5 1 11.4	149 3 0 98 2 0 3.9	599 68 7 89 10 1 21.2	470 55 7 88 10 1 22.0
crim1	27 12 50 30 13 56 83.1	45 34 45 36 27 36 91.1	59 44 39 42 31 27 89.4	67 33 67 40 20 40 79.6	83 39 30 55 26 20 71.1	281 162 231 42 24 34 82.3	281 162 231 42 24 34 82.3
crim2	36 18 35 40 20 39 79.8	43 43 38 35 35 31 100.0	66 54 22 46 38 15 91.5	74 31 62 44 19 37 74.3	89 47 16 59 31 11 72.4	308 193 173 46 29 26 82.9	308 193 173 46 29 26 82.9
crim3	46 39 4 52 44 4 92.1	55 62 7 44 50 6 105.6	88 49 5 62 35 4 72.5	99 47 21 59 28 13 68.9	110 34 8 72 22 5 50.0	398 231 45 59 34 7 75.2	398 231 45 59 34 7 75.2
inrs1	0 0 89 0 0 100 100.0	0 0 124 0 0 100 100.0	0 0 142 0 0 100 100.0	0 0 167 0 0 100 100.0	0 0 152 0 0 100 100.0	0 0 674 0 0 100 100.0	0 0 674 0 0 100 100.0
mit_lcs1	57 12 20 64 13 22 49.4	79 28 17 64 23 14 58.9	120 12 10 85 8 7 23.9	149 11 7 89 7 4 17.4	140 8 4 92 5 3 13.2	545 71 58 81 11 9 29.7	396 60 51 78 12 10 33.7
sri1	60 16 13 67 18 15 50.6	75 27 22 60 22 18 61.3	101 23 18 71 16 13 45.1	141 9 17 84 5 10 21.0	132 12 8 87 8 5 21.1	509 87 78 76 13 12 37.4	377 75 70 72 14 13 42.1
sri2	65 13 11 73 15 12 41.6	75 26 23 60 21 19 60.5	101 25 16 71 18 11 46.5	149 6 12 89 4 7 14.4	139 9 4 91 6 3 14.5	529 79 66 78 12 10 33.2	390 70 62 75 13 12 38.7
Overall Totals	458 181 251 51 20 28 68.9	614 306 320 50 25 26 75.2	837 318 265 59 22 19 63.5	1081 216 373 65 13 22 48.2	1091 198 231 72 13 15 41.2		
Foreign System Totals	423 140 238 53 17 30 64.7	526 289 301 47 26 27 78.8	708 305 265 55 24 21 68.5	932 205 366 62 14 24 51.6	820 177 219 67 15 18 47.1		

Legend:

#T #F #NA
%T %F %NA
% Weighted Error

Table 9: ATIS SLS Results: Class (A+D) by Collection Site

Multi-Site Data Collection and Evaluation in Spoken Language Understanding

L. Hirschman, M. Bates, D. Dahl, W. Fisher, J. Garofolo,
*D. Pallett, K. Hunicke-Smith, P. Price, A. Rudnicky, and E. Tzoukermann**

Contact: Lynette Hirschman
NE43-643 Spoken Language Systems Group
MIT Laboratory for Computer Science, Cambridge, MA 02139
e-mail: lynette@goldilocks.lcs.mit.edu

ABSTRACT

The Air Travel Information System (ATIS) domain serves as the common task for DARPA spoken language system research and development. The approaches and results possible in this rapidly growing area are structured by available corpora, annotations of that data, and evaluation methods. Coordination of this crucial infrastructure is the charter of the Multi-Site ATIS Data COllection Working group (MADCOW). We focus here on selection of training and test data, evaluation of language understanding, and the continuing search for evaluation methods that will correlate well with expected performance of the technology in applications.

1. INTRODUCTION

Data availability and evaluation procedures structure research possibilities: the type and amount of training data affects the performance of existing algorithms and limits the development of new algorithms; and evaluation procedures document progress, and force research choices in a world of limited resources. The recent rapid progress in spoken language understanding owes much to our success in collecting and distributing a large corpus of speech, transcriptions, and associated materials based on human-machine interactions in the air travel domain. A tight feedback loop between evaluation methodology and evaluation results has encouraged incremental extension to the evaluation methodology, to keep pace with the technology development. The paper reports on the data collection and evaluation efforts co-ordinated by MADCOW over the past year.

The multi-site data collection paradigm [3, 4] distributes the burden of data collection, provides data rapidly, educates multiple sites about data collection issues, and results in a more diverse pool of data than could be obtained with a single collection site. The resulting data represents a wide range of variability in speaker characteristics, speech style, language style and interaction style. It has allowed individual sites to experiment with data collection methods: by replacing various system components with a human, we collect the kind of data we can aim for in the future, while completely automated systems help us to focus on the major current issues in system accuracy and speed. Sites have also experimented with interface strategies: spoken output only, tabular output only, response summaries, spoken and written paraphrase, and system initiative may be more or less appropriate for different users and different tasks and all can dramatically affect the resulting data.

MADCOW's recent accomplishments include:

- Release of 14,000 utterances for training and test, including speech and transcriptions;
- Release of annotations for almost 10,000 of these utterances (7500 training utterances and three test sets of 2300 utterances total), balanced by site;
- A bug reporting and bug fix mechanism, to maintain the quality and consistency of the training data;
- An evaluation schedule that delivered training data and froze changes in the principles of interpretation[1] several months before the evaluation;
- An experiment with "end-to-end" evaluation that permits evaluation of aspects of the system not previously evaluable.

Table 1 shows the breakdown of all training data and Table 2 shows the breakdown for just the annotated data.[2]

2. CURRENT EVALUATION METHODOLOGY

When the ATIS task was developed in 1990 [9], little work had been done on formal evaluation of understanding for natural language interfaces.[3] In the absence of a generally accepted semantic representation,

*This paper was written the auspices of the Multi-Site ATIS Data Collection Working group (MADCOW). In addition to the authors, many other people, listed under the Acknowledgements section, made important contributions to this work.

[1] These are the principles that define how various vague or difficult phrases are to be interpreted; see section 2.1 below.

[2] A class A utterance can be interpreted by itself, with no additional context; a class D utterance requires an earlier "context-setting" utterance for its interpretation; and a class X utterance cannot be evaluated in terms of a reference database answer.

[3] This coincides with the beginnings of formal evaluation for written text, via the Message Understanding Conferences (MUCs)

Site	Speakers	Scenarios	Utterances
AT&T	57	200	2100
BBN	62	307	2277
CMU	47	214	2219
MIT	182	625	4910
SRI	90	148	2478
TOTAL	438	1494	13984

Table 1: Multi-site ATIS Data Summary

Site	Class A	Class D	Class X	Total
ATT	457 36.6%	497 39.8%	295 23.6%	1249 16.6%
BBN	858 56.2%	357 23.4%	312 20.4%	1527 20.3%
CMU	562 37.6%	340 22.7%	594 39.7%	1496 19.9%
MIT	663 37.7%	680 38.7%	414 23.6%	1757 23.4%
SRI	676 45.7%	618 41.8%	184 12.4%	1478 19.7%
Total	3216 42.8%	2492 33.2%	1799 24.0%	7507 100.0%

Table 2: Annotated Training Data Summary

the DARPA SLS community focused instead on "the right answer," as defined in terms of a database query task (air travel planning). This permitted evaluation by comparing "canonical" database answers to the system answers using a comparator program [1]. This approach was felt to be far easier, given proper definition of terms, than to agree on a standard semantic representation.

The original evaluation methodology was defined only for context-independent (*class A*) utterances. However, this left approximately half the data as unevaluable (see Table 2). Over the next two years, the evaluation method was extended to cover context-dependent queries (*class D* utterances), it was tightened by requiring that a correct answer lie within a minimal answer and a maximal answer (see section 2.1), and it was made more realistic by presenting utterances in scenario order, as spoken during the data collection phase, with no information about the class of an utterance. Thus, we now can evaluate on approximately 75% of the data (all but *class X* data – see Tables 2 and 4). We also introduced a *Weighted Error* metric because we believed, at least in some applications, wrong answers might be worse than "no answer":[4]

$$WeightedError = \#(No\_Answer) + 2 * \#(Wrong\_Answer).$$

2.1. The Evaluation Mechanism

The comparator-based evaluation method compares human annotator-generated canonical ("reference") database answers to system generated answers. The annotators first classify utterances into context-independent (A), context-dependent (D) and unevaluable (X) classes. Each evaluable utterance (class A or D) is then given minimal and maximal reference answers. The minimal reference answer is generated using NLParse[5] and the maximal answer is generated algorithmically from the minimal answer. A correct answer must include all of the tuples contained in the minimal answer and no more tuples than contained in the maximal answer.

The Principles of Interpretation document provides an explicit interpretation for vague natural language expressions, e.g., "red-eye flight" or "mid-afternoon," and specifies other factors necessary to define reference answers, e.g., how context can override ambiguity in certain cases, or how utterances should be classified if they depend on previous unevaluable utterances. This document serves as a point of common reference for the annotators and the system developers, and permits evaluation of sentences that otherwise would be too vague to have a well-defined database reference answer.

The initial Principles of Interpretation was implemented in 1990. The document is now about 10 pages long, and includes interpretation decisions based on some 10,000 ATIS utterances. The document continues to grow but at a significantly slower rate, as fewer new issues arise. It is remarkable that such a small document has sufficed to provide well-defined interpretations for a corpus of this size. This demonstrates that rules for the interpretation of natural language utterances, at least in the ATIS domain, can be codified well enough to support an automatic evaluation process. Because this procedure was explicit and well-documented, two new sites were able to participate in the most recent evaluation (November 1992).

2.2. Testing on the MADCOW Data

The test data selection procedure was designed to ensure a balanced test set. Test data for the November 1992 evaluation were chosen using procedures similar to those for the November 1991 test [3]. As sites submitted data to NIST, NIST set aside approximately 20% of the utterances to create a pool of potential test data; some 1200 utterances constituted the November 1991

[8]. The MUC evaluation uses a domain-specific template as the basis for evaluation. To date, the goal of a domain-independent semantic representation, perhaps analogous to the minimal bracketing of the Penn Treebank database [2] for parsing, remains elusive.

[4]A recent experiment [5] showed that for one system, subjects were able to detect a system error before making their next query in 90% of the cases. In the remaining 10%, a system error caused the subject to lose several turns before recovering, leading to a reduced estimated weighting factor of 1.25 for errors in that system.

[5]NLParse is a database access product of Texas Instruments.

test pool; 1300 utterances constituted the November 1992 test pool.

NIST's goal was to select approximately 1000 test utterances from the test data pool, evenly balanced among the five collection sites (AT&T, BBN, CMU, MIT, and SRI). Utterances were selected by session, i.e., utterances occurring in one problem-solving scenario were selected as a group, avoiding sessions that seemed to be extreme outliers (e.g., in number of class X utterances, total number of utterances, or number of repeated utterances). Because the test pool contained only marginally more utterances than were needed for the test, it was not possible to simultaneously balance the test set for number of speakers, gender, or subject-scenarios. The test set contained 1002 utterances.[6] The breakdown of the data is shown in Table 3.

NIST verified and corrected the original transcriptions. However, some uncertainty about the transcriptions remained, due to inadequacies in the specifications for the transcription of difficult-to-understand speech, such as *sotto voce* speech. After the transcriptions were verified, the data were annotated by the SRI annotation group to produce categorizations and reference answers. A period for adjudication followed the test, where testing sites could request changes to the test data categorizations, reference answers, and transcriptions. The final post-adjudication classification of the test data set is shown in Table 4. Final evaluation results are reported in [6].

Collecting Site	Speakers	Scenarios	Utterances
ATT	7; 1M/ 6F	22	200
BBN	7; 3M/ 4F	28	201
CMU	4; 4M/ 0F	12	200
MIT	10; 3M/ 7F	37	201
SRI	9; 5M/ 4F	19	200
Total	37; 16M/21F	118	1002

Table 3: Multi-site ATIS Test Data November 1992

3. LIMITATIONS OF THE CURRENT EVALUATION

The current data collection and evaluation paradigm captures important dimensions of system behavior. However, we must constantly re-assess our evaluation procedures in terms of our goals, to ensure that our evaluation procedures help us to assess the suitability of a particular technology for a particular application, and to ensure that benchmark scores will correlate well with user satisfaction and efficiency when the technology is transferred to an application.

The advantage of using a pre-recorded corpus for evaluation is clear: the same data are used as input to all systems under evaluation, and each system's set of answers is used to automatically generate a benchmark score. This approach ensures a uniform input across all systems and removes human involvement from the benchmark testing process (except that human annotators define the reference answers). Any annotated set of data can be used repeatedly for iterative training. However, some of these same strengths also impose limitations on what we can evaluate.

First, there is the issue of the match between the reference answer and the user's need for useful information. The comparator method can count answers as correct despite system misunderstanding. For example, if a system misrecognizes "Tuesday" as "Wednesday" and the user realizes that the flight information shown is for Wednesday flights, the user may appropriately believe that the answer is wrong. However, if all flights have daily departures, the database answer will be *canonically* correct. On the other hand, useful (but not strictly correct) answers will be counted wrong, because there is no "partially correct" category for answers.

Second, mixed initiative in human-machine dialogue will be required for technology transfer in many spoken language understanding applications. But the evaluation paradigm actively discourages experimentation with mixed initiative. A query that is a response to a system-initiated query is classified as unevaluable if the user's response can only be understood in the context of the system's query. During evaluation, any system response that is a query will automatically be counted as incorrect (since only database answers can be correct).

The use of pre-recorded data also preserves artifacts of the data collection system. For example, much of the test data were collected using systems or components of systems to generate responses, rather than a human alone. As a result, the data include many instances of system errors that affect the user's next query. A user may have to repeat a query several times, or may correct some error that the data collection system (but not the system under evaluation) made. These are artificial phenomena that would disappear if the data collection and evaluation systems were identical.

Finally, the current paradigm does not take into account the speed of the response, which greatly affects the overall interaction. Demonstration systems at several sites

[6] The data recorded using the Sennheiser head-mounted noise-cancelling microphone were used as the test material for "official" speech recognition (SPREC) and spoken language system (SLS, NL) testing. For a subset of the utterances in the official test sets, recordings were also made using a desk-mounted Crown microphone.

Site	Class A	Class D	Class X	Total
ATT	48 (24.0%)	41 (20.5%)	111 (55.5%)	200 (20.0%)
BBN	97 (48.3%)	27 (13.4%)	77 (38.3%)	201 (20.1%)
CMU	76 (38.0%)	66 (33.0%)	58 (29.0%)	200 (20.0%)
MIT	100 (49.8%)	67 (33.3%)	34 (16.9%)	201 (20.1%)
SRI	106 (53.0%)	46 (23.0%)	48 (24.0%)	200 (20.0%)
Total:	427 (42.6%)	247 (24.7%)	328 (32.7%)	1002 (100.0%)

Table 4: Breakdown of Test Data by Class

have begun to diverge from those used in benchmark evaluations, in part, because the requirements of demonstrating or using the system are quite different from the requirements for generating reference database answers.

These limitations of the comparator-based evaluation preclude the evaluation of certain strategies that are likely to be crucial in technology transfer. In particular, we need to develop metrics that keep human subjects in the loop and support human-machine interaction. However, the use of human subjects introduces new issues in experimental design. Over the past year, MADCOW has begun to address these issues by designing a trial *end-to-end* evaluation.

4. END-TO-END EVALUATION EXPERIMENT

The end-to-end evaluation, designed to complement the comparator-based evaluation, included 1) objective measures such as timing information, and time to task completion, 2) human-derived judgements on correctness of system answers and user solutions (*logfile evaluation*), and 3) a user satisfaction questionnaire.

The unit of analysis for the new evaluation was a scenario, as completed by a single subject, using a particular system. This kept the user in the loop, permitting each system to be evaluated on its own inputs and outputs. The use of human evaluators allowed for assessing partial correctness, and provided the opportunity to score other system actions, such as mixed initiatives, error responses and diagnostic messages. The end-to-end evaluation included both task-level metrics (whether scenarios had been solved correctly and the time it took a subject to solve a scenario) and utterance-level metrics (query characteristics, system response characteristics, the durations of individual transactions).

An experimental evaluation took place in October 1992, to assess feasibility of the new evaluation method. We defined a common experimental design protocol and a common set of subject instructions (allowing some local variation). Each site submitted to NIST four travel planning scenarios that had a well-defined "solution set". From these, NIST assembled two sets of four scenarios. Each site then ran eight subjects, each doing four scenarios, in a counter-balanced design. Five systems participated: the BBN, CMU, MIT and SRI spoken language systems, and the Paramax system using typed input.

A novel feature of the end-to-end experiment was the *logfile evaluation.* This technique, developed at MIT [7], is based on the logfile which records and timestamps all user/system interactions. A human evaluator, using an interactive program,[7] can review each user/system interaction and evaluate it by type of user request, type of system response, and correctness or appropriateness of response. For user requests, the following responses were distinguished: 1) *New Information,* 2) *Repeat,* 3) *Rephrase,* or 4) *Unevaluable.* For system responses, the evaluators categorized each response as follows:

Answer: further evaluated as *Correct, Incorrect Partially Correct or Can't Decide;*
System Initiated Directive: further evaluated as *Appropriate, Inappropriate, or Can't Decide;*
Diagnostic Message: further evaluated as *Appropriate, Inappropriate, or Can't Decide;*
Failure-to-Understand Message: no further evaluation.

The evaluator also assessed the scenario solution according to whether the subject finished and whether the answer belonged to the defined solution set.

To facilitate determination of the correctness of individual system responses, we agreed to follow the Principles of Interpretation, at least to the extent that an answer judged correct by these Principles would not be counted incorrect. For this experiment, logfile evaluation was performed independently by Bill Fisher (NIST) and Kate Hunicke-Smith (SRI Annotation), as well as by volunteers at MIT and BBN. This gave us experience in looking at the variability among evaluators of different

[7]The program was developed by David Goodine at MIT; the evaluator instructions were written by Lynette Hirschman, with help from Lyn Bates, Christine Pao and the rest of MADCOW.

levels of experience. We found that any two evaluators agreed about 90% of the time, and agreement among multiple evaluators decreased proportionally.

5. LESSONS LEARNED

The experiment provided useful feedback on the risks and advantages of end-to-end evaluation, and will guide us in refining the procedure. For the initial trial, we made methodological compromises in several areas: a small number of subjects, no control over cross-site subject variability, few guidelines in developing or selecting scenarios. These compromises seemed reasonable to get the experiment started; however, the next iteration of end-to-end evaluation will need to introduce methodological changes to provide statistically valid data.

5.1. Sources of Variability

Valid comparisons of systems across sites require control over major sources of variability, so that the differences of interest can emerge. The use of human subjects in the evaluation creates a major source of variability, due to differences in the subjects pools available at various sites and the characteristics of individuals. We can minimize some of these differences, for example, by training all subjects to the same criterion across sites (to account for differences in background and familiarity with the domain), by using many subjects from each site (so that any one subject's idiosyncrasies have less of an effect on the results), and by ensuring that procedures for subject recruitment and data collection across sites are as similar as possible (we made a serious effort in this direction, but more could be done to reduce the cross-site variability that is otherwise confounded with the system under evaluation). An alternative would be to perform the evaluation at a common site. This would allow for greater uniformity in the data collection procedure, it could increase the uniformity of the subject pool, and would allow use of powerful experimental techniques (such as within-subject designs). Such a common-site evaluation, however, would pose other challenges, including the port of each system to a common site and platform, and the complex design needed to assess potential scenario order effects, system order effects, and their interaction.

Another source of variability is the set of travel planning scenarios the subjects were asked to solve. Certain scenarios posed serious problems for all systems; a few scenarios posed particular problems for specific systems. However, the data suggest that there was a subset that could perform a reasonable diagnostic function.

5.2. Logfile Evaluation

Somewhat unexpectedly, we found that logfile evaluation was a useful tool for system developers in identifying dialogue-related problems in their systems. The evaluator interface allowed for rapid evaluation (about 5-15 minutes per scenario). However, the evaluator instructions need refinement, the interface needs minor extensions, and most important, we need to design a procedure to produce a statistically reliable logfile evaluation score by combining assessments from multiple evaluators.

A remaining thorny problem is the definition of *correct*, *partially correct*, and *incorrect answers*. For this experiment, we used the Principles of Interpretation document to define a correct answer, so that we would not need to develop a new document for these purposes. For the next evaluation, we need definitions that reflect utility to the user, not just canonical correctness.[8]

Finally, we found that we could not rely on subjects to correctly complete the scenarios presented to them. In some cases, the subject was not able to find the answer, and in other cases, the subject did not follow directions regarding what information to provide in the answer. This made it difficult to compute accurate statistics for scenario-level metrics such as task completion and task completion time; this problem was exacerbated by the limited amount of data we collected.

6. FUTURE DIRECTIONS

We view evaluation as iterative; at each evaluation, we assess our procedures and try to improve them. The comparator-based evaluation is now stable and the November 1992 evaluation ran very smoothly. The availability of an expanded database will require a new data collection effort. Increasing emphasis on portability may have an impact on evaluation technology. In addition, we plan to continue our experiments with end-to-end evaluation, to work out some of the methodological problems described in the previous section.

The ATIS *relational database* has been expanded from 11 cities to 46 cities, to provide a more realistic task supporting more challenging scenarios. The database was constructed using data from the Official Airline Guide and now includes 23,457 flights (compared to 765 flights). The set of new cities was limited to 46 because it was felt that a larger set would result in an unwieldy database

[8] Originally, we had wanted to compare logfile scores to comparator-based scores. However, for several sites, the data collection and evaluation systems had diverged and it was not possible to simultaneously interact with the subjects and provide comparator-style answers. Therefore, we were not able to perform this experiment.

and would thus require the sites to devote too many resources to issues peripheral to their research, such as database management and query optimization. Data collection on this larger database is now beginning.

The *portability* of the technology (from application to application, and from language to language) becomes an increasing challenge as the technology improves, since more potential applications become possible. It still takes many hours of data collection and several person months of system development to port an application from one domain (e.g., air travel) to another similar domain (e.g., schedule management). Evaluating portability is still more challenging. Evaluation has a significant cost: the comparator-based method requires the definition of a training corpus and its collection, defining principles of interpretation, and (most expensively) the annotation of data. Therefore, if we believe that regular evaluations play an important role in guiding research, we need to find cost-effective ways of evaluating systems. End-to-end evaluation may provide some low-overhead techniques for quickly evaluating system performance in new domains.

With the *end-to-end evaluation* experiment, we have made progress in creating a procedure that accurately assesses the usability of current spoken language technology and provides useful feedback for the improvement of this technology. The procedure needs to be further refined to reliably identify differences among systems and it must embody principles that can assess strengths and weaknesses of different systems for different purposes. In developing evaluation procedures that involve human interactions, we need to carefully assess the validity of the measures we use. For example a measure such as the number of utterances per scenario may seem relevant (e.g., the subject was frustrated with answers and had to repeat a question several times), but in fact may reflect irrelevant aspects of the process (the subject was intrigued by the system and wanted to push its limits in various ways). Meaningful evaluation will require metrics that have been systematically investigated and have been shown to measure relevant properties.

MADCOW has played a central role in developing and coordinating the multi-site data collection and evaluation paradigm. It will also play an active role in defining new methodologies, such as end-to-end evaluation, to support evaluation of interactive spoken language systems. We believe that end-to-end evaluation will allow us to assess the trade-offs among various component-level decisions (in speech recognition, natural language processing and interface design), bringing spoken language systems closer to eventual deployment.

7. ACKNOWLEDGEMENTS

We would particularly like to acknowledge the contribution of Nancy Dahlgren at NIST; prior to her accident, Nancy made important contributions to the annotation and debugging of the data. We greatly missed her participation during the final evaluation.

In addition to the authors, the following people made a valuable contribution to the process: at ATT: J. Wilpon; at BBN: R. Bobrow, R. Ingria, J. Makhoul, V. Shaked, and D. Stallard; at CMU: C. Neelan, E. Thayer, and R. Weide; at MIT: D. Goodine, J. Polifroni, C. Pao, M. Phillips, and S. Seneff; at NIST: N. Dahlgren, J. Fiscus, and B. Tjaden; at Paramax: L. Norton, and R. Nilson; and at SRI: H. Bratt, R. Moore, E. Shriberg, and E. Wade.

REFERENCES

1. Bates, M., S. Boisen, and J. Makhoul, "Developing an Evaluation Methodology for Spoken Language Systems," *Proc. Third DARPA Speech and Language Workshop*, R. Stern (ed.), Morgan Kaufmann, June 1990.
2. Black, E., *et al.*, "A Procedure for Quantitatively Comparing the Syntactic Coverage of English Grammars," *Proc. Third DARPA Speech and Language Workshop*, P. Price (ed.), Morgan Kaufmann, June 1991.
3. Hirschman, L., *et al.*, "Multi-Site Data Collection for a Spoken Language Corpus", *Proc. Fifth Speech and Natural Language Workshop*, M. Marcus (ed.), Morgan Kaufmann, Arden House, NY, February 1992.
4. Hirschman, L., *et al.*, "Multi-Site Data Collection for a Spoken Language Corpus," *Proc. of the ICSLP*, Banff, Canada, October 1992.
5. Hirschman, L. and C. Pao, "The Cost of Errors in a Spoken Language Systems," submitted to Eurospeech-93, Berlin 1993.
6. Pallett, D., Fiscus, J., Fisher, W., and J. Garofolo, "Benchmark Tests for the Spoken Language Program," *Proc. DARPA Human Language Technology Workshop*, Princeton, March 1993.
7. Polifroni, J., Hirschman, L., Seneff, S. and V. Zue, "Experiments in Evaluating Interactive Spoken Language Systems" *Proc. DARPA Speech and Natural Language Workshop*, M. Marcus (ed.), Arden House, NY, February 1992.
8. *Proc. Fourth Message Understanding Conf.*, Morgan Kaufmann, McLean, June 1992.
9. Price P., "Evaluation of Spoken Language Systems: The ATIS Domain," *Proc. Third DARPA Speech and Language Workshop*, P. Price (ed.), Morgan Kaufmann, June 1990.

THE HCRC MAP TASK CORPUS: NATURAL DIALOGUE FOR SPEECH RECOGNITION

Henry S. Thompson [1,2,3]
Anne Anderson [1,5]
Ellen Gurman Bard [1,3,4]
Gwyneth Doherty-Sneddon [1,5]
Alison Newlands [1,5]
Cathy Sotillo [1,4]

1: Human Communication Research Centre
2: Department of Artificial Intelligence
3: Centre for Cognitive Science
4: Department of Linguistics
University of Edinburgh
2 Buccleuch Place,
Edinburgh, EH12 5BB
SCOTLAND

5: Department of Psychology
University of Glasgow
56 Hillhead Street
Glasgow, G12
SCOTLAND

hthompson@edinburgh.ac.uk

ABSTRACT

The HCRC Map Task corpus has been collected and transcribed in Glasgow and Edinburgh, and recently published on CD-ROM. This effort was made possible by funding from the British Economic and Social Research Council.

The corpus is composed of 128 two-person conversations in both high-quality digital audio and orthographic transcriptions, amounting to 18 hours and 150,000 words respectively.

The experimental design is quite detailed and complex, allowing a number of different phonemic, syntactico-semantic and pragmatic contrasts to be explored in a controlled way.

The corpus is a uniquely valuable resource for speech recognition research in particular, as we move from developing systems intended for controlled use by familiar users to systems intended for less constrained circumstances and naive or occasional users. Examples supporting this claim are given, including preliminary evidence of the phonetic consequences of second mention and the impact of different styles of referent negotiation on communicative efficacy.

1. INTRODUCTION

The HCRC Map Task corpus has been collected and transcribed in Glasgow and Edinburgh, and recently published on CD-ROM (HCRC 1993). This effort was made possible by funding from the British Economic and Social Research Council.

The group which designed and collected the corpus covers a wide range of interests and the corpus reflects this, providing a resource for studies of natural dialogue from many different perspectives.

In this paper we will give a brief summary of the experimental design, and then concentrate on those aspects of the corpus which make it a uniquely valuable resource for speech recognition research in particular, as we move from developing systems intended for controlled use by familiar users to systems intended for less constrained circumstances and naive or occasional users. Some preliminary results of work on the phonetic consequences of second mention and on the impact of different styles of referent negotiation on communicative efficacy will also be presented.

2. CORPUS DESIGN AND CHARACTERISTICS

2.1. The Task

The conversations were elicited by an exercise in task-oriented cooperative problem solving. The two participants sat facing one another in a small recording studio, separated by a table on which sat back-to-back reading stands. On each stand was a schematic map, each visible only to one participant. Each map consisted of an outline and roughly a dozen labelled features (e.g. "white cottage", "Green Bay", "oak forest"). Most features are common to the two maps, but not all, and the participants were informed of this. One map had a route drawn in, the other did not. The task was for the participant without the route to draw one on the basis of discussion with the participant with the route.

2.2. Experimental Design

Using an elaboration of a design developed over a number of years (see e.g. Brown, Anderson et al. 1983), we recorded 128 two-person conversations (each talker in four conversations), employing 64 talkers (32 male, 32 female), almost all born and raised in the Glasgow area, speaking with an educated West of Scotland accent. High quality recordings were made using Shure SM10A close-talking microphones, one talker per channel on stereo DAT (Sony DTC1000ES).

The experimental design is quite detailed and complex, allowing a number of different phonemic, syntactico-semantic and pragmatic contrasts to be explored in a controlled way. In particular, maps and feature names were designed to allow for controlled exploration of phonological reductions of various kinds in a number of different referential contexts, and to provide a range of different stimuli to referent negotiation, based on matches and mis-matches between the two maps.

Among the independent variables in the design were:

- Eye-contact—in half the conversations, the participants could see one another's faces, in half, they could not.
- Familiarity—in half the conversations, the talkers were acquaintances, in half, strangers.
- Task role—Each talker participated in four conversations, two as Instruction Giver (the one with the route) and two as Instruction Follower (the one trying to draw it)

For a complete description of the experimental design, see Anderson, Bader et al. (1991).

2.3. Corpus Characteristics

Subjects accommodated easily to the task and experimental setting, and produced evidently unselfconscious and fluent speech. The syntax is largely clausal rather than sentential; showing good turn-taking, with relatively little overlap/interruption. The total corpus runs about 18 hours of speech, yielding 150,000 word tokens drawn from 2,000 word form types. Word lists containing all the feature names were also elicited from all speakers, along with a number of 'accent diagnosis' utterances.

The acoustic quality of the recordings is good but not outstanding—in particular, stereo separation is not perfect, in that it is often possible to detect the voice of one talker very faintly on the other talker's channel. A very modest amount of rumble and other non-specific background noise is occasionally detectable.

3. THE TRANSCRIPTIONS

The transcriptions are at the orthographic level, quite detailed, including filled pauses, false starts and repetitions, broken words, etc. Considerable care has been taken to ensure consistency of notation, which is thoroughly documented. Although the full complexity of overlapped regions has not been reflected in the transcriptions, such regions *are* clearly set off from the rest of the transcripts. Transcripts are connected to the acoustic sampled data by sample numbers marked every few turns.

Text Encoding Initiative-compliant SGML markup is used, both within transcripts to indicate turn boundaries and for other metatextual purposes, and also in separate corpus header and transcript header files, but this was done in a manner designed to make accessing the transcripts as plain text very easy.

We also used a very light-weight non-TEI markup for textual annotations, to mark such things as abandoned words, letter names, filled pauses and editorial uncertainties.

A brief extract from a transcript is given below as Figure 1, illustrating various aspects of the transcription, including the tags `u` for utterance, `sfo` for speech file offset, `bo` for begin overlap and `eo` for end overlap, as well as the `le` microtag for a letter name.

```
<u who=G n=3>
<sfo samp=107715>
<bo id=o75a>
About half an inch above it, we've
got an {le|x} marking start.  Have

<u who=F n=4>
<sfo samp=208987>
Yes.

<u who=G n=5>
you got that?
<eo id=o75a>
```

Figure 1. Extract from a Map Task Corpus transcript

4. THE CD-ROMS

The published version of the corpus occupies 8 CD-ROMs, and contains:

- a complete set of transcripts;
- 20KHz sampled versions of both channels of the associated speech for all the conversations;
- for each talker sampled audio for an accent diagnostic passage and a scripted reading of a list of all the feature names from the map;
- images of the maps employed;
- documentation;
- UNIX™ tools for linking the spoken and written material and other manipulations of the corpus materials.

Preparation of the corpus for publication was a much larger task than we had expected, and is described in some detail in (Thompson & Bader, 1993).

5. IMPLICATIONS FOR SPEECH RECOGNITION

5.1. High-quality unscripted dialogue

Recorded collections of natural conversation are not new—not only do many linguists have a drawer full of tapes of dinner table or staff room talk, but also more systematic and extensive collection efforts have been carried out on several occasions as part of major reference corpora building projects. But with no exceptions we are aware of, all such material is of highly varying acoustic quality, and is rarely if ever suitable for extensive computational processing.

On the other hand, to date the large development corpora collected and used to such good effect by the speech recognition community, although of a very high standard acoustically, have been exclusively monologue, and until very recently exclusively scripted.

Thus the Map Task corpus occupies a hitherto vacant position in corpus design space—it is natural, unscripted dialogue recorded to a standard suitable for digital processing. We hope the widespread availability of such a resource will help to stimulate a change in the way phonology, morphology, syntax and semantics are pursued parallel to the change which has already occurred in phonetics, that is, a change from theory development dependent on small amounts of data, often constructed by the theorist, to theory development dependent on, indeed immersed within, a large amount of naturally occurring data.

Note that this methodological change is, or at least ought to be, independent of meta-theoretical disposition, and in particular the above remarks are *not* meant to imply a bias in favour of stochastic or self-organising theoretical frameworks.

5.2. Syntax

There is modest controversy brewing about the relation between spoken and written language, particularly in a highly literate language/culture context such as obtains for English. It has been argued (see e.g. Miller 1993) that the grammar of spoken English is qualitatively different from that of written English, and demands separate treatment.

In so far as the progress of speech recognition from relatively constrained interaction situations and relatively constrained language will depend on grammars and/or models of natural English conversation, the resource provided by the Map Task has an obvious rule to play.

5.3. Prosody

It has long been assumed that there is a mutually informing relationship between prosody and discourse structure. The simple goal-oriented nature of the Map Task conversations, and the ease with which quite local, short-term goals can be identified in terms of the part of the route in question at any given time, means that the corpus provides an excellent base at attempting to explicate this relationship in some detail. Work has begun on relating the inventories of intonation on the one hand and moves within conversational games on the other, with initially encouraging results (Kowtko, Isard and Doherty 1992).

As in the case of syntax, we would hope that widespread provision of the corpus will enable comparative exploration of the numerous theories of discourse structure, prosody and their relations now being suggested.

5.4. Fast speech rules

The names associated with the landmarks drawn on the maps were designed *inter alia* to provide opportunities for various forms of phonological modification, in particular t-deletion ("vast meadow"), d-deletion ("reclaimed fields"), glottalisation ("white mountain") and nasal assimilation ("crane bay"). Furthermore, on each map one such name would be paired with another, similar name, with the intention of assessing the impact of the (putative) necessity of contrastive stress ("crane bay" vs. "green bay"). The availability in the corpus of citation form pronunciations be each speaker will provide a very useful baseline for studies in this area.

		Whole Corpus	Eye Contact	No Eye Contact
Word form types		2070	1553	1558
Word tokens	All turns	152298	69762	82536
	Instruction Giver	104828	48361	56467
	Instruction Follower	47470	21401	26069
	per conversation	1190	1090	1290
Turns	All turns	21251	9513	11738
	Instruction Giver	10678	4777	5901
	Instruction Follower	10573	4736	5837
	per conversation	166	149	183

Table 1. Summary corpus statistics

5.5. The role of eye contact

Not surprisingly, there are obvious gross effects on the conversations of the difference between the eye-contact and no-eye-contact conditions. The no-eye-contact conversations contained 22% more turns on average, but only 18% more words, i.e. more turns, but each fewer words per turn. This is presumably because of the increased need for frequent back-channel confirmations in the no-eye-contact condition.

The overall statistics for word tokens and turns are as given in Table 1. The implications of the language differences induced by the presence or absence of eye-contact are clearly significant for a range of different potential speech technology applications. See (Boyle, Anderson & Newlands, in press) for more details.

6. PRELIMINARY RESULTS

6.1. Second Mention

The duration and/or (excerpted) intelligibility of different tokens of a word uttered by the same speaker have been shown to depend on the availability of information outwith the word's acoustic shape which might help listeners to recognize it. In the context of extended discourse, this means word tokens are less intelligible when they refer to Given entities.

On the face of it, the tendency to produce degraded tokens where they are redundant seems wonderfully cooperative, in the Gricean sense of the term: when there is previous relevant material, intelligibility is reduced. The less intelligible repeated tokens are in fact helpful to listeners, for they make better prompts to earlier discourse material, either because they signal listeners to associate the word's meaning with some entity already established in a discourse model (Fowler and Housum, 1987) or because such stored information must be called into play for successful on-line word recognition (Bard et al., 1991).

The difficulty is that degraded tokens are not restricted to contexts in which the listener can recover the conditioning information. Using the Map Task corpus, we have begun to investigate how far speakers' adjustment of intelligibility is egocentrically rather than cooperatively based, that is, how far the speaker's own relevant knowledge provides his/her model for what the listener knows.

We have found the expected loss of intelligibility for excerpted second mentions as against both first mentions and citation forms. Interestingly, we found that the co-referential repetition effect found for monologue holds in dialogue: it doesn't matter who utters the word first. When it comes to the second mention of an entity either speaker may reduce intelligibility. This suggests that dialogue participants maintain a common record of textually evoked given entities.

It would also appear that once an entity is textually evoked there is no further effect of visual information. That is, it doesn't matter whether the listener or speaker can see the object they're referring to.

Also relevant is a significant intelligibility loss we found in mentions which are only 'second' for the speaker, because the relevant feature was first mentioned not in the current conversation, but in a previous conversation *with a different listener*.

Thus on the basis of our investigations to date it would appear, somewhat surprisingly, that speakers reduce articulatory effort on a purely egocentric basis, without regard to listeners' ability to share the contextual conditioning this implies.

6.2. Efficacy of New Item Introduction

The Map Task corpus presents an excellent opportunity for examining how speakers introduce new items into a discourse. Moreover, because we can measure to overall communicative effectiveness of a conversation by reference to the accuracy of the resulting map, we can go further and attempt to assess the value of particular item introduction strategies.

Definite versus indefinite article is almost certainly too simplistic a starting point for investigating this issue. This is born out by a tabulation of new item introduction over half the corpus, as shown in Table 2. 'Question' introductions are those in which the speaker queries the existence of the referent, e.g. "Right you got an extinct volcano?".

	Non-Question Introductions			Question Introductions		
Articles:	None	Definite	Indefinite	None	Definite	Indefinite
IG. Introductions	0.54	2.75	0.35	1.5	1.48	3.29
IF. Introductions	0.67	0.87	1.2	0.32	0.34	0.46

Table 2. Mean number of introductions per dialogue by form of introductions used by instruction givers (IG) and instruction followers (IF).

Overall definites and indefinites appeared with equal frequency.

If we look at listener's responses to the introduction of items they don't have on their map, we see a significant correlation of informative responses ("I haven't got an extinct volcano") with question introductions, but not with indefinite article usage as such. Also, using the accuracy of the route drawn as a measure of communicative efficacy, we found a significant correlation between use of question introductions by the IG and route accuracy. There is an independent correlation between informative IF responses and accuracy. See (Anderson & Boyle, in press) for more details.

7. CONCLUSION

The HCRC Map Task corpus has been designed to allow investigation of a range of issues relevant to both psychological models of human language production and comprehension and to speech technology, especially as the focus on effort switches to more natural, unconstrained speech. Preliminary results of studies in several areas provide encouraging evidence that the corpus will indeed yield valuable insights.

REFERENCES

1. Anderson, A. H., M. Bader, E. G. Bard, E. H. Boyle, G. M. Doherty, S. C. Garrod, S. D. Isard, J. C. Kowtko, J. M. McAllister, J. Miller, C. F. Sotillo, H. S. Thompson and R. Weinert. "The HCRC Map Task Corpus", *Language and Speech* 34(4), 1991, 351–366.
2. Anderson, A. H. and E. Boyle. "Forms of introduction in dialogue, their discourse contexts and communicative consequences", *Language and Cognitive Processes*, in press.
3. Bard, E.G., L. Cooper, J. Kowtko and C. Brew. "Psycholinguistic studies on the incremental recognition of speech: A revised and extended introduction to the messy and the sticky", University of Edinburgh: Centre for Cognitive Science DYANA Report R1.3.B, 1991.
4. Boyle, E. H., A. Anderson and A. Newlands. "The effects of visibility on dialogue & performance", *Language and Speech*, in press.
5. Brown, G., A. Anderson, G. Yule and R. Shillcock. *Teaching Talk,* Cambridge, U.K.: Cambridge University Press, 1983.
6. Fowler, C. and J. Housum. "Talkers' signalling of 'new' and 'old' words in speech and listeners' perception and use of the distinction", *Journal of Memory and Language*, 26, 1987, 489–505.
7. Human Communication Research Centre. *HCRC Map Task Corpus*, Edinburgh, U.K.: HCRC, 1993.
8. Kowtko, J., S. Isard and G. Doherty. *Conversational games within dialogue*, University of Edinburgh: HCRC Technical Report RP-31, 1992.
9. Miller, J. "Spoken and written language: language acquisition and literacy". in R. Scholes, ed., *Linguistics and Literacy*, Lawrence Erlbaum, 1993.
10. Thompson, H.S. and M. Bader. *Publishing a Spoken and Written Corpus on CD-ROM: The HCRC Map Task Experience.*, University of Edinburgh: HCRC Technical Report, 1993.

A PORTABLE APPROACH TO LAST RESORT PARSING AND INTERPRETATION

Marcia C. Linebarger, Lewis M. Norton, Deborah A. Dahl

Paramax Systems Corporation
(a Unisys Company)
70 East Swedesford Road
Paoli, PA 19301

ABSTRACT

This paper describes an approach to robust processing which is domain-independent in its design, yet which can easily take advantage of domain-specific information. Robust processing is well-integrated into standard processing in this approach, requiring essentially only a single new BNF rule in the grammar. We describe the results of implementing this approach in two different domains.

1. Introduction

For best performance, natural language processing systems must be able to extract as much information as possible from their inputs, even inputs which cannot be fully processed. In order to do this, systems must be equipped with robust processing mechanisms. In addition, cases also occur in which the system has the ability to process an input, given sufficient time, but it is not desirable to allow unlimited amounts of processing time. In this paper we describe an approach to robust processing which is domain-independent in its general architecture, but which can be easily customized to particular domains by simply listing key words and/or key concepts. The approach uses the extensive grammar already available to the system for standard processing but augments it with a special BNF rule, called "backup", which is able to prune the wordstream while it searches for key concepts. Backup can be triggered either by a failure of normal parsing or by timing out. This approach has been implemented in two distinct domains. In one of these domains, when sufficient time is allotted to attain maximal performance, backup results in an 18% improvement in score. We describe the general approach, discuss how differences in the data in each domain lead to slightly different implementations, and discuss our results.

2. Approach

The approach to robust processing which is described in this paper is implemented in the PUNDIT natural language processing system developed at Paramax Systems Corporation [6, 1]. PUNDIT includes a domain-independent, top-down parser [7] which is the primary component involved in robust processing. The key feature of robust processing in PUNDIT is that the parser is allowed to skip over words when it is unable to find a parse using every word. Skipping is an appropriate strategy for the data in the two domains we are working with, because parsing failures tend to be due to extraneous material such as interpolated irrelevant comments and false starts. Another possible strategy, relaxation of constraints as suggested by [19], is less appropriate for the data we have examined, since few parsing failures are due to violation of grammatical constraints. Skipping over words has also been implemented in the robust parsing strategies of Seneff [15] and Strzalkowski [18]; our approach differs from these in that in addition to skipping, it provides a simple way of taking domain-specific knowledge into account in the skipping process. That is, when an analysis is not possible using every word, the system begins searching through the wordstream for keywords (or words denoting key concepts), which are simply listed in a file. The use of keywords permits the system to make use of the domain-specific knowledge that certain words or concepts are important in the domain. In fact, in a mature domain, the list of keywords and concepts can be automatically generated from the system's semantic interpretation rules.

Because the backup mechanism is implemented by adding a single new BNF rule into the normal grammar, robust processing has been implemented in PUNDIT without losing the advantages of the broad-coverage syntactic grammar already in the system. This is in contrast to approaches like the template matcher discussed in [8] or the frame combiner discussed in [16] which are completely separate mechanisms from the standard linguistic processing components.

In addition to inputs for which the system cannot find a parse using the standard algorithm, there are also cases where a complete analysis would be too costly in terms of time. The system can also invoke backup in these cases, using a variation of the timeout mechanism described in [17]. The timeout mechanism in [17] allocates an absolute amount of time per sentence; in contrast, PUNDIT's timeout allocates time as a function of the number of words in the input sentence so as not to penalize relatively longer sentences.

Previous approaches to robust processing have typically either focused solely on data from one domain [8, 16, 15, 4] or have implemented a domain-independent approach [17]. Both of these alternatives have disadvantages. Approaches which have been tested on only a single domain cannot be guaranteed to be extensible to other domains. Entirely new approaches may be required when the system is ported to another domain. On the other hand, the performance of domain-independent approaches may suffer in domain-specific applications because they are not able to use domain-specific knowledge to constrain the processing. Our approach differs from previous approaches in that, while the basic architecture is domain-independent, the approach also allows domain-specific knowledge to assist in the processing. We demonstrate the general applicability of the architecture by describing implementations in two distinct domains. Although the basic mechanism is the same in each domain, we also discuss differences in the implementation which follow from basic differences in the kind of data which must be processed.

3. Domains

We now briefly describe our two application domains, with emphasis on those properties of the domains which affect the details of implementing backup "last resort" processing.

3.1. Air Traffic Control

Air traffic control (ATC) involves oral communication, as controllers interact with pilots via radio, issuing commands which govern the movements of planes both on the ground and in the air [3]. Since the controllers are already speaking into microphones, their half of this dialogue is easy to capture in a high-quality signal. If this input can be understood, possible applications will range from intelligent indexing for archival purposes to real-time monitoring for safety and planning purposes.

Utterances in the ATC domain tend to be short sequences of relatively independent commands. The range of possible commands is well-bounded, and controllers are trained to avoid expressing these commands in different phrasings. As a consequence, it is possible to separate utterances into their constituent commands with high reliability, and similarly, to resume processing at the next command if processing of the present command fails for any reason. Also, some commands may be irrelevant for a given application. For example, wind advisories could be ignored by an application only concerned with ground operations.

A sample well-formed utterance follows:

Delta seven forty six turn right heading two seven zero cleared to land runway two nine left.

3.2. Air Travel Information System

Our second domain is called ATIS (Air Travel Information System) [12, 13, 11]. This is basically a database query application. The input utterances are retrieval requests addressed to a database of information about flight schedules, fares, etc. This application has been set up by DARPA as an infrastructure for research in spoken language understanding.

DARPA has arranged for the collection of data in this domain [5]. This data is spontaneous speech from naive users, who have no idea what phrasings will work and which will not. Thus, they use an extremely wide set of variations for each request, so that the system is expected to process inputs ranging from a vanilla *Show me flights from Boston to Denver* to *I am going to have to go to Denver; I will be leaving from Boston*, etc. Disfluencies are more prevalent in this domain, since the speakers are not trained users. Another feature distinguishing ATIS from ATC is that ATIS utterances, no matter how discursive they appear, normally constitute a single request. Therefore parse fragments created by the backup mechanism seldom correspond to individual commands as they do in the ATC domain; instead, a single request may give rise to several fragments which must be integrated during semantic and pragmatic processing[1].

In both domains, since the input is spoken, there is the additional possibility of errors introduced by the speech recognition component. While the techniques discussed in this paper have obvious applicability to recovery from such errors, in what follows we will assume perfection on the part of the recognizer, and that all errors and disfluencies originate with the speaker. Note, however, that current recognizers do not include punctuation in their output, either within sentences or at the end of them. We therefore have included no punctuation in our data.

4. Implementation

Grammars used with PUNDIT have at the top level a BNF rule for the "center" node. This rule is always a disjunction of possibilities; for example, in a toy grammar, the center rule might expand to either assertion or question. In typical application domains this rule is more complex, including perhaps compounds and/or fragments. One important fact about the disjuncts for the present discussion is that they are required to consume the whole

[1] A detailed discussion of PUNDIT's general approach to fragments can be found in [9].

input word string in order to succeed.

In any grammar, our approach to robust parsing is implemented by adding one additional disjunct at the end of the center rule. We call this disjunct "backup". The BNF rule for backup has the following form:

- If positioned at a keyword, reset the time allotment if necessary, then retry the other center options, *relaxing the requirement to consume the entire word string*. If a parse is found, call the center rule on the remainder of the word string.
- If not positioned at a keyword, or if a parse is not found in the previous step, *skip to the next keyword* if any, reset the time allotment if necessary, and call the center rule on the word string starting with the keyword. If no keyword is found, fail.

The backup rule is entered either if normal parsing fails (i.e., none of the other disjuncts of the center rule produce a parse consuming the whole word string), or if timeout occurs. Users specify an amount of time in the form of a number (possibly fractional) of seconds per word, so that longer inputs are given more time. Once time has expired, no rule will execute except the backup rule, which will reallot time based on the length of the remaining word string, and then proceed as described above.

The opportunity for introducing domain knowledge to influence the behavior of the backup rule comes in the specification of the keywords. To discuss what we have done in the two domains we experimented with, we first need to introduce the PUNDIT *knowledge base*. This is simply a mapping of word tokens to a hierarchical set of concepts [10]. Synonyms usually denote the same concept. The "is-a" relation is defined over the hierarchy, so that a concorde is-a jet is-a plane, a propeller_plane also is-a plane, etc.

The keywords used by backup can be specified as word tokens or as concepts. In the latter case, the concept is taken to refer to any word token that maps to the concept or any descendant of the concept in the knowledge base. Keywords may also be specified by syntactic category, e.g., determiners or tensed verbs may function as keywords.

4.1. Air Traffic Control

In the ATC domain, we designated only word tokens as keywords. Furthermore, the list of keywords was chosen manually with great care, and is not very extensive. The choices were dictated by the semantics of the possible commands which controllers may issue, and the normal phraseology (defined by the FAA) for expressing those commands. The intent, which we were able to achieve to a large degree, was to have skipping to the next keyword be equivalent to skipping to the start of the next command. Most of the keywords are verbs, corresponding to the imperative form most often used to express commands.

4.2. Air Travel Information System

In contrast, the list of keywords for the ATIS domain is much larger, and consists mostly of concepts, which in effect makes it even larger in terms of words. The basic idea is not to skip over any word which might be useful. Thus we included prepositions, wh-introducers, and such word tokens, plus all the concepts known to the PUNDIT semantic interpreter for that domain. This list of concepts was obtained mechanically from the files driving the interpreter, followed by the removal of concepts which were descendants of other concepts in the list, for these would be redundant for the purposes of the backup procedure. As a consequence, the only words skipped are meaningless (to the semantic interpreter), including unknown words.

An ATIS utterance normally constitutes a single database retrieval request. Therefore an additional step in this domain is to integrate the parse fragments obtained by the robust parsing procedure. We delegate this responsibility to the semantic and pragmatic interpreter [14, 2]. For those fragments which are complete sentences, no extensions are necessary. The interpreter merely treats them as distinct sentences coming in sequentially in the context of the ongoing dialogue.

For true fragments we did need to add some new capability. We assume that the overall content of the utterance is either a request for some flights or some fares. For noun phrase fragments, either the head is a flight or a fare, or it is not. If it is, our normal reference resolution capabilities are sufficient to resolve the flight or fare with any other flight or fare in the context[2]. If the head is not a flight or fare, flight and fare entities are explicitly generated into the context space maintained by the semantic interpreter, and the fragment is interpreted as a modifier of either the flight or the fare. Then normal reference resolution takes over. For example, the fragment *afternoon* ends up with the same semantic representation as does *afternoon flight*, and the system proceeds as before.

[2]This is because dialogues often proceed like the following: *Show me flights from Boston to Denver.* [answer] *Show me just afternoon flights.* So in effect, *afternoon flights* is treated as *show afternoon flights* [2, 13, 11].

Prepositional phrase fragments are treated in a manner completely analogous to noun phrase fragments whose heads are not flights or fares. For example, *in the afternoon* becomes *flight in the afternoon*, and the system proceeds as before.

The data for this domain has not warranted treatment of any other fragment types.

5. Results

5.1. Air Traffic Control

We performed experiments on a set of 233 utterances in the ATC domain, incorporating utterances from two different controllers. One was guiding planes which had just landed; the other was guiding planes as they taxied in preparation for takeoff.

Substantial benefits are gained from using backup, or "last-resort" processing, after normal parsing fails or a timeout occurs. Figure 1 shows that application accuracy is improved by the use of such processing, at two different settings of the timeout parameter. In fact, performance with backup at the lower timeout setting clearly exceeds performance without backup at the higher timeout setting. The improvement comes at a cost of increased cpu time, as can be seen in Figure 2; the increase is less for the higher value of the timeout parameter, even though the benefit to accuracy remains high.

Figure 1: Effect of backup on score

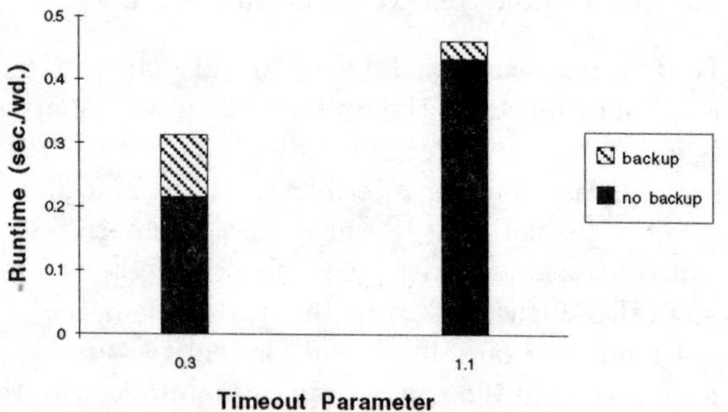

Figure 2: Effect of backup on runtime

We investigated the effects of varying the timeout parameter when backup processing is in use. Recall that this parameter is the amount of cpu time allotted for each word of an utterance before timeout. Backup processing resets this allotment, adjusted for the current position in the utterance, so that the amount of time spent processing an utterance can increase by a factor of two to four over the initial allotment, depending on the number of keywords in the utterance.

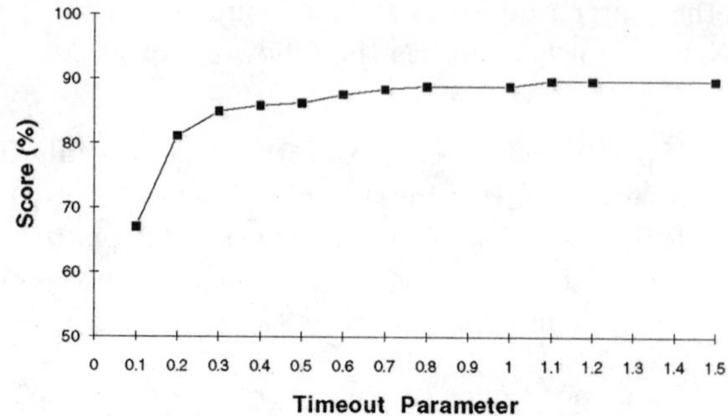

Figure 3: Effect of varying timeout

Figure 3 shows the results of our investigation. A setting of the timeout parameter below 0.3 is clearly undesirable. A setting of 0.3 enables the system to process correctly all but a handful of the utterances it could handle at a higher setting; that is, the curve changes at this point to a nearly horizontal orientation. At a setting of 1.1, the system achieves maximal performance accuracy. Somewhat surprisingly, if the utterances of each controller are considered separately, these findings remain the same, even though the content and phrasing of the utterances vary noticeably.

The optimal setting of the timeout parameter depends on the relative costs of processing time and application errors. The 0.3 setting might be optimal for archival purposes or high volume processing. The 1.1 setting might be necessary for applications which demand maximal accuracy at any cost.

5.2. Air Travel Information System

As examples of data which our system handles properly, we list some inputs which are successfully processed. All of them were previously unseen test data from the November 1992 ATIS test. None of them would result in a parse from normal parsing. These inputs include false starts, corrections, constructions not covered by our grammar, and breaks in parsing due to unknown words. Our technique contributes for all these phenomena.

I would like to do you have any flights between Philadelphia and Atlanta (false start)

Okay shoot I would have to choose the Delta flight nine seventy seven departing at twelve pm and arriving in San Francisco at two ten pm shoot and *choose* were unknown words, but the system recovers and understands the chosen flight.

Okay American Airlines does it leave Philadelphia for Dallas in the mornings Left dislocation, not in our grammar; the airline is parsed as a fragment separate from the main body of the question, and semantic processing integrates the two parses correctly.

Yes could you please give me a list of all American Airline first class flights to from Philly to Dallas Fort Worth please The correction of the preposition at *to from Philly* is successfully handled by our technique; *to* is dropped, and parse fragments are produced for the rest of the input starting at *from*.

Quantitative Results Because the semantic integration of fragmentary information is still in progress, the robust processing mechanism did not affect our final score on the ATIS evaluation. However, we did look closely at the effect of robust processing on parsing accuracy, in order to answer the following two questions:

- How much does the backup mechanism improve parsing accuracy?
- How often does the backup mechanism do the right thing?

In order to answer the first question, we compared the proportion of usable or potentially usable non-X parses which the system produced with and without backup on the subset of the 1992 ATIS test collected at BBN. Without backup, 77% of the parses were usable; with backup, 88% were usable. Thus, backup resulted in an 11% increase in the number of usable parses.

In order to answer the second question, we looked at the parses produced by backup. We found that 45% of them were usable or potentially usable by semantics. Of the parses that were not usable, we found that most of the time they were unusable because the system did not have information about some semantically important word in the sentence. Because of this missing information, the system ended up ignoring the word, and consequently the parse did not contain this important word. The fact that many of the unusable parses were due to lexical gaps was encouraging, because it means that the backup mechanism will continue to improve in this respect simply as new words are added to the system in the normal course of development.

6. Conclusion and Future Directions

We have described a domain-independent approach to robust processing which can be customized to particular domains through the simple mechanism of building a list of keywords, where keywords may correspond to specific word tokens, syntactic categories, or semantic concepts. The approach was tested in two different domains, ATC and ATIS. Differences in the way that information is conveyed in the two domains necessitated slight differences in the implementations across the two domains; in particular, additional semantic processing was required in the ATIS domain to put together information from the fragmentary outputs of the parser. Future plans include development of keyword selection techniques, both domain-independent and domain-specific; and improvements to the semantic integration process.

References

1. Deborah A. Dahl. PUNDIT – natural language interfaces. In G. Comyn, N.E. Fuchs, and M.J. Ratcliffe, editors, *Logic Programming in action*, Heidelberg, Germany, September 1992. Springer-Verlag.
2. Deborah A. Dahl and Catherine N. Ball. Reference resolution in PUNDIT. In P. Saint-Dizier and S. Szpakowicz, editors, *Logic and logic grammars for language processing*. Ellis Horwood Limited, 1990.
3. Deborah A. Dahl, Lewis M. Norton, and Nghi N. Nguyen. Air traffic control instruction monitoring using spoken language understanding. In *Proceedings of the 36th Air Traffic Control Association Meeting*, Atlantic City, NJ, November 1992.
4. Philip J. Hayes and George V. Mouradian. Flexible parsing. *American Journal of Computational Linguistics*, 7(4):232–242, 1981.
5. Charles T. Hemphill, John J. Godfrey, and George R. Doddington. The ATIS spoken language systems pilot corpus. In *Proceedings of the DARPA Speech and Language Workshop*, Hidden Valley, PA, June 1990.
6. L. Hirschman, M. Palmer, J. Dowding, D. Dahl, M. Linebarger, R. Passonneau, F.-M. Lang, C. Ball, and C. Weir. The PUNDIT natural-language processing system. In *AI Systems in Government Conf.* Computer Society of the IEEE, March 1989.
7. Lynette Hirschman and John Dowding. Restriction grammar: A logic grammar. In P. Saint-Dizier and S. Szpakowicz, editors, *Logic and Logic Grammars for Language Processing*, pages 141–167. Ellis Horwood, 1990.
8. Eric Jackson, Douglas Appelt, John Bear, Robert Moore, and Ann Podlozny. A template matcher for robust NL interpretation. In *Proceedings of the DARPA Speech and Natural Language Workshop*. Morgan Kaufmann, February 1991.
9. Marcia C. Linebarger, Deborah A. Dahl, Lynette Hirschman, and Rebecca J. Passonneau. Sentence fragments regular structures. In *Proceedings of the 26th Annual Meeting of the Association for Computational Linguistics*, Buffalo, NY, June 1988.
10. David L. Matuszek. K-Pack: A programmer's interface to KNET. Technical Memo 61, Unisys Corporation, P.O. Box 517, Paoli, PA 19301, October 1987.
11. Lewis M. Norton, Deborah A. Dahl, and Marcia C. Linebarger. Recent improvements and benchmark results for the Paramax ATIS system. In *Proceedings of the DARPA Speech and Language Workshop*, Harriman, New York, February 1992.

12. Lewis M. Norton, Deborah A. Dahl, Donald P. McKay, Lynette Hirschman, Marcia C. Linebarger, David Magerman, and Catherine N. Ball. Management and evaluation of interactive dialog in the air travel domain. In *Proceedings of the DARPA Speech and Language Workshop*, Hidden Valley, PA, June 1990.

13. Lewis M. Norton, Marcia C. Linebarger, Deborah A. Dahl, and Nghi Nguyen. Augmented role filling capabilities for semantic interpretation of natural language. In *Proceedings of the DARPA Speech and Language Workshop*, Pacific Grove, CA, February 1991.

14. Martha Palmer. *Semantic Processing for Finite Domains.* Cambridge University Press, Cambridge, England, 1990.

15. Stephanie Seneff. A relaxation method for understanding spontaneous utterances. In *Proceedings of the DARPA Speech and Natural Language Workshop.* Morgan Kaufmann, February 1992.

16. David Stallard and Robert Bobrow. Fragment processing in the DELPHI system. In *Proceedings of the Speech and Natural Language Workshop*, San Mateo, California, 1992. Morgan Kaufmann.

17. Tomek Stralkowski. TTP: a fast and robust parser for natural language. Technical report, New York University Department of Computer Science, New York, NY, 1991.

18. Tomek Strzalkowski and Barbara Vauthey. Information retrieval using robust natural language processing. In *Proceedings of the Thirtieth Annual Meeting of the Association for Computational Linguistics*, pages 104–111, 1992.

19. R. M. Weischedel and N. K. Sondheimer. Meta-rules as a basis for processing ill-formed input. *American Journal of Computational Linguistics*, 9(3-4):161–177, 1983.

THE SEMANTIC LINKER – A NEW FRAGMENT COMBINING METHOD

David Stallard and Robert Bobrow

BBN Systems and Technologies, Inc.
70 Fawcett St.
Cambridge, MA 02138

ABSTRACT

This paper presents the Semantic Linker, the fallback component used by the the DELPHI natural language component of the BBN spoken language system HARC. The Semantic Linker is invoked when DELPHI's regular chart-based unification grammar parser is unable to parse an input; it attempts to come up with a semantic interpretation by combining the fragmentary sub-parses left over in the chart using a domain-independent method incorporating general search algorithm driven by empirically determined probabilities and parameter weights. It was used in the DARPA November 92 ATIS evaluation, where it reduced DELPHI's Weighted Error on the NL test by 30% (from 32% to 22%).

1. INTRODUCTION

An important problem for natural language interfaces, as well as for other NL applications such as message processing systems, is coping with input which cannot be handled by the system's grammar. A system which depends on its input being grammatical (or on lying within the coverage of its grammar) simply will not be robust and useful. Some sort of "fallback" component is therefore necessary as a complement to regular parsing.

This paper presents the Semantic Linker, the fallback component used by the the DELPHI natural language component of the BBN spoken language system HARC. The Semantic Linker is invoked when DELPHI's regular chart-based unification grammar parser is unable to parse an input; it attempts to come up with a semantic interpretation by combining the fragmentary sub-parses left over in the chart. It was used in the DARPA November 92 ATIS evaluation, where it reduced DELPHI's Weighted Error on the NL test by 30% (from 32% to 22%).

The Semantic Linker represents an important departure from previous proposals, both our own [1] and others [2], in that it casts fragment combination as a general search problem, rather than as a problem of task model template matching (as in [4]) or as an extension to the existing parsing algorithm (as in [3]). Rather than reconstruct a parse tree, the goal of the search is to combine all the fragments into the most minimal and plausible connected graph, in which the links are not syntactic descendancy, but logical binary relations from the domain, such as "AIRLINE-OF", "ORIG-OF" etc.

States in the search space are partial connections of the fragments: in other words, a set of links. There a two types of "move" to reach a new state from an existing one. One adds a new link between fragments, and the other "hallucinates" an object to bridge two fragments that could not otherwise be linked (corresponding roughly to a notion of ellipsis). A success terminal state is one in which all the fragments have been linked. States have features associated with their constituent links and a system of weights on the features determines a score that is used to guide the search.

The advantages of this formulation are its domain-independence, flexiblity, extensibility, and ability to make use of statistical data. In particular:

- No assumption need be made about constraining task models
- The state space can be searched in any order
- New features are straightforward to add
- Probabilities of relations determined from (parseable) corpora can be used
- Weights on features are potentially derivable by automatic training

In the next sections we turn to a more detailed description of data structures and algorithms. We first give some necesary background on semantic interpretation in the DELPHI system, and on the generation and interpretation of fragmentary sub-parses in it. Next, we show how this framework is used to generate all possible connections between pairs of different fragment objects, and how probabilities and other features are assigned to these connections. We then show how we efficiently search the space of combinations of such links in order to find the minimal and plausible set of connections, and how such link combinations are turned into final interpretations. Finally, we give quantitative results, and discuss our future plans.

2. SEMANTIC INTERPRETATION OF FRAGMENTS

The central notion in DELPHI's syntactic-semantic interface is the "grammatical relation". Grammatical relations include the familar deep-structure complement relations of subject, direct-object etc., as well as other various adjunct relations, such as PP-COMP in the rule below:

```
(NP etc.)
->
HEAD (NP etc.)
PP-COMP (PP etc.)
```

The special grammatical relation "HEAD" denotes the head of the phrase. All other grammatical relations are said to "bind" a constituent they label – their "argument" – to this head to make a new object of the same category as the head. Here, a PP argument is bound to an NP head to make a new NP.

Binding operates on the semantic interpretation and subcategorization information of the head and on the semantic interpretation of the argument to produce the semantic interpretation of the new phrase. In principle, the relationship between inputs and output is completely arbitrary. In practice, however, it most often consists of an addition of a pair (RELATION, ARG-INTERP) to what are termed the "bindings" of the head input. For example, in the case of "flight on Delta" the pair added would be

```
(FLIGHT-AIRLINE-OF, DELTA)
```

In everything that follows, we will make this simplifying assumption.

We can then speak of a translation R → r from a grammatical relation to a semantic relation. For the present example, this translation would be:

```
PP-COMP(ON) -> FLIGHT-AIRLINE-OF
```

where the grammatical relation PP-COMP is further subdivided by the preposition "ON" (and the requirements on semantic type are implicit from the relation FLIGHT-AIRLINE-OF). We will term such a translation a "realization rule" because it shows how the semantic relation FLIGHT-AIRLINE-OF can be syntactically realized in terms of an on-PP. The set of all such realization rules (large in number for a non-trivial domain) is stored in a knowledge base separate from the parser and interpreter code.

The interpretation of any parse tree can now be represented as an isomorphic semantic tree, in which the nodes are the semantic interpretation objects of open-class lexical items and the links are the semantic relations between them. Such a structure can obviously also be represented as a set of n semantic objects and n-1 triples consisting of a semantic relation and head and argument semantic objects. For example, "Delta flies a 747 to Denver" would be represented in graph form as:

```
  /-------AIRCRAFT-OF -> 747
FLY---- AIRLINE-OF -> DELTA
  \-----DEST-OF -> DENVER:TO
```

where a PP such "to Denver" is represented as its NP object tagged by the preposition.

When a complete parse of an utterance cannot be performed, we are left with a set of fragmentary analyses in the chart which correspond to constituent analyses of portions of the input string. The Fragment Generator (essentially the same as was reported on in [1]) extracts the most probable fragment sub-parses associated with the longest sub-strings of the input, using probabilities associated with the producing grammar rules (as in [5].

The semantic interpretations of the parse-fragments are treated in the same way as those of a complete parse: as a set of objects and triples. As a simple example, suppose we have the three fragments "to Boston", "Denver" and "Delta flights on Monday". Then the three corresponding sub-graphs are:

```
BOSTON:TO

DENVER

FLIGHTS1------AIRLINE-OF ->  DELTA
    \--------- DAY-OF-WK -> MONDAY:ON
```

The problem of connecting the N fragments is then reduced to finding a set of relation-links which will connect a pair of objects in N-1 different fragments.

3. COMPUTING THE LINKS AND THEIR PROBABILITIES

The Semantic Linker first computes the link database, which is the set of all possible links between all pairs of objects in all pairs of different fragments. These links are computed using the same set of realization rules that drive the parser and semantic interpreter, and depend on the semantic types of the two objects and on the preposition tag (if any) of the second object. For the set of fragments in our example the link database is:

```
1a.   FLIGHTS1--- DEST-OF -> BOSTON:TO
1b.   FLIGHTS1--- ORIG-OF -> BOSTON:TO

2a.   FLIGHTS1--- DEST-OF -> DENVER
2b.   FLIGHTS1--- ORIG-OF -> DENVER

3a.   DENVER--- NEARBY-TO -> BOSTON:TO
```

where the links are grouped together in a ordered list according to the fragment-pairs they connect. Since there are three fragments there are three pairs.

Links have a set of features which are established when they are computed. The most important is the relational probability of the link, or:

```
P(r,C1,C2)
```

where r is the semantic relation of the link and C1 and C2 are semantic classes of the two argument positions, where C2 may be tagged by a preposition. This is the probability that a pair of objects of type C1 and C2 are linked by by the relation r in an interpretation (as opposed to by some different relation or by no relation at all).

A corpus of interpretations generated by hand could be used to determine these probabilities, but in our work we have chosen to work with a set of sentences that can be correctly parsed by the regular DELPHI parser. Since the semantic interpretations of these parses are just sets of triples the probabilities can be determined by counting. Approximately 3000 interpretations are currently used for our work in ATIS.

From this corpus, we can determine that the link 1a has a high (.89) probability of connecting a FLIGHT and CITY:TO object when these are present, whereas the link 3a has a near zero probability, since the relation NEARBY-CITY-OF occurs very infrequently between two cities.

We have found it convenient to use the log of these probabilities, scaled up and rounded to the lowest negative integer, as the actual value of the link probability feature. Additionally, maximum and minimum values of this number are imposed, so that even a highly likely link has a small negative score (-1), and a highly unlikely link has a finitely negative one (-70).

Links can have other features depending on assumptions made in computing them. For example, a link can be computed by ignoring the prepositional tag of the second object, in which case the link is given the feature "IGNORES-PREP". An example would be 1b above, which ignores the preposition "to". A link can also be computed by assuming a prepositional tag that is not present, giving the link the feature "ASSUMES-PREP", as in 3a, where the preposition "near" is assumed. As we shall see in the next section, these features are also assigned negative integers as penalties, balancing out any higher relational probability the link may have gained from the assumptions made by it.

4. SEARCHING THE SPACE OF COMBINATIONS

The problem of finding a connection between the N fragments is simply the problem of picking at most one link from each of the link-groups in the link database, subject to the constraints that all N fragments must be linked and that no links can be redundant.

We can formalize these constraints as follows. Let LINKED be defined as holding between two fragments if there is a link between them (in either direction), and let TC(LINKED) be the transitive closure of this relation. Then the first constraint is equivalent to the requirement that TC(LINKED) hold between all different fragments F1 and F2.

To formalize the non-redundancy constraint, let LINKED-L mean "linked except by link L". Then the non-redundancy constraint holds if there is no link L such that TC(LINKED) is the same as TC(LINKED-L).

The problem as cast implies a search space in which each state is simply the set of links chosen so far, and a transition between states is the addition of a new link. We will find it convenient, however, to include all of the following components in a state:

1. suffix of the link-database list
2. chosen-links
3. combinational features
4. state score
5. fragments-linked

The suffix of the link-database list consists of just the link-groups still available to be chosen. The combinational features are those arising from the combination of particular links, rather than from individual links themselves. The state score is the judgement of how plausible the state is, based on its features and those of its links. We want to find the most plausible success state, where a success state is one which satisfies the constraints above, as recorded on the fragments-linked slot.

Pre-success states reside on the state queue. The state queue initially consists of just the single state START. START has a pointer to the complete link-group list, an empty set of combinational features and links chosen and a score of zero. Search proceeds by selecting a state from the queue, and calling the function EXPAND-STATE on it to produce zero or more new states, adding these to the state queue and repeating until suitable success states are found or the queue becomes empty. Although this formulation allows the state space to be searched in any order, our implementation normally uses a best-first order choice. This simply means that at selection cycle, the best pre-success states are chosen for expansion.

The function EXPAND-STATE works by taking the first link-group from the link-group list suffix whose fragments are not already indirectly connected by the state and generating a new state a new state for every link L in the link-group. The links-chosen of these new states are the links-chosen of the parent state plus L, and the link-group suffix is the remainder of the parent's link-group suffix. EXPAND-STATE also generates a single new state whose link-group list suffix is the remainder but whose links-chosen are just those of the parent. This state represents the choice not to directly connect the two fragments of the link-group, and is given the feature "SKIP".

In our example, the first call to EXPAND-STATE would generate three new states from START: state S1 having the set {1a} as chosen-links, a state S2 having the set {1b} as its chosen-links and a state S3 having the empty set {} as its chosen-links, and the feature-list {SKIP}.

The score of a state is determined by summing the weighted values of its features and the features, including the log-probabilities, of its chosen links. Since the weights and log-probabilities are always negative numbers, the score of a state always decreases monotonically from the score of its parent, even in the case of a SKIP state.

At this point in our example, the state S1 has the best score, since its probability score is good (-2) and it has no "blemish" features, unlike the state S2, whose link 1b has the IGNORES-PREP feature. The SKIP state S3 is also not as good as S1, because the weight assigned to SKIP (-7) is selected so as to only be better than a link whose probability is lower than .50.

Thus, the state S1 is selected for expansion, resulting in the states S1-1, S1-2 and S1-3. The feature "CLASH", which results when a link with single-valued R (R a b) is combined with a link (R a b'), is assigned to S1-1, because it assigns the link 2a on top of 1a. The state S1-2 assigns the link 2b, which does not involve a clash. Both S1-1 and S1-2 are sucess states, and are therefore not expanded further.

Search then returns to the SKIP state S3. Its children all have lower scores than the success state S1-2, however, and given the guarantee that score decreases monotonically, any eventual success states resulting from them can never be as good as S1-2. They are therefore pruned from the search. The same happens with the descendants of other expansion candidates. The queue then becomes empty, and the best success state S1-2 is chosen as the result of fragment combination.

4.1. Hallucination

Suppose that instead of the example we have an utterance that does not include the word "flights":

Boston to Denver on Monday Delta

This utterance generates the fragments "Boston", "to Denver", "on Monday" and "Delta". Clearly, no complete set of links can be generated which would fully connect this set, without an object of semantic class FLIGHT or FARE to act as a "hub" between them.

To handle these situations, the Semantic Linker has a second type of state transition in which it is able to "hallucinate" an object of one of a pre-determined set of clases, and add link-groups between that hallucinated object and the fragment structures already present. In the ATIS domain, only objects of the classes FLIGHT, FARE, and GROUND-TRANSPORTATION may be hallucinated.

The hallucination operation is implemented by the function EXTEND-STATE. It is invoked when the function EXPAND-STATE returns the empty set (as will happen when input state's link-group list is empty) and returns states with the new link-groups added on, one for each of the allowed hallucination classes. These states are assigned a feature noting the hallucination, sub-categorized by the semantic class of the hallucinated object. Different penalty weights are associated with each such sub-categorized feature, based on the differences between probability of occurence of the classes in corpora. In ATIS, FLIGHT hallucinations are penalized least of all, FARE hallucinations more, and GROUND-TRANSPORTATION hallucinations most of all.

A state descended from one extended by hallucination cannot be extended again, and if it runs out of link-groups before connecting all fragments it is declared "dead" and removed from the queue.

4.2. Handling Corrections and Other Features

Several other combinational features influence the actions of the Semantic Linker with respect to such matters as handling speaker corrections and judging appropriate topology for the graph being built.

Speaker corrections are an important type of disfluency:

Tell me the flights to Denver uhh to Boston

This will produce the fragments "Tell me the flights to Denver" and "to Boston". Since a flight can have only one DEST-OF the fragment "to Boston" can not be connected as is. One strategy might be to ignore the "to" preposition and attempt to link "Boston" as an ORIG-OF with the IGNORE-PREP feature.

This clearly would not produce the correct interpretation, however. The Linker provides an alternative when the clashing value is to the right of the existing value in the string. In this case, the link receives the combinational feature REPLACEMENT, which is not penalized strongly. If the relational probability of the DEST-OF link is good, it will defeat its IGNORE-PREP rival, as it should.

Related to correction is the operation of *merging*, in which two nodes of a common semantic type are merged into one, and the appropriate adjustments made in the link-database and links-chosen for the state. This is appropriate for certain semantic classes where it is unlikely that separate descriptions (unless they are combined in a conjunction) will appear in an interpretation for the utterance:

Show me flights to Boston flights to Boston at 3 pm

Another feature influences the topology of the graph the Linker constructs. Nothing in the algorithm so far requires that graph structure of connections ultimately produced remain a tree, even though the input fragment interpretations themselves are trees. It is perfectly possible, in other words, for there to be two links (R a b) and (R' a' b) in which the same node is shared by two different parents.

Since we are not trying to produce a syntactic structure, but a semantic one in which the direction of relations is often irrelevant, we do not forbid this. It is discouraged, however, since it sometimes indicates an inappropriate interpretation. The combinational feature MULTI-ROLE is assigned to a state with such a combination of links, and is penalized.

Finally, we point out that the log-probability perspective is useful for assigning penalties to features. If one has a link L1 that has a high relational probability but also has a penalty feature, and another link L2 with a lower relational probability but which does not have the penalty, one can decide how far apart in probability they would have to be for the two alternatives to balance – that is, to be equally plausible. The difference in log-probabilities is the appropriate value of the penalty feature.

5. AFTER COMBINATION

After the combination phase is complete, we have zero or more success states from which to generate the utterance interpretation. If there are zero success states, an interpretation may still be generated through the mechanisms of "scavenging" and "back-off".

The Linker will find no success states either because it has searched the state-space exhaustively and not found one, or because pre-set bounds on the size of the space have been exceeded, or because the scores of all extensible frontier states have fallen below a pre-established pruning score for plausibility. In this case, the state-space which has been built up by the previous search is treated as an ordinary tree which the Linker scans recursively to find the optimum partial connection set, both in terms of fragment-percentage covered and in state score. This technique is termed "scavenging".

In some instances there may not even be partial connection states in the space. In this case, the system looks for the longest fragment to "back off" to as the interpretation.

In formal evaluation of the DELPHI system conducted under DARPA auspices[6], both scavenging and back-off were aborted in cases where there were obviously important fragments that could not be included in interpretation. This was done because of the signifigant penalty attached to a wrong answer in this evaluation.

If there is more than one success state, the Linker picks the the subset of them with the highest score. If there are more than a certain pre-set number of these (currently 2), the Linker concludes that it none of them are likely to be valid and aborts processing.

Once a suitable set of objects and triples has been produced, whether through combination, scavenging or back-off, the Linker must still decide which of the objects are to be displayed – the "topic" of the utterance. The topic-choice module for the Semantic Linker is fairly similar to the topic-choice module of the Frame Combiner reported on in [1], and so we do not go into much detail on it here. Basically, there are a number of heuristics, including whether the determiner of a nominal object is WH, whether the sort of the the nominal is a "priority" domain (in ATIS, GROUND-TRANSPORTATION is such a domain), and whether the nominal occurs only has the second argument of the triples in which it occurs (making it an unconstrained nominal). The important new feature of the Semantic Linker's topic choice module is its ability to make of use of links between a nominal object and a verb like "show" as evidence for topic choice.

6. RESULTS AND DISCUSSION

Results from the November 1992 DARPA evaluation[6] show that the Semantic Linker reduced DELPHI's Weighted Error rate on the NL-only portion of the test by 30% (from 32% to 22%). This was achieved mostly by dramaticaly lowering the No Answer rate (from 21% to 8%).

It should be noted that these results were achieved with an earlier version of the Semantic Linker than that reported here. In particular, this earlier version did not make use of empirically determined probabilities, but rather used a more ad hoc system of heuristically determined weights and features. Nevertheless, these preliminary results give us some confidence in our approach.

Several areas of future work are seen. One is the use of automatic training methods to determine feature weights. A corpus pairing sentences and sets of connecting links could be used in supervised training to adjust initial values of these weights up or down.

Another area, one in which we are already engaged, is using the Semantic Linker in ellipsis processing by treating the preceding utterance as a fragment-structure into which to link the present, elliptical one.

A third area of future work is the use of relational probabilities and search in the generation of fragments themselves. Currently, the fragment generator component is entirely separate from the rest of the Linker, which makes it difficult for combination search to recover from fragment generation. Instead of trying to combine fragments, the Linker could seek to combine the semantic objects internal to them, in a process where inter-object links found by the fragment generator would have a strong but not insurmountable advantages

A last area of future work is to more fully integrate the Semantic Linker into the regular parsing mechanism itself, and to investigate ways in which parsing can be viewed as similar to the linking process.

References

1. Stallard, D. and Bobrow, R.
Fragment Processing in the DELPHI System
Proceedings Speech and Natural Language Workshop February 1992
2. Seneff, Stephanie
A Relaxation Method for Understanding Spontaneous Speech Utterances
Proceedings Speech and Natural Language Workshop
February 1992
3. Linebarger, Marcia C., Norton, Lewis M., and Dahl, Deborah A.
A Portable Approach to Last Resort Parsing and Interpretation
(this volume)
4. Jackson, E., Appelt D., Bear J., Moore, R. and Podlozny, A.
A Template Matcher for Robust NL Interpretation
Proceedings Speech and Natural Language Workshop
February 1991
5. Bobrow, Robert
Statistical Agenda Parsing
Proceedings Speech and Natural Language Workshop
February 1991
6. Pallet, D., Fiscus, J., Fisher, W. and Garofolo, J.
Benchmark Tests for the Spoken Language Program
(this volume)

Gemini: A Natural Language System for Spoken-Language Understanding*

John Dowding, Jean Mark Gawron, Doug Appelt,
John Bear, Lynn Cherny, Robert Moore, and Doug Moran

SRI International
333 Ravenswood Avenue
Menlo Park, CA 94025

1. INTRODUCTION

Gemini is a natural language understanding system developed for spoken language applications. This paper describes the details of the system, and includes relevant measurements of size, efficiency, and performance of each of its sub-components in detail.

The demands on a natural language understanding system used for spoken language differ somewhat from the demands of text processing. For processing spoken language, there is a tension between the system being as robust as necessary, and as constrained as possible. The robust system will attempt to find as sensible an interpretation as possible, even in the presence of performance errors by the speaker, or recognition errors by the speech recognizer. In contrast, in order to provide language constraints to a speech recognizer, a system should be able to detect that a recognized string is not a sentence of English, and disprefer that recognition hypothesis from the speech recognizer. If the coupling is to be tight, with parsing and recognition interleaved, then the parser should be able to enforce as many constraints as possible for partial utterances. The approach taken in Gemini is to tightly constrain language recognition to limit overgeneration, but to extend the language analysis to recognize certain characteristic patterns of spoken utterances (but not generally thought of as part of grammar) and to recognize specific types of performance errors by the speaker.

Processing starts in Gemini when syntactic, semantic, and lexical rules are applied by a bottom-up all-paths *constituent* parser to populate a chart with edges containing syntactic, semantic, and logical form information. Then, a second *utterance* parser is used to apply a second set of syntactic and semantic rules that are required to span the entire utterance. If no semantically-acceptable utterance-spanning edges are found during this phase, a component to recognize and correct certain grammatical disfluencies is applied. When an acceptable interpretation is found, a set of parse preferences are used to choose a single best-interpretation from the chart to be used for subsequent processing. Quantifier scoping rules are applied to this best-interpretation to produce the final logical form, which is then used as input to a query answering system. The following sections will describe each of these components in detail, with the exception of the query answering subsystem, which will not be described in this paper.

Since this paper describes a component by component view of Gemini, we will provide detailed statistics on the size, speed, coverage, and accuracy of the various components. These numbers detail our performance on the subdomain of air-travel planning that is currently being used by the DARPA spoken language understanding community[13]. Gemini was trained on a 5875 utterance dataset from this domain, with another 688 utterances used as a blind test (not explicitly trained on, but run multiple times) to monitor our performance on a dataset that we didn't train on. We will also report here our results on another 756 utterance fair test set, that we ran only once. Table 1 contains a summary of the coverage of the various components on the both the training and fair test sets. More detailed explanations of these numbers are given in the relevant sections.

	Training	Test
Lexicon	99.1%	95.9%
Syntax	94.2%	90.9%
Semantics	87.4%	83.7%
Syntax (Repair Correction)	96.0%	93.1%
Semantics (Repair Correction)	89.1%	86.0%

Table 1: Domain Coverage by Component

2. SYSTEM DESCRIPTION

Gemini maintains a firm separation between the language- and domain-specific portions of the system,

*This research was supported by the Advanced Research Projects Agency under Contract ONR N00014-90-C-0085 with the Office of Naval Research. The views and conclusions contained in this document are those of the authors and should not be interpreted as necessarily representing the official policies, either expressed or implied, of the Advanced Research Projects Agency of the U.S. Government.

and the underlying infrastructure and execution strategies. The Gemini kernel consists of a set of compilers to interpret the high-level languages in which the lexicon and syntactic and semantic grammar rules are written, as well as the parser, semantic interpretation, quantifier scoping, and repair correction mechanisms, as well as all other aspects of Gemini that are not specific to a language or domain. Although this paper describes the lexicon, grammar, and semantics of English, Gemini has also been used in a Japanese spoken language understanding system [10].

2.1. Grammar Formalism

Gemini includes a midsized constituent grammar of English (described in section 2.3), a small utterance grammar for assembling constituents into utterances (described in section 2.7), and a lexicon. All three are written in a variant of the unification formalism used in the Core Language Engine [1].

The basic building block of the grammar formalism is a category with feature-constraints. Here is an example:

```
np:[wh=ynq, case=(nom∨acc),pers_num=(3rd∧sg)]
```

This category can be instantiated by any noun phrase with the value `ynq` for its `wh` feature (which means it must be a wh-bearing noun phrase like *which book*, *who*, or *whose mother*), either `acc` (accusative) or `nom` (nominative) for its case feature, and the conjunctive value `3rd∧sg` (third and singular) for its person-number feature. This formalism is related directly to the Core Language Engine, but more conceptually it is closely related to that of other unification-based grammar formalisms with a context-free skeleton, such as PATR-II [21], Categorial Unification Grammar [23], Generalized Phrase-Structure Grammar [6] and Lexical Functional Grammar [3].

We list some ways in which Gemini differs from other unification formalisms. Since many of the most interesting issues regarding the formalism concern typing, we defer discussing motivation until section 2.5.

1. Gemini uses typed-unification. Each category has a set of features declared for it. Each feature has a declared value-space of possible values (value spaces may be shared by different features). Feature structures in Gemini can be recursive, but only by having categories in their value-space, so typing is also recursive. Typed feature-structures are also used in HPSG [19]. One important difference with the use in Gemini is that Gemini has no type-inheritance.
2. Some approaches do not assume a *syntactic skeleton* of category-introducing rules (for example, Functional Unification Grammar [11]). Some make such rules implicit (for example, the various categorial unification approaches, such as Unification Categorial Grammar [24]).
3. Even when a syntactic skeleton is assumed, some approaches do not distinguish the category of a constituent (`np`, `vp`, etc.) from its other features (for example, `pers_num`, `gapsin`, `gapsout`). Thus for example, in one version of GPSG, categories were simply feature bundles (attribute-value structures) and there was a feature `MAJ` taking values like `N,V,A,P` which determined the major category of constituent.
4. Gemini does not allow rules schematizing over syntactic categories.

2.2. Lexicon

The Gemini lexicon uses the same category notation as the Gemini syntactic rules. Lexical categories are types as well, with sets of features defined for them. The lexical component of Gemini includes the lexicon of base forms, lexical templates, morphological rules, and the lexical type and feature default specifications.

The Gemini lexicon used for the air-travel planning domain contains 1,315 base entries. These expand by morphological rules to 2,019. In the 5875 utterance training set, 52 sentences contained unknown words (0.9%), compared to 31 sentences in the 756 utterance fair test (4.1%).

2.3. Constituent Grammar

A simplified example of a syntactic rule is:

```
syn(whq_ynq_slash_np,
   [s:[sentence_type=whq, form=tnsd,
      gapsin=G, gapsout=G],
   np:[wh=ynq, pers_num=N],
   s:[sentence_type=ynq, form=tnsd,
      gapsin=np:[pers_num=N],gapsout=null]]).
```

This syntax rule (named `whq_ynq_slash_np`) says that a sentence (category `s`) can be built by finding a noun phrase (category `np`) followed by a sentence. It requires that the daughter `np` have the value `ynq` for its `wh` feature and that it have the value `N` (a variable) for its `person-number` feature. It requires that the daughter sentence have a category value for its `gapsin` feature, namely an `np` with a person number value `N`, which is the same as the person number value on the wh-bearing noun phrase. The interpretation of the entire rule is that a gapless sentence with `sentence_type whq` can be built by finding a wh-phrase followed by a sentence with a noun-phrase gap in it that has the same person number as the wh-phrase.

Semantic rules are written in much the same rule format, except that in a semantic rule, each of the constituents mentioned in the phrase-structure skeleton is associated with a logical form. Thus, the semantics for the rule above is:

```
sem(whq_ynq_slash_np,
   [([whq,S], s:[]),
    (Np, np:[]),
    (S, s:[gapsin=np:[gapsem=Np]])]).
```

Here the semantics of the mother **s** is just the semantics of the daughter **s** with the illocutionary force marker **whq** wrapped around it. Also the semantics of the **s** gap's np's **gapsem** has been unified with the semantics of the wh-phrase. Through a succession of unifications this will end up assigning the wh-phrases semantics to the gap position in the argument structure of the **s**. Although each semantic rule must be keyed to a pre-existing syntactic rule, there is no assumption of rule-to-rule uniqueness. Any number of semantic rules maybe written for a single syntactic rule. We discuss some further details of the semantics in section .

The constituent grammar used in Gemini contains 243 syntactic rules, and 315 semantic rules. Syntactic coverage on the 5875 utterance training set was 94.2%, and on the 756 utterance test set was 90.9%.

2.4. Parser

Since Gemini was designed with spoken language interpretation in mind, key aspects of the Gemini parser are motivated by the increased needs for robustness and efficiency that characterize spoken language. Gemini uses essentially a pure bottom-up chart parser, with some limited left-context constraints applied to control creation of categories containing syntactic gaps.

Some key properties of the parser are:

- The parser is all-paths bottom-up, so that all possible edges admissible by the grammar are found.
- The parser uses subsumption checking to reduce the size of the chart. Essentially, an edge is not added to the chart if it is less general than a pre-existing edge, and pre-existing edges are removed from the chart if the new edge is more general.
- The parser is *on-line* [7], essentially meaning that all edges that end at position i are constructed before any that end at position $i+1$. This feature is particularly desirable if the final architecture of the speech-understanding system couples Gemini tightly with the speech recognizer, since it guarantees for any partial recognition input that all possible constituents will be built.

An important feature of the parser is the mechanism used to constrain the construction of categories containing syntactic gaps. In earlier work [17], we showed that approximately 80% of the edges built in an all-paths bottom-up parser contained gaps, and that it is possible to use prediction in a bottom-up parser only to constrain the gap categories, without requiring prediction for non-gapped categories. This limited form of left context constraint greatly reduces the total number of edges built for a very low overhead. In the 5875 utterance training set, the chart for the average sentence contained 313 edges, but only 23 predictions.

2.5. Typing

The main advantage of typed-unification is for grammar development. The type information on features allows the lexicon, grammar, and semantics compilers to provide detailed error analysis regarding the flow of values through the grammar, and warn if features are assigned improper values, or variables of incompatible types are unified. Since the type-analysis is performed statically at compile-time, there is no run-time overhead associated with adding types to the grammar.

Syntactic categories play a special role in the typing-scheme of Gemini. For each syntactic category, Gemini makes a set of declarations stipulating its allowable features and the relevant value spaces. Thus, the distinction between the syntactic category of a constituent and its other features can be cashed out as follows: the syntactic category can be thought of as the feature-structure type. The only other types needed by Gemini are the value-spaces used by features. Thus for example, the type **v** (verb) admits a feature **vform**, whose value-space **vform-types** can be instantiated with values like present participle, finite, and past participle. Since all recursive features are category-valued, these two kinds of types suffice.

2.6. Interleaving Syntactic and Semantic Information

Sortal Constraints Selectional restrictions are imposed in Gemini through the sorts mechanism. Selectional restrictions include both highly domain specific information about predicate-argument and very general predicate restrictions. For example, in our application

	Edges	Time
Syntax Only	197	3.4 sec.
Syntax + Semantics	234	4.47 sec.
Syntax + Semantics + Sorts	313	13.5 sec.

Table 2: Average number of edges built by interleaved processing

the object of the transitive verb *depart* (as in *flights departing Boston*) is restricted to be an airport or a city, obviously a domain-specific requirement. But the same machinery also restricts a determiner like *all* to take two propositions, and an adjective like *further* to take distances as its measure-specifier (as in *thirty miles further*). In fact, sortal constraints are assigned to every atomic predicate and operator appearing in the logical forms constructed by the semantic rules.

Sorts are located in a conceptual hierarchy and are implemented as Prolog terms such that more general sorts subsume more specific sorts [16]. This allows the subsumption checking and packing in the parser to share structure whenever possible. Semantic coverage when applying sortal constraints was 87.4% on the training set, and on the test set was 83.7%.

Interleaving Semantics with Parsing In Gemini syntactic and semantic processing is fully interleaved. Building an edge requires that syntactic constraints be applied, which results in a tree structure, to which semantic rules can be applied, which results in a logical form to which sortal contraints can be applied.

Table 2 contains average edge counts and parse timing statistics[1] statistics for the 5875 utterance training set.

2.7. Utterance Grammar and Utterance Parser

The constituent parser uses the constituent grammar to build all possible categories bottom-up, independent of location within the string. Thus, the constituent parser does not force any constituent to occur either at the beginning of the utterance, or at the end. The utterance parser is a top-down back-tracking parser that uses a different grammar called the utterance grammar to glue the constituents found during constituent parsing together to span the entire utterance.

Many systems [4], [9], [20], [22] have added robustness with a similar post-processing phase. The approach taken in Gemini differs in that the utterance grammar uses the same syntactic and semantic rule formalism used by the constituent grammar. Thus the same kinds of logical forms built during constituent-parsing are the output of utterance-parsing, with the same sortal constraints enforced. For example, an utterance consisting of a sequence of modifier fragments (like *on Tuesday at 3'o'clock on United*) is interpreted as a conjoined property of a flight, because the only sort of thing in the ATIS domain which can be on Tuesday at 3'o'clock on United is a flight.

The utterance grammar is significantly smaller than the constituent grammar, only 37 syntactic rules and 43 semantic rules.

2.8. Repairs

Grammatical disfluencies occur frequently in spontaneous spoken language. We have implemented a component to detect and correct a large sub-class of these disfluencies (called repairs, or self-corrections) where the speaker intends that the meaning of the utterance be gotten by deleting one or more words. Often, the speaker gives clues of their intention by repeating words or adding cue words that signal the repair:

(1) a. How many American airline flights leave Denver on June June tenth.
    b. Can you give me information on all the flights from San Francisco no from Pittsburgh to San Francisco on Monday.

The mechanism used in Gemini to detect and correct repairs is currently applied as a fall-back mechanism if no semantically acceptable interpretation is found for the complete utterance. The mechanism finds sequences of identical or related words, possibly separated by a cue word indicating a repair, and attempts to interpret the string with the first of the sequences deleted. This approach is presented in detail in [2].

The repair correction mechanism helps increase the syntactic and semantic coverage of Gemini (as reported in Table 1), at the cost miscorrecting some sentences that do not contain repairs. In the 5875 utterance training set, there were 178 sentences containing nontrivial repairs[2], of which Gemini found 89 (50%). Of the sentences Gemini corrected, 81 were analyzed correctly (91%), 8 contained repairs, but were corrected wrongly.

[1]Gemini is implemented primarily in Quintus Prolog version 3.1.1. All timing numbers given in this paper were run on a lightly loaded Sun Sparcstation 2 with at least 48MB of memory. Under normal conditions, Gemini runs in under 12MB of memory.

[2]For these results, we ignored repairs consisting of only an isolate fragment word, or sentence-initial filler words like "yes" and "okay".

In the entire training set, Gemini only misidentified 15 sentences (0.25%) as containing repairs when they did not. Similarly, the 756 utterance test set contained 26 repairs, of which Gemini found 11 (42%). Of those 11, 8 were analyzed correctly (77%), and 3 were analysed incorrectly. In the training set, 2 sentences were misidentified as containing repairs (0.26%).

2.9. Parse Preference Mechanism

The parse preference mechanism used in Gemini begins with a simple strategy to disprefer parse trees containing specific "marked" syntax rules. As an example of a dispreferred rule, consider: *Book those three flights to Boston.* This sentence has a parse on which *those three* is a noun phrase with a missing head (consider a continuation of the discourse *Three of our clients have sufficient credit*). After penalizing such dispreferred parses, the preference mechanism applies attachment heuristics based on the work by Pereira [18].

Pereira's paper shows how the heuristics of Minimal Attachment and Right Association [12] can both be implemented using a bottom-up shift-reduce parser.

(2) (a) John sang a song for Mary.
(b) John canceled the room Mary reserved yesterday.

Minimal Attachment selects for the tree with the fewest nodes, so in (2a), the parse which makes *for Mary* a complement of *sings* is preferred. Right Association selects for the tree which incorporates a constituent A into the rightmost possible constituent (where rightmost here means *beginning* the furthest to the right). Thus, in (2b) the parse in which *yesterday* modifies *reserved* is preferred.

The problem with these heuristics is that when they are formulated loosely, as in the previous paragraph, they appear to conflict. In particular, in (2a), Right Association seems to call for the parse which makes *for Mary* a modifier of *song.*

Pereira's goal is to show how a shift-reduce parser can enforce both heuristics without conflict and enforce the desired preferences for examples like (2a) and (2b). He argues that Minimal Attachment and Right Association can be enforced in the desired way by adopting the following heuristics for the oracle to resolve conflicts with:

1. Right Association: In a shift-reduce conflict, prefer shifts to reduces.
2. Minimal Attachment: In a reduce-reduce conflict, prefer longer reduces to shorter reduces.

Since these two principles never apply to the same choice, they never conflict.

In Gemini, Pereira's heuristics are enforced when *extracting* syntactically and semantically well-formed parse-trees from the chart. In this respect, our approach differs from many other approaches to the problem of parse preferences, which make their preference decisions as parsing progresses, pruning subsequent parsing paths [5], [8], [14]. Applying parse preferences requires comparing two subtrees spanning the same portion of the utterance. For purposes of invoking Pereira's heuristics, the derivation of a parse can be represented as the sequence of S's (Shift) and R's (Reduce) needed to construct the parse's unlabeled bracketing. Consider, for example, the choice between two unlabeled bracketings of (2a):

```
(a)  [John [sang [a song ] [for Mary ] ] ]
      S     S    S S   R S  S      RRR
(b)  [John [sang [ [a song ] [for Mary ] ] ] ]
      S     S      S S   R S  S      RRRR
```

There is a shift for each word and a reduce for each right bracket. Comparison of the two parses consists simply of pairing the moves in the shift-reduce derivation from left to right. Any parse making a shift move that corresponds to a reduce move loses by Right Association. Any parse making a reduce move that corresponds to a longer reduce loses by Minimal Attachment. In derivation (b) above the third reduce move builds the constituent *a song for Mary* from two constituents, while the corresponding reduce in (a) builds *sang a song for Mary* from three constituents. Parse (b) thus loses by Minimal Attachment.

Questions about the exact nature of parse preferences (and thus about the empirical adequacy of Pereira's proposal) still remain open, but the mechanism sketched does provide plausible results for a number of examples.

2.10. Scoping

The final logical form produced by Gemini is the result of applying a set of quantifier scoping rules to the best-interpretation chosen by the parse preference mechanism. The semantic rules build *quasi-logical forms*, which contain complete semantic predicate-argument structure, but do not specify quantifier scoping. The scoping algorithm that we use combines syntactic and semantic information with a set of quantifier scoping preference rules to rank the possible scoped logical forms consistent with the quasi-logical form selected by parse preferences. This algorithm is described in detail in [15].

3. CONCLUSION

This paper describes the approach we have taken to resolving the tension between overgeneration and robustness in a spoken language understanding system. Some aspects of Gemini are specifically oriented towards limiting overgeneration, such as the on-line property for the parser, and fully interleaved syntactic and semantic processing. Other components, such as the fragment and run-on processing provided by the utterance grammar, and the correction of recognizable grammatical repairs, increase the robustness of Gemini. We believe a robust system can still recognize and disprefer utterances containing recognition errors.

We have described the current state of the research in the construction of the Gemini system. Research is ongoing to improve the speed and coverage of Gemini, as well as examining deeper integration strategies with speech recognition, and integration of prosodic information into spoken language disambiguation.

References

1. Alshawi, H. (ed) (1992). *The Core Language Engine*, MIT Press, Cambridge.
2. Bear, J., Dowding, J., and Shriberg, E. (1992). "Integrating Multiple Knowledge Sources for the Detection and Correction of Repairs in Human-Computer Dialog", *30th Annual Meeting of the Association for Computational Linguists*, Newark, DE, pp. 56-63.
3. Bresnan, J. (ed) (1982) *The Mental Representation of Grammatical Relations.* MIT Press, Cambridge.
4. Carbonell, J. and P. Hayes, P., (1983). "Recovery Strategies for Parsing Extragrammatical Language," *American Journal of Computational Linguistics*, Vol. 9, Numbers 3-4, pp. 123-146.
5. Frazier, L. and Fodor,J.D. (1978). "The Sausage Machine: A New Two-Stage Parsing Model", *Cognition*, Vol. 6, pp. 291-325.
6. Gazdar, G., Klein, E., Pullum, G., Sag, I. (1982). *Generalized Phrase Structure Grammar.* Harvard University Press, Cambridge.
7. Graham, S., Harrison, M., Ruzzo, W. (1980). "An Improved Context-Free Recognizer", in *ACM Transactions on Programming Languages and Systems*, Vol. 2, No. 3, pp. 415-462.
8. Hobbs,J., Bear, J. (1990). "Two Principles of Parse Preference", in *Proceedings of the 13th International Conference on Computational Linguistics*, Helsinki, Vol. 3, pp. 162-167.
9. Hobbs, J., Appelt, D., Bear, J., Tyson, M., Magerman, D. (1992). "Robust Processing of Real-World Natural-Language Texts", in *Text Based Intelligent Systems*, ed. P. Jacobs, Lawrence Erlbaum Associates, Hillsdale, NJ, pp. 13-33.
10. Kameyama, M., (1992). "The syntax and semantics of the Japanese Language Engine." forthcoming. In *Mazuka, R. and N. Nagai Eds. Japanese Syntactic Processing* Hillsdale, NJ: Lawrence Erlbaum Associates.
11. Kay, M. (1979). "Functional Grammar". In *Proceedings of the 5th Annual Meeting of the Berkeley Linguistics Society.* pp. 142-158.
12. Kimball, J. (1973) "Seven Principles of Surface Structure Parsing in Natural Language," *Cognition*, Vol. 2, No. 1, pp. 15-47.
13. MADCOW (1992). "Multi-site Data Collection for a Spoken Language Corpus," *Proceedings of the DARPA Speech and Natural Language Workshop*, February 23-26, 1992.
14. Marcus, M. (1980). *A Theory of Syntactic Recognition for Natural Language*, MIT Press, Cambridge, Massachusetts.
15. Moran, D. (1988). "Quantifier Scoping in the SRI Core Language Engine", *Proceedings of the 26th Annual Meeting of the Association for Computational Linguistics*, State University of New York at Buffalo, Buffalo, NY, pp. 33-40.
16. Mellish, C. (1988). "Implementing Systemic Classification by Unification". *Computational Linguistics* Vol. 14, pp. 40-51.
17. Moore, R. and J. Dowding (1991). "Efficient Bottom-up Parsing," *Proceedings of the DARPA Speech and Natural Language Workshop*, February 19-22, 1991, pp. 200-203.
18. Pereira, F. (1985). "A New Characterization of Attachment Preferences.", in *Natural Language Parsing*, Ed. by Dowty, D., Karttunen, L., and Zwicky, A., Cambridge University Press, Cambridge, pp. 307-319.
19. Pollard, C. and Sag, I. (in press) *Information-Based Syntax and Semantics, Vol. 2*, CSLI Lecture Notes.
20. Seneff, S. (1992) "A Relaxation Method for Understanding Spontaneous Speech Utterances", in *Proceedings of the Speech and Natural Language Workshop*, Harriman, NY, pp. 299-304.
21. Shieber, S., Uszkoreit, H., Pereira, F., Robinson, J., and Tyson, M. (1983). "The Formalism and Implementation of PATR-II", In Grosz,B. and Stickel,M. (eds) *Research on Interactive Acquisition and Use of Knowledge*, SRI International. pp. 39-79.
22. Stallard, D. and Bobrow, R. (1992) "Fragment Processing in the DELPHI System", in *Proceedings of the Speech and Natural Language Workshop*, Harriman, NY, pp. 305-310.
23. Uszkoreit, H. (1986) "Categorial Unification Grammars". In *Proceedings of the 11th International Conference on Computational Linguistics and the the 24th Annual Meeting of the Association for Computational Linguistics*, Institut fur Kummunikkationsforschung und Phonetik, Bonn University.
24. Zeevat, H., Klein, E., and Calder, J. (1987) "An Introduction to Unification Categorial Grammar". In Haddock, N.,Klein,E., Merrill, G. (eds.) *Edinburgh Working Papers in Cognitive Science*, Volume 1: *Categorial Grammar, Unification Grammar, and Parsing.*

A Bilingual VOYAGER System[1]

J. Glass, D. Goodine, M. Phillips, S. Sakai[2], S. Seneff, and V. Zue[3]

Spoken Language Systems Group
Laboratory for Computer Science
Massachusetts Institute of Technology
Cambridge, Massachusetts 02139

ABSTRACT

This paper describes our initial efforts at porting the VOYAGER spoken language system to Japanese. In the process we have reorganized the structure of the system so that language dependent information is separated from the core engine as much as possible. For example, this information is encoded in tabular or rule-based form for the natural language understanding and generation components. The internal system manager, discourse and dialogue component, and database are all maintained in language transparent form. Once the generation component was ported, data were collected from 40 native speakers of Japanese using a wizard collection paradigm. A portion of these data was used to train the natural language and segment-based speech recognition components. The system obtained an overall understanding accuracy of 52% on the test data, which is similar to our earlier reported results for English [1].

INTRODUCTION

In the fall of 1989, our group first demonstrated VOYAGER, a system that can engage in verbal dialogues with users about a geographical region within Cambridge, Massachusetts [2]. The system can provide users with information about distances, travel times, or directions between objects located within this area (e.g., restaurants, hotels, post offices, subway stops), as well as information such as addresses or telephone numbers of the objects themselves. While VOYAGER is constrained both in its capabilities and domain of knowledge, it contains all the essential components of a spoken-language system, including discourse maintenance and language generation. The VOYAGER application provided us with our first experience with the development of spoken language systems, helped us understand the issues related to this endeavor, and provided a framework for our subsequent system development efforts [3, 4].

Over the past few years, we have become increasingly interested in developing multilingual spoken language systems. There are several ongoing international spoken language *translation* projects whose goal is to enable humans to communicate with each other in their native tongues [5, 6]. Our objective, however, is somewhat different. Specifically, we are interested in developing multilingual human-*computer* interfaces, such that the information stored in the database can be accessed and received in multiple spoken languages. We believe that there is great utility in having such systems, since information is fast becoming globally accessible. Furthermore, we suspect that this type of multilingual system may be easier to develop than speech translation systems, since the system only needs to anticipate the diversity of one side of the conversation, i.e., the human side. During the past year, we have begun to develop a multilingual version of VOYAGER. This paper will describe our work in extending VOYAGER's capability from English to Japanese.

Since VOYAGER was originally designed only for English, a number of changes were necessary to accommodate multiple languages. In the next section, we describe our approach to developing multilingual systems, and the modifications made to the original system. A discussion of the specific implementation of the various components for Japanese will follow. Finally, performance evaluation of the Japanese VOYAGER system will be presented, followed by a brief description of future plans.

SYSTEM DESCRIPTION

Figure 1 shows a block diagram of a prototypical MIT spoken language system. The speech signal is converted to words using our SUMMIT segment-based speech recognition system [7]. Language understanding makes use of TINA, a probabilistic natural language system that interleaves syntactic and semantic information in the parse tree [8]. Data exchange between SUMMIT and TINA is currently achieved via an N-best interface, in which the recognizer produces the top-N sentence hypotheses, and TINA screens them for syntactic and semantic well-formedness within the domain [1]. The parse-tree produced

[1]This research was supported by DARPA under Contract N00014-89-J-1332, monitored through the Office of Naval Research.

[2]Currently a visiting scientist from NEC Corp, Kawasaki, Japan.

[3]The authors are listed in alphabetical order.

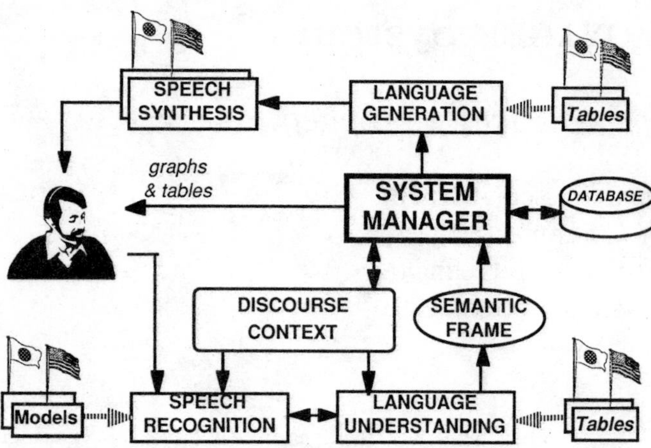

Figure 1: Schematic of prototypical MIT spoken-language system.

by TINA is subsequently converted to a *semantic frame* which is intended to capture the meaning of the input utterance in a language *independent* form [4].

The semantic frame is passed to the system manager which uses it, along with contextual information stored in the discourse component, to access information stored in the database, and provide a response [2]. The VOYAGER application uses an object-oriented database, although we have also accessed data in SQL and other configurations [3]. Responses to the user consist of displays, text, and synthetic speech. The latter two are derived via a language generation component which generates noun-phrases from the internal semantic representation and embeds them into context-dependent messages.

In order to develop a multilingual capability for our spoken language systems, we have adopted the approach that each component in the system be as language transparent as possible. In the VOYAGER system for instance, the system manager, discourse component, and the database are all structured so as to be independent of the input or output language. Where language-dependent information is required we have attempted to isolate it in the form of external tables or rules, as illustrated in Figure 1 for both the language understanding and generation components. As will be described in more detail in the next section, we trained a version of the basic SUMMIT system for both Japanese and English, using data recorded from native speakers for each language. The current user interface is very similar to that of the original VOYAGER system, except that a separate recording icon is used for each language. For text-to-speech synthesis we use a DECtalk system for English, and an NEC text-to-speech system for Japanese.

If we are to attain a multilingual capability within a single system framework, the task of porting to a new language should involve only adapting existing tables or models, without requiring any modification of the individual components. By incrementally porting the system to new languages we hope to slowly generalize the architecture of each component to achieve this result. The following sections provide more detailed descriptions of the work done in the different areas to achieve a bilingual status of VOYAGER.

JAPANESE IMPLEMENTATION

To allow VOYAGER to converse with a user in Japanese, the following steps were taken. We first converted the system so that it could generate responses in Japanese. This enabled us to collect data from native speakers of Japanese in a *wizard* mode whereby an experimentor would *translate* the subjects' spoken input and type the resulting English queries to the system [3, 9]. Once data were available we were able to port the speech recognition and language understanding components. In the process of augmenting the system components to handle Japanese, we made many changes to the system core structure, separating out the language-dependent aspects into external tables and rules.

Data Collection

One of the most time-consuming aspects of the porting process was the acquisition of appropriate user data capturing the many different ways users can ask questions within the VOYAGER domain. We started with translations from available English sentences, but these alone are not nearly adequate for closure on coverage of actual data. Although in theory a grammar developer can use his/her innate knowledge of the language to write appropriate grammar rules, in practice such an approach falls far short of complete coverage of actual user utterances.

For data collection from Japanese subjects we recorded data from 40 native speakers, recruited from the general MIT community. In a manner similar to data collection techniques used for the ATIS domain [3], subjects were asked to solve four problem scenarios. At the end of the session subjects were also allowed to ask random questions of the system. The resulting corpus of 1426 utterances was partitioned into a 34 speaker training set and a 6 speaker test set which was subsequently used to evaluate system components.

Speech Recognition

Major tasks in porting SUMMIT to Japanese include acoustic-phonetic, lexical-phonological and language modeling. In an earlier paper, we described these components and reported on a speaker-dependent evaluation [10]. Will briefly summarize our previous work, and describe all subsequent developments, including improved language modeling and speaker-independent training.

Phonetic Modeling In the current version, we use a context-independent mixture (up to 16) diagonal Gaussian model to represent each label in the lexical network [7]. Starting from seed models, the phonetic models are iteratively trained using a segmental K-means-like procedure whereby the forced alignments of the previous iteration are used to train the current iteration. In the English version, the seed models were trained from the manually-aligned phonetic transcriptions of the TIMIT corpus [11]. Rather than obtaining aligned phonetic transcriptions for a Japanese corpus, we found that we could achieve reasonable initial alignments by seeding our Japanese phonetic models from their phonetically most similar English counterparts. Based on an inspection of the alignments, we confirmed that the resulting Japanese models were converging to the intended labels after a few training iterations.

Phonological Modeling Words in the lexicon must be mapped from the abstract phonemic representation to the possible acoustic realizations, taking into account contextual variations. We have adopted the procedure of modeling some of these variations through a set of phonological transformation rules, some of which are unique to Japanese. One of the typical phonological effects that we must account for in Japanese is the different phonetic realizations of the so-called mora (syllabic) phonemes /Q/ and /N/. For example, the phoneme /Q/ is regarded to occupy one higher-level temporal unit (mora) and is realized as a lengthening of the closure interval before stop consonants. When it is followed by fricatives, it may be realized instead as a lengthening of the following frication. Another major phonological phenomenon is the devoicing of /i/ and /u/, which typically occurs when they are preceded and followed by voiceless consonants.

In the English version of SUMMIT, phonological transformation rules have been used to generate alternative pronunciations based on low-level phonological effects such as flapping, palatalization, and gemination. For the Japanese version, we have been able to use the same framework for the conversion of mora phonemes into different phonetic realizations as well as describing lower-level phonological effects such as gemination and devocalization. A set of approximately 60 phonological rules has been developed to account for the possible acoustic realizations of word sequences. These rules produce a total of 56 distinct acoustic labels in the resulting lexical network.

Language Modeling Language modeling is an important aspect of speech recognition since it can dramatically reduce the difficulty of a task. Many speech recognition systems developed for English, particularly those developed for spontaneous speech, employ n-gram language models which capture local word constraints in an utterance [4, 12]. On the other hand, most speech recognition systems for Japanese speech currently employ only small and rather constrained context-free grammars which may not be well suited to spontaneous speech [13].

Word ID	Pronunciation	Left Category	Right Category
ta	t a	aux-tai	adj-r
tara	t a r a	aux-tara	aux-tara
Q	q	inf-v-soku	v-p-soku
te	t e	aux-te	aux-te
de	d e	p-c-de	p-c-de
desu	d e s u	aux-desu	aux-desu-f
to	t o	p-c-to	p-c-to
to(p-j)	t o	p-j-to	p-j-to

Figure 2: Example lexical entries. Each lexical entry consists of a word ID, a pronunciation, and left and right morphological categories.

Compared to English, the choice of lexical units for Japanese speech recognition is less clear. In particular, Japanese orthography does not have spacing between words, making it difficult to have a common agreement on where word boundaries are in a sentence, especially in the case of certain function word sequences. The choice of units impacts both the compactness of the lexical representation and the effectiveness of local grammatical constraints. If we choose units that are too large, the lexicon will need many redundant entries to capture the linguistic variation. On the other hand, choosing smaller units weakens the constraint available from local language models such as statistical bigrams. We have addressed this to some degree by carefully choosing a set of morphological units along with left and right adjacency categories for these units. For example, lexical entries are fully separated into root and inflectional suffixes, except for words with irregular inflections, thus providing a system flexible enough to cope with various expressions in spontaneous speech.

In order to develop sufficiently general grammatical constraints to be used for continuous speech recognition, we developed a category bigram grammar, where the classes are defined by morphological categories. As illustrated in Figure 2, each lexical entry is given a left and right morphological adjacency category. The probability of the word w_j given word w_i is defined to be

$$\begin{aligned} p(w_j|w_i) &\approx \hat{p}(l(w_j)|w_i)\ \hat{p}(w_j|l(w_j)) \\ &\approx \hat{p}(l(w_j)|r(w_i))\ \hat{p}(w_j|l(w_j)) \\ \hat{p}(w_j|l(w_j)) &= \frac{1}{L(l(w_j))} \end{aligned}$$

where $l(w)$ and $r(w)$ are the categories of word w as viewed from the left and right respectively, and $L(l)$ is the number of distinct words in a category l. By this definition, all words within a category are assumed to be equally probable.

As we and others have done previously [4, 12], the category bigram probability is smoothed by interpolating the bigram estimate with the prior probabilities of each category:

$$\hat{p}(l|r) = \lambda(r)\,\frac{c(r,l)}{c(r)} + (1-\lambda(r))\,\frac{c(l)}{c(all\ word\ tokens)}$$

$$\lambda(r) = \frac{c(r)}{c(r)+K}$$

where $c(x)$ is the count of tokens of category x in the corpus.

Language Understanding

The grammar for the English VOYAGER had been entered in the form of context-free rules plus constraints. A trace mechanism was used to handle movement phenomena, and syntactic and semantic features were unified during parsing to invoke agreement constraints. Japanese was in many respects easier than English – we found that it was unnecessary to mark any syntactic or semantic features, and Japanese, unlike European languages, appears not to make use of constituent movement. The only difficulty with Japanese was that parse trees tend to be left-recursive, which can cause infinite-loop problems in a top-down parser. Noun phrase modifiers are positioned to the left of the modified object, and, furthermore, the preposition indicating the relationship *follows* the modifier. Thus a top-down depth-first parser can keep seeking a noun modifier as the next constituent, at the end of an infinite series of recursive modifiers.

Since the main reason for parsing top-down was the trace mechanism, which Japanese does not use, our solution was to implement a simple bottom-up parser without trace. Rules were entered by hand, based on all of the training material we had collected. Figure 3 shows an example parse for the sentence, *"Sentoraru Eki no chikaku no toshokan wa doko desu ka?"* (*"Where is a library in the vicinity of Central Station?"*). The left-recursion is apparent from the shape of the parse tree, and the potential for infinite recursion is clear from the category labels on the left-most branch, since "A-PLACE" can rewrite as ("A-PLACE" ...).

Meaning Representation

The Japanese parse tree must be converted to a semantic representation in order to access the information in the VOYAGER knowledge base. To do this, we designed the grammar rules for the Japanese grammar such that the resulting parse tree could easily be converted to a semantic frame essentially identical to that of the corresponding English sentence. A table-driven procedure is used to convert the parse tree to the semantic frame for both languages. The functions that carry out the conversion are essentially language independent, with the language-dependent information being stored in separate tables for each language. We have found that the original semantic frame designed for English can accommodate Japanese with only minor modifications.

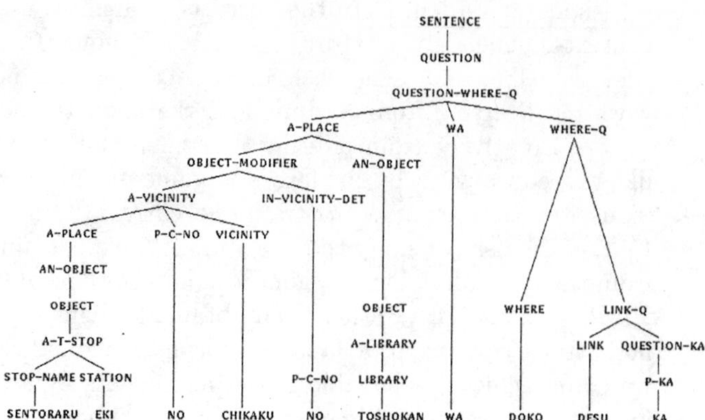

Figure 3: Parse tree for the sentence, *"Sentoraru Eki no chikaku no toshokan wa doko desu ka?"* (*"Where is a library in the vicinity of Central Station?"*).

Semantic Associations for Relevant Parse Nodes:

Parse Category	Semantic Category	Function
question-where-q	locate	set-sentype
a-t-stop	station	noun-phrase
library	public-building	noun-phrase
stop-name	stop-name	proper-name
vicinity	j-near	j-operator

Terminal Translations:

toshokan	library
Sentoraru	central

Table 1: Control tables required to convert from parse tree of Figure 3 to semantic frame of Figure 4. These include mappings from parse tree categories to semantic categories to functional types, as well as translations for critical content words.

Given a well-constructed grammar, it is a relatively simple process to define the conversions from a parse tree to a semantic frame. Semantic encoding is defined at the level of the grammatical category, identified with each node in the parse tree, rather than at the level of an entire rule. All of the semantic encoding instructions are entered in the form of simple association lists. Each semantically active category (preterminal or nonterminal) in the parse tree is associated with a corresponding semantic name, which is often the same as its given name. Each unique semantic name is in turn associated with a functional type, defining what function to call when this node is encountered in the parse tree during the stage of converting the parse to a semantic frame. There are fewer than twenty distinct functional types.

The function that converts a parse tree to a semantic frame visits each node once in a top-down left-to-right fashion, calling the appropriate functions as dictated by the mappings. Table 1 gives the complete set of category correspondences required in order to produce a semantic frame from the parse tree in Figure 3. Notice that most of the nodes in the parse tree are ignored. The semantic categories shown in the table are all identical to those for English except for the special category "j-near" corresponding to the function "j-operator," specialized to handle Japanese postpositional particles. The "j-operator" function renames the generic key "topic" in the semantic frame under construction to the specific semantic relationship defined by the particular operator, in our case, "near." In addition to these mappings, a translation table must also be provided for those words that carry semantic information. Only two words in this sentence need to be provided, as shown in the table.

Ultimately, upon complete analysis of a parse tree, a nested semantic frame is produced – a structure with a name, a type, and a set of [key–value] pairs, where the value could be a string, a symbol, a list of values, a number, or another semantic frame. The semantic frame for our example sentence is shown in Figure 4. Entries in the frame are order-independent, and the same semantic frame is produced from a large pool of questions with different phrasings but equivalent meanings, such as "*What is the distance between MIT and Harvard,*" and "*How far is it from MIT to Harvard.*" Likewise, Japanese versions of this question produce a semantic frame that is essentially identical to the one produced for English.

We had anticipated that the very different order of constituents between Japanese and English might make it hard to produce an equivalent semantic frame from a Japanese sentence to that produced by an English sentence with the same meaning. This did not turn out to be the case. Except for the additional special functions to handle post-positional particles, along with a few other minor adaptations, we were able to use the same functional procedures for converting Japanese parse trees to semantic frames as those used for English. By carefully choosing grammar rules with correspondences to their English equivalents, we were able to exploit the same protocol for producing a semantic frame, thus feeding into the main system with a common interlingual representation. We feel that the success of this approach is largely attributable to the fact that we have intentionally designed our semantic interpretation procedure to operate at the level of independent parse tree nodes, rather than to be explicitly associated with grammar rules or with complex patterns found in the parse tree.

System Manager & Discourse Component

The system manager and discourse components attempt to process an input semantic frame in the context of a discourse and provide an appropriate response to the user [2]. Normally this will involve accessing the database for the set of objects satisfying the input constraints, although in the case where a query is ambiguous, some

```
(LOCATE CLAUSE
      TOPIC: [library] REFERENCE
            REFTYPE: PUBLIC-BUILDING
            PREDICATE: NEAR  PREDICATE
                      TOPIC: [central] REFERENCE
                            REFTYPE: STATION)
```

Figure 4: Semantic frame produced by parse tree of Figure 3 using mappings defined in Table 1.

sort of clarification might be appropriate. In the example shown in Figures 3 and 4 for instance, the result would be the set of libraries having the property that they are near a station named "Central". These components are structured so that they are language independent (i.e., the resulting set would be identical no matter what the input language was). The net effect is that the input and output languages are completely isolated from each other so that a user could speak in one language and have the system respond in another. Additionally, since contextual information is stored in a language independent form, linguistic references to objects in focus can be generated based on the output language of the current query. This means that a user can carry on a dialogue in mixed languages, with the system producing the appropriate responses to each query.

Language Generation

Once the system manager has determined an appropriate response for the user it will display the result on the map, and use the language generation component to produce a verbal answer. The language generation component has the ability to generate noun phrases describing object sets produced by the system manager. The noun phrase can be singular or plural, and can contain a definite or indefinite article. For the example of the set of libraries near Central Station, the English noun-phrase generator could produce "*library near Central Station*", or "*libraries near Central Station*", along with the articles "*a*" or "*the*" depending on the need. These conditions can be specified by the system manager at the moment of generation since the precise context of the response is known.

The noun phrases produced by the generator are embedded in language-dependent message strings which are stored in a table. Each string is given a unique label so it can be referenced by the system manager. Each language thus requires an association list of the message label and string pattern. To produce a response, the system manager calls the language generation component with a particular message label, and the noun phrases associated with the response. In the library example for instance, the system knows of one library near Central Station. It would therefore call the language generation component with an *only* message, and pass as arguments the noun-phrase "*library near Central Station*" or "*Sen-*

toraru Eki no chikaku ni aru toshokan" depending on whether the output language were English or Japanese. The respective unknown messages consist of "*I know of only one <noun-phrase>.*" or "*<noun-phrase> wa hitotsu dake shitte imasu.*"

Although the language generation process has been presented as a two-stage process, it is actually recursive since as is the case for our example, a noun-phrase can itself consist of many embedded noun-phrases. To build up the noun-phrase for the set of libraries near Central Station, the generator would start with the basic vocabulary value for library, and embed this string using the *near* message and the string value of the noun-phrase Central Station. In English, the near message would be of the form "*<noun> near <object>*". Using this procedure, the language generation component can create arbitrarily complicated noun-phrases in the domain.

EVALUATION

For the Japanese VOYAGER system, we defined a vocabulary of 495 words comprised of words in the training set and words determined by translating 2000 sentences from the English VOYAGER training corpus. This vocabulary covered 99% of the words in the test set (96% of unique words). The category bigram was also trained using the training data and had perplexities of 25.9 and 27.5 on the training and test sets respectively. First choice word and sentence error rates were 14.9% and 53.3%, respectively, on the test set.

The parser covers 82% percent of the training data, and 65% of the test data. An inspection of the answers generated by the system using text input showed that 60% of the responses for the test set was correct. The performance of the system dropped by 8%, to 52%, when the input is spoken rather than typed ($N = 10$ for the N-best interface). Note that the system's understanding ability actually exceeds its sentence recognition accuracy by 5%, which suggests that a full transcription is not always necessary for understanding. Finally, this performance is similar to that initially reported for our English system when using context-independent phone models with a word-pair grammar of similar perplexity (22) [1].

FUTURE PLANS

In this paper we described our recent effort at converting VOYAGER to a bilingual platform. We are encouraged by our preliminary results, and will continue to improve its capabilities in all directions, including context-dependent phonetic models, a robust parsing capability modeled after our ATIS system, and an expansion of its knowledge domain. We are currently porting the VOYAGER system to other languages including French, Italian, and German. We plan to collect data for all languages in scenario collection format in order to acquire more goal-oriented speech. We would also like to incorporate a pointing mechanism into the system, since the VOYAGER application lends itself to this kind of multi-modal input.

REFERENCES

[1] Zue, V., Glass, J., Goddeau, D., Goodine, D., Leung, H., McCandless, M., Phillips, M., Polfroni, J., Seneff, S., and Whitney, D., "Recent Progress on the MIT VOYAGER Spoken Language System," *Proc. ICSLP*, 1317–1320, Kobe, Japan, November 1990.

[2] Zue, V., Glass, J., Goodine, D., Leung, H., Phillips, M., Polifroni, J. and Seneff, S. "Preliminary Evaluation of the VOYAGER Spoken Language System," *Proc. DARPA Speech and NL Workshop*, 160–167, Harwichport, MA, October 1989.

[3] Seneff, S., Glass, J., Goddeau, D., Goodine, D., Hirschman, L., Leung, H., Phillips, M., Polifroni, J., and Zue, V., "Development and Preliminary Evaluation of the MIT ATIS System," *Proc. DARPA Speech and NL Workshop*, 88–93, Pacific Grove, CA., February 1991.

[4] Zue, V., Glass, J., Goddeau, D., Goodine, D., Hirschman, L., Phillips, M., Polfroni, J., Seneff, S. "The MIT ATIS System: February 1992 Progress Report," *Proc. DARPA Speech and NL Workshop*, 84–88, Harriman, NY, February 1992.

[5] Roe, D. B., Pereira, F., Sproat, R. W., Riley, M. D., Moreno, P. J., and Macarron, A., "Toward a Spoken Language Translator for Restricted-domain Context-free Languages," *Proc. Eurospeech*, 1063-1066, Genova, Italy, September 1991.

[6] Morimoto, T., Takezawa, T., Ohkura, K., Nagata, M., Yato, F., Sagayama, S., and Kurematsu, A., "Enhancement of ATR's Spoken Language Translation System: SL-TRANS2," *Proc. ICSLP*, 397–400, Banff, Canada, October 1992.

[7] Phillips, M., Glass, J., and Zue, V., "Automatic Learning of Lexical Representations for Sub-Word Unit Based Speech Recognition Systems," *Proc. Eurospeech*, 577–580, Genova, Italy, September 1991.

[8] Seneff, S., "TINA: A Natural Language System for Spoken Language Applications," *Computational Linguistics*, Vol. 18, No. 1, 61–86, 1992.

[9] Zue, V., Daly, N., Glass, J., Goodine, D., Leung, H., Phillips, M., Polifroni, J., Seneff, S. and Soclof, M. "The Collection and Preliminary Analysis of a Spontaneous Speech Database," *Proc. DARPA Speech and NL Workshop*: 126–134, October 1989.

[10] Sakai, S., and Phillips, M., "J-SUMMIT: A Japanese Segment-Based Speech Recognition System,", *Proc. ICSLP*, 1515–1518, Banff, Alberta, Canada, October 1992.

[11] Lamel, L., Kassel, R., and Seneff, S., "Speech Database Development: Design and Analysis of the Acoustic-Phonetic Corpus," *Proc. DARPA Speech Recognition Workshop*, Report No. SAIC-86/1546, 100–109, February 1986.

[12] Kubala F., et al. "BBN BYBLOS and HARC February 1992 ATIS Benchmark Results", *Proc. DARPA Speech and NL Workshop*, 72–77, Harriman, NY, February 1992.

[13] Itou, K., Hayamizu, S., Tanaka, H., "Continuous Speech Recognition by Context-Dependent Phonetic HMM and an Efficient Algorithm for Finding N-best Sentence Hypotheses," *Proc. ICASSP*, 21–24, San Francisco, CA, March 1992.

SESSION 2: INVITED OVERVIEWS

Madeleine Bates

BBN Systems & Technologies
70 Fawcett Street
Cambridge, MA 02138

By adopting the name Human Language Technology for one of its flagship programs, ARPA intended to included everything that is involved in understanding and/or generating natural human language. In the Information Age, more and more resources are being devoted to collecting, retrieving, and using information (text and speech) in digital form. The time is ripe to multiply the power of human-machine problem solving systems by automating ways to cope with the information explosion we are all experiencing.

The scope of this workshop, expanded from a previous concentration on spoken language systems to include all spoken and written language work at ARPA, meant that many of the attendees were coming into contact for the first time with researchers from related but different disciplines. Several invited overview presentations helped to set the context for what was to come later in the workshop.

Beth Sundheim of the Naval Command, Control & Ocean Surveillance Center described the series of four MUCs (Message Understanding Conferences) that have taken place since 1987. These conferences, each involving a highly structured evaluation of message processing systems, have served to quantify the state of the art in this field, and to provide a forum for studying and modifying the evaluation methodology. Participation in the MUCs has risen from 6 sites to 17, demonstrating increased interest in message processing as a task, and increased willingness to evaluate systems using a common task for which training data is available.

Donna Harman of the National Institute of Science and Technology (NIST) presented the background leading up to the first Text REtrieval Conference (TREC-1), and the results of that conference. The TREC participants were eager to test a variety of retrieval techniques in a common, challenging evaluation. Approaches ranging from pattern matching to term weighting to natural language processing competed in what was probably the best modern information retrieval test, and certainly the largest. Papers by several of the TREC participants appear in this proceedings (particularly in Session 12, Information Retrieval).

Thomas Crystal from ARPA presented an overview of the TIPSTER program, including both the message detection and data extraction tasks. By "detection" is meant two variants of information retrieval: retrospective retrieval and routing. The detection problem is to process queries in the form of user-need statements and finding messages that meet the needs (e.g, are on a particular topic) from among a huge set of messages, some of which are similar but not on the desired topic, and some of which are completely irrelevant. By "extraction" is meant extracting specific types of information from messages that are likely to be relevant to the particular topic. Extraction systems typically apply text understanding techniques to process the text, and then produce database fill from the results of that understanding.

Part of the challenge of the TIPSTER program has been to provide a harder problem than has been worked on before, one that can be solved only by applying very advanced technology; to this end, TIPSTER detection and extraction work has been pursued in both English and Japanese. The current TIPSTER contractors' work is represented throughout this proceedings. Because Tom Crystal will be leaving ARPA shortly, questions about this program should be directed to George Doddington.

George Doddington of ARPA provided an overview of the Spoken Language Systems (SLS) program, which is also well-represented in this proceedings, particularly in Sessions 1 and 3. The SLS program is concerned with all aspects of human-machine communication by voice, and has been using ATIS (Air Travel Information System) as a common domain for development and evalulation. The paper by David Pallett gives a summary of the most recent benchmark evaluations in this program.

Inquires about the SLS program or any other aspect of the ARPA HLT program should be addressed to:

Dr. George Doddington
ARPA / SISTO Room 744
3701 N. Fairfax Drive
Arlington, VA 22303-1714
gdoddington@darpa.mil
703-696-2259

SURVEY OF THE MESSAGE UNDERSTANDING CONFERENCES

Beth M. Sundheim

Naval Command, Control & Ocean Surveillance Ctr.
RDT&E Division (NRaD), Code 444
San Diego, CA 92152-7420

Nancy A. Chinchor

Science Applications International Corporation
10260 Campus Point Drive, M/S A2-F
San Diego, CA 92121

ABSTRACT

In this paper, the Message Understanding Conferences are reviewed, and the natural language system evaluation that is underway in preparation for the next conference is described. The role of the conferences in the evaluation of information extraction systems is assessed in terms of the purposes of three broad classes of evaluation: *progress*, *adequacy*, and *diagnostic*. The conferences have measured system performance primarily to assess progress and the state of the art, but they have also been influenced by the concerns associated with assessing adequacy and providing diagnostics. Challenges for the future of similar evaluations are also discussed.

1. INTRODUCTION

Much has happened since the last time a paper appeared in the ARPA workshop proceedings about the Message Understanding Conferences [11]. The evaluation methodology has been changing steadily, and more demanding information extraction tasks have been defined. In response to the challenges of the evaluation task and metrics, researchers have developed robust and efficient methods for working with large corpora and have confronted prevalent text analysis issues that have so far constrained performance.

These challenges have also resulted in a critical rethinking of assumptions concerning the ideal system to submit for evaluation. Is it a "generic" natural language system with in-depth analysis capabilities and a well-defined internal representation language designed to accomodate the translation of various kinds of textual input into various kinds of output? Or is it one that uses only shallow processing techniques and does not presume to be suitable for language processing tasks other than information extraction?

2. REVIEW OF PAST MUCs

The first Message Understanding Conference (MUC) was held in 1987, used ten narrative paragraphs from naval messages as a training corpus and two others as test data, and had no defined evaluation task or metrics. Researchers from six organizations ran their systems on the test data during the conference, then demonstrated and explained how the systems analyzed the texts. Two years later, the second MUC was held [10]. It made use of a training corpus of 105 naval message narratives of four different types, a dry-run test set of 20 narratives, and a final test set of five. An information extraction task was defined that consisted of identifying ten different pieces of information and representing them as slot fillers in a *template* resembling a semantic frame. This task emulates an information management application requiring the culling of facts from a large body of free text as a means to generate updates to a formatted database.

A rudimentary set of scoring standards was developed, and the templates produced by the eight systems (including four of the six systems represented at the 1987 evaluation) were scored by hand by comparison with a hand-generated answer key. The nature of the corpus used for the second MUC was difficult enough that grammar coverage and parsing efficiency were serious issues. The domain was complex enough that the knowledge engineering job was greatly facilitated by the availability of documentation presenting much of the essential, declarative domain knowledge in a structured format.

After another two-year interval, MUC-3 was held in May, 1991, followed by MUC-4 in June, 1992. There are published proceedings for the third and fourth conferences [8, 9], including descriptions and test results of the participating systems (15 for MUC-3, 17 for MUC-4). A new corpus of 1,400 texts on the subject of Latin American terrorism was used that includes 16 text types (transcribed speeches, newspaper articles, editorial reports, etc.). The template developed for MUC-3 contained slots for 17 pieces of information; the number of information-bearing slots increased to 22 for MUC-4. The scoring metrics were refined and implemented for MUC-3 and MUC-4 in a semiautomated scoring program.

For MUC-3, a study was carried out to measure the complexity of the MUC-3 terrorism task vis-a-vis the naval task, and the scores obtained in the 1989 evaluation were recomputed using the MUC-3 method of scoring [5]. Although these scores were lower, the conclusion was that significant progress had been made, because the increase in difficulty in the task more than offset the decrease in scores.

It was possible to conduct a more refined study of the progress from MUC-3 to MUC-4 [12] that showed that higher levels of performance by nearly all veteran systems were achieved despite the relative difficulty of the MUC-4 test set that was used in the comparison and despite increased strictness of the scoring with respect to spurious data generation. The results of MUC-4 show that higher recall is usually correlated with higher precision[1], which is consistent with the results of previous evaluations and suggests that there is still a variety of techniques with potential for attaining even higher levels of performance in the future. In absolute terms, however, recall and precision scores were still only moderate.

According to an analysis of the effectiveness of techniques used by MUC-3 systems [4], pattern-matching techniques (with hand-crafted or automatically acquired patterns) and probabilistic text categorization techniques proved successful only when combined with linguistic techniques. The use of robust processing including robust parsing was shown to correlate with the success of the system. In a comparison of MUC-3 and MUC-4 systems, minimal improvement from MUC-3 to MUC-4 was demonstrated by the two systems that did not use linguistically-based processing [12]. Several linguistically-based MUC-3 systems improved considerably via extensions made for MUC-4, as did one MUC-3 system that was converted from a generic text understanding system to an information extraction system that maintains its basis in linguistics but is streamlined for speed and geared specifically to the demands of information extraction. However, other systems which underwent a complete overhaul for MUC-4 showed only slight progress or even a degradation in performance.

Error analyses point to the critical need for further research in areas such as discourse reference resolution and inferencing. For example, the inability to reliably determine whether a description found in one part of the text refers or does not refer to something previously described inhibits both recall and precision because it could result in the system either missing information or generating spurious information; the inability to pick up subtle relevance indications (e.g., that persons described as being "in" a place that was attacked could be targets of the attack) and not-so-subtle ones (e.g., that a vehicle whose roof collapsed as a result of a bomb explosion was damaged by the explosion) places a limitation on recall because it results in missed information. The ability to take advantage of sophisticated approaches to discourse that have already received computational treatment is limited by a dependence on error-free outputs from earlier stages of processing. Thus, there is a need for renewed attention to robust processing at the sentence level.

3. MUC-5

We are in another one-year cycle this year, with MUC-5 scheduled for August, 1993. Over 20 organizations are currently planning to participate in the evaluation. Among the expected participants are the organizations already working on the Tipster Text extraction program, other MUC-4 veteran organizations, and six additional participants, four of whom are from outside the United States.

The final evaluation of the Tipster contractors' systems will be the MUC-5 evaluation. There are four tasks, each with its own corpus: joint ventures in English and in Japanese and microelectronics in English and in Japanese. The Tipster-sponsored organizations will be evaluated on all tasks that they are contracted to work on; other MUC-5 participants are allowed to work on both languages if they want to but have been required to choose between the two domains to keep them from spreading their efforts too thin.

The joint ventures task (in both languages) appears to pose significantly greater challenges than the microelectronics task, largely because the joint ventures articles are less technical and more varied in style, are generally longer, and often discuss more than one joint venture. The template includes over 40 content-bearing slots identifying and interrelating various facts about the joint venture and the entities involved. The microelectronics template has fewer slots; it covers features of microchip fabrication processes and the organizations mentioned in association with those processes.

4. ROLES IN EVALUATION

Three broad types or purposes of evaluation have been identified and described by H. Thompson and M. King[2]: *progress evaluation*, *adequacy evaluation*, and *diagnostic evaluation*. The MUC evaluations have been primarily examples of progress evaluation, which is defined as "assessing the actual state of a system with respect to some desired state of the same system, as when progress of a project towards some goal is assessed." However,

---

[1] Recall is the ratio of correctly generated fills to the total number of expected fills; precision is the ratio of the correctly generated fills to the total number of generated fills. Thus, shortfalls in recall reflect the amount of missing fills as well as incorrect fills, and shortfalls in precision reflect the amount of spurious fills as well as incorrect fills. See [2] for detailed information on the formulation of these and other metrics, which are under review for MUC-5.

[2] These were outlined by Henry Thompson (University of Edinburgh) at the Association for Machine Translation in the Americas Evaluation Workshop in San Diego, CA, in November, 1992, and further discussed in a subsequent personal communication from Margaret King (ISSCO, Geneva).

the information extraction tasks that have been used for MUC are quite realistic in some respects, and there are ways in which the evaluation metrics and scoring procedures reflect the concern that the interests of technology consumers be accomodated to the extent possible. Their interest is in adequacy evaluation, which is defined as "assessing the adequacy of a system with respect to some intended use of that system, as exemplified by a potential customer investigating whether a system, either in its current state or after modification, will do what he requires, how well it will do it and at what cost." The third type, diagnostic evaluation, is defined as "assessing the state of a system with the intention of discovering where it fails and why, as exemplified by a research group examining their own system." There are ways in which the MUC evaluations partially support this purpose as well, by providing quantitative data and by facilitating the collection of qualitative data.

4.1. Progress Evaluation

There are at least three ways we look at progress: as an assessment of the current state of the art, as a measure of progress relative to the previous evaluation, and as a measure of progress toward matching human performance on the same task. We expect the metrics to be applicable to both machines and humans, to provide a useful way to look at how much of the expected data the system is finding and at the classes and numbers of errors it is making, and to offer a means for comparing performance across systems.

Using the metrics that have been developed so far, we can say how systems are doing on particular information extraction tasks with respect to correct, incorrect, spurious and missing data at various levels of granularity, and we can tell how a system's performance on the parts of the task that it tried to do compares to its performance on the total task. Repeated over time, the assessments measure progress of the systems as a group and as individuals, although precise measurement has been complicated by the changes to the evaluation methodology, task domain, and template design, and by the radical system design changes made by some groups. Overall cross-system comparisons are possible given a single-value metric [2] and statistical significance tests [3]. The most compelling research problems posed by the task, e.g., suprasentential processing [7], are dramatically revealed.

In the context of ARPA's Tipster program, human performance studies have been carried out with the analysts who filled the answer-key templates. One of these studies [13], which was conducted in the English joint ventures domain, used 20 templates generated independently by four analysts and compared with a key prepared by a fifth "expert" partly on the basis of the other four. The results showed that the best performance achieved was 82% recall and 84% precision, that a fairly small amount of variability existed between the two top-scoring humans, and that there was a sizable performance difference between the top-scoring and the lowest-scoring humans.

An error analysis of these results showed that about half of the approximately 20% total disagreement among the analysts could be attributed to human error (misinterpretation, oversight, data-entry error). The rest was attributed to problems outside the human's control (gaps in template-filling guidelines, legitimate analytical differences in text and guideline interpretation, and bugs in the template-filling tool). Although human performance in this study is far from perfect, it nonetheless represents a challenging performance objective for computer systems.

4.2. Adequacy Evaluation

Although the evaluation tasks emulate actual or hypothesized real-life tasks, they are unrealistic in certain crucial respects, such as the complete autonomy of the extraction process. Since the tasks are constrained in ways such as this for the purposes of evaluation, it is not possible to translate the evaluation results directly into terms that reflect the specific requirements of any particular real-life applications, even applications that bear strong resemblances to the evaluation tasks. Nonetheless, we can consider the relevance of the MUC evaluation methodology to the problem of assessing the adequacy of systems and methods for real-life tasks.

Decisions concerning choice of evaluation metrics have been motivated in part by an interest in establishing good communications with technology consumers. As communications have improved, misconceptions concerning the presumed needs of technology consumers in terms of evaluation metrics have surfaced and are being addressed. The result should be a small set of easily-understood metrics that provide insightful performance data for consumers as well as producers.

One example concerns the treatment of missing and spurious fills, which has been left as a variable so that technology consumers can decide to what extent they are concerned with absent or excess data in the database. However, it now appears that a strict and equal treatment of both types of error is more meaningful to the technology consumers as well as to the technology producers. Another example concerns the overall metric that is computed primarily to enable systems to be ranked. The current metric was designed with the presumed interests of technology consumers in mind, by incorporating variable weights for recall and precision and by including a factor that rewards systems for balanced performance on those two measures. However, there is strong interest among some technology users and others in replacing the current metric with the error rate (number wrong divided by total possible).

In addition to influencing the development of evaluation metrics, the concerns of adequacy evaluation have affected some of the decisions programmed into the scoring software. All in all, the MUC evaluations have quite consciously responded to some of the presumed needs of technology consumers; it now appears that one of our priorities should be to eliminate some of the embellishments and complexities that have been introduced over the last few years.

4.3. Diagnostic Evaluation

The primary metrics of recall and precision and the secondary ones of undergeneration and overgeneration provide diagnostic information in the sense that they show how accurate system performance is at the system's current level of task coverage. We rely on the evaluation participants for error analyses and qualitative assessments of their system's performance, using the metrics as one starting point. Attempts that have been made to use the information extraction task to reveal language analysis capabilities directly have so far met with limited success. Although these attempts have stayed within the "black-box" information extraction evaluation paradigm by examining only textual inputs in relation to template-filler outputs, they are diagnostic evaluations in the sense that they seek to isolate specific aspects of text analysis from the information extraction task, making use of test suites of examples selected from the overall extraction task.

One of the studies examined the results of information extraction at the local level of processing (apposition handling), and the other looked at the global level of processing (discourse handling). The former was carried out for MUC-3 [1] and the latter for MUC-4 [6]. In both studies, there were conditions where the results conformed to expectations and conditions where they did not. Both studies suffered from small test suites and a number of uncontrolled variables. Although there seems to be no theoretical impediment to conducting successful, fine-grained, task-oriented tests, these two efforts seem to show that such tests cannot be designed as *adjuncts* to the basic evaluation but rather require independent specification in order to ensure adequate test samples and an appropriately designed information extraction task.

5. CHALLENGES FOR THE FUTURE

A major challenge for the immediate future of the MUC evaluations is to make the results more intuitively meaningful and more directly usable by the various interested parties -- those doing the research and development, those watching, and those contemplating use. To date, the results seem to have served those doing the research and development well and the others not so well. Of benefit to all, however, have been the development of the shared tasks and the large prototype systems, which have provided the basis for effective communication.

The pressures of the information extraction evaluation tasks and the pressures of the evaluations themselves have resulted in increased attention to task-specific processing techniques. These techniques are often designed not only to improve the quantity and quality of extracted information but also to shorten the development cycle and reduce the human effort associated with porting and extending the system. At the extreme end of the spectrum is a class of systems that exploit various shallow processing techniques. The performance objective of such systems is to at least come close to the estimated potential performance of an in-depth understanding system and to reach that level with much less time and effort. Thus, the contrasts in system design philosophy and system architecture have grown, and the foundation has been laid for an evaluation that could reveal a lot about the near-term transition potential of some technologies and about the strategies for addressing the significant, longer-term research issues associated with the information extraction task.

Although information extraction has served as an excellent vehicle for elucidating the application potential of current technology, its utility as a vehicle for focusing attention on solving the hard, general problems of natural language processing is not as great. Many insights have been gained into the nature of natural language processing by experience in developing the large-scale systems required to participate in the evaluation. Nevertheless, so much effort is involved simply to make it through the evaluation that it takes a disciplined effort to resist implementing quick solutions to all the major issues involved, whether they are well understood problems or not. This is especially true of the many MUC participants with severely limited resources, but it is also true to some extent for those with more extensive resources, who may feel the pressure of competition for high performance more keenly. It is clearly of little use to anyone to ask a large number of research-oriented groups to productize their systems and fine-tune them to a particular domain, just for the purposes of evaluation. The challenge to play a role in solving the hard natural language processing problems is a challenge for the evaluators and participants alike.

ACKNOWLEDGEMENTS

The authors are especially indebted to the other members of the MUC-5 program committee: Sean Boisen, Lynn Carlson, Jim Cowie, Ralph Grishman, Jerry Hobbs, Joe McCarthy, Mary Ellen Okurowski, Boyan Onyshkevych, and Carl Weir. The authors' work is funded by ARPA/SISTO under ARPA order 6359.

REFERENCES

1. Chinchor, N., MUC-3 Linguistic Phenomena Test Experiment, in *Proceedings of the Third Message Understanding Conference (MUC-3)*, May, 1991, Morgan Kaufmann, pp. 31-45.

2. Chinchor, N., MUC-4 Evaluation Metrics, in *Proceedings of the Fourth Message Understanding Conference (MUC-4)*, June, 1992, Morgan Kaufmann Publishers, pp. 22-29.

3. Chinchor, N., Statistical Significance of MUC-4 Results, in *Proceedings of the Fourth Message Understanding Conference (MUC-4)*, June, 1992, Morgan Kaufmann Publishers, pp. 30-50.

4. Chinchor, N., Hirschman, L., and Lewis, D.D., Evaluating Message Understanding Systems: An Analysis of the Third Message Understanding Conference (MUC-3), to appear in *Computational Linguistics*, 19(3).

5. Hirschman, L., Comparing MUCK-II and MUC-3: Assessing the Difficulty of Different Tasks, in *Proceedings of the Third Message Understanding Conference (MUC-3)*, May, 1991, Morgan Kaufmann Publishers, pp. 25-30.

6. Hirschman, L., An Adjunct Test for Discourse Processing in MUC-4, in *Proceedings of the Fourth Message Understanding Conference (MUC-4)*, June, 1992, Morgan Kaufmann Publishers, pp. 67-84.

7. Iwanska, L., et al., Computational Aspects of Discourse in the Context of MUC-3, in *Proceedings of the Third Message Understanding Conference (MUC-3)*, May, 1991, Morgan Kaufmann Publishers, pp. 256-282.

8. *Proceedings of the Third Message Understanding Conference (MUC-3)*, May, 1991, Morgan Kaufmann Publishers.

9. *Proceedings of the Fourth Message Understanding Conference (MUC-4)*, June, 1992, Morgan Kaufmann Publishers.

10. Sundheim, B., Plans for a Task-Oriented Evaluation of Natural Language Understanding Systems, in *Proceedings of the Speech and Natural Language Workshop*, February, 1989, Morgan Kaufmann Publishers, pp. 197-202.

11. Sundheim, B., Third Message Understanding Evaluation and Conference (MUC-3): Phase 1 Status Report, in *Proceedings of the Speech and Natural Language Workshop*, February, 1991, Morgan Kaufmann Publishers, pp. 301-305.

12. Sundheim, B., Overview of the Fourth Message Understanding Evaluation and Conference, in *Proceedings of the Fourth Message Understanding Conference (MUC-4)*, June, 1992, Morgan Kaufmann Publishers, pp. 3-21.

13. Will, C. and Onyshkevych, B., Human Performance for Information Extraction, unpublished presentation given at the Tipster 12-month meeting in San Diego, CA, September, 1992.

OVERVIEW OF TREC-1

Donna Harman

National Institute of Standards and Technology
Gaithersburg, Md. 20899

ABSTRACT

The first Text REtrieval Conference (TREC-1) was held in early November 1992 and was attended by about 100 people working in the 25 participating groups. The goal of the conference was to bring research groups together to discuss their work on a new large test collection. There was a large variety of retrieval techniques reported on, including methods using automatic thesaurii, sophisticated term weighting, natural language techniques, relevance feedback, and advanced pattern matching. As results had been run through a common evaluation package, groups were able to compare the effectiveness of different techniques, and discuss how differences among the systems affected performance.

1. INTRODUCTION

There is a long history of experimentation in information retrieval. Research started with experiments in indexing languages, such as the Cranfield I tests [1], and has continued with over 30 years of experimentation with the retrieval engines themselves. The Cranfield II studies [2] showed that automatic indexing was comparable to manual indexing, and this and the availability of computers created a major interest in the automatic indexing and searching of texts. The Cranfield experiments also emphasized the importance of creating test collections and using these for comparative evaluation. The Cranfield collection, created in the late 1960's, contained 1400 documents and 225 queries, and has been heavily used by researchers since then. Subsequently other collections have been built, such as the CACM collection [3], and the NPL collection [4].

In the thirty or so years of experimentation there have been two missing elements. First, although some research groups have used the same collections, there has been no concerted effort by groups to work with the same data, use the same evaluation techniques, and generally compare results across systems. The importance of this is not to show any system to be superior, but to allow comparison across a very wide variety of techniques, much wider than only one research group would tackle. Karen Sparck Jones in 1981 [5] commented that:

> Yet the most striking feature of the test history of the past two decades is its lack of consolidation. It is true that some very broad generalizations have been endorsed by successive tests: for example...but there has been a real failure at the detailed level to build one test on another. As a result there are no explanations for these generalizations, and hence no means of knowing whether improved systems could be designed (p. 245).

This consolidation is more likely if groups can compare results across the same data, using the same evaluation method, and then meet to discuss openly how methods differ.

The second missing element, which has become critical in the last ten years, is the lack of a realistically-sized test collection. Evaluation using the small collections currently available may not reflect performance of systems in large full-text searching, and certainly does not demonstrate any proven abilities of these systems to operate in real-world information retrieval environments. This is a major barrier to the transfer of these laboratory systems into the commercial world. Additionally some techniques such as the use of phrases and the construction of automatic thesaurii seem intuitively workable, but have repeatedly failed to show improvement in performance using the small collections. Larger collections might demonstrate the effectiveness of these procedures.

The overall goal of the Text REtrieval Conference (TREC) is to address these two missing elements. It is hoped that by providing a very large test collection, and encouraging interaction with other groups in a friendly evaluation forum, a new thrust in information retrieval will occur. There is also an increased interest in this field within the DARPA community, and TREC is designed to be a showcase of the state-of-the-art in retrieval research. NIST's goal as co-sponsor of TREC is to encourage communication and technology transfer among academia, industry, and government.

The following description was excerpted from a more lengthy overview published in the conference proceedings [6]. The full proceedings also contain papers by all participants and results for all systems.

2. THE TASK

2.1 Introduction

TREC is designed to encourage research in information retrieval using large data collections. Two types of retrieval are being examined -- retrieval using an "ad-hoc" query such as a researcher might use in a library environment, and retrieval using a "routing" query such as a profile to filter some incoming document stream. It is assumed that potential users need the ability to do both high precision and high recall searches, and are willing to look at many documents and repeatedly modify queries in order to get high recall. Obviously they would like a system that makes this as easy as possible, but this ease should be reflected in TREC as added intelligence in the system rather than as special interfaces.

Since TREC has been designed to evaluate system performance both in a routing (filtering or profiling) mode, and in an ad-hoc mode, both functions need to be tested. The test design was based on traditional information retrieval models, and evaluation used traditional recall and precision measures. The following diagram of the test design shows the various components of TREC (Figure 1).

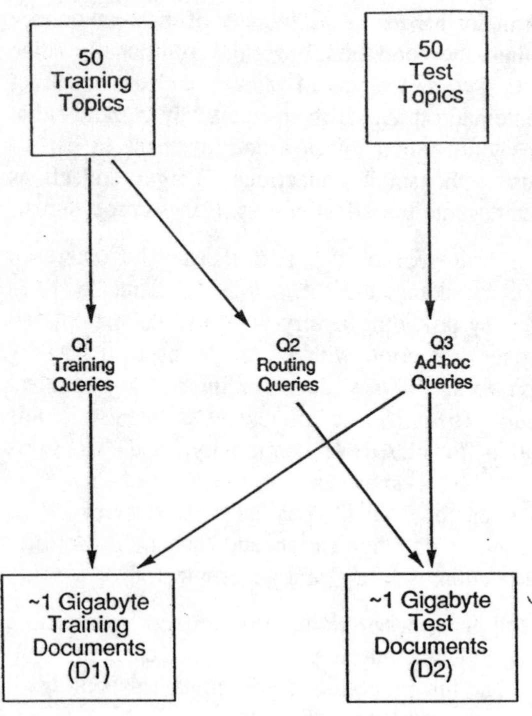

Figure 1 -- The TREC Task

This diagram reflects the four data sets (2 sets of topics and 2 sets of documents) that were provided to participants. These data sets (along with a set of sample relevance judgments for the 50 training topics) were used to construct three sets of queries. Q1 is the set of queries (probably multiple sets) created to help in adjusting a system to this task, create better weighting algorithms, and in general to train the system for testing. The results of this research were used to create Q2, the routing queries to be used against the test documents. Q3 is the set of queries created from the test topics as ad-hoc queries for searching against the combined documents (both training documents and test documents). The results from searches using Q2 and Q3 were the official test results. The queries could be constructed using one of three alternative methods. They could be constructed automatically from the topics, with no human intervention. Alternatively they could be constructed manually from the topic, but with no "retries" after looking at the results. The third method allowed "retries", but under constrained conditions.

2.2 The Participants

There were 25 participating systems in TREC-1, using a wide range of retrieval techniques. The participants were able to choose from three levels of participation: Category A, full participation, Category B, full participation using a reduced dataset (25 topics and 1/4 of the full document set), and Category C for evaluation only (to allow commercial systems to protect proprietary algorithms). The program committee selected only twenty category A and B groups to present talks because of limited conference time, and requested that the rest of the groups present posters. All groups were asked to submit papers for the proceedings.

Each group was provided the data and asked to turn in either one or two sets of results for each topic. When two sets of results were sent, they could be made using different methods of creating queries (methods 1, 2, or 3), or by using different parameter settings for one query creation method. Groups could chose to do the routing task, the adhoc task, or both, and were requested to submit the top 200 documents retrieved for each topic for evaluation.

3. THE TEST COLLECTION

Critical to the success of TREC was the creation of the test collection. Like most traditional retrieval collections, there are three distinct parts to this collection. The first is the documents themselves -- the training set (D1) and the test set (D2). Both were distributed as CD-ROMs with about 1 gigabyte of data each, compressed to fit. The training topics, the test topics and the relevance judgments were supplied by email. These components of the test collection -- the documents, the topics, and the relevance judgments, are discussed in the rest of this section.

3.1 The Documents

The documents came from the following sources.

Disk 1
- WSJ -- Wall Street Journal (1986, 1987, 1988, 1989)
- AP -- AP Newswire (1989)
- ZIFF -- Information from Computer Select disks (Ziff-Davis Publishing)
- FR -- Federal Register (1989)
- DOE -- Short abstracts from Department of Energy

Disk 2
- WSJ -- Wall Street Journal (1990, 1991, 1992)
- AP -- AP Newswire (1988)
- ZIFF -- Information from Computer Select disks (Ziff-Davis Publishing)
- FR -- Federal Register (1988)

The particular sources were selected because they reflected the different types of documents used in the imagined TREC application. Specifically they had a varied length, a varied writing style, a varied level of editing and a varied vocabulary. All participants were required to sign a detailed user agreement for the data in order to protect the copyrighted source material. The documents were uniformly formatted into an SGML-like structure, as can be seen in the following example.

<DOC>
<DOCNO> WSJ880406-0090 </DOCNO>
<HL> AT&T Unveils Services to Upgrade Phone Networks Under Global Plan </HL>
<AUTHOR> Janet Guyon (WSJ Staff) </AUTHOR>
<DATELINE> NEW YORK </DATELINE>
<TEXT>

American Telephone & Telegraph Co. introduced the first of a new generation of phone services with broad implications for computer and communications equipment markets.

AT&T said it is the first national long-distance carrier to announce prices for specific services under a world-wide standardization plan to upgrade phone networks. By announcing commercial services under the plan, which the industry calls the Integrated Services Digital Network, AT&T will influence evolving communications standards to its advantage, consultants said, just as International Business Machines Corp. has created de facto computer standards favoring its products.

.
.
.

</TEXT>
</DOC>

All documents had beginning and end markers, and a unique DOCNO id field. Additionally other fields taken from the initial data appeared, but these varied widely across the different sources. The documents also had different amounts of errors, which were not checked or corrected. Not only would this have been an impossible task, but the errors in the data provided a better simulation of the real-world tasks. Table 1 shows some basic document collection statistics.

TABLE 1
DOCUMENT STATISTICS

Subset of collection	WSJ	AP	ZIFF	FR	DOE
Size of collection (megabytes)					
(disk 1)	295	266	251	258	190
(disk 2)	255	248	188	211	
Number of records					
(disk 1)	98,736	84,930	75,180	26,207	226,087
(disk 2)	74,520	79,923	56,920	20,108	
Median number of terms per record					
(disk 1)	182	353	181	313	82
(disk 2)	218	346	167	315	
Average number of terms per record					
(disk 1)	329	375	412	1017	89
(disk 2)	377	370	394	1073	

Note that although the collection sizes are roughly equivalent in megabytes, there is a range of document lengths from very short documents (DOE) to very long (FR). Also the range of document lengths within a collection varies. For example, the documents from AP are similar in length (the median and the average length are very close), but the WSJ and ZIFF documents have a wider range of lengths. The documents from the Federal Register (FR) have a very wide range of lengths.

What does this mean to the TREC task? First, a major portion of the effort for TREC-1 was spent in the system engineering necessary to handle the huge number of documents. This means that little time was left for system tuning or experimental runs, and therefore the TREC-1 results can best be viewed as a baseline for later research. The longer documents also required major adjustments to the algorithms themselves (or loss of performance). This is particularly true for the very long documents in FR. Since a relevant document might contain only one or two relevant sentences, many algorithms needed adjustment from working with the abstract length documents found in the old collections. Additionally many documents were composite stories, with different topics, and this caused problems for most algorithms.

3.2 The Topics

In designing the TREC task, there was a conscious decision made to provide "user need" statements rather than more traditional queries. Two major issues were involved in this decision. First there was a desire to allow a wide range of query construction methods by keeping the topic (the need statement) distinct from the query (the actual text submitted to the system). The second issue was the ability to increase the amount of information available about each topic, in particular to include with each topic a clear statement of what criteria make a document relevant. The topics were designed to mimic a real user's need, and were written by people who are actual users of a retrieval system. Although the subject domain of the topics was diverse, some consideration was given to the documents to be searched. The following is one of the topics used in TREC.

<top>
<head> Tipster Topic Description
<num> Number: 066
<dom> Domain: Science and Technology
<title> Topic: Natural Language Processing
<desc> Description: Document will identify a type of natural language processing technology which is being developed or marketed in the U.S.
<narr> Narrative: A relevant document will identify a company or institution developing or marketing a natural language processing technology, identify the technology, and identify one or more features of the company's product.
<con> Concept(s):
1. natural language processing
2. translation, language, dictionary, font
3. software applications
<fac> Factor(s):
<nat> Nationality: U.S.
</fac>
<def> Definition(s):
</top>

3.3 The Relevance Judgments

The relevance judgments are of critical importance to a test collection. For each topic it is necessary to compile a list of relevant documents; hopefully as comprehensive a list as possible. Relevance judgments were made using a sampling method, with the sample constructed by taking the top 100 documents retrieved by each system for a given topic and merging them into a pool for relevance assessment. This sampling, known as pooling, proved to be an effective method. There was little overlap among the 25 systems in their retrieved documents. For example, out of a maximum of 3300 unique documents (33 runs times 100 documents), over one-third were actually unique. This means that the different systems were finding different documents as likely relevant documents for a topic. One reason for the lack of overlap is the very large number of documents that contain many of the same keywords as the relevant documents, but probably a larger reason is the very different sets of keywords in the constructed queries. This lack of overlap should improve the coverage of the relevance set, and verifies the use of the pooling methodology to produce the sample.

The merged list of results was then shown to the human assessors. Each topic was judged by a single assessor to insure the best consistency of judgment and varying numbers of documents were judged relevant to the topics (with a median of about 250 documents).

4. PRELIMINARY RESULTS

An important element of TREC was to provide a common evaluation forum. Standard recall/precision figures were calculated for each system and the tables and graphs for the results are presented in the proceedings. The results of the TREC-1 conference can be viewed only as a preliminary baseline for what can be expected from systems working with large test collections. There are several reasons for this. First, the deadlines for results were very tight, and most groups had minimal time for experiments. Additionally groups were working blindly as to what constitutes a relevant document. There were no reliable relevance judgments for training, and the use of the structured topics was completely new. It can be expected that the results seen at the second TREC conference will be much better, and also more indicative of how well a method works.

However there were some clear trends that emerged. Automatic construction of queries proved to be as effective as manual construction of queries. Figure 2 shows a comparison of four sets of results, two using automatic query construction and two using manual query construction, and it can be seen that there is relatively little difference between the results.

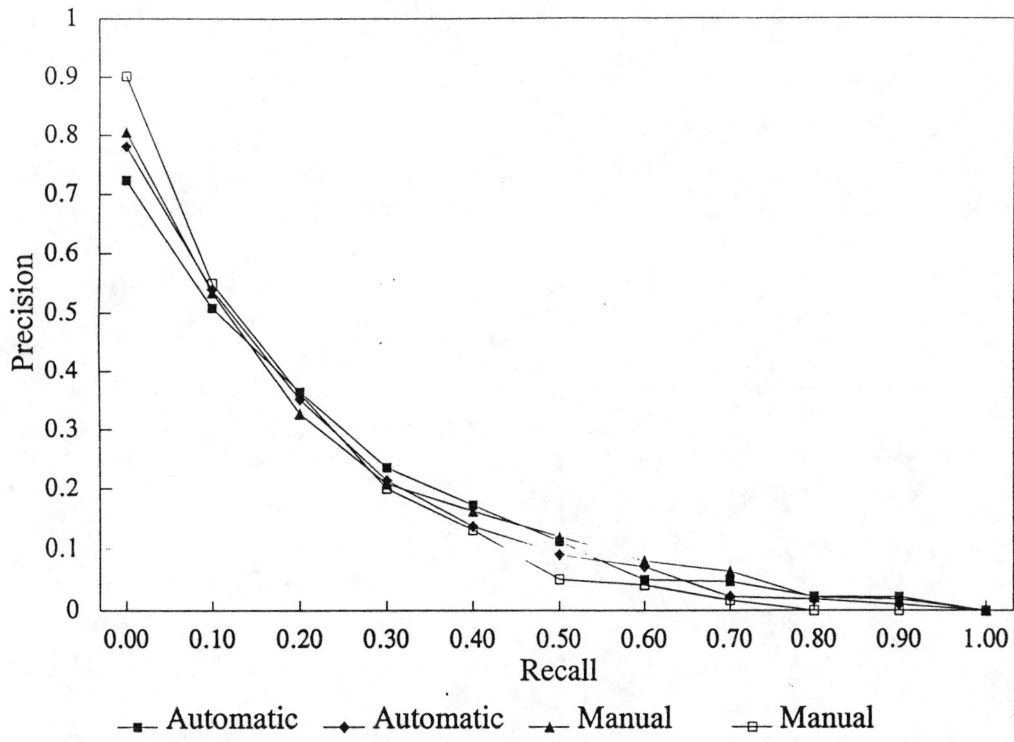

Figure 2 -- A Comparison of Adhoc Results using Different Query Construction Methods

The two automatic systems shown used basically all the terms in the topic as query terms, and relied on automatic term weighting and sophisticated ranking algorithms for performance. The manual systems also used sophisticated term weighting and algorithms, but manually selected which terms to include in a query.

Several minor trends were also noticeable. Systems that worked with subdocuments, or used local term context to improve term weighting, seemed particularly successful in handling the longer documents in TREC. More systems may investigate this approach in TREC-2. Also systems that attempted to expand a topic beyond its original terms (either manually or automatically) seemed to do well, although it was often hard to properly control this expansion (particularly for automatically expanded queries). These trends may continue in TREC-2 and it is expected that clearer trends will emerge as groups have more time to work at this new task.

5. REFERENCES

[1] Cleverdon C.W., (1962). *Report on the Testing and Analysis of an Investigation into the Comparative Efficiency of Indexing Systems*. College of Aeronautics, Cranfield, England, 1962.

[2] Cleverdon C.W., Mills, J. and Keen E.M. (1966). *Factors Determining the Performance of Indexing Systems, Vol. 1: Design, Vol. 2: Test Results.* Aslib Cranfield Research Project, Cranfield, England, 1966.

[3] Fox E. (1983). Characteristics of Two New Experimental Collections in Computer and Information Science Containing Textual and Bibliographic Concepts. *Technical Report TR 83-561*, Cornell University: Computing Science Department.

[4] Sparck Jones K. and C. Webster (1979). *Research in Relevance Weighting*, British Library Research and Development Report 5553, Computer Laboratory, University of Cambridge.

[5] Sparck Jones K. (1981). *Information Retrieval Experiment.* London, England: Butterworths.

[6] Harman D. "The First Text REtrieval Conference (TREC1)." *National Institute of Standards and Technology Special Publication 500-207*, Gaithersburg, Md. 20899 (in press, available in May 1993).

SESSION 3: CONTINUOUS SPEECH RECOGNITION*

Douglas B. Paul, Chair

MIT Lincoln Laboratory
Lexington, MA, 02173

The papers in this session focus on techniques for and applications of large-vocabulary continuous speech recognition. The technique oriented papers discuss techniques for channel compensation, fast search, acoustic modeling, and adaptive language modeling. The applications oriented papers discuss methods for using recognizers for language identification, speaker identification, speaker-sex identification, and keyword spotting.

In "Efficient Cepstral Normalization for Robust Speech Recognition," Liu et al. discuss several preprocessors for channel (including microphone) compensation. Several of these techniques cover only channel equalization and several also account for additive noise. The authors obtained the their best unknown-microphone performance using a technique that accounts for both the equalization and the additive noise.

In "Comparative Experiments on Large Vocabulary Speech Recognition," Schwartz et al. describe several aspects of the BBN recognition system. They briefly describe their use of forward-backward N-best search. They also found a number of small modeling improvements which add up to a significant total improvement in performance. Finally, they describe their results on channel compensation—which are not completely in agreement with the results of the previous paper.

"An Overview of the SPHINX-II Speech Recognition System" by Huang et al. describes the CMU SPHINX-II recognition system. It describes their feature set, their use of tied-mixture (semicontinuous) pdfs, their statewise-clustered phone models (senones) and their search strategy. It also describes a technique for combination of the acoustic and language model probabilities which does not assume statistical independence between the two information sources.

Murveit et al. describe the search strategy used in the SRI recognizer in "Progressive-Search Algorithms for Large Vocabulary Speech Recognition." This progressive search strategy performs the search several times, initially using inexpensive coarse models and then progressively more detailed and expensive models on each iteration. Information from each iteration is used to produce a smaller word network to constrain the search space of the next iteration.

In "Search Algorithms for Software-Only Real-Time Recognition with Very Large Vocabularies," Nguyen et al. describe the techniques used at BBN to achieve real-time recognition of a 20K word task. The techniques center on using a very fast approximate forward search. Information saved from this forward search is then used to constrain a backwards A* search. This backwards search is inherently fast and can provide an N-best sentence list for more detailed reevaluation.

Gauvain and Lamel, in "Identification on Non-Linguistic Speech Features," apply a phonetic recognizer to several other purposes. By using multiple phone sets running independently in parallel, they use the output likelihoods to identify speaker sex, speaker identity, and the language. In each case the phone sets are matched to the aspect to be identified.

"On the Use of Tied-Mixture Distributions" by Kimball and Ostendorf discusses the use of tied Gaussian-mixture pdfs, which have been shown to yield good recognition performance in standard HMM recognizers at a number of sites. They discuss the application of tied mixtures to their stochastic segment recognition models and show improved performance over a non-mixture based system.

In "Adaptive Language Modeling Using the Maximum Entropy Principle," Lau et al. describe a new method for recognition-time adaptation of the of the language model based upon the recent past. The technique uses "trigger" words that signal an increased probability for other words in the near future. They report a greater reduction in perplexity than that obtained by the use of a "caching" adaptive language model.

In "Improved Keyword-Spotting Using SRI's DECIPHER (TM) Large-Vocabulary Speech-Recognition Sys-

*This work was sponsored by the Advanced Research Projects Agency. The views expressed are those of the author and do not reflect the official policy or position of the U.S. Government.

tem," Weintraub describes use of a large-vocabulary recognizer to a keyword-spotting task. He shows significantly improved performance over the traditional technique of searching for only the keywords against a background of unknown words.

Peskin et al., in "Topic and Speaker Identification via Large Vocabulary Continuous Speech Recognition," describe the use of the Dragon large-vocabulary recognizer to perform both topic and speaker identification. The technique described here uses a topic and speaker-independent recognizer to produce a word sequence. This word sequence can then be economically rescored using topic-dependent language models for topic identification or speaker-dependent acoustic models for speaker identification. The authors report good performance on both tasks.

EFFICIENT CEPSTRAL NORMALIZATION FOR ROBUST SPEECH RECOGNITION

Fu-Hua Liu, Richard M. Stern, Xuedong Huang, Alejandro Acero

Department of Electrical and Computer Engineering
School of Computer Science
Carnegie Mellon University
Pittsburgh, PA 15213

ABSTRACT

In this paper we describe and compare the performance of a series of cepstrum-based procedures that enable the CMU SPHINX-II speech recognition system to maintain a high level of recognition accuracy over a wide variety of acoustical environments. We describe the MFCDCN algorithm, an environment-independent extension of the efficient SDCN and FCDCN algorithms developed previously. We compare the performance of these algorithms with the very simple RASTA and cepstral mean normalization procedures, describing the performance of these algorithms in the context of the 1992 DARPA CSR evaluation using secondary microphones, and in the DARPA stress-test evaluation.

1. INTRODUCTION

The need for speech recognition systems and spoken language systems to be robust with respect to their acoustical environment has become more widely appreciated in recent years (*e.g.* [1]). Results of many studies have demonstrated that even automatic speech recognition systems that are designed to be speaker independent can perform very poorly when they are tested using a different type of microphone or acoustical environment from the one with which they were trained (*e.g.* [2,3]), even in a relatively quiet office environment. Applications such as speech recognition over telephones, in automobiles, on a factory floor, or outdoors demand an even greater degree of environmental robustness.

Many approaches have been considered in the development of robust speech recognition systems including techniques based on autoregressive analysis, the use of special distortion measures, the use of auditory models, and the use of microphone arrays, among many other approaches (as reviewed in [1,4]).

In this paper we describe and compare the performance of a series of cepstrum-based procedures that enable the CMU SPHINX-II speech recognition system to maintain a high level of recognition accuracy over a wide variety of acoustical environments. The most recently-developed algorithm is *multiple fixed codeword-dependent cepstral normalization* (MFCDCN). MFCDCN is an extension of a similar algorithm, FCDCN, which provides an additive environmental compensation to cepstral vectors, but in an environment-specific fashion [5]. MFCDCN is less computationally complex than the earlier CDCN algorithm, and more accurate than the related SDCN and BSDCN algorithms [6], and it does not require domain-specific training to new acoustical environments. In this paper we describe the performance of MFCDCN and related algorithms, and we compare it to the popular RASTA approach to robustness.

2. EFFICIENT CEPSTRUM-BASED COMPENSATION TECHNIQUES

In this section we describe several of the cepstral normalization techniques we have developed to compensate simultaneously for additive noise and linear filtering. Most of these algorithms are completely data-driven, as the compensation parameters are determined by comparisons between the testing environment and simultaneously-recorded speech samples using the DARPA standard closetalking Sennheiser HMD-414 microphone (referred to as the CLSTLK microphone in this paper). The remaining algorithm, *codeword-dependent cepstral normalization* (CDCN), is model-based, as the speech that is input to the recognition system is characterized as speech from the CLSTLK microphone that undergoes unknown linear filtering and corruption by unknown additive noise.

In addition, we discuss two other procedures, the RASTA method, and cepstral mean normalization, that may be referred to as cepstral-filtering techniques. These procedures do not provide as much improvement as CDCN, MFCDCN and related algorithms, but they can be implemented with virtually no computational cost.

2.1. Cepstral Normalization Techniques

SDCN. The simplest compensation algorithm, *SNR-Dependent Cepstral Normalization* (SDCN) [2,4], applies an additive correction in the cepstral domain that depends exclusively on the instantaneous SNR of the signal. This correction vector equals the average difference in cepstra between simultaneous "stereo" recordings of speech samples from both the training and testing environments at each SNR of speech in the testing environment. At high SNRs, this correction vector primarily compensates for differences in spectral tilt between the training and testing environments (in a manner similar to the blind deconvolution procedure first proposed by Stockham *et al.* [7]), while at low SNRs the vector provides a form of noise subtraction (in a manner similar to the spectral subtraction algorithm first proposed by Boll [8]). The SDCN algorithm is simple and effective, but it requires environment-specific training.

FCDCN. *Fixed codeword-dependent cepstral normalization* (FCDCN) [4,6] was developed to provide a form of compensation that provides greater recognition accuracy than SDCN but in a more computationally-efficient fashion than the CDCN algorithm which is summarized below.

The FCDCN algorithm applies an additive correction that depends on the instantaneous SNR of the input (like SDCN), but that can also vary from codeword to codeword (like CDCN)

$$\hat{\mathbf{x}} = \mathbf{z} + \mathbf{r}[k, l]$$

where for each frame $\hat{\mathbf{x}}$ represents the estimated cepstral vector of the compensated speech, $\mathbf{z}$ is the cepstral vector of the incoming speech in the target environment, k is an index identifying the VQ codeword, l is an index identifying the SNR, and $\mathbf{r}[k, l]$ is the correction vector.

The selection of the appropriate codeword is done at the VQ stage, so that the label k is chosen to minimize

$$\|\mathbf{z} + \mathbf{r}[k, l] - \mathbf{c}[k]\|^2$$

where the $\mathbf{c}[k]$ are the VQ codewords of the speech in the training database. The new correction vectors are estimated with an EM algorithm that maximizes the likelihood of the data.

The probability density function of $\mathbf{x}$ is assumed to be a mixture of Gaussian densities as in [2,4].

$$p(x) = \sum_{k=0}^{K-1} P[k] \, (N_x c[k], \Sigma_k)$$

The cepstra of the corrupted speech are modeled as Gaussian random vectors, whose variance depends also on the instantaneous SNR, l, of the input.

$$p(z| k, r, l) = \frac{C'}{\sigma[l]} \exp\left(-\frac{1}{2\sigma^2} \|z + r[k, l] - c[k]\|^2\right)$$

In [4] it is shown that the solution to the EM algorithm is the following iterative algorithm. In practice, convergence is reached after 2 or 3 iterations if we choose the initial values of the correction vectors to be the ones specified by the SDCN algorithm.

1. Assume initial values for $\mathbf{r}'[k, l]$ and $\sigma^2[l]$.

2. **Estimate** $f_i[k]$, the *a posteriori* probabilities of the mixture components given the correction vectors $\mathbf{r}'[k, l_i]$, variances $\sigma^2[l_i]$, and codebook vectors $\mathbf{c}[k]$

$$f_i[k] = \frac{\exp\left(-\frac{1}{2\sigma^2[l_i]} \|z_i + \mathbf{r}'[k, l] - \mathbf{c}[k]\|^2\right)}{\sum_{p=0}^{K-1} \exp\left(-\frac{1}{2\sigma^2[l_i]} \|z_i + \mathbf{r}'[p, l_i] - \mathbf{c}[p]\|^2\right)}$$

where l_i is the instantaneous SNR of the ith frame.

3. **Maximize** the likelihood of the complete data by obtaining new estimates for the correction vectors $\mathbf{r}'[k, l]$ and corresponding $\sigma[l]$:

$$\mathbf{r}[k, l] = \frac{\sum_{i=0}^{N-1} (x_i - z_i) f_i[k] \, \delta[l - l_i]}{\sum_{i=0}^{N-1} f_i[k] \, \delta[l - l_i]}$$

$$\sigma^2[l] = \frac{\sum_{i=0}^{N-1} \sum_{k=0}^{K-1} \|x_i - z_i - \mathbf{r}[k, l]\|^2 f_i[k] \, \delta[l - l_i]}{\sum_{i=0}^{N-1} \sum_{k=0}^{K-1} f_i[k] \, \delta[l - l_i]}$$

4. Stop if convergence has been reached, otherwise go to Step 2.

In the current version of FCDCN the SNR is varied over a range of 30 dB in 1-dB steps, with the lowest SNR set equal to the estimated noise level. At each SNR compensation vectors are computed for each of 8 separate VQ clusters.

Figure 1 illustrates some typical compensation vectors obtained with the FCDCN algorithm, computed using the standard closetalking Sennheiser HMD-414 microphone and the unidirectional desktop PCC-160 microphone used as the target environment. The vectors are computed at the extreme SNRs of 0 and 29 dB, as well as at 5 dB. These curves are obtained by calculating the cosine transform of the cepstral compensation vectors, so they provide an estimate of the effective spectral profile of the compensation vectors. The horizontal axis represents frequency, warped nonlinearly according to the mel scale [9]. The maximum frequency corresponds to the Nyquist frequency, 8000 Hz. We note that the spectral profile of the compensation vector varies with SNR, and that especially for the intermediate SNRs the various VQ clusters require compensation vectors of different spectral shapes. The compensation curves for 0-dB SNR average to zero dB at low frequencies by design.

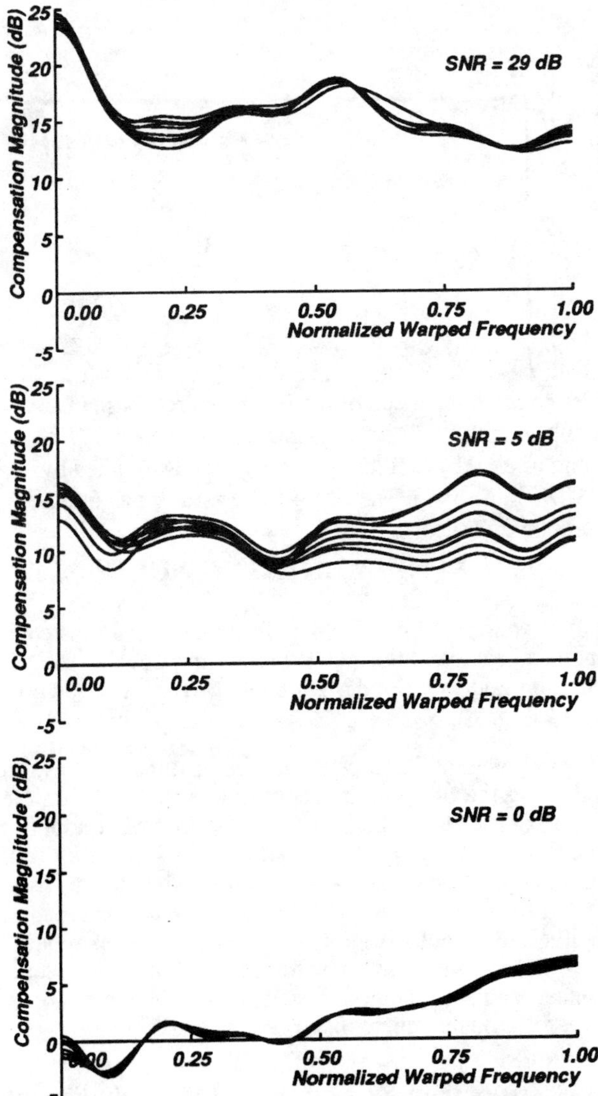

Figure 1: Comparison of compensation vectors using the FCDCN method with the PCC-160 unidirectional desktop microphone, at three different signal-to-noise ratios. The maximum SNR used by the FCDCN algorithm is 29 dB.

The computational complexity of the FCDCN algorithm is very low because the correction vectors are precomputed. However, FCDCN does require simultaneously-recorded data from the training and testing environments. In previous studies [6] we found that the FCDCN algorithm provided a level of recognition accuracy that exceeded what was obtained with all other algorithms, including CDCN.

MFCDCN. *Multiple fixed codeword-dependent cepstral normalization* (MFCDCN) is a simple extension to the FCDCN algorithm, with the goal of exploiting the simplicity and effectiveness of FCDCN but without the need for environment-specific training.

In MFCDCN, compensation vectors are precomputed in parallel for a set of target environments, using the FCDCN procedure as described above. When an utterance from an unknown environment is input to the recognition system, compensation vectors computed using each of the possible target environments are applied successively, and the environment is chosen that minimizes the average residual VQ distortion over the entire utterance,

$$\| z + r[k, l, m] - c[k] \|^2$$

where k refers to the VQ codeword, l to the SNR, and m to the target environment used to train the ensemble of compensation vectors. This general approach is similar in spirit to that used by the BBN speech system [13], which performs a classification among six groups of secondary microphones and the CLSTLK microphone to determine which of seven sets of phonetic models should be used to process speech from unknown environments.

The success of MFCDCN depends on the availability of training data with stereo pairs of speech recorded from the training environment and from a variety of possible target environments, and on the extent to which the environments in the training data are representative of what is actually encountered in testing.

IMFCDCN. While environment selection for the compensation vectors of MFCDCN is generally performed on an utterance-by-utterance basis, the probability of a correct selection can be improved by allowing the classification process to make use of cepstral vectors from previous utterances in a given session as well. We refer to this type of unsupervised incremental adaptation as *Incremental Multiple Fixed Codeword-Dependent Cepstral Normalization* (IMFCDCN).

CDCN. One of the best known compensation algorithms developed at CMU is *Codeword-Dependent Cepstral Normalization* (CDCN) [2,4]. CDCN uses EM techniques to compute ML estimates of the parameters characterizing the contributions of additive noise and linear filtering that when applied in inverse fashion to the cepstra of an incoming utterance produce an ensemble of cepstral coefficients that best match (in the ML sense) the cepstral coefficients of the incoming speech in the testing environment to the locations of VQ codewords in the training environment.

The CDCN algorithm has the advantage that it does not require *a priori* knowledge of the testing environment (in the form of any sort of simultaneously-recorded "stereo" training data in the training and testing environments). However, it has the disadvantage of a somewhat more computationally demanding compensation process than MFCDCN and the other algorithms described above. Compared to MFCDCN and similar algorithms, CDCN uses a greater amount of structural knowledge about the nature of the degradations to the speech signal in order to improve recognition accuracy. Liu *et al.* [5] have shown that the structural knowledge embodied in the CDCN algorithm enables it to adapt to new environments much more rapidly than an algorithm closely related to SDCN, but this experiment has not yet been repeated for FCDCN.

2.2. Cepstral Filtering Techniques

In this section we describe two extremely simple techniques, RASTA and cepstral mean normalization, which can achieve a considerable amount of environmental robustness at almost negligible cost.

RASTA. In *RASTA* filtering [10], a high-pass filter is applied to a log-spectral representation of speech such as the cepstral coefficients. The SRI DECIPHER™ system, for example, uses the highpass filter described by the difference equation

$$y[n] = x[n] - x[n-1] + 0.97y[n-1]$$

where $x[n]$ and $y[n]$ are the time-varying cepstral vectors of the utterance before and after RASTA filtering, and the index n refers to the analysis frames [11].

Cepstral mean normalization. *Cepstral mean normalization* (CMN) is an alternate way to high-pass filter cepstral coefficients. In cepstral mean normalization the mean of the cepstral vectors is subtracted from the cepstral coefficients of that utterance on a sentence-by-sentence basis:

$$y[n] = x[n] - \frac{1}{N}\sum_{n=1}^{N} x[n]$$

where N is the total number frames in an utterance.

Figure 2 shows the low-frequency portions of the transfer functions of the RASTA and CMN filters. Both curves exhibit a deep notch at zero frequency. The shape of the CMN curve depends on the duration of the utterance, and is plotted in Figure 2 for the average duration in the DARPA Wall Street Journal task, 7 seconds. The Nyquist frequency for the time-varying cepstral vectors is 50 frames per second.

Algorithms like RASTA and CMN compensate for the effects of unknown linear filtering because linear filters produce a static compensation vector in the cepstral domain that is the average difference between the cepstra of speech in the training and testing environments. Because the RASTA and CMN filters are highpass, they force the average values of cepstral coefficients to be zero in both the training and testing domains. Nevertheless, neither CMN nor RASTA can compensate directly for the combined effects of additive noise and linear filtering. It is seen in Figure 1 that the compensation vectors that maximize the likelihood of the data vary as a function of the SNR of individual frames of the utterance. Hence we expect compensation algorithms like MFCDCN (which incorporate this knowledge) to be more effective than RASTA or CMN (which do not).

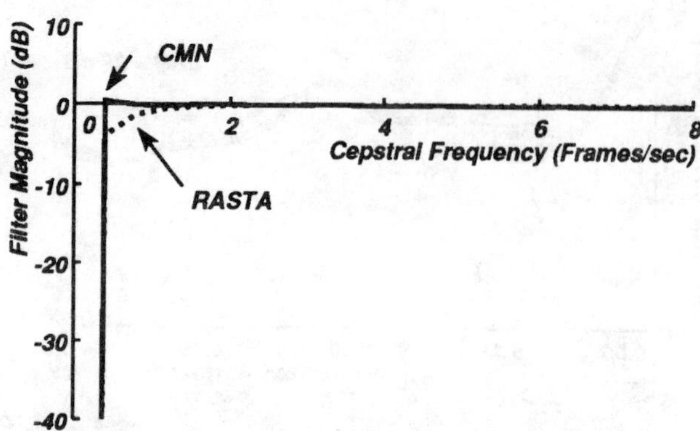

Figure 2: Comparison of the frequency response of the highpass cepstral filters implemented by the RASTA algorithm as used by SRI (dotted curve), and as implied by CMN (solid curve). The CMN curve assumes an utterance duration of 7 seconds.

3. EXPERIMENTAL RESULTS

In this section we describe the ability of the various environmental compensation algorithms to improve the recognition accuracy obtained with speech from unknown or degraded microphones.

The environmental compensation algorithms were evaluated using the SPHINX-II recognition system [12] in the context of the November, 1992, evaluations of continuous speech recognition systems using a 5000-word closed-vocabulary task consisting of dictation of sentences from the Wall Street Journal. A component of that evaluation involved utterances from a set of unknown "secondary" microphones, including desktop microphones, telephone handsets and speakerphones, stand-mounted microphones, and lapel-mounted microphones.

3.1. Results from November CSR Evaluations

We describe in this section results of evaluations of the MFCDCN and CDCN algorithms using speech from secondary microphones in the November, 1992, CSR evaluations.

Because of the desire to benchmark multiple algorithms under several conditions in this evaluation combined with limited resources and the severe time constraints imposed by the evaluation protocol, this evaluation was performed using a version of SPHINX-II that was slightly reduced in performance, but that could process the test data more rapidly than the system described in [12]. Specifically, the selection of phonetic models (across genders) was performed by minimizing mean VQ distortion of the cepstral vectors before recognition was attempted, rather than on the basis of *a posteriori* probability after classification. In addition, neither the unified stochastic engine (USE) described in [12] nor the cepstral mean normalization algorithms were applied. Finally, the CDCN evaluations were conducted without making use of the CART decision tree or alternate pronunciations in the recognition dictionary. The effect of these computational shortcuts was to increase the baseline error rate for the 5000-word task from 6.9% as reported in [12] to 8.1% for the MFCDCN evaluation, and to 8.4% for the CDCN evaluation.

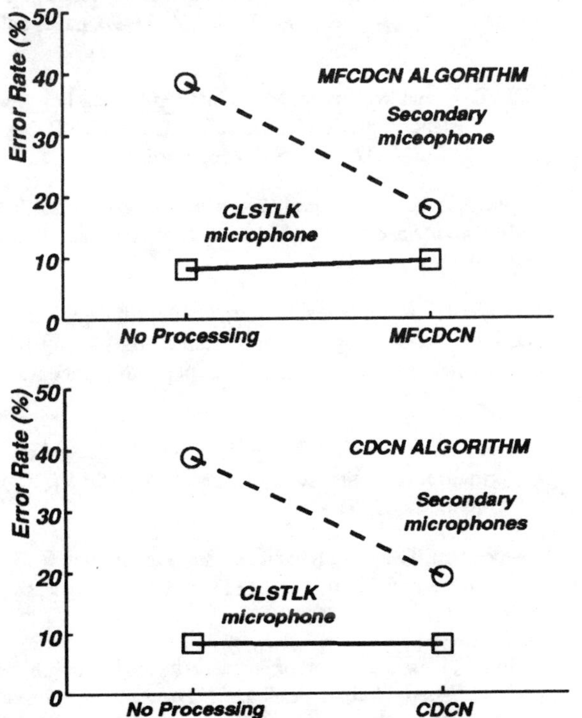

Figure 3: Performance of the MFCDCN algorithm (upper panel) and the CDCN algorithm (lower panel) on the official DARPA CSR evaluations of November, 1992

Figure 3 summarizes the results obtained in the official November, 1992, evaluations. For these experiments, the MFCDCN algorithm was trained using the 15 environments in the training set and developmental test set for this evaluation. It is seen that both the CDCN and MFCDCN algorithms significantly improve the recognition accuracy obtained with the secondary microphones, with little or no loss in performance when applied to speech from the closetalking Sennheiser HMD-414 (CLSTLK) microphone. The small degradation in recognition accuracy observed for speech from the CLSTLK microphone using the MFCDCN algorithm may be at least in part a consequence of errors in selecting the environment for the compensation vectors. Environment-classification errors occurred on 48.8% of the CLSTLK utterances and on 28.5% of the utterances from secondary microphone. In the case of the secondary microphones, however, recognition accuracy was no better using the FCDCN algorithm which presumes knowledge of the correct environment, so confusions appear to have taken place primarily between acoustically-similar environments.

In a later study we repeated the evaluation using MFCDCN compensation vectors obtained using only the seven categories of microphones suggested by BBN rather than the original 15 environments. This simplification produced only a modest increase in error rate for speech from secondary microphones (from 17.7% to 18.9%) and actually improved the error rate for speech from the CLSTLK microphone (from 9.4% to 8.3%).

Figure 4 summarizes the results of a series of (unofficial) experiments run on the same data that explore the interaction between MFCDCN and the various cepstral filtering techniques. The vertical dotted line identifies the system described in [12].

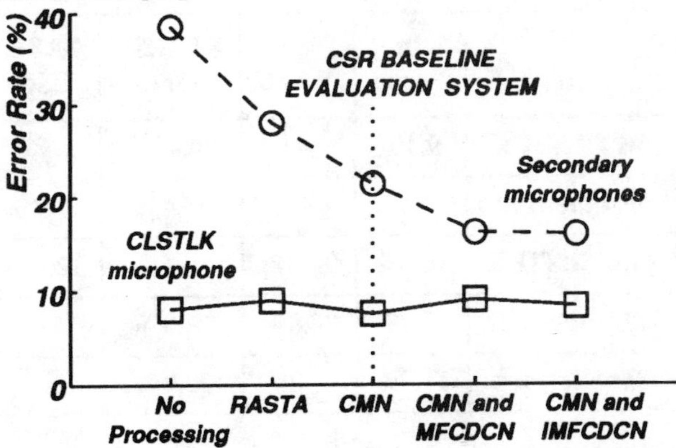

Figure 4: Comparison of the effects of MFCDCN, IMFCDCN, cepstral mean normalization (CMN), and the RASTA algorithm on recognition accuracy of the Sennheiser HMD-414 microphone (solid curve) and the secondary microphones (dashed curve). from the November 1992 DARPA CSR evaluation data.

It can be seen in Figure 4 that RASTA filtering provides only a modest improvement in errors using secondary microphones, and degrades speech from the CLSTLK microphone. CMN, on the other hand, provides almost as much improvement in recognition accuracy as MFCDCN, without degrading speech from the CLSTLK microphone. We do not yet know why our results using CMN are so much better than the results obtained using RASTA. In contrast, Schwartz *et al.* obtained approximately comparable results using these two procedures [13].

Finally, adding MFCDCN to CMN improves the error rate from 21.4% to 16.2%, and the use of IMFCDCN provides a further reduction in error rate to 16.0% for this task.

3.2. Results from the "Stress Test" Evaluation

In addition to the evaluation described above, a second unofficial "stress-test" evaluation was conducted in December, 1992, which included spontaneous speech, utterances containing out-of-vocabulary words, and speech from unknown microphones and environments, all related to the Wall Street Journal domain.

The version of SPHINX-II used for this evaluation was configured to maximize the robustness of the recognition process. It was trained on 13,000 speaker-independent utterances from the Wall Street Journal task and 14,000 utterances of spontaneous speech from the ATIS travel planning domain. The trigram grammar for the system was derived from 70.0 million words of text without verbalized punctuation and 11.6 million words with verbalized punctuation. Two parallel versions of the SPHINX-II system were run, with and without IMFCDCN. Results obtained are summarized in the Table I below.

	In Vocab	Out of Vocab	STRESS TOTAL	BASE CSR
5K CLSTLK	9.4%	–	**9.4%**	5.3%
5K other mic	13.4%	–	**13.4%**	17.7%
20K CLSTLK	16.8%	22.8%	**18.1%**	12.4%
20K other mic	23.7%	24.8%	**24.0%**	–
Spontaneous	11.9%	27.2%	**22.4%**	–

Table 1: Error rates obtained by SPHINX-II in the December, 1992, "Stress-Test" Evaluation. The baseline CSR results are provided for comparison only, and were not obtained using a comparably-configured system.

We also compared these results with the performance of the baseline SPHINX-II system on the same data. The baseline system achieved a word error rate of 22.9% using only the bigram language model. Adding IMFCDCN reduced the error rate only to 22.7%, compared to 20.8% for the stress-test system using IMFCDCN. We believe that the IMFCDCN algorithm provided only a small benefit because only a small percentage of data in this test was from secondary microphones.

In general, we are very encouraged by these results, which are as good or better than the best results obtained only one year ago under highly controlled conditions. We believe that the stress-test protocol is a good paradigm for future evaluations.

ACKNOWLEDGMENTS

This research was sponsored by the Department of the Navy, Naval Research Laboratory, under Grant No. N00014-93-2005. The views and conclusions contained in this document are those of the authors and should not be interpreted as representing the official policies, either expressed or implied, of the U.S. Government. We thank Raj Reddy and the rest of the speech group for their contributions to this work.

REFERENCES

1. Juang, B. H. "Speech Recognition in Adverse Environments". Comp. Speech and Lang. **5**:275-294, 1991.

2. Acero, A. and Stern, R. M. "Environmental Robustness in Automatic Speech Recognition". *ICASSP-90*, pages 849-852. April, 1990.

3. Erell, A. and Weintraub, M. Estimation "Using Log-Spectral-Distance Criterion for Noise-Robust Speech Recognition". *ICASSP-90*, pages 853-856. April, 1990.

4. Acero, A. *Acoustical and Environmental Robustness in Automatic Speech Recognition*. Kluwer Academic Publishers, Boston, MA, 1993.

5. Liu, F.-H., Acero, A., and Stern, R. M. "Efficient Joint Compensation of Speech for the Effects of Additive Noise and Linear Filtering". *ICASSP-92*, pages 865-868. March, 1992.

6. Acero, A. and Stern, R. M. "Robust Speech Recognition by Normalization of the Acoustic Space". *ICASSP-91*, pages 893-896. May, 1991.

7. Stockham, T. G., Cannon, T. M,. and Ingebretsen, R. B. "Blind Deconvolution Through Digital Signal Processing". *Proc. IEEE*. **63**:678-692, 1975.

8. Boll, S. F. "Suppression of Acoustic Noise in Speech Using Spectral Subtraction". *IEEE Trans. Acoust. Speech. and Sig. Proc.* **2**:113-120, 1979.

9. Davis, S.B, Mermelstein, P. "Comparison of Parametric Representations of Monosyllabic Word Recognition in Continuously Spoken Sentences", *IEEE Trans. Acoust. Speech. and Sig. Proc.* **28**:357-366, 1980.

10. Hermansky, H., Morgan, N., Bayya, A., Kohn, P. "RASTA-PLP Speech Analysis Technique". *ICASSP-92*, pages 121-124. March, 1992

11. Murveit, H., Weintraub, M. "Speaker-Independent Connected-Speech Recognition Using Hidden Markov Models". *Proc. DARPA Speech and Natural Language Workshop*. February, 1992.

12. Huang, X.,Alleva, F., Hwang. M.-Y., Rosenfeld, R. "An Overview of the SPHINX-II Speech Recognition System". *Proc. DARPA Human Language Technology Workshop*. March, 1993.

13. Schwartz, R., Anastasakos,A., Kubala, F., Makhoul, J., Nguyen, L., Zavaliagkos, G. "Comparative Experiments on Large Vocabulary Speech Recognition". *Proc. DARPA Human Language Technology Workshop*, March, 1993.

COMPARATIVE EXPERIMENTS ON LARGE VOCABULARY SPEECH RECOGNITION

Richard Schwartz, Tasos Anastasakos, Francis Kubala, John Makhoul, Long Nguyen, George Zavaliagkos

BBN Systems & Technologies
70 Fawcett Street, Cambridge, MA 02138

ABSTRACT

This paper describes several key experiments in large vocabulary speech recognition. We demonstrate that, counter to our intuitions, given a fixed amount of training speech, the number of training speakers has little effect on the accuracy. We show how much speech is needed for speaker-independent (SI) recognition in order to achieve the same performance as speaker-dependent (SD) recognition. We demonstrate that, though the N-Best Paradigm works quite well up to vocabularies of 5,000 words, it begins to break down with 20,000 words and long sentences. We compare the performance of two feature preprocessing algorithms for microphone independence and we describe a new microphone adaptation algorithm based on selection among several codebook transformations.

1. INTRODUCTION

During the past year, the DARPA program has graduated from medium vocabulary recognition problems like Resource Management and ATIS into the large vocabulary dictation of Wall Street Journal (WSJ) texts. With this move comes some changes in computational requirements and the possibility that the algorithms that worked best on smaller vocabularies would not be the same ones that work best on larger vocabularies. We found that, while the required computation certainly increased, the programs that we had developed on the smaller problems still worked efficiently enough on the larger problems. However, while the BYBLOS system achieved the lowest word error rate obtained by any site for recognition of ATIS speech, the error rates for the WSJ tests were the second lowest of the six sites that tested their systems on this corpus. The reader will find more details on the evaluation results in [1].

In the sections that follow, we will describe the BBN BYBLOS system briefly. Then we enumerate several modifications to the BBN BYBLOS system. Following this we will describe four different experiments that we performed and the results obtained.

2. BYBLOS

All of the experiments that will be described were performed using the BBN BYBLOS speech recognition system. This system introduced an effective strategy for using context-dependent phonetic hidden Markov models (HMM) and demonstrated their feasibility for large vocabulary, continuous speech applications [2]. Over the years, the core algorithms have been refined with improved algorithms for estimating robust speech models and using them effectively to search for the most likely sentence.

The system can be trained using the pooled speech of many speakers or by training separate models for each speaker and then averaging the resulting models.

The system can be constrained by any finite-state language model, which includes probabilistic n-gram models as a special case. Nonfinite-state models can also be used in a post process through the N-best Paradigm.

The BYBLOS speech recognition system uses a multi-pass search strategy designed to use progressively more detailed models on a correspondingly reduced search space. It produces an ordered list of the N top-scoring hypotheses which is then reordered by several detailed knowledge sources.

1. A forward pass with a bigram grammar and discrete HMM models saves the top word-ending scores and times [6].
2. A fast time-synchronous backward pass produces an inital N-best list using the Word-Dependent N-best algorithm[5].
3. Each of the N hypotheses is rescored with cross-word-boundary triphones and semi-continuous density HMMs.
4. The N-best list can be rescored with a trigram grammar (or any other language model).

Each utterance is decoded with each gender-dependent model. For each utterance, the N-best list with the highest top-1 hypothesis score is chosen. The top choice in the final list constitutes the speech recognition results reported below. This N-best strategy [3, 4] permits the use of otherwise computationally prohibitive models by greatly reducing the search space to a few (N=20-100) word sequences. It has enabled us to use cross-word-boundary triphone models and trigram language models with ease.

During most of the development of the system we used the 1000-Word RM corpus [8] for testing. More recently, the system has been used for recognizing spontaneous speech from the ATIS corpus, which contains many spontaneous speech effects, such as partial words, nonspeech sounds, extraneous noises, false starts, etc. The vocabulary of the ATIS domain was about twice that of the RM corpus. So there were no significant new problems having to do with memory and computation.

2.1. Wall Street Journal Corpus

The Wall Street Journal (WSJ) pilot CSR corpus contains training speech read from processed versions of the Wall Street Journal. The vocabulary is inherently unlimited. The text of 35M words available for language modeling contains about 160,000 different words. The data used for speech recognition training and test was constrained to come from sentences that contained only the 64,000 most frequent words.

There are two speech training sets. One has 600 sentences from each of 12 speakers (6 male and 6 female). The other has a total of 7,200 sentences from 84 different speakers. The total vocabulary in the training set is about 13,000 words. There are two different standard bigram language models that are typically used – one with 5,000 (5K) words and one with 20,000 (20K) words. The 5K language models were designed to include all of the words in the 5K test set. The 20K language models contain the most likely 20K words in the corpus. As a result, about 2% of the words in the test speech are not in this vocabulary. In addition, there are two variants depending on whether the punctuation is read out loud: verbalized punctuation (VP) and nonverbalized punctuation (NVP).

Most of the test speech is read. In addition to test sets for 5K-word and 20K-word vocabularies, there is also spontaneous speech collected from journalists who were instructed to dictate a newspaper story.

3. IMPROVEMENTS IN ACCURACY

In this section, we describe several modifications that each resulted in an improvement in accuracy on the WSJ corpus. In all cases, we used the same training set (SI-12) and the standard bigram grammars. The initial word error rate when testing on a 5K-word closed-vocabulary VP language model was 12.0%. Each of these methods is described below.

3.1. Silence Detection

Even though the training speech is read from prompts, there are often short pauses either due to natural sentential phrasing, reading disfluency, or running out of breath on long sentences. Naturally, the orthographic transcription that is provided with each utterance does not indicate these pauses. But it would be incorrect to model the speech as if there were no pauses. In particular, phonetic models that take into account acoustic coarticulation between words (cross-word models) do not function properly if they are confounded by unmarked pauses between words.

We developed a two-stage training process to deal with this problem. First we train HMM models assuming there are no pauses between words. Then we mark the missing silence locations automatically by running the recognizer on the training data constrained to the correct word sequence, but allowing optional silence between words. Then we retrain the model using the output of the recognizer as *corrected* transcriptions.

We find that this two-stage process increases the gain due to using cross-word phonetic models. The word error was reduced by 0.6% which is about a 5% reduction in word error.

3.2. Phonetic Dictionary

Two distinct phonetic dictionaries were supplied for training and testing purposes. We found the dictionaries for training and testing were not consistent. That is, there were many words that appeared in both dictionaries, but had different spellings. We also modified the spellings of several words that we judged to be wrong. However, after correcting all of these mistakes, including the inconsistency between the training and testing dictionary, the improvement was only 0.2%, which is statistically insignificant.

One inadequacy of the supplied dictionary was that it did not contain any schwa phonemes to represent reduced vowels. It did, on the other hand, distinguish three levels of stress. But we traditionally remove the stress distinction before using the dictionary. So we translated all of the lowest stress level of the UH and IH phonemes into AX and IX (We will use Random House symbols here). This resulted in another 0.2% reduction in word error.

Another consideration in designing a phonetic dictionary is the tradeoff between the number of parameters and the accuracy of the estimates. Finer phonetic distinctions in the dictionary can result in improved modeling, but they also increase the need for training data. Lori Lamel had previously reported [7] that the error rate on the RM corpus was reduced when the number of phonemes was reduced, ignoring some phonetic distinctions. In particular, she suggested replacing some diphthongs, affricates, and syllabic consonants with two-vowel sequences. She also suggested removing some phonetic distinctions. The list of substitutions is listed in Table 1 below.

Original	New
AY	AH-EE
OY	AWH-EE
OW	AH-OOH
CH	T-SH
IX	AX
UN	AX-N
UM	AX-M
UL	AX-L
AE	EY
OO	UH
ZH	Z
AH	AW

Table 1: These phonemes were removed by mapping them to other phonemes or sequences.

When we made these substitutions, we found that the word error rate decreased by 0.2% again. While this change is not significant, the size of the system was subtantially decreased due to the smaller number of triphone models.

Finally, we reinstated the last three phonemes in the list, since we were uncomfortable with removing too many distinctions. Again, the word error rate was reduced by another 0.2%.

While each of the above improvements was miniscule, the total improvement from changes to the phonetic dictionary was 0.8%, which is about a 7% reduction in word error. At the same time, we now only have a single phonetic dictionary to keep track of, and the system is substantially smaller.

3.3. Weight Optimization

After making several changes to the system, we reoptimized the relative weights for the acoustic and language models, as well as the word and phoneme insertion penalties. These weights were optimized on the development test set automatically using the N-best lists [4]. Optimization of these weights reduced the word error by 0.4%.

3.4. Cepstral Mean Removal

One of the areas of interest is recognition when the microphone for the test speech is unknown. We tried a few different methods to solve this problem, which will be described in a later section. However, during the course of trying different methods, we found that the simplest of all methods, which is to subtract the mean cepstrum from every frame's cepstrum vector actually resulted in a very small improvement in recognition accuracy even when the microphone was the same for training and test. This resulted in a 0.3% reduction in word error rate.

3.5. 3-Way Gender Selection

It has become a standard technique to model the speech of male and female speakers separately, since the speech of males and females is so different. This typically results in a 10% reduction in error relative to using a single speaker-independent model. However, we have found that there are occassional speakers who do not match one model much better than the other. In fact, there are some very rare sentences in which the model of the wrong gender is chosen. Therefore we experimented with using a third "gender" model that is the simple gender-independent model, derived by averaging the male and the female models. During recognition, we find the answer independently using each of these models and then we choose the answer that has the highest overall score. We find that about one out of 10 speakers will typically score better using the gender-independent model than the model for the correct gender. In addition, with this third model, we no longer ever see sentences that are misclassified as belonging to the wrong gender. The reduction error associated with using a third gender model was 0.4%.

3.6. Improvement Summary

The methods we used and the corresponding improvements are summarized in Table 2 below.

Improvement	Method
0.6%	silence-detection
0.8	improvements to phonetic dictionary
0.2	consistent dictionary
0.2	addition of schwa
0.2	reduced phoneme set
0.2	less reduced phoneme set
0.4	Automatic optimization of weights
0.3	Removing mean cepstrum, and
0.4	3-way gender selection
2.5%	Total improvement

Table 2: Absolute reduction in word error due to each improvement.

All the gains shown were additive, resulting in a total of 2.5% reduction in absolute word error, or about a 20% relative change.

4. COMPARATIVE EXPERIMENTS

In this section we describe several controlled experiments comparing the accuracy when using different training and recognition scenarios, and different algorithms.

4.1. Effect of Number of Training Speakers

It has always been assumed that for speaker independent recognition to work well, we must train the system on as many speakers as possible. We reported in [9] that when we trained a speaker-independent system on 600 sentences from each of 12 different speakers (a total of 7,200 sentences), the word error rate was only slightly higher than when the system was trained on a total of 3,990 sentences from 109 speakers. These experiments were performed on the 1000-word Resource Management (RM) Corpus. The results were difficult to interpret because the number of sentences were not exactly the same for both conditions, the data for the 109 speakers covered a larger variety of phonetic contexts than the data for the 12 speakers, and the 12 speakers were carefully selected to cover the various dialectic regions of the country (as well as is possible with only 7 male and 5 female speakers).

For the first time we were able to perform a well-controlled experiment to answer this question on the large vocabulary WSJ corpus. The amount of training data is the same in both cases. In one condition, there are 12 speakers (6 male and 6 female) with 600 sentences each. In the other case, there are 84 speakers with a total of 7,200 sentences. In both cases, all of the sentence scripts are unique. The speakers in both sets were selected randomly, without any effort to cover the general population. In both cases, we used separate models for male and female speakers.

In a second experiment, we repeated another experiment that had previously been run only on the RM corpus. Instead of pooling all of the training data (for one gender) and estimating a single model, we trained on the speech of each speaker separately, and then combined all of the resulting models simply by averaging the densities of the resulting models. We had previously found that this method worked well when each speaker had a substantial amount of training speech (enough to estimate a speaker-dependent model), and all of the speakers had the same sentences in their training. But in this experiment, we also computed separate speaker-dependent models for the speakers with 50-100 utterances, and each speaker had different sentences.

The results of these comparisons are shown in Table 3.

Training	Pooled	Averaged
SI-84	11.2	12.3
SI-12	11.6	12.0

Table 3: Word error rate for few (SI-12) vs many (SI-84) speakers, and for a single (Pooled) model vs separately trained (Averaged) models. The experiments were run on the 5K VP closed-vocabulary development test set of the WSJ pilot corpus using the standard bigram grammar.

We found, to our surprise, that there is almost no advantage for having more speakers if the total amount of speech is fixed. We also that the performance when we trained the system separately on each of the speakers and averaged the resulting models, was quite similar to that when we trained jointly on all of the speakers together. This result was particularly surprising for the SI-84 case, in which each speaker had very little training data.

More recently we ran this experiment again on the 5K NVP closed-vocabulary development test set with an improved system, and found that the results for a pooled model from 84 speakers were almost identical to those with an averaged model from 12 speakers (10.9% vs 11.3

Both of these results have important implications for practical speech corpus collection. There are many advantages for having a small number of speakers. We call this paradigm the *SI-few paradigm* as opposed to the *SI-many paradigm*. There are also practical advantages for being able to train the models for the different speakers separately.

1. It is much more efficient to collect the data; there are far fewer people to recruit and train.
2. In SI-few training, we get speaker-dependent models for the training speakers for free.
3. When new speakers are added to the training data, we just develop the models for the new speakers and average their models in with the model for all of the speakers, without having to retrain on all of the speech from scratch.
4. The computation for the average model method is easy to parallelize across several machines.
5. Perhaps the most compelling argument for SI-few training is that having speaker-specific models available for each of the training speakers allows us to experiment with speaker adaptation techniques that would not be possible otherwise.

Our conclusion is that there is little evidence that having a very large number of speakers is significantly better than a relatively small number of speakers – if the total amount of training is kept the same. Actually, if we equalize the cost of collecting data under the SI-few and SI-many conditions, then the SI-few paradigm would likely yield better recognition performance than the SI-many paradigm.

4.2. Speaker-Dependent vs Speaker-Independent

It is well-known that, for the same amount of training speech, a system trained on many speakers and tested on new speakers (i.e. speaker-independent recognition) results in significantly worse performance than when the system is trained on the speaker who will use it. However, it is important to know what the trade-off is between the amount of speech and whether the system is speaker-independent or not, since for many applications, it would be practical to collect a substantial amount of speech from each user.

Below we compare the recognition error rate between SI and SD recognition. The SI models were trained with 7,200 sentences, while the SD were trained with only 600 sentences, each. Two different sets of test speakers were used for the SI model, while for the SD case, the test and training speakers were the same, but we compare two different test sets from these same speakers. These experiments were performed using the 5K-word NVP test sets, using the standard bigram language models and also rescoring using a trigram language model.

Training / Test	SI-12 (7200)	SD-1 (600)
Dev. Test	10.9	7.9
Nov. 92 Eval	8.7	8.2

Table 4: Speaker-dependent vs Speaker-independent training

As can be seen, the word error rate for the SI model is only somewhat higher than for the SD model, depending on which SI test set is used. We estimate that, on the average, if the amount of training speech for the SI model were 15-20 times that used for the SD model, then the average word error rate would be about the same.

One might mistakenly conclude from the above results that if there is a large amount of speaker-independent training available, there is no longer any reason to consider speaker-dependent recognition. However, it is extremely important to remember that these results only hold for the case where all of the speakers are native speakers of English. We have previously shown [10] that when the test speakers are not native speakers, the error rate goes up by an astonishing factor of eight! In this case, we must clearly use either a speaker-dependent or speaker-adaptive model in order to obtain usable performance. Of course each speaker can use the type of model that is best for him.

4.3. N-Best Paradigm

In 1989 we developed the N-best Paradigm method for combining knowledge sources mainly as a way to integrate speech recognition with natural language processing. Since then, we have found it to be useful for applying other expensive speech knowledge sources as well, such as cross-word models, tied-mixture densities, and trigram language models. The basic idea is that we first find the top N sentence hypotheses using a less expensive model, such as a bigram grammar with discrete densities, and within-word context models. And then we rescore each of the resulting hypotheses with the more complex models, and finally we pick the highest scoring sentence as the answer.

One might expect that there would be a severe problem with this approach if the latter knowledge sources were much more powerful than those used in the initial N-best pass. However, we have found that this is not the case, as long as the initial error rate is not too high and the sentences are not too long.

In tests on the ATIS corpus (class A+D sentences only), we obtained a 40% reduction in word error rate by rescoring the N-best sentence hypotheses with a trigram language model. In this test, we used a value of 100 for N. This shows that the trigram language model is much more powerful than the bigram language model used in finding the N-best sentences. But there were many utterances for which the correct answer was not found within the N-best hypotheses. It was important to determine whether the system was being hampered by restricting its consideration to the N-best sentences before using the trigram language model. Therefore, we artificially added the correct sentence to the N-best list before rescoring with the trigram model. We found that the word error only decreased by another 7%. We must remember that in this experiment, the performance with the correct sentence added was an optimistic estimate, since we did not add all of the other sentence hypotheses that scored worse than the 100th hypothesis, but better than the correct answer.

The question is whether this result would hold up when the vocabulary is much larger, thereby increasing the word error rate, and the sentences are much longer, thereby increasing the number of possible permutations of word sequences exponentially. In experiments with the 5K-word WSJ sentences with word error rates around 14% during the initial pass, and with average sentence lengths around 18 words we still found little loss.

However, on the 20K-word development test set, we observed a significant loss for trigram rescoring, but not for other less powerful knowledge sources. The experiment was limited to those sentences that contained only words that were inside the recognition vocabulary. (It is impossible to correct errors due to words that are outside of the recognition vocabulary.) This included about 80% of the development test set. The results are shown below in Table 5 for the actual N-best list and with the correct utterance artificially inserted into the list.

Knowledge Used	Actual N-best	With Correct Answer Added
Initial N-best	19.5	19.5
Cross-word rescoring	16.1	15.6
Trigram rescoring	13.9	10.2

Table 5: Effect of N-best Paradigm on 20K-word recognition with trigram Language model rescoring

While this result is a lower bound on the error rate, it indicates that much of the potential gain for using the trigram language model is being lost due to the correct answer not being included in the N-best list. As a result we are modifying the N-best rescoring to alleviate this problem.

5. MICROPHONE INDEPENDENCE

DARPA has placed a high priority on microphone independence. That is, if a new user plugs in any microphone (e.g., a lapel microphone or a telephone) without informing the system of the change, the recognition system is expected to work as well as it does with the microphone that was used for training.

We considered two different types of methods to alleviate this problem. The first attempts to use features that are independent of the microphone, while the second attempts to adapt the system or the input to observed differences in the incoming signal in order to make the speech models match better.

5.1. Cepstrum Preprocessing

The RASTA algorithm [11] smoothes the cepstral vector with a five-frame averaging window, and also removes the effect of a slowly varying multiplicative filter, by subtracting an estimate of the average cepstrum. This average is estimated with an exponential filter with a constant of 0.97, which results in a time constant of about one third of a second. The blind deconvolution algorithm estimates the simple mean of each cepstral value over the utterance, and then subtracts this mean from the value in each frame. In both cases, speech frames are not distinguished from noise frames. The processing is applied to all frames equally. In addition, there was no dependence on estimates of SNR.

Every test utterance was recorded simultaneously on the same microphone used in the training (a high-quality noise-cancelling Sennheiser microphone) and on some other microphone which was not known, but which ranged from an omni-directional boom-mounted microphone or table-mounted microphone, a lapel microphone, or a speaker-phone. We present the error rates for the baseline and for the two preprocessing methods in Table 6 below.

Preprocessing	Sennheiser	Alternate-Mic
Mel cepstra vectors	12.0	37.7
RASTA preprocessing	12.5	27.8
Cepstral Mean Removal	11.8	27.2

Table 6: Comparison of simple preprocessing algorithms. The results were obtained on the 5K-word VP development test set, using the bigram language model.

The results show that the word error rates increase by a factor of three when the microphone is changed radically. The RASTA algorithm reduced the degradation to a factor of 2.3, while degrading the performance on the Sennheiser microphone just slightly. The blind deconvolution also reduced the degradation, but did not degrade the performance on the training microphone. (In fact, it seemed to improve it very slightly, but not significantly.) This shows that the five-frame averaging used in the RASTA algorithm is not necessary for this problem, and that the short-term exponential averaging used to estimate the long-term cepstrum might vary too quickly.

5.2. Known Microphone Adaptation

We decided to attack the problem of accomodating an unknown microphone by considering another problem that seemed simpler and more generally useful. It would be very useful to be able to adapt a system trained on one microphone so that it works well on another particular microphone. The microphone would not have been known at the time the HMM training data was collected, but it *is* known before it is to be used. In this case, we can collect a small sample of stereo data with the microphone used for training and the new microphone simultaneously. Then using the stereo data we can adapt the system to work well on the new microphone.

For microphone adaptation, we assume we have the VQ index of the cepstrum of the Sennheiser signal, and the cepstrum of the alternate microphone. Given this stereo data, we accumulate the mean and variance of the cepstra of the alternate microphone of the frames whose Sennheiser data falls into each of the bins of the VQ codebook. Now, we can use this to define a new set of Gaussians for data that comes from the new microphone. The new Gaussians have means that are shifted relative to the original means, where the shift can be different for each bin. In addition, the variances are typically wider for the new microphone, due to some nondeterministic differences between the microphones. Thus the distributions typically overlap more, but only to the degree that they should. The new set of means and variances represents a codebook transformation that accomodates the new microphone.

5.3. Microphone Selection

In the problem we were trying to solve the test microphone is not known, and is not even included in any data that we might have seen before. In this case, how can we estimate a codebook transformation like the one described above? One technique is to estimate a transformation for many different types of microphones and then use one of those transformations.

We had available stereo training data from several microphones that were not used in the test. We grouped the alternate microphones in the training into six broad categories, such as lapel, telephone, omni-directional, directional microphones, and two specific desk-mounted microphones. Then, we estimated a transformed codebook for each of the microphones using stereo data from that microphone and the Sennheiser, being sure that the adaptation data included both male and female speakers.

To select which microphone transformation to use, we tried simply using each of the transformed codebooks in turn, recognizing the utterance with each, and then choosing the answer with the highest score. Unfortunately, we found that this method did not work well, because data that really came from the Sennheiser microphone was often misclassified as belonging to another microphone. We believe this was due to the radically different nature of the Gaussians for the Sennheiser and the alternate microphones. The alternate microphone Gaussians overlapped much more.

Instead we developed a much simpler, less costly method to select among the microphones. For each of the seven microphone types (Sennheiser plus six alternate types) we estimated a mixture density consisting of eight Gaussians. Then, given a sentence from an unknown microphone, we computed the probability of the data being produced by each of the seven mixture densities. The one with the highest likelihood was chosen, and we then used the transformed codebook corresponding to the chosen microphone type. We found that on development data this microphone selection algorithm was correct about 98% of the time, and had the desirable property that it *never* misclassified the Sennheiser data.

After developing this algorithm, we found that a similar algorithm had been developed at CMU [12]. There were four differences between the MFCDCN method and our method. First, we grouped the several different microphones into six microphone types rather than modeling them each separately. Second, we modified the covariances as well as the means of each Gaussian, in order to reflect the increased uncertainty in the codebook transformation. Third, we used an independent microphone classifier, rather than depend on the transformed codebook itself to perform microphone selection. And fourth, the CMU algorithm used an SNR-dependent transformation, whereas we used only a single transformation. The first difference is probably not important. We believe that the second and third differences favor our algorithm, and the fourth difference clearly favors the MFCDCN algorithm. Further experimentation will be needed to determine the best combination of algorithm features.

We then compared the performance of the baseline system with blind deconvolution and the microphone adaptation algorithm described above. Since these experiments were performed after improvements described in Section 1, and the test sets and language models were different the results in Table 7 are not directly comparable to those in Table 6 above.

Preprocessing	Sennheiser	Alternate-Mic
Mel cepstra vectors	11.6	
Cepstral Mean Removal	11.3	32.4
Microphone Adaptation	11.3	21.3

Table 7: Microphone Adaptation vs Mean Removal. These experiments were performed on the 5K-word NVP development test set using a bigram language model.

6. SUMMARY

We have reported on several methods that result in some reduction in word error rate on the 5K-word WSJ test. In addition, we have described several experiments that answer questions related to training scenarios, recognition search strategies, and microphone independence. In particular, we verified that there is no reason to collect speech from a large number of speakers for estimating a speaker-independent model. Rather, the same results can be obtained with less effort by collecting the same amount of speech from a smaller number of speakers. We determined that the N-best rescoring paradigm can degrade somewhat when the error rate is very high and the sentences are very long. We showed that a simple blind deconvolution preprocessing of the cepstral features results in a better microphone independence method than the more complicated RASTA method. And finally, we introduced a new microphone adaptation algorithm that achieves improved accuracy by adapting to one of several codebook transformations derived from several known microphones.

Acknowledgement

This work was supported by the Defense Advanced Research Projects Agency and monitored by the Office of Naval Research under Contract Nos. N00014-91-C-0115, and N00014-92-C-0035.

REFERENCES

[1] Pallett, D., Fiscus, J., Fisher, W., and J. Garofolo, "Benchmark Tests for the Spoken Language Program", *DARPA Human Language Technology Workshop*, Princeton, NJ, March, 1993.

[2] Chow, Y., M. Dunham, O Kimball, M. Krasner, G.F. Kubala, J. Makhoul, P. Price, S. Roucos, and R. Schwartz (1987) "BYBLOS: The BBN Continuous Speech Recognition System," *IEEE ICASSP-87*, pp. 89-92

[3] Chow, Y-L. and R.M. Schwartz, "The N-Best Algorithm: An Efficient Procedure for Finding Top N Sentence Hypotheses", ICASSP90, Albuquerque, NM S2.12, pp. 81-84.

[4] Schwartz, R., S. Austin, Kubala, F., and J. Makhoul, "New Uses for the N-Best Sentence Hypotheses Within the BYBLOS Speech Recognition System", ICASSP92, San Francisco, CA, pp. I.1-I.4.

[5] Schwartz, R. and S. Austin, "A Comparison Of Several Approximate Algorithms for Finding Multiple (N-Best) Sentence Hypotheses", ICASSP91, Toronto, Canada, pp. 701-704.

[6] Austin, S., Schwartz, R., and P. Placeway, "The Forward-Backward Search Algorithm", ICASSP91, Toronto, Canada, pp. 697-700.

[7] Lamel, L., Gauvain, J., "Continuous Speech Recognition at LIMSI", *DARPA Neural Net Speech Recognition Workshop*, September, 1992.

[8] Price, P., Fisher, W.M., Bernstein, J., and D.S. Pallett (1988) "The DARPA 1000-Word Resource Management Database for Continuous Speech Recognition," *IEEE Int. Conf. Acoust., Speech, Signal Processing*, New York, NY, April 1988, pp. 651-654.

[9] Kubala, F., R. Schwartz, C. Barry, "Speaker Adaptation from a Speaker-Independent Training Corpus", *IEEE ICASSP-90*, Apr. 1990, paper S3.3.

[10] Kubala, F., R. Schwartz, Makhoul, J., "Dialect Normalization through Speaker Adaptation", *IEEE Workshop on Speech Recognition* Arden House, Harriman, NY, Dec. 1991.

[11] Hermansky, H., Morgan, N., Bayya, A., Kohn, P., "Compensation for the Effect of the Communication Channel in Auditory-Like Analysis of Speech (RASTA-PLP), *Proc. of the Second European Conf. on Speech Comm. and Tech.* September, 1991.

[12] Liu, F-H., Stern, R., Huang, X., Acero, A., "Efficient Cepstral Normalization for Robust Speech Recognition", *DARPA Human Language Technology Workshop*, Princeton, NJ, March, 1993.

[13] Placeway, P., Schwartz, R., Fung, P., and L. Nguyen, "The Estimation of Powerful Language Models from Small and Large Corpora", To be presented at ICASSP93, Minneapolis, MN.

An Overview of the SPHINX-II Speech Recognition System

Xuedong Huang, Fileno Alleva, Mei-Yuh Hwang, and Ronald Rosenfeld

School of Computer Science
Carnegie Mellon University
Pittsburgh, PA 15213

ABSTRACT

In the past year at Carnegie Mellon steady progress has been made in the area of acoustic and language modeling. The result has been a dramatic reduction in speech recognition errors in the SPHINX-II system. In this paper, we review SPHINX-II and summarize our recent efforts on improved speech recognition. Recently SPHINX-II achieved the lowest error rate in the November 1992 DARPA evaluations. For 5000-word, speaker-independent, continuous, speech recognition, the error rate was reduced to 5%.

1. INTRODUCTION

At Carnegie Mellon, we have made significant progress in large-vocabulary speaker-independent continuous speech recognition during the past years [16, 15, 3, 18, 14]. In comparison with the SPHINX system [23], SPHINX-II offers not only significantly fewer recognition errors but also the capability to handle a much larger vocabulary size. For 5,000-word speaker-independent speech recognition, the recognition error rate has been reduced to 5%. This system achieved the lowest error rate among all of the systems tested in the November 1992 DARPA evaluations, where the testing set has 330 utterances collected from 8 new speakers. Currently we are refining and extending these and related technologies to develop practical unlimited-vocabulary dictation systems, and spoken language systems for general application domains with larger vocabularies and reduced linguistic constraints.

One of the most important contributions to our systems development has been the availability of large amounts of training data. In our current system, we used about 7200 utterances of read Wall Street Journal (WSJ) text, collected from 84 speakers (half male and half female speakers) for acoustic model training; and 45-million words of text published by the WSJ for language model training. In general, more data requires different models so that more detailed acoustic-phonetic phenomena can be well characterized. Towards this end, our recent progress can be broadly classified into feature extraction, detailed representation through parameter sharing, search, and language modeling. Our specific contributions in SPHINX-II include normalized feature representations, multiple-codebook semi-continuous hidden Markov models, between-word senones, multi-pass search algorithms, long-distance language models, and unified acoustic and language representations. The SPHINX-II system block diagram is illustrated in Figure 1, where feature codebooks, dictionary, senones, and language models are iteratively reestimated with the semi-continuous hidden Markov model (SCHMM), albeit not all of them are jointly optimized for the WSJ task at present. In this paper, we will characterize our contributions

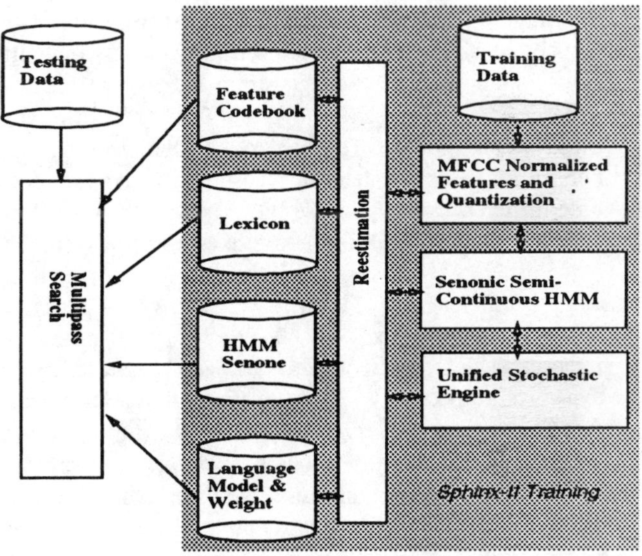

Figure 1: Sphinx-II System Diagram

by percent error rate reduction. Most of these experiments were performed on a development test set for the 5000-word WSJ task. This set consists of 410 utterances from 10 new speakers.

2. FEATURE EXTRACTION

The extraction of reliable features is one of the most important issues in speech recognition and as a result the training data plays a key role in this research. However the curse of dimensionality reminds us that the amount of training data will always be limited. Therefore incorporation of additional features may not lead to any measurable error reduction. This does not necessarily mean that the additional features are poor ones, but rather that we may have insufficient data to reliably model those features. Many systems that incorporate environmentally-robust [1] and speaker-robust [11] models face similar constraints.

2.1. MFCC Dynamic Features

Temporal changes in the spectra are believed to play an important role in human perception. One way to capture this information is to use delta coefficients that measure the change in coefficients over time. Temporal information is particularly suitable for HMMs, since HMMs assume each frame is independent of the past, and these dynamic features broaden the scope of a frame. In the past, the SPHINX system has utilized three codebooks containing [23]: (1) 12 LPC cepstrum coefficients $x_t(k)$, $1 <= k <= 12$; (2) 12 differenced LPC cepstrum coefficients (40 msec. difference) $\Delta x_t(k)$, $1 <= k <= 12$; (3) Power and differenced power (40 msec.) $x_t(0)$ and $\Delta x_t(0)$. Since we are using a multiple-codebook hidden Markov model, it is easy to incorporate new features by using an additional codebook. We experimented with a number of new measures of spectral dynamics, including: (1) second order differential cepstrum and power ($\Delta\Delta x_t(k)$, $1 <= k <= 12$, and $\Delta\Delta x_t(0)$) and third order differential cepstrum and power. The first set of coefficients is incorporated into a new codebook, whose parameters are second order differences of the cepstrum. The second order difference for frame t, $\Delta\Delta x_t(k)$, where t is in units of 10ms, is the difference between $t+1$ and $t-1$ first order differential coefficients, or $\Delta\Delta x_t(k) = \Delta x_{t-1}(k) - \Delta x_{t+1}(k)$. Next, we incorporated both 40 msec. and 80 msec. differences, which represent short-term and long-term spectral dynamics, respectively. The 80 msec. differenced cepstrum $\Delta x'_t(k)$ is computed as: $\Delta x'_t(k) = x_{t-4}(k) - x_{t+4}(k)$. We believe that these two sources of information are more complementary than redundant. We incorporated both Δx_t and $\Delta x'_t$ into one codebook (combining the two into one feature vector), weighted by their variances. We attempted to compute optimal linear combination of cepstral segment, where weights are computed from linear discriminants. But we found that performance deteriorated slightly. This may be due to limited training data or there may be little information beyond second-order differences. Finally, we compared mel-frequency cepstral coefficients (MFCC) with our bilinear transformed LPC cepstral coefficients. Here we observed a significant improvement for the SCHMM model, but nothing for the discrete model. This supported our early findings about problems with modeling assumptions [15]. Thus, the final configuration involves 51 features distributed among four codebooks, each with 256 entries. The codebooks are: (1) 12 mel-scale cepstrum coefficients; (2) 12 40-msec differenced MFCC and 12 80-msec differenced MFCC; (3) 12 second-order differenced MFCC; and (4) power, 40-msec differenced power, second-order differenced power. The new feature set reduced errors by more than 25% over the baseline SPHINX results on the WSJ task.

3. DETAILED MODELING THROUGH PARAMETER SHARING

We need to model a wide range of acoustic-phonetic phenomena, but this requires a large amount of training data. Since the amount of available training data will always be finite one of the central issues becomes that of how to achieve the most detailed modeling possible by means of parameter sharing. Our successful examples include SCHMMs and senones.

3.1. Semi-Continuous HMMs

The semi-continuous hidden Markov model (SCHMM) [12] has provided us with an an excellent tool for achieving detailed modeling through parameter sharing. Intuitively, from the continuous mixture HMM point of view, SCHMMs employ a shared mixture of continuous output probability densities for each individual HMM. Shared mixtures substantially reduce the number of free parameters and computational complexity in comparison with the continuous mixture HMM, while maintaining, reasonably, its modeling power. From the discrete HMM point of view, SCHMMs integrate quantization accuracy into the HMM, and robustly estimate the discrete output probabilities by considering multiple codeword candidates in the VQ procedure. It mutually optimizes the VQ codebook and HMM parameters under a unified probabilistic framework [13], where each VQ codeword is regarded as a continuous probability density function.

For the SCHMM, an appropriate acoustic representation for the diagonal Gaussian density function is crucial to the recognition accuracy [13]. We first performed exploratory semi-continuous experiments on our three-codebook system. The SCHMM was extended to accommodate a multiple feature front-end [13]. All codebook means and covariance matrices were reestimated together with the HMM parameters except the power covariance matrices, which were fixed. When three codebooks were used, the diagonal SCHMM reduced the error rate of the discrete HMM by 10-15% for the RM task [16]. When we used our improved 4-codebook MFCC front-end, the error rate reduction is more than 20% over the discrete HMM.

Another advantage of using the SCHMM is that it requires less training data in comparison with the discrete HMM. Therefore, given the current limitations on the size of the training data set, more detailed models can be employed to improve the recognition accuracy. One way to increase the number of parameters is to use speaker-clustered models. Due to the smoothing abilities of the SCHMM, we were able to train multiple sets of models for different speakers. We investigated automatic speaker clustering as well as explicit male, female, and generic models. By using sex dependent models with the SCHMM, the error rate is further reduced by 10% on the WSJ task.

3.2. Senones

To share parameters among different word models, context-dependent subword models have been used successfully in many state-of-the-art speech recognition systems [26, 21, 17]. The principle of parameter sharing can also be extended to subphonetic models [19, 18]. We treat the state in phonetic hidden Markov models as the basic subphonetic unit — *senone*. Senones are constructed by clustering the state-dependent output distributions across different phonetic models. The total number of senones can be determined by clustering all the triphone HMM states as the shared-distribution models [18]. States of different phonetic models may thus be tied to the same senone if they are close according to the distance measure. Under the senonic modeling framework, we could also use a senonic decision tree to predict unseen triphones. This is particularly important for *vocabulary-independence* [10], as we need to find subword models which are detailed, consistent, trainable and especially generalizable. Recently we have developed a new senonic decision-tree to predict the subword units not covered in the training set [18]. The decision tree classifies senones by asking questions in a hierarchical manner [7]. These questions were first created using speech knowledge from human experts. The tree was automatically constructed by searching for simple as well as composite questions. Finally, the tree was pruned using cross validation. When the algorithm terminated, the leaf nodes of the tree represented the senones to be used. For the WSJ task, our overall senone models gave us 35% error reduction in comparison with the baseline SPHINX results.

The advantages of senones include not only better parameter sharing but also improved pronunciation optimization. Clustering at the granularity of the state rather than the entire model (like generalized triphones [21]) can keep the dissimilar states of two models apart while the other corresponding states are merged, and thus lead to better parameter sharing. In addition, senones give us the freedom to use a larger number of states for each phonetic model to provide more detailed modeling. Although an increase in the number of states will increase the total number of free parameters, with senone sharing redundant states can be clustered while others are uniquely maintained.

Pronunciation Optimization. Here we use the forward-backward algorithm to iteratively optimize a senone sequence appropriate for modeling multiple utterances of a word. To explore the idea, given the multiple examples, we train a word HMM whose number of states is proportional to the average duration. When the Baum-Welch reestimation reaches its optimum, each estimated state is *quantized* with the senone codebook. The closest one is used to label the states of the word HMM. This sequence of senones becomes the senonic baseform of the word. Here arbitrary sequences of senones are allowed to provide the flexibility for the automatically learned pronunciation. When the senone sequence of every word is determined, the parameters (senones) may be re-trained. Although each word model generally has more states than the traditional phoneme-concatenated word model, the number of parameters remains the same since the size of the senone codebook is unchanged. When senones were used for pronunciation optimization in a preliminary experiment, we achieved 10-15% error reduction in a speaker-independent continuous spelling task [19].

4. MULTI-PASS SEARCH

Recent work on search algorithms for continuous speech recognition has focused on the problems related to large vocabularies, long distance language models and detailed acoustic modeling. A variety of approaches based on Viterbi beam search [28, 24] or stack decoding [5] form the basis for most of this work. In comparison with stack decoding, Viterbi beam search is more efficient but less optimal in the sense of MAP. For stack decoding, a fast-match is necessary to reduce a prohibitively large search space. A reliable fast-match should make full use of detailed acoustic and language models to avoid the introduction of possibly unrecoverable errors. Recently, several systems have been proposed that use Viterbi beam search as a fast-match [27, 29], for stack decoding or the N-best paradigm [25]. In these systems, N-best hypotheses are produced with very simple acoustic and language models. A multi-pass rescoring is subsequently applied to these hypotheses to produce the final recognition output. One problem in this paradigm is that decisions made by the initial phase are based on simplified models. This results in errors that the N-best hypothesis list cannot recover. Another problem is that the rescoring procedure could be very expensive per se as many hypotheses may have to be rescored. The challenge here is to design a search that makes the appropriate compromises among memory bandwidth, memory size, and computational power [3].

To meet this challenge we incrementally apply all available acoustic and linguistic information in three search phases. Phase one is a left to right Viterbi Beam search which produces word end times and scores using right context between-word models with a bigram language model. Phase two, guided by the results from phase one, is a right to left Viterbi Beam search which produces word beginning times and scores based on left context between-word models. Phase three is an A* search which combines the results of phases one and two with a long distance language model.

4.1. Modified A* Stack Search

Each theory, *th*, on the stack consists of five entries. A partial theory, *th.pt*, a one word extension *th.w*, a time *th.t* which denotes the boundary between *th.pt* and *th.w*, and two scores *th.g*, which is the score for *th.pt* up to time *th.t* and *th.h* which is the best score for the remaining portion of the input starting with *th.w* at time *th.t+1* through to the end. Unique theories are determined by *th.pt* and *th.w*. The algorithm proceeds as follows.

1. Add initial states to the stack.
2. According to the evaluation function $th.g+th.h$, remove the best theory, th, from the stack.
3. If th accounts for the entire input then output the sentence corresponding to th. Halt if this is the *N*th utterance output.
4. For the word $th.w$ consider all possible end times, t as provided by the left/right lattice.
   (a) For all words, w, beginning at time $t+1$ as provided by the right/left lattice
      i. Extend theory th with w. Designate this theory as th'. Set $th'.pt = th.pt + th.w$, $th'.w ::= w$ and $th'.t = t$.
      ii. Compute scores $th'.g = th.g + w\_score(w, th.t+1, t)$, and $th'.h$. See following for definition of w_score and $th'.h$ computation.
      iii. If th' is already on the stack then choose the best instance of th' otherwise push th' onto the stack.
5. Goto step 2.

4.2. Discussion

When *th* is extended we are considering all possible end times *t* for *th.w* and all possible extensions *w*. When extending *th* with *w* to obtain *th'* we are only interested in the value for *th'.t* which gives the best value for *th'.h + th'.g*. For any *t* and *w*, *th'.h* is easily determined via table lookup from the right/left lattice. Furthermore the value of *th'.g* is given by *th.g + w_score (w, th.t+1, t)*. The function *w_score(w,b,e)* computes the score for the word *w* with begin time *b* and end time *e*.

Our objective is to maximize the recognition accuracy with a minimal increase in computational complexity. With our decomposed, incremental, semi-between-word-triphones search, we observed that early use of detailed acoustic models can significantly reduce the recognition error rate with a negligible increase computational complexity as shown in Figure 2.

By incrementally applying knowledge we have been able to decompose the search so that we can efficiently apply detailed acoustic or linguistic knowledge in each phase. Further more, each phase defers decisions that are better made by a subsequent phase that will apply the appropriate acoustic or linguistic information.

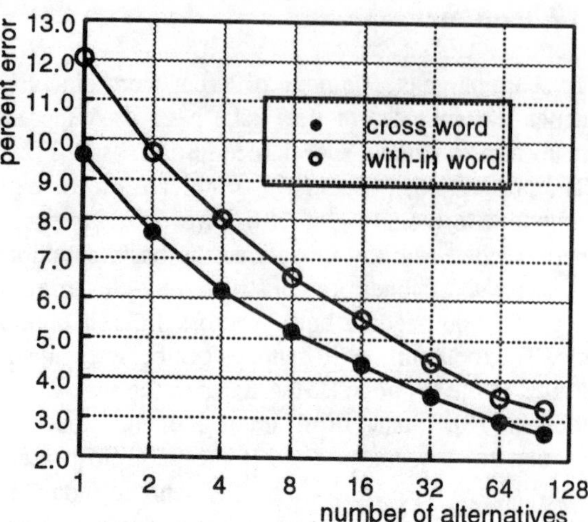

Figure 2: Comparison between early and late use of knowledge.

5. UNIFIED STOCHASTIC ENGINE

Acoustic and language models are usually constructed separately, where language models are derived from a large text corpus without consideration for acoustic data, and acoustic models are constructed from the acoustic data without exploiting the existing text corpus used for language training. We recently have developed a unified stochastic engine (USE) that jointly optimizes both acoustic and language models. As the true probability distribution of both the acoustic and language models can not be accurately estimated, they can not be considered as real probabilities but scores from two different sources. Since they are scores instead of probabilities, the straightforward implementation of the Bayes equation will generally not lead to a satisfactory recognition performance. To integrate language and acoustic probabilities for decoding, we are forced to weight acoustic and language probabilities with a so called language weight [6]. The constant language weight is usually tuned to balance the acoustic probabilities and the language probabilities such that the recognition error rate can be minimized. Most HMM-based speech recognition systems have one single constant language weight that is independent of any specific acoustic or language information, and that is determined using a hill-climbing procedure on development data. It is often necessary to make many runs with different language weights on the development data in order to determine the best value.

In the unified stochastic engine (USE), not only can we iteratively adjust language probabilities to fit our given acoustic representations but also acoustic models. Our multi-pass search algorithm generates N-best hypotheses which are used to optimize language weights or implement many discriminative training methods, where recognition errors can be used as the objective function [20, 25]. With the progress of new database construction such as DARPA's CSR Phase II, we believe acoustically-driven language modeling will eventually provide us with dramatic performance improvements.

In the N-best hypothesis list, we can assume that the correct hypothesis is always in the list (we can insert the correct answer if it is not there). Let hypothesis be a sequence of words $w_1, w_2, ...w_k$ with corresponding language and acoustic probabilities. We denote the correct word sequence as θ, and all the incorrect sentence hypotheses as $\overline{\theta}$. We can assign a variable weight to each of the n-gram probabilities such that we have a weighted language probability as:

$$W(\mathcal{W}) = \prod_i Pr(w_i|w_{i-1}w_{i-2}...)^{\alpha(\mathcal{X}_i, w_i, w_{i-1}, ...)} \quad (1)$$

where the weight $\alpha()$ is a function of acoustic data, $\mathcal{X}_i$, for w_i, and words $w_i, w_{i-1}, ...$ For a given sentence k, a very general objective function can be defined as

$$\begin{aligned} L_k(\lambda) &= \sum_{\overline{\theta}} Pr(\overline{\theta})\{-\sum_{i\in\theta}[logPr(\mathcal{X}_i|w_i) + \\ &\quad +\alpha(\mathcal{X}_i, w_iw_{i-1}...)logPr(w_i|w_{i-1}w_{i-2}...)] + \\ &\quad +\sum_{i\in\overline{\theta}}[logPr(\mathcal{X}_i|w_i) + \\ &\quad +\alpha(\mathcal{X}_i, w_iw_{i-1}...)logPr(w_i|w_{i-1}...)]\}. \quad (2) \end{aligned}$$

where λ denotes acoustic and language model parameters as well as language weights, $Pr(\overline{\theta})$ denotes the a priori probability of the incorrect path $\overline{\theta}$, and $Pr(\mathcal{X}_i|w_i)$ denotes acoustic probability generated by word model w_i. It is obvious that when $L_k(\lambda) > 0$ we have a sentence classification error. Minimization of Equation 2 will lead to minimization of sentence recognition error rate. To jointly optimize the whole training set, we first define a nondecreasing, differentiable cost function $l_k(\lambda)$ (we use the sigmoid function here) in the same manner as the adaptive probabilistic decent method [4, 20]. There exist many possible gradient decent procedures for the proposed problems.

The term $\alpha(\mathcal{X}_i, w_iw_{i-1}...)logPr(w_i|w_{i-1}...)$ could be merged as one item in Equation 2. Thus we can have language probabilities directly estimated from the acoustic training data. The proposed approach is fundamentally different from traditional stochastic language modeling. Firstly, conventional language modeling uses a text corpus only. Any acoustical confusable words will not be reflected in language probabilities. Secondly, maximum likelihood estimation is usually used, which is only loosely related to minimum sentence error. The reason for us to keep $\alpha()$ separate from the language probability is that we may not have sufficient acoustic data to estimate the language parameters at present. Thus, we are forced to have $\alpha()$ shared across different words so we may have n-gram-dependent, word-dependent or even word-count-dependent language weights. We can use the gradient decent method to optimize all of the parameters in the USE. When we jointly optimize $L(\lambda)$, we not only obtain our unified acoustic models but also the unified language models. A preliminary experiment reduced error rate by 5% on the WSJ task [14]. We will extend the USE paradigm for joint acoustic and language model optimization. We believe that the USE can further reduce the error rate with an increased amount of training data.

6. LANGUAGE MODELING

Language Modeling is used in Sphinx-II at two different points. First, it is used to guide the beam search. For that purpose we used a conventional backoff bigram for that purpose. Secondly, it is used to recalculate linguistic scores for the top N hypotheses, as part of the N-best paradigm. We concentrated most of our language modeling effort on the latter.

Several variants of the conventional backoff trigram language model were applied at the reordering stage of the N-best paradigm. (Eventually we plan to incorporate this language model into the A* phase of the multi-pass search with the USE). The best result, a 22% word error rate reduction, was achieved with the simple, non-interpolated "backward" trigram, with the conventional forward trigram finishing a close second.

7. SUMMARY

Our contributions in SPHINX-II include improved feature representations, multiple-codebook semi-continuous hidden Markov models, between-word senones, multi-pass search algorithms, and unified acoustic and language modeling. The key to our success is our data-driven unified optimization approach. This paper characterized our contributions by percent error rate reduction on the 5000-word WSJ task, for which we reduced the word error rate from 20% to 5% in the past year [2].

Although we have made dramatic progress there remains a large gap between commercial applications and laboratory systems. One problem is the large number of out of vocabulary (OOV) words in real dictation applications. Even for a 20000-word dictation system, on average more than 25% of the utterances in a test set contain OOV words. Even if we exclude those utterance containing OOV words, the error rate is still more than 9% for the 20000-word task due to the limitations of current technology. Other problems are illustrated by the November 1992 DARPA stress test evaluation, where testing data comprises both spontaneous speech with many OOV words but also speech recorded using several different microphones. Even though we augmented our system with more than 20,000 utterances in the training set and a noise normalization component [1], our augmented system only reduced the error rate of our 20000-word baseline result from 12.8% to 12.4%, and the error rate for the stress test was even worse when compared with the baseline (18.0% vs. 12.4%). To summarize, our current word error rates under different testing conditions are listed in Table 1. We can see from this

Systems	Vocabulary	Test Set	Error Rate
Baseline	5000	330 utt.	5.3%
Baseline	20000	333 utt.	12.4%
Stress Test	20000	320 utt.	18.0%

Table 1: Performance of SPHINX-II in real applications.

table that improved modeling technology is still needed to make speech recognition a reality.

8. Acknowledgements

This research was sponsored by the Defense Advanced Research Projects Agency and monitored by the Space and Naval Warfare Systems Command under Contract N00039-91-C-0158, ARPA Order No. 7239.

The authors would like to express their gratitude to Raj Reddy and other members of CMU speech group for their help.

References

1. Acero, A. *Acoustical and Environmental Robustness in Automatic Speech Recognition.* Department of Electrical Engineering, Carnegie-Mellon University, September 1990.
2. Alleva, F., Hon, H., Huang, X., Hwang, M., Rosenfeld, R., and Weide, R. *Applying SPHINX-II to the DARPA Wall Street Journal CSR Task.* in: **DARPA Speech and Language Workshop**. Morgan Kaufmann Publishers, San Mateo, CA, 1992.
3. Alleva, F., Huang, X., and Hwang, M. *An Improved Search Algorithm for Continuous Speech Recognition.* in: **IEEE International Conference on Acoustics, Speech, and Signal Processing**. 1993.
4. Amari, S. *A Theory of Adaptive Pattern Classifiers.* **IEEE Trans. Electron. Comput.**, vol. EC-16 (1967), pp. 299–307.
5. Bahl, L. R., Jelinek, F., and Mercer, R. *A Maximum Likelihood Approach to Continuous Speech Recognition.* **IEEE Transactions on Pattern Analysis and Machine Intelligence**, vol. PAMI-5 (1983), pp. 179–190.
6. Bahl, L., Bakis, R., Jelinek, F., and Mercer, R. *Language-Model/Acoustic Channel Balance Mechanism.* **IBM Technical Disclosure Bulletin**, vol. 23 (1980), pp. 3464–3465.
7. Breiman, L., Friedman, J., Olshen, R., and Stone, C. **Classification and Regression Trees**. Wadsworth, Inc., Belmont, CA., 1984.
8. Hon, H. and Lee, K. *CMU Robust Vocabulary-Independent Speech Recognition System.* in: **IEEE International Conference on Acoustics, Speech, and Signal Processing**. Toronto, Ontario, CANADA, 1991, pp. 889–892.
9. Huang, X. *Minimizing Speaker Variations Effects for Speaker-Independent Speech Recognition.* in: **DARPA Speech and Language Workshop**. Morgan Kaufmann Publishers, San Mateo, CA, 1992.
10. Huang, X. *Phoneme Classification Using Semicontinuous Hidden Markov Models.* **IEEE Transactions on Signal Processing**, vol. 40 (1992), pp. 1062–1067.
11. Huang, X., Ariki, Y., and Jack, M. **Hidden Markov Models for Speech Recognition**. Edinburgh University Press, Edinburgh, U.K., 1990.
12. Huang, X., Belin, M., Alleva, F., and Hwang, M. *Unified Stochastic Engine (USE) for Speech Recognition.* in: **IEEE International Conference on Acoustics, Speech, and Signal Processing**. 1993.
13. Huang, X., Hon, H., Hwang, M., and Lee, K. *A Comparative Study of Discrete, Semicontinuous, and Continuous Hidden Markov Models.* **Computer Speech and Language, in press**, 1993.
14. Huang, X., Lee, K., Hon, H., and Hwang, M. *Improved Acoustic Modeling for the SPHINX Speech Recognition System.* in: **IEEE International Conference on Acoustics, Speech, and Signal Processing**. Toronto, Ontario, CANADA, 1991, pp. 345–348.
15. Hwang, M., Hon, H., and Lee, K. *Modeling Between-Word Coarticulation in Continuous Speech Recognition.* in: **Proceedings of Eurospeech**. Paris, FRANCE, 1989, pp. 5–8.
16. Hwang, M. and Huang, X. *Shared-Distribution Hidden Markov Models for Speech Recognition.* **IEEE Transactions on Speech and Audio Processing**, vol. 1 (1993).
17. Hwang, M. and Huang, X. *Subphonetic Modeling with Markov States — Senone.* in: **IEEE International Conference on Acoustics, Speech, and Signal Processing**. 1992.
18. Juang, B.-H. and Katagiri, S. *Discriminative Learning for Minimum Error Classification.* **IEEE Trans on Signal Processing, to appear**, December 1992.
19. Lee, K. *Context-Dependent Phonetic Hidden Markov Models for Continuous Speech Recognition.* **IEEE Transactions on Acoustics, Speech, and Signal Processing**, April 1990, pp. 599–609.
20. Lee, K., Hon, H., and Reddy, R. *An Overview of the SPHINX Speech Recognition System.* **IEEE Transactions on Acoustics, Speech, and Signal Processing**, January 1990, pp. 35–45.
21. Lowerre, B. and Reddy, D. *The Harpy Speech Understanding System.* in: **The Harpy Speech Understanding System**, by B. Lowerre and D. Reddy, edited by W. Lee. Prentice-Hall, Englewood Cliffs, NJ, 1980.
22. Schwartz, R., Austin, S., Kubala, F., and Makhoul, J. *New Uses for the N-Best Sentence Hypotheses Within the Byblos Speech Recognition System.* in: **IEEE International Conference on Acoustics, Speech, and Signal Processing**. 1992, pp. 1–4.
23. Schwartz, R., Chow, Y., Kimball, O., Roucos, S., Krasner, M., and Makhoul, J. *Context-Dependent Modeling for Acoustic-Phonetic Recognition of Continuous Speech.* in: **IEEE International Conference on Acoustics, Speech, and Signal Processing**. 1985, pp. 1205–1208.
24. Soong, F. and Huang, E. *A Tree-Trellis Based Fast Search for Finding the N-Best Sentence Hypothesis.* in: **DARPA Speech and Language Workshop**. 1990.
25. Viterbi, A. J. *Error Bounds for Convolutional Codes and an Asymptotically Optimum Decoding Algorithm.* **IEEE Transactions on Information Theory**, vol. IT-13 (1967), pp. 260–269.

PROGRESSIVE-SEARCH ALGORITHMS FOR LARGE-VOCABULARY SPEECH RECOGNITION

Hy Murveit
John Butzberger
Vassilios Digalakis
Mitch Weintraub

SRI International

ABSTRACT

We describe a technique we call *Progressive Search* which is useful for developing and implementing speech recognition systems with high computational requirements. The scheme iteratively uses more and more complex recognition schemes, where each iteration constrains the search space of the next. An algorithm, the *Forward-Backward Word-Life Algorithm,* is described. It can generate a word lattice in a progressive search that would be used as a language model embedded in a succeeding recognition pass to reduce computation requirements. We show that speed-ups of more than an order of magnitude are achievable with only minor costs in accuracy.

1. INTRODUCTION

Many advanced speech recognition techniques cannot be developed or used in practical speech recognition systems because of their extreme computational requirements. Simpler speech recognition techniques can be used to recognize speech in reasonable time, but they compromise word recognition accuracy. In this paper we aim to improve the speed/accuracy trade-off in speech recognition systems using progressive search techniques.

We define *progressive search* techniques as those which can be used to efficiently implement other, computationally burdensome techniques. They use results of a simple and fast speech recognition technique to constrain the search space of a following more accurate but slower running technique. This may be done iteratively—each progressive search pass uses a previous pass' constraints to run more efficiently, and provides more constraints for subsequent passes.

We will refer to the faster speech recognition techniques as "earlier-pass techniques", and the slower more accurate techniques as "advanced techniques." Constraining the costly advanced techniques in this way can make them run significantly faster without significant loss in accuracy.

The key notions in progressive search techniques are:

1. An early-pass speech recognition phase builds a lattice, which contains all the likely recognition unit strings (e.g. word sequences) given the techniques used in that recognition pass.
2. A subsequent pass uses this lattice as a grammar that constrains the search space of an advanced technique (e.g., only the word sequences contained in a word lattice of pass p would be considered in pass p+1).

Allowing a sufficient breadth of lattice entries should allow later passes to recover the correct word sequence, while ruling out very unlikely sequences, thus achieving high accuracy and high speed speech recognition.

2. PRIOR ART

There are three important categories of techniques that aim to solve problems similar to the ones the progressive search techniques target.

2.1. Fast-Match Techniques

Fast-match techniques[1] are similar to progressive search in that a coarse match is used to constrain a more advanced computationally burdensome algorithm. The fast match, however, simply uses the local speech signal to constrain the costly advanced technique. Since the advanced techniques may take advantage of non-local data, the accuracy of a fast-match is limited and will ultimately limit the overall technique's performance. Techniques such as progressive search can bring more global knowledge to bear when generating constraints, and, thus, more effectively speed up the costly techniques while retaining more of their accuracy.

2.2. N-Best Recognition Techniques

N-best techniques[2] are also similar to progressive search in that a coarse match is used to constrain a more computationally costly technique. In this case, the coarse matcher is a complete (simple) speech recognition system. The output of the N-best system is a list of the top N most likely sentence hypotheses, which can then be evaluated with the slower but more accurate techniques.

Progressive search is a generalization of N-best—the earlier-pass technique produces a graph, instead of a list of N-best sentences. This generalization is crucial because N-best is only computationally effective for N in the order of tens or hundreds. A progressive search word graph can effectively account for orders of magnitude more sentence hypotheses. By limiting the advanced techniques to just searching the few top N sentences, N-best is destined to limit the effectiveness of the advanced techniques and, consequently, the overall system's accuracy. Furthermore, it does not make much sense to use N-best in an iterative fashion as it does with progressive searches.

2.3. Word Lattices

This technique is the most similar to progressive search. In both approaches, an initial-pass recognition system can generate a lattice of word hypotheses. Subsequent passes can search through the lattice to find the best recognition hypothesis. It should be noted that, although we refer to lattices as word lattices, they could be used at other linguistic level, such as the phoneme, syllable, e.t.c.

In the traditional word-lattice approach, the word lattice is viewed as a scored graph of possible segmentations of the input speech. The lattice contains information such as the acoustic match between the input speech and the lattice word, as well as segmentation information.

The progressive search lattice is not viewed as a scored graph of possible segmentations of the input speech. Rather, the lattice is simply viewed as a word-transition grammar which constrains subsequent recognition passes. Temporal and scoring information is intentionally left out of the progressive search lattice.

This is a critical difference. In the traditional word-lattice approach, many segmentations of the input speech which could not be generated (or scored well) by the earlier-pass algorithms will be eliminated for consideration before the advanced algorithms are used. With progressive-search techniques, these segmentations are implicit in the grammar and can be recovered by the advanced techniques in subsequent recognition passes.

3. Building Progressive Search Lattices

The basic step of a progressive search system is using a speech recognition algorithm to make a lattice which will be used as a grammar for a more advanced speech recognition algorithm. This section discusses how these lattices may be generated. We focus on generating word lattices, though these same algorithms are easily extended to other levels.

3.1. The Word-Life Algorithm

We implemented the following algorithm to generate a word-lattice as a by-product of the beam search used in recognizing a sentence with the DECIPHER™ system[4-7].

1. For each frame, insert into the table *Active(W, t)* all words *W* active for each time t. Similarly construct tables *End(W, t)* and *Transitions*(W_1, W_2, t) for all words ending at time t, and for all word-to-word transition at time t.

2. Create a table containing the word-lives used in the sentence, *WordLives*(W, T_{start}, T_{end}). A *word-life* for word *W* is defined as a maximum-length interval (frame T_{start} to T_{end}) during which some phone in word *W* is active. That is,
$$W \in Active(W, t), T_{start} \le t \le T_{end}$$

3. Remove word-lives from the table if the word never ended between T_{start} and T_{end}, that is, remove *WordLives*(W, T_{start}, T_{end}) if there is time *t* between T_{start} and T_{end} where *End(W, t)* is true.

4. Create a finite-state graph whose nodes correspond to word-lives, whose arcs correspond to word-life transitions stored in the *Transitions* table. This finite state graph, augmented by language model probabilities, can be used as a grammar for a subsequent recognition pass in the progressive search.

This algorithm can be efficiently implemented, even for large vocabulary recognition systems. That is, the extra work required to build the "word-life lattice" is minimal compared to the work required to recognize the large vocabulary with a early-pass speech recognition algorithm.

This algorithm develops a grammar which contains all whole-word hypotheses the early-pass speech recognition algorithm considered. If a word hypothesis was active and the word was processed by the recognition system until the word finished (was not pruned before transitioning to another word), then this word will be generated as a lattice node. Therefore, the size of the lattice is directly controlled by the recognition search's beam width.

This algorithm, unfortunately, does not scale down well—it has the property that small lattices may not contain the best recognition hypotheses. This is because one must use small beam widths to generate small lattices. However, a small beam width will likely generate pruning errors.

Because of this deficiency, we have developed the Forward/Backward Word-Life Algorithm described below.

3.2. Extending the Word-Life Algorithm Using Forward And Backward Recognition Passes

We wish to generate word lattices that scale down gracefully. That is, they should have the property that when a lattice is reduced in size, the most likely hypotheses remain and the less likely ones are removed. As was discussed, this is not the case if lattices are scaled down by reducing the beam search width.

The forward-backward word-life algorithm achieves this scaling property. In this new scheme, described below, the size of the lattice is controlled by the *LatticeThresh* parameter.

1. A standard beam search recognition pass is done using the early-pass speech recognition algorithm. (None of the lattice building steps from Section 3.1 are taken in this forward pass).

2. During this forward pass, whenever a transition leaving word *W* is within the beam-search, we record that probability in *ForwardProbability(W,frame)*.

3. We store the probability of the best scoring hypothesis from the forward pass, *Pbest*, and compute a pruning value
Pprune = Pbest / LatticeThresh.

4. We then recognize the same sentence over again using the same models, but the recognition algorithm is run backwards[1].

5. The lattice building algorithm described in Section 3.1 is used in this backward pass with the following exception. During the backward pass, whenever there is a transition between words W_i and W_j at time t, we compute the overall hypothesis probability P_{hyp} as the product of *ForwardProbability*$(W_j,t-1)$, the language model probability $P(W_i|W_j)$, and the Backward pass probability that W_i ended at time t (i.e. the probability of starting *word* W_i at time t and finishing the sentence). If $P_{hyp} < P_{prune}$, then the backward transition between W_i and W_j at time t is blocked.

Step 5 above implements a backwards pass pruning algorithm. This both greatly reduces the time required by the backwards pass, and adjusts the size of the resultant lattice.

4. Progressive Search Lattices

We have experimented with generating word lattices where the early-pass recognition technique is a simple version of the DECIPHER™ speech recognition system, a 4-feature, discrete density HMM trained to recognize a 5,000 vocabulary taken from DARPA's WSJ speech corpus. The test set is a difficult 20-sentence subset of one of the development sets.

We define the number of errors in a single path p in a lattice, *Errors(p)*, to be the number of insertions, deletions, and substitutions found when comparing the words in p to a reference string. We define the number of errors in a word lattice to be the minimum of *Errors(p)* for all paths p in the word lattice.

The following tables show the effect adjusting the beam width and *LatticeThresh* has on the lattice error rate and on the lattice size (the number of nodes and arcs in the word lattice). The grammar used by the has approximately 10,000 nodes and 1,000,000 arcs. The the simple recognition system had a 1-best word error-rate ranging from 27% (beam width 1e-52) to 30% (beam width 1e-30).

Table 1: Effect Of Pruning On Lattice Size

Beam Width 1e-30

Lattice Thresh	nodes	arcs	# errors	%word error
1e-5	60	278	43	10.57
1e-9	94	541	34	8.35
1e-14	105	1016	30	7.37
1e-18	196	1770	29	7.13
1e-32	323	5480	23	5.65
1e-45	372	8626	23	5.65
inf	380	9283	23	5.65

1. Using backwards recognition the sentence is processed from last frame to first frame with all transitions reversed.

Beam Width 1e-34

Lattice Thresh	nodes	arcs	# errors	%word error
1e-5	64	299	28	6.88
1e-9	105	613	20	4.91
1e-14	141	1219	16	3.93
1e-18	260	2335	15	3.69
1e-23	354	3993	15	3.69
1e-32	537	9540	15	3.69

Beam Width 1e-38

Lattice Thresh	nodes	arcs	# errors	%word error
1e-14	186	1338	14	3.44
1e-18	301	2674	13	3.19
1e-23	444	4903	12	2.95

Beam Width 1e-42

Lattice Thresh	nodes	arcs	# errors	%wd error
1e-14	197	1407	13	3.19
1e-18	335	2926	11	2.70
1e-23	520	5582	10	2.46

Beam Width 1e-46

Lattice Thresh	nodes	arcs	# errors	%word error
1e-14	201	1436	13	3.19
1e-18	351	3045	10	2.46
1e-23	562	5946	10	2.46

Beam Width 1e-52

Lattice Thresh	nodes	arcs	# errors	%word error
1e-14	216	1582	12	2.95
1e-18	381	3368	9	2.21

The two order of magnitude reduction in lattice size has a significant impact on HMM decoding time. Table 2 shows the per-sentence computation time required for the above test set when computed using a Sparc2 computer, for both the original grammar, and word lattice grammars generated using a *LatticeThresh* of 1e-23.

Table 2: Lattice Computation Reductions

Beam Width	Forward pass recognition time (secs)	Lattice recognition time (secs)
le-30	167	10
le-34	281	16
le-38	450	24
le-46	906	57
le-52	1749	65

5. Applications of Progressive Search Schemes

Progressive search schemes can be used in the same way N-best schemes are currently used. The two primary applications we've had at SRI are:

5.1. Reducing the time required to perform speech recognition experiments

At SRI, we've been experimenting with large-vocabulary tied-mixture speech recognition systems. Using a standard decoding approach, and average decoding times for recognizing speech with a 5,000-word bigram language model were 46 times real time. Using lattices generated with beam widths of le-38 and a *LatticeThresh* of le-18 we were able to decode in 5.6 times real time). Further, there was no difference in recognition accuracy between the original and the lattice-based system.

5.2. Implementing recognition schemes that cannot be implemented with a standard approach.

We have implemented a trigram language model on our 5,000-word recognition system. This would not be feasible using standard decoding techniques. Typically, continuous-speech trigram language models are implemented either with fastmatch technology or, more recently, with N-best schemes. However, it has been observed at BBN that using an N-best scheme (N=100) to implement a trigram language model for a 20,000 word continuous speech recognition system may have significantly reduced the potential gain from the language model. That is, about half of the time, correct hypotheses that would have had better (trigram) recognition scores than the other top-100 sentences were not included in the top 100 sentences generated by a bigram-based recognition system[8].

We have implemented trigram-based language models using word-lattices, expanding the finite-state network as appropriate to unambiguously represent contexts for all trigrams. We observed that the number of lattice nodes increased by a factor of 2-3 and the number of lattice arcs increased by a factor of approximately 4 (using lattices generated with beam widths of le-38 and a *LatticeThresh* of le-18). The resulting decoding times increased approximately by 50% when using trigram lattices instead of bigram lattices.

ACKNOWLEDGEMENTS

We gratefully acknowledge support for this work from DARPA through Office of Naval Research Contract N00014-92-C-0154. The Government has certain rights in this material. Any opinions, findings, and conclusions or recommendations expressed in this material are those of the authors and do not necessarily reflect the views of the government funding agencies.

REFERENCES

1. Bahl, L.R., de Souza, P.V., Gopalakrishnan, P.S., Nahamoo, D., and M. Picheny, "A Fast Match for Continuous Speech Recognition Using Allophonic Models," *1992 IEEE ICASSP*, pp. I-17-21.
2. Schwartz, R., Austin, S., Kubala, F., Makhoul, J., Nguyen, L., Placeway, P., and G. Zavaliagkos, "New uses for the N-Best Sentence Hypotheses Within the BYBLOS Speech Recognition System", *1992 IEEE ICASSP*, pp. I-1-4.
3. Chow, Y.L., and S. Roukos, "Speech Understanding Using a Unification Grammar", *1989 IEEE ICASSP*, pp. 727-730
4. H. Murveit, J. Butzberger, and M. Weintraub, "Performance of SRI's DECIPHER Speech Recognition System on DARPA's CSR Task," 1992 DARPA Speech and Natural Language Workshop Proceedings, pp 410-414
5. Murveit, H., J. Butzberger, and M. Weintraub, "Reduced Channel Dependence for Speech Recognition," 1992 DARPA Speech and Natural Language Workshop Proceedings, pp. 280-284.
6. H. Murveit, J. Butzberger, and M. Weintraub, "Speech Recognition in SRI's Resource Management and ATIS Systems," 1991 DARPA Speech and Natural Language Workshop, pp. 94-100.
7. Cohen, M., H. Murveit, J. Bernstein, P. Price, and M. Weintraub, "The DECIPHER™ Speech Recognition System," *1990 IEEE ICASSP*, pp. 77-80.
8. Schwartz, R., BBN Systems and Technologies, Cambridge MA, Personal Communication

Search Algorithms for Software-Only Real-Time Recognition with Very Large Vocabularies

Long Nguyen, Richard Schwartz, Francis Kubala, Paul Placeway

BBN Systems & Technologies
70 Fawcett Street, Cambridge, MA 02138

ABSTRACT

This paper deals with search algorithms for real-time speech recognition. We argue that software-only speech recognition has several critical advantages over using special or parallel hardware. We present a history of several advances in search algorithms, which together, have made it possible to implement real-time recognition of large vocabularies on a single workstation without the need for any hardware accelerators. We discuss the Forward-Backward Search algorithm in detail, as this is the key algorithm that has made possible recognition of very large vocabularies in real-time. The result is that we can recognize continuous speech with a vocabulary of 20,000 words strictly in real-time entirely in software on a high-end workstation with large memory. We demonstrate that the computation needed grows as the cube root of the vocabulary size.

1. Introduction

The statistical approach to speech recognition requires that we compare the incoming speech signal to our model of speech and choose as our recognized sentence that word string that has the highest probability, given our acoustic models of speech and our statistical models of language. The required computation is fairly large. When we realized that we needed to include a model of understanding, our estimate of the computational requirement was increased, because we assumed that it was necessary for all of the knowledge sources in the speech recognition search to be tightly coupled.

Over the years DARPA has funded major programs in special-purpose VLSI and parallel computing environments specifically for speech recognition, because it was taken for granted that this was the only way that real-time speech recognition would be possible. However, these directions became major efforts in themselves. Using a small number of processors in parallel was easy, but efficient use of a large number of processors required a careful redesign of the recognition algorithms. By the time high efficiency was obtained, there were often faster uniprocessors available.

Design of special-purpose VLSI obviously requires considerable effort. Often by the time the design is completed, the algorithms implemented are obsolete and much faster general purpose processors are available in workstations. The result is that neither of these approaches has resulted in real-time recognition with vocabularies of 1,000 words or more.

Another approach to the speech recognition search problem is to reduce the computation needed by changing the search algorithm. For example, IBM has developed a flexible stack-based search algorithm and several *fast match* algorithms that reduce the search space by quickly eliminating a large fraction of the possible words at each point in the search. In 1989 we, at BBN [1], and others [2, 3] developed the N-best Paradigm, in which we use a powerful but inexpensive model for speech to find the top N sentence hypotheses for an utterance, and then we rescore each of these hypotheses with more complex models. The result was that the huge search space described by the complex models could be avoided, since the space was constrained to the list of N hypotheses. Even so, an exact algorithm for the N-best sentence hypotheses required about 100 times more computation than the simple Viterbi search for the most likely sentence.

In 1990 we realized that we could make faster advances in the algorithms using off-the-shelf hardware than by using special hardware. Since then we have gained orders of magnitude in speed in a short time by changing the search algorithms in some fundamental ways, without the need for additional or special hardware other than a workstation. This has resulted in a major paradigm shift. We no longer think in terms of special-purpose hardware – we take it for granted that recognition of any size problem will be possible with a software-only solution.

There are several obvious advantages to software-based recognizers: greater flexibility, lower cost, and the opportunity for large gains in speed due to clever search algorithms.

1. Since the algorithms are in a constant state of flux, any special-purpose hardware is obsolete before it is finished.
2. Software-only systems are key to making the technology broadly usable.
   - Many people will simply not purchase extra hardware.
   - Integration is much easier.

- The systems are more flexible.

3. For those people who already have workstations, software is obviously less expensive.

4. Most importantly, it is possible to obtain much larger gains in speed due to clever search algorithms than from faster hardware.

We have previously demonstrated real-time software-only recognition for the ATIS task with over 1,000 words. More recently, we have developed new search algorithms that perform recognition of 20,000 words with fully-connnected bigram and trigram statistical grammars in strict real-time with little loss in recognition accuracy relative to research levels.

First, we will very briefly review some of the search algorithms that we have developed. Then we will explain how the Forward-Backward Search can be used to achieve real-time 20,000-word continuous speech recognition.

2. Previous Algorithms

The two most commonly used algorithms for speech recognition search are the time-synchronous beam search [4] and the best-first stack search [5]. (We do not consider "island-driven" searches here, since they have not been shown to be effective.)

2.1. Time-Synchronous Search

In the time-synchronous Viterbi beam search, all the states of the model are updated in lock step frame-by-frame as the speech is processed. The computation required for this simple method is proportional to the number of states in the model and the number of frames in the input. If we discard any state whose score is far below the highest score in that frame we can reduce the computation by a large factor.

There are two important advantages of a time-synchronous search. First, it is necessary that the search be time-synchronous in order for the computation to be finished at the same time that the speech is finished. Second, since all of the hypotheses are of exactly the same length, it is possible to compare the scores of different hypotheses in order to discard most hypotheses. This technique is called the *beam search*. Even though the beam search is not theoretically admissible, it is very easy to make it arbitrarily close to optimal simply by increasing the size of the beam. The computational properties are fairly well-behaved with minor differences in speech quality.

One minor disadvantage of the Viterbi search is that it finds the state sequence with the highest probability rather than the word sequence with the highest probability. This is only a minor disadvantage because the most likely state sequence has been empirically shown to be highly correlated to the most likely word sequence. (We have shown in [6] that a slight modification to the Viterbi computation removes this problem, albeit with a slight approximation. When two paths come to the same state at the same time, we add the probabilities instead of taking the maximum.) A much more serious problem with the time-synchronous search is that it must follow a very large number of theories in parallel even though only one of them will end up scoring best. This can be viewed as wasted computation.

We get little benefit from using a fast match algorithm with the time-synchronous search because we consider starting all possible words at each frame. Thus, it would be necessary to run the fast match algorithm at each frame, which would be too expensive for all but the least expensive of fast match algorithms.

2.2. Best-First Stack Search

The true best-first search keeps a sorted stack of the highest scoring hypotheses. At each iteration, the hypothesis with the highest score is advanced by all possible next words, which results in more hypotheses on the stack. The best-first search has the advantage that it can theoretically minimize the number of hypotheses considered if there is a good function to predict which theory to follow next. In addition, it can take very good advantage of a fast match algorithm at the point where it advances the best hypothesis.

The main disadvantage is that there is no guarantee as to when the algorithm will finish, since it may keep backing up to shorter theories when it hits a part of the speech that doesn't match well. In addition it is very hard to compare theories of different length.

2.3. Pseudo Time-Synchronous Stack Search

A compromise between the strict time-synchronous search and the best-first stack search can be called the Pseudo Time-Synchronous Stack Search. In this search, the shortest hypothesis (i.e. the one that ends earliest in the signal) is updated first. Thus, all of the active hypotheses are within a short time delay of the end of the speech signal. To keep the algorithm from requiring exponential time, a beam-type pruning is applied to all of the hypotheses that end at the same time. Since this method advances one hypothesis at a time, it can take advantage of a powerful fast match algorithm. In addition, it is possible to use a higher order language model without the computation growing with the number of states in the language model.

2.4. N-best Paradigm

The N-best Paradigm was introduced in 1989 as a way to integrate speech recognition with natural language processing. Since then, we have found it to be useful for applying the more expensive speech knowledge sources as well, such as cross-word models, tied-mixture densities, and trigram language models. We also use it for parameter and weight optimization. The N-best Paradigm is a type of fast match at the sentence level. This reduces the search space to a short list of likely whole-sentence hypotheses.

The Exact N-best Algorithm [1] has the side benefit that it is also the only algorithm that guarantees finding the most likely sequence of words. Theoretically, the computation required for this algorithm cannot be proven to be less than exponential with the length of the utterance. However, this case only exists when all the models of all of the phonemes and words are identical (which would present a more serious problem than large computation). In practice, we find that the computation required can be made proportional to the number of hypotheses desired, by the use of techniques similar to the beam search.

Since the development of the exact algorithm, there have been several approximations developed that are much faster, with varying degrees of accuracy [2, 3, 7, 8]. The most recent algorithm [9] empirically retains the accuracy of the exact algorithm, while requiring little more computation than that of a simple 1-best search.

The N-best Paradigm has the potential problem that if a knowledge source is not used to find the N-best hypotheses, the answer that would ultimately have the highest score including this knowledge source may be missing from the top N hypotheses. This becomes more likely as the error rate becomes higher and the utterances become longer. We have found empirically that this problem does not occur for smaller vocabularies, but it does occur when we use vocabularies of 20,000 words and trigram language models in the rescoring pass.

This problem can be avoided by keeping the lattice of all sentence hypotheses generated by the algorithm, rather than enumerating independent sentence hypotheses. Then the lattice is treated as a grammar and used to rescore all the hypotheses with the more powerful knowledge sources [10].

2.5. Forward-Backward Search Paradigm

The Forward-Backward Search algorithm is a general paradigm in which we use some inexpensive approximate time-synchronous search in the forward direction to speed up a more complex search in the backwards direction. This algorithm generally results in two orders of magnitude speedup for the backward pass. Since it was the key mechanism that made it possible to perform recognition with a 20,000-word vocabulary in real time, we discuss it in more detail in the next section.

3. The Forward-Backward Search Algorithm

We developed the Forward-Backward Search (FBS) algorithm in 1986 as a way to greatly reduce the computation needed to search a large language model. While many sites have adopted this paradigm for computation of the N-best sentence hypotheses, we feel that its full use may not be fully understood. Therefore, we will discuss the use of the FBS at some length in this section.

The basic idea in the FBS is to perform a search in the forward direction to compute the probability of each word ending at each frame. Then, a second more expensive search in the backward direction can use these word-ending scores to speed up the computation immensely. If we multiply the forward score for a path by the backward score of another path ending at the same frame, we have an estimate of the total score for the combined path, given the entire utterance. In a sense, the forward search provides the ideal fast match for the backward pass, in that it gives a good estimate of the score for each of the words that can follow in the backward direction, including the effect of all of the remaining speech.

When we first introduced the FBS to speed up the N-best search algorithm, the model used in the forward and backward directions were identical. So the estimate of the backward scores provided by the forward pass were exact. This method has also been used in a best-first stack search [8], in which it is very effective, since the forward-backward score for any theory covers the whole utterance. The forward-backward score solves the primary problem with the best-first search, which is that different hypotheses don't span the same amount of speech.

However, the true power of this algorithm is revealed when we use different models in the forward and backward directions. For example, in the forward direction we can use approximate acoustic models with a bigram language model. Then, in the backward pass we can use detailed HMM models with a trigram language model. In this case, the forward scores still provide an excellent (although not exact) estimate of the ranking of different word end scores. Because both searches are time-synchronous, it does not matter that the forward and backward passes do not get the same score. (This is in contrast to a backward best-first or A* search, which depends on the forward scores being an accurate prediction of the actual scores that will result in the backward pass.)

In order to use these approximate scores, we need to modify the algorithm slightly. The forward scores are normalized relative to the highest forward score at that frame. (This happens automatically in the BYBLOS decoder, since we normalized the scores in each frame in order to prevent underflow.) We multiply the normalized forward score by the normalized backward score to produce a normalized forward-backward score. We can compare these normalized forward-backward scores to the normalized backward scores using the usual beam-type threshold. This causes us to consider more than one path in the backwards direction. The best path (word sequence) associated with each word end may not turn out to be the highest, but this does not matter, because the backward search will rescore all the allowed paths anyway.

We find that the backward pass can run about 1000 times faster than it would otherwise, with the same accuracy. For example, when using a vocabulary of 20,000 words a typical beam search that allows for only a small error rate due to pruning requires about 20 times real time. In contrast, we find that the backward pass runs at about 1/60 real time! This makes it fast enough so that it can be performed at the end of the utterance with a delay that is barely noticeable.

But the FBS also speeds up the forward pass indirectly! Since we know there will be a detailed backward search, we need not worry about the accuracy of the forward pass to some extent. This allows us the freedom to use powerful approximate methods to speed up the forward pass, even though they may not be as accurate as we would like for a final score.

4. Sublinear Computation

Fast match methods require much less computation for each word than a detailed match. But to reduce the computation for speech recognition significantly for very large vocabulary problems, we must change the computation from one that is linear with the vocabulary to one that is essentially independent of the vocabulary size.

4.1. Memory vs Speed Tradeoffs

One of the classical methods for saving computation is to trade increased memory for reduced computation. Now that memory is becoming large and inexpensive, there are several methods open to us. The most obvious is various forms of fast match. We propose one such memory-intensive fast match algorithm here. Many others could be developed.

Given an unknown word, we can make several orthogonal measures on the word to represent the acoustic realization of that word as a single point in a multi-dimensional space. If we quantize each dimension independently, we determine a single (quantized) cell in this space. We can associate information with this cell that gives us a precomputed estimate of the HMM score of each word. The computation is performed only once, and is therefore very small and independent of the size of the vocabulary. (Of course the precompilation of the scores of each of the words given a cell in the space can be large.) The precision of the fast match score is limited only by the amount of memory that we have, and our ability to represent the scores efficiently.

4.2. Computation vs Vocabulary Size

To learn how the computation of our real-time search algorithm grows with vocabulary size we measured the computation required at three different vocabulary sizes: 1,500 words, 5,000 words, and 20,000 words. The time required, as a fraction of real time, is shown plotted against the vocabulary size in Figure 1.

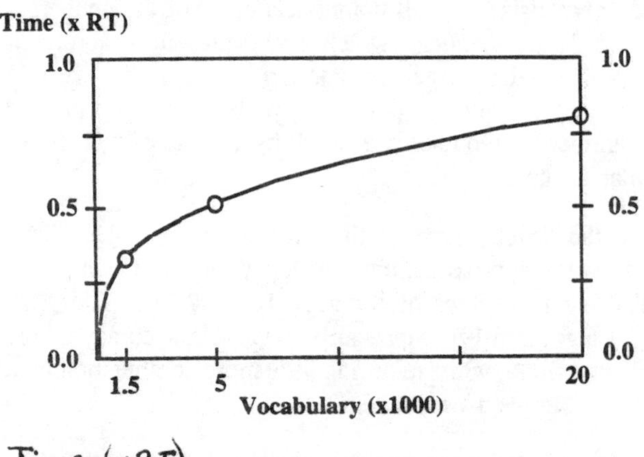

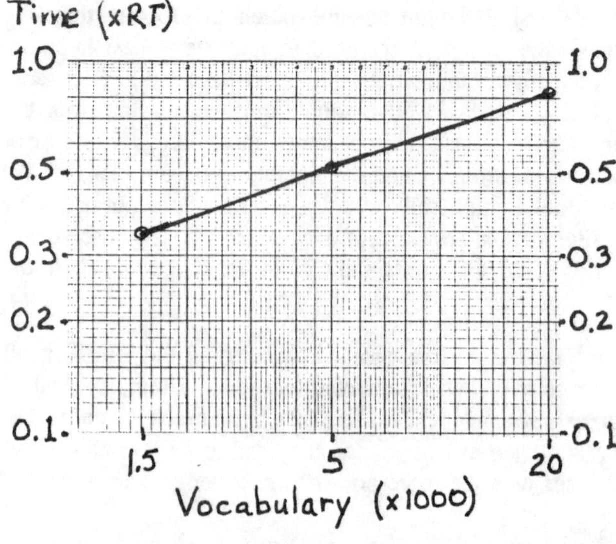

Figure 1: Run time vs vocabulary size. Plotted on a linear and a log-log scale.

As can be seen, the computation increases very slowly with increased vocabulary. To understand the behavior better we plotted the same numbers on a log-log scale as shown above.

Here we can see that the three points fall neatly on a straight line, leading us to the conclusion that the computation grows as a power of the vocabulary size, V. Solving the equation gives us the formula

$$time = 0.04 \quad V^{1/3} \tag{1}$$

This is very encouraging, since it means that if we can decrease the computation needed by a small factor it would be feasible to increase the vocabulary size by a much larger factor, making recognition with extremely large vocabularies possible.

5. Summary

We have discussed the search problem in speech recognition and concluded that, in our opinion, it is no longer worth considering parallel or special purpose hardware for the speech problem, because we have been able to make faster progress by modifying the basic search algorithm in software. At present, the fastest recognition systems are based entirely on software implementations. We reviewed several search algorithms briefly, and discussed the advantage of time-synchronous search algorithms over other basic strategies. The Forward-Backward Search algorithm has turned out to be an algorithm of major importance in that it has made possible the first real-time recognition of 20,000-word vocabularies in continuous speech. Finally, we demonstrated that the computation required by this algorithm grows as the cube root of the vocabulary size, which means that real-time recognition with extremely large vocabularies is feasible.

Acknowledgement

Some of this work was supported by the Defense Advanced Research Projects Agency and monitored by the Office of Naval Research under Contract Nos. N00014-91-C-0115, and N00014-92-C-0035.

References

1. Schwartz, R. and Y.L. Chow (1990) "The N-Best Algorithm: An Efficient and Exact Procedure for Finding the N Most Likely Sentence Hypotheses", ICASSP-90, April 1990, Albuquerque S2.12, pp. 81-84. Also in *Proceedings of the DARPA Speech and Natural Language Workshop*, Cape Cod, Oct. 1989.
2. V. Steinbiss (1989) "Sentence-Hypotheses Generation in a Continuous-Speech Recognition System," *Proc. of the European Conf. on Speech Communication and Technology, Paris, Sept. 1989, Vol. 2, pp. 51-54*
3. Mariño, J. and E. Monte (1989) "Generation of Multiple Hypothesis in Connected Phonetic-Unit Recognition by a Modified One-Stage Dynamic Programming Algorithm", *Proc. of the European Conf. on Speech Communication and Technology, Paris, Sept. 1989, Vol. 2, pp. 408-411*
4. Lowerre, B. (1977) "The Harpy Speech Recognition System", *Doctoral Thesis* CMU 1977.
5. Bahl, L.R., de Souza, P., Gopalakrishnan, P.S., Kanevsky, D., and D. Nahamoo (1990) "Constructing Groups of Acoustically Confusable Words". *Proceedings of the ICASSP 90*, April, 1990.
6. Schwartz, R.M., Chow, Y., Kimball, O., Roucos, S., Krasner, M., and J. Makhoul (1985) "Context-Dependent Modeling for Acoustic-Phonetic Recognition of Continuous Speech", *Proceedings of the ICASSP 85*, pp. 1205-1208, March, 1985.
7. R.M. Schwartz and S.A. Austin, "Efficient, High-Performance Algorithms for N-Best Search," *Proc. DARPA Speech and Natural Language Workshop*, Hidden Valley, PA, Morgan Kaufmann Publishers, pp. 6-11, June 1990.
8. Soong, F., Huang, E., "A Tree-Trellis Based Fast Search for Finding the N Best Sentence Hypotheses in Continuous Speech Recognition". *Proceedings of the DARPA Speech and Natural Language Workshop*, Hidden Valley, June 1990.
9. Alleva, F., Huang, X., Hwang, M-Y., Rosenfeld, R., "An Improved Search Algorithm Using Incremental Knowledge for Continuous Speech Recognition and An Overview of the SPHINX-II Speech Recognition System", *DARPA Human Language Technology Workshop*, Princeton, NJ, March, 1993.
10. Murveit, H., Butzberger, J., Digalakis, V., Weintraub, M., "Progressive-Search Algorithms for Large Vocabulary Speech Recognition", *DARPA Human Language Technology Workshop*, Princeton, NJ, March, 1993.

Identification of Non-Linguistic Speech Features

Jean-Luc Gauvain and Lori F. Lamel

LIMSI-CNRS, BP 133
91403 Orsay cedex, FRANCE
{lamel,gauvain}@limsi.fr

ABSTRACT

Over the last decade technological advances have been made which enable us to envision real-world applications of speech technologies. It is possible to foresee applications where the spoken query is to be recognized without even prior knowledge of the language being spoken, for example, information centers in public places such as train stations and airports. Other applications may require accurate identification of the speaker for security reasons, including control of access to confidential information or for telephone-based transactions. Ideally, the speaker's identity can be verified continually during the transaction, in a manner completely transparent to the user. With these views in mind, this paper presents a unified approach to identifying non-linguistic speech features from the recorded signal using phone-based acoustic likelihoods.

This technique is shown to be effective for text-independent language, sex, and speaker identification and can enable better and more friendly human-machine interaction. With 2s of speech, the language can be identified with better than 99% accuracy. Error in sex-identification is about 1% on a per-sentence basis, and speaker identification accuracies of 98.5% on TIMIT (168 speakers) and 99.2% on BREF (65 speakers), were obtained with one utterance per speaker, and 100% with 2 utterances for both corpora. An experiment using unsupervised adaptation for speaker identification on the 168 TIMIT speakers had the same identification accuracies obtained with supervised adaptation.

INTRODUCTION

As speech recognition technology advances, so do the aims of system designers, and the prospects of potential applications. One of the main efforts underway in the community is the development of speaker-independent, task-independent large vocabulary speech recognizers that can easily be adapted to new tasks. It is becoming apparent that many of the portability issues may depend more on the specification of the task, and the ergonomy, than on the performance of the speech recognition component itself. The acceptance of speech technology in the world at large will depend on how well the technology can be integrated in systems which simplify the life of the users. This in turns means that the service provided by such a system must be easy to use, and as fast as other providers of the service (i.e., such as using a human operator).

While the focus has been on improving the performance of the speech recognizers, it is also of interest to be able to identify what we refer to as some of the "non-linguistic" speech features present in the acoustic signal. For example, it is possible to envision applications where the spoken query is to be recognized without prior knowledge of the language being spoken. This is the case for information centers in public places, such as train stations and airports, where the language may change from one user to the next. The ability to automatically identify the language being spoken, and to respond appropriately, is possible.

Other applications, such as for financial or banking transactions, or access to confidential information, such as financial, medical or insurance records, etc., require accurate identification or verification of the user. Typically security is provided by the human who "recognizes" the voice of the client he is used to dealing with (and often will also be confirmed by a fax), or for automated systems by the use of cards and/or codes, which must be provided in order to access the data. With the widespread use of telephones, and the new payment and information retrieval services offered by telephone, it is a logical extension to explore the use of speech for user identification. An advantage is that if text-independent speaker verification techniques are used, the speaker's identity can be continually verified during the transaction, in a manner completely transparent to the user. This can avoid the problems encountered by theft or duplication of cards, and pre-recording of the user's voice during an earlier transaction.

With these future views in mind, this paper presents a unified approach for identifying non-linguistic speech features, such as the language being spoken, and the identity or sex of the speaker, using phone-based acoustic likelihoods. The basic idea is similar to that of using sex-dependent models for recognition, but instead of the output being the recognized string, the output is the characteristic associated with the model set having the highest likelihood. This approach has been evaluated for French/English language identification, and speaker and sex identification in both languages.

PHONE-BASED ACOUSTIC LIKELIHOODS

The basic idea is to train a set of large phone-based ergodic hidden Markov models (HMMs) for each non-linguistic feature to be identified (language, gender, speaker, ...). Feature identification on the incoming signal $\mathbf{x}$ is then performed by computing the acoustic likelihoods $f(\mathbf{x}|\lambda_i)$ for all the models λ_i of a given set. The feature value corresponding to the model with the highest likelihood is then hypothesized. This decoding procedure can efficiently be implemented by processing all the models in parallel using a time-synchronous beam search strategy.

This approach has the following advantages:

- It can perform text-independent feature recognition. (Text-dependent feature recognition can also be performed.)
- It is more precise than methods based on long-term statistics such as long term spectra, VQ codebooks, or probabilistic acoustic maps[26, 28].
- It can easily take advantage of phonotactic constraints. (These are shown to be useful for language identification.)
- It can easily be integrated in recognizers which are based on phone models as all the components already exist.

A disadvantage of the approach is that, at least in the current formulation, phonetic labels are required for training the models. However, there is in theory no absolute need for phonetic labeling of the speech training data to estimate the HMM parameters. Labeling of a small portion of the training data can be enough to bootstrap the training procedure and insure the phone-based nature of the resulting models. (In this case, phonotactic constraints must be obtained only from speech corpora.) We have sucessfully experimented with this approach for speaker identification.

In our implementation, each large ergodic HMM is built from small left-to-right phonetic HMMs. The Viterbi algorithm is used to compute the joint likelihood $f(\mathbf{x}, \mathrm{s}|\lambda_i)$ of the incoming signal and the most likely state sequence instead of $f(\mathbf{x}|\lambda_i)$. This implementation is therefore nothing more than a slightly modified phone recognizer with language-, sex-, or speaker- dependent model sets used in parallel, and where the output phone string is *ignored*[1] and only the acoustic likelihood for each model is taken into account.

The phone recognizer can use either context-dependent or context-independent phone models, where each phone model is a 3-state left-to-right continuous density hidden Markov model (CDHMM) with Gaussian mixture observation densities. The covariance matrices of all Gaussian components are diagonal. Duration is modeled with a gamma distribution per phone model. As proposed by Rabiner et al.[23], the HMM and duration parameters are estimated separately and combined in the recognition process for the Viterbi search.

Maximum likelihood estimators are used to derive language specific models whereas maximum a posteriori (MAP) estimators are used to generate sex- and speaker- specific models as has already been proposed in [11]. The MAP estimates are obtained with the segmental MAP algorithm [16, 9, 10] using speaker-independent seed models. These seed models are used to estimate the parameters of the prior densities and to serve as an initial estimate for the segmental MAP algorithm. This approach provides a way to incorporate prior information into the model training process and is particularly useful to build the speaker specific models when using only a small amount of speaker specific data.

In our earlier reported results using this approach for language- and speaker-identification[13, 14, 7], the acoustic likelihoods were computed sequentially for each of the models. As mentioned earlier, the Viterbi decoder is now implemented as a one-pass beam search procedure applied on all the models in parallel, resulting in an efficient decoding procedure which saves a lot of computation.

[1]The likelihood computation can in fact be simplified since there is no need to maintain the backtracking information necessary to know the recognized phone sequence.

EXPERIMENTAL CONDITIONS

Four corpora have been used to carry out the experiments reported in this paper: BDSONS[2] and BREF[15, 8] for French; and TIMIT[4] and WSJ0[22] for English. From the BDSONS corpus only the phonetically equilibrated sentence sub-corpus (CDROM 6) has been used for testing, whereas depending on experiment, the 3 other corpora have been used for training and testing.

The BDSONS Corpus: BDSONS, Base de Données des Sons du Français[2], was designed to provide a large corpus of French speech data for the study of the sounds in the French language and to aid speech research. The corpus contains an "evaluation" subcorpus consisting primarily of isolated and connected letters, digits and words from 32 speakers (16m/16f), and an "acoustic" subcorpus which includes phonetically balanced words and sentences from 12 speakers (6m/6f).

The BREF Corpus: BREF is a large read-speech corpus, containing over 100 hours of speech material, from 120 speakers (55m/65f)[15]. The text materials were selected verbatim from the French newspaper *Le Monde*, so as to provide a large vocabulary (over 20,000 words) and a wide range of phonetic environments[8]. Containing 1115 distinct diphones and over 17,500 triphones, BREF can be used to train vocabulary-independenet phonetic models. The text material was read without verbalized punctuation.

The DARPA WSJ0 Corpus: The DARPA Wall Street Journal-based Continuous-Speech Corpus (WSJ)[22] has been designed to provide general-purpose speech data (primarily, read speech data) with large vocabularies. Text materials were selected to provide training and test data for 5K and 20K word, closed and open vocabularies, and with both verbalized and non-verbalized punctuation. The recorded speech material supports both speaker-dependent and speaker-independent training and evaluation.

The DARPA TIMIT Corpus: The DARPA TIMIT Acoustic-Phonetic Continuous Speech Corpus[4] is a corpus of read speech designed to provide speech data for the acquisition of acoustic-phonetic knowledge and for the development and evaluation of automatic speech recognition systems. TIMIT contains a total of 6300 sentences, 10 sentences spoken by each of 630 speakers from 8 major dialect regions of the U.S. The TIMIT CDROM[4] contains a training/test subdivision of the data that ensures that there is no overlap in the text materials. All of the utterances in TIMIT have associated time-aligned phonetic transcriptions.

Since the identification of non-linguistic speech features is based on phone recognition, some phone recognition results for the above corpora are given here. The speaker-independent (SI) phone recognizers use sets of context-dependent (CD) models which were automatically selected based on their frequencies in the training data. There are 428 sex-dependent CD models for BREF, 1619 for WSJ and 459 for TIMIT. Phone errors rates are given in Table 1. For BREF and WSJ phone errors are reported after removing silences, whereas for TIMIT silences are included as transcribed. Scoring without the sentence initial/final silence increases the phone error by about 1.5%. The phone error for BREF is 21.3%, WSJ (Feb-92 5knvp) is 25.7% and TIMIT (complete testset) is 27.6% scored using the 39 phone set proposed by[18]. These results are provided to calibrate the recognizers used in the experiments in this paper, and observe differences in the corpora. It appears that the BREF data is easiest to recognize at the phone level, and that TIMIT is more difficult than WSJ.

Condition	*Correct*	*Subs.*	*Del.*	*Ins.*	*Errors*
BREF	81.7	13.7	4.6	3.0	21.3
WSJ nvp	79.3	16.2	4.5	5.0	25.7
TIMIT	77.3	17.3	5.4	4.9	27.6

Table 1: Phone error (%) with CD models and phone bigram.

SEX IDENTIFICATION

It is well known that the use of sex-dependent models gives improved performance over one set of speaker-independent models. However, this approach can be costly in terms of computation for medium-to-large-size tasks, since recognition of the unknown sentence is typically carried out twice, once for each sex. A logical alternative is to first determine the speaker's sex, and then to perform word recognition using the models of selected sex. This is the approach used in our Nov-92 WSJ system[6]. In these experiments the standard SI-84 training material, containing 7240 sentences from 84 speakers (42m/42f) is used to build speaker-independent phone models. Sex-dependent models are then obtained using MAP estimation[11] with the SI seed models. The phone likelihoods using context-dependent male and female models were computed, and the sex of the speaker was selected as the sex associated with the models that gave the highest likelihood. Since these CD male and female models are the same as are used for word recognition, there is no need for additional training material or effort. No errors were observed in sex identification for WSJ on the Feb92 or Nov92 5k test data containing 851 sentences, from 18 speakers (10m/8f).

For BREF, sex-dependent models were also obtained from SI seeds by MAP estimation. The training data consisted of 2770 sentences from 57 speakers (28m/29f). No errors in sex-identification were observed on 109 test sentences from 21 test speakers (10m/11f).

To further investigate sex identification based on acoustic likelihoods on a larger set of speakers, the approach was evaluted on the 168 speakers of the TIMIT test corpus. The SI seed models were trained using all the available training data, i.e., 4620 sentences from 462 speakers, and adapted using data from the 326 males speakers and 136 females to form gender-specific models. The test data consist of 1344 sentences, comprised of 8 sentences from each of the 168 test speakers (112m/56f). Results are shown in the first row of Table 2 where the error rate is given as a function of the speech duration. Each speech segment used for the test is part of a single sentence, and always starts at the beginning of the sentence, preceeded by about 100ms of silence[2]. These results on this more significant test show that sex identification error rate using phone-based acoustic likelihoods is 2.8% with 400ms of speech and is under 1% with 2s of speech. The 400ms of speech signal (which includes about 100ms of silence) represents about 4 phones, about the number found in a typical word (avg. 3.9 phones/word) in TIMIT. This implies that before the speaker has finished enunciating the first word, one is fairly certain of the speaker's sex. Sentences misclassified with regards to the speaker's sex had better phone recognition accuracies with the cross-sex models.

Using exactly the same test data and the same phone models, an experiment of text-dependent sex identification was carried out in order to assess if by adding linguistic information the speaker's gender can be more easily identified. To do this a long left-to-right HMM is built for each sex by concatenating the sex-dependent CD phone models corresponding to the TIMIT transcriptions. The basic idea is to measure the lower bound on the error rate that would be obtained if higher order knowledge such as lexical information were provided. The acoustic likelihoods are then computed for the two models. These likelihood values are lower than are obtained for text-independent identification. The results are given in the second row of Table 2 where it can be seen that the error rate is not any better than the error rate obtained with the text-independent method. This shows that acoustic-phonetic knowledge is sufficient to accomplish this task.

Duration	*0.4s*	*0.8s*	*1.2s*	*1.6s*	*2.0s*	*EOS*
Text indep.	2.8	1.9	1.5	1.2	0.9	1.2
Text dep.	3.4	2.2	1.0	1.0	1.2	1.3

Table 2: Error rate in sex identification as a function of duration. (EOS is End Of Sentence identification error rate.)

While in our previous work[6], sex-identification was used primarily as a means to reduce the computation, sex identification can permit the synthesis module of a system to respond appropriately to the unknown speaker. In French, where the

[2] The initial and final silences of each test sentence have been automatically reduced to 100ms.

formalities are used perhaps more than in English, the system acceptance may be easier if the familiar "Bonjour Madame" or "Je vous en prie Monsieur" is foreseen.

Since sex-identification is not perfect, some fall-back mechanism must be integrated to avoid including the signs of politeness if the system is unsure of the sex. This can be accomplished by comparing the likelihoods of the model sets, or by being wary of speakers for whom the better likelihood jumps back and forth between models.

LANGUAGE IDENTIFICATION

Language identification is another feature that can be identified using the same approach. In this case language-dependent models are used instead of sex-dependent ones. The basic idea is to process in parallel the unknown incoming speech by different sets of phone models (each set is a large ergodic HMM) for each of the languages under consideration, and to choose the language associated with the model set providing the highest normalized likelihood.[3] In this way, it is no longer necessary to ask the speaker to select the language, before using the system. If the language can be accurately identified, it simplifies using speech recognition for a variety of applications, from selecting an appropriate operator, or aiding with emergency assistance. Language identification can also be done using word recognition, but it is much more efficient to use phone recognition, which has the added advantage of being task independent.

Experimental results for language identification for English/French were given in [13, 14], where models trained on TIMIT [4] and BREF [15], were tested on different sentences taken from the same corpus. While these results gave high identification accuracies (100% if an entire sentence is used, and greater than 97% with 400ms, and error free with 1.6s of speech signal), it is difficult to discern that the language and not the corpus are being identified. Identification of independent data taken from the WSJ0 corpus was less accurate: 85% with 400ms, and 4% error with 1.6s of speech signal.

In these experiments we attempted to avoid the bias due to corpus, by testing on data from the same corpora from which the models are built, and on independent test data from different corpora. The language-dependent models are trained from similar-style corpora, BREF for French and WSJ0 for English, both containing read newspaper texts and similar size vocabularies[8, 15, 22]. For each language a set of context-independent phone models were built, 35 for French and 46 for English.[4] Each phone model has 32 gaussians per mixture, and no duration model is used. In order to minimize influences due to the use of different microphones and recording conditions a 4 kHz bandwidth is used. The training data were the same as for sex-identification on BREF (2770 sentences from 57 speakers) and WSJ (standard SI-84 training: 7240 sentences from 84 speakers).

Language identification accuracies are given in Tables 3 and 4 without and with phonotactic constraints provided by a phone bigram. Results are given for 4 test corpora, WSJ and TIMIT for English, and BREF and BDSONS for French, as a function of the duration of the speech signal which includes approximately 100ms of silence. As for speaker-identification, the initial and final silences were automatically removed based on HMM segmentation, so as to be able to compare language identification as a function of duration without biases due to long initial silences. The test data for WSJ are the first 10 sentences for each of the 10 speakers (5m/5f) in the Feb92-si5knvp (speaker-independent, 5k, non-verbalized punctuation) test data. For TIMIT, the 192 sentences in the "coretest" set containing 8 sentences from each of 24 speakers (16m/8f) was used. The BREF test data consists of 130 sentences from 20 speakers (10m/10f) and for BDSONS the data is comprised of 121 sentences from 11 speakers (5m/6f).

Duration	*0.4s*	*0.8s*	*1.2s*	*1.6s*	*2.0s*	*2.4s*
Eng. WSJ	7.0	3.0	2.0	2.0	1.0	1.0
Eng. TIMIT	10.9	6.3	3.1	2.1	0	0
Fr. BREF	10.8	2.3	2.3	0.8	0.8	0.8
Fr. BDSONS	7.5	4.1	1.7	1.7	0.8	0
Overall	9.4	4.2	2.4	1.7	0.5	0.4

Table 3: Language identification error rates as a function of duration and language (without phonotactic constraints).

Duration	*0.4s*	*0.8s*	*1.2s*	*1.6s*	*2.0s*	*2.4s*
Eng. WSJ	5.0	3.0	1.0	2.0	1.0	1.0
Eng. TIMIT	9.4	5.7	2.6	2.1	0.5	0
Fr. BREF	8.5	1.5	0.8	0	0.8	0.8
Fr. BDSONS	7.4	2.5	2.5	1.7	0.8	0
Overall	7.9	3.5	1.8	1.5	0.7	0.4

Table 4: Language identification error rates as a function of duration and language (with phonotactic constraints).

While WSJ sentences are more easily identified as English for short durations, errors persist longer than for TIMIT. In contrast for French with 400ms of signal, BDSONS data is better identified than BREF, perhaps because the sentences are phonetically balanced. For longer durations, BREF is slightly better identified than BDSONS. The performance indicates that language identification is task independent.

Using phonotactic constraints is seen to improve language identification, particularly for short signals. The smallest improvement is seen for TIMIT, probably due to the nature

[3] In fact, this is not a new idea: House and Neuberg (1977)[12] proposed a similar approach for language identification using models of broad phonetic classes, where we use phone models. Their experimental results, however, were synthetic, based on phonetic transcriptions derived from texts.

[4] The 35 phones used to represent French include 14 vowels (including 3 nasal vowels), 20 consonants (6 plosives, 6 fricatives, 3 nasals, and 5 semivowels), and silence. The phone table can be found in [5]. For English, the set of 46 phones include 21 vowels (including 3 diphthongs and 3 schwas), 24 consonants (6 plosives, 8 fricatives, 2 affricates, 3 nasals, 5 semivowels), and silence.

of the selected sentences which emphasized rare phone sequences. The error rate with 2s of speech is less than 1% and with 1s of speech (not shown in the tables) is about 2%. With 3s of speech, language identification is almost error free.

Due to the source of the BREF and WSJ data, language identification is complicated by the inclusion of foreign words. One of the errors on BREF involved such a sentence. The sentence was identified as French at the beginning and then all of a sudden switched to English. The sentence was "Durant mon adolescence, je dévorais les récits *westerns de Zane Grey, Luke Short*, et *Max Brand...*", where the italicized words were pronounced in correct English.

We are in the process of obtaining corpora for other languages to extend our language identification work. However, there are variety of applications where a bilingual system, just French/English would be of use, including air traffic control (where both French and English are permitted languages for flights within France), telecommunications applications, and many automated information centers, ticket distributors, and tellers, where already you can select between English and French with the keyboard or touch screen.

SPEAKER IDENTIFICATION

Speaker identification has been the topic of active research for many years (see, for example, [3, 21, 26]), and has many potential applications where propriety of information is a concern. In our experiments with speaker identification, a set of CI phone models were built for each speaker, by supervised adaptation of SI models[11], and the unknown speech was recognized by all of the speakers models in parallel.[5] Speaker-identification experiments were performed using BREF for French and TIMIT for English. TIMIT has recently been used in a few studies on speaker identification[1, 20, 27, 14] with high speaker identification rates reported using subsets of 100 to all 462 speakers.

For the experiments with TIMIT, a speaker-independent set of 40 CI models were built using data from all of the 462 training speakers with 8kHz Mel frequency-based cepstral coefficients and their first order differences. 31-phone model sets were then adapted to each of the 168 test speakers using 8 sentences (2 SA, 3 SX, and 3 SI) for adaptation. We chose this set for identification test so as to evaluate the performance for speakers not in the original SI training material, which greatly simplifies the enrollment procedure for new speakers. A reduced number of phones was used so as to minimize subtle distinctions, and to reduce the number of models to be adapted. The remaining 2 SX sentences for each speaker were reserved for the identification test. While the original CI models had a maximum of 32 Gaussians, the adapted models were limited to 4 mixture components, since the amount of adaptation data was relatively limited.

[5]Using HMM for speaker recognition has been previously proposed, see [26] for a review, and also [24, 25].

The unknown speech was recognized by all of the speakers models in parallel by building one large HMM. Error rates are shown as a function of the speech signal duration in Table 5, for text-independent speaker identification. As for sex and language identification, the initial and final silences were adjusted to have a maximum duration of 100ms according to the provided time-aligned transcriptions. Using the entire utterance the identification accuracy is 98.5%. With 2.5s of speech the speaker identification accuracy is 98.3%. For the small number of sentences longer than 3s, speaker identification was correct, suggesting that with longer sentences performance will improve. This is also supported by the result that speaker-identification using both sentences for identification was 100%.

Duration	*0.5s*	*1.0s*	*1.5s*	*2.0s*	*2.5s*	EOS
TIMIT	36.9	19.6	7.8	3.9	1.7	1.5
BREF	33.8	13.1	7.8	3.3	2.6	0.8

Table 5: Text-independent speaker identification error rate as a function of duration for 168 test speakers of TIMIT, and 65 speakers from BREF. (EOS is End Of Sentence identification error rate.)

For French, the acoustic seed models were 35 SI CI models, built using data from 57 BREF training speakers, excluding 10 sentences to be used for adaptation and test. In order to have a similar situation to English, these models were adapted to each of 65 speakers (including 8 new speakers not used in training) using only 8 sentences for adaptation, and reserving 2 sentences for identification test. Using only one sentence per speaker for identification, there is one error, giving an identification accuracy of 99.2%, and when 2 sentences are used all speakers are correctly identified (as observed for TIMIT). Speaker-identification results are given in Table 5 for 65 speakers (27m/38f) as a function of signal duration. It can be noted that the identification accuracies as a function of time are similar for both corpora. However, since BREF sentences are somewhat longer than TIMIT sentences, the overall identification error rate per sentence is lower for BREF (EOS), even though the error for BREF at 2.5s is greater. For both TIMIT and BREF, when there was a confusion, the speaker was always identified by another speaker of the same sex.

Experiments for text-dependent speaker identification using exactly the same models and test sentences were performed. For both TIMIT and BREF a performance degradation was observed (on the order of 4% using the accuracy at the end of the sentence.) These results were contrary to our expectations, in that typically text-dependent speaker verification is considered to outperform text-independent[3, 19].

An experiment was also performed in which speaker-adapted models were built for each of the 168 test speakers from TIMIT *without* knowledge of the phonetic transcription, using the same 8 sentences for adaptation. Performing text-independent speaker identification as before on the remaining 2 sentences give the results shown in Table 6. As before if both sentences are used for identification, the speaker identification accuracy is 100%. This experimental result indicates that the time consuming step of providing phonetic transcriptions is not needed for accuracte text-independent speaker identification.

Duration	*0.5s*	*1.0s*	*1.5s*	*2.0s*	*2.5s*	EOS
TIMIT	37.5	21.2	6.6	4.0	2.1	1.5

Table 6: Text-independent speaker identification error rate as a function of duration for 168 test speakers of TIMIT with unsupervised adaptation. (EOS is End Of Sentence identification error rate.)

SUMMARY

In this paper we have reported on recent work on the identification of non-linguistic speech features from recorded signals using phone-based acoustic likelihoods. The inclusion of this technique in speech-based systems, can broaden the scope of applications of speech technologies, and lead to more user-friendly systems.

The approach is based on training a set of large phone-based ergodic HMMs for each non-linguistic feature to be identified (language, gender, speaker, ...), and identifying the feature as that associated with the model having the highest acoustic likelihood of the set. The decoding procedure is efficiently implemented by processing all the models in parallel using a time-synchronous beam search strategy.

This has been shown to be a powerful technique for sex-, language-, and speaker-identification, and has other possible applications such as for dialect identification (including foreign accents), or identification of speech disfluencies. Sex-identification for BREF and WSJ was error-free, and 99% accurate for TIMIT with 2s of speech. With 2s of speech the language is correctly identified as English or French with over 99% accuracy. Speaker identification accuracies of 98.5% on TIMIT (168 speakers) and 99.1% on BREF (65 speakers) were obtained with one utterance per speaker, and 100% if 2 utterances were used for identification. The same identification accuracy was obtained on the 168 speakers of TIMIT using unsupervised adaptation, verifying that it is not necessary to provide phonetic transcription for accurate speaker identification. Being independent of the spoken text, and requiring only a small amount of speech (on the order of 2.5s), this technique is promising for a variety of applications, particularly those for which continual verification is preferable.

In conclusion, we propose a unified approach to identifying non-linguistic speech features from the recorded signal using phone-based acoustic likelihoods. This technique has been shown to be effective for language, sex, and speaker identification and can enable better and more friendly human machine interaction.

REFERENCES

[1] Y. Bennani, "Speaker Identification through a Modular Connectionist Architecture: Evaluation on the TIMIT Database," *ICSLP-92*.

[2] R. Carré, R. Descout, M. Eskénazi, J. Mariani, M. Rossi, "The French language database: defining, planning, and recording a large database," *ICASSP-84*.

[3] G.R. Doddington, "Speaker Recognition - Identifying People by their Voices," *Proc. IEEE*, **73**,(11), Nov. 1985.

[4] J.S. Garofolo, L.F. Lamel, W.M. Fisher, J.G. Fiscus, D.S. Pallett, N.L. Dahlgren, "The DARPA TIMIT Acoustic-Phonetic Continuous Speech Corpus CDROM" NTIS order number PB91-100354.

[5] J.L. Gauvain, L.F. Lamel, "Speaker-Independent Phone Recognition Using BREF," *DARPA Speech & Nat. Lang. Workshop*, Feb. 1992.

[6] J.L. Gauvain, L.F. Lamel, G. Adda, "LIMSI Nov92 WSJ Evaluation," presented at the *DARPA Spoken Language Systems Technology Workshop*, MIT, Cambridge, MA, Jan., 1993.

[7] J.L. Gauvain, L.F. Lamel, G. Adda, J. Mariani, "Speech-to-Text Conversion in French," to appear in *Int. J. Pat. Rec. & A.I.*, 1993.

[8] J.L. Gauvain, L.F. Lamel, M. Eskénazi, "Design considerations & text selection for BREF, a large French read-speech corpus," *ICSLP-90*.

[9] J.L. Gauvain, C.H. Lee, "Bayesian Learning of Gaussian Mixture Densities for Hidden Markov Models," *DARPA Speech & Nat. Lang. Workshop*, Feb. 1991.

[10] J.L. Gauvain, C.H. Lee, "MAP Estimation of Continuous Density HMM: Theory and Applications," *DARPA Speech & Nat. Lang. Workshop*, Feb. 1992.

[11] J.L. Gauvain, C.H. Lee, "Bayesian Learning for Hidden Markov Model with Gaussian Mixture State Observation Densities," *Speech Communication*, **11**(2-3), 1992.

[12] A.S. House, E.P. Neuburg, "Toward automatic identification of the language of an utterance. I. Preliminary methodological considerations," *JASA*, **62**(3).

[13] L.F. Lamel, J.L. Gauvain, "Continuous Speech Recognition at LIMSI," *DARPA Speech & Nat. Lang. Workshop*, Sep. 1992.

[14] L.F. Lamel, J.L. Gauvain, "Cross-Lingual Experiments with Phone Recognition," *ICASSP-93*.

[15] L.F. Lamel, J.L. Gauvain, M. Eskénazi, "BREF, a Large Vocabulary Spoken Corpus for French," *EUROSPEECH-91*.

[16] C.H. Lee, C.H. Lin, B.H. Juang, "A Study on Speaker Adaptation of the Parameters of Continuous Density Hidden Markov Models," *IEEE Trans. on ASSP*, April 1991.

[17] C.H. Lee, L.R. Rabiner, R. Pieraccini, J.G. Wilpon, "Acoustic modeling for large vocabulary speech recognition," *Computer Speech & Language*, 4, 1990.

[18] K.F. Lee, H.W. Hon, "Speaker-Independent Phone Recognition Using Hidden Markov Models," *IEEE Trans. ASSP*, 37(11), 1989.

[19] T. Matsui, S. Furui, "Speaker Recognition using Concatenated Phoneme Models," *ICSLP-92*.

[20] C. Montacié, J.L. Le Floch, "AR-Vector Models for Free-Text Speaker Recognition," *ICSLP-92*.

[21] J.M. Naik, "Speaker Verification: A Tutorial," *IEEE Communications Magazine*, **28**(1), 1990.

[22] D. Paul, J. Baker, "The Design for the Wall Street Journal-based CSR Corpus" *DARPA Speech & Nat. Lang. Workshop*, Feb. 1992.

[23] L.R. Rabiner, B.H. Juang, S.E. Levinson, M.M. Sondhi, "Recognition of Isolated Digits Using Hidden Markov Models with Continuous Mixture Densities," *AT&T Technical Journal*, 64(6), 1985.

[24] R.C. Rose and D.A. Reynolds, "Text Independent Speaker Identification using Automatic Acoustic Segmentation," *ICASSP-90*.

[25] A.E. Rosenberg, C.H. Lee, F.K. Soong, "Sub-Word Unit Talker Verification Using Hidden Markov Models," *ICASSP-90*.

[26] A.E. Rosenberg, F.K. Soong, "Recent Research in Automatic Speaker Recognition," in *Advances in Speech Signal Processing*, (Eds. Furui, Sondhi), Marcel Dekker, NY, 1992.

[27] M. Savic, J. Sorenson, "Phoneme Based Speaker Verification," *ICASSP-92*.

[28] B.L. Tseng, F.K. Soong, A.E. Rosenberg, "Continuous Probabilistic Acoustic MAP for Speaker Recognition," *ICASSP-92*.

ON THE USE OF TIED-MIXTURE DISTRIBUTIONS

Owen Kimball, Mari Ostendorf

Electrical, Computer and Systems Engineering
Boston University, Boston, MA 02215

ABSTRACT

Tied-mixture (or semi-continuous) distributions are an important tool for acoustic modeling, used in many high-performance speech recognition systems today. This paper provides a survey of the work in this area, outlining the different options available for tied mixture modeling, introducing algorithms for reducing training time, and providing experimental results assessing the trade-offs for speaker-independent recognition on the Resource Management task. Additionally, we describe an extension of tied mixtures to segment-level distributions.

1. INTRODUCTION

Tied-mixture (or semi-continuous) distributions have rapidly become an important tool for acoustic modeling in speech recognition since their introduction by Huang and Jack [1] and Bellegarda and Nahamoo [2], finding widespread use in a number of high-performance recognition systems. Tied mixtures have a number of advantageous properties that have contributed to their success. Like discrete, "non-parametric" distributions, tied mixtures can model a wide range of distributions including those with an "irregular shape," while retaining the smoothed form characteristic of simpler parametric models. Additionally, because the component distributions of the mixtures are shared, the number of free parameters is reduced, and tied-mixtures have been found to produce robust estimates with relatively small amounts of training data. Under the general heading of tied mixtures, there are a number of possible choices of parameterization that lead to systems with different characteristics. This paper outlines these choices and provides a set of controlled experiments assessing trade-offs in speaker-independent recognition on the Resource Management corpus in the context of the stochastic segment model (SSM). In addition, we introduce new variations on training algorithms that reduce computational requirements and generalize the tied mixture formalism to include segment-level mixtures.

2. PREVIOUS WORK

A central problem in the statistical approach to speech recognition is finding a good model for the probability of acoustic observations conditioned on the state in hidden-Markov models (HMM), or for the case of the SSM, conditioned on a region of the model. Some of the options that have been investigated include discrete distributions based on vector quantization, as well as Gaussian, Gaussian mixture and tied-Gaussian mixture distributions. In tied-mixture modeling, distributions are modeled as a mixture of continuous densities, but unlike ordinary, non-tied mixtures, rather than estimating the component Gaussian densities separately, each mixture is constrained to share the same component densities with only the weights differing. The probability density of observation vector $\mathbf{x}$ conditioned on being in state i is thus

$$\mathrm{p}(\mathbf{x} \mid s = i) = \sum_k w_{ik} \mathrm{p}_k(\mathbf{x}). \tag{1}$$

Note that the component Gaussian densities, $\mathrm{p}_k(\mathbf{x}) \sim N(\mu_k, \Sigma_k)$, are not indexed by the state, i. In this light, tied mixtures can be seen as a particular example of the general technique of tying to reduce the number of model parameters that must be trained [3].

"Tied mixtures" and "semi-continuous HMMs" are used in the literature to refer to HMM distributions of the form given in Equation (1). The term "semi-continuous HMMs" was coined by Huang and Jack, who first proposed their use in continuous speech recognition [1]. The "semi-continuous" terminology highlights the relationship of this method to discrete and continuous density HMMs, where the mixture component means are analogous to the vector quantization codewords of a discrete HMM and the weights to the discrete observation probabilities, but, as in continuous density HMMs, actual quantization with its attendant distortion is avoided. Bellegarda and Nahamoo independently developed the same technique which they termed "tied mixtures" [2]. For simplicity, we use only one name in this paper, and choose the term tied mixtures, to highlight the relationship to other types of mixture distributions and because our work is based on the SSM, not the HMM.

Since its introduction, a number of variants of the tied mixture model have been explored. First, different assumptions can be made about feature correlation within individual mixture components. Separate sets of tied mixtures have been used for various input features including cepstra, derivatives of cepstra, and power and its derivative, where each of these feature sets have been treated as independent observation streams. Within an observation stream, different assumptions about feature correlation have been explored, with some researchers currently favoring diagonal covariance matrices [4, 5] and others adopting full covariance matrices [6, 7].

Second, the issue of parameter initialization can be important, since the training algorithm is an iterative hill-climbing technique that guarantees convergence only to a local optimum. Many researchers initialize their systems with parameters estimated from data subsets determined by K-means clustering, e.g. [6], although Paul describes a different, bootstrapping initialization [4]. Often a large number of mixture components are used and, since the parameters can be overtrained, contradictory results are reported on the benefits of parameter re-estimation. For example, while many researchers find it useful to reestimate all parameters of the mixture models in training, BBN reports no benefit for updating means and covariances after the initialization from clustered data [7].

Another variation, embodied in the CMU senone models [8], involves tying mixture weights over classes of context-dependent models. Their approach to finding regions of mixture weight tying involves clustering discrete observation distributions and mapping these clustered distributions to the mixture weights for the associated triphone contexts.

In addition to the work described above, there are related methods that have informed the research concerning tied mixtures. First, mixture modeling does not require the use of Gaussian distributions. Good results have also been obtained using mixtures of Laplacian distributions [9, 10], and presumably other component densities would perform well too. Ney [11] has found strong similarities between radial basis functions and mixture densities using Gaussians with diagonal covariances. Recent work at BBN has explored the use of elliptical basis functions which share many properties with tied mixtures of full-covariance Gaussians [12]. Second, the positive results achieved by several researchers using non-tied mixture systems [13] raise the question of whether tied-mixtures have significant performance advantages over untied mixtures when there is adequate training data. It is possible to strike a compromise and use limited tying: for instance the context models of a phone can all use the same tied distributions (e.g. [14, 15]).

Of course, the best choice of model depends on the nature of the observation vectors and the amount of training data. In addition, it is likely that the amount of tying in a system can be adjusted across a continuum to fit the particular task and amount of training data. However, an assessment of modeling trade-offs for speaker-independent recognition is useful for providing insight into the various choices, and also because the various results in the literature are difficult to compare due to differing experimental paradigms.

3. TRAINING ALGORITHMS

In this section we first review properties of the SSM and then describe the training algorithm used for tied mixtures with the SSM. Next, we describe an efficient method for training context-dependent models, and lastly we describe a parallel implementation of the trainer that greatly reduces experimentation time.

3.1. The SSM and "Viterbi" Training with Tied Mixtures

The SSM is characterized by two components: a family of length-dependent distribution functions and a deterministic mapping function that determines the distribution for a variable-length observed segment. More specifically, in the work presented here, a linear time warping function maps each observed frame to one of m regions of the segment model. Each region is described by a tied Gaussian mixture distribution, and the frames are assumed conditionally independent given the length-dependent warping. The conditional independence assumption allows robust estimation of the model's statistics and reduces the computation of determining a segment's probability, but the potential of the segment model is not fully utilized. Under this formulation, the SSM is similar to a tied-mixture HMM with a phone-length-dependent, constrained state trajectory. Thus, many of the experiments reported here translate to HMM systems.

The SSM training algorithm [16] iterates between segmentation and maximum likelihood parameter estimation, so that during the parameter estimation phase of each iteration, the segmentation of that pass gives a set of known phonetic boundaries. Additionally, for a given phonetic segmentation, the assignment of observations to regions of the model is uniquely determined. SSM training is similar to HMM "Viterbi training", in which training data is segmented using the most likely state sequence and model parameters are updated using this segmentation. Although it is possible to define an SSM training algorithm equivalent to the Baum-Welch algorithm for HMMs, the computation is prohibitive for the SSM because of the large effective state space.

The use of a constrained segmentation greatly simplifies parameter estimation in the tied mixture case, since there is only one unobserved component, the mixture mode. In this case, the parameter estimation step of the iterative segmentation/estimation algorithm involves the standard iterative expectation-maximization (EM) approach to estimating the parameters of a mixture distribution [17]. In contrast, the full EM algorithm for tied mixtures in an HMM handles both the unobserved state in the Markov chain and the unobserved mixture mode [2].

3.2. Tied-Mixture Context Modeling

We have investigated two methods for training context-dependent models. In the first, weights are used to combine the probability of different types of context. These weights can be chosen by hand [18] or derived automatically using a deleted-interpolation algorithm [3]. Paul evaluated both types of weighting for tied-mixture context modeling and reported no significant performance difference between the two [4]. In our experiments, we evaluated just the use of hand-picked weights.

In the second method, only models of the most detailed context (in our case triphones) are estimated directly from the data and simpler context models (left, right, and context-independent models) are computed as marginals of the triphone distributions. The computation of marginals is negligible since it involves just the summing and normalization of mixture weights at the end of training. This method reduces the number of model updates in training in proportion to the number of context types used, although the computation of observation probabilities conditioned on the mixture component densities, remains the same. In recognition with marginal models, it is still necessary to combine the different context types, and we use the same hand-picked weights as before for this purpose. We compared the two training methods and found that performance on an independent test set was essentially the same for both methods (marginal training produced 2 fewer errors on the Feb89 test set) and the marginal trainer required 20 to 35% less time, depending on the model size and machine memory.

3.3. Parallel Training

To reduce computation, our system prunes low probability observations, as in [4], and uses the marginal training algorithm described above. However, even with these savings, tied-mixture training involves a large computation, making experimentation potentially cumbersome. When the available computing resources consist of a network of moderately powerful workstations, as is the case at BU, we would like to make use of many machines at once to speed training. At the highest level, tied mixture training is inherently a sequential process, since each pass requires the parameter estimates from the previous pass. However, the bulk of the training computation involves estimating counts over a database, and these counts are all independent of each other. We can therefore speed training by letting machines estimate the counts for different parts of the database in parallel and combine and normalize their results at the end of each pass.

To implement this approach we use a simple "bakery" algorithm to assign tasks: as each machine becomes free, it reads and increments the value of a counter from a common location indicating the sentences in the database it should work on next. This approach provides load balancing, allowing us to make efficient use of machines that may differ in speed. Because of the coarse grain of parallelism (one task typically consists of processing 10 sentences), we can use the relatively simple mechanism of file locking for synchronization and mutual exclusion, with no noticeable efficiency penalty. Finally, one processor is distinguished as the "master" processor and is assigned to perform the collation and normalization of counts at the end of each pass. With this approach, we obtain a speedup in training linear with the number of machines used, providing a much faster environment for experimentation.

4. MODELING & ESTIMATION TRADE-OFFS

Within the framework of tied Gaussian mixtures, there are a number of modeling and training variations that have been proposed. In this section, we will describe several experiments that investigate the performance implications of some of these choices.

4.1. Experimental Paradigm

The experiments described below were run on the Resource Management (RM) corpus using speaker-independent, gender-dependent models trained on the standard SI-109 data set. The feature vectors used as input to the system are computed at 10 millisecond intervals and consist of 14 cepstral parameters, their first differences, and differenced energy (second cepstral differences are not currently used). In recognition, the SSM uses an N-best rescoring formalism to reduce computation: the BBN BYBLOS system [7] is used to generate 20 hypotheses per sentence, which are rescored by the SSM and combined with the number of phones, number of words, and (optionally) the BBN HMM score, to rerank the hypotheses. The weights for recombination are estimated on one test set and held fixed for all other test sets. Since our previous work has indicated problems in weight estimation due to test-set mismatch, we have recently introduced a simple time normalization of the scores that effectively reduces the variability of scores due to utterance length and leads to more robust performance across test sets.

Although the weight estimation test set is strictly speaking part of the training data, we find that for most experiments, the bias in this type of testing is small enough to allow us to make comparisons between systems when both are run on the weight-training set. Accordingly some of the experiments reported below are only run on the weight training test set. Of course, final evaluation of a system must be on an independent test set.

4.2. Experiments

We conducted several series of experiments to explore issues associated with parameter allocation and training. The results are compared to a baseline, non-mixture SSM that uses full covariance Gaussian distributions.

The first set of experiments examined the number of component densities in the mixture, together with the choice of full- or diagonal-covariance matrices for the mixture component densities. Although the full covariance assumption provides a more detailed description of the correlation between features, diagonal covariance models require substantially less computation and it may be possible to obtain very detailed models using a larger number of diagonal models.

In initial experiments with just female speakers, we used diagonal covariance Gaussians and compared 200- versus 300-density mixture models, exploring the range typically reported by other researchers. With context-independent models, after several training passes, both systems got 6.5% word error on the Feb89 test set. For context-dependent models, the 300-density system performed substantially better, with a 2.8% error rate, compared with 4.2% for the 200 density system. These results compare favorably with the baseline SSM which has an error rate on the Feb89 female speakers of 7.7% for context-independent models and 4.8% for context-dependent models.

For male speakers, we again tried systems of 200 and 300 diagonal covariance density systems, obtaining error rates of 10.9% and 9.1% for each, respectively. Unlike the females, however, this was only slightly better than the result for the baseline SSM, which achieves 9.5%. We tried a system of 500 diagonal covariance densities, which gave only a small improvement in performance to 8.8% error. Finally, we tried using full-covariance Gaussians for the 300 component system and obtained an 8.0% error rate. The context-dependent performance for males using this configuration showed similar improvement over the non-mixture SSM, with an error rate of 3.8% for the mixture system compared with 4.7% for the baseline. Returning to the females, we found that using full-covariance densities gave the same performance as diagonal. We have adopted the use of full-covariance models for both genders for uniformity, obtaining a combined word error rate of 3.3% on the Feb89 test set. In the RM SI-109 training corpus, the training data for males is roughly 2.5 times that for females, so it is not unexpected that the optimal parameter allocation for each may differ slightly.

Unlike other reported systems which treat cepstral parameters and their derivatives as independent observation streams, the BU system models them jointly using a single output stream, which gives better performance than independent streams with a single Gaussian distribution (non-mixture system). Presumably, the result would also hold for mixtures.

Since the training is an iterative hill climbing technique, initialization can be important to avoid converging to a poor solution. In our system, we choose initial models, using one of the two methods described below. These models are used as input to several iterations of context-independent training followed by context-dependent training. We add a small padding value to the weight estimates in the early training passes to delay premature parameter convergence.

We have investigated two methods for choosing the initial models. In the first, we cluster the training data using the *K-means* algorithm and then estimate a mean and covariance from the data corresponding to each cluster. These are then used as the parameters of the component Gaussian densities of the initial mixture. In the second method, we initialize from models trained in a non-mixture version of the SSM. The initial densities are chosen as means of triphone models, with covariances chosen from the corresponding context-independent model. For each phone in our phone alphabet we iteratively choose the triphone model of that phone with the highest frequency of occurrence in training. The object of this procedure is to attempt to cover the space of phones while using robustly estimated models.

We found that the *K-means* initialized models converged slower and had significantly worse performance on independent test data than that of the second method. Although it is possible that with a larger padding value added to the weight estimates and more training passes, the *K-means* models might have "caught up" with the

System	Test set	
	Oct 89	Sep 92
Baseline SSM	4.8	8.5
T.M. SSM	3.6	7.3
T.M. SSM + HMM	3.2	6.1

Table 1: Word error rate on the Oct89 and Sep92 test sets for the baseline non-mixture SSM, the tied-mixture SSM alone and the SSM in combination with the BYBLOS HMM system.

other models, we did not investigate this further.

The various elements of the mixtures (means, covariances, and weights) can each be either updated in training, or assumed to have fixed values. In our experiments, we have consistently found better performance when all parameters of the models are updated.

Table 1 gives the performance on the RM Oct89 and Sept92 test set for the baseline SSM, the tied-mixture SSM system, and the tied-mixture system combined in N-best rescoring with the BBN BYBLOS HMM system. The mixture SSM's performance is comparable to results reported for many other systems on these sets. We note that it may be possible to improve SSM performance by incorporating second difference cepstral parameters as most HMM systems do.

5. SEGMENTAL MIXTURE MODELING

In the version of the SSM described in this paper, in which observations are assumed conditionally independent given model regions, the dependence of observations over time is modeled implicitly by the assumption of time-dependent stationary regions in combination with the constrained warping of observations to regions. Because segmentation is explicit in this model, in principle it is straightforward to model distinct segmental trajectories over time by using a mixture of such segment-level models, and thus take better advantage of the segment formalism. The probability of the complete segment of observations, $\mathbf{Y}$, given phonetic unit α is then

$$\mathrm{p}(\mathbf{Y} \mid \alpha) = \sum_k w_k \, \mathrm{p}(\mathbf{Y} \mid \alpha_k),$$

where each of the densities $\mathrm{p}(\mathbf{Y} \mid \alpha_k)$ is an SSM. The component models could use single Gaussians instead of tied mixtures for the region dependent distributions and they would remain independent frame models, but in training all the observations for a phone would be updated jointly, so that the mixture components capture distinct trajectories of the observations across a complete segment. In practice, each such trajectory is a point in a very high-dimensional feature space, and it is necessary to reduce the parameter dimension in order to train such models. There are several ways to do this. First, we can model the trajectories within smaller, subphonetic units, as in the microsegment model described in [19, 20]. Taking this approach and assuming microsegments are independent, the probability for a segment is

$$\mathrm{p}(\mathbf{Y} \mid \alpha) = \prod_j \sum_k w_{jk} \, \mathrm{p}(\mathbf{Y}_j \mid \alpha_{jk}), \qquad (2)$$

where α_{jk} is the kth mixture component of microsegment j and $\mathbf{Y}_j$ is the subset of frames in $\mathbf{Y}$ that map to microsegment j. Given the SSM's deterministic warping and assuming the same number of distributions for all mixture components of a given microsegment, the extension of the EM algorithm for training mixtures of this type is straightforward. The tied-mixture SSM discussed in previous sections is a special case of this model, in which we restrict each microsegment to have just one stationary region and a corresponding mixture distribution.

A different way to reduce the parameter dimension is to continue to model the complete trajectory across a segment, but assume independence between subsets of the features of a frame. This case can be expressed in the general form of (2) if we reinterpret the $\mathbf{Y}_j$ as vectors with the same number of frames as the complete segment, but for each frame, only a specific subset of the original frame's features are used. We can of course combine these two approaches, and assume independence between observations representing feature subsets of different microsegmental units. There are clearly a large number of possible decompositions of the complete segment into time and feature subsets, and the corresponding models for each may have different properties. In general, because of constraints of model dimensionality and finite training data, we expect a trade-off between the ability to model trajectories across time and to model the correlation of features within a local time region.

Although no single model of this form may have all the properties we desire, we do not necessarily have to choose one to the exclusion of all others. All the models discussed here compute probabilities over the same observation space, allowing for a straightforward combination of different models, once again using the simple mechanism of non-tied mixtures:

$$\mathrm{p}(\mathbf{Y} \mid \alpha) = \sum_i \prod_j \sum_k w_{ijk} \, \mathrm{p}(\mathbf{Y}_j \mid \alpha_{ijk}).$$

In this case, each of the i components of the leftmost summation is some particular realization of the general model expressed in Equation (2). Such a mixture can combine component models that individually have beneficial properties for modeling either time or frequency correlation, and the combined model may be able to model both aspects well. We note that, in principle, this model can also be extended to larger units, such as syllables or words.

6. SUMMARY

This paper provided an overview of work using tied-mixture models for speech recognition. We described the use of tied mixtures in the SSM as well as several innovations in the training algorithm. Experiments comparing performance for different parameter allocation choices using tied-mixtures were presented. The performance of the best tied-mixture SSM is comparable to HMM systems that use similar input features. Finally, we presented a general method we are investigating for modeling segmental dependence with the SSM.

ACKNOWLEDGMENTS

The authors gratefully acknowledge BBN Inc. for their help in providing the N-best sentence hypotheses. We thank J. Robin Rohlicek of BBN for many useful discussions. This research was jointly funded by NSF and DARPA under NSF grant number IRI-8902124, and by DARPA and ONR under ONR grant number N00014-92-J-1778.

References

1. Huang, X. D. and Jack, M. A., "Performance comparison between semi-continuous and discrete hidden Markov models," *IEE Electronics Letters*, Vol. 24 no. 3, pp. 149-150.
2. Bellegarda, J. R. and Nahamoo, D., "Tied Mixture Continuous Parameter Modeling for Speech Recognition," *IEEE Trans. on Acoust., Speech and Signal Processing*, Dec 1990, pp. 2033–2045.
3. Jelinek, F. and Mercer, R.L., "Interpolated Estimation of Markov Source Parameters from Sparse Data," in *Proc. Workshop Pattern Recognition in Practice*, May 1980, pp. 381-397.
4. Paul, D.B., "The Lincoln Tied-Mixture HMM Continuous Speech Recognizer," *Proc. IEEE Int. Conf. Acoust., Speech, Signal Processing*, May 1991, pp. 329–332.
5. Murveit, H., Butzberger, J., Weintraub, M., "Speech Recognition in SRI's Resource Management and ATIS Systems," *Proc. of the DARPA Workshop on Speech and Natural Language*, June 1990, pp. 94–100.
6. Huang, X.D., Lee, K.F., Hon, H.W., and Hwang, M.-Y., "Improved Acoustic Modeling with the SPHINX Speech Recognition System," *Proc. IEEE Int. Conf. Acoust., Speech, Signal Processing*, May 1991, pp. 345–348.
7. Kubala, F., Austin, S., Barry, C., Makhoul, J. Placeway, P., and Schwartz, R., "BYBLOS Speech Recognition Benchmark Results," *Proc. of the DARPA Workshop on Speech and Natural Language*, Asilomar, CA, Feb. 1991, pp. 77-82.
8. Hwang, M.-Y., Huang, X. D., "Subphonetic Modeling with Markov States - Senone," *Proc. IEEE Int. Conf. Acoust., Speech, Signal Processing*, March 1992, pp. I-33–36.
9. Ney, H., Haeb-Umbach, R., Tran, B.-H., Oerder, M., "Improvements in Beam Search for 10000-Word Continuous Speech Recognition," *Proc. IEEE Int. Conf. Acoust., Speech, Signal Processing*, April 1992, pp. I-9–12.
10. Baker, J. K., Baker, J. M., Bamberg, P., Bishop, K., Gillick, L., Helman, V., Huang, Z., Ito, Y., Lowe, S., Peskin, B., Roth, R., Scattone, F., "Large Vocabulary Recognition of Wall Street Journal Sentences at Dragon Systems," *Proc. of the DARPA Workshop on Speech and Natural Language*, February 1992, pp. 387-392.
11. H. Ney, "Speech Recognition in a Neural Network Framework: Discriminative Training of Gaussian Models and Mixture Densities as Radial Basis Functions," *Proc. IEEE Int. Conf. Acoust., Speech, Signal Processing*, May 1991, pp. 573–576.
12. Zavaliagkos, G., Zhao, Y., Schwartz, R., and Makhoul,J., to appear in *Proc. of the DARPA Workshop on Artificial Neural Networks and CSR*, Sept. 1992.
13. Pallett, D., Results for the Sept. 1992 Resource Management Benchmark, presented at the DARPA Workshop on Artificial Neural Networks and CSR, Sept. 1992.
14. Lee, C., Rabiner, L., Pieraccini, R., and Wilpon, J., "Acoustic Modeling for Large Vocabulary Speech Recognition," *Computer Speech and Language*, April. 1990, pp. 127–165.
15. Paul, D. B., "The Lincoln Robust Continuous Speech Recognizer," *Proc. IEEE Int. Conf. Acoust., Speech, Signal Processing*, May 1989, pp. 449–452.
16. Ostendorf, M. and Roukos, S. , "A Stochastic Segment Model for Phoneme-Based Continuous Speech Recognition," *IEEE Trans. on Acoust., Speech and Signal Processing*, Dec. 1989, pp. 1857–1869.
17. Dempster, A., Laird, N. and Rubin, D., "Maximum Likelihood from Incomplete Data via the EM Algorithm," *J. Royal Statist. Soc. Ser. B*, Vol. 39 No. 1, pp. 1–22, 1977.
18. Schwartz, R., Chow, Y. L., Kimball, O., Roucos, S., Krasner, M. and Makhoul, J., "Context-Dependent Modeling for Acoustic-Phonetic Recognition of Continuous Speech," *Proc. IEEE Int. Conf. Acoust., Speech, Signal Processing*, March 1985, pp. 1205–1208.
19. Digalakis, V. *Segment-Based Stochastic Models of Spectral Dynamics for Continuous Speech Recognition*, Boston University Ph.D. Dissertation, 1992.
20. Kannan, A., and Ostendorf, M., "A Comparison of Trajectory and Mixture Modeling in Segment-Based Word Recognition," *Proc. IEEE Int. Conf. Acoust., Speech, Signal Processing*, April 1993.

ADAPTIVE LANGUAGE MODELING USING THE MAXIMUM ENTROPY PRINCIPLE

Raymond Lau, Ronald Rosenfeld, Salim Roukos*

IBM Research Division
Thomas J. Watson Research Center
Yorktown Heights, NY 10598

ABSTRACT

We describe our ongoing efforts at adaptive statistical language modeling. Central to our approach is the Maximum Entropy (ME) Principle, allowing us to combine evidence from multiple sources, such as long-distance triggers and conventional short-distance trigrams. Given consistent statistical evidence, a unique ME solution is guaranteed to exist, and an iterative algorithm exists which is guaranteed to converge to it. Among the advantages of this approach are its simplicity, its generality, and its incremental nature. Among its disadvantages are its computational requirements. We describe a succession of ME models, culminating in our current Maximum Likelihood / Maximum Entropy (ML/ME) model. Preliminary results with the latter show a 27% perplexity reduction as compared to a conventional trigram model.

1. STATE OF THE ART

Until recently, the most successful language model (given enough training data) was the trigram [1], where the probability of a word is estimated based solely on the two words preceding it. The trigram model is simple yet powerful [2]. However, since it does not use anything but the very immediate history, it is incapable of adapting to the style or topic of the document, and is therefore considered a *static* model.

In contrast, a dynamic or *adaptive* model is one that changes its estimates as a result of "seeing" some of the text. An adaptive model may, for example, rely on the history of the current document in estimating the probability of a word. Adaptive models are superior to static ones in that they are able to improve their performance after seeing some of the data. This is particularly useful in two situations. First, when a large heterogeneous language source is composed of smaller, more homogeneous segments, such as newspaper articles. An adaptive model trained on the heterogeneous source will be able to hone in on the particular "sublanguage" used in each of the articles. Secondly, when a model trained on data from one domain is used in another domain. Again, an adaptive model will be able to adjust to the new language, thus improving its performance.

The most successful adaptive LM to date is described in [3]. A cache of the last few hundred words is maintained, and is used to derive a "cache trigram". The latter is then interpolated with the static trigram. This results in a 23% reduction in perplexity, and a 5%–24% reduction in the error rate of a speech recognizer.

*This work is now continued by Ron Rosenfeld at Carnegie Mellon University.

In what follows, we describe our efforts at improving our adaptive statistical language models by capitalizing on the information present in the document history.

2. TRIGGER-BASED MODELING

To extract information from the document history, we propose the idea of *a trigger pair as the basic information bearing element*. If a word sequence A is significantly correlated with another word sequence B, then $(A \rightarrow B)$ is considered a "trigger pair", with A being the *trigger* and B the *triggered sequence*. When A occurs in the document, it triggers B, causing its probability estimate to change.

Before attempting to design a trigger-based model, one should study what long distance factors have significant effects on word probabilities. Obviously, some information about $P(B)$ can be gained simply by knowing that A had occurred. But exactly how much? And can we gain significantly more by considering how recently A occurred, or how many times?

We have studied these issues using the a Wall Street Journal corpus of 38 million words. Some illustrations are given in figs. 1 and 2. As can be expected, different trigger pairs give different answers, and hence should be modeled differently. More detailed modeling should be used when the expected return is higher.

Once we determined the phenomena to be modeled, one main issue still needs to be addressed. Given the part of the document processed so far (h), and a word w considered for the next position, there are many different estimates of $P(w|h)$. These estimates are derived from the various triggers of w, from the static trigram model, and possibly from other sources. how do we combine them all to form one optimal estimate? We propose a solution to this problem in the next section.

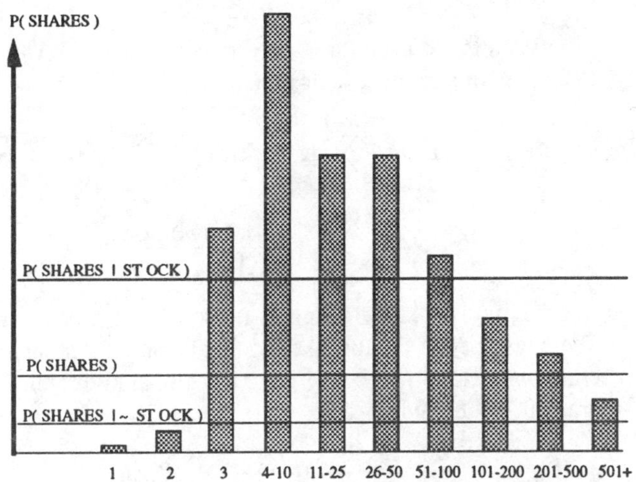

Figure 1: Probability of 'SHARES' as a function of the distance from the last occurrence of 'STOCK' in the same document. The middle horizontal line is the unconditional probability. The top (bottom) line is the probability of 'SHARES' given that 'STOCK' occurred (did not occur) before in the document.

3. MAXIMUM ENTROPY SOLUTIONS

Using several different probability estimates to arrive at one combined estimate is a general problem that arises in many tasks. We use the maximum entropy (ME) principle ([4, 5]), which can be summarized as follows:

1. Reformulate the different estimates as constraints on the expectation of various functions, to be satisfied by the target (combined) estimate.
2. Among all probability distributions that satisfy these constraints, choose the one that has the highest entropy.

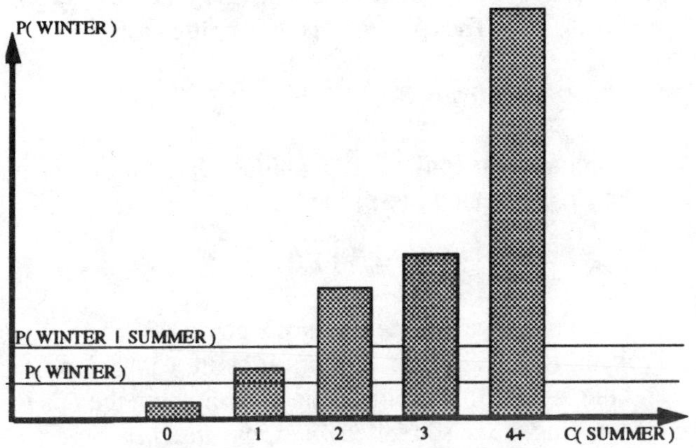

Figure 2: Probability of 'WINTER' as a function of the number of times 'SUMMER' occurred before it in the same document. Horizontal lines are as in fig. 1.

In the next 3 sections, we describe a succession of models we developed, all based on the ME principle. We then expand on the last model, describe possible future extensions to it, and report current results. More details can be found in [6, 7].

4. MODEL I: EARLY ATTEMPTS

Assume we have identified for each word w in a vocabulary, V, a set of n_w trigger words $t_{w1}t_{w2}\ldots t_{wn_w}$; we further assume that we have the relative frequency of observing a trigger word, t, occurring somewhere in the history, h, (in our case we have used a history length, K, of either 25, 50, 200, or 1000 words) and the word w just occurs after the history from some training text; denote the observed relative frequency of a trigger and a word w by

$$d(t,w) = \frac{c(t \in h \textit{ and } w \textit{ immediately follows } h)}{N}$$

where $c(.)$ is the count in the training data. We use $\{t,w\}$ to indicate the event that trigger t occurred in the history and word w occurs next; the term *long-distance* bigram has been used for this event.

Assume we have a joint distribution $p(h,w)$ of the history of K words and the next word w. We require this joint model to assign to the events $\{t,w\}$ a probability that matches the observed relative frequencies. Assuming we have R such constraints we find a model that has Maximum Entropy:

$$p^*(h,w) = \arg\max - \sum_{h,w} p(h,w) \lg p(h,w)$$

subject to the R trigger constraints[1]:

$$p(t,w) = \sum_{h:t\in h} p(h,w) = d(t,w)$$

We also include the case that none of the triggers of word w occur in the history (we denote this event by $\{t_0,w\}$.) Using Lagrange multipliers, one can easily show that the Maximum Entropy model is given by:

$$p(h,w) = \prod_{t:t\in h} \mu_{wt}$$

i.e., the joint probability is the product of $l_h(w)$ factors one factor for each trigger t_{wi} of word w that occurs in the history h (or one factor if none of the triggers occur.) The Maximum Entropy joint distribution over a space of $|V|^{K+1}$ is given by R parameters, one for each constraint. In our case, we used a maximum of 20 triggers per word for a 20k vocabulary with an average of 10 resulting in 200,000 constraints.

[1] we also imposed unigram constraints to match the unigram distribution of the vocabulary

4.1. How to determine the factors?

One can use the "Brown" algorithm to determine the set of factors. At each iteration, one updates the factor of one constraint and as long as one cycles through all constraints repeatedly the factors will converge to the optimal value. At the *i-th* iteration, assume we are updating the factor that corresponds to the $\{t, w\}$-constraint. Then the update is given by:

$$\mu_{wt}^{new} = \mu_{wt}^{old} \frac{d(t,w)}{m(t,w)}$$

where the model predicted value $m(t, w)$ is given by:

$$m(t,w) = \sum_{h:t\in h} p^{old}(h,w) \quad (1)$$

where p^{old} uses the old factor values.

Using the ME joint model, we define a conditional *unigram* model by:

$$p(w|h) = \frac{p^*(h,w)}{\sum_w p^*(h,w)}$$

This is a "time-varying" unigram model where the previous K words determine the relative probability that w would occur next. The perplexity of the resulting model was about 2000 much higher than the perplexity of a static unigram model. In particular, the model underestimated the probability of the frequent words. To ease that problem we disallowed any triggers for the most frequent L words. We experimented with L ranging from 100 to 500 words. The resulting model was better though its perplexity was still about 1100 which is 43% higher than the static unigram perplexity of 772. One reason that we conjecture was that the ME model gives a rather high probability for histories that are quite unlikely in reality and the trigger constraints are matched using those unrealistic histories. We tried an ad hoc computation where the summation over the histories in Equation 1 was weighed by a crude estimate, $w(h)$, of the probability of the history i.e. we used

$$m(t,w) = \sum_{h:t\in h} w(h)p^{old}(h,w)$$

The resulting model had a much lower perplexity of 559, about 27% lower than the static unigram model on a test set of (1927 words). This ad hoc computation indicates that we need to model the histories more realistically. The model we propose in the next section is derived from the viewpoint that ME indicates that R factors define a conditional model that captures the "long-distance" bigram constraints and that using this parametric form with Maximum Likelihood estimation may allow us to concentrate on typical histories that occur in the data.

5. MODEL II: ML OF CONDITIONAL ME

The ME viewpoint results in a conditional model that belongs to the exponential family with K parameters when K constraints are contemplated. We can use Maximum Likelihood estimation to estimate the K factors of the model. The log likelihood of a training set is given by:

$$\begin{aligned} L &= \sum_{t=0}^{N-1} \lg p(w_{t+1}|h_t) \\ &= \sum_{t=0}^{N-1} \lg \frac{\prod_{i\in I_{h_t}(w_{t+1})} \mu_i}{\sum_w \prod_{j\in J_{h_t}(w)} \mu_j} \end{aligned}$$

where $I_h(w)$ is the set of triggers for word w that occur in h. The convexity of the log likelihood guarantees that any hill climbing method will converge to the global optimum. The gradient can be shown to be:

$$\frac{\partial}{\partial \mu_{wt}} L = \frac{1}{\mu_{wt}}(d(t,w) - \sum_{h:t\in h} p(w|h))$$

one can use the gradient to iteratively re-estimate the factors by:

$$\mu_{wt}^{new} = \mu_{wt}^{old} + \frac{1}{\mu_{wt}^{old}}(d(t,w) - m'(t,w))$$

where the model predicted value $m'(t, w)$ for a constraint is:

$$m'(t,w) = \sum_{h:t\in h} p(w|h))$$

The training data is used to estimate the gradient given the current estimate of the factors. The size of the gradient step can be optimized by a line search on a small amount of training data.

Given the "time-varying" unigram estimate, we use the methods of [8] to obtain a bigram LM whose unigram matches the time-varying unigram using a window of the most recent L words.

6. CURRENT MODEL: ML/ME

For estimating a probability function $P(\mathbf{x})$, each constraint i is associated with a *constraint function* $f_i(\mathbf{x})$ and a *desired expectation* c_i. The constraint is then written as:

$$E_P f_i \stackrel{\text{def}}{=} \sum_{\mathbf{x}} P(\mathbf{x}) f_i(\mathbf{x}) = c_i \,. \quad (2)$$

Given consistent constraints, a unique ME solutions is guaranteed to exist, and to be of the form:

$$P(\mathbf{x}) = \prod_i \mu_i^{f_i(\mathbf{x})} \,, \quad (3)$$

where the μ_i's are some unknown constants, to be found. Probability functions of the form (3) are called *log-linear*, and the family of functions defined by holding the f_i's fixed and varying the μ_i's is called *an exponential family*.

To search the exponential family defined by (3) for the μ_i's that will make $P(\mathbf{x})$ satisfy all the constraints, an iterative algorithm, "Generalized Iterative Scaling", exists, which is guaranteed to converge to the solution ([9]).

6.1. Formulating Triggers as Constraints

To reformulate a trigger pair $A \rightarrow B$ as a constraint, define the constraint function $f_{A \rightarrow B}$ as:

$$f_{A \rightarrow B}(h, w) = \begin{cases} 1 & \text{if } A \in h, w = B \\ 0 & \text{otherwise} \end{cases} \tag{4}$$

Set $c_{A \rightarrow B}$ to $\tilde{E}[f_{A \rightarrow B}]$, the *empirical expectation* of $f_{A \rightarrow B}$ (ie its expectation in the training data). Now impose on the desired probability estimate $P(h, w)$ the constraint:

$$E_P\, [f_{A \rightarrow B}] = \tilde{E}\, [f_{A \rightarrow B}] \tag{5}$$

6.2. Estimating Conditionals: The ML/ME Solution

Generalized Iterative Scaling can be used to find the ME estimate of a simple (non-conditional) probability distribution over some event space. But in our case, we need to estimate conditional probabilities of the form $P(w|h)$. How should this be done more efficiently than in the previous models?

An elegant solution was proposed by [10]. Let $P(h, w)$ be the desired probability estimate, and let $\tilde{P}(h, w)$ be the empirical distribution of the training data. Let $f_i(h, w)$ be any constraint function, and let c_i be its desired expectation. Equation 5 can be rewritten as:

$$\sum_h P(h) \cdot \sum_w P(w|h) \cdot f_i(h, w) = c_i \tag{6}$$

We now modify the constraint to be:

$$\sum_h \tilde{P}(h) \cdot \sum_w P(w|h) \cdot f_i(h, w) = c_i \tag{7}$$

One possible interpretation of this modification is as follows. Instead of constraining the expectation of $f_i(h, w)$ with regard to $P(h, w)$, we constrain its expectation with regard to a different probability distribution, say $Q(h, w)$, whose conditional $Q(w|h)$ is the same as that of P, but whose marginal $Q(h)$ is the same as that of $\tilde{P}$. To better understand the effect of this change, define H as the set of all possible histories h, and define H_{f_i} as the partition of H induced by f_i. Then the modification is equivalent to assuming that, for every constraint f_i, $P(H_{f_i}) = \tilde{P}(H_{f_i})$. Since typically H_{f_i} is a very small set, the assumption is reasonable.

The unique ME solution that satisfies equations like (7) or (6) can be shown to also be the Maximum Likelihood (ML) solution, namely that function which, among the exponential family defined by the constraints, has the maximum likelihood of generating the data. The identity of the ML and ME solutions, apart from being aesthetically pleasing, is extremely useful when estimating the conditional $P(w|h)$. It means that hillclimbing methods can be used in conjunction with Generalized Iterative Scaling to speed up the search. Since the likelihood objective function is convex, hillclimbing will not get stuck in local minima.

6.3. Incorporating the trigram model

We combine the trigger based model with the currently best static model, the N-Gram, by reformulating the latter to fit into the ML/ME paradigm. The usual unigram, bigram and trigram ML estimates are replaced by unigram, bigram and trigram constraints conveying the same information. Specifically, the constraint function for the unigram w_1 is:

$$f_{w_1}(h, w) = \begin{cases} 1 & \text{if } w = w1 \\ 0 & \text{otherwise} \end{cases} \tag{8}$$

and its associated constraint is:

$$\sum_h \tilde{P}(h) \sum_w P(w|h) f_{w_1}(h, w) = \tilde{E} f_{w_1}(h, w). \tag{9}$$

Similarly, the constraint function for the bigram w_1, w_2 is

$$f_{w_1, w_2}(h, w) = \begin{cases} 1 & \text{if } h \text{ ends in } w_1 \text{ and } w = w2 \\ 0 & \text{otherwise} \end{cases} \tag{10}$$

and its associated constraint is

$$\sum_h \tilde{P}(h) \sum_w P(w|h) f_{w_1, w_2}(h, w) = \tilde{E} f_{w_1, w_2}(h, w). \tag{11}$$

and similarly for higher-order ngrams.

The computational bottleneck of the Generalized Iterative Scaling algorithm is in constraints which, for typical histories h, are non-zero for a large number of w's. This means that bigram constraints are more expensive than trigram constraints. Implicit computation can be used for unigram constraints. Therefore, the time cost of bigram and trigger constraints dominates the total time cost of the algorithm.

7. ME: PROS AND CONS

The ME principle and the Generalized Iterative Scaling algorithm have several important advantages:

1. The ME principle is simple and intuitively appealing. It imposes all of the constituent constraints, but assumes nothing else. For the special case of constraints derived from marginal probabilities, it is equivalent to assuming a lack of higher-order interactions [11].

2. ME is extremely general. Any probability estimate of any subset of the event space can be used, including estimates that were not derived from the data or that are

inconsistent with it. The distance dependence and count dependence illustrated in figs. 1 and 2 can be readily accommodated. Many other knowledge sources, including higher-order effects. can be incorporated. Note that constraints need not be independent of nor uncorrelated with each other.

3. The information captured by existing language models can be absorbed into the ML/ME model. We have shown how this is done for the conventional N-gram model. Later on we will show, how it can be done for the cache model of [3].

4. Generalized Iterative Scaling lends itself to incremental adaptation. New constraints can be added at any time. Old constraints can be maintained or else allowed to relax.

5. A unique ME solution is guaranteed to exist for consistent constraints. The Generalized Iterative Scaling algorithm is guaranteed to converge to it.

This approach also has the following weaknesses:

1. Generalized Iterative Scaling is computationally very expensive. When the complete system is trained on the entire 50 million words of Wall Street Journal data, it is expected to require many thousands of MIPS-hours to run to completion.

2. While the algorithm is guaranteed to converge, we do not have a theoretical bound on its convergence rate.

3. It is sometimes useful to impose constraints that are not satisfied by the training data. For example, we may choose to use Good-Turing discounting [12], or else the constraints may be derived from other data, or be externally imposed. Under these circumstances, the constraints may no longer be consistent, and the theoretical results guaranteeing existence, uniqueness and convergence may not hold.

8. INCORPORATING THE CACHE MODEL

It seems that the power of the cache model, described in section 1, comes from the "bursty" nature of language. Namely, infrequent words tend to occur in "bursts", and once a word occurred in a document, its probability of recurrence is significantly elevated.

Of course, this phenomena can be captured by a trigger pair of the form $A \rightarrow A$, which we call a "self trigger". We have done exactly that in [13]. We found that self triggers are responsible for a disproportionately large part of the reduction in perplexity. Furthermore, self triggers proved particularly robust: when tested in new domains, they maintained the correlations found in the training data better than the "regular" triggers did.

Thus self triggers are particularly important, and should be modeled separately and in more detail. The trigger model we currently use does not distinguish between one or more occurrences of a given word in the history, whereas the cache model does. For self-triggers, the additional information can be significant (see fig. 3).

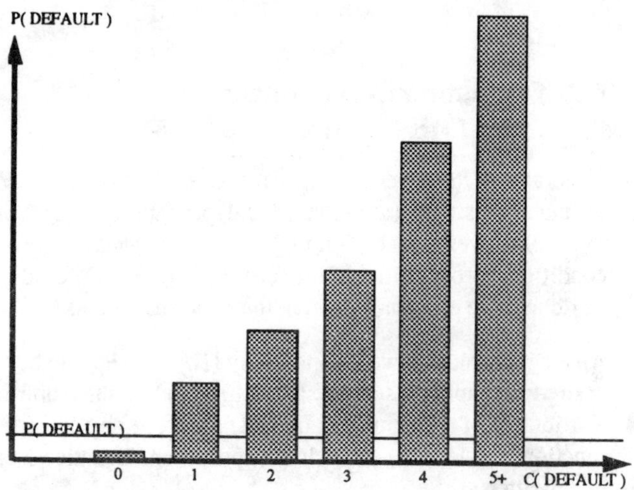

Figure 3: Behavior of a self-trigger: Probability of 'DEFAULT' as a function of the number of times it already occurred in the document. The horizontal line is the unconditional probability.

We plan to model self triggers in more detail. We will consider explicit modeling of frequency of occurrence, distance from last occurrence, and other factors. All of these aspects can easily be formulated as constraints and incorporated into the ME formalism.

9. RESULTS

The ML/ME model described above was trained on 5 million words of Wall Street Journal text, using DARPA's official "20o" vocabulary of some 20,000 words. A conventional trigram model was used as a baseline. The constraints used by the ML/ME model were: 18,400 unigram constraints, 240,000 bigram constraints, and 414,000 trigram constraints. One experiment was run with 36,000 trigger constraints (best 3 triggers for each word), and another with 65,000 trigger constraints (best 6 triggers per word). All models were trained on the same data, and evaluated on 325,000 words on independent data. The Maximum Entropy models were also interpolated with the conventional trigram, using yet unseen data for interpolation. Results are summarized in table 1.

model	Test-set Perplexity	% improvement over baseline
trigram	173	—
ML/ME-top3	134	23%
+trigram	129	25%
ML/ME-top6	130	25%
+trigram	127	27%

Table 1: Improvement of Maximum Likelihood / Maximum Entropy model over a conventional trigram model. Training is on 5 million words of WSJ text. Vocabulary is 20,000 words.

The trigger constraints used in this run were selected very crudely, and their number was not optimized. We believe much more improvement can be achieved. Special modeling of self triggers has not been implemented yet. Similarly, we expect it to yield further improvement.

10. ACKNOWLEDGEMENTS

We are grateful to Peter Brown, Stephen Della Pietra, Vincent Della Pietra and Bob Mercer for many suggestions and discussions.

Research by Ron Rosenfeld was sponsored by the Defense Advanced Research Projects Agency and monitored by the Space and Naval Warfare Systems Command under Contract N00039-91-C-0158, ARPA Order No. 7239. The views and conclusions contained in this document are those of the authors and should not be interpreted as representing the official policies, either expressed or implied, of the U.S. Government.

References

1. Bahl, L., Jelinek, F., Mercer, R.L., "A Statistical Approach to Continuous Speech Recognition," *IEEE Trans. on PAMI,* 1983.
2. Jelinek, F., "Up From Trigrams!" Eurospeech 1991.
3. Jelinek, F., Merialdo, B., Roukos, S., and Strauss, M., "A Dynamic Language Model for Speech Recognition." *Proceedings of the Speech and Natural Language DARPA Workshop,* pp.293–295, Feb. 1991.
4. Jaines, E. T., "Information Theory and Statistical Mechanics." *Phys. Rev.* **106**, pp. 620–630, 1957.
5. Kullback, S., *Information Theory in Statistics.* Wiley, New York, 1959.
   [6, 7].
6. Rosenfeld, R., "Adaptive Statistical Language Modeling: a Maximum Entropy Approach," *Ph.D. Thesis Proposal, Carnegie Mellon University,* September 1992.
7. Lau, R., Rosenfeld, R., Roukos, S., "Trigger-Based Language Models: a Maximum Entropy Approach," *Proceedings of ICASSP-93,* April 1993.
8. Della Pietra,S., Della Pietra, V., Mercer, R. L., Roukos, S., "Adaptive Language Modeling Using Minimum Discriminant Estimation," *Proceedings of ICASSP-92,* pp. I-633-636, San Francisco, March 1992.
9. Darroch, J.N. and Ratcliff, D., "Generalized Iterative Scaling for Log-Linear Models", *The Annals of Mathematical Statistics,* Vol. 43, pp 1470–1480, 1972.
10. Brown, P., Della Pietra, S., Della Pietra, V., Mercer, R., Nadas, A., and Roukos, S., "Maximum Entropy Methods and Their Applications to Maximum Likelihood Parameter Estimation of Conditional Exponential Models," *A forthcoming IBM technical report.*
11. Good, I. J., "Maximum Entropy for Hypothesis Formulation, Especially for Multidimensional Contingency Tables." *Annals of Mathematical Statistics,* Vol. 34, pp. 911–934, 1963.
12. Good, I. J., "The Population Frequencies of Species and the Estimation of Population Parameters." *Biometrika,* Vol. 40, no. 3, 4, pp. 237–264, 1953.
13. Rosenfeld, R., and Huang, X. D., "Improvements in Stochastic Language Modeling." *Proceedings of the Speech and Natural Language DARPA Workshop,* Feb. 1992.

IMPROVED KEYWORD-SPOTTING USING SRI'S DECIPHER™ LARGE-VOCABUARLY SPEECH-RECOGNITION SYSTEM

Mitchel Weintraub

SRI International
Speech Research and Technology Program
Menlo Park, CA, 94025

ABSTRACT

The word-spotting task is analogous to text-based information retrieval tasks and message-understanding tasks in that an exhaustive accounting of the input is not required: only a useful subset of the full information need be extracted in the task. Traditional approaches have focussed on the keywords involved. We have shown that accounting for more of the data, by using a large-vocabulary recognizer for the wordspotting task, can lead to dramatic improvements relative to traditional approaches. This result may well be generalizable to the analogous text-based tasks.

The approach described makes several novel contributions, including: (1) a method for dramatic improvement in the FOM (figure of merit) for word-spotting results compared to more traditional approaches; (2) a demonstration of the benefit of language modeling in keyword spotting systems; and (3) a method that provides rapid porting of to new keyword vocabularies.

1. INTRODUCTION

Although both continuous speech recognition and keyword-spotting tasks use the very similar underlying technology, there are typically significant differences in the way in which the technology is developed and used for the two applications (e.g. acoustic model training, model topology and language modeling, filler models, search, and scoring). A number of HMM-based systems have previously been developed for keyword-spotting [1-5]. One of the most significant differences between these keyword-spotting systems and a CSR system is the type of non-keyword model that is used. It is generally thought that very simple non-keyword models (such as a single 10-state model [2], or the set of monophone models [1]) can perform as well as more complicated non-keyword models which include words or triphones.

We describe how we have applied CSR techniques to the keyword-spotting task by using a speech recognition system to generate a transcription of the incoming spontaneous speech which is searched for the keywords. For this task we have used SRI's DECIPHER™ system, a state-of-the-art large-vocabulary speaker-independent continuous-speech recognition system [6-10]. The method is evaluated on two domains: (1) the Air Travel Information System (ATIS) domain [13], and (2) the "credit card topic" subset of the Switchboard Corpus [11], a telephone speech corpus consisting of spontaneous conversation on a number of different topics.

In the ATIS domain, for 78 keywords in a vocabulary of 1200, we show that the CSR approach significantly outperforms the traditional wordspotting approach for all false alarm rates per hour per word: the figure of merit (FOM) for the CSR recognizer is 75.9 compared to only 48.8 for the spotting recognizer. In the Credit Card task, the spotting of 20 keywords and their 58 variants on a subset of the Switchboard corpus, the system's performance levels off at a 66% detection rate, limited by the system's ability to increase the false alarm rate. Additional experiments show that varying the vocabulary size from medium- to large-vocabulary recognition systems (700 to 7000) does not affect the FOM performance.

A set of experiments compares two topologies: (1) a topology for a fixed vocabulary for the keywords and the N most common words in that task (N varies from Zero to Vocabulary Size), forcing the recognition hypothesis to choose among the allowable words (traditional CSR), and (2) a second topology in which a background word model is added to the word list, thereby allowing the recognition system to transcribe parts of the incoming speech signal as background. While including the background word model does increase the overall likelihood of the recognized transcription, the probability of using the background model is highly likely (due to the language model probabilities of out of vocabulary words) and tended to replace a number of keywords that had poor acoustic matches.

Finally, we introduce an algorithm for smoothing language model probabilities. This algorithm combines small task-specific language model training data with large task-independent language training data, and provided a 14% reduction in test set perplexity.

2. TRAINING

2.1. Acoustic Modeling

DECIPHER™ uses a hierarchy of phonetic context-dependent models, including word-specific, triphone, generalized-triphone, biphone, generalized-biphone, and context independent models. Six spectral features are used to model the speech signal: the cepstral vector (C1-CN) and its first and second derivatives, and cepstral energy (C0) and its first and second derivatives. These features are computed from an FFT filterbank and subsequent high-pass RASTA filtering of the filterbank log energies, and are modeled either with VQ and scalar codebooks or with tied-mixture Gaussian models. The acoustic models used for the Switchboard task use no cross word acoustic constraints.

2.2. Language Modeling

The DECIPHER™ system uses a probabilistic finite state grammar (PFSG) to constrain allowable word sequences. In the ATIS, WSJ, and Credit Card tasks, we use a word-based bigram grammar, with the language model probabilities estimated using Katz's back-off bigram algorithm [12]. All words that are not in the specified vocabulary that are in the language model training data are mapped to the *background* word model. The *background* word model is treated like all the other words in the recognizer, with bigram language model probabilities on the grammar transitions between words.

Two topologies are used for the experiments described in this paper. One topology is to use a fixed vocabulary with the keywords and the N most common words in that task (N varies from Zero to VocabSize), forcing the recognition hypothesis to choose among the allowable words. A second topology is to add the *background* word model to the above word list, thereby allowing the recognition system to transcribe parts of the incoming speech signal as *background*. A sample *background* word with 60 context-independent phones is shown below in Figure 1.

Figure 1: A sample topology for the *background* word model. The minimum duration is 2 phones and the self loop allows for an infinite duration.

2.3. Task-Specific Language Model Estimation

The Switchboard Corpus [11] is a telephone database consisting of spontaneous conversation on a number of different topics. The Credit Card task is to spot 20 keywords and their variants where both the keywords and the test set focus on a subset of the Switchboard conversations pertaining to credit cards. To estimate the language model for this task, we could (1) use a small amount of task-specific training data that focuses only on the credit card topic, (2) use a large amount of task-independent training data, or (3) combine the task-specific training with the task-independent training data.

For combining a small amount of task-specific (TS) training with a very large amount of task-independent (TI) training data, we modified the Katz back-off bigram estimation algorithm [12]. A weight was added to reduce the effective size of the task-independent training database as shown in Equation 1:

$$C(w2, w1) = C_{TS}(w2, w1) + \gamma \bullet C_{TI}(w2, w1)$$

where $C(w2, w1)$ is the counts of the number of occurrences of word w1 followed by w2, $C_{TS}(w2, w1)$ are the counts from the task-specific database and $C_{TI}(w2, w1)$ are the counts from the task-independent database. The weight γ reduces the effective size of the task-independent database so that these counts don't overwhelm the counts of the task-specific database.

Table 1 shows both the training set and test set perplexity for the credit card task as a function of γ. The task-specific training consisted of 18 credit card conversations (59 K words) while the task-independent training consisted of 1123 general conversations (17 M words).

Table 1: Perplexity of Credit Card Task as a Function of Task Independent-Specific Smoothing

γ	Effective Task Indep. Training Size	Training Set Perplexity	Test Set Perplexity
1.0	17,611,159	174.7	380.0
0.5	8,805,579	154.5	358.3
0.2	3,352,223	131.0	332.0
0.1	1,761,116	117.5	321.8
0.05	880,558	109.7	328.8
0.02	352,223	102.6	360.4
0.01	176,111	98.8	396.9
0.005	88,055	96.2	443.4
0.002	35,222	94.5	521.5
0.001	17,611	94.0	592.3

3. SEARCH

The DECIPHER™ system uses a time-synchronous beam search. A partial Viterbi backtrace [6] is used to locate the most-likely Viterbi path in a continuous running utterance. The Viterbi backtrace contains both language model information (grammar transition probabilities into and out of the keyword), acoustic log likelihood probabilities for the keyword, and the duration of the keyword hypothesis.

A duration-normalized likelihood score for each keyword is computed using the following Equation 2:

$$KeyScore = \frac{AP + GP + \text{Constant}}{Duration}$$

where AP is the acoustic log-likelihood score for the keyword, and GP is the log probability of the grammar transition into the keyword, and Constant is a constant added to the score to penalize keyword hypotheses that have a short duration. None of the earlier HMM keyword systems used a bigram language in either the decoding or the scoring. Many previous systems did use weights on the keywords to adjust the operating location on the ROC curve.

A hypothesized keyword is scored as correct if its midpoint falls within the endpoints of the correct keyword. The keyword scores are used to sort the occurrences of each keyword for computing the probability of detection at different false-alarm levels. The overall figure-of-merit is computed as the average detection rate over all words and over all false alarm rates up to ten false alarms per word per hour.

4. EXPERIMENTS

4.1. ATIS Task

The ATIS task [13] was chosen for keyword-spotting experiments because (1) the template-based system that interprets the queries of the airline database focuses on certain keywords that convey the meaning of the query, and ignores many of the other filler words (e.g. "I would like...", "Can you please ..."), (2) the task uses spontaneous speech, and (3) we have worked extensively on this recognition task over the last two years. Sixty-six keywords and their variants were selected as keywords based on the importance of each of the words to the SRI template-matcher which interprets the queries.

SRI applied two different recognition systems to the ATIS keyword spotting task. The first system was SRI's large-vocabulary speaker-independent speech recognition system that we have used for the ATIS speech-recognition task [3]. The vocabulary used in this system is about 1200 words, and a back-off bigram language model was trained using the ATIS MADCOW training data [13]. Many of the words in the vocabulary use word-specific or triphone acoustic models, with biphone and context-independent models used for those words that occur infrequently.

The second system is a more traditional word-spotting system. There are 66 keywords plus 12 variants of those keywords for a total of 78 keyword models. There is a *background* model (see Figure 1) that tries to account for the rest of the observed acoustics, making a total of 79 words in this second system. This second system also uses a back-off bigram grammar, but all non-keywords are replaced with the *background* word when computing language model probabilities.

The acoustic models for the keywords and their variants were identical in the two systems. The only difference between the two systems is that the first system uses ~1100 additional words for the *background* model, while the second system uses one *background* model with 60 context-independent phones. The resulting FOM and ROC curves are show in Figure 2 for the two systems.

Table 2: ATIS Keyword Spotting Results

System Description	Number of Filler Models	FOM
ATIS Recognizer	1100	75.9
Spotting Recognizer	1	48.8

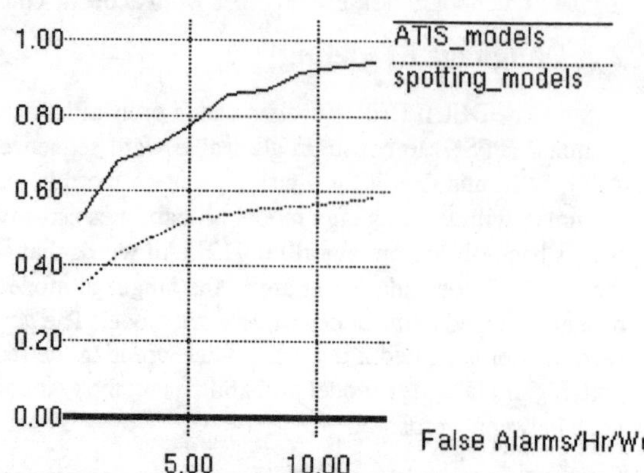

Figure 2: Probability of detection as a function of the false alarm rate for the above two CSR systems on the ATIS Task.

There are two possible explanations for the experimental results in Figure 2 and Table 2. The first explanation is that the ATIS recognizer has a much larger vocabulary, and this larger vocabulary is potentially better able at matching the non-keyword acoustics than the simple *background* model. The second explanation is that for the larger vocabulary ATIS system, the back-off bigram grammar can provide more interword constraints to eliminate false alarms than the back-off bigram grammar that maps all non-keywords to the filler model. Additional experiments are planned to determine the extent of these effects.

4.2. Credit Card Task

The Credit Card task is to spot 20 keywords and their 58 variants on a subset of the Switchboard database. The keywords were selected to be content words relevant to the credit card topic and based on adequate frequency of occurrence of each keyword for training and testing.

Acoustic models were trained on an 11,290 hand-transcribed utterances subset of the Switchboard database. A back-off bigram language model was trained as described in Section 2.3, using the text transcriptions from 1123 non-credit-card conversations and 35 credit card conversations. The most common 5,000 words in the non-credit-card conversations were combined with the words in the credit card conversations, the keywords, and their variants to bring the recognition vocabulary size to 6914 words (including the *background* word model).

The resulting CSR system was tested on 10 credit-card conversations from the Switchboard database. Each conversation consisted of two stereo recordings (each talker was recorded separately) and was approximately 5 minutes long. Each of the two channels is processed independently. The resulting ROC curve is shown in Figure 3. The ROC curve levels out at 66% because the CSR system hypothesized 431 keywords out of a total of 498 true keyword locations. Our current CSR approach, which uses the Viterbi backtrace, does not allow us to increase the keyword false alarm rate.

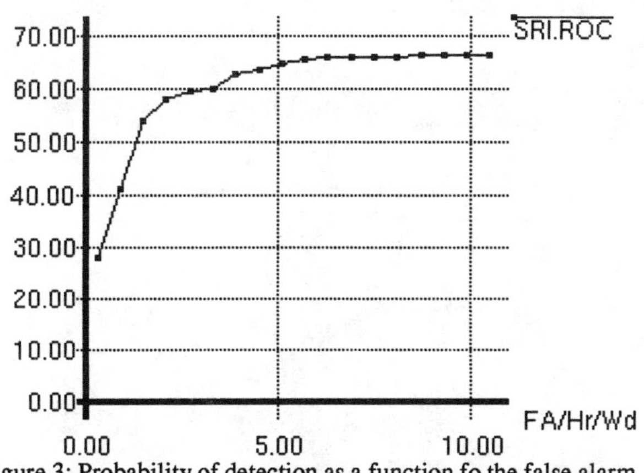

Figure 3: Probability of detection as a function fo the false alarm rate for the 6914 word CSR system on the Credit Card Task.

The effect of using different scoring formulas is shown in Table 3. If only the duration-normalized acoustic log-likelihoods are used, an average probability of detection (FOM) of 54% is achieved. When the grammar transition log-probability into this keyword is added to the score (Eqn 2), the FOM increases to 59.9%. In addition, if a constant is added to the score before normalization, the FOM increases for both cases. This has the effect of reducing the false-alarm rate for shorter-duration keyword hypotheses. We have not had a chance to experiment with the grammar transition leaving the keyword, nor with any weighting of grammar scores relative to acoustic scores.

Table 3: Credit Card FOM Scoring

	Acoustic Likelihood + Grammar Transition	Acoustic Likelihood
Keyword Score	59.9	54.0
Optimized Score	60.5	57.1

We then varied the recognition vocabulary size and determined its effect on the keyword-spotting performance. These experiments show that varying the vocabulary size from medium- to large-vocabulary recognition systems (700 to 7000) does not affect the FOM performance.

Table 4: Credit Card FOM as a Function of CSR Vocabulary Size

Vocabulary Size	FOM
725	59.3
1423	59.5
6914	59.9

Finally, we experimented with including or excluding the *background* word model in the CSR lexicon. While including the *background* word model does increase the overall likelihood of the recognized transcription, the probability of using the *background* model is highly likely (due to the language model probabilities of OOV words) and tended to replace a number of keywords that had poor acoustic matches. Table 5 shows that a slight improvement can be gained by eliminating this *background* word model.

Table 5: FOM With and Without *Background* Model for Large Vocabulary CSR System

Vocabulary Size	FOM
6914	59.9
6913 (No Background)	61.6

5. SUMMARY

This paper describes how SRI has applied our speaker-independent large-vocabulary CSR system (DECIPHER™) to the keyword-spotting task. A transcription is generated for the incoming spontaneous speech by using a CSR system, and any keywords that occur in the transcription are hypothesized. We show that the use of improved models of non-keyword speech with a CSR system can yield significantly improved keyword spotting performance.

The algorithm for computing the score of a keyword combine information from acoustic, language, and duration. One key limitation of this approach is that keywords are only hypothesized if they are included in the Viterbi backtrace. This does not allow the system builder to operate effectively at high false alarm levels if desired. We are considering other algorithms for hypothesizing "*good score*" keywords that are on high scoring paths.

We introduced an algorithm for smoothing language model probabilities. This algorithm combines small task-specific language model training data with large task-independent language training data, and provided a 14% reduction in test set perplexity.

The use of a large-vocabulary continuous-speech recognition system allows the system designer a great deal of flexibility in choosing the keywords that they would like to select for the particular application. If the desired keyword is already in the lexicon, then searching for the keyword can be achieved by looking for the word in the transcription generated by the recognizer. If the word is not in the lexicon, the word can be easily added to the system since triphone models have already been trained.

The ability to transcribe spontaneous speech and search for relevant keywords will play an important role in the future development of simple spoken language applications. Such systems will be easily portable to new domains. Since the operating point for our speech recognizer is typically one which has a low insertion rate, there is little chance for a keyword false alarm. Future experimentation will determine the effectiveness of such understanding systems for human-computer interaction.

REFERENCES

1. R. Rose and D. Paul, "A Hidden Markov Model Based Keyword Recognition System," 1990 *IEEE ICASSP*, pp. 129-132.
2. J.G. Wilpon, L.R. Rabiner, C.H. Lee, and E.R. Goldman, "Automatic Recognition of Keywords in Unconstrained Speech Using Hidden Markov Models," 1990 *IEEE Trans. ASSP*, Vol 38. No. 11, pp. 1870-1878.
3. J.G. Wilpon, L.G. Miller, and P. Modi, "Improvements and Applications for Key Word Recognition Using Hidden Markov Modeling Techniques," 1991 *IEEE ICASSP*, pp. 309-312.
4. R. Rohlicek, W. Russell, S. Roukos, H. Gish, "Continuous Hidden Markov Modeling for Speaker-Independent Word Spotting," 1989 *IEEE ICASSP*, pp. 627-630.
5. L.D. Wilcox, and M.A. Bush, "Training and Search Algorithms for an Interactive Wordsptting System," 1992 *IEEE ICASSP*, pp. II-97-II-100.
6. H. Murveit, J. Butzberger, and M. Weintraub, "Performance of SRI's DECIPHER Speech Recognition System on DARPA's CSR Task," 1992 DARPA Speech and Natural Language Workshop Proceedings, pp 410-414
7. Murveit, H., J. Butzberger, and M. Weintraub, "Reduced Channel Dependence for Speech Recognition," 1992 DARPA Speech and Natural Language Workshop Proceedings, pp. 280-284.
8. Butzberger, J., H. Murveit, E. Shriberg, and P. Price, "Spontaneous Speech Effects in Large Vocabulary Speech Recognition Applications," 1992 DARPA Speech and Natural Language Workshop Proceedings, pp. 339-343.
9. H. Murveit, J. Butzberger, and M. Weintraub, "Speech Recognition in SRI's Resource Management and ATIS Systems," 1991 DARAP Speech and Natural Language Workshop, pp. 94-100.
10. Cohen, M., H. Murveit, J. Bernstein, P. Price, and M. Weintraub, "The DECIPHER™ Speech Recognition System," *1990 IEEE ICASSP*, pp. 77-80.
11. J.J. Godfrey, E.C. Holliman, and J.McDaniel, "SWITCHBOARD: Telephone Speech Corpus for Research and Development," 1992 *IEEE ICASSP*, pp. I-517-I-520.
12. S.M. Katz, "Estimation of Probabilities from Sparse Data for the Language Model Component of a Speech Recognizer," 1987 *IEEE ASSP*, Vol. 35, No. 3. pp.400-401.
13. MADCOW, "Multi-Site Data Collection for a Spoken Language Corpus," 1992 DARPA Speech and Natural Language Workshop Proceedings, pp. 7-14.

Topic and Speaker Identification via Large Vocabulary Continuous Speech Recognition

Barbara Peskin, Larry Gillick, Yoshiko Ito, Stephen Lowe, Robert Roth, Francesco Scattone, James Baker, Janet Baker, John Bridle, Melvyn Hunt, Jeremy Orloff

Dragon Systems, Inc.
320 Nevada Street
Newton, Massachusetts 02160

ABSTRACT

In this paper we exhibit a novel approach to the problems of topic and speaker identification that makes use of a large vocabulary continuous speech recognizer. We present a theoretical framework which formulates the two tasks as complementary problems, and describe the symmetric way in which we have implemented their solution. Results of trials of the message identification systems using the Switchboard corpus of telephone conversations are reported.

1. INTRODUCTION

The task of topic identification is to select from a set of possibilities the topic that is most likely to represent the subject matter covered by a sample of speech. Similarly, speaker identification requires selecting from a list of possibilities the speaker most likely to have produced the speech. In this paper, we present a novel approach to the problems of topic and speaker identification which uses a large vocabulary continuous speech recognizer as a preprocessor of the speech messages.

The motivation for developing improved message identification systems derives in part from the increasing reliance on audio databases such as arise from voice mail, for example, and the consequent need to extract information from them. Technology that is capable of searching such a database of recorded speech and classifying material by subject matter or by speaker would have substantial value, much as text-based information retrieval technology has for textual corpora. Several approaches to the problems of topic and speaker identification have already appeared in the literature. For example, an approach to topic identification using wordspotting is described in [1] and approaches to the speaker identification problem are reported in [2] and [3].

Dragon Systems' approach to the message identification tasks depends crucially on the existence of a large vocabulary continuous speech recognition system. We view the tasks of topic and speaker identification as complementary problems: for topic identification, the speaker is irrelevant and only the subject matter is of interest; for speaker identification, the reverse is true. For efficiency of computation, in either case we first use a speaker-independent topic-independent recognizer to transcribe the speech messages. The resulting output is then scored using topic-sensitive or speaker-sensitive models.

This approach to the problem of message identification is based on the belief that the contextual information used in a full-scale recognition is invaluable in extracting reliable data from difficult speech channels. For example, unlike standard approaches to topic identification through spotting a small collection of topic-specific words, the approach via continuous speech recognition should more reliably detect keywords because of the acoustic and language model context available to the recognizer. Moreover, with large vocabulary recognition, the list of keywords is no longer limited to a small set of highly topic-specific (but generally infrequent) words, and instead can grow to include much (or even all) of the recognition vocabulary. The use of contextual information makes the message systems sufficiently robust that they are able to operate even with vocabulary sizes and noise environments that would make speech recognition extremely difficult for other applications.

To test our message identification systems, we have been using the "Switchboard" corpus of recorded telephone messages [4] collected by Texas Instruments and now available through the Linguistic Data Consortium. This collection of roughly 2500 messages includes conversations involving several hundred speakers. People who volunteered to participate in this program were prompted with a subject to discuss (chosen from a set that they had previously specified as acceptable) and were expected to talk for at least five minutes. We report results of topic identification tests involving messages on ten different topics using four and a half minutes of speech and speaker identification tests involving 24 speakers with test intervals containing as little as 10 seconds of speech.

In the next section, we describe the theoretical framework on which our message identification systems are based and discuss the dual nature of the two problems. We then describe how this theory is implemented in the current message processing systems. Preliminary tests of the systems using the Switchboard corpus are reported in Section 4. We close with a discussion of the test results and plans for further research.

2. THEORETICAL FRAMEWORK

Our approach to the topic and speaker identification tasks is based on modelling speech as a stochastic process. For each of the two problems, we assume that a given stream of speech is generated by one of several possible stochastic sources, one corresponding to each of the possible topics or to each of the possible speakers in question. We are required to judge from the acoustic data which topic (or speaker) is the most probable source.

Standard statistical theory provides us with the optimal solution to such a classification problem. We denote the string of acoustic observations by A and introduce the random variable T to designate which stochastic model has produced the speech, where T may take on the values from 1 to n for the n possible sources. If we let p_i denote the prior probability of stochastic source i and assume that all classification errors have the same cost, then we should choose the source $T = \hat{i}$ for which

$$\hat{i} = \operatorname*{argmax}_i \; p_i \; P(A \mid T = i).$$

We assume, for the purposes of this work, that all prior probabilities are equal, so that the classification problem reduces simply to choosing the source i for which the conditional probability of the acoustics given the source is maximized.

In principle, to compute each of the probabilities $P(A \mid T = i)$ we would have to sum over all possible transcriptions W of the speech:

$$P(A \mid T = i) = \sum_W P(A, W \mid T = i).$$

In practice, such a collection of computations is unwieldy and so we make several simplifying approximations to limit the computational burden. First, we estimate the above sum only by its single largest term, i.e. we approximate the probability $P(A \mid T = i)$ by the joint probabiltiy of A and the single most probable word sequence $W = W^i_{\text{max}}$. Of course, generating such an optimal word sequence is exactly what speech recognition is designed to do. Thus, for the problem of topic identification, we could imagine running n different speech recognizers, each modelling a different topic, and then compare the resulting probabilities $P(A, W^i_{\text{max}} \mid T = i)$ corresponding to each of the n optimal transcriptions W^i_{max}. Similarly, for speaker identification, we would run n different speaker-dependent recognizers, each trained on one of the possible speakers, and compare the resulting scores.

This approach, though simpler, still requires us to make many complete recognition passes across the speech sample. We further reduce the computational burden by instead producing only a single transcription of the speech to be classified, by using a recognizer whose models are both topic-independent and speaker-independent. Once this single transcription $W = W_{\text{max}}$ is obtained, we need only compute the probabilities $P(A, W_{\text{max}} \mid T = i)$ corresponding to each of the stochastic sources $T = i$.

Rewriting $P(A, W_{\text{max}} \mid T = i)$ as

$$P(A \mid W_{\text{max}}, T = i) \, * \, P(W_{\text{max}} \mid T = i),$$

we see that the problem of computing the desired probability factors into two components. The first, $P(A \mid W, T)$, we can think of as the contribution of the acoustic model, which assigns probabilities to acoustic observations generated from a given string of words. The second factor, $P(W \mid T)$, encodes the contribution of the language model, which assigns probabilities to word strings without reference to the acoustics.

Now for the problem of topic identification, we wish to determine which of several possible topics is most likely the subject of a given sample of speech. Nothing is known about the speaker. We therefore assume that the same speaker-independent acoustic model holds for all topics; i.e. for the topic identification task, we assume that $P(A \mid W, T)$ does not depend on T. But we need n different language models $P(W \mid T = i)$, $i = 1, \ldots, n$. From the above factorization, it is then clear that in comparing scores from the different sources, only this latter term matters.

Symmetrically, for the speaker identification problem, we must choose which of several possible speakers is most likely to have produced a given sample of speech. While in practice, different speakers may well talk about different subjects and in different styles, we assume for the speaker identification task that the language model $P(W \mid T)$ is independent of T. But n different acoustic models $P(A \mid W, T = i)$ are required. Thus only the first factor matters for speaker identification.

As a result, once the speaker-independent topic-independent recognizer has generated a transcript of the speech message, the task of the topic classifier is simply to score the transcription using each of n different language models. Similarly, for speaker identification the task reduces to computing the likelihood of the acoustic data given the transcription, using each of n different acoustic models.

3. THE MESSAGE IDENTIFICATION SYSTEM

We now examine how this theory is implemented in each of the major components of Dragon's message identification system: the continuous speech recognizer, the speaker classifier, and the topic classifier.

3.1. The Speech Recognizer

In order to carry out topic and speaker identification as described above, it is necessary to have a large vocabulary continuous speech recognizer that can operate in either speaker-independent or speaker-dependent mode. Dragon's speech recognizer has been described extensively elsewhere ([5], [6]). Briefly, the recognizer is a time-synchronous hidden Markov model (HMM) based system. It makes use of a set of 32 signal-processing parameters: 1 overall amplitude term, 7 spectral parameters, 12 mel-cepstral parameters, and 12 mel-cepstral differences. Each word pronunciation is represented as a sequence of phoneme models called PICs (phonemes-in-context) designed to capture coarticulatory effects due to the preceding and succeeding phonemes. Because it is impractical to model all the triphones that could in principle arise, we model only the most common ones and back off to more generic forms when a recognition hypothesis calls for a PIC which has not been built. The PICs themselves are modelled as linear HMMs with one or more nodes, each node being specified by an output distribution and a double exponential duration distribution. We are currently modelling the output distributions of the states as tied mixtures of double exponential distributions. The recognizer employs a rapid match module which returns a short list of words that might begin in a given frame whenever the recognizer hypothesizes that a word might be ending. During recognition, a digram language model with unigram backoff is used.

We have recently begun transforming our basic set of 32 signal-processing parameters using the IMELDA transform [7], a transformation constructed via linear discriminant analysis to select directions in parameter space that are most useful in distinguishing between designated classes while reducing variation within classes. For the speaker-independent recognizer, we sought directions which maximize average variation between phonemes while being relatively insensitive to differences within the phoneme class, such as might arise from different speakers, telephone channels, etc. Since the IMELDA transform generates a new set of parameters ordered with respect to their value in discriminating classes, directions with little discriminating power between phonemes can be dropped. We use only the top 16 IMELDA parameters for speaker-independent recognition. A different IMELDA transform, in many ways dual to this one, was employed by the speaker classifier, as described below.

For speaker-independent recognition, we also normalize the average speech spectra across conversations via blind deconvolution prior to performing the IMELDA transform, in order to further reduce channel differences. A fixed number of frames are removed from the beginning and end of each speech segment before computing the average to minimize the effect of silence on the long-term speech spectrum.

Finally, we are now building separate male and female acoustic models and using the result of whichever model scores better. While in principle, one would have to perform a complete recognition pass with both sets of models and choose the better scoring, we have found that one can fairly reliably determine the model which better fits the data after recognizing only a few utterances. The remainder of the speech can then be recognized using only the better model.

3.2. The Speaker Classifier

Given the transcript generated by the speaker-independent recognizer, the job of the speaker classifier is to score the speech data using speaker-specific sets of acoustic models, assuming that the transcript provides the correct text; i.e. it must calculate the probabilities $P(A \mid W, T = i)$ discussed above. Dragon's continuous speech recognizer is capable of running in such a "scoring" mode. This step is much faster than performing a full recognition, since the recognizer only has to hypothesize different ways of mapping the speech data to the required text – a frame-by-frame phonetic labelling we refer to as a "segmentation" of the script – and need not entertain hypotheses on alternate word sequences.

In principle, the value of $P(A \mid W, T)$ should be computed as the sum over all possible segmentations of the acoustic data, but, as usual, we approximate this probability using only the largest term in the sum, corresponding to the maximum likelihood segmentation. While one could imagine letting each of the speaker-dependent models choose the segmentation that is best for them, in our current version of the speaker classifier we have chosen to compute this "best" segmentation once and for all using the same speaker-independent recognizer responsible for generating the initial transcription. This ensures that the comparison of different speakers is relative to the same alignment of the speech and may yield an actual advantage in performance, given the imprecision of our probability models.

Thus, the job of the speaker classifier reduces to scoring the speech data given both a fixed transcription and a specified mapping of individual speech frames to PICs. To perform this scoring, we use a "matched set" of tied mixture acoustic models – a collection of speaker-dependent models each trained on speech from one of the target speakers but constructed with exactly the same collection of PICs to keep the scoring directly comparable. Running in "scoring" mode, we then produce a set of scores corresponding to the negative log likelihood of generating the acoustics given the segmentation for each of the speaker-dependent acoustic models. The speech sample is assigned to the lowest scoring model.

In constructing speaker scoring models, we derived a new "speaker sensitive" IMELDA transformation, designed to enhance differences between speakers. The transform was computed using only voiced speech segments of the test speakers (and, correspondingly, only voiced speech was used in the scoring). As is common in using the IMELDA strategy, we dropped parameters with the least discriminating power, reducing our original 32 signal-processing parameters to a new set of 24 IMELDA parameters. These were the parameters used to build the speaker scoring models. It is worth remarking that, because these parameters were constructed to emphasize differences between speakers rather than between phonemes, it was particularly important that the phoneme-level segmentation used in the scoring be set by the original recognition models.

3.3. The Topic Classifier

Once the speaker-independent recognizer has generated a transcription of the speech, the topic classifier need only score the transcript using language models trained on each of the possible topics. The current topic scoring algorithm uses a simple (unigram) multinomial probability model based on a collection of topic-dependent "keywords". Thus digrams are not used for topic scoring although they are used during recognition. For each topic, the probability of occurrence of each keyword is estimated from training material on that topic. Non-keyword members of the vocabulary are assigned to a catch-all "other" category whose probability is also estimated. Transcripts are then scored by adding in a negative log probability for every recognized word, and running totals are kept for each of the topics. The speech sample is assigned to the topic with the lowest cumulative score.

We have experimented with two different methods of keyword selection. The first method is based on computing the chi-squared statistic for homogeneity based on the number of times a given word occurs in the training data for each of the target topics. This method assumes that the number of occurrences of the word within a topic follows a binomial distribution, i.e. that there is a "natural frequency" for each word within each topic class. The words of the vocabulary can then be ranked according to the P-value resulting from this chi-squared test. Presumably, the smaller the P-value, the more useful the word should be for topic identification. Keyword lists of different lengths are obtained by selecting all words whose P-value falls below a given threshold.

Unfortunately, this method does not do a good job of excluding function words and other high frequency words, such as "uh" or "oh", which are of limited use for topic classification. Consequently, this method requires the use of a human-generated "stop list" to filter out these unwanted entries. The problem lies chiefly in the falsity of the binomial assumption: one expects a great deal of variability in the frequency of words, even among messages on the same topic, and natural variations in the occurrence rates of these very high frequency words can result in exceptionally small P-values.

The second method is designed to address this problem by explicitly modelling the variability in word frequency among conversations in the same topic instead of only variations between topics. It also uses a chi-squared test to sort the words in the vocabulary by P-value. But now for each word we construct a two-way table sorting training messages from each topic into classes based on whether the word in question occurs at a low, a moderate, or a high rate. (If the word occurs in only a small minority of messages, it becomes necessary to collapse the three categories to two.) Then we compute the P-value relative to the null hypothesis that the distribution of occurrence rates is the same for each of the topic classes. Hence this method explicitly models the variability in occurrence rates among documents in a nonparametric way. This method does seem successful at automatically excluding most function words when stringent P-value thresholds are set, and as the threshold is relaxed and the keyword lists allowed to grow, function words are slowly introduced at levels more appropriate to their utility in topic identification. Hence, this method eliminates the need for human editing of the keyword lists.

4. TESTING ON SWITCHBOARD DATA

To gauge the performance of our message classification system, we turned to the Switchboard corpus of recorded telephone conversations. The recognition task is particularly challenging for Switchboard messages, since they involve spontaneous conversational speech across noisy phone lines. This made the Switchboard corpus a particularly good platform for testing the message identification systems, allowing us to assess the ability of the continuous speech recognizer to extract information useful to the message classifiers even when the recognition itself was bound to be highly errorful.

To create our "Switchboard" recognizer, male and female speaker-independent acoustic models were trained using a total of about 9 hours of Switchboard messages (approximately 140 message halves) from 8 male and 8 female speakers not involved in the test sets. We found that it was necessary to hand edit the training messages in order to remove such extraneous noises as cross-talk, bursts of static, and laughter. We also corrected bad transcriptions and broke up long utterances into shorter, more manageable pieces.

Models for about 4800 PICs were constructed. We chose to construct only one-node models for the Switchboard task, both to reduce the number of parameters to be estimated given the limited training data and to minimize the penalty for reducing or skipping phonemes in the often rapid speech of many Switchboard speakers. A vocabulary of 8431 words (all words occurring at least 4 times in the training data) and a digram language model were derived from a set of 935 transcribed Switchboard messages involving roughly 1.4 million words of text and covering nearly 60 different topics. Roughly a third of the language model training messages were on one of the 10 topics used for the topic identification task.

For the speaker identification trials, we used a set of 24 test speakers, 12 male and 12 female. Speaker-dependent scoring models were constructed for each of the 24 speakers using the same PIC set as for the speaker-independent recognizer. PIC models were trained using 5 to 10 hand-edited message halves (about 16 minutes of speech) from each speaker.

The speaker identification test material involved 97 message halves and included from 1 to 6 messages for each test speaker. We tested on speech segments from these messages that contained 10, 30, and 60 seconds of speech. The results of the speaker identification tests were surprisingly constant across the three duration lengths. Even for segments containing as little as 10 seconds of speech, 86 of the 97 message halves, or 88.7%, were correctly classified. When averaged equally across speakers, this gave 90.3% accuracy. The results from the three trial runs are summarized in Table 1. It is worth remarking that even the few errors that were made tended to be concentrated in a few difficult speakers; for 17 of the 24 speakers, the performance was always perfect, and for only 2 speakers was more than one message ever misclassified.

Given the insensitivity of these results to speech duration, we decided to further limit the amount of speech available to the speaker classifier. The test segments used in the speaker test were actually concatenations of smaller speech intervals, ranging in length from as little as 1.5 to as much as 50.2 seconds. We rescored using these individual fragments as the test pieces.[1] Results remained excellent. For example, when testing only the pieces of length under 3 seconds, 42 of the 46 pieces, or 91.3%, were correctly classified (90.9% when speakers were equally weighted). These pieces represented only 19 of the 24 speakers, but did include our most problematic speakers. For segments of length less than 5 seconds, 177 of the 201 pieces (88.1%, or 89.4% when the 24 speakers were equally weighted) were correctly classified.

speech interval (seconds)	weighted by message (%)	weighted by speaker (%)
10	88.7	90.3
30	88.7	90.6
60	87.6	89.9

Table 1: Speaker identification accuracy for 97-message Switchboard test.

For the topic identification task, we used a test set of 120 messages, 12 conversations on each of 10 different topics. Topics included such subjects as "air pollution", "pets", and "public education", and involved several topics (for example, "gun control" and "crime") with significant common ground. For topic identification, we planned to use the entire speech message, but for uniformity all messages were truncated after 5 minutes and the first 30 seconds of each was removed because of concern that this initial segment might be artificially rich in keywords.

Keywords were selected from the same training messages used for constructing the recognizer's language model. This collection yielded just over 30 messages on each of the ten topics, for a total of about 50,000 words of training text per topic. Because this is relatively little for estimating reliable word frequencies, word counts for each topic were heavily smoothed using counts from all other topics. We found that it was best to use a 5-to-1 smoothing ratio; i.e. data specific to the topic were counted five times as heavily as data from the other nine topics.

Keyword lists of lengths ranging from about 200 words to nearly 5000 were generated using the second method of keyword selection. We also tried using the entire 8431-

[1] The initial speaker-independent recognition and segmentation were not, however, re-run so that such decisions as gender determination were inherited from the larger test.

word recognition vocabulary as the "keyword" list. The results of the initial runs, given in the second column of Table 2, were disappointing: performance fell between 70% and 75% in all cases.

#keywords	original (%)	recalibrated (%)
203	70.0	71.7
1127	71.7	85.0
2655	72.5	87.5
4658	74.2	87.5
8431	72.5	88.3

Table 2: Topic identification accuracy for 120-message Switchboard test.

It is worth noting that, as it was designed to, the new keyword selection routine succeeded in automatically excluding virtually all function words from the 203-word list. For comparison, we also ran some keyword lists selected using our original method and filtered through a human-generated "stop list". The performance was similar: for example, a list of 211 keywords resulted in an accuracy of 67.5%.

The problem for the topic classifier was that scores for messages from different topics were not generally comparable due to differences in the acoustic confusability of the keywords. When tested on the true transcripts of the speech messages, the topic classifier did extremely well, missing only 2 or 3 messages out of the 120 with any of the keyword lists. Unfortunately, when run on the recognized transcriptions, some topics (most notably "pets", with its preponderance of monosyllabic keywords) never received competitive scores.

In principle, this problem could be corrected by estimating keyword frequencies not from true transcriptions of training data but from their recognized counterparts. Unfortunately, this is a fairly expensive approach, requiring that the full training corpus be run through the recognizer. Instead, we took a more expedient course. In the process of evaluating our Switchboard recognizer, we had run recognition on over a hundred messages on topics other than the ten used in the topic identification test. For each of these off-topic messages, we computed scores based on each of the test topic language models to estimate the (per word) handicap that each test topic should receive. When the 120 test messages were rescored using this adjustment, the results improved dramatically for all but the smallest list (where the keywords were too sparse for scores to be adequately estimated). The improved results are given in the last column of Table 2.

5. CONCLUSIONS

As the Switchboard testing demonstrates, message identification via large vocabulary continuous speech recognition is a successful strategy even in challenging speech environments. Although the quality of the recognition as measured by word accuracy rates was very low for this task – only 22% of the words were correctly transcribed – the recognizer was still able to extract sufficient information to reliably identify speech messages. This supports our belief in the advantages of using articulatory and language model context.

We were surprised not to find a more pronounced benefit from using large numbers of keywords for the topic identification task. Our prior experience had indicated that there were small but significant gains as the number of keywords grew and, although such a pattern is perhaps suggested by the results in Table 2, the gains (beyond those in the recalibration estimates) are too small to be considered significant. It is possible that with better modelling of keyword frequencies or by introducing acoustic distinctiveness as a keyword selection criterion, such improvements might be realized.

Given the strong performance of both of our identification systems, we also look forward to exploring how much we can restrict the amount of training and testing material and still maintain the quality of our results.

References

1. R.C. Rose, E.I. Chang, and R.P. Lipmann, "Techniques for Information Retrieval from Voice Messages," *Proc. ICASSP-91*, Toronto, May 1991.
2. A.L. Higgins and L.G. Bahler, "Text Independent Speaker Verification by Discriminator Counting," *Proc. ICASSP-91*, Toronto, May 1991.
3. L.P. Netsch and G.R. Doddington, "Speaker Verification Using Temporal Decorrelation Post-Processing," *Proc. ICASSP-92*, San Francisco, March 1992.
4. J.J. Godfrey, E.C. Holliman, and J. McDaniel, "SWITCHBOARD: Telephone Speech Corpus for Research and Development," *Proc. ICASSP-92*, San Francisco, March 1992.
5. J.K. Baker *et al.*, "Large Vocabulary Recognition of Wall Street Journal Sentences at Dragon Systems," *Proc. DARPA Speech and Natural Language Workshop*, Harriman, New York, February 1992.
6. R. Roth *et al.*, "Large Vocabulary Continuous Speech Recognition of Wall Street Journal Data," *Proc. ICASSP-93*, Minneapolis, Minnesota, April 1993.
7. M.J. Hunt, D.C. Bateman, S.M. Richardson, and A. Piau, "An Investigation of PLP and IMELDA Acoustic Representations and of their Potential for Combination," *Proc. ICASSP-91*, Toronto, May 1991.

SESSION 4: NATURAL LANGUAGE

Robert C. Moore, Chair

Artificial Intelligence Center
SRI International
Menlo Park, CA 94025

Collectively, the papers in this session are mainly concerned with parsing, semantic interpretation, and inference. Interest in these processes can be motivated if we recognize that the overall goal of the field of NLP is the manipulation of natural language in ways that depend on meaning. Parsing, the recovery of the linguistic or grammatical structure of a natural-language utterance, is of concern to NLP because, in general, the meaning of a natural-language utterance depends on its structure. An example that illustrates this point is the sentence *The man with the umbrella opened the door.* If we tried to process this sentence without paying attention to its grammatical structure, we could easily be misled by the fact that it contains the substring *the umbrella opened.* But this sentence has nothing to do with umbrellas opening. Because of the structure of the sentence, the *umbrella* must be grouped with *with* and not with *opened.*

If the central concern of NLP is the manipulation of natural language in ways that depend on meaning, then semantic interpretation would naturally be expected to play a central role. In practice, semantic interpretation in NLP usually means recovering a representation of the meaning of an utterance that encodes that meaning in a more transparent way than does the utterance itself. How does this contribute to the goal of manipulating language in meaning-dependent ways? We want to have algorithms that manipulate language according to meaning, but meaning is ultimately an abstraction that algorithms can have no direct access to. Algorithms can directly manipulate expressions only according to their structure. Thus we need expressions whose structure corresponds in a very direct way to their meaning. While, as we have argued above, the meaning of a natural-language expression is dependent on its structure, this dependence can be very indirect. By recovering an expression that encodes the meaning of an utterance more directly, we can create modular algorithms that consist of interacting pieces that each look only at a small piece of the structure of the meaning representation. If the pieces of the meaning representation fit together in a natural way that reflects the overall meaning of the utterance, then the algorithms that manipulate them will also be able to fit together in a natural way that reflects the overall meaning of the utterance.

Finally, inference is the pay-off for the previous phases of parsing and semantic interpretation, being the canonical example of a form of manipulation of natural-language that depends on the meaning of utterances. In fact, a strong argument could be made that inference is a process on meanings and not on natural-language expressions per se.

With this as background, we can briefly consider some of the major issues raised by the papers in this session. Some of the most important issues currently being raised about parsing are how complete it needs to be and how complex a structure needs to be recovered for different applications. The paper by McCord takes a fairly traditional view, attempting to recover a complete structural description of any sentence presented to the parser. In the paper by Hobbs, et al., parsing is much more fragmentary, attempting only to recover the structure of pieces of a text that are critical for the particular application. Moreover, the structures recovered in the Hobbs paper are simple enough to be characterized by finite-state automata, while the structures described in the McCord paper are more complex. A second parsing issue, which forms the focus of the McCord paper, is the problem of ambiguity. In parsing, we are given a string of words or tokens, and we have to recover the grammatical structure, but there may be many structures compatible with a given string. McCord, then, addresses the issue of how to find the most likely stucture out of all the ones that are possible.

Issues of semantic interpretation are of greatest concern in the paper by Hwang and Schubert. The type of work reported in this paper can perhaps be best appreciated by keeping in mind some central methodological principles that are ofter used to guide work on semantics. Having such principles is important because of the lack of clear intuititive agreement about the adequacy of semantic representations. Speech recognition, in contrast, is methodologically much simpler than semantics because of the enormous intersubjective agreement as to what strings of words most speech signals correspond to. While there are particular cases where the proper transcription of a signal can be argued about, in most cases this is simply not a problem. No such intuitive agreement exists in the field of semantics. It is something like speech recognition might be if there were no written languages and no general agreement on segmentation of speech into words.

So, in semantic interpretation, there are two methodological principles that have come to be used as a means of evaluating the adequacy of proposed analyses. The first is that one should be able to give a mathematical, "model theoretic" interpretation of the formal expressions used to represent the meaning of natural-language expressions. This gives a way to decide whether there is really any basis for the claim that the representations in question actually do capture the meaning of the corresponding natural-language. The main alternative seems to be what is sometimes referred to as "pretend it's English" semantics, where one reads the tokens that appear in the representation as if they are English words and sees whether it sounds like it means what is desired—not a very satisfactory state of affairs. A second methodological principle in semantic interpretation is that of compositionality—the slogan being, "the meaning of the whole must be a function of the meaning of the parts." This principle reflects the fact that it is not sufficient just to be able to represent formally the meaning of natural-language expressions; it must be possible to produce them in a systematic way from the natural language. In the Hwang and Schubert paper, the representations used may seem quite complex to someone outside the field, but that complexity is motivated by the need to satisfy these methodological constraints.

In Vilain's paper, the major issue adressed is the tradeoff between expressiveness in a representation formalism and the tractability of the inference problem for that formalism. It is notorious that the more expressive a representation language is, the more computationally complex the inference problem for it is. Vilain looks at whether for a certain type of application, the expressions in the representation language can be limited to a normal form which is known to be computationally tractable.

There are also a number of issues that cut across all phases of processing. One such issue is to what degree systems can be made language and domain independent. The ideal is for the algorithms to be both language and domain independent, with a declaratively specified grammar and lexicon that is language dependent but domain independent, and a final domain-dependent module that interfaces the language processing to the application. The paper by Aone, et al., explores how well this model works in a real multi-lingual data extraction system. A second issue is that of hand coding versus automatic extraction of the knowledge required for NLP systems. Almost all the knowledge embodied in the systems described in this session is hand-coded, while the emphasis in Session 8 is on systems that use methods for automatic extraction. Often this issue is conflated with the issue of whether the knowledge in question is represented by symbolic rules or by numerical parameters such as probabilities, but it is worth pointing out that the paper by Brill in Session 8 uses symbolic rules, but extracts them automatically from a corpus. Finally, several of these papers raise the question of how to evaluate the work reported on. This has come to be recognized as a central methodological issue in the field, and the McCord, Hobbs, and Vilain papers all address the problem in one way or another.

HEURISTICS FOR BROAD-COVERAGE NATURAL LANGUAGE PARSING

Michael C. McCord

IBM T. J. Watson Research Center
POB 704 Yorktown Heights, NY 10598

ABSTRACT

The Slot Grammar system is interesting for natural language applications because it can deliver parses with deep grammatical information on a reasonably broad scale. The paper describes a numerical scoring system used in Slot Grammar for ambiguity resolution, which not only ranks parses but also contributes to parsing efficiency through a parse space pruning algorithm. Details of the method of computing parse scores are given, and test results for the English Slot Grammar are presented.

1. INTRODUCTION

As everyone who has tried it knows, the hardest part of building a broad-coverage parser is not simply covering all the constructions of the language, but dealing with ambiguity.

One approach to ambiguity resolution is to "understand" the text well enough – to have a good semantic interpretation system, to use real-world modeling, inference, etc. This can work well in small domains, and it is, in this author's opinion, ultimately necessary for the highest quality of natural language processing in any domain; but it is probably not feasible on a broad scale today. So some kind of heuristic method is needed for disambiguation, some way of ranking analyses and choosing the best. Even in the ideal model of human language processing (which would use a great deal of knowledge representation and inference), ranking heuristics seem appropriate as a mechanism since humans must work with incomplete knowledge most of the time.

Two major questions that can be asked about a heuristic method for ambiguity resolution are these:

1. What level of representation is used for disambiguation and is involved in the statements of the heuristic rules – lexical/morphological, surface syntactic, deep syntactic, or logical/semantic?
2. Where do the heuristic rules come from? Are they largely created through human linguistic insight, or are they induced by processing corpora?

This paper describes the heuristic method used in the Slot Grammar (SG) system [10, 11, 13, 16, 17] for ambiguity resolution – the SG parse scoring system. This scoring system operates during parsing (with a bottom-up chart parser), assigning real number scores to partial analyses as well as to analyses of the complete sentence. The scores are used not only for ranking the final analyses but also for pruning the parse space during parsing, thus increasing time and space efficiency.

The level of representation being disambiguated is thus the level of SG parses. SG parse structures are dependency- or head-oriented, and include, in a single tree, both surface structure and deep syntactic information such as predicate-argument structure, remote dependencies, control information, and unwinding of passives. [1]

SG parse structures also include a choice of *word senses*. The extent to which these represent semantic sense distinctions depends on the lexicon. The SG system is set up to deal with semantic word-sense distinctions and to resolve them by doing semantic type-checking during parsing. However, in the lexicon for **ESG** (English Slot Grammar), nearly all word sense distinctions are a matter of part of speech or syntactic slot frame. Some semantic types are shown in the lexicon and are used in parsing, but generally very few. Thus one would say that **ESG** parse structures are basically *syntactic* structures, although the deep information like argument structure, passive unwinding, etc., counts for "semantics" in some people's books.

Where do the SG scoring rules come from – human linguistic insight or induction from corpus processing? The score of an SG parse, which will be described in Section 4, is the sum of several components. Most of these come completely from human linguistic insight, though some of them get their numeric values from corpus processing. In the tests reported in the final section, only the "linguistic-insight" rules are used. Some previous tests using the corpus-based heuristic rules together with the main SG heuristic rules showed that the former could improve the parse rate by a few percentage points. It is definitely worth pursuing both approaches, and more work will be done with a combination of the two.

[1] No attempt is made to resolve quantifier scoping in SG parses, although there is a post-processing system that produces a logical form with scope resolution for quantifiers and other "focalizers"[12]. Anaphora resolution [8, 9] is also done by post-processing SG parses.

In the next section we give a brief overview of Slot Grammar. In Section 3 we describe the scoring system generally and its use in parse space pruning, and in Section 4 we give some details of the computation of scores. Finally, Section 5 presents the results of some tests of **ESG**.

2. OVERVIEW OF SLOT GRAMMAR

The *slots* that figure in Slot Grammar rules and parsing come in two varieties: *complement slots* and *adjunct slots*. Analysis is word-oriented, and slots are associated with word senses. The complement slots for a word sense are associated with it in the lexicon. The adjunct slots depend only on the part of speech of the word sense and are listed for that part of speech in the grammar. Slots have names like *subj* and *obj* and should be thought of basically as *syntactic* relations, though complement slot frames in the lexicon can be viewed as corresponding to arguments in logical form.

The notion that a phrase *fills* a slot of a word (sense) is primitive in the grammar, and the conditions under which this can happen are given by the *slot-filler* rules. Grammatical analysis of a phrase consists basically of choosing, for each word of the phrase, (1) a word sense, (2) a feature structure, and (3) filler subphrases for its slots. A slot is *obligatory* or *optional* according as it must be, or need not be, filled in order for the analysis to be complete. Adjunct slots are normally optional. A complement slot can be filled at most once, but adjunct slots can, by default, be filled multiply.

The parser works bottom-up, beginning with one-word phrases and attaching other phrases as left and right modifiers as they can fill slots. As a phrase is built up in this way, it retains a distinguished head word, and the slots associated with this head word are considered slots of the phrase.

An example of a slot-filler rule is the following for the subject slot (in simplified form):

$$subj \Longrightarrow f(noun(nom, Num))\ \&\ hf(verb(fin(Num))).$$

A goal $f(Feat)$ on the right hand side of a filler rule tests that the feature structure of the filler phrase matches $Feat$. A goal $hf(Feat)$ tests the feature structure of the *higher* phrase – the phrase (with possibly other modifiers attached) with which the slot is associated. The SG formalism includes a rich set of special predicates like f and hf that can be used for examining any aspects of the filler phrase and higher phrase for a slot filling.

Slot-filler rules normally do not constrain left-to-right ordering of the phrases involved. Instead, there are modularly stated ordering rules, which are applied as constraints in parsing after slot-filler rules apply.

Generally, there is a modular treatment of different grammatical phenomena in a Slot Grammar. There are separate rule systems not only for slot-filling and ordering, but also for coordination, unbounded dependencies, obligatory slots, adjunct slot declaration, "or-slots", punctuation, and parse scoring. All these rule types make use of the same system of special predicates (mentioned above for slot-filler rules) for examining the phrases involved in slot filling. Modularization of the rule system makes large grammars more manageable and also makes it easier to adapt a grammar for one language to another language.

There are currently Slot Grammars (in various states of completeness) for English, German, Spanish, Danish, Norwegian, and Hebrew. A great deal of attention has been paid to the development of a large, language-universal component of the system, the Slot Grammar *shell*. For a particular language, the shell represents roughly 65% of the rules/facts, not counting lexicons. All of the rule types mentioned above have part of their treatment in the shell, but there are especially large language-universal components for coordination, unbounded dependencies, punctuation, and parse scoring. Nevertheless, for all of these, there can be rules in the language-specific grammar that override or augment the language-universal rules.

The lexicon for **ESG** consists of a hand-coded portion for approximately 6,000 lemmas (basically most frequent words), plus a large back-up lexicon of approximately 60,000 lemmas derived from UDICT [1, 7] and other sources. Mary Neff is working on improvements of the large **ESG** lexicon through extraction from standard dictionaries.

Slot Grammars are used for source analysis in the MT system **LMT** [14, 15].

For a more detailed description of current version of the SG system, see [16, 17, 18]. In this paper we concentrate on the scoring system, in its latest form.

3. SCORING AND PARSE SPACE PRUNING

During parsing, each analysis P of a subphrase is assigned a real number $score(P)$. A larger number represents a worse score. As described in the next section, most of the ingredients that go into scores are positive numbers that are like penalties for unusual structure, and total scores are normally positive.

Parse space pruning involves comparison of scores of partial analyses and pruning away analyses that have relatively bad scores; but the comparisons are made only within certain equivalence classes of analyses. Two partial analyses are *equivalent* when they have the same boundaries, the same head word, and the same *basic feature*. For most categories, the basic feature is just the part of speech, but for verbs a finer distinction is made according to the inflection type (finite, infinitive, etc.) of the verb. The notion of equivalence is loosened in certain ways for coordinated phrases that will not be described here.

Pruning is done as follows. Suppose P is a new, candidate partial analysis obtained in parsing. Let $compar(P)$ denote the set of existing partial analyses that are equivalent to P (not including P itself). Because of previous pruning, all members of $compar(P)$ have the same score; call this number $scompar(P)$. (If $compar(P) = \emptyset$ then consider $scompar(P) = +\infty$.) The system stores this best score $scompar(P)$ for the equivalence class of P in a way that can immediately be computed from P without searching the chart.

Now three things can happen: (1) If $score(P) > scompar(P)$, then P is discarded. (2) If $score(P) = scompar(P)$, then P is simply added to the chart. (3) If $score(P) < scompar(P)$, then P is added to the chart and all members of $compar(P)$ are discarded.

This parse space pruning can be turned on or off at run time, but scoring is done in any case, and final parses are ranked by the scoring system whether pruning is on or off. Generally, parse space pruning is crucial to the running of the system for large sentences because of space and time problems if it is not used. When pruning is turned on, there are generally very few final parses obtained for a sentence – on average about 1.3 (per successfully parsed sentence).

When parsing of a sentence fails, the system pieces together a "fitted parse" in a manner somewhat similar to that in [5]. The scores obtained for partial analyses figure heavily in choosing the pieces for this result.

4. COMPUTATION OF SCORES

The score of a partial analysis is obtained incrementally in building up the analysis. The initial score, for a one-word analysis, is associated with the word sense, and the score is incremented whenever a slot is filled or a coordinate structure is formed. All in all, there are eight main components of the total score (the score is the sum of them). We first list them with a brief description and then discuss them individually. The list is in decreasing order of "importance" – the amount of effort put into the rules/data for the component and roughly the current contribution of the component to successful parsing. Components 1, 2, 3, 4, 5, 8 are totally "human-coded", and components 6, 7 get their data from corpus processing.

Most of the heuristics described in [4] are covered by these rules (and were developed independently).

1. *SlotPref*. Computed when a modifier is attached by filling a slot. Measures the preference for using that slot *vs.* other slots for attaching the given modifier to the given higher phrase.
2. *ParallelCoord*. Favors parallelism in coordination.
3. *CloseAttach*. Favors close attachment.
4. *PhrasePref*. Tests the characteristics of a "completed" phrase – a phrase that becomes a modifier or is taken as an analysis of the complete input segment. Similar to *SlotPref*, but independent of the slot.
5. *WordSensePref*. Favors one sense of a word over other senses.
6. *HeadSlotFiller*. Used, like *SlotPref*, when a slot is filled, but tests for specific choices for the head words of the higher phrase and the filler phrase, as well their parts of speech, and tests only these things.
7. *POSPref*. Similar to *WordSensePref*, but tests only for part of speech.
8. *LexSlotPref*. Another score associated with filling a given slot, but coded in the lexicon in a given slot frame and can test semantic type conditions on the filler.

In the following more detailed description of the scoring components, we will use "XSG" to refer to the language-specific part of the Slot Grammar of language X. Thus the rules for grammar of X reside in both the SG shell and XSG.

SlotPref The rules for *SlotPref* are coded in both the shell and XSG. The default score, given in the shell, is +1 for an adjunct slot and 0 for a complement slot, so that complement slots are preferred over adjuncts.

For an example, consider the sentence *John sent the file to Bill.* The PP *to Bill* can attach to *file* by an adjunct slot or to *sent* by a complement slot (its indirect object), but the default *SlotPref* score is 1 for the adjunct and 0 for the complement, [2] so the analysis with the complement wins and the other is pruned away. [3]

Slot-scoring rules in XSG can override the default. Currently, out of a total of 678 rules of various types in **ESG**, 216 are slot-scoring rules. Most of the day-to-day effort in improving **ESG** consists of work on these scoring rules.

A slot-scoring rule is of the form:

$$Slot + E \ (\leftarrow Body).$$

E is normally a real number and is the contribution of this rule to *SlotPref*. The *Body*, if present, can contain special predicates like those mentioned in Section 2 for slot-filler

[2] Actually, a slot-scoring rule in **ESG** gives the adjunct a score of 2 in this instance.

[3] The *CloseAttach* component by itself favors the closer attachment of the PP to *file*, but this score component is dominated by *SlotPref*.

rules that test any characteristics of the filler phrase and the higher phrase.

Two examples of slot-scoring rules in **ESG** are as follows (given in simplified form).

$$ndet + 0 \leftarrow hf(noun(T, *, *))\&(T = cn|T = gerund).$$

$$vadv + 0 \leftarrow f(noun(*, *, *))\&st(tm).$$

The first says that the determiner slot for nouns is rewarded if the higher noun is a common noun or a gerund. The second says that the *vadv* slot for verbs is rewarded when it is filled by a time noun phrase. The special goal $st(Type)$ says that *Type* is a semantic type of the (sense of) the filler phrase, and *tm* is a semantic type used in **ESG** for time words.

A slot-scoring rule might be used to penalize the use of a complement slot under certain conditions, by assigning it a score higher than the default 0. An example of this in **ESG** is

$$comp(binf) + 1 \leftarrow headf(noun(*, *, *))\&hrmods(nil).$$

Here $comp(binf)$ is a verb complement slot filled by a bare infinitive VP. This is penalized if the head word of the filler is *also* a noun and the higher verb has (so far) no right modifiers. This is to discourage use of the $comp(binf)$ analysis when the phrase may really be an NP, maybe an object. Several of the slot-scoring rules in **ESG** involve checks on existing *alternative* analyses of words, as in this example. It is quite useful to have such heuristics because of the great ambiguity of English in part of speech of words.

Slot-scoring may use conditions on punctuation. For example, for the slot *nprep* that finds adjunct PP modifiers of nouns, we might have:

$$nprep + 2 \leftarrow \neg sep(nil)\&\neg hrmodf(*, prep(*, *, *)).$$

This penalizes *nprep* if the separator is not nil (say, if there is a comma separator) and there is no other PP postmodifier already. Thus, in an example like *John noticed his neighbor, from across the street*, there will be a preference for the PP to modify *noticed* instead of *neighbor*.

ParallelCoord Most of the rules for this score component are in the shell. Parallelism in coordinate structures is measured by similarity of the conjuncts with respect to several different characteristics. Explicitly, when a coordinate structure is formed, the increment in the total score due to the *ParallelCoord* component is currently given by a formula (slightly simplified):

$$PFea + PFrame + PSense + PMods + PLen + PConj + PXSG.$$

Here the first five ingredients measure similarity of the conjuncts with respect to the following: (1) $PFea$: feature structures; (2) $PFrame$: complement slot frames; (3) $PSense$: word senses; (4) $PMods$: modifier list lengths; (5) $PLen$: word list lengths.

The ingredient $PConj$ tests for certain characteristics of the conjunction itself (which can include punctuation).

The ingredient $PXSG$ represents a contribution from language-specific coordination rules in XSG.

CloseAttach This score is essentially the same as that developed by Heidorn [3], and is designed to favor close attachment, although *SlotPref* and *ParallelCoord* can easily override it.

For a phrase P, the default for $CloseAttach(P)$ is defined recursively as the sum of all terms

$$0.1 * (CloseAttach(Mod) + 1),$$

where Mod varies over the modifiers of P. (One need not state the base of this recursive formula separately, since one arrives eventually at phrases with no modifiers, and then the sum over the empty list is understood to be zero.) The factor 0.1 used in the recursive formula is the default, and it can be overridden by an option in slot-scoring rules. Also, a slot-scoring rule can change the basic formula applied, in a way that will not be described here.

The combination of *SlotPref* and *CloseAttach* is closely related to preference rules discussed in [19].

PhrasePref Some rules for this component are coded in the shell and have to do with preferences for the feature structure of the analysis of a complete input phrase, for example preference of finite clauses over noun phrases (except in certain environments).

Phrase-scoring rules in XSG contribute to *PhrasePref*, and are of a form similar to slot-scoring rules – without mentioning a slot:

$$+E \leftarrow Body.$$

The real number E is added to the total score whenever a phrase satisfying *Body* fills any slot, or is used as a conjunct in a coordinate structure, or is taken as a top-level analysis.

A sample phrase-scoring rule in **ESG** is

$$+1 \leftarrow f(noun(*, *, *))\&\neg lmod(ndet, *)\& lmod(nadj, P)\&headst(P, quantadv).$$

This penalizes (by +1) a complete noun phrase that has no determiner but does have an adjective modifier which has *some* analysis with the feature *quantadv*. This rule penalizes for example the analysis of *even Bill* in which *even* is an adjective.

WordSensePref All of the rules for this component are coded in the lexicon. An example is a lexical entry for the word *man*:

$$man < n(human\&male, nil) < v(ev(2), *, obj1).$$

The first lexical analysis element shows *man* as a noun with features *human* and *male*. The second analysis shows a verb word sense with a *WordSensePref* penalty of +2.

These scores for word sense choices can also be coded *conditionally* on subject area codes, and there is an if-then-else formalism for expressing this.

The *WordSensePref* score is added when an initial (one-word) phrase analysis is formed.

HeadSlotFiller Following a method due largely to Ido Dagan [2], counts of head-slot-filler occurrences are obtained by parsing a corpus with **ESG**. Actually parts of speech are stored along with the head words of the higher and modifier phrases, so the counts are of quintuples:

$$(HWord, HPOS, Slot, MWord, MPOS).$$

These counts are then used (with certain coefficients) to add a reward (a negative number) to the score each time a modifier is attached with a match to a stored quintuple.

POSPref Using an idea of Ido Dagan and Herbert Leass, **ESG** corpus parsing is used to obtain counts of occurrences of pairs

$$(Word, PartOfSpeech).$$

When an initial (one-word) phrase analysis is formed, and the word and its part of speech match an entry in the table just mentioned, then the count, with a certain negative coefficient, is added as the *POSPref* contribution to the phrase score. This is of course similar to *WordSensePref*, taken from the lexicon, and there is an overlap.

LexSlotPref Rules for this component are coded in the lexicon. A slot appearing in a slot frame in a lexical entry can have an associated semantic type test on its filler. For example consider the following entry for *give* (not an actual entry for **ESG**):

$$give < v(obj\ .\ iobj : human).$$

Here the *iobj* slot requires a filler with the semantic type *human*. (In general, any Boolean combination of type tests can be coded.) If this analysis is used, then a *LexSlotPref* score of -1 is added. As it is stated, this semantic type requirement is absolute. But if one writes

$$give < v(obj\ .\ iobj : pref(human)).$$

then the test is not an absolute requirement, but merely gives a score increment of -1 if it is satisfied. In both the absolute and the "failsoft" forms of semantic type tests, the formalism allows one to specify arbitrary score increments.

5. TESTS OF ESG

Three recent tests of **ESG** coverage will be described, two on computer manual text and one on *Wall Street Journal (WSJ)* text. In all of the tests, there were no restrictions placed on vocabulary or length of test segments. Only the *first* parse given by **ESG** for each segment was considered. [4]

For each segment, parse output was rated with one of three categories – *p*: perfect parse, *pa*: *approximate parse*, or *bad*: not *p* or *pa*. To get a *p* rating, all of the SG structure had to be correct, including for example slot labels; so this is a stricter requirement than just getting surface structure or bracketing correct. An *approximate parse* is a non-perfect one for which nevertheless all the feature structures are correct and surface structure is correct except for level of attachment of modifiers. In MT applications, one can often get reasonable translations using approximate parses.

This way of rating parses is not an ideal one, because a parse for a very long sentence can be rated *bad* even when it has a single word with a wrong feature or slot. A combination of measures of partial success, such as those obtained by counting bracketing crossings, would be reasonable, since partially correct parses may still be useful. I can make up for this partially by reporting results as a function of segment length.

Test 1 This was done using a set of approximately 88,000 segments from computer manuals on which no training of **ESG** had been done. Half of the corpus, simply consisting of the odd-numbered segments, was used for some lexical training. Slava Katz's terminology identification program [6] was run on this portion as well as a program that finds candidate terms by looking (roughly) for sequences of capitalized words. About one day was spent editing this auxiliary multiword lexicon; the edited result consisted of 2176 entries. Then 100 segments were selected (automatically) at random from the (blind) even-numbered segments. The segments ranged in token list length from 2 to 38. The following table shows rating percentages for the segments of token list length $\leq N$ for selected N.

N	% *p*	% *p* or *pa*
10	75	75
17	71	79
25	66	76
38	61	73

[4] This first parse had the best score, but when more than one parse had the best, only the first one output by the system was used.

Test 2 From a set of about 2200 computer manual segments, 20% had been selected automatically at random, removed, and kept as a blind test set, and some **ESG** grammatical and lexical work had been done on the remaining. The test was on 100 of the blind test sentences, which happened to have the same range in token list length, 2 to 38, as in the preceding test. The following table, similar in form to the preceding, shows results.

N	% *p*	% *p* or *pa*
10	72	75
17	74	84
25	70	80
38	67	80

Test 3 This used a corpus of over 4 million segments from the *WSJ*. No attempt was made to isolate a blind test set. However, little work on **ESG** has been done for *WSJ* text – maybe looking at a total of 500 sentences over the span of work on **ESG**, with most of these obtained in other ways (I do not know if they were in the corpus in question). At any rate, automatic random choice from the 4M-segment corpus presumably resulted in segments that **ESG** had never seen in its life.

Prior to selection of the test set, Katz's terminology identification was run on approximately 40% of the corpus. A portion of the results (based on frequency) underwent about a day's worth of editing, giving an auxiliary multiword lexicon with 1513 entries.

Then 100 segments were selected at random from the 4M-segment corpus. They ranged in token list length from 6 to 57. **ESG** was run, with the following results, shown again as percentages for segments of length $\leq N$:

N	% *p*	% *p* or *pa*
10	75	75
17	48	56
25	45	55
38	33	48
57	29	45

ESG delivered some kind of analysis for all of the segments in the three tests, with about 11% fitted parses for the computer manual texts, and 26% fitted parses for the *WSJ*. The average parse time per segment was 1.5 seconds for the computer manuals and 5.6 seconds for the *WSJ* – on an IBM mainframe with a Prolog interpreter (not compiled).

References

1. Byrd, R. J. "Word Formation in Natural Language Processing Systems," *Proceedings of IJCAI-VIII*, 1983, pp. 704-706.
2. Dagan, I. and Itai, A. "Automatic Acquisition of Constraints for the Resolution of Anaphoric References and Syntactic Ambiguities," *Proceedings of Coling-90*, vol. 3, 1990, pp. 162-167.
3. Heidorn, G. E. "Experience with an Easily Computed Metric for Ranking Alternative Parses," *Proceedings of the 20th Annual Meeting of the ACL*, 1982, pp. 82-84.
4. Hobbs, J. R. and Bear, J. "Two Principles of Parse Preference," *Proceedings of Coling-90*, vol. 3, 1990, pp. 162-167.
5. Jensen, K. and Heidorn, G. E. "The Fitted Parse: 100% Parsing Capability in a Syntactic Grammar of English," Research Report RC9729, 1982, IBM T.J. Watson Research Center, Yorktown Heights, NY 10598.
6. Justeson, J.S. and Katz, S.M. "Technical Terminology: Its Linguistic Properties and an Algorithm for Identification in Text" (to appear).
7. Klavans, J. L. and Wacholder, N. "Documentation of Features and Attributes in UDICT," Research Report RC14251, 1989, IBM T.J. Watson Research Center, Yorktown Heights, N.Y.
8. Lappin, S. and McCord, M.C. "A Syntactic Filter on Pronominal Anaphora in Slot Grammar" in *Proceedings of the 28th Annual Meeting of the Association for Computational Linguistics*, 1990, pp. 135-142.
9. Lappin, S. and McCord, M.C. "Anaphora Resolution in Slot Grammar," *Computational Linguistics* 16, 1990, pp. 197-212.
10. McCord, M. C. "Slot Grammars," *Computational Linguistics*, vol. 6, 1980, pp. 31-43.
11. McCord, M. C. "Using Slots and Modifiers in Logic Grammars for Natural Language," *Artificial Intelligence*, vol. 18, 1982, pp. 327-367.
12. McCord, M. C. "Natural Language Processing in Prolog," in Walker, A. (Ed.), McCord, M., Sowa, J. F., and Wilson, W. G., *Knowledge Systems and Prolog: A Logical Approach to Expert Systems and Natural Language Processing*, Addison-Wesley, Reading, Mass., 1987.
13. McCord, M. C. "A New Version of Slot Grammar," Research Report RC14506, 1989, IBM T.J. Watson Research Center, Yorktown Heights, NY.
14. McCord, M. C. "Design of **LMT**: A Prolog-based Machine Translation System," *Computational Linguistics*, 15, 1989, pp. 33-52.
15. McCord, M. C. "**LMT**," *Proceedings of MT Summit II*, 1989, pp. 94-99, Deutsche Gesellschaft für Dokumentation, Frankfurt.
16. McCord, M. C. "Slot Grammar: A System for Simpler Construction of Practical Natural Language Grammars," In R. Studer (ed.), *Natural Language and Logic: International Scientific Symposium*, Lecture Notes in Computer Science, Springer Verlag, Berlin, 1990, pp. 118-145.
17. McCord, M. C. "The Slot Grammar System," Research Report RC17313, 1991, IBM T.J. Watson Research Center, Yorktown Heights, NY. To appear in J. Wedekind and C. Rohrer (Eds.), *Unification in Grammar*, MIT Press.
18. McCord, M. C., Bernth, A., Lappin, S., and Zadrozny, W. "Natural Language Processing within a Slot Grammar Framework," *International Journal on Artificial Intelligence Tools*, vol. 1, 1992, pp. 229-277.
19. Wilks, Y., Huang, X-M., and Fass, D. "Syntax, Preference and Right-Attachment," *Proceedings of the 9th International Joint Conference on Artificial Intelligence*, 1985, pp. 779-784.

FASTUS: A System for Extracting Information from Text*

Jerry R. Hobbs, Douglas Appelt, John Bear, David Israel, Megumi Kameyama, and Mabry Tyson

SRI International
333 Ravenswood Avenue
Menlo Park, CA 94025

INTRODUCTION

FASTUS is a (slightly permuted) acronym for Finite State Automaton Text Understanding System. It is a system for extracting information from free text in English (Japanese is under development), for entry into a database, and potentially for other applications. It works essentially as a set of cascaded, nondeterministic finite state automata.

FASTUS is most appropriate for *information extraction* tasks, rather than full text understanding. That is, it is most effective for text-scanning tasks where

- Only a fraction of the text is relevant.
- There is a pre-defined, relatively simple, rigid target representation that the information is mapped into.
- The subtle nuances of meaning and the writer's goals in writing the text are of no interest.

THE STRUCTURE OF THE MUC-4 FASTUS SYSTEM

The operation of FASTUS is comprised of four steps.

1. Triggering: Sentences are scanned for key words to determine whether they should be processed further.
2. Recognizing Phrases: Sentences are segmented into noun groups, verb groups, and particles.
3. Recognizing Patterns: The sequence of phrases produced in Step 2 is scanned for patterns of interest, and when they are found, corresponding "incident structures" are built.
4. Merging Incidents: Incident structures from different parts of the text are merged if they provide information about the same incident.

*This research was supported in part by the Defense Advanced Research Projects Agency under Contract ONR N00014-90-C-0220 with the Office of Naval Research, in part by NTT Data, and in part by an SRI internal research and development grant. The views and conclusions contained in this document are those of the authors and should not be interpreted as necessarily representing the official policies, either expressed or implied, of the Defense Advanced Research Projects Agency of the U.S. Government.

Many systems have been built to do pattern matching on strings of words. One crucial innovation in the FASTUS system has been separating that process into the two steps of recognizing phrases and recognizing patterns. Phrases can be recognized reliably with purely syntactic information, and they provide precisely the elements that are required for stating the patterns of interest.

The system is implemented in CommonLisp and runs on both Sun and Symbolics machines.

AN EXAMPLE

The task in the MUC-3 and MUC-4 (Message Understanding Conference) evaluations of text processing systems was to scan news reports and extract information about terrorist incidents, in particular, who did what to whom. The following sentence occurred in one report:

> Salvadoran President-elect Alfredo Cristiani condemned the terrorist killing of Attorney General Roberto Garcia Alvarado and accused the Farabundo Marti National Liberation Front (FMLN) of the crime.

1. Triggering: This sentence is triggered because it has a number of key words, including "terrorist", "killing", and "FMLN".

2. Recognizing Phrases: Step 2 segments the sentence into the following phrases:

Noun Group:	Salvadoran President-elect
Name:	Alfredo Cristiani
Verb Group:	condemned
Noun Group:	the terrorist killing
Preposition:	of
Noun Group:	Attorney General
Name:	Roberto Garcia Alvarado
Conjunction:	and
Verb Group:	accused
Noun Group:	the Farabundo Marti National Liberation Front (FMLN)
Preposition:	of
Noun Group:	the crime

The phrases that are recognized are names, the noun group, or the noun phrase up through the head noun, the verb group, or the verb together with its auxilliaries and any trapped adverbs, and various particles, including prepositions, conjunctions, relative pronouns, the word "ago", and the word "that" which is treated specially because of the ambiguities it gives rise to. Essentially the full complexity of English noun groups and verb groups is accommodated.

This phase of the processing gives very reliable results—better than 96% accuracy on the data we have examined.

3. Recognizing Patterns: In the example, two patterns are recognized in the sequence of phrases:

<Perpetrator> <Killing> of <HumanTarget>

and

<GovtOfficial> accused <PerpOrg> of <Incident>

Two corresponding incident structures are constructed:

Incident:	KILLING
Perpetrator:	"terrorist"
Confidence:	–
Human Target:	"Roberto Garcia Alvarado"

and

Incident:	INCIDENT
Perpetrator:	FMLN
Confidence:	Suspected or Accused by Authorities
Human Target:	–

Altogether for the MUC-4 application, about one hundred patterns were recognized.

4. Merging Incidents: These two incident structures are merged into a single incident structure, containing the most specific information from each.

Incident:	KILLING
Perpetrator:	FMLN
Confidence:	Suspected or Accused by Authorities
Human Target:	"Roberto Garcia Alvarado"

In the MUC-4 system, there are fairly elaborate rules for merging the noun groups that appear in the Perpetrator, Physical Target, and Human Target slots. A name can be merged with a description, as "Garcia" with "attorney general", provided the description is consistent with the other descriptions for that name. A precise description can be merged with a vague description, such as "person", with the precise description as the result. Two precise descriptions can be merged if they are semantically compatible. The descriptions "priest" and "Jesuit" are compatible, while "priest" and "peasant" are not. When precise descriptions are merged, the longest string is taken as the result. If merging is impossible, both noun groups are listed in the slot.

SKIPPING COMPLEMENTS

Pattern-matching approaches have often been tried in the past, without much success. We believe that our success was due to two key ideas. The first, as stated above, is the use of *cascaded* finite-state automata, dividing the task at the noun group and verb group level. The second is our approach to skipping over complements.

One significant problem in pattern-matching approaches is linking up arguments with their predicates when they are distant in the sentence, for example, linking up the subject noun group with the main verb when the subject has a number of nominal complements. One technique that has been tried is to skip over up to some number of words, say, five, in looking for the subject's verb. One trouble with this is that there are often more than five words in the subject's nominal complement. Another trouble is that in a sentence like

> The police reported that terrorists bombed the Parliament today.

this technique would find "the police" as the subject of "bombed".

Our approach is to implement knowledge of the grammar of nominal complements directly into the finite-state pattern recognizer. The material between the end of the subject noun group and the beginning of the main verb group must be read over. There are patterns to accomplish this. Two of them are as follows:

Subject {Preposition NounGroup}*
VerbGroup

Subject Relpro {NounGroup | Other}*
VerbGroup {NounGroup | Other}*
VerbGroup

The first of these patterns reads over prepositional phrases. The second over relative clauses. The verb group at the end of these patterns takes the subject noun group as its subject. There is another pattern for capturing the content encoded in relative clauses:

Subject Relpro {NounGroup | Other}*
VerbGroup

Since the finite-state mechanism is nondeterministic, the full content can be extracted from the sentence

The mayor, who was kidnapped yesterday, was found dead today.

One branch discovers the incident encoded in the relative clause. Another branch marks time through the relative clause and then discovers the incident in the main clause. These incidents are then merged.

A similar device is used for conjoined verb phrases. The pattern

Subject VerbGroup {NounGroup | Other}* Conjunction VerbGroup

allows the machine to nondeterministically skip over the first conjunct and associate the subject with the verb group in the second conjunct. This is how, in the above example, we were able to recognize Cristiani as the one who was accusing the FMLN of the crime.

THE PERFORMANCE OF FASTUS

On the MUC-4 evaluation in June 1992, FASTUS was among to top few systems, even though it had only been under development for five months. On the TST3 set of one hundred messages, FASTUS achieved a recall of 44% and a precision of 55%. The full results of the MUC-4 evaluation can be found in Sundheim (1992).

Moreover, FASTUS is an order of magnitude faster than any other comparable system. In the MUC-4 evaluation it was able to process the entire test set of 100 messages, ranging from a third of a page to two pages in length, in 11.8 minutes of CPU time on a Sun SPARC-2 processor. The elapsed real time was 15.9 minutes. In more concrete terms, FASTUS can read 2,375 words per minute. It can analyze one text in an average of 9.6 seconds. This translates into 9,000 texts per day.

This fast run time translates directly into fast development time. FASTUS became operational on May 6, 1992, and we did a run on a set of messages that we had not trained on, obtaining a score of 8% recall and 42% precision. At that point we began to train the system on 1300 development texts, adding patterns and doing periodic runs on the fair test to monitor our progress. This effort culminated three and a half weeks later on June 1 in a score of 44% recall and 57% precision. (Recall is percent of the possible answers the system got correct; precision is percent of the system's answers that were correct.) Thus, in less than a month, recall went up 36 points and precision 15 points.

A more complete description of FASTUS and its performance is given in Hobbs et al. (1992).

RECENT EXTENSIONS

We are currently extending the FASTUS system in three ways:

- We are developing a convenient interface that will allow users to define patterns more easily.
- We are implementing a Japanese language version of FASTUS.
- We are applying the system to a new domain—extracting information about joint ventures from news articles.

The last of these will be the subject of our MUC-5 paper. The other two are described here.

THE INTERFACE

The original version of FASTUS has been augmented with a convenient graphical user interface for implementing or extending an application, employing SRI's Grasper system (Karp et al., 1993). We expect this to speed up development time for a new application by a factor of three or four. Moreover, whereas before now only a system developer could implement a new application, now virtually anyone should be able to.

In a specification interface for FASTUS, there needs to be convenient means for performing four tasks:

1. Defining target structures.
2. Defining word classes.
3. Defining state transitions.
4. Defining merge conditions.

We have done nothing yet in the first two areas, since everyone currently working with the system is fluent in Lisp. Target structures are defined with defstruct, word classes with defvar. As we acquire users who are not programmers, it will be straightforward to implement convenient means for these tasks.

The Grasper-based graphical interface provides a convenient means for creating, examining, editing, and destroying nodes and links in the graphs representing the finite-state automata. Each link is labelled with the tokens that cause that transition to take place. Nodes have associated with them sequences of instructions that are executed when that node is reached. These instructions typically fill slots in the target structures, and they can be conditionalized on what link the node was reached from, allowing greater economy in the finite-state machines.

In addition, the interface allows the graphs at each level to be modularized in whatever fashion the user desires, so that at any given time, the user can focus on only a small portion of the total graph. There are also convenient means for saving and compiling the graphs after changes have been made.

Perhaps the hardest problem in the information extraction task is defining when two target structures can be merged. This is, after all, the coreference problem in discourse, well-known to be "AI-complete". We have developed a kind of algebra on the target structures. The user can define abstract data types, including number ranges, date ranges, locations, and strings. Comparison operations can then be defined for each of these data types, returning values of Equal, Subsumes, Inconsistent, and Incomparable. Combination operations can also be defined. For example, the combination of two number or date ranges is the more restrictive range. For strings, the combination depends on the semantic categories of the heads of the strings. If one is more specific than the other, the more specific term is the result of the combination. There are three types of actions that be performed after doing a comparison. The items can be merged or combined. If they are incomparable and if the slot in the target structure admits compound entries, the two can simply be added together. Or the unification of the two items can be rejected.

This algebra of target structures gives us a very clean treatment of what in the MUC-4 system was often very ad hoc.

FASTUS has been restructured somewhat as well since MUC-4. A Tokenizer Phase has been added. Its input consists of ascii characters and it output is tokens, usually words, numerals, and punctuation marks. This phase gives the user control over the lowest level of input, so that special rules can be encoded for abbreviations, numbers with radix other than 10, and other such phenomena. The most common tokenizations are, of course, already implemented.

A Preprocessor Phase has also been added. This incorporates the multiword handling that was done in the Phrase Recognition phase of the first version of FASTUS. It also allows the user to customize automata for dealing, for example, with names that have a different given-name family-name order and with names of nonhuman entities that have internal structure significant to the domain, such as company names.

The treatment of appositives, conjunctions, and "of" prepositional phrases was originally done in the Pattern Recognition phase. This has now been separated out into a Combining Phase for a treatment that is more perspicuous and hence more convenient for the user.

JAPANESE FASTUS

We are also developing a Japanese version of FASTUS. The initial application is for extracting a summary of spoken dialogues, input in Roman characters, in the domain of conference room reservations. Summarizing goal-oriented dialogues can be achieved by filling a predefined summary template, and any digressions in the dialogue content can be ignored. Summarization is then an example of expectation-driven information extraction performed by FASTUS.

Despite the dissimilarity between the English and Japanese languages, the basic FASTUS architecture consisting of four phases can be applied to the processing of Japanese. The phrase recognition phase (phase II) recognizes noun groups, verb groups, and particles. The phrase combination phase (phase III) recognizes the "NG no NG" phrases (similar to the English "of" phrases) and NG conjunctions that are of interest to the given domain. The incident recognition phase (phase IV) recognizes those utterance patterns that contain key information relevant to the summary template. Because the input is spontaneous dialogues rather than written news reports, we will have a dialogue managing module after the incident recognition phase in order to combine information contained in successive dialogue turns—for instance, question-answer pairs and request-confirmation pairs. We have implemented phases II and III, and phase IV will be in place shortly.

The main complexity of summarization in this room reservation domain is in the use of temporal expressions and in the dynamics of negotiation between the two speakers. Written news reports typically report past events whose resulting states are already known. Spoken dialogues, however, progress through a sequence of negotiations where the speakers express their desires, possibilities, impossibilities, concessions, acceptances, and so forth. This is a considerable challenge to the structure merging routine of FASTUS.

For the MUC-5 participation, the Japanese FASTUS system will be extended for the new domain of joint ventures and the new input type of written news reports in Japanese characters.

SUMMARY

The advantages of the FASTUS system are as follows:

- It is conceptually simple. It is a set of cascaded finite-state automata.
- The basic system is relatively small, although the dictionary and other lists are potentially very large.
- It is effective. It was among the top few systems in the MUC-4 evaluation.
- It has very fast run time. The average time for analyzing one message is less than 10 seconds. This is nearly an order of magnitude faster than comparable systems.
- In part because of the fast run time, it has a very fast development time. This is also true because the system provides a very direct link between the texts being analyzed and the data being extracted.

We believe that the FASTUS technology can achieve a level of 60% recall and 60% precision on information extraction tasks like that of MUC-4. Human coders do not agree on this task more than 80% of the time. Hence, a system working ten times as fast as humans do can achieve 75% of human performance. We believe that combining this system with a good user interface could increase the productivity of analysts by a factor of five or ten in this task.

This of course raises the question about the final 25%. How can we achieve that? We believe this will not be achieved until we make substantial progress on the long-term problem of full text understanding. This cannot happen until there is a long-term commitment that makes resources available for innovative research on the problem, research that will almost surely not produce striking results on large bodies of text in the near future.

Absent such an environment, our immediate plans are to spend about two months bringing our MUC-5 system to and beyond the level of our MUC-4 system, and then to explore the important research question of how much of full text understanding can be approximated by the finite-state approach. The following observations are very suggestive in this regard.

We believe that the most promising approach for full text understanding is the "Interpretation as Abduction" approach elaborated in Hobbs et al. (1993). There are three basic operations in this approach, and each of them can be approximated in FASTUS technology. First, the syntactic structure is recognized and a logical form is produced. The corresponding operation in FASTUS is the recognition of phrases, that part of syntax that can be done reliably. Second, the logical form is proven abductively by back-chaining on axioms of the form

$$(\forall a, b)Y(a, b) \supset X(a, b)$$

This can be approximated by adding further patterns: In addition to having a pattern for

A X'ed B

we would also have a pattern for

A Y'ed B

Third, redundancies are spotted and merged to solve the coreference problem. As pointed out above, this is approximated in FASTUS by the operation of merging incidents.

However, it must be realized that much of the success of the FASTUS approach is in the clever ways it ignores much of the irrelevant information in the text. As we deal with texts in which more and more of the information is relevant, this advantage could well be lost, and a genuine, full text-understanding system will be required.

REFERENCES

1. Hobbs, Jerry R., Douglas E. Appelt, John Bear, David Israel, and Mabry Tyson, 1992. "FASTUS: A System for Extracting Information from Natural-Language Text", SRI Technical Note 519, SRI International, Menlo Park, California, November 1992.

2. Hobbs, Jerry R., Mark Stickel, Douglas Appelt, and Paul Martin, 1993. "Interpretation as Abduction", to appear in *Artificial Intelligence Journal*. Also published as SRI Technical Note 499, SRI International, Menlo Park, California. December 1990.

3. Karp, Peter D., John D. Lowrance, Thomas M. Strat, David E. Wilkins, 1993. "The Grasper-CL Graph Management System", Technical Note No. 521, Artificial Intelligence Center, SRI International, January 1993.

4. Sundheim, Beth, ed., 1992. *Proceedings*, Fourth Message Understanding Conference (MUC-4), McLean, Virginia, June 1992. Distributed by Morgan Kaufmann Publishers, Inc., San Mateo, California.

INTERPRETING TEMPORAL ADVERBIALS*

Chung Hee Hwang & Lenhart K. Schubert
Department of Computer Science, University of Rochester
Rochester, New York 14627-0226

Abstract

We take for granted that sentences describe situations [2, 12]. One of the most important properties of situations are then their temporal locations, which are indicated by tense and aspect and temporal adverbials in the surface form. In [10, 22], we offered a formal theory for English tense and aspect and an algorithm that computes the temporal relationships between the situations implicitly introduced by a text. In the present paper, we propose a systematic approach to temporal adverbials, fully integrated with our tense-aspect theory and the interpretive algorithms, using the Episodic Logic (EL) formalism [9, 11, 12, 21].

1. INTRODUCTION

Previous theoretical work on temporal adverbials has mostly concentrated on adverbials specifying temporal locations (e.g., "yesterday"), durations (e.g., "for a month") and time spans (e.g., "in three hours"). It appears that interest in the first kind of adverbial originated from the desire to correct the erroneous analyses provided by Priorean tense logics, in particular, their treatment of the interaction between time adverbials and tense. The second and third kinds of adverbials were often considered in connection with the aspectual classes of the VPs or sentences those adverbials modify (e.g., durative adverbials may modify only stative sentences, whereas adverbials of time span may modify only accomplishment sentences). However, other kinds of temporal adverbials have received little attention, including ones specifying *repetition*:

> The engineer shut down the motor *twice* yesterday.
> The engine *frequently* broke down.
> The operator checked the level of oil *every half hour*.
> The inspector visits the lab *every Monday*.

On our analysis, these sentences describe complex events, consisting of a sequence of subevents of specified types, and the given adverbials modify the structure of these complex events: the cardinality of component events ("twice"), the frequency or distribution pattern of component events ("frequently," "regularly," "every half hour," etc.), and the temporal location of cyclic events that occur synchronously with other recurrent time frames or events ("every Monday" or "every time the alarm went off").

Other issues that deserve further investigation are the interactions between multiple temporal adverbials, and various kinds of aspectual class shift due to aspectual class constraints on the use of adverbials (occurring singly or jointly with others). The following sentences illustrate these issues.

> John ran *for half an hour every morning for a month.*
> John stepped out of his office *for fifteen minutes.*
> Mary is going to Boston *for three days.*
> Mary won the competition *for four years.*
> John saw Mary *twice in two years.*

Our aim is to provide a uniform analysis for all kinds of temporal adverbials. Our approach is compositional in that the lexicon supplies meanings at the word level (or possibly at the morpheme level, e.g., for '-ly' adverbs), and the meanings of adverbials are computed from the lexical entries by our GPSG-like grammar rules. The grammar rules take care of aspectual compatibility of adverbials with the VPs they modify. The resulting indexical logical form is then "deindexed" (converted to an explicit, context-independent form) by a set of recursive rules. The resultant episodic logical form (ELF) is formally interpretable and lends itself to effective inference. We now consider the syntax and the semantics of temporal adverbials. We first show logical form representations of temporal adverbials, in both indexical and deindexed form, and how to obtain them from the surface structure, together with a brief discussion of semantics. Then, we discuss an extension of our system that accommodates aspectual class shifts to properly handle the interaction between temporal adverbials and aspectual classes.

2. SYNTAX AND SEMANTICS OF TEMPORAL ADVERBIALS

We first discuss the basic interpretive mechanism, using *yesterday* as an example, and then generalize to other types of temporal adverbials.

2.1. The Basic Mechanism

As indicated in the following fragment of a GPSG-like sentence grammar, we treat all adverbial adjuncts as VP-adjuncts at the level of syntax.[1] (Aspectual feature agreement is assumed, but not discussed till section 3.)

> NP ← *Mary*; Mary
> V[1bar, past] ← *left*; <past leave>
> VP ← V[1bar]; V′
> VP ← VP ADVL[post-VP]; (ADVL′ VP′)
> S ← NP VP; [NP′ VP′]

However, despite this surface syntax, the semantic rule (ADVL′ VP′), specifying functional application of the ADVL-translation to the VP-translation, may lead to either predicate modification or sentence modification at the level of immediate logical form. In particular, manner adverbials (e.g., *with*

*This research was supported in part by NSF Research Grant IRI-9013160 and ONR/DARPA Research Contracts No. N00014-82-K-0193 and No. N00014-92-J-1512. The authors benefited from example sentences by Greg Carlson and Phil Harrison.

[1] In sentences like "Yesterday Mary left," we treat the preposed ADVL as topicalized, i.e., as "extracted" from post-VP position. However, we may want to treat modal and attitude adverbials (as in "Oddly, Mary left") as sentence-modifying. This does not affect our discussion here.

a brush, hastily, etc.) are uniformly interpreted as predicate modifiers at the level of immediate LF, while temporal (and locative) adverbials are all interpreted as sentence modifiers. How such sentence-modifier interpretations are formed from VP adjuncts is easily seen from rules such as the following:

NP[def-time] ← *yesterday* ; *Yesterday*
PP[post-VP] ← NP[def-time] ; (during NP′)
ADVL ← PP[e-mod, post-VP] ; λPλx((adv-e PP′) [x P]).

(adv-e stands for 'episode-modifying adverbial'.[2] More on this later.) From these rules it is clear that the logical translation of *yesterday*, as an adverbial adjunct, is

λPλx((adv-e (during *Yesterday*)) [x P]).

In the interpretation of a sentence such as "Mary left yesterday," this λ-abstract would be applied to predicate leave (initially paired with unscoped tense operator past), yielding

λx((adv-e (during *Yesterday*)) [x <past leave>]),

and this in turn would be applied to term Mary (translating the NP *Mary*), yielding the formula

((adv-e (during *Yesterday*)) [Mary <past leave>]).

Here, (during *Yesterday*) is a 1-place predicate (the result of applying the 2-place predicate during to the indexical constant *Yesterday*, allowable in the "curried function" semantics of EL). adv-e maps this 1-place predicate into a *sentence* modifier; i.e., (adv-e (during *Yesterday*)) denotes a function from sentence meanings to sentence meanings. In the present case, the operand is the sentence [Mary <past leave>], written in the square-bracketed, infixed form that is the preferred sentence syntax in EL.[3]

The above *indexical* (context-dependent) logical form is obtained quite directly as a byproduct of parsing, and is subsequently further processed—first, by scoping of ambiguously scoped quantifiers, logical connectives, and tense operators, and then by applying a set of formal *deindexing rules*, which introduce explicit *episodic variables* into the LF, and temporally relate these based on tense operators, temporal adverbials, and context structures called *tense trees*. These tense trees, described in [10, 22], supply "orienting relations" between episodes introduced by different clauses, such as the relation that exists between successively reported events in a narrative. We should emphasize that our treatment of time adverbials is fully compatible and integrated with the treatment of tense, but we will neglect tense operators and tense trees herein as far as possible. We do need to mention, though, that tense operators are generally assumed to take wide scope over adverbials in the same clause. Thus, after scoping, we get

(past ((adv-e (during *Yesterday*)) [Mary leave])).

Since the deindexing rules "work their way inward" on a given indexical LF, starting with the outermost operator, the past tense operator in the sentence under consideration will already have been deindexed when the adv-e construct is encountered. In fact we will have

$(\exists e_1{:}\,[e_1 \text{ before } u_1]$
$\quad [((\text{adv-e (during } \textit{Yesterday})) \text{ [Mary leave]})_{\mathrm{T}} ** e_1])$,

where u_1 denotes the utterance event for the sentence concerned, and T denotes the current tense tree. Note that we use restricted quantifiers of form $(Q\alpha{:}\,\Phi\,\Psi)$, where Q is a quantifier, α is a variable, and restriction Φ and matrix Ψ are formulas. At this point the following deindexing rule for adv-e is brought to bear (we omit the second half of the rule, specifying the transformation of the tense tree T ; see [9, 11]):

For π a monadic predicate, and Φ a formula,
adv-e: $((\text{adv-e } \pi)\ \Phi)_{\mathrm{T}} \leftrightarrow [{}^{\vee}\pi_{\mathrm{T}} \wedge \Phi_{\pi\cdot\mathrm{T}}]$

This rule essentially splits the formula into a conjunction of two subformulas: one for the adverbial itself, the other for the sentence modified by the adverbial, much as in Dowty's system [4, 5]. To provide an intuitive explanation of how this works, we need to mention the operators '*' and '**', which are central to EL. Roughly, $[\Phi * \eta]$ means that Φ is true in episode η (or, Φ describes η), and $[\Phi ** \eta]$ means that Φ, and only Φ, is true in episode η (or, Φ characterizes η). (For details, see [9, 11, 12].) Now the expression ${}^{\vee}\pi_{\mathrm{T}}$ on the RHS of the deindexing rule for adv-e is a sentential formula (formed from predicate π_{T}) which can be read as "π_{T} is true of the current episode (i.e., the one at which ${}^{\vee}\pi_{\mathrm{T}}$ is evaluated)." In view of this, the combination

$[[{}^{\vee}\pi_{\mathrm{T}} \wedge \Phi_{\pi\cdot\mathrm{T}}] ** \eta]$

is equivalent to $[[[\eta\ \pi_{\mathrm{T}}] \wedge \Phi_{\pi\cdot\mathrm{T}}] ** \eta]$. Note that π_{T} is now predicated directly of episode η. In the example above, we obtain

$(\exists e_1{:}\,[e_1 \text{ before } u_1]$
$\quad [[[e_1 \text{ during } \textit{Yesterday}_{\mathrm{T}}] \wedge \text{[Mary leave]}] ** e_1])$,

and this leaves only $\textit{Yesterday}_{\mathrm{T}}$ to be deindexed to a specific day (that is, (*yesterday-rel-to* u_1)).

To make the semantics of '∨', '*' and '**' a little more precise, we mention two clauses from the truth-conditional semantics:

1. For Φ a formula, and η a term,
$[\![\Phi * \eta]\!]^s = 1$ only if $\mathit{Actual}([\![\eta]\!], s)$ and $[\![\Phi]\!]^{[\![\eta]\!]} = 1$;
$= 0$ only if $\mathit{Nonactual}([\![\eta]\!], s)$ or $[\![\Phi]\!]^{[\![\eta]\!]} \neq 1$,
where these conditionals become biconditionals (iffs) for s an *exhaustive* (informationally maximal) situation.
2. For $s \in \mathcal{S}$, and π a predicate over situations,
$[\![{}^{\vee}\pi]\!]^s = [\![\pi]\!]^{s,s}$, i.e., $[\![\pi]\!](s)(s)$,
where $\mathcal{S}$ is the set of possible situations.

Also, a few relevant axioms are (for π, π' 1-place predicates, η a term, and Φ a formula):

---

[2] Certain feature principles are assumed in the grammar—namely, certain versions of the head feature principle, the control agreement principle, and the subcategorization principle. Notice that in our system, features are treated as trees; e.g., the subtree rooted by feature mod-vp has daughters pre-vp and post-vp, and the subtree rooted by feature e-mod has daughters temp-loc, dur, time-span, freq, card, cyc-time, etc., where temp-loc in turn has daughters def-time, indef-time, etc.

[3] In general, $[\tau_n\ \pi\ \tau_1 \ldots \tau_{n-1}]$ is an equivalent way of writing $(\pi\ \tau_1 \ldots \tau_n)$, which is in turn equivalent to $(\ldots((\pi\ \tau_1)\tau_2)\ldots\tau_n)$. See [9, 11].

$\Box$ $[\Phi ** \eta]$
$\leftrightarrow [[\Phi * \eta] \wedge \neg(\exists e{:}\, [e \text{ proper-subep-of } \eta]\, [\Phi * e])]$
$\Box$ $[{}^{\vee}\pi \wedge {}^{\vee}\pi'] \leftrightarrow {}^{\vee}\lambda e[[e\ \pi] \wedge [e\ \pi']]$
$\Box$ $[[{}^{\vee}\pi \wedge \Phi] ** \eta] \leftrightarrow [[[\eta\ \pi] \wedge \Phi] ** \eta]$

2.2. Adverbials of Duration, Time-span, and Repetition

Like adverbials of temporal location, durative adverbials are also translated as (adv-e π). For instance, "John slept for two hours" becomes (with tense neglected)

((adv-e (lasts-for (K ((num 2) (plur hour))))) [John sleep]).

Like `during`, `lasts-for` is a 2-place predicate. Here it has been applied to a term (K...), leaving a 1-place predicate. Just as in the case of (during *Yesterday*), the deindexed LF will contain a predication stating that the episode characterized by *John sleeping* lasts for two hours. (The details of the term (K...), denoting the abstract kind of quantity, two hours, need not concern us here. K as used here corresponds to K1 in [9, 11].) Time-span adverbials (as in "John ran the race *in two hours*") are treated in much the same way, using predicate `in-span-of`.

The translation of cardinal and frequency adverbials involves the sentence-modifying construct (adv-f π). π is a predicate which applies to a *collection* of temporally separated episodes. It may describe the cardinality of the episodes or their frequency (i.e., their relative density), periodicity or distribution pattern. So, for instance, we have

((adv-f ((num 2) (plur episode))) [John see Movie3])

for "John saw the movie twice," and

((adv-f ((attr frequent) (plur episode))) [John call Mary])

for "John called Mary frequently." (`num` is an operator that maps numbers into predicate modifiers, and `plur` ('*plural*') is a function that maps predicates applicable to individuals into predicates applicable to collections; cf., Link [13]. `attr` ('*attributive*') is an operator that maps predicates into predicate modifiers.) Table 1 shows lexical rules and PP and ADVL rules handling large classes of frequency adverbials, including periodic ones such as *every two hours* and synchronized cyclic ones such as *every spring*.

The deindexing rule for `adv-f` is as follows:

For π a monadic predicate, and Φ a formula,
`adv-f:` $((\text{adv-f } \pi)\ \Phi)_T \leftrightarrow [{}^{\vee}\pi_T \wedge (\text{mult } \Phi_{\pi \cdot T})]$

As illustrated in Table 1, π could take various forms. `mult` on the RHS side of the rule is a function that transforms sentence intensions, and is defined as follows.

For η an episode, and Φ a formula,
$\Box$ $[(\text{mult } \Phi) ** \eta]$
$\leftrightarrow [[\eta\ (\text{plur episode})] \wedge$
$(\forall e{:}\, [e \text{ member-of } \eta]$
$[[\Phi ** e] \wedge \neg(\exists e' [[e' \neq e] \wedge [e' \text{ member-of } \eta] \wedge$
$[e' \text{ overlaps } e]])])]$,

Table 1: GPSG Fragment (Adverbials)

% VP Adjunct Rules
ADVL ← PP[e-mod, post-VP] ; λPλx((adv-e PP′) [x P])
ADVL ← ADV[e-mod, mod-VP] ; λPλx(ADV′ [x P])
VP ← VP ADVL[mod-vp] ; (ADVL′, VP′)

% Temporal ADV, PP Rules
NP[def-time] ← *yesterday*; *Yesterday*
PP[post-VP] ← NP[def-time] ; (during NP′)
e.g., yesterday′ = λPλx((adv-e (during *Yesterday*)) [x P])

N[time-unit, plur] ← *hours*; (plur hour)
ADJ[number, plur] ← *two*; (num 2)
N[1bar, time-length] ← ADJ[number] N[time-unit] ; (ADJ′ N′)
NP ← N[1bar, time-length] ; (K N′)
P[dur] ← *for* ; lasts-for
P[span] ← *in*; in-span-of
PP[e-mod, post-VP] ← P NP[time-length] ; (P′ NP′)
e.g., for two hours′ = λPλx((adv-e (lasts-for
(K ((num 2) (plur hour))))) [x P])
e.g., in two hours′ = λPλx((adv-e (in-span-of
(K ((num 2) (plur hour))))) [x P])

ADV[card, post-VP] ← *twice*; (adv-f ((num 2) (plur episode)))
N.B. 'adv-n' used in [9] is no longer used.
ADV[freq, mod-VP] ← *frequently*;
(adv-f ((attr frequent) (plur episode)))
ADV[freq, mod-VP] ← *periodically*;
(adv-f ((attr periodic) (plur episode)))
ADV[freq, post-VP] ← Det[every] N[1bar, time-length] ;
(adv-f λ*s*[[*s* ((attr periodic) (plur episode))] ∧
[(period-of *s*) = (K N′)]])
e.g., twice′ = λPλx((adv-f ((num 2) (plur episode))) [x P])
e.g., frequently′ = λPλx((adv-f ((attr frequent) (plur episode))) [x P])
e.g., every two hours′
= λPλ*x*((adv-f λ*s*[[*s* ((attr periodic) (plur episode))] ∧
[(period-of *s*) = (K ((num 2) (plur hour)))]]) [x P])

N[indef-time] ← *spring*; spring
NP[cyc-time] ← Det[every] N[1bar, indef-time] ; <Det′ N′>
PP[post-VP] ← NP[cyc-time] ; (during NP′)
ADV ← PP[cyc-time, post-VP] ;
(adv-f λ*s*(∃*e* [[*e* member-of *s*] ∧ [*e* PP′]]))
e.g., every spring′
= λPλx((adv-f λ*s*(∃*e* [[*e* member-of *s*] ∧ [*e* during <∀ spring>]]))
[x P])

Sentences (1)–(5) below illustrate the rules stated in Table 1. The (a)-parts are the English sentences, the (b)-parts their immediate indexical LFs, and the (c)-parts the deindexed ELFs. (1) should be fairly transparent at this point. (2c) says that "some time before the utterance event, there was a 2 month-long (multi-component) episode, that consists three episodes of type 'John date Mary'." (3c) reads similarly. (4c) reads as "there was a 10 day-long episode that consists of periodically occurring subepisodes of type 'John take medicine', where the period was 4 hours." (5c) is understood as "at the generic present there is a collection of episodes of type 'Mary bake cake', such that during each Saturday within the time spanned by the collection,[4] there is such an episode." (We take verbs of creation such as *bake* as predicate modifiers.)

(1) a. John worked *for three hours yesterday*.
b. (past ((adv-e (during *Yesterday*))
((adv-e (lasts-for (K ((num 3) (plur hour))))) [John work])))
c. ($\exists e_1$: [e_1 before u_1]
[[[e_1 during (yesterday-rel-to u_1)] $\wedge$
[e_1 lasts-for (K ((num 3) (plur hour)))] $\wedge$
[John work]] ** e_1])

(2) a. Mary visited Paris *three times in two months*.
b. (past ((adv-e (in-span-of (K ((num 2) (plur month)))))
((adv-f ((num 3) (plur episode))) [Mary visit Paris])))
c. ($\exists e_2$: [e_2 before u_2]
[[[e_2 in-span-of (K ((num 2) (plur month)))] $\wedge$
[e_2 ((num 3) (plur episode))] $\wedge$
(mult [Mary visit Paris])] ** e_2])

(3) a. John *regularly* dated Mary *for two years*.
b. (past ((adv-e (lasts-for (K ((num 2) (plur year)))))
((adv-f ((attr regular) (plur episode))) [John date Mary])))
c. ($\exists e_3$: [e_3 before u_3]
[[[e_3 lasts-for (K ((num 2) (plur year)))] $\wedge$
[e_3 ((attr regular) (plur episode))] $\wedge$
(mult [John date Mary])] ** e_3])

(4) a. John took medicine *every four hours for ten days*.
b. (past ((adv-e (lasts-for (K ((num 10) (plur day)))))
((adv-f λs [[s ((attr periodic) (plur episode))] $\wedge$
[(period-of s) = (K ((num 4) (plur hour)))]])
[John take (K medicine)])))
c. ($\exists e_4$: [e_4 before u_4]
[[[e_4 lasts-for (K ((num 10) (plur day)))]
[e_4 ((attr periodic) (plur episode))] $\wedge$
[(period-of e_4) = (K ((num 4) (plur hour)))] $\wedge$
(mult [John take (K medicine)])]
** e_4])

(5) a. Mary bakes a cake *every Saturday*.
b. (gpres ((adv-f λs($\forall d$: [d Saturday]
($\exists e$ [[e member-of s] $\wedge$ [e during d]])))
[Mary (bake cake)]))
c. ($\exists e_5$: [e_5 gen-at u_5]
[[($\forall d$: [d Saturday]
($\exists e$ [[e member-of e_5] $\wedge$ [e during d]])) $\wedge$
(mult [Mary (bake cake)])]
** e_5])

We emphasize again that ELFs are completely deindexed, and so allow effective inference. EPILOG [20], the computer implementation of EL, makes inferences very efficiently, based on such ELFs and world knowledge, aided by a "time specialist." For instance, given "There is a train to Boston every two hours," "A train left for Boston at 2:30," and appropriate axioms, EPILOG can infer that the next train would be at 4:30.[5]

[4]This constraint on the Saturdays under consideration is assumed to be added by the deindexing process for time- or event-denoting nominals, but has been omitted from (5c).

[5]The following kind of meaning postulates are assumed:

a. ($\forall s$: [s ((attr periodic) (plur episode))]
($\exists n$: [[n number] $\wedge$ [$n \geq 2$]] [s ((num n) (plur episode))]))
A periodic collection of episodes has at least two component episodes.

b. ($\forall k$: [k kind-of-timelength] ($\forall e$: [[e episode] $\wedge$ [[e lasts-for k]]
($\exists t$: [[t time] $\wedge$ [(timelength-of t) = k]] [e throughout t])))
An episode lasting for a certain length of time means there is a time of that length such that the temporal projections of the time and the episode are identical.

c. ($\forall e$($\forall s$: [[s ((attr periodic) (plur episode))] $\wedge$ [s throughout e]]
($\forall p$: [(period-of s) = p] ($\forall e1$: [$e1$ member-of s]
[[($\exists e2$:[$e2$ immed-successor-in $e1$ s]
[(dist (begin-of $e1$) (begin-of $e2$)) = p]) $\vee$
[(dist (begin-of $e1$) (end-of e)) < p]] $\wedge$
[($\exists e3$:[$e3$ immed-predecessor-in $e1$ s]
[(dist (begin-of $e1$) (begin-of $e3$)) = p]) $\vee$
[(dist (begin-of $e1$) (begin-of e)) < p]]]))))
A component episode of a sequence of episodes with period p has an immediate predecessor/successor that is apart from it by p unless it is the first/last element of the sequence. The distance between the first/last element and the begin/end point of the episode the sequence permeates is less than p.

This kind of reasoning is very important in the TRAINS project [1], one of our target applications.

We also have a tentative account of adverbials such as *consecutively* and *alternately*, and some non-PP adverbials, but cannot elaborate within the present space limitations.

3. AN EXTENSION: TEMPORAL ADVERBIALS AND ASPECTUAL CLASS SHIFTS

So far, we have assumed aspectual category agreement between temporal adverbials and VPs they modify. We now discuss our aspectual class system and our approach to apparent aspectual class mismatch between VPs and adverbials, based on certain aspectual class transformations.

We make use of two aspectual class feature hierarchies, `stativeness` and `boundedness` as below:[6]

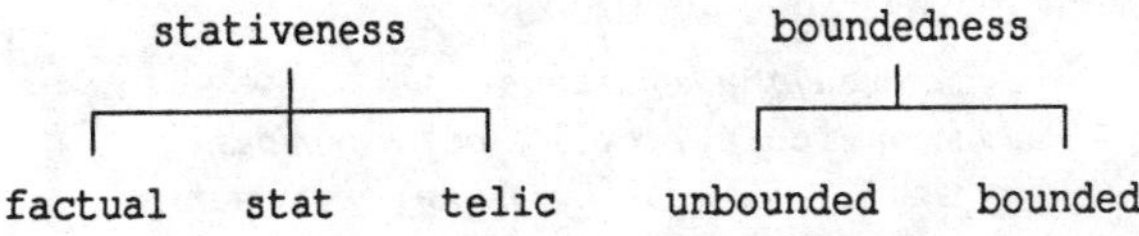

Atemporal (or, unlocated) sentences whose truth value does not change over space and time are assigned the feature `factual`. Every tensed English sentence, e.g., "Mary left before John arrived," in combination with a *context*, is considered factual. Untensed sentences may be stative or telic, depending on the type of the predicate (i.e., achievement/accomplishment versus state/process predicates) and on the object and subject (e.g., count versus mass). Sentences describing states or processes are assigned the feature `stat`, while those describing achievements or accomplishments are assigned the feature `telic`.

By a co-occurrence restriction, factual formulas are unbounded, and telics are bounded. Statives are *by default* unbounded. Intuitively, a formula is *bounded* if the episode it characterizes terminates in a distinctive result state (result states are formally defined in [11].) This is a property we ascribe to all telic episodes as well as to some stative episodes (such as an episode of John's being ill, at the end of which he

[6]Our aspectual class system resembles Passonneau's [18] in that it makes use of two orthogonal feature hierarchies, although the actual division of features is different from hers.

is *not* ill). Conversely, a formula is *unbounded* if the episode it characterizes does not terminate in a distinctive result state. For instance, *was ill* in "John was ill when I saw him last week" is unbounded as the sentence does not entail that John was not ill right after the described episode. However, when we say "John was ill twice last year," we are talking about bounded "ill" episodes.[7]

As has been discussed by many authors (e.g., in [3, 6, 15, 17, 26, 27]), VPs and temporal adverbials may not arbitrarily combine. Normally, durative adverbials combine with unbounded VPs; cardinal and frequency adverbials with bounded VPs; and adverbials of time-span with telic VPs. Thus, for instance,

Mary studied *for an hour*.[8]
*Mary finished the homework *for a second*.
Mary called John *twice | repeatedly | every five minutes*.
Mary wrote the paper *in two weeks*.

Note, however, that we also say

Mary sneezed *for five minutes*.
Mary stepped out of her office *for five minutes*.
Mary was ill *twice | repeatedly | every two months*.

The latter group of sentences show that VPs often acquire an interpretation derived from their original, primitive meaning. More specifically, when "stative" adverbials are applied to telic VPs, usually iteration is implied, as in the first sentence. However, in the case of the second sentence, the preferred reading is one in which the adverbial specifies the duration of the resultant episode, i.e., "the *result state* of Mary's stepping out of her office" (i.e., her being *outside* of her office), rather than a reading involving iteration. Next, when cardinal or frequency adverbials (i.e., "bounded" adverbials) are applied to unbounded-stative VPs, those VPs are interpreted as bounded-statives. Thus, the third sentence above means that the kind of episode in which Mary becomes ill and then ceases to be ill occurred twice, repeatedly, etc.

To be able to accommodate such phenomena, the syntactic parts of our grammar use `stat` and bounded as agreement features. The semantic parts introduce, as needed, operators for aspectual class transformation such as `result-state`, `iter` (iteration), bounded, etc. (In place of `iter`, we may sometimes use a habitual operator, H.)

Adverbials of temporal location like *yesterday* or *last week* may combine with either bounded or unbounded formulas (with unbounded ones, these imply a *throughout* reading; with bounded ones, a *sometime during* reading). For instance, in "John left last month," the "leaving" episode took place *sometime during* last month, but in case of "Mary was ill last month," Mary's "ill" episode may be either *sometime during* or *throughout* last month (corresponding to bounded and unbounded readings of the VP). Synchronized cyclic adverbials like *every spring* or *every time I saw Mary* may combine with bounded or unbounded formulas.

Secondly, an application of certain temporal adverbials often induces shifts in the aspectual classes of the resultant VPs. Frequency adverbials transform bounded sentences into unbounded-stative ones, while durative adverbials normally yield bounded VPs and synchronized cyclic ones yield unbounded-statives. Thus,

John {{*was ill twice*} *in three years*}.
?John {{*was ill twice*} *for three years*}.
John {{*was frequently ill*} *for three years*}.
?John {{*was frequently ill*} *in three years*}.
John {{*worked for five hours*} *three times*} last week.

We now rewrite the VP adjunct rules introduced earlier to accommodate the interaction between VPs and adverbials and possible shifts in aspectual classes.[9] We also show VP rules that perform aspectual class shifts. Note that aspectual class features (`stat`, bounded, etc.) are head features.

VP ← VP[stat, unbounded] ADVL[dur] ; (ADVL′ VP′)
VP[bounded] ← VP[stat, unbounded] ADVL[dur] ; (ADVL′ VP′)
VP ← VP[bounded] ADVL[span] ; (ADVL′ VP′)
VP ← VP[bounded] ADVL[card] ; (ADVL′ VP′)
VP[stat, unbounded] ← VP[bounded] ADVL[freq] ; (ADVL′ VP′)
VP[stat, unbounded] ← VP ADVL[cyc-time] ; (ADVL′ VP′)

VP[bounded] ← VP[stat, unbounded] ; (bounded VP′)
VP[stat, unbounded] ← VP[bounded] ; (iter VP′)
VP[stat, unbounded] ← VP[telic] ; (result-state VP′)

These rules allow transitions in aspectual class and VP-adverbial combinations somewhat too liberally. We assume, however, that undesirable transitions and combinations may be ruled out on semantic grounds. We now show some additional sentences and their initial translations (with tense neglected) to illustrate the above rules.

(6) a. Mary was ill twice in December
b. ((adv-e (during (in-time *December*)))
((adv-f ((num 2) (plur episode))) [Mary (*bounded* ill)]))

(7) a. Mary received an award for three years
b. ((adv-e (lasts-for (K ((num 3) (plur year)))))
[Mary (*iter* λx($\exists y$: [y award] [x receive y]))])

(8) a. Mary became unconscious for five minutes
b. ((adv-e (lasts-for (K ((num 5) (plur minute)))))
[Mary (*result-state* (become unconscious))])

(9) a. Nobody slept for eight hours for a week
b. ((adv-e (lasts-for (K week))) (No x: [x person]
((adv-e (lasts-for (K ((num 8) (plur hour))))) [x sleep])))
c. ((adv-e (lasts-for (K week))) (No x: [x person]
[x (*iter* λy((adv-e (lasts-for (K ((num 8) (plur hour)))))
[y sleep]))]))
d. (No x: [x person] ((adv-e (lasts-for (K week)))
[x (*iter* λy((adv-e (lasts-for (K ((num 8) (plur hour)))))
[y sleep]))])))

[7] Semantically, `stativeness` and `boundedness` play an important role with respect to the persistence of a formula. In general, stative formulas are inward persistent (modulo granularity), and bounded formulas are outward persistent. (Polarized ones are exceptional, however.) See [11] for further discussion.

[8] However, **Mary resembled her mother for five years*, even though "resembling" is a typical stative VP. This indicates that compatibility between predicates and adverbials involves more than just the aspectual class compatibility; that is, pragmatics and world knowledge need to be considered.

[9] Similar kinds of shift in aspectual classes have previously been discussed in the literature; first in [24], and subsequently in [15, 23].

Notice that (9) has at least three readings: first, during a certain week-long event, nobody had an 8-hour snooze; second, a situation in which nobody slept regularly for 8 hours persisted for a week[10]; and third, there is no one who slept daily for 8 hours for a week. (9b), (9c) and (9d) provide these three readings (distinguished by the scope of the quantifier No and the adverbial *for a week*). Note now that in (9a), the inner durative adverbial *for eight hours* transforms the unbounded VP to a bounded one. Being another durative adverbial, however, the outer *for a week* requires that its argument be unbounded. This is not a problem as shown in ELFs (9b, c, d). That is, in (9b), the argument is a negated formula which is normally considered to be stative-unbounded, and in (9c) and (9d), the *iter* operator produces stative-unbounded formulas.

4. CONCLUSION

Much theoretical work has been done on temporal adverbials (e.g., [4, 5, 7, 14, 16, 19]). There is also some computationally oriented work. For instance, Hobbs [8] provided simple rules for some temporal adverbials, including frequency ones. Moens and Steedman [15], among others, discussed the interaction of adverbials and aspectual categories. Our work goes further, in terms of (1) the scope of syntactic coverage, (2) interaction of adverbials with each other and with tense and aspect, (3) systematic (and compositional) transduction from syntax to logical form (with logical-form deindexing), (4) formal interpretability of the resulting logical forms, and (5) demonstrable use of the resulting logical forms for inference.

Our initial focus in the analysis of temporal adverbials has been PP-adverbials. Remaining work includes the analysis of clausal adverbials. Also, interactions with negation and aspect (perfect and progressive) have not been completely worked out. Negations of statives are statives, but negations of bounded sentences may be either bounded or unbounded (cf., "We *haven't* met *for three years*" versus "I have friends I *haven't* met *in three years*"). The interaction between present perfect and multiple adverbials of temporal location also creates some subtle difficulties. E.g., in "Mary has jogged {*at dawn*} {*this month*}," the inner time adverbial modifies the "jogging" episode, while the outer one modifies the interval that contains the "jogging" episode as well as the utterance time. See [11] for some relevant points. Another issue that requires thought is adverbials involving implicit anaphoric referents. Consider, e.g., "*Shortly*, Mary came in," "John came back *in ten minutes*," and "*After three years*, John proposed to Mary." These adverbials involve an implicit reference episode. Such implicit referents may often be identified from our tense trees, but at other times require inference. Another important remaining issue is the interaction between event nominals and frequency adjectives (along the lines of [25]).

[10] Here, iterated sleep is understood as daily sleep — something that must be determined by pragmatics.

References

1. J. Allen and L. K. Schubert. The TRAINS Project. TR 382, U. of Rochester, 1991.
2. J. Barwise and J. Perry. *Situations and Attitudes*. MIT Press, Cambridge, MA, 1983.
3. Ö. Dahl. On the definition of the telic-atelic (bounded-nonbounded) distinction. *Tense and Aspect (Syntax and Semantics, V.14)*, 79-90. Academic Press, New York. 1981.
4. D. Dowty. *Word Meaning and Montague Grammar*. Reidel, Dordrecht, 1979.
5. D. Dowty. Tense, time adverbs and compositional semantic theory. *Linguistics and Philosophy*, 5:23–55, 1982.
6. E. W. Hinrichs. *A Compositional Semantics for Aktionsarten and NP Reference in English*. PhD thesis, Ohio State U., 1985.
7. E. W. Hinrichs. Tense, quantifiers, and contexts. *Computational Linguistics*, 14:3–14, 1988.
8. J. R. Hobbs. Ontological promiscuity. In *Proc. 23rd Annual Meeting of the ACL*, 61–69. Chicago, IL, July 8–12, 1985.
9. C. H. Hwang. *A Logical Approach to Narrative Understanding*. PhD thesis, U. of Alberta, Canada, 1992.
10. C. H. Hwang and L. K. Schubert. Tense trees as the "fine structure" of discourse. In *Proc. 30th Annual Meeting of the ACL*, 232–240. Newark, DE, June 29–July 2, 1992.
11. C. H. Hwang and L. K. Schubert. *Episodic Logic: A comprehensive semantic representation and knowledge representation for language understanding*. In preparation.
12. C. H. Hwang and L. K. Schubert. Episodic Logic: A situational logic for natural language processing. In *Situation Theory and its Applications, V. 3*, CSLI, Stanford, CA, In print.
13. G. Link. The logical analysis of plurals and mass terms: A lattice-theoretical approach. In *Meaning, Use, and Interpretation of Language* (editors Bäuerle, Schwarze, and von Stechow), Walter de Gruyter, Germany. 302–323, 1983.
14. A. Mittwoch. Aspects of English aspect: On the interaction of perfect, progressive and durational phrases. *Linguistics and Philosophy*, 11:203–254, 1988.
15. M. Moens and M. Steedman. Temporal ontology and temporal reference. *Computational Linguistics*, 14:15–28, 1988.
16. F. Moltmann. Measure adverbials. *Linguistics and Philosophy*, 14:629–660, 1991.
17. A. P. D. Mourelatos. Events, processes and states. *Tense and Aspect (Syntax and Semantics, V.14)*, 191-212. Academic Press, New York. 1981.
18. R. J. Passonneau. A computational model of the semantics of tense and aspect. *Computational Linguistics*, 14:44–60, 1988.
19. B. Richards and F. Heny. Tense, aspect, and time adverbials. *Linguistics and Philosophy*, 5:59–154, 1982.
20. S. Schaeffer, C. H. Hwang, J. de Haan, and L. K. Schubert. *The User's Guide to* EPILOG (Prepared for Boeing Co.). 1991.
21. L. K. Schubert and C. H. Hwang. An Episodic knowledge representation for narrative texts. In *KR '89*, 444–458, Toronto, Canada, May 15-18, 1989.
22. L. K. Schubert and C. H. Hwang. Picking reference events from tense trees: A formal, implementable theory of English tense-aspect semantics. *Proc. Speech and Natural Language, DARPA*, 34–41, Hidden Valley, PA, June 24-27, 1990.
23. C. Smith. *The Parameter of Aspect*. Kluwer, Dordrecht, 1991.
24. M. J. Steedman. Reference to past time. In *Speech, Place and Action*, 125–157. John Wiley and Sons, New York, 1982.
25. G. T. Stump. The interpretation of frequency adjectives. *Linguistics and Philosophy*, 4:221–257, 1981.
26. Z. Vendler. *Linguistics in Philosophy*: Chapter 4, Verbs and Times. Ithaca, Cornell U. Pr., 1967.
27. H. J. Verkuyl. Aspectual classes and aspectual composition. *Linguistics and Philosophy*, 12:39–94, 1989.

THE MURASAKI PROJECT: MULTILINGUAL NATURAL LANGUAGE UNDERSTANDING

Chinatsu Aone, Hatte Blejer, Sharon Flank, Douglas McKee, Sandy Shinn

Systems Research and Applications (SRA)
2000 15th Street North
Arlington, VA 22201

ABSTRACT

This paper describes a multilingual data extraction system under development for the Department of Defense (DoD). The system, called Murasaki, processes Spanish and Japanese newspaper articles reporting AIDS disease statistics. Key to Murasaki's design is its language-independent and domain-independent architecture. The system consists of shared processing modules across the three languages it currently handles (English, Japanese, and Spanish), shared general and domain-specific knowledge bases, and separate data modules for language-specific knowledge such as grammars, lexicons, morphological data and discourse data. This data-driven architecture is crucial to the success of Murasaki as a language-independent system; extending Murasaki to additional languages can be done for the most part merely by adding new data. Some of the data can be added with user-friendly tools, others by exploiting existing on-line data or by deriving relevant data from corpora.

1. INTRODUCTION

Project Murasaki is a 30-month project for DoD to design and develop a data extraction prototype, operative in Spanish and Japanese and extensible to other languages. Using SRA's core natural language processing (NLP) software, SOLOMON, Project Murasaki extracts information from newspaper articles and TV transcripts in Japanese and from newspaper articles from a variety of Spanish-speaking countries. The topic of the articles and transcripts is the disease AIDS. The extracted information – some in a canonical form and some as it appears in the input texts – is stored in an object-oriented database schema implemented in a recently released multilingual version of the Sybase RDBMS.

Project Murasaki has been under development since October 1990 and will be delivered to DoD in June 1993. The goal of the project was to extend SOLOMON's data extraction capabilities, hitherto used for English texts, to Spanish and Japanese. It was explicitly requested that Murasaki be as language-independent and domain-independent as possible and be extensible to additional languages and domains ultimately.

SOLOMON reflects six years of development. From its inception, language and domain independence have been deliberate design goals. Murasaki was our first extensive use of SOLOMON for languages other than English and thus the first testing-ground for its claimed language independence. SOLOMON had been used and continues to be used across a variety of domains over the past six years. In the MUC-4 conference, SRA demonstrated a single system extracting information about Latin American terrorism from newspaper articles in all three languages, using Spanish and Japanese data modules developed for Murasaki and terrorism vocabulary in Spanish and Japanese acquired in the two weeks prior to the demonstration (cf. [1, 2]).

SOLOMON's architecture did not change significantly during the course of Murasaki. For the most part, its claim to language independence was borne out. Below, we will discuss how we have extended it to increase its language independence.

2. UNIQUE FEATURES OF MURASAKI

2.1. Modular Architecture

Murasaki is composed of shared processing modules across the three languages supported by separate data modules, as shown in Figure 1. Murasaki has six processing modules: PREPROCESSING, SYNTAX, SEMANTICS, DISCOURSE, PRAGMATICS, and EXTRACT. Each of these modules has associated data. For example:

PREPROCESSING:	lexicons, patterns, morphological data
SYNTAX:	grammars
SEMANTICS:	knowledge bases
DISCOURSE:	discourse knowledge sources
PRAGMATICS:	inference rules
EXTRACT:	extract data

Modularity is crucial to the *reusability* and *extensibility* of Murasaki. It facilitates, on the one hand, reuse of parts of Murasaki and on the other hand replacement of parts of the system.

We have been able to reuse portions of SOLOMON in the past, and expect to be able to pull modules out of Murasaki and use them separately as warranted in the future. For instance, PREPROCESSING could be used in isolation in multilingual information retrieval applications.

Conversely, modules – both processing and data modules –

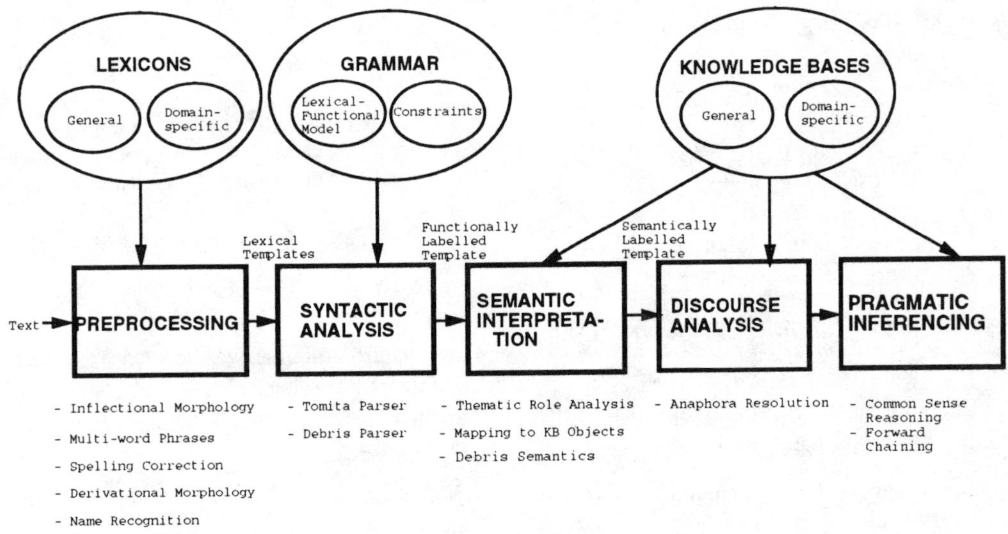

Figure 1: Murasaki Architecture

can be replaced as technology improves or in order to port to a new language or new domain. In order to port Murasaki to MUC-4 Latin American terrorism domain, we replaced the Japanese and Spanish AIDS domain lexicons with Japanese and Spanish terrorism domain lexicons, resulting in a system which understood Spanish and Japanese newspaper articles on terrorism in a matter of weeks. Since the terrorism domain knowledge bases (KB's) were developed for English for MUC-4 already, and since the KB's can be shared across languages, there was no need to change or add KB's in this case.

In addition to plugging in new data modules, we have successfully replaced single processing modules, (separately) at various times, such as PREPROCESSING, SEMANTICS, DISCOURSE and EXTRACT without changes to the other modules. In addition, we added an entirely new module PRAGMATICS in the past year. In no case were extensive changes to other parts of the system required.

Finally, in developing NLP systems it is crucial to be able to isolate the source of system errors during development and testing. While black-box testing can indicate how the system is performing overall, only glass-box (module-level) testing can focus on the source of errors in such a way as to aid the developers. Murasaki's modular architecture has facilitated such glass-box testing.

2.2. Data-driven Architecture

Each Murasaki processing module is data-driven. Data modules are specific to the language, domain, or application. Keeping the data modules separate is an essential factor in the system's success as a multilingual system. We have been able to isolate the majority of the language-specific knowledge to the data modules associated with PREPROCESSING (i.e. lexicons, patterns, morphological data) and SYNTAX (i.e. grammars). SEMANTICS is entirely language-independent, and DISCOURSE isolates the small amount of language-specific information to the discourse data module (i.e. discourse knowledge sources).

Thus, in order to port to a new language, the following subset of the data modules are necessary:

PREPROCESSING:	lexicons, patterns, morphological data
SYNTAX:	grammars
DISCOURSE:	discourse knowledge sources

To facilitate data acquisition in multiple languages, we have been developing language-independent automatic data acquisition algorithms [3, 4]. Also, in order to improve the quality of grammars, we have adapted a grammar evaluation tool (PARSEVAL) to evaluate the performance of our Spanish and Japanese grammars on texts bracketed by the Penn Treebank bracketing tool.

3. MULTILINGUAL MODULES

In this section, we discuss what we have done to the processing modules in Murasaki in order for them to handle multilingual input.

3.1. Preprocessing

Murasaki replaced its original morphological analyzer with a multilingual morphological analyzer. The new analyzer consists of a morphological processing engine and morphological data for each language, as shown in Figure 2. In order to add a new language, one only has to add morphological data for

VSTEM TENUMPERS ER-VERB PRETERIT

com er

yo	com	!'i
t!'u	com	iste
ella	com	i!'o
nosotros	com	imos
vosotros	com	isteis
ellos	com	ieron

Figure 2: An Example of Spanish Morphological Data

the language. This approach is especially useful for highly inflected languages like Spanish and Japanese.

After morphological analysis, pattern matching is performed to recognize multi-word phrases like numbers, date, personal names, organization names, and so on. Although specific patterns to recognize, for example, Japanese and Spanish personal names are different, the same pattern matching engine and pattern specification language are used for all the languages. Examples of phrases recognized by Spanish patterns are shown in Figure 3, using SGML markers.

3.2. Syntax

In order to make the syntax module language-independent, Murasaki extended the Tomita parsing algorithm [5] to deal with ambiguous word boundaries in Japanese. These boundaries are problematic because there is no space between words in a Japanese sentence, and it can be segmented in more than one way. Our implementation of the algorithm was originally token-based, where a token was a word or phrase. The extended algorithm is character-based, and now allows variable length input.

The same X-bar-based grammar specification language for English has been used to write the Spanish and Japanese grammars. In addition, all the grammars call the same constraint functions to check syntactic subcategorization and semantic type restrictions during parsing. Skeletal rules can be provided for a new language to start with especially when the new language is structurally similar to the languages of the existing grammars (e.g. Portuguese). In fact, much of

```
##054 09ago89 Excelsior-Jalapa palabras 218
     El nu'mero de casos de sida en la entidad
aumento' a 326, con los 15 detectados durante
<time>el mes de julio</time>, aseguro' hoy
<name>el doctor Jose' Rodri'guez Domi'nguez</name>,
jefe de <org>los Servicios Coordinados de Salud
Pu'blica</org> en el estado.
```

Figure 3: Spanish Text with Pattern Examples

Head-Initial	Head-Final
V1 → *V NP	V1 → NP *V
P1 → *P NP	P2 → NP PARTP
GMOD → SUBCONJP S	GMOD → S SUBCONJP
N4 → N4 GMOD	N4 → GMOD N4
N4 → N4 NCOMPS	N4 → NCOMPS N4

Figure 4: Examples of Basic X-Bar Rules

the Spanish grammar was derived from the English grammar. A few basic X-bar rules for head-initial (e.g. English and Spanish) and head-final languages (e.g. Japanese) are shown in Figure 4.[1]

The output of the parser is a structure called a functionally labeled template (FLT), which is similar to LFG's f-structure. The FLT specification language is language-independent. It uses grammatical functions like subject, object, etc. as registers, but no language-specific information such as precedence is present at this level. Thus, while Spanish texts often use inversion as in "... y en total se han registrado cuarenta y siete casos con treinta víctimas", it is not the case with English, e.g. ".. and in total 47 cases with 30 victims were recorded." However, such differences are normalized in FLT's.

The FLT specification has been extended and tested to cover phenomena in three languages as Spanish and Japanese grammars are developed. It must be general and expressive enough to cover linguistic phenomena in multiple languages because the semantic interpretation expects its input in any language to follow this specification. For example, quantity phrases (QP's) in any languages now have a *unit* register in the FLT. In English and Spanish, measure units in measure phrases fill the unit values (e.g. "3 *pints* of blood", "62 *por ciento* de las personas con sida"). In Japanese, so-called classifiers fill in the unit values. Classifiers are used to count any objects in Japanese, including discrete objects such as people and companies. Such unit information is sometimes important for semantic disambiguation.

Once broad-coverage grammars are developed, they can be used to process texts in any domain (unless the domain uses a sublanguage) without much modification, since linguistic structures of languages do not change from domain to domain. The only difference between domains is the weights on each rule because the frequency of using particular rules changes, just as the frequency of particular words changes in different domains. Thus, the same Spanish and Japanese grammars developed for the AIDS domain were used to process Spanish and Japanese texts in the MUC-4 (terrorism) domain with a

[1] GMOD stands for General MODifier, NCOMPS for Noun COMPlementS, and PARTP for PARTicle Phrase. The Arabic numerals indicate bar levels.

few additional rules.

3.3. Semantics

Murasaki has a single semantics processing module for all the languages. It takes as input output of the syntax module in the FLT format. Thus, so long as the input to the semantics processing module conforms to the FLT specification, Murasaki can use different grammars or parsers. The semantics processing module uses core and domain-specific knowledge bases (KB's) common to all languages to perform semantic disambiguation and inference, and outputs language-independent KB objects.

In moving from English to multiple languages, English specific information was moved from the KB's to the lexicons. Our KB's originally encoded both semantic and English-specific syntactic information (e.g. subcategorization information). We moved the language-specific syntactic information from the KB's to English lexicons, and left the language-independent semantic type information in the KB's.

In addition, the semantics processing module itself has become more data-driven to be more language-independent. For example, interpretation of the complements of nominalized verbs among three languages became language-independent by classifying pre/postpositions of these languages into common semantic classes. Thus, AGENT roles of nominalized verbs are typically expressed by AGENT markers (e.g. "by", "por", "niyoru") of given languages, and THEME roles by NEUTRAL markers (e.g. "of", "de", "no").

	AGENT	THEME
Eg	investigation *by* WHO	transmission *of* AIDS
Sp	investigación *por* WHO	transmisión *de* SIDA
Jp	WHO-*niyoru* chousa	AIDS-*no* kansen

A more general, data-driven approach has been also taken for semantic disambiguation necessary to interpret pre/postpositional phrases, compound nouns, appositives etc. which are common for all the languages. In all cases of semantic disambiguation, the same knowledge-based strategy is used to determine the most plausible relations between two semantic objects. For example, for noun phrases like "AIDS/cancer patients", "afectados de SIDA" (Spanish), or "AIDS kanja" (Japanese), a relation **Has-Disease** is chosen from the KB's for the two nouns. Semantics of ambiguous pre/postpositions (e.g. "in", "en") is determined in a similar way. For sentences in (1) below, a relation **Location** is chosen, while for those in (2) a relation **Time** is chosen.

(1) a. 500 men were infected with AIDS in China.
b. En China se han infectado 500 hombres con SIDA.

(2) a. 500 men were infected with AIDS in March.
b. En marzo se han infectado 500 hombres con SIDA.

```
(WAKARU
      ((CATEGORY . V)
       (INFLECTION-CLASS . CR)
       (GLOSS . UNDERSTAND)
       (PREDICATE #UNDERSTAND#)
       (SITUATION-TYPE INVERSE-STATE)
       (IDIOSYNCRASIES
         (GOAL (MAPPING (LITERAL ''NI'')
                        (SURFACE SUBJECT))))
       (TRANSCRIPTION . WAKARU)))
```

Figure 5: A Lexical Entry for "wakaru"

The Murasaki semantics module uses four basic language-independent predicate-argument mapping rules called *situation types*, which map syntactic arguments of verbs in FLT's (e.g. subject, object, etc.) to thematic roles of verb predicates in the KB's (e.g. agent, theme, etc.), as shown in Table 1. Such mapping rules, along with any idiosyncratic mapping information, for each verb are derived from corpora automatically (see [4] for more detail).

For example, the English word "understand" uses what we call INVERSE-STATE mapping, where the subject maps to GOAL and and the object THEME of the predicate #UNDERSTAND#. The Japanese semantic equivalent "wakaru" also uses the INVERSE-STATE mapping. However, the language-specific idiosyncratic information that the GOAL role can be also specified by a particle "ni" is stated in the lexicon. As shown in Figure 5, the lexical entry for "wakaru" has pointers to its semantic predicate in a KB (i.e. #UNDERSTAND#) and its mapping rule (i.e. INVERSE-STATE), and specifies its word-specific idiosyncrasy information about "ni" in addition.

3.4. Discourse

The Murasaki discourse module needed the most work to be language-independent. A discourse module is generally least developed in any NLP system, and our system was no exception. In addition, some part of the module was designed to be English specific. For example, since grammatical genders and natural genders usually coincide in English, the original discourse module paid attention only to natural genders. However, in Spanish, grammatical genders of an anaphor and its antecedent, not the natural genders, must be compatible for them to co-refer. For example, the third person feminine pronoun "la" in the following sentence refers to "la transmisión", which is not a semantic object with a female gender: "En otras entidades como Baja California y Veracruz la transmisión en este grupo es 1.2 veces mayor que la que ocurre a nivel nacional."

Moreover, different languages have different types of anaphora (e.g. zero pronouns in Spanish and Japanese). In

Situation Types		English/Spanish Mapping	Japanese Mapping
CAUSED-PROCESS	AGENT THEME	(SURFACE SUBJECT) (SURFACE OBJECT)	(SURFACE SUBJECT) (SURFACE OBJECT)
PROCESS-OR-STATE	THEME	(SURFACE SUBJECT)	(SURFACE SUBJECT)
AGENTIVE-ACTION	AGENT	(SURFACE SUBJECT)	(SURFACE SUBJECT)
INVERSE-STATE	GOAL THEME	(SURFACE SUBJECT) (SURFACE OBJECT)	(SURFACE SUBJECT) (SURFACE OBJECT) (PARTICLE "GA")

Table 1: Predicate-Argument Mapping Rules (Situation Types)

addition, languages differ in the distribution patterns of each type of anaphora (e.g. the antecedent of a Japanese anaphor "uchi" is found in the adjacent *discourse clause*). Furthermore, constraints on the antecedents differ from language to language (e.g. a Japanese third person masculine pronoun "kare" must refer to a male person, but not Spanish third person masculine pronouns).

We achieved the multilingual capability of the discourse module by dividing the anaphora resolution process into multiple knowledge sources and using subsets of the knowledge sources to handle different discourse phenomena (cf. [6]). Both the discourse knowledge sources and discourse phenomena are represented as objects in the KB's. Thus, the discourse processing module called *Resolution Engine* has become strictly data-driven (cf. Figure 6).

The discourse knowledge source KB consists of *generators* (i.e. various ways to generate antecedent hypotheses), *filters* (e.g. syntactic number filter, syntactic gender filter, semantic amount filter, semantic gender filter, semantic type filter, etc.), and *orderers* (e.g. focus orderer, recency orderer, etc.). Language-independence of the knowledge sources has been achieved by dividing each knowledge source into language-specific data and language-independent processing functions. For example, the semantic gender filter has associated data for English and Japanese, which specifies constraints on genders of semantic objects imposed by certain pronouns (e.g. English "he" cannot refer to semantic objects with female gender like "girl"). As explained above, Spanish does not use the semantic gender filter but uses the syntactic gender filter.

Finally, we wanted to be able to evaluate the performance of the Murasaki discourse module so that we can train it and maximize its performance in different languages and domains. Our architecture allows anaphora resolution performance to be evaluated and trained. We use corpora tagged with discourse relations, as shown in Figure 7, for such evaluation.

4. CONCLUSION

We have described a multilingual system, Murasaki, focusing on specifics of its language-independent architecture and describing how language-specific data is integrated with general processing modules. While this architecture is currently operating for data extraction from Japanese, Spanish, and English texts, it has been designed to be extended to additional languages in the future. Murasaki also has associated multilingual data acquisition tools and algorithms, which have been used to extend its data modules. In addition, we have developed preliminary multilingual training and evaluation tools for the syntax and discourse modules of Murasaki.

Planned future enhancements include addition of new data modules (e.g. multilingual "WordNets"), extension of the Spanish and Japanese data sources to new domains, and improved multilingual tools for automatic data acquisition from corpora. We would also like to extend the system to a new, typologically different language such as Arabic in order to further test and refine its language independence.

References

1. Aone, C., McKee, D., Shinn, S., and Blejer, H., "SRA: Description of the SOLOMON System as Used for MUC-4," in *Proceedings of Fourth Message Understanding Conference (MUC-4)*, Morgan Kaufmann Publishers, Inc., San Mateo, CA, 1992.
2. Aone, C., McKee, D., Shinn, S., and Blejer, H., "SRA SOLOMON: MUC-4 Test Results and Analysis," in *Proceedings of Fourth Message Understanding Conference (MUC-4)*, Morgan Kaufmann Publishers, Inc., San Mateo, CA, 1992.
3. McKee, D., and Maloney, J., "Using Statistics Gained From Corpora in a Knowledge-Based NLP System," in *Proceedings of The AAAI Workshop on Statistically-Based NLP Techniques*, 1992.
4. Aone, C., and McKee, D., "Three-Level Knowledge Representation of Predicate-Argument Mapping for Multilingual Lexicons," in *AAAI Spring Symposium Working Notes on "Building Lexicons for Machine Translation"*, 1993.
5. Tomita, M., "An Efficient Context-free Parsing Algorithm for Natural Language," in *Proceedings of IJCAI*, 1985.
6. Aone, C., and McKee, D., "Language-Independent Anaphora Resolution System for Understanding Multilingual Texts," to appear in *Proceedings of 31st Annual Meeting of the ACL"*, 1993.

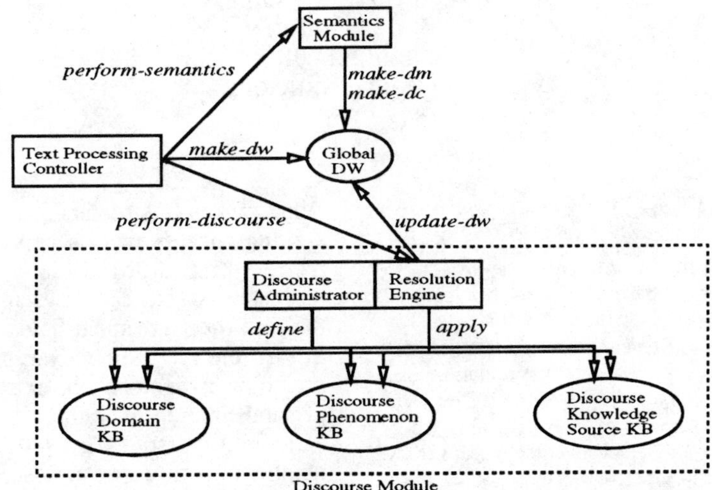

Figure 6: Discourse Architecture

```
La Comisio'n de Te'cnicos del SIDA informo' ayer de que existen
<DM ID=2000>196 enfermos de <DM ID=2001>SIDA</DM></DM> en la Comunidad
Valenciana.  De <DM ID=2002 Type=PRO Ref=2000>ellos</DM>, 147
corresponden a Valencia; 34, a Alicante; y 15, a Castello'n.
Mayoritariamente <DM ID=2003 Type=DNP Ref=2001>la enfermedad</DM>
afecta a <DM ID=2004 Type=GEN>los hombres</DM>, con 158 casos.  Entre
<DM ID=2005 Type=DNP Ref=2000>los afectados</DM> se encuentran nueve
nin'os menores de 13 an'os.
```

Figure 7: Discourse Tagged Corpora

VALIDATION OF TERMINOLOGICAL INFERENCE IN AN INFORMATION EXTRACTION TASK

Marc Vilain

The MITRE Corporation
Burlington Rd.
Bedford, MA 01730
mbv@linus.mitre.org

ABSTRACT

This paper is concerned with an inferential approach to information extraction, reporting in particular on the results of an empirical study that was performed to validate the approach. The study brings together two lines of research: (1) the RHO framework for tractable terminological knowledge representation, and (2) the *Alembic* message understanding system. There are correspondingly two principal aspects of interest to this work. From the knowledge representation perspective, the present study serves to validate experimentally a normal form hypothesis that guarantees tractability of inference in the RHO framework. From the message processing perspective, this study substantiates the utility of limited inference to the information extraction task.

1. SOME BACKGROUND

Alembic is a natural language-based information extraction system that has been under development for about one year. As with many such systems, the information extraction process in *Alembic* occurs through pattern matching against the semantic representation of sentences. These representations are themselves derived from parsing the input text, in our case with a highly lexicalized neo-categorial grammar [1].

Experience has shown that this kind of approach can yield impressive performance levels in the data extraction task (see [18]). We have found—as have others—that meaningful results can be obtained despite only having sketchy sentence semantics (as can happen when there are widespread gaps in the lexicon's semantic assignments). In addition, because the parsing process normalizes the sentence semantics to a significant degree, the number of extraction patterns can be relatively small, especially compared to approaches that use only rudimentary parsing.

Strict semantic pattern-matching is unattractive, however, in cases that presume some degree of inference. Consider the following example of an East-West joint venture:

> [...] Samsung signed an agreement with Soyuz, the external-trade organization of the Soviet Union, to swap Korean TV's and VCR's for pig iron from the Soviet Union

What makes this sentence an example of the given joint venture concept is an accumulation of small inferences: that Soyuz is a Soviet entity, that signing an agreement designates agreement between the signing parties, and that the resulting agreement holds between a Soviet and non-Soviet entity. Such examples suggest that it is far preferable to approach the extraction problem through a set of small inferences, rather than through some monolithic extraction pattern. This notion has been embodied in a number of earlier approaches, e.g. [11] or [17].

The inferential approach we were interested in bringing to bear on this problem is the RHO framework. RHO is a terminological classification framework that ultimately descends from KL-ONE. Unlike most recent such systems, however, RHO focuses on terminological inference (rather than subsumption). And whereas most KL-ONE descendants sacrifice completeness for computational tractability, inference in RHO is complete in polynomial time if terminological axioms meet a normal form criterion.

Nevertheless, before embarking on a significant development effort to implement the RHO framework under *Alembic*, we wanted to verify that the framework was up to the data extraction task. In particular, we were keen to ensure that the theoretical criterion that guarantees polynomial time completeness for RHO was actually met in practice. Towards this end, my colleagues and I undertook an extensive empirical study whose goal was, among others, to validate this criterion.

The present paper is a summary of our findings, with a special focus on RHO itself and on the validation task. We provide some suggestive interpretations of these findings, and touch on current and ongoing work towards bringing RHO to bear on the extraction task in *Alembic*.

2. THE RHO FRAMEWORK

The RHO framework, as noted above, arose in reaction to standard approaches to terminological reasoning, as embodied in most descendants of KL-ONE, e.g., CLASSIC [4], BACK [13], LOOM [12], and many others. This line of work has come to place a major emphasis on computing concept subsumption, i.e., the determination of whether a representational description (a concept) necessarily entails another description. In our view, this emphasis is mistaken.

Indeed, this emphasis ignores the way in which practical applications have successfully exploited the terminological framework. These systems primarily rely on the operation of classification, especially instance classification. Although subsumption helps to provide a semantic model of classification, it does not necessarily follow that it should provide its computational underpinnings.

In addition, the emphasis on complete subsumption algorithms has led to restricted languages that are representationally weak. As is well-known, these languages have been the subject of increasingly pessimistic theoretical results, from intractability of subsumption [5], to undecidability of subsumption [15, 16], to intractability of the fundamental normalization of a terminological KB [14].

Against this background, RHO was targeted to support instance classification, and thus departs in significant ways from traditional terminological reasoners. The most draconian departure is in separating the normal terminological notion of necessary and sufficient definitions into separate sufficiency axioms and necessity axioms. The thrust of the former is to provide the kind of antecedent inference that is the hallmark of classification, e.g.,

$$\text{western-corp}(x) \leftarrow \text{corporation}(x) \ \& \ \text{hq-in}(x, y) \ \& \ \text{western-nation}(y) \quad (1)$$

The role of necessity conditions is to provide consequent inference such as that typically associated with inheritance and sort restrictions on predicates, e.g.,

$$\text{organization}(x) \leftarrow \text{corporation}(x) \quad (2)$$
$$\text{corporation}(x) \leftarrow \text{western-corp}(x) \quad (3)$$
$$\text{organization}(x) \leftarrow \text{agreement}(x, y, z) \quad (4)$$

Although both classes of axioms are expressed in the same syntactic garb, namely function-free Horn clauses, they differ with respect to their inferential import. If one thinks of predicates as being organized according to some taxonomy (see Fig. 1), then necessity axioms encode inference that proceeds up the hierarchy (i.e., inheritance), while sufficiency axioms encode inference that proceeds down the hierarchy (i.e., classification).

The most interesting consequence of RHO's uniform language for necessity and sufficiency is that it facilitates the formulation of a criterion under which classification is guaranteed to be tractable. For a knowledge base to be guaranteed tractable, the criterion requires that there be a tree shape to the implicit dependencies between the variables in any given axiom in the knowledge base.

For the sample axioms above, Fig. 2 informally illustrates this notion of variable dependencies. Axiom (1), for

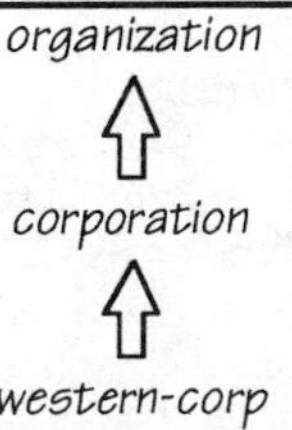

Figure 1: A predicate taxonomy

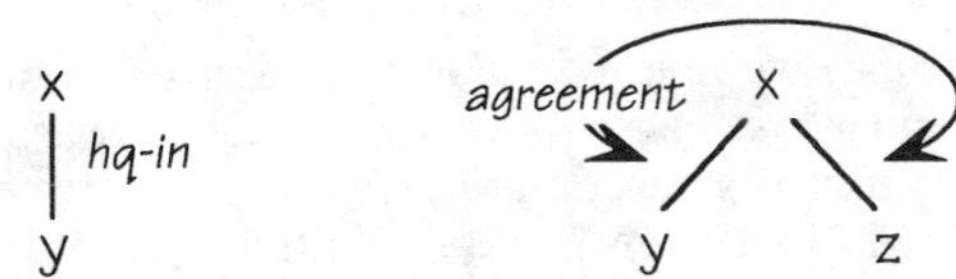

Figure 2: Dependency trees for variables in axioms (1), on the left, and (4), on the right.

example, mentions two variables, x and y. A dependency between these variables is introduced by the predicative term hq-in(x,y): the term makes the two variables dependent by virtue of mentioning them as arguments of the same predicate. As the axiom mentions no other variables, its dependency graph is the simple tree on the left of Fig. 1. Similarly, in axiom (4) the agreement predicate makes both y and z dependent on x, also yielding a tree. Finally, axioms (2) and (3) lead to degenerate trees containing only x. Since all the dependency relations between these variables are tree-shaped, the knowledge base formed out of their respective axioms is tractable under the criterion. A formal proof that tractability follows from the criterion appears in an appendix below, as well as in [19].

3. VALIDATING RHO

This formal tractability result is appealing, especially in light of the overwhelming number of intractability claims that are usually associated with terminological reasoning. Its correctness, however, is crucially dependent on a normal form assumption, and as with all such normal form criteria, it remains of little more than theoretical interest unless it is validated in practice. As we mentioned above, we strove to achieve such a validation by determining through a paper study whether the RHO framework could be put to use in the data extraction phase of *Alembic*.

Towards this end, my colleagues and I assembled a set of unbiased texts on Soviet economics. The validation task then consisted of deriving a set of terminological rules that would allow RHO to perform the inferential pattern matching necessary to extract from these texts all instances of a pre-determined class of target concepts. The hypothesis that RHO's tractability criterion can be met in practice would thus be considered validated just in case this set of inference rules was tractable under the criterion.

3.1. Some assumptions

At the time that we undertook the study, however, the *Alembic* implementation was still in its infancy. We thus had to make a number of assumptions about what could be expected out of *Alembic*'s parsing and semantic composition components. In so doing, we took great pain not to require superhuman performance on the part of the parser, and restricted our expected syntactic coverage to phenomena that we felt were well within the state of the art.

In particular, we rejected the need to derive S. As with many similar systems, *Alembic* uses a fragment parser that produces partial syntactic analyses when its grammar is insufficient to derive S. In addition, we exploited *Alembic*'s hierarchy of syntactic categories, and postulated a number of relatively fine-grained categories that were not currently in the system. This allowed us for example to assume we could obtain the intended parse of "Irish-Soviet airline" on the basis of the pre-modifiers being both adjectives of geographic origin (and hence co-ordinable).

We also exploited the fact that the *Alembic* grammar is highly lexicalized (being based on the combinatorial categorial framework). This allowed us to postulate some fairly detailed subcategorization frames for verbs and their nominalizations. As is currently the case with our system, we assumed that verbs and their nominalizations are canonicalized to identical semantic representations.

Elsewhere at the semantic level, we assumed basic competence at argument-passing, a characteristic already in place in the system. This allowed us, for example, to assume congruent semantics for the phrases "Samsung was announced to have X'd" and "Samsung has X'd."

3.2. The validation corpus

With these assumptions in mind, we assembled a corpus of data extraction inference problems in the area of Soviet economics. The corpus consisted of text passages that had been previously identified for an evaluation of information retrieval techniques in this subject area. The texts were drawn from over 6200 Wall Street Journal articles from 1989 that were released through the ACL-DCI. These articles were filtered (by extensive use of GREP) to a subset of 300-odd articles mentioning the then-extant Soviet Union. These articles were read in detail to locate all passages on a set of three pre-determined economic topics:

1. East-West joint ventures, these being any business arrangements between Soviet and non-Soviet agents.
2. Hard currency, being any discussion of attempts to introduce a convertible unit of monetary value in the former USSR.
3. Private cooperatives, i.e., employee-owned enterprises within the USSR.

We found 85 such passages in 74 separate articles (1.2% of the initial set of articles under consideration).

Among these, 47 passages were eliminated from consideration because they were just textual mentions of the target concepts (e.g. the string "joint venture") or of some simple variant. These passages could easily be identified by Boolean keyword techniques, and as such were not taken to provide a particularly insightful validation of a complex NL-based information-extraction process! Unfortunately, this eliminated all instances of private cooperatives from the corpus, because in these texts, the word "cooperative" is a perfect predictor of the concept.

An additional four passages were also removed during a cross-rater reliability verification. These were all amplifications of an earlier instance of one of the target concepts, e.g., "U.S. and Soviet officials hailed the joint project." These passages were eliminated because the corpus collectors had differing intuitions as to whether they were sufficient indications in and of themselves of the target concepts, or were somehow pragmatically "parasitic" upon earlier instances of the target concept. The remaining 34 passages required some degree of terminological inference, and formed the corpus for this study.

4. INFERENTIAL DATA EXTRACTION

We then set about writing a collection of terminological axioms to handle this corpus. As these axioms are propositional in nature, and the semantic representations produced by *Alembic* are not strictly propositional, this required specifying a mapping from the language of interpretations to that of the inference axioms.

4.1. Semantic representation in *Alembic*

Alembic produces semantic representations at the increasingly popular interpretation level [2, 10]. That is, instead of generating fully scoped and disambiguated logical forms, *Alembic* produces representations that are ambiguous with respect to quantifier scoping. For example, the noun phrase "a gold-based ruble" maps into something akin to the following interpretation:

```
[ [head ruble]
  [quant :exists]
  [args NIL]
  [proxy P117]
  [mods { [ [head basis-of]
            [args { P117 [ [head gold]
                           [quant :kind]] }]]}]]
```

Semantic heads of phrases are mapped to the head slot of the interpretation, arguments are mapped to the args slot, modifiers to the mods slot, and generalized quantifiers to the quant slot. The proxy slot contains a unique variable designating the individuals that satisfy the interpretation. If this interpretation were to be fully mapped to a sorted first-order logical form, it would result in the following sentence, where gold is treated as a kind individual:

∃ P117 : ruble basis-of(P117, gold)

Details of this semantic framework can be found in [3].

4.2 Conversion to propositional form

Axioms in RHO are strictly function-free Horn clauses, and as such are intended to match neither interpretations nor first-order logical forms. As a result, we needed to specify a mapping from interpretations to some propositional encoding that can be exploited by RHO's terminological axioms. In brief, this mapping hyper-Skolemizes the proxy variables in the interpretation and then recursively flattens the interpretation's modifiers.[1]

For example, the interpretation for "a gold-based ruble" is mapped to the following propositions:

ruble(P117)
basis-of(P117, gold)

The interpretation has been flattened by pulling its modifier to the same level as the head proposition (yielding an implicit overall conjunction). In addition, the proxy variable has been interpreted as a Skolem constant, in this case the "gensymed" individual P117.

This interpretation of proxies as Skolem constants is actually hyper-Skolemization, because we perform it on universally quantified proxies as well as on existentially quantified ones. Ignoring issues of negation and disjunction, this unorthodox Skolemization process has a curious model-theoretic justification (which is beyond our present scope). Intuitively, however, one can think of these hyper-Skolemized variables as designating the individuals that would satisfy the interpretation, once it has been assigned some unambiguously scoped logical form.

To see this, say we had the following inference rule:

m-loves-w(x,y) ← loves (x, y) & man (x) & woman(y)

Now say this rule were to be applied against the semantics of the infamously ambiguous case of "every man loves a woman." In propositionalized form, this would be:

man(P118)
woman(P119)
loves(P118,P119)

[1]This glosses over issues of event reference, which we address through a partly Davidsonian framework, as in [9].

target	occurrences, n	sufficiency rules, r	rule density, r/n
joint venture	12	17	1.4
hard curr.	22	13	.59

Table 1: Summary of experimental findings.

From this, the rule will infer m-loves-w(P118,P119). If we think of P118 and P119 as designating the individuals that satisfy the logical form of "every man loves a woman" in some model, then we can see that indeed the m-loves-w relation necessarily must hold between them. This is true regardless of whether the model itself satisfies the standard ∀-∃ scoping of the sentence or the notorious ∃-∀ scoping. This demonstrates a crucial property of this approach, namely that it enables inferential extraction over ambiguously scoped text, without requiring resolution of the scope ambiguity (and without expensive theorem proving).

5. FINDINGS

Returning to our validation study, we took this propositionalized representation as the basis for writing the set of axioms necessary to cover our corpus of data extraction problems. In complete honesty, we expected that the resulting axioms would not all end up meeting the tractability criterion. Natural language is notoriously complex, and even such classic simple KL-ONE concepts as Brachman's arch [6] do not meet the criterion.

What we found took us by surprise. We came across many examples that were challenging at various levels: complex syntactic phenomena, nightmares of reference resolution, and the ilk. However, once the corpus passages were mapped to their corresponding interpretations, the terminological axioms necessary to perform data extraction from these interpretations all met the criterion.

Table 1, above, summarizes these findings. To cover our corpus of 34 passages, we required between two and three dozen sufficiency rules, depending upon how one encoded certain economic concepts, and depending on what assumptions one made about argument-passing in syntax. We settled on a working set of thirty such rules.

Note that this inventory does not include any necessity rules. We ignored necessity rules for the present purposes in part because they only encode inheritance relationships. The size of their inventory thus only reflects the degree to which one chooses to model intermediate levels of the domain hierarchy. For this study, we could arguably have used none. In addition, necessity rules are guaranteed to meet the tractability criterion, and were consequently of only secondary interest to our present objectives.

5.1. Considerations for data extraction

From a data extraction perspective, these results are clearly preliminary. Looking at the positive side, we are encouraged that the rules for our hard currency examples were shared over multiple passages, as follows from their fractional rule density of .59 (see Table 1). The joint venture rules fared less well, mainly because the concept they encode is fairly complex, and can be described in many ways.

Given our restricted data set, however, it is not possible to conclude how well either set of rules will generalize if presented with a larger corpus. What is clearly needed is a larger corpus of examples. This would allow us to estimate generalizability of the rules by considering the asymptotic growth of the rule set as it is extended to cover more examples. Unfortunately, constructing such a corpus is a laborious task, since the examples we are interested in are precisely those that escape simple automated search techniques such as Boolean keyword patterns. The time and expense that were incurred in constructing the MUC3/4 and TIPSTER corpora attest to this difficulty.

We soon hope to know more about this question of rule generalizability. We are currently in the process of implementing a version of RHO in the context of the *Alembic* system, which is now considerably more mature than when we undertook the present study. We intend to exploit this framework for our participation in MUC5, as well as retool our system for the MUC4 task. As the TIPSTER and MUC4 data sets contain a considerably greater number of training examples than our Soviet economics corpus, we expect to gain much better insights into the ways in which our rule sets grow and generalize.

5.2. Considerations for RHO

From the perspective of our terminological inference framework, however, these preliminary results are quite encouraging indeed. We started with a very simple tractable inference framework, and studied how it could be applied to a very difficult problem in natural language processing. And it appears to work.

Once again, one should refrain from reaching overly general conclusions based on a small test sample. And admittedly RHO gets a lot of help from other parts of *Alembic*, especially the parser and a rudimentary inheritance taxonomy. Further analyses, however, reveal some additional findings that suggest that RHO's tractability criterion may be of general validity to this kind of natural language inference.

Most interestingly, the tractability result can be understood in the context of some basic characteristics of natural language sentence structure. In particular, axioms that violate the tractability criterion can only be satisfied by sentences that display anaphora or definite reference. For example, an axiom with the following right hand side:

own(x, z) & scorn(x, y) & dislike(y, z)

matches the sentences "the man who owns a Ferrari scorns anyone who dislikes it/his car/that car/the car." It is impossible, however, to satisfy this kind of circular axiom without invoking one of these referential mechanisms (at least in English). This observation, which was made in another context in [8], suggests a curious alignment between tractable cases of terminological natural language inference and non-anaphoric cases of language use.

It is particularly tantalizing that the cases where these terminological inferences are predicted to become computationally expensive are just those for which heuristic interpretation methods seem to play a large role (e.g., discourse structure and other reference resolution strategies). Though one must avoid the temptation to draw too strong a conclusion form such coincidences, one is still left thinking of Alice's ineffable words, "Curiouser and curiouser."

∽ Acknowledgments ∽

Much gratitude is owed John Aberdeen for preparing our corpus through tireless perusal of the Wall Street Journal. Many thanks also to those who served as technical inspiration or as sounding boards: Bill Woods, Remko Scha, Steve Minton, Dennis Connolly, and John Burger.

REFERENCES

[1] Aberdeen, J., Burger, J., Connolly, D., Roberts, S., & Vilain, M. (1992). "Mitre-Bedford: Description of the Alembic system as used for MUC-4". In [18].

[2] Alshawi, H.& Van Eijck, J. (1989). "Logical forms in the core language engine". In *Prcdgs. of ACL89*. Vancouver, BC, 25-32.

[3] Bayer, S. L. & Vilain, M. B. (1991). "The relation-based knowledge representation of King Kong". *Sigart Bulletin* 2(3), 15-21.

[4] Brachman, R. J., Borgida, A., McGuiness, D. L., & Patel-Schneider, P. F. (1991). "Living with CLASSIC". In Sowa, J., *ed., Principles of Semantic Networks*. San Mateo, CA: Morgan-Kaufmann.

[5] Brachman, R. J. & Levesque, H. (1984). "The tractability of subsumption in frame-based description languages". In *Prcdgs. of AAAI84*. Austin, Texas, 34-37.

[6] Brachman, R. J. & Schmolze, J. K. (1985). "An overview of the KL-ONE knowledge representation system". *Cognitive Science* 9(2), 171-216.

[7] Garey, M. R. & Johnson, D. S. (1979). *Computers and Intractability*. New York: W. H. Freeman.

[8] Haddock, N. J., (1992). "Semantic evaluation as constraint network consistency". In *Prcdgs. of AAAI92*. San Jose, CA, 415-420.

[9] Hobbs, J. R. (1985). "Ontological promiscuity". In *Prcdgs. of ACL85*. Chicago, IL, 119–124.

[10] Hobbs, J. R. & Shieber, S. M. (1987). "An algorithm for generating quantifier scopings". *Computational Linguistics* 13(1-2), 47-63.

[11] Jacobs, P. S. (1988). "Concretion: Assumption-based understanding". In *Prcdgs. of the 1988 Intl. Conf. on Comput. Linguistics (COLING88)*. Budapest, 270-274.

[12] MacGregor, R. (1991). "Inside the LOOM description classifier". *Sigart Bulletin* 2(3), 88-92.

[13] Nebel, B. (1988). "Computational complexity of terminological reasoning in BACK". *Artificial Intelligence* **34**(3), 371-383.

[14] Nebel, B. (1990). "Terminological reasoning in inherently intractable". *Artificial Intelligence* **43**, 235-249.

[15] Patel-Schneider, P. F. (1989). Undecidability of subsumption in NIKL. *Artificial Intelligence* 39: 263–272.

[16] Schmidt-Schauß, M. (1989). "Subsumption in KL-ONE is undecidable". In *Prcdgs. of KR89*. Toronto, ON.

[17] Stallard, D. G. (1986). "A terminological simplification transformation for natural language question-answering systems". In *Prcdgs. of ACL86*. New York, NY, 241-246.

[18] Sundheim, B., *ed.* (1992). *Prcdgs. of the Fourth Message Understanding Conf.* (MUC-4), McLean, VA, 215-222.

[19] Vilain, M. (1991). "Deduction as parsing: Tractable classification in the KL-ONE framework". In *Prcdgs. of AAAI91*. Anaheim, CA, 464-470

APPENDIX: PROOF OF TRACTABILITY

To demonstrate the validity of the tractability criterion, we only need consider the computational cost of finding all instantiations of the right-hand side of an axiom. In general, finding a single such instantiation is NP-complete, by reduction to the conjunctive Boolean query problem (see [7]). Intuitively, this is because general function-free Horn clauses can have arbitrary interactions between the variables on the right-hand side, i.e., their dependency graphs are fully cross-connected, as in:

$$R(v_1,v_2) \,\&\, R(v_1,v_3) \,\&\, R(v_2,v_3) \,\&\, R(v_1,v_4) \,\&\, R(v_2,v_4)\ldots$$

Intuitively again, verifying the instantiation of a given variable in a rule may require (in the worst case) checking all instantiations of all other variables in the rule. Under the usual assumptions of NP-completeness, no known algorithm exists that performs better in the worst case than enumerating all these instantiations. As each variable may take on as many as κ instantiations, where κ is the number of constants present in the knowledge base, the overall cost of finding a single globally consistent instantiation is $O(\kappa^{\xi})$, where ξ is the number of variables in the rule. The resulting complexity is thus exponential in ξ, which itself varies in the worst case with the length of the rule.

Consider now an axiom that satisfies the tractability criterion, yielding a graph such as that in Fig. 3. By

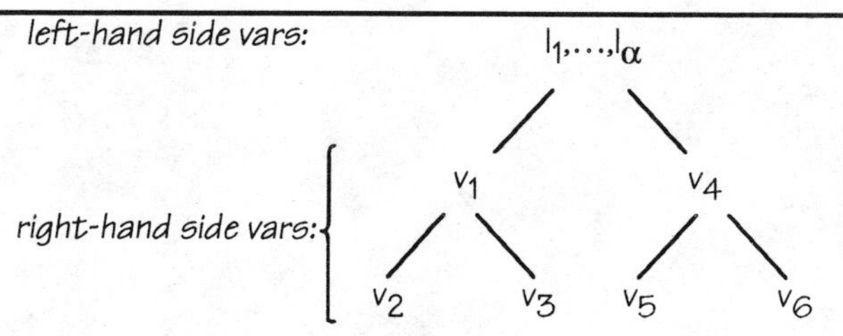

Figure 3: A dependency graph.

definition, the root of the graph corresponds to all the variables on the left-hand side, and all other nodes correspond to some variable introduced on the right-hand side. The cost of finding all the instantiations of the root variables is bounded by κ^{α}, where α is the maximal predicate valence for all the predicates appearing in the database. The cost of instantiating each non-root variable v is in turn bounded by $\alpha\kappa^{\alpha}$, corresponding to the cost of enumerating all possible instantiations of any predicate relating v to its single parent in the graph.

The topological restriction of the criterion leads directly to the fact that the exponent of these terms is a low-magnitude constant, α, rather than a parameter, ξ, that can be allowed to grow arbitrarily with the complexity of inference rules. The topological restriction also leads to the fact that these terms contribute *additively* to the overall cost of finding all instantiations of a rule. This overall cost is thus bounded by $\kappa^{\alpha} + \underbrace{\alpha\kappa^{\alpha}+\ldots+\alpha\kappa^{\alpha}}_{\xi}$, or $O(\xi\alpha\kappa^{\alpha})$.

Finally, we note that with the appropriate indexing scheme, finding all consequents of all rules only adds a multiplicative cost of ρ, where ρ is the total number of rules, yielding a final overall cost of $O(\rho\xi\alpha\kappa^{\alpha})$. It is often assumed that predicates in natural languages have no more than three arguments, so this formula approximately reduces to $O(\kappa^3)$.

This is of course a worst-case estimate. We are looking forward to measuring run-time performance figures on the MUC5 task, and are of course hoping to find actual performance to lie well below this cubic upper bound.

SESSION 5: DISCOURSE

Jerry R. Hobbs, Chair

Artificial Intelligence Center
SRI International
Menlo Park, California 94025

The fundamental problem in discourse is "What structure is there in discourse above the level of the sentence?" This question can be asked in terms of text versus dialogue. Is there a kind of structure that is exhibited in text but not in dialogue, or in dialogue but not in text? What are the appropriate structural descriptions of text and of dialogue?

The question can also be asked from the perspective of recognition and from the perspective of generation. There is the structure that the speaker puts there and the structure the hearer discovers there. Are these the same? Does one have primacy over the other? For example, does the speaker impose the structure so that it is the job of the hearer to discover it, no matter what it is, or is it necessary for the speaker to design his discourse in a way that makes it as easy as possible for the hearer to interpret?

The four papers in this session discuss various aspects of this family of questions.

The first paper, by Liddy and her colleagues at Syracuse University, is concerned with text rather than dialogue, and recognition rather than generation. Structure in text can be studied from a general point of view or from a genre-specific point of view. This paper examines the structure specific to the genre of newspaper articles. The structure found can be in the form of a hierarchy, a tree-like structure, much like the syntactic structure of sentences, or it can consist of a division of the text into segments of various kinds, performing various functions, such as the Lead, the Main Body, and so on. Liddy and her colleagues argue that the latter kind of structure is more appropriate for newspaper articles.

Among the questions addressed in this paper are

- What are the structural elements or possibilities?
- How can they be recognized, computationally?
- Once recognized, how can they be used?

The remaining papers are concerned with dialogue. The key idea in investigations of discourse from an artificial intelligence perspective is that the structure of a dialogue is, or is at least derived from, the structure of the participants' plans. "Plan" here is meant in the AI sense of a hierarchical structure of causal relations, decomposing goals into subgoals, and these subgoals into further subgoals, and so on. An utterance in a dialogue is an action in a larger plan to achieve some goal. Generation is a matter of finding the right such actions. Recognition is a matter of discovering the role that action plays in the overall plan.

Moore's paper examines a problem that arises in generation. We don't like to be told too much. If we already know something, we don't like to hear it again. If the speaker does not take this into account, the result is what my children used to refer to as "talking to me like I'm a retard." It is also an inefficient way of conveying a plan or some other structured body of information. The problem that Moore addresses is "How should we use knowledge gained from the previous discourse to convey a plan as efficiently as possible?"

The paper by Ferguson and Allen take the perspective of recognition. Part of understanding an utterance is discovering the role it plays in the speaker's larger plan. But the speaker's plan, or intentions, are inaccessible to us. All we have to go on is what he or she said. From that we have to hypothesize a plan in which the observable utterances would make the most sense. This is the problem that Ferguson and Allen address: "How can we recognize the speaker's plan, given only sparse information about it?"

In stretches of dialogue larger than a single utterance, neither participant is exclusively a speaker or exclusively a hearer. They are each executing their own plan, and their plans change as they are impacted by the actions of the other participant. In very focused, collaborative, problem-solving dialogues, they are working together to come up with a single plan for solving the problem. How can a single shared plan arise out of the interaction? This is the problem addressed in the paper by Biermann and his colleagues at Duke University. Each participant has pieces of a plan; how can they be combined into a single, agreed-upon plan? The particular situation described is a very common one. One participant, in this case, the tutoring system, has control over general knowledge about the domain. The other participant, here, the user, has the knowledge of the specific problematic situation. How can these be combined into a solution of the problem?

DEVELOPMENT, IMPLEMENTATION AND TESTING OF A DISCOURSE MODEL FOR NEWSPAPER TEXTS

Elizabeth D. Liddy [1], *Kenneth A. McVearry* [2], *Woojin Paik* [1], *Edmund Yu* [3], *Mary McKenna* [1]

[1] Syracuse University
School of Information Studies
Syracuse, NY 13244

[2] Coherent Research, Inc.
1 Adler Drive
East Syracuse, NY 13057

[3] Syracuse University
College of Engineering and Computer Science
Syracuse, NY 13244

ABSTRACT

Texts of a particular type evidence a discernible, predictable schema. These schemata can be delineated, and as such provide models of their respective text-types which are of use in automatically structuring texts. We have developed a Text Structurer module which recognizes text-level structure for use within a larger information retrieval system to delineate the discourse-level organization of each document's contents. This allows those document components which are more likely to contain the type of information suggested by the user's query to be selected for higher weighting. We chose newspaper text as the first text type to implement. Several iterations of manually coding a randomly chosen sample of newspaper articles enabled us to develop a newspaper text model. This process suggested that our intellectual decomposing of texts relied on six types of linguistic information, which were incorporated into the Text Structurer module. Evaluation of the results of the module led to a revision of the underlying text model and of the Text Structurer itself.

1. DISCOURSE-LEVEL TEXT MODELS

A discourse-level model of a text type can be likened to an interpretation model [Breuker & Wielinga, 1986] in that it specifies the necessary classes of knowledge to be identified in order to develop the skeletal conceptual structure for a class of entities. The establishment of text-type models derives from research in discourse linguistics which has shown that writers who repeatedly produce texts of a particular type are influenced by the schema of that text-type and, when writing, consider not only the specific content they wish to convey but also what the usual structure is for that type of text based on the purpose it is intended to serve [Jones, 1983]. As a result, one basic tenet of discourse linguistics is that texts of a particular type evidence the schema that exists in the minds of those who produce the texts. These schemata can be delineated, and as such provide models of their respective text-types which we suggest would be of use in automatically structuring texts.

The existence of and need for such predictable structures in texts is consistent with findings in cognitive psychology suggesting that human cognitive processes are facilitated by the ability to 'chunk' the vast amounts of information encountered in daily life into larger units of organized data [Rumelhart, 1977]. Schema theories posit that during chunking we recode individual units of perception into increasingly larger units, until we reach the level of a schema. Humans are thought to possess schema for a wide range of concepts, events, and situations [Rumelhart, 1980]. Discourse linguists have extended this notion to suggest that schema exist for text-types that participate regularly in the shared communication of a particular community of users.

What is delineated when a text schema is explicated is its discernible, predictable structure, referred to as the text's Superstructure. Superstructure is the text-level syntactic organization of semantic content; the global schematic structure; the recognizable template that is filled with different meaning in each particular example of that text-type [van Dijk, 1980]. Among the text-types for which schemas or models have been developed with varying degrees of detail are: folk-tales [Propp, 1958], newspaper articles [van Dijk, 1980], arguments [Cohen, 1987], historical journal articles [Tibbo, 1989], and editorials [Alvarado, 1990], empirical abstracts [Liddy, 1991], and theoretical abstracts [Francis & Liddy, 1991].

The goal of our current effort is to develop a component that can recognize text-level structure within a larger document detection system (DR-LINK) to enable the system to produce better retrieval results. For this system, we have focused our first efforts on newspaper texts, since the corpus we must process includes both the Wall Street Journal and the Associated Press Newswire.

2. DR-LINK

DR-LINK is a multi-stage document detection system being developed under the auspices of DARPA's TIPSTER Project. The purpose of TIPSTER is to significantly advance the state of the art in document detection and data extraction from large, real-world data collections. The document detection part of the project focuses on retrieving relevant documents from gigabyte-sized document collections, based on descriptions of users' information needs called topic statements. The data extraction part processes a much smaller set of documents, presumed to be relevant to a topic, in order to extract information which is used to fill a database.

The overall goal of DR-LINK is to simultaneously 1) focus the flow of texts through the system by selecting a subset of texts on the basis of subject content and then highlighting those sub-parts of a document which are likely spots of relevant text while 2) enriching the semantic representation of text content by: a) delineating each text's discourse-level structure; b) detecting relations among concepts; c) expanding lexical representation with semantically-related terms; and d) representing concepts and relations in Conceptual Graphs.

The purpose of the Text Structurer component in DR-LINK is to delineate the discourse-level organization of documents' contents so that processing at later stages can focus on those components where the type of information suggested in a query is most likely to be found. For example, in newspaper texts, opinions are likely to be found in EVALUATION components, basic facts of the news story are likely to be found in MAIN EVENT, and predictions are likely to be found in EXPECTATION. The Text Structurer produces an enriched representation of each document by decomposing it into smaller, conceptually labelled components. Operationally, DR-LINK evaluates each sentence in the input text, comparing it to the known characteristics of the prototypical sentence of each component of the text-type model, and then assigns a component label to the sentence.

In a form of processing parallel to the Text Structurer, the Topic Statement Processor evaluates each topic statement to determine if there is an indication that a particular text model component in the documents should be more highly weighted when matched with the topic statement representation. For example, topic statement indicator terms such as *predict* or *anticipate* or *proposed* reveal that the time frame of the event in question must be in the future in order for the document to be relevant. Therefore, documents in which this event is reported in a piece of text which has been marked by the Text Structurer as being EXPECTATION would be ranked more highly than those in which this event is reported in a different text model component

3. DEVELOPMENT OF THE NEWS SCHEMA MODEL

The need for a text model specifically for newspaper text is necessitated by the fact that the journalistic style forsakes the linear logic of storytelling and presents the various categories of information in a recurrent cyclical manner whereby categories and the topics contained within them are brought up, dropped, and then picked up again for further elaboration later in the news article. This internal topical disorganization makes a story grammar, as well as the expository text models [Britton & Black, 1985] not appropriate as text models.

Therefore, we took as a starting point, the uniquely journalistic, hierarchical newspaper text model proposed by van Dijk [1988]. With this as a preliminary model, several iterations of coding of a sample of 149 randomly chosen Wall Street Journal articles from 1987-1988 resulted in a revised News Schema which took from van Dijk's model the terminal node categories and organized them according to a more temporally oriented perspective, to support the computational task for which our model was to be used. We retained the segmentation of the overall structure into van Dijk's higher level categories, namely: Summary, Story and Comment, but added several terminal components as warranted by the data.

The News Schema Components which comprise the model are the categories of information which account for all the text in the sample of articles. The components are:

CIRCUMSTANCE - context in which main event occurs

CONSEQUENCE - definite causal result of main event

CREDENTIAL - credentials of author

DEFINITION - definition of special terminology

ERROR - mention of error that was made (in a correction)

EVALUATION - author's comments on events

EXPECTATION - likely or possible result of main event

HISTORY - non-recent past history of main event

LEAD - first sentence or paragraph which introduces or summarizes article

MAIN EVENT - text which advances the plot or main thread of the story

NO COMMENT - refusal or unavailability of source to comment

PREVIOUS EVENT - immediate past context for main event

REFERENCE - reference to related article (title and date)

VERBAL REACTION - quoted reaction from source to main event

While coding the sample, we developed both defining features and properties for each component. The defining features convey the role and purpose of that component within the News Schema while the properties provide suggestive clues for the recognition of that component in a news article. The manual coding suggested to us that we were in fact relying on six different types of linguistic information during our coding. The data which would provide these evidence sources was then analyzed statistically and translated into computationally recognizable text characteristics. Briefly defined, the six sources of evidence used in the original Text Structurer are:

Likelihood of Component Occurring - The unit of analysis for the first source of evidence is the sentence and is based on the observed frequency of each component in our coded sample set.

Order of Components - This source of evidence relies on the tendency of components to occur in a particular, relative order. For this source of evidence, we calculated across the coded files we had of each of the sample documents, looking not at the content of the individual documents, but the component label. We used this data to compute the frequency with which each component followed every other component and the frequency with which each component preceded every other component. The results are contained in two 19 by 19 matrices (one for probability of which component follows a given component and one for probability of which component precedes a given component). These two can be used in conjunction when there is a sentence lying between two other sentences which have already been coded for component or even when only the component of the preceding or following sentence is known. For example, if a series of sentences, *a-b-c*, the component label for sentence *b* is unknown, but the labels for sentence *a* and *c* are known, these matrices provide evidence of the likelihood that *b* might be any of the components in the model.

Lexical Clues - The third source of evidence is a set of one, two and three word phrases for each component. The set of lexical clues for each component was chosen based on observed frequencies and distributions. We were looking for words with sufficient occurrences, statistically skewed observed frequency of occurrence in a particular component, and semantic indication of the role or purpose of each component. For example, all the clues for VERBAL REACTION reveal the distinctly informal nature of quoted comments and the much more personal nature of this component when compared to the other components in a newspaper text.

Syntactic Sources - We make use of two types of syntactic evidence: 1) typical sentence length as measured in average number of words per sentence for each component; 2) individual part-of-speech distribution based on the output of the part-of-speech tagging of each document, using POST. This evidence helps to recognize those components which, because of their nature, tend to have a disproportionate number of their words be of a particular part of speech. For example, EVALUATION component sentences tend to have more adjectives than sentences in other components.

Tense Distribution - Some components, as might be expected by their name alone, tend to contain verbs of a particular tense more than verbs of other tenses. For example, DEFINITION sentences seldom contain past tense, whereas the predominate tense in HISTORY and PREVIOUS EVENT sentences is the past tense, based on POST tags.

Continuation Clues - The sixth and final source of evidence is based on the conjunctive relations suggested in Halliday and Hasan's Cohesion in English. The continuation clues are lexical clues which occur in a sentence-initial position and were observed in our coded sample data to predictably indicate either that the current sentence continues the same component as the prior sentence (e.g. *And* or *In addition*) or that there is a change in the component (e.g. *However* or *Thus*).

4. EMPIRICAL TESTING OF THE MODEL

The above computational method of instantiating a discourse-level model of the newspaper text-model has been incorporated in an operational system (DR-LINK). The original Text-Structurer evaluated each sentence of an input newspaper article against these six evidence sources for the purpose of assigning a text-level label to each sentence. This implementation uses the Dempster-Shafer Theory of Evidence Combination [Shafer, 1976] to coordinate information from some very complex matrices of statistical values for the various evidence sources which were generated from the intellectual analysis of the sample of 149 Wall Street Journal articles.

Operationally, the text is processed a sentence at a time, and each source of evidence assigns a number between 0 and 1 to indicate the degree of support that evidence source provides to the belief that a sentence is of a particular news-text component. Then, a simple supporting function for each component is computed and the component with the greatest support is selected.

The Text Structurer was tested using five of the six evidence sources. (The algorithms for incorporating evidence from the continuation clues were not complete at the time of testing, so that evidence source was not added to the system.) We tested the Text Structurer on a set of 116 Wall Street Journal articles, consisting of over two thousand sentences.

The first run and evaluation of the original Text Structurer resulted in 72% of the sentences being correctly identified. A manual simulation of one small, heuristic adjustment was tested and improved the system's performance to 74% of the sentences correctly identified. A second manual adjustment for a smaller sample of sentences resulted in 80% correct identification of components for sentences.

5. ATTRIBUTE MODEL

After evaluating the preliminary results from the Text Structurer, we became dissatisified with some aspects of the model we developed and the processing based on that model. We needed a more precise way to define the components in the model, and we saw that frequently a sentence contained information for more than one component.

As a result, we developed a set of attributes of newspaper text in order to first better distinguish between similar components, and then to assign the attributes to text independent of component labels. These attributes are usually binary in nature. We identified eight attributes: Time, Tense, Importance, Attribution, Objectivity, Definiteness, Completion, and Causality.

For example, the Importance attribute has two possible values: "foreground" and "background". Components which are in the foreground include LEAD and MAIN EVENT; background components include CIRCUMSTANCE, DEFINITION, PREVIOUS EVENT, HISTORY, VERBAL REACTION, and NO COMMENT. The Objectivity attribute is also binary: its possible values are "objective" and "subjective". Objective components include CIRCUMSTANCE, MAIN EVENT, PREVIOUS EVENT, and HISTORY; subjective components include VERBAL REACTION, EVALUATION, and EXPECTAION. The Time attribute is multi-valued: its possible values are "past", "present", "past or present", and "future".

6. CURRENT MODEL

As a result of our analysis of text based on its attributes, we revised both the text-type model and the algorithms used by the Text Structurer. Revisions to the model focused primarily on subdividing components and adding new components to fill in gaps in the model and make it more precise. Revisions to the processing algorithms include: 1) restricting the sources of evidence used to lexical clues only; 2) establishing an order of precedence for components; 3) moving from a single lexicon to a lexicon for each component; 4) discontinuing the use of the Dempster-Shafer method of evidence combination; 5) moving the level of analysis from the sentence to the clause level.

The new components:

CIRCUMSTANCE-STOCK - closing price of stock mentioned in the article

CONSEQUENCE-PAST/PRESENT - past or present causal result of main event

CONSEQUENCE-FUTURE - future causal result of main event

EVALUATION - opinion attributed to a source

EVALUATION-JOURNALIST - opinion not attributed to a source

EXPECTATION-JOURNALIST - likely or possible result of main event not attributed to a source

FIGURE DESCRIPTION - text which describes a nearby figure, table, etc.

LEAD-ATTENTION - attention-getting lead (does not summarize)

LEAD-FUTURE - lead which refers to the future

LEAD-HISTORY - lead which refers to the non-recent past

LEAD-PREVIOUS - lead which refers to the recent past

MAIN-EXAMPLE - specific instance or example of main event

MAIN-FUTURE - main event set in the future

MAIN2 - alternate main event (new story)

PAST - undated past context of main event

---

7. FUTURE WORK

There are several areas we would like to explore, both in improving the operation of the Text Structurer and in demonstrating its applicability. One obvious way to improve the accuracy and coverage of the Text Structurer is to expand the lexicons for each component, via corpus-guided acquisition of synonyms. Another possibility is that ordering and continuation evidence can in fact be used to augment lexical evidence, e.g. for sentences which should be labeled HISTORY and which follow a HISTORY lexical clue but which themselves do not contain any HISTORY clues. One area which needs improvement is distinguishing between foreground and background components, e.g. MAIN EVENT vs. CIRCUMSTANCE. It is clear that purely lexical information is not sufficient to make the distinction, and that patterns of verbs and other words, ordering, and other information are required, if not some internal understanding of the subject of the text.

There are several possible uses of the Text Structurer module in a document detection system. Within DR-LINK, it can be used as a focusing mechanism (filter or weighting) for other modules, e. g. the Relation-Concept Detector, which identifies concepts and relations between concepts in text. For example, the Relation-Concept Detector can be set to emphasize those sentences which are labeled with a foreground component (LEAD, MAIN EVENT, etc.) by the Text Structurer. Another application outside of DR-LINK is as an intermeditate process between document detection and data extraction. Once a document is determined to be relevant, the Text Structurer can focus the data extraction process on those sentences or sentence fragments which are most likely to contain the information required to fill the database.

8. CONCLUSIONS

Although we are clearly in the early stages of development of the Text Structurer, we find these results quite promising and are eager to share our empirical results and experiences in creating an operational system with other computational linguists. To our knowledge, no similar, operational discourse structuring system has yet been reported in the literature.

We have applied the newspaper text-type model to text from a different source, by coding a sample of AP Newswire articles. This effort verified that the model was general enough to handle news text from various sources; in fact, a subset of the model covered all cases seen in the AP text.

We are in the process of evaluating the latest version of the Text Structurer based on the current newspaper text model. We will next apply a similar methodology to the development of a model and processing component for automatically structuring full-length, technical journal articles.

REFERENCES

1. Alvarado, S. J. (1990). Understanding editorial text: A computer model of argument comprehension. Boston, MA: Kluwer Academic Publishers.
2. Breuker & Wielinga. (1986). Models of expertise. ECAI.
3. Britton, B. & Black, J. (1985). "Understanding expository text: From structure to process and world knowledge." In B. Britton & J. Black (Eds.), Understanding expository texts: A theoretical and practical handbook for analyzing explanatory text. (pp. 1-9). Hillsdale, NJ: Lawrence Erlbaum Associates.
4. Cohen, R. (1987). "Analyzing the structure of argumentative discourse." Computational Linguistics. 13, pp. 11-24.
5. Francis, H. & Liddy, E. D. (1991). "Structured representation of theoretical abstracts: Implications for user interface design." In Dillon, M. (Ed.), Interfaces for information retrieval and online systems. NY: Greenwood Press.
6. Halliday, M. A. K. & Hasan, R. (1976). Cohesion in English. London, Longmans.
7. Jones, L. B. (1983). Pragmatic aspects of English text structure. Arlington, TX: Summer Institute of Linguistics.
8. Liddy, E. D. (1991). "The discourse-level structure of empirical abstracts: An exploratory study." Information Processing & Management. (pp. 55-81).
9. Meteer, M., Schwartz, R. & Weischeidel, R. (1991). "POST: Using probabilities in language processing." Proceedings of the Twelfth International Conference on Artificial Intelligence. Sydney, Australia.
10. Propp, V. (1958). Morphology of the folk-tale. (L. Scott, Trans.). Bloomington: Indiana University Press. (Original work published 1919).
11. Rumelhart, D. (1977). "Understanding and summarizing brief stories." In D. LaBerge & S. J. Samuels (Eds.), Basic processes in reading: Perception and comprehension (pp. 265-303). Hillsdale, NJ: Lawrence Earlbaum Associates.
12. Rumelhart, D. (1980). "Schemata: the building blocks of cognition." In R. Spiro, B. Bruce, & W. Brewer (Eds.), Theoretical issues in reading comprehension: Perspectives from cognitive psychology, linguistics, artificial intelligence and education (pp. 33-58). Hillsdale, NJ: Lawrence Earlbaum Associates.

13. Shafer, G. (1976). A mathematical theory of evidence. Princeton, NJ: Princeton University Press.

14. Tibbo, H. R. (1989). Abstracts, online searching, and the humanities: An analysis of the structure and content of abstracts of historical discourse. Ph.D. Dissertation, College of Library and information Science.

15. van Dijk, T. A. (1980). Macrostructures: An interdisciplinary study of global structures in discourse, interaction, and cognition. Hillsdale, NJ: Lawrence Earlbaum Associates.

16. van Dijk, T. A. (1988). News analysis: Case studies of international and national news in the press. Hillsdale, NJ: Lawrence Earlbaum Associates.

INDEXING AND EXPLOITING A DISCOURSE HISTORY TO GENERATE CONTEXT-SENSITIVE EXPLANATIONS

*Johanna D. Moore**

Department of Computer Science, and LRDC
University of Pittsburgh
Pittsburgh, PA 15260

ABSTRACT

A striking difference between the interactions that students have with human tutors and those they have with computer-based instruction systems is that human tutors frequently refer to their own previous explanations. Based on a study of human-human instructional interactions, we are categorizing the uses of previous discourse and are developing a computational model of this behavior. In this paper, I describe the strategies we have implemented for identifying relevant prior explanations, and the mechanisms that enable our text planner to exploit the information stored in its discourse history in order to omit information that has previously been communicated, to point out similarities and differences between entities and situations, and to mark re-explanations in circumstances where they are deemed appropriate.

1. Introduction

To reap the benefits of natural language interaction, user interfaces must be endowed with the properties that make human natural language interaction so effective. One such property is that human speakers freely exploit all aspects of the mutually known context, including the previous discourse. Computer-generated utterances that do not draw on the previous discourse seem awkward, unnatural, or even incoherent. The effect of the discourse history is especially important in instructional applications because explanation is essentially incremental and interactive. To provide missing information in a way that facilitates understanding and learning, the system must have the capability to relate new information effectively to recently conveyed material, and to avoid repeating old material that would distract the student from what is new. Strategies for using the discourse history in generating utterances are therefore crucial for building computer systems intended to engage in instructional dialogues with their users.

The goal of our work is to produce a computational model of the effects of discourse context on explanations in instructional dialogues, and to implement this model in an intelligent explanation facility. Based on a study of human-human instructional dialogues, we are developing a taxonomy that classifies the types of contextual effects that occur in our data according to the explanatory functions they serve [1]. Thus far, we have focused on four categories from our taxonomy

- explicit reference to a previous explanation (or portion thereof) in order to point out similarities (differences) between the material currently being explained and material presented in earlier explanation(s),
- omission of previously explained material to avoid distracting student from what is new,
- explicit marking of repeated material to distinguish it from new material (e.g., "As I said before, ...")
- elaboration of previous material in the form of generalizations, more detail, or justifications.[1]

Building on previous work [2, 3] we have implemented an explanation facility that maintains a discourse history and uses it in planning subsequent explanations. We are using this explanation facility as part of two intelligent systems. The first is a patient education system intended to provide patients with information about their disease, possible therapies, and medications [4, 5]. The second is an intelligent coached practice environment for training avionics technicians to troubleshoot complex electronic equipment [6].

In order to generate texts that exploit previous discourse, a system must have the following capabilities:

1. It must understand its own previous explanations.
2. It must be able to find prior explanations (or parts thereof) that are relevant to generating the current explanation, *in an efficient manner*.
3. It must have strategies for exploiting the relevant prior texts in pedagogically useful ways when generating the current explanation.

In this paper, I describe how we have realized these three requirements in the two instructional systems.

2. Background

To achieve the first requirement, our explanation system uses an extended version of the text planner developed by Moore

*The research described in this paper was supported by the Office of Naval Research, Cognitive and Neural Sciences Division, and the National Science Foundation, Research Initiation Award.

[1]This category breaks up into number of subcategories in our taxonomy.

and Paris [2]. Briefly, the text planner works in the following way. When the user provides input to the system, the query analyzer interprets the question and forms a *communicative goal* representing the system's intended effect on the hearer's mental state, e.g., "achieve the state where the hearer believes that action A is suboptimal" or "achieve the state where the hearer knows about the side effects of drug X." A linear planner synthesizes responses to achieve these goals using a library of explanation operators that map communicative goals to linguistic resources (speech acts and rhetorical strategies) for achieving them. In general, there may be many operators available to achieve a given goal, and the planner has a set of *selection heuristics* for choosing among them. Planning is complete when all goals have been refined into speech acts, such as INFORM and RECOMMEND.

In this system, a text plan represents the effect that each part of the text is intended to have on the hearer's mental state, the linguistic strategies that were used to achieve these effects, and how the complete text achieves the overall communicative goal. When a text plan is complete, the system presents the explanation to the user, retaining the plan that produced it in a *discourse history*.

In previous work, I showed how a system could support a limited range of dialogue capabilities using the information recorded in its discourse history [3]. In particular, I devised interpretation and recovery heuristics that examine the text plan that produced the immediately preceding explanation in order to interpret and respond to the follow-up questions "Why?" and "Huh?". In addition, the system is able to avoid producing the same answer to a question asked a second time by searching the discourse history to determine if the communicative goal corresponding to the question was ever posted before. If so, the system notes which strategy was used in the previous case and employs recovery heuristics to choose an alternative strategy.

The work reported in this paper is aimed at augmenting the ways in which the information recorded in the discourse history affects each new explanation as it is planned. In general, previous dialogue should potentially influence the answer to *every* subsequent question, not just explicit follow-up questions, such as "Why?" and "Huh?", or questions that are literally asked twice. Supporting this capability requires recognizing when prior explanations are relevant and how they should affect the current response.

3. Examples

Examples of the types of contextual effects we are interested in appear in Figures 1 and 2. The dialogue in Figure 1 is taken from our corpus of human-human written instructional dialogues in the SHERLOCK domain. SHERLOCK is an intelligent training system that teaches avionics technicians to troubleshoot complex electronic equipment. It is built within the "learning by doing" paradigm, in which students solve problems with minimal tutor interaction and then review their troubleshooting behavior in a post-problem *reflective follow-up* session (RFU) where the tutor replays each student action and provides a critique (here the tutor marks each action as "good" (<+>) or as "could be improved" (<->)). To collect protocols for study, the system was used to replay each step during RFU, but the human tutor provided the assessment and answered any questions the student posed.

In Figure 1, the student performs three actions that are assessed negatively for reasons that are related. Testing pin 28 is bad for one of the same reasons as testing pin 38, and testing pin 36 is bad for precisely the same reason as testing pin 28. In the figure, italics are used to highlight what we categorize as contextual effects on the explanations given. For example, when explaining why testing pin 28 is bad (turn 6), the tutor refers back to one of the reasons given in the explanation in turn 3, and reiterates the fact that the main data inputs are highly suspect (signalled by "As explained before"). In turn 6, the tutor offers an elaboration that introduces the notions of main and secondary data control signals and justifies why the main data signal should be tested first. Later, when explaining why testing pin 36 is bad in turn 9, the tutor refers back to the explanation he gave for testing pin 28 and states a generalization explaining why all three of these actions are considered suboptimal. The tutor expects the student to be able to make use of the explanations given in turn 6 (and therefore turn 3) by indicating that it is relevant to the current situation ("for the same reasons given ..." serves this purpose). Accordingly, the tutor does not repeat the detailed explanation of why the main control data signals should be tested first. By generating the explanation in turn 9 in such a way that it 'meshes' with the previous two, not only does the tutor correct student's error, but he forces the student to consider how the three situations are similar. Pointing out this similarity may facilitate the student in forming the domain generalization and recognizing how the three instances fit this generalization.

Figure 2 shows an actual dialogue with our patient education system, and is based upon phenomena we observed in naturally occurring interviews with physicians. The responses shown in this example are automatically generated, and typify the type of interaction a patient can have with our system. Patients construct questions via a direct manipulation interface that allows users to combine menu selection and highlighting portions of previous explanations on the screen. This interface extends our previous work [7]. Note that although the user asks exactly the same type of question in turns 1 and 3, the system's answers are quite different. This is because the answer in turn 4 (R4) is affected by the context created in turns 1–3. For example, the first sentence of R4 points out that Elavil is used for the same type of therapy as Inderal. Further

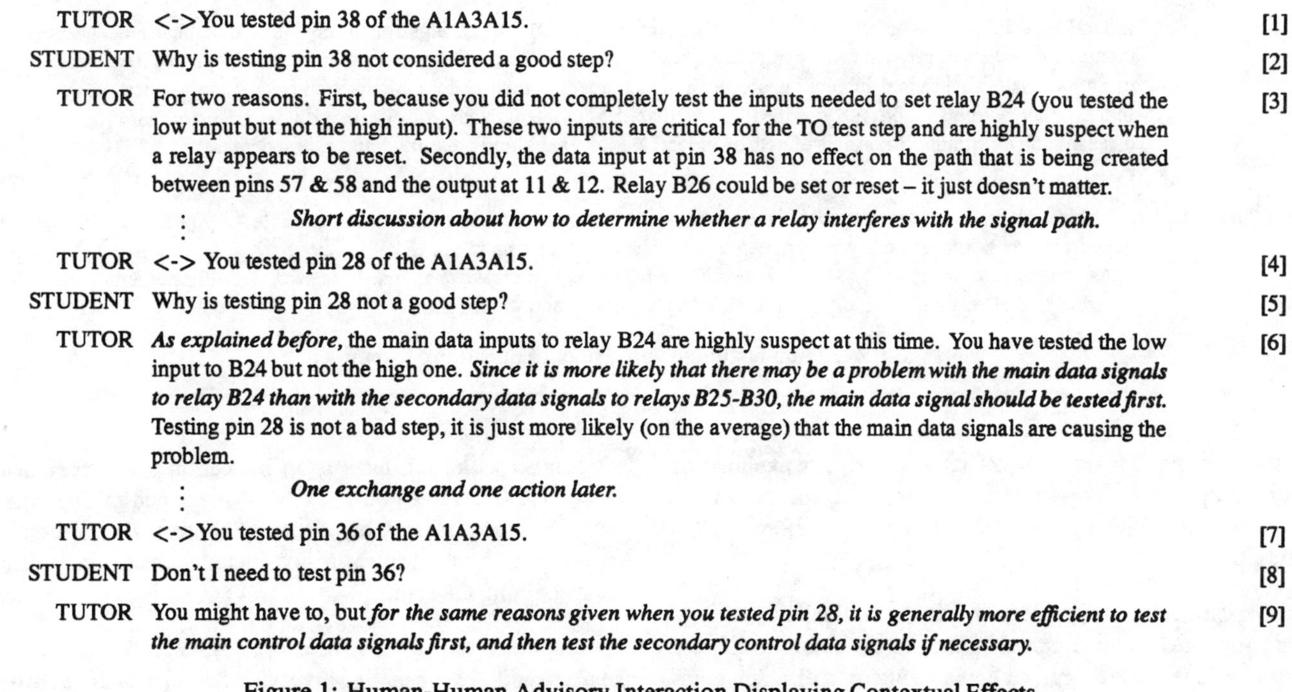

TUTOR <->You tested pin 38 of the A1A3A15. [1]

STUDENT Why is testing pin 38 not considered a good step? [2]

TUTOR For two reasons. First, because you did not completely test the inputs needed to set relay B24 (you tested the low input but not the high input). These two inputs are critical for the TO test step and are highly suspect when a relay appears to be reset. Secondly, the data input at pin 38 has no effect on the path that is being created between pins 57 & 58 and the output at 11 & 12. Relay B26 could be set or reset – it just doesn't matter. [3]

⋮ *Short discussion about how to determine whether a relay interferes with the signal path.*

TUTOR <-> You tested pin 28 of the A1A3A15. [4]

STUDENT Why is testing pin 28 not a good step? [5]

TUTOR *As explained before,* the main data inputs to relay B24 are highly suspect at this time. You have tested the low input to B24 but not the high one. *Since it is more likely that there may be a problem with the main data signals to relay B24 than with the secondary data signals to relays B25-B30, the main data signal should be tested first.* Testing pin 28 is not a bad step, it is just more likely (on the average) that the main data signals are causing the problem. [6]

⋮ *One exchange and one action later.*

TUTOR <->You tested pin 36 of the A1A3A15. [7]

STUDENT Don't I need to test pin 36? [8]

TUTOR You might have to, but *for the same reasons given when you tested pin 28, it is generally more efficient to test the main control data signals first, and then test the secondary control data signals if necessary.* [9]

Figure 1: Human-Human Advisory Interaction Displaying Contextual Effects

note that in R4 the system does not explain what prophylactic treatment means because it has done so previously in R2, i.e, the system omits information that has been presented in a previous explanation. Finally, in the penultimate sentence of R4, Elavil's contraindications and side effects are contrasted with those of Inderal.

4. Finding Relevant Prior Explanations

In order to produce the types of behavior exemplified above, a system must be able to determine which prior explanation(s) should be referred to when constructing an explanation. Although it is convenient for expository purposes to think of the tasks of finding relevant prior explanations and exploiting them in the construction of the current explanation as conceptually distinct, they may be interleaved in the actual text generation process, as discussed in the next section.

In our systems, the discourse history is a simple stack. Explanation plans are large, complex structures and they will accumulate rapidly as the dialogue progresses. Exhaustively searching the discourse history for relevant prior explanations is computationally prohibitive. Therefore, we require indexing strategies that allow the system to find possibly relevant prior explanations in an efficient manner. We have found that two factors influence the identification of relevant prior explanations:

- what was conveyed in prior explanations, i.e., the relationship of the domain content to be conveyed to the domain content presented in prior explanation(s)
- why a previous explanation was given, i.e., the relationship between the communicative goal(s) of the current and prior explanation(s)

Therefore, to facilitate the search for relevant prior explanations, we index each segment of an explanation by the communicative goal(s) the text is intended to achieve, and the domain entities and situations that are discussed in that segment.[2]

Let us consider how these indices can be used to facilitate the identification of a relevant prior explanation for generating the tutor's response in turn 6 of Figure 1. When the student asks why testing pin 28 is not a good step (turn 5), the system forms the communicative goal: `(BEL H (SUBOPTIMAL-STEP (MEAS-TEST (PIN28 OF A1A3A15))))`. One of strategies for answering this question looks to see if there is a previous student action, ?A, that is similar to the test of pin 28 and that was involved in a previous explanation segment satisfying the goal `(BEL H (SUBOPTIMAL-STEP ?A))`. Using an algorithm described below, the system determines that in this case, the action of testing pin 38 is similar to the test of pin 28 and there is an explanation (turn 3) satisfying the communicative goal `(BEL H (SUBOPTIMAL-STEP`

[2]Following Grosz and Sidner [8], in our model intentions are the basic determiner of segmentation, and therefore each communicative goal indicates a segment boundary.

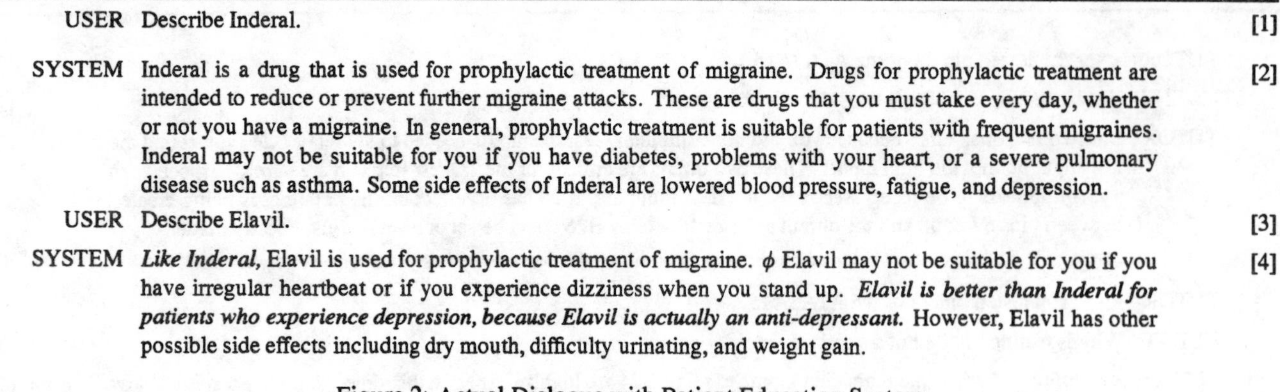
USER Describe Inderal. [1]

SYSTEM Inderal is a drug that is used for prophylactic treatment of migraine. Drugs for prophylactic treatment are intended to reduce or prevent further migraine attacks. These are drugs that you must take every day, whether or not you have a migraine. In general, prophylactic treatment is suitable for patients with frequent migraines. Inderal may not be suitable for you if you have diabetes, problems with your heart, or a severe pulmonary disease such as asthma. Some side effects of Inderal are lowered blood pressure, fatigue, and depression. [2]

USER Describe Elavil. [3]

SYSTEM *Like Inderal,* Elavil is used for prophylactic treatment of migraine. ϕ Elavil may not be suitable for you if you have irregular heartbeat or if you experience dizziness when you stand up. ***Elavil is better than Inderal for patients who experience depression, because Elavil is actually an anti-depressant.*** However, Elavil has other possible side effects including dry mouth, difficulty urinating, and weight gain. [4]

Figure 2: Actual Dialogue with Patient Education System

(MEAS-TEST (PIN38 OF A1A3A15)))). The explanation strategy points out the similarity between the prior and current explanation, generating the text "As explained before, ..." in turn 6.

Other strategies cover cases in which an identical communicative goal was attempted before, or the action itself or a similar action was discussed but in service of a different communicative goal. These strategies use the two types of indices to quickly determine if there are prior explanations that satisfy the constraints on their applicability. I provide examples from the patient education domain in the Section .

Determining Relationships between Domain Entities

In the patient education system, domain knowledge is represented in LOOM [9], a term-subsumption language. Therefore, domain entities and relationships between them are well defined and determined simply by queries written in LOOM's query language.

In the Sherlock system, much of the knowledge used in troubleshooting and assessing student's actions is represented procedurally, and therefore other techniques for computing relationships between domain entities are needed. In RFU interactions, the most commonly asked question is to justify the tutor's assessment of a step (32% of all questions asked during RFU), and 27% of the answers to such questions involve references to previously assessed actions. Therefore, an efficient algorithm for computing similarity of student actions was considered essential for producing the types of context-sensitive explanations that are required in this domain. To compute similarity between actions, the system uses a technique adapted from Ashley's work in case-based legal reasoning [10]. This algorithm, developed by James Rosenblum, makes use of a set of facets that SHERLOCK employs to evaluate each student action. These facets were derived from a cognitive task analysis aimed at identifying the factors that expert avionics tutors use in assessing student's troubleshooting actions [11]. Associated with each facet is an indication of whether that facet contributes to a good (+), bad (–), or neutral (n) evaluation in the current problem-solving context. The system's representation of a student action includes the list of facets characterizing the action.

Treating each student action as a "case", the algorithm builds a *similarity DAG* representing a partial ordering of actions based on the similarity of each action to a given action. The system can compute overall similarity, or similarity with respect to a certain class of facets (+, –, or n). For example, when answering a question about why the current action received a negative assessment, the similarity DAG is built so that it indicates similarity of previous actions to the current action with respect to the – facets. The root of the DAG represents the current action and the facets that apply to it. Each node in the graph represents a set of actions that share the same set of facets. The more facets that a node has in common with the current action (the root node), the closer it will be to the root node.

Initial results using this algorithm are quite promising. The algorithm is both efficient (complexity $O(n^2)$ where n is the number of student actions) and accurate. In a corpus of 8 student-tutor protocols involving 154 student actions and 30 requests to justify the tutor's assessment of the student's action, the human tutor produced 8 responses that explicitly pointed out similarity(ies) to action(s) whose assessment had previously been explained. These 8 responses involved 11 similar actions in total. In all 8 situations the algorithm correctly selected as most similar the same actions used in the tutor's explanations. In 3 cases the algorithm suggested a similarity not used by the tutor. However, when presented with these similarities, our expert tutor judged them as correct and stated that explanations that explicitly pointed out these similarities would have been pedagogically useful. In all other cases in which the human tutor did not make reference to a previous explanation as part of an answer, our algorithm reported that no prior action was similar.

NAME: Op1
EFFECT: (KNOW-ABOUT H ?d))
CONSTRAINTS: (AND (ISA ?d DRUG)
(USE ?d ?t))
NUCLEUS: (BEL H (USE ?d ?t))
SATELLITES:
(((BEL H (SOMEREF (contraindication ?d))) *required*)
((BEL H (SOMEREF (other-use ?d))) *optional*)
((BEL H (SOMEREF (side-effect ?d))) *required*)
((BEL H (SOMEREF (warning ?d))) *optional*))

NAME: Op3
EFFECT: (BEL H (?r ?arg1 ?arg2))
CONSTRAINTS: (IN-DH (BEL H (?r ?x ?arg2)))
NUCLEUS: (BEL H (SAME-AS (?r ?x ?arg2)
(?r ?arg1 ?arg2)))
SATELLITES: nil

NAME: Op6
EFFECT: (BEL H ?p)
CONSTRAINTS: nil
NUCLEUS: (INFORM H ?p)
SATELLITES: nil

Figure 3: Sample Plan Operators from Patient Education System

5. Exploiting Prior Explanations

With the capability to identify relevant prior discourse, our systems are able to exploit this information when planning explanations using three mechanisms: plan operators that implement context-sensitive strategies, domain-independent planning heuristics (e.g., prefer operators that refer to previous explanations), and plan modification rules that alter a plan based on information from the discourse history (e.g., if an optional communicative goal has already been achieved, don't plan text to achieve it).

We now consider how the patient education system can produce the behavior illustrated in the sample dialogue in Figure 2. When the user asks the system to 'Describe Inderal' (turn 1), the system posts the goal (KNOW-ABOUT H INDERAL). The planner searches its operator library to find an operator capable of achieving this goal, and finds Op1 shown in Figure 3. This operator encodes a strategy for describing a drug derived from our analysis of transcripts of doctor-patient interactions and interviews with physicians.

To determine whether this operator can be used in the current situation, the planner checks its constraints. If a constraint predicate includes only bound variables, then the planner verifies the constraint against the knowledge base. For example, the first constraint in Op1 (ISA ?d DRUG) checks the domain knowledge to verify that INDERAL is of type DRUG. Alternatively, if a constraint predicate contains variables that are not yet bound, the planner searches the system's knowledge bases for acceptable bindings for such variables. For example, to check the constraint (USE ?d ?t) where ?d is bound to INDERAL, but ?t is not bound, the planner searches the medical knowledge base and finds that the variable ?t can be bound to PROPHYLACTIC-MIGRAINE-TREATMENT. Therefore, all the constraints on Op1 are verified, and the operator is chosen. To expand the operator, the planner posts the subgoal appearing in the nucleus[3] field of the operator, (BEL H (USE INDERAL PROPHYLACTIC-MIGRAINE-TREATMENT)), and then the subgoals appearing in the satellite. Expanding the satellites of Op1 posts up to four additional subgoals.

[3]The terms *nucleus* and *satellite* come from Rhetorical Structure Theory (RST). For more details about RST, see [12].

The planner must then find operators for achieving each of the subgoals. To achieve the first subgoal, (BEL H (USE INDERAL PROPHYLACTIC-MIGRAINE-TREATMENT)), the planner uses Op6 which encodes the simple strategy: to make the hearer believe any proposition ?p, simply inform her of ?p. Speech acts, e.g., INFORM and RECOMMEND, are the primitives of our text planning system. When a subgoal has been refined to a speech act, the system constructs a *functional description (FD)* for the speech act. When text planning is complete, these FDs are passed to the FUF sentence generator [13] which produces the actual English text.

In the process of building an FD, new text planning goals may be posted as side effects. This occurs because it is only when building FDs that the planner considers how concepts will be realized in text. To provide informative and understandable explanations, the system uses the plan modification heuristic: "Post optional subgoals to explain unfamiliar terms introduced in explanation". During the process of building FDs, this heuristic causes the system to check its user model to see if each term that will be mentioned in the text is known to the user. In transforming (INFORM H (USE INDERAL PROPHYLACTIC-MIGRAINE-TREATMENT)), the interface notes that the user does not already know the concept PROPHYLACTIC-MIGRAINE-TREATMENT, therefore it posts a subgoal to describe this term, as shown in the system's utterance in turn 2 of the sample dialogue.

The rest of the explanation in turn 2 results from expanding the remaining satellite subgoals in a similar manner. The user then asks the system to describe Elavil (turn 3). Op1 is again chosen, however, this time the planner finds two applicable operators for achieving the subgoal (INFORM H (USE ELAVIL PROPHYLACTIC-MIGRAINE-TREATMENT)), namely Op3 and Op6. Note that the constraint of Op3 (IN-DH (BEL H (?r ?x ?arg2))) (where ?r is bound to USE and ?arg2 to PROPHYLACTIC-MIGRAINE-TREATMENT) is satisfied by binding ?x to INDERAL because the system achieved the goal (BEL H (USE INDERAL PROPHYLACTIC-MIGRAINE-TREATMENT))) in its previous explanation. The system can determine this efficiently using the indices described in the previous section.

The system has a selection heuristic that guides it to prefer operators that refer to previous explanations, and thus Op3 is chosen to achieve the current goal. Refining this operator leads the system to generate the text "Like Inderal, Elavil is used for ...". Another context-sensitive operator applies when the system expands the subgoal (BEL H (OTHER-USE ELAVIL DEPRESSION)), and leads to the text "Elavil is better than Inderal ...". In addition, note that the system did not explain the term PROPHYLACTIC-MIGRAINE-TREATMENT when describing Elavil. This is because when the system attempts to determine whether this term is known to the user, it finds that the term was explained in the previous text (i.e., the goal (KNOW-ABOUT H PROPHYLACTIC-MIGRAINE-TREATMENT) appears in a previous text plan), and therefore it does not re-explain this term.

Thus we see that, by checking for the existence of certain communicative goals in the discourse history, context-sensitive plan operators, plan selection heuristics, and plan modification rules enable the system to generate context-sensitive responses.

6. Related Work

Computational linguists have investigated how the context provided by the previous discourse should affect the generation of referring expressions, including pronominalization decisions (e.g., [14, 15]). Others have studied how a more extensive discourse history could affect other aspects of the response. Swartout's XPLAIN system can suggest simple analogies with previous explanations and omit portions of a causal chain that have been presented in an earlier explanation. However, this is the only type of contextual effect implemented in XPLAIN, and it was done so using an ad hoc technique to provide this one effect. We are attempting to provide a more general approach.

McKeown carried out a preliminary analysis of how previous discourse might affect a system's response to users' requests to describe an object or compare two objects [16]. She found that by simply maintaining a list of the questions that had been asked, it was possible to avoid certain types of repetition. She further found that if the system were to keep track of the exact information that was provided previously, it could create a text that contrasts or parallels an earlier one. While McKeown's analysis was fairly detailed, no discourse history was maintained in the implementation, and none of the suggestions for how responses could be altered, if such a history existed, were actually implemented or tested. We are devising a way for explanation strategies to make use of the information stored in a discourse history, and are implementing these strategies.

Finally, our work bears some resemblance to work in *plan adaptation* [17]. Systems using plan adaptation often use CBR techniques to index a library of previously synthesized plans. However, plan adaptation is concerned with indexing plans so that they can be retrieved and reused, perhaps with modification, in later situations. Our emphasis is not on reusing plans, but rather on exploiting prior plans as one of many knowledge sources affecting explanation generation.

References

1. J. A. Rosenblum and J. D. Moore. A field guide to contextual effects in instructional dialogues. Technical report, University of Pittsburgh, Computer Science Department, forthcoming.
2. J. D. Moore and C. L. Paris. Planning text for advisory dialogues. In *Proc. of the 27th Annual Meeting of the ACL*, pp. 203–211, 1989.
3. J. D. Moore. *A Reactive Approach to Explanation in Expert and Advice-Giving Systems*. PhD thesis, University of California, Los Angeles, 1989.
4. B. G. Buchanan, J.D. Moore, D. E. Forsythe, G. E. Banks, and S. Ohlsson. Involving patients in health care: Using medical informatics for explanation in the clinical setting. In *Proc. of the Symposium on Computer Applications in Medical Care*, pp. 510–514. McGraw-Hill Inc., 1992.
5. G. Carenini and J. D. Moore. Generating explanations in context. *Proceedings of the International Workshop on Intelligent User Interfaces*, pp. 175–182, 1993. ACM Press.
6. A. Lesgold, S. Lajoie, M. Bunzo, and G. Eggan. Sherlock: A coached practice environment for an electronics troubleshooting job. In *Computer Assisted Instruction and Intelligent Tutoring Systems: Shared Goals and Complementary Approaches*, pp. 201–238. LEA Hillsdale, New Jersey, 1992.
7. J. D. Moore and W. R. Swartout. Pointing: A way toward explanation dialogue. In *Proc. of AAAI-90*, pp. 457–464, 1990.
8. B. J. Grosz and C. L. Sidner. Attention, intention, and the structure of discourse. *Computational Linguistics*, 12(3):175–204, 1986.
9. R. MacGregor and M. H. Burstein. Using a description classifier to enhance knowledge representation. *IEEE Expert*, 6(3):41–4, 1991.
10. K. D. Ashley. *Modeling Legal Argument: Reasoning with Cases and Hypotheticals*. MIT Press, Cambridge, MA, 1990.
11. R. Pokorny and S. Gott. The evaluation of a real-world instructional system: Using technical experts as raters. Technical report, Armstrong Laboratories, Brooks Air Force Base, 1990.
12. W. C. Mann and S. A. Thompson. Rhetorical Structure Theory: Towards a functional theory of text organization. *TEXT*, 8(3):243–281, 1988.
13. M. Elhadad. FUF: the universal unifier user manual version 5.0, October 1991.
14. R. Granville. Controlling lexical substitution in computer text generation. In *Proc. of COLING*, pp. 381–384, 1984.
15. R. Dale. Cooking up referring expressions. In *Proc. of the 27th Annual Meeting of the ACL*, pp. 68–75, 1989.
16. K. R. McKeown. *Text Generation: Using Discourse Strategies and Focus Constraints to Generate Natural Language Text*. Cambridge University Press, Cambridge, England, 1985.
17. R. Alterman. Adaptive planning. In Stuart Shapiro, editor, *The Encyclopedia of Artificial Intelligence*, pp. 5–15. Wiley, New York, 1992.

Generic Plan Recognition for Dialogue Systems

George Ferguson, James F. Allen

University of Rochester
Rochester, NY, 14627-0226

ABSTRACT

We describe a general framework for encoding rich domain models and sophisticated plan reasoning capabilities. The approach uses graph-based reasoning to address a wide range of tasks that typically arise in dialogue systems. The graphical plan representation is independent of but connected to the underlying representation of action and time. We describe types of plan recognition that are needed, illustrating these with examples from dialogues collected as part of the TRAINS project. The algorithms for the tasks are presented, and issues in the formalization of the reasoning processes are discussed.

1. Introduction

Plan recognition is an essential part of any dialogue system. Traditional approaches to plan recognition are inadequate in one of two ways. Those that are formally well-specified tend to be highly restricted in the phenomena they can accomodate and are therefore unsuitable for a general purpose dialogue system. On the other hand, the heuristically-motivated systems have been difficult to formalize and hence to understand. In both cases, the representation of plans is insufficient for a collaborative dialogue-based system.

The research reported here is part of the TRAINS project [1]. The goal of this project is an intelligent planning assistant that is conversationally proficient in natural language. In this paper we concentrate on the plan recognition procedures of the domain plan reasoner component of the system.

As examples of the phenomena that arise in discourse and affect plan recognition, consider the following utterances gathered from TRAINS dialogues:

1. Utterances that suggest courses of action, *e.g.*,
   (a) Send engine E3 to Dansville.
   (b) Move the oranges to Avon and unload them.

   This is the prototypical case studied in the literature, and most systems are limited to handling only this case.

2. Utterances that identify relevant objects to use, *e.g.*,
   (a) Let's use engine E3.
   (b) There's an OJ factory at Dansville.

   The second sentence is an example of an indirect suggestion to use the OJ factory.

3. Utterances that identify relevant constraints, *e.g.*,
   (a) We must get the oranges there by 3 PM.
   (b) Engine E2 cannot pull more than 3 carloads at a time.

4. Utterances that identify relevant lines of inference, *e.g.*,
   (a) The car will be there because is it attached to engine E1.

5. Utterances that identify goals of the plan, *e.g.*,
   (a) We have to make OJ.

6. Utterances that introduce complex relations, *e.g.*, purpose clauses such as
   (a) Use E3 to pick up the car.
   (b) Send engine E3 to Dansville to pick up the oranges.

Our approach to plan reasoning is motivated by examples such as these. It is a *generic* approach because the details of the algorithms do not depend directly on properties of the underlying knowledge representation. Rather, the approach assumes that certain operations are exported by the underlying reasoner (such as entailment, $\models$), and it uses these to validate plan reasoning steps.

We first describe our representation of plans and its connection to the underlying knowledge representation scheme. We then present plan recognition algorithms for the dialogue phenomena and we discuss how they interact with other modules of the system. Finally, we discuss related and future work.

2. Plan Graphs

We assume that the underlying knowledge representation formalism can be effectively partitioned into two types of formulas:

- *Event formulas* state that something happened that (possibly) resulted in a change in the world.
- *Fact formulas* are everything else, but typically describe properties of the world (possibly temporally qualified).

In our temporal logic,[1] the former are of the form *Occurs*(e) and the latter are, for example, *At*(*eng*3, *dansville*, *now*). For formalisms where there are no explicit events (*e.g.*, the situation calculus), we can extend the language—an example of this is given below.

We then define a graphical notion of plans, based on viewing them as *arguments* that a certain course of events under certain explicit conditions will achieve certain explicit goals. A *plan graph* is a graph over two types of nodes: *event nodes* are labelled with event formulas, *fact nodes* are labeled with fact formulas. These can be connected by four types of arcs:

event-fact: Achievement

fact-event: Enablement

event-event: Generation

fact-fact: Inferential

The link types correspond roughly to an intuitive classification of the possible relations between events and facts (*c.f.*, [5]). The *goal nodes* of a plan graph are its sinks, the *premise nodes* are its sources.

For example, using the temporal logic, we might have a plan graph like that shown in Figure 1(a). The functions *blk*1 and *blk*2 are *role functions* that denote objects participating in the event; the functions *pre*1 and *eff*1 are *temporal* role functions denoting intervals related to the time of the event. In a formalism such as the situation calculus, actions are terms and there is no equivalent of the *Occurs* predicate. However, we can introduce one as a placeholder, and then we might get a plan graph like that shown in Figure 1(b).

A plan graph makes no claim to either correctness or completeness. It represents an argument from its premises to its goals, and as such can be "correct," "incorrect," or neither. The previous examples are intuitively correct, for example, but are incomplete since they don't specify that the block being stacked must also be clear for the stacking to be successful.

A translation of plan graphs into a first-order logic with quotation is straightforward. With this, one can declaratively define properties of plans represented by plan graphs (such as "correct") relative to the underlying representation's entailment relation. For example, a node n in a plan graph P might be *supported* if its preconditions (nodes with arcs incident on n) are sufficient to ensure the truth of n, formally:

$$\mathit{supported}(n, P) \equiv$$
$$\bigwedge \{\pi \mid \exists n'.\langle n', n\rangle \in P \wedge \pi = \mathit{Label}(n')\} \models \mathit{Label}(n)$$

[1] Space precludes a detailed description of this representation, see [2, 3, 4]. In what follows, we will rely on intuitive descriptions of the relevant aspects of the logic.

The antecent of the entailment must, of course, also be consistent.

Unfortunately, such an analysis is not particularly illuminating in the case of plans arising from dialogue since such plans are often too poorly specified to meet such criteria. In particular, they are often based on assumptions that the system makes in the course of its interpretation of the manager's statements. We feel that making such assumptions explicit is crucial since they often drive the discourse. To illustrate this, we will present the algorithms used by the TRAINS plan reasoner to reason with plan graphs. We will return to the issue of axiomatizing them in the final section.

3. Plan Graph Algorithms

We characterize plan reasoning for dialogue systems as search through a space of plan graphs. The termination criterion for the search depends on the type of recognition being done, as will be described presently. Since the plan graph formalism sanctions arbitrarily complex graphs labelled with arbitrarily complex formulas, searching all possible plan graphs is impossible. We therefore rely on additional properties of the underlying representation to restrict the search.

First, we assume the ability to test whether two objects (including events and facts) unify and, optionally, to determine assumptions under which they would unify. Simple objects use simple equality. In the temporal logic, two events are equal if their roles are equal. Two facts unify if there are assumptions that make them logically equivalent. This use of equality and inequality corresponds to the posting of *codesignation* constraints in traditional planners.

Second, we assume that events be defined using relations corresponding to *enablers*, *effects*, and *generators*. This should not be controversial. In the temporal logic, these descriptions can be obtained from the event definition axioms. For a STRIPS system, they correspond to the add- and delete-lists. Existing plan recognition systems use an event taxonomy, which corresponds to the generators slot. There can be multiple definitions of an event type, thereby allowing alternative decompositions or conditional effects.

The search then only considers plan graphs that reflect the structure of the event definitions, we call such plan graphs *acceptable*. In this respect, the search will only find plan graphs that agree with the assumed-shared "event library." However, information returned from failed searches can be used to guide the repair of apparent incompatibilities at the discourse level.

3.1. Incorporation

Plan recognition using plan graphs operates by searching the space of acceptable plan graphs breadth-first. The search

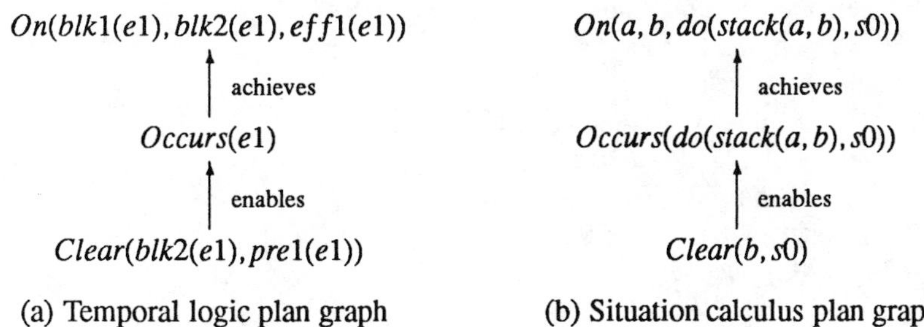

(a) Temporal logic plan graph

(b) Situation calculus plan graph

Figure 1: Simple example plan graphs

frontier is expanded by the function `expand-graph`, shown in Figure 2. The use of breadth-first search implements a "shortest-path" heuristic—we prefer the simplest connection to the existing plan. The plan reasoner exports several interfaces to the basic search routine, each motivated by the discourse phenomena noted at the outset. The discourse module of the system invokes these procedures to perform domain reasoning.

The procedure `incorp-event` takes as parameters a plan graph and an event (a term or a lambda expression representing an event type). For example, sentence (1a) results in the following call:

```
(incorp-event
  (lambda ?e*Move-Engine
        (And (Eq (eng ?e) ENG3)
             (Eq (dst ?e) DANSVILLE)))
  THE-PLAN)
```

where `?e*Move-Engine` is an event variable of type `Move-Engine`.

The plan reasoner first checks if the given event unifies with an event already in the plan. If so, the plan reasoner signals that nothing needed to be added to the plan (except possibly unifying assumptions, which are also indicated). Otherwise, it attempts to add an event node to the plan graph labelled with (an instance of) the event. The search continues until one or more unifying event nodes are found.[2] An example of the search in progress for the previous call is given in Figure 3, assuming that the plan already includes moving some oranges to Dansville (event `e1`). At this point (two levels of search), the given `Move-Engine` event unfies uniquely with a leaf node, so the search terminates successfully. The connecting path (double arrows) indicates that moving the engine is done to move a car that will contain the oranges, thus moving them. Note that we do not know yet which car this will be.

[2]In fact, we also use a depth bound, based on the intuition that if the connection is not relatively short, the user's utterance has probably been misinterpreted.

If more than one match is found at the same depth, the plan reasoner signals the ambiguity to the discourse module for resolution. Otherwise the connecting path is returned as a list of things that need to be added to the plan to incorporate the given event. These are usually interpreted by the discourse module as being implicatures of the user's utterance. They are added to a plan context and are used both for subsequent planning and plan recognition steps and to generate utterances when the system gets the turn.

The procedure `incorp-role-filler` is used for statements that mention objects to be used in the plan (example (2) previously). In this case, the termination criterion for the search is an event node labelled by an event that has a role that unifies with the given object (a term or lambda expression). For example, the sample sentences result in the following calls:

```
(2a) (incorp-role-filler ENG3 THE-PLAN)
(2b) (incorp-role-filler
       (lambda ?x*OJ-Factory (At ?x DANSVILLE NOW))
       THE-PLAN)
```

Finally, there is the procedure `incorp-fact` that searches for a fact node that would unify with the given one. This is used for utterances like the examples (3) and (4), since the plan graph representation supports inferential (fact-fact) links. Again however, the search space of potential unifying formulas is infinite. We therefore only consider certain candidates, based on syntactic considerations. These include facts that the underlying reasoning system is particularly good at, such as temporal constraints or location reasoning. Continued use of the system will identify which inferences need to be made at this level, and which are best left to management by higher-level discourse manager routines.

3.2. Goals

These `incorp-` routines all take an existing plan graph as argument and expand it. This could come from an initial specification, but utterances like example (5) require that the plan reasoner be able to incorporate goals. There is therefore an `incorp-goal` procedure that takes a sentence and a (possibly

```
function expand-graph (g p)
  foreach n ∈ leaf nodes of g
    if n is an event node
    then e ← Label(n)
         foreach f ∈ Enablers(Type(e))
           add (plan-enabler f_e e p) to g
         foreach e' ∈ Generators(Type(e))
           add (plan-generates e' e p) to g
    else f ← Label(n)
         foreach event type T
           foreach f' ∈ Effects(T) s.t. Unify(f,f',φ)
             add (plan-enables (lambda T φ) f p) to g
```

Figure 2: Function expand-graph (subscript *e* indicates substitution)

empty) plan graph as arguments. If the sentence is *Occurs*(*e*), then the plan graph is searched for a matching event node. If one is found, then the plan reasoner returns relevant assumptions and marks the node as a goal. Otherwise, a new event node is added to the plan and marked as a goal. Similar processing is done for fact goals. In our dialogues, the user often begins by communicating a goal that the rest of the dialogue is concerned with achieving. There is no point in doing much work for goals (beyond checking consistency) since it is likely to be immediately elaborated upon in subsequent utterances. Proper treatment of subgoals expressed as goals is part of our current work on subplans.

3.3. Purpose clauses

One construction that uses subgoals and subplans and that arises repeatedly in collaborative dialogue is the use of purpose clauses, such as example sentences (6). To accomodate these, the incorp- functions all accept an optional "purpose" argument (an event). For example, the sample sentences result in the following calls:

```
(6a) (incorp-role-filler ENG3 THE-PLAN
       :purpose (lambda ?e*Move-Car
                  (Eq (car ?e) THE-CAR)))
(6b) (incorp-event
       (lambda ?el*Move-Engine
         (And (Eq (eng ?el) ENG3)
              (Eq (dst ?el) DANSVILLE)))
       THE-PLAN
       :purpose (lambda ?e2*Load
                  (Eq (obj ?e2) THE-ORANGES)))
```

If the purpose argument is present, it is first incorporated using incorp-event. If this fails, then the discourse module is notified—presumably this is some kind of presupposition failure requiring discourse-level action. If it succeeds, then the original item is incorporated but with the search *restricted* to the (sub-)plan graph rooted at the purpose event.

This simple modification of the basic plan recognition algorithms is effective at reducing the ambiguity that would otherwise be detected if the entire plan graph were searched. It is likely not adequate for all types of purpose or rationale clause, in particular those that involve the mental state of the agent rather than domain events. However, the generality of the plan graph formalism does allow it to handle many of the cases arising in our dialogues.

4. Example

To further illustrate our approach to plan reasoning, we present a sample TRAINS dialogue and describe how it is processed by the system. This dialogue was gathered from simulations where a person played the role of the system. A previous version of the TRAINS system processed the dialogue correctly—the current implementation will also once it is completed.

The manager starts by communicating her goals, making several statements, and asking a question. The system replies and makes a proposal, which is then accepted by the manager. The complete transcript is as follows:

1. M: We have to make OJ.
2. M: There are oranges at Avon and an OJ factory at Bath.
3. M: Engine E3 is scheduled to arrive at Avon at 3pm.
4. M: Shall we ship the oranges?
5. S: Ok.
6. S: Shall I start loading the oranges into the empty car at Avon?
7. S: Ok.

The manager's first utterance results in the following call to the plan reasoner:

```
(incorp-goal (lambda ?e*Make-OJ
               (Eq (agent ?e) SYSHUM))
             THE-PLAN)
```

As described above, this results in an event node begin added to the (formerly empty) plan.

Utterance (2) could be interpreted simply as statements about the world. However, since the system already knows these

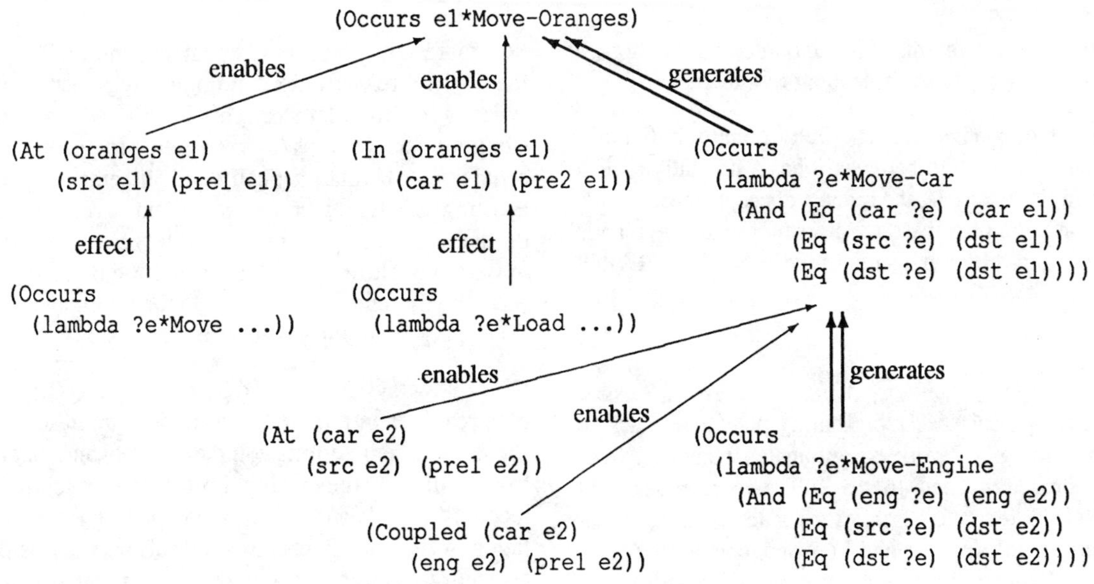

Figure 3: Incorporating moving the engine

facts (and assumes the manager knows it knows, *etc.*), the utterance is interpreted as suggesting use of the objects, resulting in the following calls:

```
(incorp-role-filler o1 THE-PLAN)
(incorp-role-filler f1 THE-PLAN)
```

The constants o1 and f1 are determined by the scope and reference module.

For the first call, the Make-OJ event has a role for some oranges, but there is a constraint that they must be at the location of the factory. While the system does not yet know which factory this will be, it can deduce that Avon cannot be that city since there is no factory there. Since the system knows only that the oranges are at Avon now (by assumption), they cannot be used directly for the Make-OJ. The plan reasoner therefore searches the space of acceptable plan graphs breadth-first, as described above. A connection is found by assuming that the oranges will be moved from Avon to the factory (wherever it turns out to be) via a Move-Oranges event. A description of this path (with assumptions) is returned to the discourse module. For the second call, the factory is acceptable as a role of the Make-OJ event, so only the required equality assumption is returned. This has the additional effect of determining to where the oranges are shipped (Bath).

Utterance (3) is also non-trivial to connect to the plan. We presume that the system already knows of E3's imminent arrival in the form of a sentence like (Occurs e0*Arrive). Again therefore, the statement is therefore taken to suggest the use of E3 in the plan. The system can reason about the effects of the Arrive event, in this case that E3 will be at Avon at 3pm. Even so, there is no event with a role for an engine in the plan yet, so the space of acceptable plans is again searched breadth-first. In this case, a connection is possible by postulating a MoveCar event that generates the previously-added Move-Oranges event, and a Move-Engine event that generates the Move-Car.

The manager then makes the query (4), thereby relinquishing the turn. The dialogue module evaluates the query by calling the plan reasoner with:

```
(incorp-event (lambda ?e*Move-Oranges
                (Eq? (oranges ?e) o1)) THE-PLAN)
```

The plan reasoner finds the Move-Oranges event added a result of utterance (2), and indicates this to the discourse module. The system therefore replies with utterance (5), implicitly accepting the rest of the plan as well.

The plan reasoner is then called to elaborate the plan, during which it performs fairly traditional means-ends planning to attempt to flesh out the plan. In so doing, it attempts to satisfy or assume preconditions and bind roles to objects in order to generate a supported plan. It freely makes consistent persistence assumptions by assuming inclusion of one unconstrained temporal interval within another known one. It can ignore some details of the plan, for example the exact route an engine should take. These can be reasoned about if necessary (*i.e.*, if the human mentions them) but can be left up to the agents otherwise.

In the example scenario, many things can be determined unambiguously. For example, the oranges should be unloaded at Bath at the appropriate time, leading to an event of type Unload. The choice of car for transporting the oranges, however, is ambiguous: in the scenario, there is an empty car at Avon as well as one attached to E3. The plan reasoner signals the ambiguity to the discourse module, which chooses one alternative and proposes it, leading to utterance (6).

At this point the manager regains the turn and the dialogue continues until the system believes it has a mutually agreed upon plan. In this example, the manager accepts the system's suggestion, and the plan reasoner determines that the plan is ready for execution by the agents in the simulated TRAINS world.

5. Discussion

Graph-based approaches to representing plans date back to the very beginnings of work on automated planning, from Sacerdoti's procedural nets [6] to SIPE's representation of plans [7]. Often these representations reflected a combination of temporal information and knowledge about the plan. In our view, the temporal reasoning is provided by the underlying knowledge representation and the plan graph represents an *argument* that a certain course of action under conditions will achieve certain explicit goals. The earlier systems' inability to separate the plan representations from their use as data structures in planners made it difficult to predict and explain their behaviour. The plan graph formalism achieves such a separation, but the price we pay is the inability to use directly the efficient algorithms developed previously. Some of the results from the planning community on efficient algorithms can be adapted to the temporally explicit logic of events (*c.f.*, [2]). We are developing a theory of plan graphs that will provide a formal basis for many of the heuristic procedures developed previously.

With respect to plan recognition, Kautz's work [8, 9] provides a formal basis for plan recognition but only dealt with observed events fitting into a hierarchy of event types. Pollack [10] uses a formalism similar to our underlying temporal logic, but includes representations of belief and intention that are not the focus of this paper. We believe that there is a structure to plans independent of the intentions of agents, and that plan graphs seen as arguments provide the proper perspective for reasoning about them at that level.

Carberry [11] describes a model for incremental plan inference in task-related information-seeking dialogues. It uses a "context model" consisting of a tree of goals, with associated plans. Since we see the overall structure of a plan as an argument, there is no such separation in our approach, although we do treat goals specially as described previously. Her "current focused" goal and plan are analogous to our `:purpose` mechanism and to the techniques used by the language and discourse modules for determining focus. The system also uses breadth-first search with "focusing heuristics," several of which correspond to our heuristics described previously. However, the approach lacks a formal description that we believe can be provided by the plan graph formalism.

Several recent approaches to plan recognition [12, 13] rely on the use of a powerful terminological reasoner to place event types in a virtual lattice. This has the advantage that subsumption relationships (corresponding to our unification procedure) can be automatically and incrementally computed. Existing terminological reasoners, however, typically either do not allow complex objects (roles) and equality, or draw only the conclusions about subsumption that are deductively (necessarily) entailed. Neither do they compute the assumptions that would unify facts.

No existing system is as ambitious as the TRAINS domain plan reasoner in providing services required to support dialogue, from representing complex, partial and incorrect plans to providing incremental and interleaved planning and plan recognition. We are currently completing a new implementation of the procedures based on this paper. It is part of our current research to apply work on argument systems directly to justifying these plan graph algorithms in terms of a formal theory of plan graphs.

References

1. James F. Allen and Lenhart K. Schubert. The TRAINS project. TRAINS Technical Note 91-1, Dept. of Computer Science, University of Rochester, Rochester, NY, 1991.
2. James F. Allen. Temporal reasoning and planning. In *Reasoning about Plans*, pages 1–68. Morgan Kaufmann, 1991.
3. George Ferguson. Explicit representation of events, actions, and plans for assumption-based plan reasoning. Technical Report 428, Dept. of Computer Science, University of Rochester, Rochester, NY, June 1992.
4. James F. Allen and George Ferguson. Action in interval temporal logic. In *Proceedings of the Second Symposium on Logical Formalizations of Commonsense Reasoning*, pages 12–22, Austin, TX, 11–13 January 1993.
5. A.I. Goldman. *A Theory of Human Action*. Prentice-Hall, 1970.
6. E.D. Sacerdoti. *A Structure for Plans and Behaviour*. Elsevier, North-Holland, 1977.
7. D.E. Wilkins. *Practical Planning: Extending the Classical AI Planning Paradigm*. Morgan Kaufmann, 1988.
8. Henry A. Kautz. *A Formal Theory of Plan Recognition*. PhD thesis, Dept. of Computer Science, University of Rochester, Rochester, NY, May 1987. Available as TR 215.
9. Henry A. Kautz. A formal theory of plan recognition and its implementation. In *Reasoning about Plans*, pages 69–126. Morgan Kaufmann, 1991.
10. Martha E. Pollack. Plans as complex mental attitudes. In P.R. Cohen, J. Morgan, and M.E. Pollack, editors, *Intentions in Communication*. MIT Press, 1990.
11. Sandra Carberry. *Plan Recgnition in Natural Language*. MIT Press, 1990.
12. Barbara Di Eugenio and Bonnie Webber. Plan recognition in understanding instructions. In *Proceedings of the First Intl. Conf. on AI Planning Systems*, pages 52–61, 15–17 June 1992.
13. Robert Weida and Diane Litman. Terminological reasoning with constraint networks and an application to plan recognition. In *Proceedings of KR92*, pages 282–293, Boston, MA, 25–29 October 1992.

Efficient Collaborative Discourse: A Theory and Its Implementation

Alan W. Biermann, Curry I. Guinn, D. Richard Hipp, Ronnie W. Smith

Computer Science Department
Duke University
Durham, NC 27706

ABSTRACT

An architecture for voice dialogue machines is described with emphasis on the problem solving and high level decision making mechanisms. The architecture provides facilities for generating voice interactions aimed at cooperative human-machine problem solving. It assumes that the dialogue will consist of a series of local self-consistent subdialogues each aimed at subgoals related to the overall task. The discourse may consist of a set of such subdialogues with jumps from one subdialogue to the other in a search for a successful conclusion. The architecture maintains a user model to assure that interactions properly account for the level of competence of the user, and it includes an ability for the machine to take the initiative or yield the initiative to the user. It uses expectation from the dialogue processor to aid in the correction of errors from the speech recognizer.

1. Supporting the Voice Technologies

Dialogue theory is the implementing science for the voice technologies. The many successes in voice recognition and generation will have value only to the extent that they become incorporated into practical systems that deliver service to users. This paper reports on a dialogue system design that attempts to implement a variety of behaviors that we believe to be necessary for efficient human-machine interaction. These behaviors include:

1. Collaborative problem-solving: The system must have the ability for the machine to problem-solve and collaborate with the human user in the process. Specifically, the machine must be able to formulate queries to the user and process responses that will enable progress toward the goal.
2. Subdialogue processing: It must be able to participate in locally coherent subdialogues to solve subgoals and to jump in possibly unpredictable ways from subdialogue to subdialogue in an aggressive search for the most effective path to success. Such jumps may emanate from the system's own processing strategy or they may be initiated by the user and tracked through plan recognition by the system.
3. User modeling: It needs to maintain a user model that enables it to formulate queries appropriate to the user and that will inhibit outputs that will not be helpful.
4. Variable initiative: The machine must be able to take the initiative and lead the interaction at places where it has information implying that it can do this effectively. It also needs to be able to yield the initiative completely or in part at times when data is available indicating that it should do so. It needs to be able to negotiate with the user to either take or release the initiative when appropriate.
5. The use of expectation: It needs to be able to use the expectation implicit in the dialogue to support the voice recognition stage in error correction.

2. A Dialogue System Architecture

Despite the variety of the target behaviors and their seeming structural disjointness, an architecture has been found that supports them all in a relatively uniform and natural way [1, 2, 3, 4]. The design is based on the model of a Prolog processor but includes a variety of special capabilities to address the needs of this application. This section will describe the fundamental theory of the system and the next section will describe its performance in a series of tests with human subjects.

The basic operation of the architecture is illustrated in Figure 1 where problem-solving is to achieve top level goal G. Prolog-style theorem proving proceeds in the usual way and if G can be proven from available information there will be no interaction with the user. However, if information is not sufficient to allow completion of the proof, the system can attempt to provide "missing axioms" through interaction with the user. In the figure, this process is illustrated in the subtree C where P has been proven from an existing assertion but Q is not known. Then the system may be able to resort to a voice interaction with the user to discover Q. Thus the architecture organizes interactions with the user to directly support the theorem proving process. This organization gives the dialogue the task-oriented coherent ([5]) organization that is needed for effective cooperative problem-solving. It provides the **intentional structure** described by Grosz and Sidner[6].

The example continues with the illustrated rule

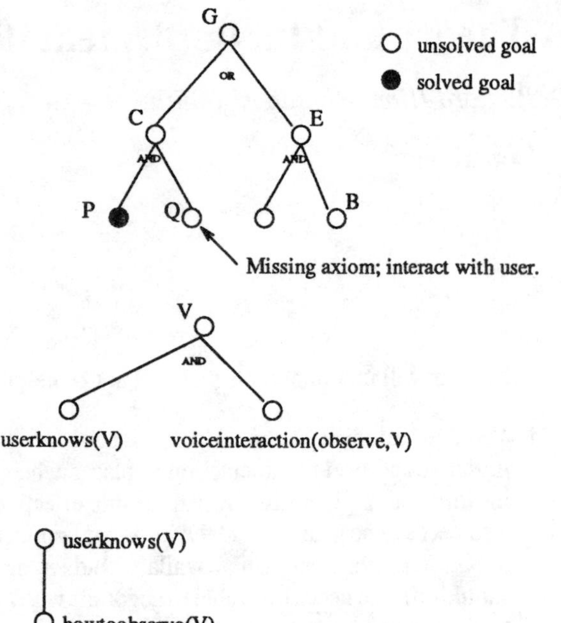

Figure 1: The theorem proving tree associated with a voice dialogue.

V :- userknows(V), voiceinteraction(observe,V)

which is also shown in Figure 1. Specifically, it asserts that if, according to the user model[7, 8, 9, 10], the user knows V, then a voice interaction could be initiated to try to obtain that information. Our approach effectively enables V to unify with any goal to enable the interaction. This could yield an exchange between computer and user of the type

C: Is the switch on?
U: Yes.

But the situation might not be as simple as a single question and answer. It may be that the user does not know how to observe Q but could be told. This is illustrated by the rules

userknows(V) :- howtoobserve(V)
howtoobserve(V) :- . . .

which could lead to a lengthy interaction involving locating other objects, carrying out actions, and making other observations. Thus a series of voice interactions could ensue with the goal of eventually observing Q. The set of all interactions aimed at the completion of a given goal is defined by this project to be a **subdialogue**. Notice that the subdialogue accounts at every step for the user's knowledge through invocation of the user modeling assertions. The dialogue asks only questions that the user model indicates are appropriate and explains concepts either extensively, briefly, or not at all depending on the assertions contained in the model. Subdialogues by one name or another have been studied by a variety of authors [11, 12, 13, 14].

The system allows for the possibility of unpredictable jumps from one subdialogue to another. In the above example, the user might be locally uncooperative and respond as follows:

C: Is the switch up?
U: B is true.

Here we assume that B is an assertion related to another subgoal on the theorem proving tree as shown in Figure 1. The user may initiate such a change in subdialogue in an attempt to pursue another path to the global goal. Here the machine first must track the user's intention (in a process called "plan recognition" [15, 16, 17, 18, 19]) and then evaluate whether to follow the move or not. This decision is based upon the current level of the initiative of the system as described below. If the system follows the user's initiative, it will apply its internal theorem proving system to the subgoal E and pursue voice interactions related to it. If it rejects the user's indicated path, it will simply store the received fact and reaffirm its own path:

C: Is the switch up?

The system may also abandon a subdialogue for reasons of its own. For example, processing during the dialogue could yield the unexpected result that the current path is no longer likely to yield an efficient path to the global goal. Then the system could abruptly drop a line of interactions and jump to a new subgoal which is momentarily evaluated as more attractive.

Efficient dialogue often requires regular changes of initiative depending on which participant currently has the key information[20, 21, 22, 23]. When a subject is opened where one participant is knowledgeable and the other is not, that participant should lead the interaction to its completion and the other should be supportive and respond cooperatively. Our project implements four levels of initiative, directive, suggestive, declarative, and passive. These levels result in, respectively, uncompromising control on the part of the machine, control but only at a weaker level, the yielding of control to the user but with a willingness to make assertions about the problem-solving process, and quiet acceptance of the user's initiative. The level of initiative sets the strength at which the machine will prefer its own best evaluated solution path when it selects the subdialogue to be followed. The initiative level also adjusts the assertiveness of the spoken outputs and may affect the way inputs are processed. (See [1]).

Expectation at each point in a dialogue is derived from the proof tree and other dialogue information in a manner similar to that explained by Young[24]. Concepts that would be appropriate in the context of the current local interaction are "unparsed" into expected syntactic inputs and voice recognition is biased to receive one of these expected inputs. If the recognition phase fails to achieve a good match with a local expectation, comparisons are made to nonlocal expectations at increasing distances from the local context until an acceptable match is found or an error message is reported. Recognition of a nonlocal expectation amounts to the discovery that the user is following a different path; this is a process called "plan recognition" in the literature. If the system is following the user initiative at this point, it may shift its theorem proving efforts to that subtree and cooperate with the user.

3. The Implementation

The major system developed by this project is known as "The Circuit Fix-It Shoppe" [1, 25]. It is implemented with a domain modeller to guide the process of debugging an electric circuit and to present appropriate subgoals for possible examination. A complex dialogue controller overviews the processing of decisions related to which subgoal to select and level of initiative issues.

The coding has been done primarily in Quintus Prolog on a Sun 4 workstation. The parser is coded in C and uses a nearest neighbor algorithm to find the best match between the error prone recognition system output and the set of expected inputs. The speech recognizer is a Verbex 6000 user-dependent connected speech recognizer running on an IBM PC, and the vocabulary is currently 125 words. Users are required to begin each utterance with the word "verbie" and end with the word "over."

The implemented domain processor is loaded with a model of a particular experimental circuit that was constructed on a Radio Shack 160-in-One Electronic Project Kit. The model is complete enough to do any problem of the circuit that involves missing wires. For example, if the system is asked to debug the circuit with no wires at all, it will systematically discover every missing wire and ask the user to install it.

Speech output is done by a DECtalk DTC01 text-to-speech converter.

4. Experimental Results

The system was tested with human subjects solving missing wire problems. Subjects were trained to use the system and given some guidance on acceptable sentence syntax. They were required to register their pronunciation of all of the vocabulary words and they spoke 239 sentences to train the recognizer on coarticulation. They were provided with a list of vocabulary words and charts on a poster board suggesting implemented syntax. They were told not to address the experimenter during the test but the experimenter had a set of eleven standard messages that he or she would give to the subject under certain specified conditions. These included such things as "The system is ready for your next utterance" or "Please restrict your utterances to one sentence." On two later days, subjects were given up to ten problems per session, one session with the machine at the strongest initiative level and one at a moderately passive level.

A transcript of one such dialogue follows here. This interaction was in moderately passive mode so the system tends to suggest rather than demand action. The user inserted two missing wires during the interaction and made two changes in subdialogue (marked as **) that were each correctly tracked by the system. The total time of the interaction was 160 seconds.

C: This is the circuit fix it shop. How may I help you?
U: RS111 is not working.
C: I am familiar with that circuit.
C: The LED is supposed to be displaying alternately flashing one and seven.
U: The LED is off.
C: The power is on when the switch is up.
U: The switch is up.
C: The switch is connecting to the battery when there is a wire between connector one one one and connector one two zero.
U: LED is displaying one and seven. **
C: Is the one on the LED flashing?
U: No.
C: Is the seven on the LED flashing?
U: No.
C: There is supposed to be a wire between connector three zero and connector seven zero.
U: RS111 is working. **
C: Glad to have been of assistance. Good-bye.

Eight subjects attempted 141 dialogues, 75 with the machine in mildly passive mode and 66 with it in directive mode. The average problem completion time in the two modes was 270.6 seconds and 511.3 seconds respectively. The longer sessions in the directive mode were because the system required the user to pedantically go through every step of a debugging procedure while in the more passive mode, the user could often jump to the correct subgoal and solve it quite quickly. The average number of utterances spoken per dialogue was 10.7 and 27.6, respectively. The experimenter needed to give error messages to the subject about one every six sentences with the machine in passive mode and one every eighteen sentences in directive mode. This indicates that with the greater freedom allowed by the more passive mode, subjects tended to get into more difficulty using the system. The exact sentence recognition rate by the Verbex machine in the two modes was 44.3 and 53.1 percents, respectively. These were corrected to 75.3 and 85.0 respectively by the expectation-based nearest neighbor error correction system.

5. Current Research

Our newest dialogue algorithm by Guinn[3] features a set of real numbers on the proof tree paths that are continuously updated to reflect estimates of the nearness to a solution. The algorithm follows paths using a best first strategy, and it includes automatic mechanisms to change mode, negotiate initiative, and other efficiency improving behaviors. This algorithm has not been incorporated into the voice interactive system and is instead being tested separately.

This algorithm allows a more complicated interaction to occur involving negotiation if the machine and user differ on who should control the initiative. Suppose the machine adamantly demands its own path (Is the switch up?) and the user is equally as uncompromising and demands information related to the E subgoal as shown in Figure 1. With Guinn's strategy the system negotiates with the user to try to convince the user to follow its path. Specifically, it presents the user with part of the proof tree leading to the goal to show the user how quickly the goal can be achieved. For example, in the case of Figure 1, it might assert

> C: If the switch is up, then since P is true, then C will be true; consequently G will be true.

Alternatively, the user could present his or her own path to the goal in a negotiation and conceivably convince the system to lower its evaluation of its own path.

This newer theory of initiative bases subdialogue decisions on a real number and biases the number with an initiative parameter which can take on any value between 0 and 1. In this system, the level of initiative is defined over a continuous range rather than a discrete set of initiative values.

Tests on the newer dialogue algorithm have been in machine-to-machine problem-solving sessions. The methodology has been to randomly distribute facts about a murder mystery between the two participants and then observe the conversations that lead to a solution of the mystery. The transmitted information between the participants is in the form of Prolog-style predicates since the machines gain nothing through a translation to natural language. Detailed results have been extremely encouraging and will be given later. For example, in one test involving 85 dialogues, the average number of interactions required to solve the problems was 123 without the negotiation feature described above and 103 with it.

6. Comparisons with Other Dialogue Systems

The system that most resembles the one we describe here is the MINDS system of Young *et al.* [26]. Their system maintains and AND-OR tree much like our Prolog tree and engages in dialogue similarly to try to achieve subgoals. It similarly uses expectations generated by subgoals and enhanced by a user model to predict incoming utterances for the purpose of error correction. The resulting system demonstrated dramatic improvements. For example, the effective perplexity in one test was reduced from 242.4 to 18.3 using dialogue level constraints while word recognition accuracy was increased from 82.1 percent to 97.0. We employ Prolog-style rules for the knowledge base and the associated proofs for directing the goal-oriented behavior. This leads to the "missing axiom theory" we describe above and some rather simple methods for handling the user model, multiple subdialogues, variable initiative, negotiation and a variety of other features.

Another dialogue system, by Allen *et al.* ([27]), uses a blackboard architecture to store representations of sentence processing and dialogue structures. Processing is done by a series of subroutines that function at the syntactic, semantic, and dialogue levels. This system models detailed interactions between the sentence and dialogue levels that are beyond anything we attempt but does not support problem-solving, variable initiative and voice interactions as we do.

A third interesting project has produced the TINA system[28]. This system uses probabilistic networks to parse token sequences provided by a speech recognition system, SUMMIT by Zue *et al.* [29]. The networks and their probabilities are created automatically from grammatical rules and text samples input by the designer. Their main utility is to provide expectation for error correction as we do in our system. However, their expectation is primarily syntax-based while ours uses structure from all levels, subdialogue (or focus-based), semantic and syntactic. Their semantics is built directly into the parse trees which is translated into SQL for access to a database. Our system is task-oriented, emphasizes problem-solving, and employs a user model to assure effectiveness of the interaction.

References

1. R.W. Smith, D.R. Hipp and A.W. Biermann. A Dialog Control Algorithm and its Performance. *Proc. of the Third Conf. on Applied Natural Language Processing*, Trento, Italy, 1992.
2. D.R. Hipp. *A New Technique for Parsing Ill-formed Spoken Natural-language Dialog*. Ph.D. thesis. Duke University, Durham, North Carolina. 1992.
3. C.I. Guinn. Ph.D. thesis. Duke University. Durham, North Carolina. To appear. 1993.
4. R.W. Smith. *A Computational Model of Expectation-Driven Mixed-Initiative Dialog Processing*. Ph.D. thesis, Duke University, Durham, North Carolina, 1991.
5. J.R. Hobbs. "Coherence and coreference." *Cognitive Science* 3:67–90, 1979.
6. B.J. Grosz and C.L. Sidner. Attentions, intentions, and the structure of discourse. *Computational Linguistics*, 12(3):175–204, 1986.
7. A. Kobsa and W. Wahlster, editors. *Special Issue on User Modeling*. MIT Press, Cambridge, Mass., September 1988. A special issue of *Computational Linguistics*.
8. R. Cohen and M. Jones. Incorporating user models into expert systems for educational diagnosis. In A. Kobsa and W. Wahlster, editors, *User Models in Dialog Systems*, pages 313–333. Springer-Verlag, New York, 1989.

9. T.W. Finin. GUMS: A general user modeling shell. In A. Kobsa and W. Wahlster, editors, *User Models in Dialog Systems*, pages 411–430. Springer-Verlag, New York, 1989.

10. S. Carberry. Modeling the user's plans and goals. *Computational Linguistics*, 14(3):23–37, 1988.

11. B.J. Grosz. Discourse analysis. In D.E. Walker, editor, *Understanding Spoken Language*, pages 235–268. North-Holland, New York, 1978.

12. C. Linde and J. Goguen. Structure of planning discourse. *J. Social Biol. Struct.* pages 1:219–251, 1978.

13. L. Polanyi and R. Scha. On the recursive structure of discourse. In *Connectedness in Sentence, Discourse and Text*, ed. by K. Ehlich and H. van Riemsdijk. Tilburg University. pages 141-178, 1983.

14. R. Reichman. *Getting Computers to Talk Like You and Me*. MIT Press, Cambridge, Mass., 1985.

15. J.F. Allen. Recognizing intentions from natural language utterances. In M. Brady and R.C. Berwick, editors, *Computational Models of Discourse*, pages 107–166. MIT Press, Cambridge, Mass., 1983.

16. H.A. Kautz. A formal theory of plan recognition and its implementation. in *Reasoning about Plans*, ed. by J.F. Allen, H.A. Kautz, R.N. Pelavin, and J.D. Tenenberg. San Mateo, California: Morgan Kaufmann, pages 69–125, 1991.

17. D.J. Litman and J.F. Allen. A plan recognition model for subdialogues in conversations. *Cognitive Science*, 11(2):163–200, 1987.

18. M.E. Pollack. A model of plan inference that distinguishes between the beliefs of actors and observers. In *Proceedings of the 24th Annual Meeting of the Association for Computational Linguistics*, pages 207–214, 1986.

19. S. Carberry. *Plan Recognition in Natural Language Dialogue*. MIT Press, Cambridge, Mass., 1990.

20. H. Kitano and C. Van Ess-Dykema. Toward a plan-based understanding model for mixed-initiative dialogues. In *Proceedings of the 29th Annual Meeting of the Association for Computational Linguistics*, pages 25–32, 1991.

21. D.G. Novick. *Control of Mixed-Initiative Discourse Through Meta-Locutionary Acts: A Computational Model*. PhD thesis, University of Oregon, 1988.

22. M. Walker and S Whittaker. Mixed initiative in dialogue: An investigation into discourse segmentation. In *Proceedings of the 28th Annual Meeting of the Association for Computational Linguistics*, pages 70–78, 1990.

23. S. Whittaker and P. Stenton. Cues and control in expert-client dialogues. In *Proceedings of the 26th Annual Meeting of the Association for Computational Linguistics*, pages 123–130, 1988.

24. S.R. Young. Use of dialogue, pragmatics and semantics to enhance speech recognition. *Speech Communication*, 9:551–564, 1990.

25. D.R. Hipp and R.W. Smith. *A Demonstration of the 'Circuit Fix-It Shoppe'*. Twelve minute video tape, Department of Computer Science, Duke University, Durham, North Carolina. 1991.

26. S.R. Young, A.G. Hauptmann, W.H. Ward, E.T. Smith, and P. Werner. High level knowledge sources in usable speech recognition systems. *Communications of the ACM*, pages 183–194, February 1989.

27. J. Allen, S. Guez, L. Hoebel, E. Hinkelman, K. Jackson, A. Kyburg, and D. Traum. The discourse system project. Technical Report 317, University of Rochester, November 1989.

28. S. Seneff. TINA: A Natural Language System for Spoken Language Applications. *Computational Linguistics*, 18(1):61-86, 1992.

29. V. Zue, J. Glass, M. Phillips and S. Seneff. The MIT SAUMMIT speech recognition system: a program report. *Proceedings, DARPA Speech and Natural Language Workshop*, Philadelphia, pages 21–23, 1989.

Acknowledgment

This research was supported by National Science Foundation grant number NSF-IRI-88-03802 and by Duke University.

Machine Translation

Alex Waibel

School of Computer Science
Carnegie Mellon University
Pittsburgh PA 15213

Machine Translation was one of the declared highlights and focal points of the Human Language Technology Workshop. Machine Translation, or MT for short, has seen a renaissance in recent years, brought about by the availability of faster and more powerful computing, and several decades of advances in speech and language processing. ARPA now sponsors a machine translation initiative and companies and governments, domestic and overseas, view it as a growth area and devote significant efforts to this problem. Indeed, as nations are growing increasingly intertwined with each other, and as economies, defense, travel, and the media grow increasingly internationalized and globalized, handling and overcoming language barriers effectively, becomes an ever more pressing issue.

The session at the ARPA workshop attempted to do justice to the various blossoming avenues that make up machine translationa as we see it today. First and perhaps foremost is the question of how MT is to be done. Two approaches have attracted considerable scientific interest and debate: the knowledge based and statistical approaches. The knowledge based approach is perhaps the more classical approach, based on linguistic theory and in its most purist incarnation relying on rule based systems for syntactic and semantic analysis and generation. The statistical approach, in contrast, attempts to achieve solutions to machine translation by finding suitable mappings between two languages via statistical analysis based on large corpora. Critcs of the former will argue that a knowledge based approach will lack the ability to make soft decisions, deal with uncertainty and ambiguity and cannot learn. Critics of the latter will see the lack of structure and simplicity of the statistical model as too simplistic and limited, given the intricacies and rich structure of language. The two views were highlighted and well argued by Ed Hovy and Peter Brown in two eloquent, enlightening as well as entertaining tutorials. Both cases were well delivered and the discussion that ensued highlighted perhaps the commonalities more than the differences. Indeed, as knowledge based approaches adopt statistical techniques and as proponents pf statistical MT discover structure in language, the two approaches appear to be growing toward a common middle ground. Learning and handling uncertainty as well as taking advantage of structural universals of human languages will guide progress in years to come. Along he way, better tools, better principles of evaluation and a better understanding of what the ultimate needs in MT would be will drive advances.

Tools, dictionaries and knowledgebases of various kinds make up important parts of the translation task (human or by machine). Short of academic squabbles over the "right" approach, a number of efforts are aiming to improve and expand these supporting technologies to achieve better quality translations more effectively and more efficiently by humans and/or machines. Acknowledging that accurate automatic translation of any unrestricted texts may still be a research item for a while, researchers attempt to develop tools that help the human translator in "Machine Aided Translation" (MAT), to do the job more effectively. Unlike speech recognition, a partial solution here can provide significant help or save costs. A paper by Kevin Knight entitled "Building a Large Ontology for Machine Translation" and by Peter Brown et al. entitled "But Dictionaries are Data too", address ways by which dictionaries and ontologies can be automatically or semi-automatically generated and how they can be applied and used in MT. The papers "LINGSTAT: and Interactive, Machine-Aided Translation System" by Jonathan Yamron et al. and "An MAT Tool and Its Effectiveness" by Robert Frederking et al. address the question of how tools for generating translated documents semi-automatically can improve effectiveness of translation.

In the light of these different streams of activity it is particularly difficult to define commonly useful and accepted evaluation procedures. Since there is no clear definition of a "correct" translation, it is not a simple matter of counting the number correct or error rate. Translation fidelity is subjective in part and is determined by various schemes in which panels of judges decide on the naturalness and intelligibility of translations. No doubt, the cost of performing such evaluations is considerable and different schemes are being discussed. The paper "Evaluation of Machine Translation" by John White et al. addresses this thorny issue and gives evaluation results using current evaluation measures used under the ARPA MT-program.

Finally, two papers on Speech Translation address the questions that arise, when text is not the input medium, but if an input sentence is spoken in one language and should be translated into another. Applications for this kind of MT system abound (telecommunication, media, conferences, etc.). The problem of translation is made harder by the fact that the input to the MT-system is now corrupted by syntactic ill-formedness produced by the speaker, colloquialisms, acoustic noise, and speech recognition error. While a speech translation system may at first glance combine speech-to-text recognition with text based machine translation, its long term viability demands a tighter coupling as translation and recognition need to derive the intended meaning, not a perfect textual transcription and need to involve conextual cues in a cross-lingual dialog. Attempts at answering some of these still open questions are under way and described in two papers: "Recent Advances in Speech Translation" by Monika Woszczyna et al. and "A Speech to Speech Translation

System built from Standard Components" by Manny Rayner et al. They describe currently operational speech translation systems.

In summary, a good number of the outstanding issues in Machine Translation have been touched by the papers presented at the workshop. It is our hope that they pave the way for a rich ongoing debate between proponents of different approaches, applications and deployment considerations to our collective benefit. Indeed, the academic efforts are well warranted by the urgent needs in an increasingly internationalized but linguistically splintered world.

Session 8: Machine Translation Summary

Machine Translation was one of the declared highlights and focal points of the Human Language Technology Workshop. Machine Translation, or MT for short, has seen a renaissance in recent years, brought about by the availability of faster and more powerful computing, and several decades of advances in speech and language processing. ARPA now sponsors a machine translation initiative and companies and governments, domestic and overseas, view it as a growth area and devote significant efforts to this problem. Indeed, as nations are growing increasingly intertwined with each other, and as economies, defense, travel, and the media grow increasingly internationalized and globalized, handling and overcoming language barriers effectively, becomes an ever more pressing issue. The session at the ARPA workshop attempted to do justice to the various blossoming avenues that make up machine translationa as we see it today. First and perhaps foremost is the question of how MT is to be done. Two approaches have attracted considerable scientific interest and debate: the knowledge based and statistical approaches. The knowledge based approach is perhaps the more classical approach, based on linguistic theory and in its most purist incarnation relying on rule based systems for syntactic and semantic analysis and generation. The statistical approach, in contrast, attempts to achieve solutions to machine translation by finding suitable mappings between two languages via statistical analysis based on large corpora. Critcs of the former will argue that a knowledge based approach will lack the ability to make soft decisions, deal with uncertainty and ambiguity and cannot learn. Critics of the latter will see the lack of structure and simplicity of the statistical model as too simplistic and limited, given the intricacies and rich structure of language. The two views were highlighted and well argued by Ed Hovy and Peter Brown in two eloquent, enlightening as well as entertaining tutorials. Both cases were well delivered and the discussion that ensued highlighted perhaps the commonalities more than the differences. Indeed, as knowledge based approaches adopt statistical techniques and as proponents pf statistical MT discover structure in language, the two approaches appear to be growing toward a common middle ground. Learning and handling uncertainty as well as taking advantage of structural universals of human languages will guide progress in years to come. Along he way, better tools, better principles of evaluation and a better understanding of what the ultimate needs in MT would be will drive advances. Tools, dictionaries and knowledgebases of various kinds make up important parts of the translation task (human or by machine). Short of academic squabbles over the right approach, a number of efforts are aiming to improve and expand these supporting technologies to achieve better quality translations more effectively and more efficiently by humans and/or machines. Acknowledging that accurate automatic translation of any unrestricted texts may still be a research item for a while, researchers attempt to develop tools that help the human translator in Machine Aided Translation (MAT), to do the job more effectively. Unlike speech recognition, a partial solution here can provide significant help or save costs. A paper by Kevin Knight entitled Building a Large Ontology for Machine Translation and by Peter Brown et al. entitled But Dictionaries are Data too, address ways by which dictionaries and ontologies can be automatically or semi-automatically generated and how they can be applied and used in MT. The papers LINGSTAT: and Interactive, Machine-Aided Translation System by Jonathan Yamron et al. and An MAT Tool and Its Effectiveness by Robert Frederking et al. address the question of how tools for generating translated documents semi-automatically can improve effectiveness of translation. In the light of these different streams of activity it is particularly difficult to define commonly useful and accepted evaluation procedures. Since there is no clear definition of a correct translation, it is not a simple matter of counting the number correct or error rate. Translation fidelity is subjective in part and is determined by various schemes in which panels of judges decide on the naturalness and intelligibility of translations. No doubt, the cost of performing such evaluations is considerable and different schemes are being discussed. The paper Evaluation of Machine Translation by John White et al. addresses this thorny issue and gives evaluation results using current evaluation measures used under the ARPA MT-program. Finally, two papers on Speech Translation address the questions that arise, when text is not the input medium, but if an input sentence is spoken in one language and should be translated into another. Applications for this kind of MT system abound (telecommunication, media, conferences, etc.). The problem of translation is made harder by the fact that the input to the MT-system is now corrupted by syntactic ill-formedness produced by the speaker, colloquialisms, acoustic noise, and speech recognition error. While a speech translation system may at first glance combine speech-to-text recognition with text based machine translation, its long term viability demands a tighter coupling as translation and recognition need to derive the intended meaning, not a perfect textual transcription and need to involve conextual cues in a cross-lingual dialog. Attempts at answering some of these still open questions are under way and described in two papers: Recent Advances in Speech Translation by Monika Woszczyna et al. and A Speech to Speech Translation System built from Standard Components by Manny Rayner et al. They describe currently operational speech translation systems. In summary, a good number of the outstanding issues in Machine Translation have been touched by the papers presented at the workshop. It is our hope that they pave the way for a rich ongoing debate between proponents of different approaches, applications and deployment considerations to our collective benefit. Indeed, the academic efforts are well warranted by the urgent needs in an increasingly internationalized but linguistically splintered world.

BUILDING A LARGE ONTOLOGY FOR MACHINE TRANSLATION

Kevin Knight

USC/Information Sciences Institute
4676 Admiralty Way
Marina del Rey, CA 90292

ABSTRACT

This paper describes efforts underway to construct a large-scale ontology to support semantic processing in the PANGLOSS knowledge-base machine translation system. Because we are aiming at broad semantic coverage, we are focusing on automatic and semi-automatic methods of knowledge acquisition. Here we report on algorithms for merging complementary online resources, in particular the LDOCE and WordNet dictionaries. We discuss empirical results, and how these results have been incorporated into the PANGLOSS ontology.

1. Introduction

The PANGLOSS project is a three-site collaborative effort to build a large-scale knowledge-based machine translation system. Key components of PANGLOSS include New Mexico State University's ULTRA parser [Farwell and Wilks, 1991], Carnegie Mellon's interlingua representation format [Nirenburg and Defrise, 1991], and USC/ISI's PENMAN English generation system [Penman, 1989]. Another key component currently under construction at ISI is the PANGLOSS ontology, a large-scale conceptual network intended to support semantic processing in other PANGLOSS modules. This network will contain 50,000 nodes representing commonly encountered objects, entities, qualities, and relations.

The upper (more abstract) region of the ontology is called the Ontology Base (OB) and contains approximately 400 items that represent generalizations essential for the various PANGLOSS modules' linguistic processing during translation. The middle region of the ontology, approximately 50,000 items, provides a framework for a generic world model, containing items representing many English word senses. The lower (more specific) regions of the ontology provide anchor points for different application domains. Both the middle and domain model regions of the ontology house the open-class terms of the MT interlingua. They also contain specific information used to screen unlikely semantic and anaphoric interpretations.

The Ontology Base is a synthesis of USC/ISI's PENMAN Upper Model [Bateman, 1990] and CMU's ONTOS concept hierarchy [Carlson and Nirenburg, 1990]. Both of these high-level ontologies were built by hand, and they were merged manually. Theoretical motivations behind the OB and its current status are described in [Hovy and Knight, 1993].

The problem we focus on in this paper is the construction of the large middle region of the ontology. Because large-scale knowledge resources are difficult to build by hand, we are pursuing primarily automatic methods applied in several stages. During the first stage we created several tens of thousands of nodes, organized them into sub/superclass taxonomies, and subordinated those taxonomies to the 400-node Ontology Base. This work we describe below. Later stages will address the insertion of additional semantic information such as restrictions on actors in events, domain/range constraints on relations, and so forth.

For the major node creation and taxonomization stage, we have primarily used two on line sources of information: (1) the Longman Dictionary of Contemporary English (LDOCE)[Group, 1978], and (2) the lexical database WordNet [Miller, 1990].

2. Merging LDOCE and WordNet

LDOCE is a learner's dictionary of English with 27,758 words and 74,113 word senses. Each word sense comes with:

- A short definition. One of the unique features of LDOCE is that its definitions only use words from a "control vocabulary" list of 2000 words. This makes it attractive from the point of view of extracting semantic information by parsing dictionary entries.
- Examples of usage.
- One or more of 81 syntactic codes.
- For nouns, one of 33 semantic codes.
- For nouns, one of 124 pragmatic codes.

WordNet is a semantic word database based on psycholinguistic principles. Its size is comparable to LDOCE, but its information is organized in a completely different manner. WordNet groups synonymous word senses into single units ("synsets"). Noun senses are organized into a deep hierarchy, and the database also contains part-of links, antonym links, and others. Approximately 55% of WordNet synsets have brief informal definitions.

Each of these resources has something to offer a large-scale natural language system, but each is missing important features present in the other. What we need is a combination of the features of both.

Our most significant project to date has been to merge LDOCE and WordNet. This involves producing a list of matching pairs of word senses, e.g.:

```
    LDOCE          WORDNET

(abdomen_0_0   ABDOMEN-1)
(crane_1_2     CRANE-1)
(crane_1_1     CRANE-2)
(abbess_0_0    ABBESS-1)
(abbott_0_0    ABBOTT-1)
    ...            ...
```

Section 4 describes how we produced this list semi-automatically. Solving this problem yields several benefits:

- It allows us to taxonomize tens of thousands of LDOCE word senses and subordinate them quickly to the Ontology Base. Section 5 describes how we did this.
- It provides a syntactic and pragmatic lexicon for WordNet, as well as careful definitions.
- It groups LDOCE senses into synonyms sets and taxonomies.
- It allows us to identify and correct errors in the original resources.

3. Related Work

Our ontology is a symbolic model for fueling semantic processing in a knowledge-based MT system. We are aiming at broader coverage (dictionary-scale) than has previously been available to symbolic MT systems. Also, we are committed to automatic and semi-automatic methods of knowledge acquisition from the start. This, and the fact that we are concentrating on a particular language-processing application, distinguishes the PANGLOSS work from the CYC knowledge base [Lenat and Guha, 1990]. We also believe that dictionaries and corpora are imperfect sources of knowledge, so we still employ human effort to check the results of our semi-automatic algorithms. This is in contrast to purely statistical systems (e.g., [Brown *et al.*, 1992]), which are difficult to inspect and modify.

There has been considerable use in the NLP community of both WordNet (e.g., [Lehman *et al.*, 1992; Resnik, 1992]) and LDOCE (e.g..., [Liddy *et al.*, 1992; Wilks *et al.*, 1990]), but no one has merged the two in order to combine their strengths. The next section describes our approach in detail.

4. Algorithms and Results

We have developed two algorithms for merging LDOCE and WordNet. Both algorithms generate lists of sense pairs, where each pair consists of one sense from LDOCE and the proposed matching sense from WordNet, if any.

4.1. Definition Match

The Definition Match algorithm is based on the idea that two word senses should be matched if their two definitions share words. For example, there are two noun definitions of "batter" in LDOCE:

- (batter_2_0) "mixture of flour, eggs, and milk, beaten together and used in cooking"
- (batter_3_0) "a person who bats, esp in baseball — compare BATSMAN"

and two definitions in WordNet:

- (BATTER-1) "ballplayer who bats"
- (BATTER-2) "a flour mixture thin enough to pour or drop from a spoon"

The Definition Match Algorithm will match (batter_2_0) with (BATTER-2) because their definitions share words like "flour" and "mixture." Similarly (batter_3_0) and (BATTER-1) both contain the word "bats," so they are also matched together.

Not all senses in WordNet have definitions, but most have synonyms and superordinates. For this reason, the algorithm looks not only at WordNet definitions, but also at locally related words and senses. For example, if synonyms of WordNet sense x appear in the definition of LDOCE sense y, then this is evidence that x and y should be matched.

Here is the algorithm:

Definition-Match

For each English word w found in both LDOCE and WordNet:

1. Let n be the number of senses of w in LDOCE.
2. Let m be the number of senses of w in WordNet.
3. Identify and stem all open-class, content words in the definitions (and example sentences) of all senses of w in both resources.
4. Let ULD be the union of all stemmed content words appearing in LDOCE definitions.
5. Let UWN be the same for WordNet, plus all synonyms of the senses, their direct superordinates, siblings, super-superordinates, as well as stemmed content words from the definitions of direct superordinates.
6. Let CW=(ULD ∩ UWN) − w. These are definition words common to LDOCE and WordNet.
7. Create matrix L of the n LDOCE senses and the words from CW. For all $0 \leq i < n$ and $0 \leq x < |CW|$:

$$L[i,x] = \begin{cases} 1.00 & \text{if the definition of sense } i \text{ in LDOCE contains word } x \\ 0.01 & \text{otherwise} \end{cases}$$

8. Create matrix W of the m WordNet senses and the words from CW. For all $0 \leq j < m$ and $0 \leq x < |CW|$:

$$W[x,j] = \begin{cases} 1.00 & \text{if } x \text{ is a synonym or superordinate of sense } j \text{ in WordNet} \\ 0.80 & \text{if } x \text{ is contained in the definition of sense } j \text{ or the definition of its superordinate} \\ 0.60 & \text{if } x \text{ is a sibling or super-superordinate of sense } j \text{ in WordNet} \\ 0.01 & \text{otherwise} \end{cases}$$

9. Create similarity matrix SIM of LDOCE and WordNet senses. For all $0 \leq i < n$ and $0 \leq j < m$:

$$\mathrm{SIM}[i,j] = \left[\sum_{x=0}^{|CW|-1} (L[i,x] \cdot W[x,j]) \right] \; / \; |CW|$$

10. Repeat until SIM is a zero matrix:
    (a) Let SIM[y, z] be the largest value in the SIM matrix.
    (b) Generate matched pair of LDOCE sense y and WordNet sense z.
    (c) For all $0 \leq i < n$, set SIM[i, z] = 0.0.
    (d) For all $0 \leq j < m$, set SIM[y, j] = 0.0.

In constructing the SIM matrix the algorithm comes up with a similarity measure between each of the $n \cdot m$ possible pairs of LDOCE and WordNet senses. This measure, SIM[i, j], is a number from 0 to 1, with 1 being as good a match as possible. Thus, every matching pair proposed by the algorithm comes with a confidence factor.

Empirical results are as follows. We ran the algorithm over all nouns in both LDOCE and WordNet. We judged the correctness of its proposed matches, keeping records of the confidence levels and the degree of ambiguity present.

For low-ambiguity words (words with exactly two senses in LDOCE and two in WordNet), the results are:

confidence level	pct. correct	pct. coverage
≥ 0.0	75%	100%
≥ 0.4	85%	53%
≥ 0.8	90%	27%

At confidence levels ≥ 0.0, 75% of the proposed matches are correct. If we restrict ourselves to only matches proposed at confidence ≥ 0.8, accuracy increases to 90%, but we only get 27% of the possible matches.

For high-ambiguity words (more than five senses in LDOCE and WordNet), the results are:

confidence level	pct. correct	pct. coverage
≥ 0.0	47%	100%
≥ 0.1	76%	44%
≥ 0.2	81%	20%

Accuracy here is worse, but increases sharply when we only consider high confidence matches.

The algorithm's performance is quite reasonable, given that 45% of WordNet senses have no definitions and that many existing definitions are brief and contain misspellings. Still, there are several improvements to be made—e.g., modify the "greedy" strategy in which matches are extracted from SIM matrix, weigh rare words in definitions more highly than common ones, and/or score senses with long definitions lower than ones with short definitions. These improvements yield only slightly better results, however, because most failures are simply due to the fact that matching sense definitions have no words in common. For example, "seal" has 5 noun senses in LDOCE, one of which is:

> (seal_1_1) "any of several types of large fish-eating animals living mostly on cool seacoasts and floating ice, with broad flat limbs (FLIPPERs) suitable for swimming"

WordNet has 7 definitions of "seal," one of which is:

> (SEAL-7) "any of numerous marine mammals that come on shore to breed; chiefly of cold regions"

The Definition Match algorithm cannot see any similarity between (seal_1_1) and (SEAL-7), so it does not match them. However, we have developed another match algorithm that can handle cases like these.

4.2. Hierarchy Match

The Hierarchy Match algorithm dispenses with sense definitions altogether. Instead, it uses the various sense hierarchies inside LDOCE and WordNet.

WordNet noun senses are arranged in a deep is-a hierarchy. For example, SEAL-7 is a PINNIPED-1, which is on AQUATIC-MAMMAL-1, which is a EUTHERIAN-1, which is a MAMMAL-1, which is ultimately an ANIMAL-1, and so forth.

LDOCE has two fairly flat hierarchies. The *semantic code* hierarchy is induced by a set of 33 semantic codes drawn up by Longman lexicographers. Each sense is marked with one of these codes, e.g., "H" for human "P" for plant, "J" for movable object. The other hierarchy is the *genus sense* hierarchy. Researchers at New Mexico State University have built an automatic algorithm [Bruce and Guthrie, 1992] for locating and disambiguating genus terms (head nouns) in sense definitions. For example, (bat_1_1) is defined as "any of the several types of specially shaped wooden stick used for ..." The genus term for (bat_1_1) is (stick_1_1). As another example, the genus sense of (aisle_0_1) is (passage_0_7). The genus sense and the semantic code hierarchies were extracted automatically from LDOCE. The semantic code hierarchy is fairly robust, but since the genus sense hierarchy was generated heuristically, it is only 80% correct.

The idea of the Hierarchy Match algorithm is that once two senses are matched, it is a good idea to look at their respective ancestors and descendants for further matches. For example, once (animal_1_2) and ANIMAL-1 are matched, we can look into the respective animal-subhierarchies. We find that the word "seal" is locally unambiguous—only one sense of "seal" refers to an animal (in both LDOCE and WordNet). So we feel confident to match those seal-animal senses. As another example, suppose we know that (swan_dive_0_0) is the same concept as (SWAN-DIVE-1). We can then match their superordinates (dive_2_1) and (DIVE-3) with high confidence; we need not consider other senses of "dive."

Here is the algorithm:

Hierarchy-Match

1. Initialize the set of matches:
    (a) Retrieve all words that are unambiguous in both LDOCE and WordNet. Match their corresponding senses, and place all the matches on a list called M1.
    (b) Retrieve a prepared list of hand-crafted matches. Place these matches on a list called M2. We created 15 of these, mostly high-level matches like (person_0_1, PERSON-2) and (plant_2_1, PLANT-3). This step is not strictly necessary, but provides guidance to the algorithm.
2. Repeat until M1 and M2 are empty:
    (a) For each match on M2, look for words that are unambiguous within the hierarchies rooted at the two matched senses. Match the senses of locally unambiguous words and place the matches on M1.
    (b) Move all matches from M2 to a list called M3.
    (c) For each match on M1, look upward in the two hierarchies from the matched senses. Whenever a word appears in both hierarchies, match the corresponding senses, and place the match on M2.

(d) Move all matches from M1 to M2.

The algorithm operate in phases, shifting matches from M1 to M2 to M3, placing newly-generated matches on M1 and M2. Once M1 and M2 are exhausted, M3 contains the final list of matches proposed by the algorithm.

Again, we can measure the success of the algorithm along two dimensions, coverage and correctness:

phase	pct. correct	matches proposed
Step 1	99%	7563
Step 2(a)	94%	876
Step 2(c)	85%	530
Step 2(a)	93%	2018
Step 2(c)	83%	40
Step 2(a)	92%	99
Step 2(c)	100%	2

In the end, the algorithm produced 11,128 matches at 96% accuracy. We expected 100% accuracy, but the algorithm was foiled at several places by errors in one or another of the hierarchies. For example, (savings_bank_0_0) is mistakenly a subclass of river-bank (bank_1_1) in the LDOCE genus hierarchy, rather than (bank_1_4), the money-bank. "Savings bank" senses are matched in step 1(a), so step 2(c) erroneously goes on to match the river-bank of LDOCE with the money-bank of WordNet.

Fortunately, the Definition and Hierarchy Match algorithms complement one another, and there are several ways to combine them. Our practical experience has been to run the Hierarchy Match algorithm to completion, remove the matched senses from the databases, then run the Definition Match algorithm. The Definition Match algorithm's performance improves slightly after hierarchy matching removes some word senses. Once the high confidence definition matches have been verified, we use them as fuel for another run of the Hierarchy Match algorithm.

We have built an interface that allows a person to verify matches produced by both algorithms, and to reject or correct faulty matches. So far, we have 15,000 correct matches, with 10,000 to follow shortly. The next section describes what we do with them in our ontology.

5. The Current Ontology

The ontology currently contains 15,000 noun senses from LDOCE and 20,000 more from WordNet. Its purpose is to support semantic processing in the PANGLOSS analysis and generation modules. Because we have not yet taxonomized adjective and verb senses (see Section 6) semantic support is still very limited.

On the generation side, the PENMAN system requires that all concepts be subordinated to the PENMAN Upper Model, which is part of the Ontology Base (OB). It is difficult to subordinate tens of thousands of LDOCE word senses to the OB individually, but if we instead subordinate various WordNet hierarchies to the OB, the LDOCE senses will follow automatically via the WordNet-LDOCE merge.

Subordinating the WordNet noun hierarchy to the OB required about 100 manual operations. Each operation either merged a WordNet concept with an OB equivalent, inserted one or more WordNet concepts between two OB concepts, or attached a WordNet concept below an OB concept. The noun senses from WordNet (and their matches from LDOCE) fall under all three of the OB's primary top-level categories of `OBJECT`, `PROCESS`, and `QUALITY`. The PENMAN generator now has access to the semantic knowledge it needs to generate a broad range of English.

To support parsing, we have manually added about 20 mutual-disjoint assertions into the ontology. One of these assertions states that no individual can be both an **INANIMATE-OBJECT** and an **ANIMATE-OBJECT**, another states that **PERSON** and **NON-HUMAN-ANIMAL** are mutually disjoint, and so forth. A parser can use such information to disambiguate sentences like "this crane is my pet," where "crane" and "pet" have several senses in LDOCE (crane_1_1, a machine; crane_1_2, a bird; pet_1_1, a domestic animal; pet_1_2, a favorite person; etc.). The only pair of senses that are not mutually disjoint in our ontology is (crane_1_2)/(pet_1_1), so this is the preferred interpretation. So far, all mutual-disjoint links are between OB concepts. We plan a study of our lexicon to determine which nouns have senses that are not distinguishable on the basis of mutual-disjointness, and this will drive further knowledge acquisition of these assertions.

We are now integrating the ontology with ULTRA, the Prolog-based parsing component of the PANGLOSS translator. Although ULTRA parses Spanish input for PANGLOSS, the lexical items have already been semantically tagged with LDOCE sense keys, so no large-scale knowledge acquisition is necessary. Our first step has been to produce a Prolog version of the ontology, with inference rules for inheritance and propagation of mutual-disjoint links.

Another use of the ontology has been to help us refine LDOCE and WordNet themselves. For example, any sample of the automatically-generated LDOCE genus-sense hierarchy has approximately 20% errors. Using our merged LDOCE-WordNet-OB ontology as a standard, we have been able to locate and fix a large number of these errors automatically.

6. Future Work

There are several items on our immediate agenda:

- Ontologize adjective, verb, and adverb senses from LDOCE. Most adjective senses either pertain to objects (e.g., atomic_1_1) or represent slot-value pairs in the ontology (e.g.,green_1_1 refers to `COLOR/GREEN-COLOR` as pertaining to `PHYSICAL-OBJECTs`). Most verb senses refer to `PROCESSes`, whose participants have class restrictions, and so forth. Much of this information can be mined from WordNet and LDOCE, as well as from online corpora.
- Extract a large Spanish lexicon for the ontology. We plan to use a bilingual Spanish-English dictionary (and merging techniques similar in spirit to the ones, described in this paper) in order to roughly annotate the ontology with Spanish words and phrases.
- Incrementally flesh out the ontology to improve the quality of PANGLOSS translations. We will focus on acquiring relations like `SIZE`, `PURPOSE`, `PART-OF`, `POSTCONDITION`, etc., through primarily automatic methods, including parsing of LDOCE definitions and processing corpora.

7. Acknowledgments

I would like to thank Richard Whitney for significant assistance in programming and verification. The Ontology Base was built by Eduard Hovy, Licheng Zeng, Akitoshi Okumura, Richard Whitney, and the author. I wish to express gratitude to Longman Group, Ltd., for making the machine readable version of LDOCE, 2nd edition, available to us. Louise Guthrie assisted in LDOCE extraction and kindly provided us with the LDOCE genus sense hierarchy. This work was carried out under ARPA Order No. 8073, contract MDA904-91-C-5224.

References

Bateman, J. 1990. Upper modeling: Organizing knowledge for natural language processing. In *Proc. Fifth International Workshop on Natural Language Generation, Pittsburgh, PA.*

Brown, P., V. Della Pietra, P. deSouza, J. Lai, and R. Mercer. 1992. Class-based n-gram models of natural language. *Computational Linguistics* 18(4).

Bruce, Rebecca and Louise Guthrie. 1992. Genus disambiguation: A study in weighted preference. In *Proceedings of the 15th International Conference on Computational Linguistics (COLING-92).*

Carlson, L. and S. Nirenburg. 1990. *World Modeling for NLP.* Tech. Rep. CMU-CMT-90-121, Center for Machine Translation, Carnegie Mellon University.

Farwell, D. and Y. Wilks. 1991. Ultra: A multilingual machine translator. In *Proceedings of the 3rd MT Summit.*

Longman Group. 1978. *Longman Dictionary of Contemporary English.* Essex, UK: Longman.

Hovy, E. and K. Knight. 1993. Motivating shared knowledge resources: An example from the pangloss collaboration. *(Submitted to: Theoretical and Methodological Issues in Machine Translation).*

Lehman, J., A. Newell, T. Polk, and R. Lewis. 1992. The rule of language in cognition. In *Conceptions of the Human Mind*, ed. G. Harman. Hillsdale, NJ: Lawrence Erlbaum. (Forthcoming).

Lenat, D. and R.V. Guha. 1990. *Building Large Knowledge-Based Systems.* Reading, MA: Addison-Wesley.

Liddy, E., W. Paik, and J. Woelfel. 1992. Use of subject field codes from a machine-readable dictionary for automatic classification of documents. In *Advances in Classification Research: Proc. 3rd ASIS SIG/CR Classification Research Workshop.*

Miller, George. 1990. Wordnet: An on-line lexical database. *International Journal of Lexicography* 3(4). (Special Issue).

Nirenburg, S. and C. Defrise. 1991. Aspects of text meaning. In *Semantics and the Lexicon*, ed. J. Pustejovsky. Dordrecht, Holland: Kluwer.

Penman. 1989. *The Penman Documentation.* Tech. rep., USC/Information Sciences Institute.

Resnik, P. 1992. Wordnet and distributional analysis: A class-based approach to lexical discovery. In *Proc. AAAI Workshop on Statistically-Based NLP techniques.*

Wilks, Y., D. Fass, C. Guo, J. McDonald, T. Plate, and B. Slator. 1990. Providing machine tractable dictionary tools. *Machine Translation* 5.

LINGSTAT: AN INTERACTIVE, MACHINE-AIDED TRANSLATION SYSTEM*

Jonathan Yamron, James Baker, Paul Bamberg, Haakon Chevalier, Taiko Dietzel, John Elder, Frank Kampmann, Mark Mandel, Linda Manganaro, Todd Margolis, and Elizabeth Steele

Dragon Systems, Inc., 320 Nevada Street, Newton, MA 02160

ABSTRACT

In this paper we present the first implementation of LINGSTAT, an interactive machine translation system designed to increase the productivity of a user, with little knowledge of the source language, in translating or extracting information from foreign language documents. In its final form, LINGSTAT will make use of statistical information gathered from parallel and single-language corpora, and linguistic information at all levels (lexical, syntactic, and semantic).

1. INTRODUCTION

The DARPA initiative in machine translation supports three very different avenues of research, including CANDIDE's fully automatic system [1,2], the interactive, knowledge-based system of the PANGLOSS group [3–6], and LINGSTAT, also an interactive system. LINGSTAT, as its name implies, incorporates both linguistic and statistical knowledge representations. It is intended for users who are native speakers of the target language, and is designed to be useful to those with little knowledge of the source (by providing access to foreign language documents), as well as those with a greater knowledge of the source (by improving productivity in translation). Although a future implementation will suggest translations of phrases and sentences, high quality automatic translation is not a goal; LINGSTAT's purpose is to relieve users of the most tedious and difficult translation tasks, but may well leave problems that the user is better suited to solve.

Initial efforts have been focused on the translation of Japanese to English in the domain of mergers and acquisitions, and a first version of a translator's workstation has been assembled. Work has also begun on a Spanish version of the system. As resources become available, particularly parallel corpora, the Spanish system will be further developed and work will be extended to include other European languages. This paper describes the Japanese system.

Japanese poses special challenges in translation that are not seen in European languages. The most striking are that Japanese text is not divided into words, and that the number of writing symbols is very large. These symbols can be divided into at least four sets: kanji, hiragana, katakana, and, occasionally, the Latin alphabet. The general-use kanji number about 2000. They are not phonetic symbols (most have several pronunciations, depending on context), but carry meaning and often appear two or three to a word. Hiragana and katakana, on the other hand, are phonetic alphabets; hiragana is usually used for important function words in Japanese grammar (sentence particles, auxiliary verbs) and to indicate inflection of verbs, adjectives, and nouns, while katakana is used almost exclusively for borrowed foreign words.

Another difficulty of Japanese is that it lacks many grammatical features taken for granted in English, such as plurals, articles, routine use of pronouns, and a future tense. Conversely, there are many Japanese concepts that have no analog in English, including the many levels of politeness, the notion of a sentence topic distinct from its subject, and exclusive *vs.* non-exclusive listings. In addition, Japanese word order and sentence structure are very different from English.

This paper is organized as follows. Section 2 lists the dictionaries and text resources used in assembling LINGSTAT. Section 3 presents an outline of the system components, some of which are described in greater detail in section 4. Section 5 describes the results of the DARPA July 1992 evaluation of the Japanese system, as well some informal results on the Spanish system. Section 6 discusses some improvements planned for future versions of the workstation.

2. RESOURCES

LINGSTAT currently makes use of a number of dictionaries and text sources of Japanese. As yet, there is no high-quality source of parallel Japanese-English text.

Dictionaries

- EDR Dictionary
  Approximately 400,000 words defined in both En-

*This work was sponsored by the Defense Advanced Research Projects Agency under contract number J-FBI-91-239.

glish and Japanese (about 200,000 distinct definitions)

- Japanese-English CD-ROM Dictionary
  Pronunciations and glosses for approximately 50,000 Japanese words
- ICOT morphological dictionary
  Pronunciations and parts of speech for approximately 150,000 Japanese words

Text

- TIPSTER articles
  Japanese newspaper articles on joint ventures
- Technical abstracts
  10,000 scientific abstracts in Japanese, with English summaries or low-quality translations
- Asahi Sinbun CD-ROM
  Seven years of Japanese newspaper articles, all subjects

3. OVERVIEW OF SYSTEM ARCHITECTURE

An initial implementation of the interactive translation system for Japanese has been completed, running under MS-DOS on PC (486) hardware. In its current form, lexical and syntactic analyses are done in a pre-processing step (initiated by the user) that produces an annotated source document and a document-specific dictionary, which are then presented to the user in a customized word-processing environment.

The pre-processing step consists of a number of subtasks, including:

1. Breaking the Japanese character stream into words using a maximum-likelihood tokenizer in conjunction with a morphological analyzer (de-inflector) that recognizes all inflected forms of Japanese verbs, adjectives, and nouns
2. Attaching lexical information to the identified words, including inflection codes and roots (for inflected forms), pronunciation, English glosses (some automatically generated from parallel text), and English definitions
3. Finding "best guess" transliterations of katakana words using dynamic-programming techniques
4. Translating numbers with following counters (eliminating a large source of user errors arising from the unusual numbering conventions in Japanese)
5. Using a finite-state parser to identify modifying phrases
6. Creating the annotated document and document-specific dictionary

The user's word-processing environment consists normally of two windows, one containing the original Japanese broken into words and annotated with pronunciation and "best guess" glosses, the other for entry of the English translation. Information extracted during pre-processing but not available in the annotated document (longer definitions, inflection information, *etc.*) can be accessed instantly from the document-specific dictionary using the keyboard or mouse, and is presented in a pop-up window. The interface also allows easy access to browsing resources such as on-line dictionaries and proper name lists.

4. IMPLEMENTATION DETAILS

Tokenization. Tokenization is done using a maximum-likelihood algorithm that finds the "best" way to break up a given sentence into words. Conceptually, the idea is to find all ways to tokenize a sentence, score each tokenization, then choose the one with the best score. The tokenizer uses a master list of Japanese words with unigram frequencies.

The score of a tokenization is defined to be the sum of the scores assigned to the words it contains, and the score of a word is taken to be proportional to the log of its unigram probability. Any character sequence not in the master list is considered infinitely bad, although to guarantee that a tokenization is always found, an exception is made for single character tokens not in the master list, which are assigned a very low, but finite, score. The tokenizer also assigns a moderate score to unfamiliar strings of ASCII or katakana, as well as to numbers.

The search for the best tokenization is done using a simple dynamic programming algorithm. Let $score(w)$ and $length(w)$ denote the score and length of the character sequence w. For a sentence of N characters numbered from 0 to $N-1$, let $best[i]$ denote the score of the best tokenization of the character sequence from 0 to $i-1$, and initialize $best[0] = 0$, $best[i] = -\infty$ for $1 < i < N$. The best tokenization score for the sentence is then given by $best[N]$ after:

```
FOR i = 0 to N - 1 DO
  FOR all sequences w that start at position i DO
    IF best[i] + score(w) > best[i + length(w)]
    THEN best[i + length(w)] = best[i] + score(w)
```

Note that when two tokenizations both have a word ending at a given position, only the higher scoring solution up to that position is used in subsequent calculations.

Currently the most serious tokenization errors are caused by kanji proper nouns in the incoming document. Unlike European languages, there is no lexical cue (such as capitalization) to identify such nouns, and since most kanji can appear as words in isolation, the tokenizer will always find some way to break up a multi-kanji name into legal, but probably not sensible, pieces.

De-inflection. In order to keep the master list relatively small, only root forms of words that inflect have an entry. To recognize inflected forms, the tokenizer calls a de-inflector whenever it fails to find a candidate token in the master list.

In Japanese there are three classes of words that inflect: verbs (no person or number, but negatives and many tenses), adjectives (no cases or plurals, but negatives, adverbial, and tense), and *nani*-nouns (adjectival and adverbial). De-inflection is typically a multi-step process, as in

tabetakunakatta (didn't want to eat)
→ *tabetakunai* (doesn't want to eat)
→ *tabetai* (wants to eat)
→ *taberu* (eats).

It may also happen that a particular form can de-inflect along multiple paths to different roots.

The engine of the LINGSTAT de-inflection module is language-independent (to the extent that words inflect by transformation of their endings), driven by a language-specific de-inflection table. It handles multi-step and multi-path de-inflections, and for a given candidate will return all possible root forms to the tokenizer, along with the probability of the particular inflection for incorporation into the word score. The de-inflector also returns information about the de-inflection path for use by the annotation module. De-inflection tables have been developed for Japanese, Spanish, and English.

Annotation. The annotation module attaches pronunciations, English glosses, English definitions, and inflection information to each word identified by the tokenizer.

Pronunciation information might seem superfluous but is often of value to a Japanese translator. One of the consequences of the difficulty of written Japanese is that most students of the language can speak much better than they can read (recall that the pronunciation of a kanji cannot be deduced from its shape). The verbal cue that LINGSTAT provides through the pronunciation may therefore be enough to allow a user to identify an otherwise unfamiliar kanji word. In any case, having the pronunciation allows the user access to supplementary paper dictionaries ordered by pronunciation, which are much faster to use than radical-and-stroke dictionaries ordered by character shape information.

The glosses used by LINGSTAT come from three sources: hand entry, the Japanese-English CD-ROM dictionary, and automatic extraction from the definitions in the EDR dictionary. There are two methods of automatic extraction:

- Pull the gloss out of the definition—for example, *A type of financial transaction named leveraged buyout* becomes *leveraged buyout.*
- Use the English and Japanese definitions in the EDR dictionary as sentenced-aligned parallel text and apply CANDIDE's word alignment algorithm (Model 1) [1] to determine which English words correspond to each Japanese word.

The first method is moderately successful because many of the definitions adhere to a particular style. The second method gives good glosses for those Japanese words that occur frequently in the text of the definitions.

Katakana Transliteration. Words are borrowed so frequently from other languages, particularly English, that their transliterations into katakana rarely appear in even the largest dictionaries. The best way to determine their meaning, therefore, is to transliterate them back into English. This is made difficult by the fact that the transformation to katakana is not invertible: for example, English *l* and *r* both map to the Japanese *r*, *r* following a vowel is sometimes dropped, and vowels are inserted into consonant clusters.

The LINGSTAT katakana transliterator attempts to guess what English words might have given rise to an unfamiliar katakana word. It converts the katakana pronunciation into a representation intermediate between Japanese and English, then compares this to a list of 80,000 English words in the same representation. A dynamic programming algorithm is used to identify the English words that most closely match the katakana. These words are then attached to the katakana token in the annotation step.

This procedure fails for non-English foreign words, and for most proper names (since they rarely appear in the master English list).

Number Translation. In traditional Japanese, numbers up to 10^4 are formed by using the kanji digits in conjunction with the kanji symbols for the various powers of ten up to 1000, *e.g.,* 6542 would be written

$$(6)(1000)(5)(100)(4)(10)(2),$$

with each number in parentheses replaced by the appropriate kanji symbol. Notice that the powers of ten are explicitly represented, rather than being implied by position.

There are special kanji for the large numbers 10^4, 10^8, *etc.* These may be preceded by expressions like that above to form very large numbers, such as

$$\begin{aligned}&(2)(10^8)(5)(1000)(5)(100)(10^4)\\&= 2 \times 10^8 + 5500 \times 10^4\\&= 255,000,000.\end{aligned}$$

Modern Japanese often mixes the traditional Japanese representation with the "place-holding" representation used in English. Arabic numerals are freely mixed with kanji symbols in both formats. To ease the burden on the translator LINGSTAT has a function that recognizes numbers in all their styles, including following counters, and translates them into conventional English notation. These translations are then attached to the number token in the annotation step. Comparison of manual and LINGSTAT-aided translations has demonstrated that this feature eliminates a large source of critical errors, particularly in the evaluation domain, which frequently references large monetary transactions.

Finite-state parser. As a first pass at helping the user with Japanese sentence structure, LINGSTAT incorporates a simple finite-state parser designed to identify modifying phrases in Japanese sentences. An interface function has also been added to display this information in a structured way. At this stage, the quality of the parse is only fair. This function has not yet been tested for its effect on translation speed.

5. RESULTS

The system as described here (without the finite-state parser) was evaluated by DARPA in July 1992. The performance of two Level 2 translators was measured on a test set of 18 Japanese documents, each translator translating 9 with the aid of the system and 9 by hand. In general, the quality of translation with and without the system was found to be comparable, but the system provided a speedup of approximately 30%.

Since the tested system provided no help with the analysis of the Japanese sentences, this savings was achieved by drastically reducing the time spent doing tokenization and lookup. It might appear surprising that so much time could be saved from these activities alone, but the many unusual features of Japanese described above conspire to produce a large overhead in this phase of translation compared to other languages. This result is also consistent with an analysis of how the translators allocated their time: without the system, their principal effort involved dictionary lookup, but with the system most of their time was spent analyzing sentence structure.

Productivity tests have also been conducted on the rudimentary Spanish version of the workstation. This system incorporates a Spanish de-inflector, provides word for word translation to English, and has fast access to an on-line dictionary. On a scaled down version of the DARPA test (6 documents instead of 18, including 3 by hand and 3 with the aid of the system), a fluent speaker of Italian (a language very similar to Spanish) showed no productivity gain. At the other extreme, a user with no Spanish knowledge and no recent training in any European language was about 50% faster using the system's on-line tools than with a paper dictionary.

6. CURRENT AND FUTURE WORK

There are currently two programs underway to improve the translation system. The first is an effort to expand the Japanese and Spanish dictionaries, which requires not only adding words, but also glosses, pronunciations (for Japanese), and multi-word objects. Part of this task involves updating the Japanese and Spanish word frequency statistics, which will improve the performance of the tokenizer in Japanese and the de-inflector in both languages. Part of speech information is also being added, in anticipation of the use of grammatical tools.

The second program is the development of a probabilistic grammar to parse the source and provide grammatical information to the user. This will supplement or replace the current rule-based finite-state parser currently implemented in the system. In the current phase, we have chosen a lexicalized context-free grammar, which has the property that the probability of choosing a particular production rule in the grammar is dependent on headwords associated with each non-terminal symbol. Lexicalization is a useful tool for resolving attachment questions and in sense disambiguation. This grammar will be trained using the inside-outside algorithm [7] on Japanese and Spanish newspaper articles.

One use of the grammar will be to provide more accurate glossing of the source by making use of co-occurrence statistics among the phrase headwords. This requires developing an English word list with frequency and part of speech information, as well as constructing an English inflector-deinflector. These tools, along with an English grammar, will enable the system to construct candidate translations of Japanese phrases and simple Spanish sentences.

A longer term goal of the syntactic analysis (particularly when more languages are incorporated) is to generate a probability distribution in a space of data structures in which the order of representation of the component grammatical elements is language neutral. This can regarded as a kind of syntactic interlingua. There will also be a deeper semantic analysis of the source which will be less dependent on the syntactic analysis, and will use a probabilistic model to fill in the components of a case-frame semantic interlingua. These kinds of structures will allow faster inclusion of new languages and domains.

References

1. P.F. Brown, S.A. DellaPietra, V.J. DellaPietra, and R.L. Mercer, "The Mathematics of Machine Translation: Parameter Estimation," submitted to Computational Linguistics, 1991.
2. P.F. Brown, S.A. DellaPietra, V.J. DellaPietra, J. Lafferty, and R.L. Mercer, "Analysis, Statistical Transfer, and Synthesis in Machine Translation," submitted to TMI-92, Fourth International Conference on Theoretical and Methodological Issues in Machine Translation, 1992.
3. D. Farwell and Y. Wilkes, "ULTRA: A Multi-lingual Machine Translator," Proceedings of the Third MT Summit, pp. 19–24, 1991.
4. E. Hovy and S. Nirenburg, "Approximating an Interlingua in a Principled Way," Proceedings of the Speech and Natural Language Workshop, pp. 261–266, 1992.
5. K. Knight, "Building a Large Ontology for Machine Translation," Proceedings of the ARPA Workshop on Human Language Technology, 1993.
6. R. Frederking, D. Grannes, P. Cousseau, and S. Nirenburg, "A MAT Tool and Its Effectiveness," Proceedings of the ARPA Workshop on Human Language Technology, 1993.
7. J.K. Baker, "Trainable Grammars for Speech Recognition," Speech Communication Papers for the 97th Meeting of the Acoustical Society of America (D.H. Klatt and J.J. Wolf, eds.), pp. 547–550, 1979.

An MAT Tool and Its Effectiveness

Robert Frederking, Dean Grannes, Peter Cousseau, Sergei Nirenburg

Carnegie Mellon University
Center for Machine Translation
Pittsburgh, PA 15213

ABSTRACT

Although automatic machine translation (MT) of unconstrained text is beyond the state of the art today, the need for increased translator productivity is urgent. The PANGLOSS system addresses this dilemma by integrating MT with machine-aided translation (MAT). The main measure of progress in the development of the PANGLOSS system is a gradual increase in the level of automation. The current PANGLOSS MT system typically generates sub-sentence-length units of the target text. Any remaining gaps are treated by lexicon lookup. A mixture of these two kinds of *components* is presented to the user using the CMAT (Component Machine-Aided Translation) editor, which was designed to facilitate the transformation of this output into a high-quality text. An experiment evaluating the utility of the CMAT editor demonstrated its usefulness in this task, and provides useful guidance for further development.

1. Introduction

Fully automated machine translation of unconstrained texts is beyond the state of the art today. The need for mechanizing the translation process is, however, very urgent. It is desirable, therefore, to seek ways of both speeding up the process of translating texts and making it less expensive. In this paper we describe an environment that facilitates the integration of automatic machine translation (MT) and machine-aided translation (MAT).

This environment, called the Translator's Workstation (TWS)[5], has been developed in the framework of the PANGLOSS machine translation project.[1] The main goal of this project is to develop a system that will, from the very beginning, produce high-quality output. This can only be attained currently by keeping the human being in the translation loop. The main measure of progress in the development of the Pangloss system is the gradual increase in the level of automation.

PANGLOSS MARK I translates from Spanish into English, although additional source languages are planned. The analyzer used in this configuration is a version of the ULTRA Spanish analyzer from NMSU[2], while generation is carried out by the PENMAN generator from ISI[4]. The Translator's Workstation provides the user interface and the integration platform. It is similar in spirit to systems such as the Translator's Workbench[3].

The processing in PANGLOSS goes as follows:

1. an input passage is broken into sentences;
2. a fully-automated translation of each full sentence is attempted; if it fails, then
3. a fully-automated translation of smaller chunks of text is attempted (currently, these are noun phrases);
4. the material that does not get covered by noun phrases is treated in a "word-for-word" mode, whereby translation suggestions for each word (or phrase) are sought in the system's MT lexicons, an online bilingual dictionary, and a set of user-supplied glossaries;
5. The resulting list of translated noun phrases and translation suggestions for words and phrases is displayed in a special editor window, where the human user finalizes the translation.

This entire process can be viewed as helping a human translator, by doing parts of the job automatically and making the rest less time-consuming.

We have designed and implemented an intelligent post-editing environment, the CMAT (Component Machine-Aided Translation) editor.

2. The User's View

The CMAT editor allows the user to move, replace or delete output text elements, called *components*, with at most two mouse actions. The main user interface tool is a dynamically-changing popup menu available for each component. The ordering of alternate selections in the menus changes as the tool is used, to reflect the most recent user choices.

Suppose the user selects a region of source text by highlighting it and submits it to be machine-translated. The result appears in a target window as a string of components, each

[1]PANGLOSS is a joint project of the Center for Machine Translation at Carnegie Mellon University (CMU), the Computing Research Laboratory of New Mexico State University (NMSU), and the Information Sciences Institute of the University of Southern California (ISI).

surrounded by "≪" and "≫" characters.[2] A mouse click anywhere within a single component brings up a CMAT menu for that component. In Figure 1, the user has clicked on the word "increase". A CMAT menu consists of three regions, each separated by a horizontal line. From top to bottom these are:

- The LABEL region, which contains the word or phrase in the source text that produced this particular component.[3]
- The FUNCTION region, which contains the post-editing **Move**, **Delete**, **Modify**, and **Finish** functions. When the user selects **Move**, the component disappears, and the mouse pointer changes shape, indicating that a **Move** is in progress. The component is reinserted into the text at the nearest word break to the point where the user clicks the mouse again. **Delete** simply deletes the component. **Modify** pops up a window that allows the user to type in a new alternative (see next bullet). **Finish** removes the component markers, indicating that CMAT editing for this component is finished.[4]
- The ALTERNATIVE region contains alternative translations of the source word or phrase. The source word or phrase is also present as an alternative, when available, as translators may wish to leave some source language words temporarily in the target text, and return to them later. Selecting one of the alternatives replaces the original selection for this component with the alternative, while the latter becomes an alternative in the alternative region.

An additional menu-base editing feature allows the user to change the morphology of a word with a single mouse action (Figure 2). This menu changes verb inflection or the determiner on a noun phrase, stripping any old morphological features before adding the new one.

Using these popup menus, the user can move, replace, modify, or delete an output component with one or two mouse actions, rapidly turning the string of translated words and phrases into a coherent, high-quality target language text. Note that the user is not forced to use the CMAT editor at any particular time. Its use can be intermingled with other translation activities, according to the user's preferences.

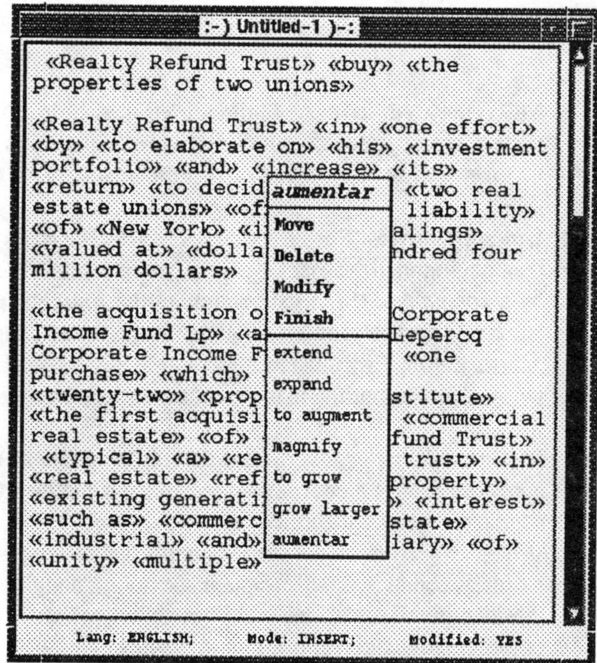

Figure 1: A typical CMAT menu

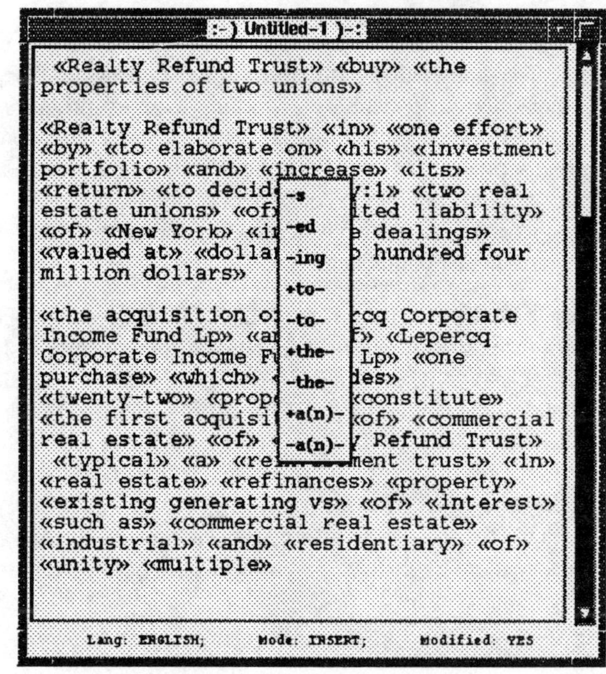

Figure 2: A typical CMAT morphology menu

3. The CMAT Editor

As part of the TWS, the CMAT editor is implemented in Common LISP. It communicates through CLM (the Common LISP-Motif interface)[1] to use Motif widgets inside of the X11 window system.

The CMAT editor views text as a list of components. These

[2] If two components with different internal forms have the same string, it is followed by a colon and an integer.

[3] Note that this information is not always available in noun phrase translation.

[4] The user may also choose to wait and remove all the markers at once, for either a selected region or the whole buffer, using a selection in the TWS's main menu bar or a special keystroke.

components are of three types:

1. **MT-generated strings.** Phrases translated by the MT system are represented simply as the generated target language string, and are not further processed by CMAT.

2. **Glossary entries.** Phrases not translated by the MT system, but found in the user glossaries, are each represented by a *component list*, a list containing the *source string* (source language phrase), the identifier `:GLOSS`, and a *glossary entry list*: a list of the possible target language phrases corresponding to the source language phrase.

3. **Dictionary entries.** Words not covered by either of the above are represented by a component list containing the source string, the identifier `:MT` and a *target language string list*: a list of the corresponding target language words as found in the MT system's lexicons; and finally the identifier `:DICT` and a *dictionary entry list*: a list of target language words found in the machine-readable dictionary.

The CMAT editor uses a knowledge base and a working memory. The knowledge base stores static information for a component's menu, while the working memory provides a mapping between the knowledge base and the components currently present in the target buffer. This separation is necessary because any given component generally occurs more than once in a given text, but there is only one menu associated with a particular component.

Knowledge base structures are indexed by their component source strings. These structures contain four slots, one slot each for `:GLOSS`, `:MT`, and `:DICT` lists, plus a fourth slot containing the *candidate list*. This list is a union of the first three lists, with the elements' positions varying to reflect current estimates of their likelihood of being chosen by the user. Initially, the items from the target language string list appear first in the list and glossary entries appear second, since these items are more likely to be the correct translations of a source string in our domain.

When a component list is passed to the CMAT editor to be displayed, the latter first checks to see if a structure for the component already exists in the knowledge base. If an entry does not exist, one is created. Then the first component is chosen from the candidate list and displayed with brackets in the editor window. In the working memory, a pointer to the knowledge base entry is stored, indexed by the displayed component.

When the user clicks the mouse within a CMAT component, the system must use the actual character string as the index into the working memory, and from there get the index into the knowledge base.[5] The list of alternative translations for the component can then be obtained from the knowledge base structure.

If a component is **Moved** in the editor window, nothing changes in the internal representation of the CMAT editor. When a component is **Deleted**, the pointer in the working memory is removed. If an alternative translation is chosen from the candidate list, the old component is replaced with a new component in the CMAT editor. The pointer in the working memory is removed from its old location and stored under the new component. The new candidate is also moved to the front of the candidate list as the most likely candidate for future use. When a component is **Modified**, the new alternative entered by the user is stored in the knowledge base, and then treated as if it had just been chosen.

When the component's markers are removed, either singly or *en masse*, the component's pointer in the working memory is removed, but the entry in the knowledge base remains. These are retained in order to provide a summary of the user's preferences, for the frequent case where future translations contain these components. This summary can be saved as a file, which can be loaded into the knowledge base in a later editing session, or analyzed by system developers.

4. The Evaluation of the Tool

In order to evaluate the effectiveness of this tool, we compared editing with the CMAT editor versus editing with just the basic Emacs-like text editor in which it is embedded. We conducted two experiments comparing CMAT and non-CMAT editing efficiency, one using monolinguals and one using translators.

4.1. Experiment I

Method. The monolingual task was to take the output of the MT system and, using as reference an English translation that was previously produced manually, produce the "same" text using either the CMAT editor or the regular editor. The time required for each text-editing session was recorded. Keystrokes and mouse actions were automatically counted by the interface.

As test texts, we used two of the texts from the 1992 DARPA MT evaluation. To shorten total experiment time and provide a reasonable number of sample texts, we broke each text into two halves of roughly equal size, at paragraph breaks, resulting in four text samples.

Two subjects were presented with the samples in the same order. Their use of the CMAT or the plain Emacs editor on

[5] This is due to details of the CLM interface, and is the reason for marking identical components that have different internal data structures with a colon and an integer: otherwise there would be no way to locate the correct associated data structure.

different samples was arranged to provide as much variation as possible in practice effects and acclimatization, so that these could be cancelled out during analysis. A few days later, subjects repeated the procedure, reversing the use or non-use of the CMAT editor. Since practice effects should be more uniform in a simple editing task than in translation (the task is much less intellectually challenging), we felt that texts could be reused if practice effects are taken into account in analysis.

Subjects were instructed to produce a "close paraphrase" of the example translation, since any two translators will produce slightly different correct translations of the same text. Subjects were also instructed not to use the CMAT **Modify** function, since it causes the editor to learn during use, making analysis even harder.

Analysis. Given the above ordering of test runs, one can balance practice effects, subject differences, and text differences simply by normalizing the total editing times for a subject on each run through the texts. That is, if we divide the editing time for each text by the total time for the entire set of texts in the given run, the variation between normalized editing times *between subjects* should reflect variations in the efficiency of editing. For example, in Figure 3, we see that for Session 1, Subject 1 spent a greater fraction of time using CMAT (0.2413) than Subject 2 spent editing it in a regular editor (0.2198), while for Session 2, the fraction of total time was the same with either editor.

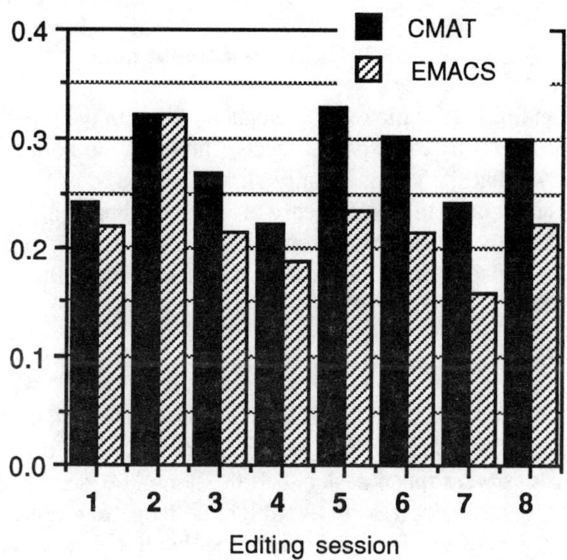

Figure 3: Normalized editing times

From comparing these normalized times, it appears that the CMAT actually slows subjects down. This contradicts the universal subjective impression of all CMAT users that it is quite helpful. It could be the case that the CMAT makes the job *easier* without making it *faster*, but we had the definite impression that it makes translating faster as well as easier. We therefore investigated further.

Normalized keystroke and mouse action counts are shown in Figures 4 and 5. Here we see that while the CMAT editing sessions had 1/2 to 1/3 the number of keystrokes, they had between 2 and 9 times as many mouse operations. This is significant, since mouse actions are slower than keystrokes.

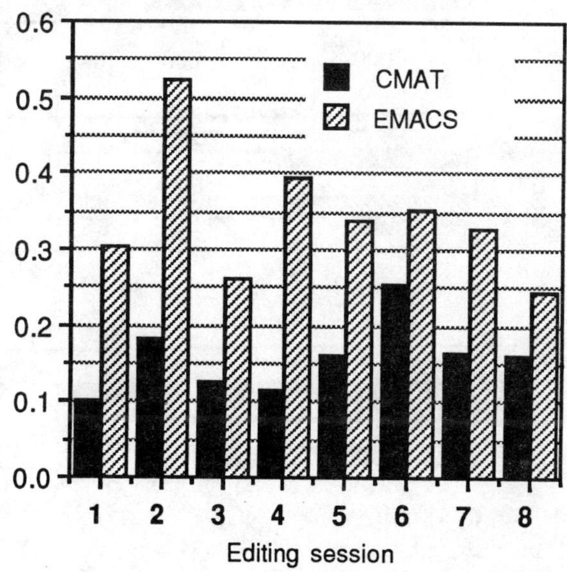

Figure 4: Normalized keystroke counts

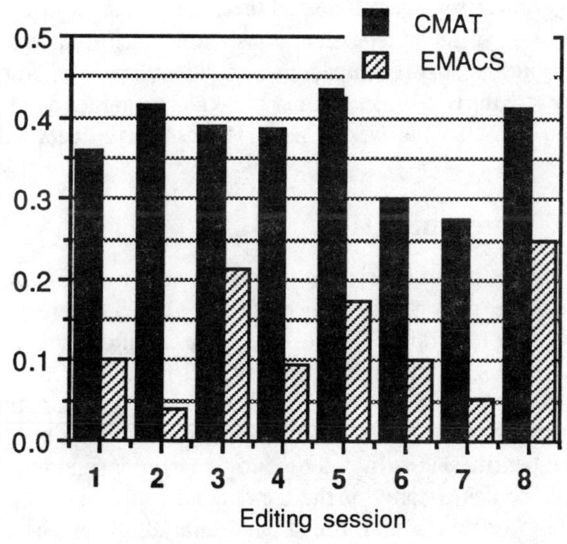

Figure 5: Normalized mouse action counts

Figure 6 shows that Subject 1 has roughly the same speed with or without CMAT, while Subject 2 is about 50% slower editing with the CMAT (top chart). Subject 2 also increases his mouse usage much more during CMAT editing than Subject 1 (bottom chart). Thus all the slow down of the CMAT might be attributable to mouse usage.[6]

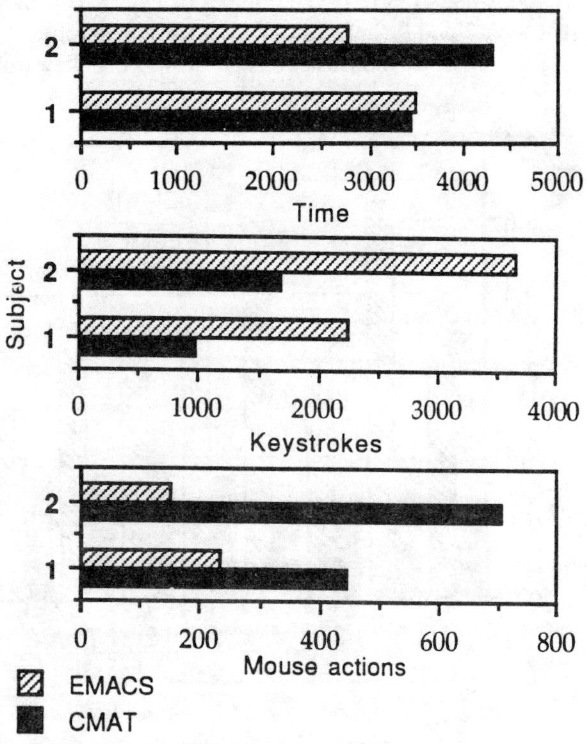

Figure 6: Total times and counts

Experiment I suggested that all the value of the CMAT editor comes from its assistance to translation, since it had either a negligible positive impact or a negative impact on editing times for the two subjects. Emacs is widely regarded as a very good editor, so this hypothesis made sense, but still needed to be tested.

4.2. Experiment II

Method. In this experiment, actual Spanish to English translation was performed. Subjects practiced on a different text until they felt comfortable using the CMAT editor. This time, subjects used the original Spanish text for reference, as is usual when using the TWS. Since translation takes more time, fewer texts were done. Also, each text could only be used once per translator. In order to provide more insight into the exact benefit, if any, of the CMAT editor, times and counts were recorded for both "rough" and "final" drafts of the translations, as judged by the translators. In all other respects, the experiment was conducted like the first one.

[6] It may also be significant that Subject 2 is a touch-typist. His non-CMAT times are faster than Subject 1's, even with roughly 50% more keystrokes.

Analysis. Three translators took part in this test, but one (Subject 4) clearly had not acclimated to using the CMAT, and his data point had to be discarded. He took much longer than anyone else when using the CMAT editor.

Since there had been three subjects, Subject 5 used the CMAT for both texts. Therefore these results had to be analyzed differently than the first experiment: the normalized times for Subject 5 were used to determine the intrinsic difficulty of the two different texts. So if the other subject spent more time on a text than Subject 5, this should have been due to more difficult editing conditions.

As shown in Figure 7, the use of the CMAT editor resulted in an editing time of 89.74% of what would have been expected with Emacs, or in other words a 10.3% speedup compared to non-CMAT editing (top bar). While this number obviously cannot be taken too literally, it does provide an initial indication of a significant speed improvement through the use of the CMAT editor, which should be verified with further testing.

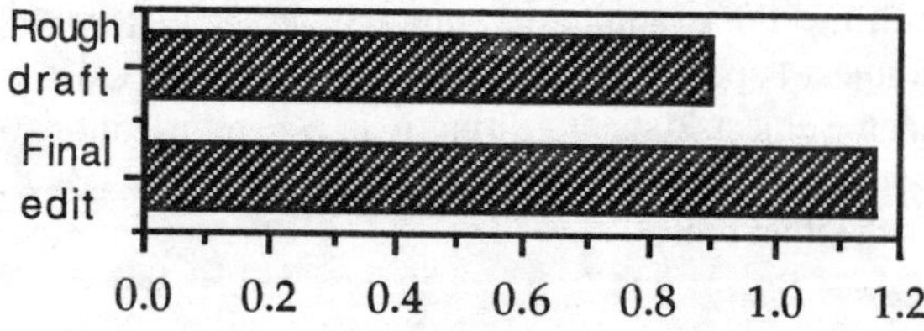

Figure 7: CMAT/Emacs time ratio

In addition, the ratio of the time taken *between* the rough and final drafts by these two subjects, shown in the bottom bar, shows that the CMAT actually slowed editing down a bit in this interval. This makes sense given the earlier results, since essentially all the translation was finished, and only editing remained to be done. So all 10% of the speed-up is attributable to faster translating.

4.3. Discussion

Users of the CMAT editor all indicate that it is helpful in translating. The current test subjects also reported that the CMAT sessions were much easier than the non-CMAT sessions. In fact, one subject tried to avoid taking the second non-CMAT test. Part of this benefit seems to be due to the easy on-line access to relevant dictionary entries. Another benefit is that the brackets provided by the CMAT help the user to segment (and then interpret) the fragmentary English output, and to locate untranslated words. These experiments did not attempt to measure quality differences between test conditions. We intend to carry out further experiments that look for quality enhancement from using the CMAT editor, due to the additional information available to translators, and that measure any trade-off between quality and speed of translation.

In the second experiment, the normalized total-edit time ratios between the two texts for Subject 5 were essentially identical to the rough draft ratios, indicating that this ratio is indeed a good indicator of the relative difficulty of the two passages.

It is interesting to note that Subject 4, whose data point had to be thrown out because his CMAT times were twice the length of his non-CMAT times, corresponds closely to the level of familiarity our translators had with the CMAT editor in the first MT evaluation in 1992. An important part of our preparation for the 1993 MT evaluation will be training the test subjects in the most efficient use of our tools.

5. Conclusion and Future Work

The CMAT editor, in conjunction with often fragmentary MT and word-for-word translation, allows the translator to produce high-quality translations more quickly and easily than the simple combination of a text editor and an online dictionary. It will remain a crucial module in PANGLOSS until the MT system reaches the point of translating full sentences on a regular basis.

These experiments provide initial evidence that the CMAT editor is indeed effective, and have been very useful in pointing out areas for improvement:

- The current CMAT design requires the use of the mouse. Since mouse actions are often slower than keystrokes, we will provide keybindings for *all* CMAT commands, including viewing and selecting alternative translations. This should not be technically difficult.
- The users need to be taught the most effective strategies for using the CMAT, such as only using the mouse if they are fast with it, and generally not using the CMAT after their rough draft is finished.
- Currently the CMAT menu often does not contain the correct answer, due to the low-quality of the online dictionary. This dictionary is currently being replaced, and we expect the coverage to be much improved for the next MT evaluation.

References

1. Bäcker, A., C. Beilken, T. Berlage, A. Genau, M. Spenke, 1992. CLM – A Language Binding for Common Lisp and OSF/Motif: User Guide and Reference Manual, Version 2.1, Technical report, German National Research Center for Computer Science.
2. Farwell, D., Y. Wilks, 1990. ULTRA: a Multi-lingual Machine Translator. Memoranda in Computing and Cognitive Science MCCS-90-202, Computing Research Laboratory, New Mexico State University, Las Cruces, NM, USA.
3. Kugler, M., G. Heyer, R. Kese, B. von Kleist-Retzow, G. Winkelmann, 1991. The Translator's Workbench: An Environment for Multi-Lingual Text Processing and Translation. In Proceedings of MT Summit III, Washington, DC.
4. Mann, W., 1983. An Overview of the Penman Text Generation System. In Proceedings of the Third AAAI Conference (261-265). Also available as USC/Information Sciences Institute Research Report RR-83-114.
5. Nirenburg, S., P. Shell, A. Cohen, P. Cousseau, D. Grannes, C. McNeilly, 1992. Multi-purpose Development and Operation Environments for Natural Language Applications, In Proceedings of the 3rd Conference on Applied Natural Language Processing (ANLP-92), Trento, Italy.

But Dictionaries Are Data Too

Peter F. Brown, Stephen A. Della Pietra, Vincent J. Della Pietra, Meredith J. Goldsmith, Jan Hajic, Robert L. Mercer, and Surya Mohanty

IBM Thomas J. Watson Research Center
Yorktown Heights, NY 10598

ABSTRACT

Although empiricist approaches to machine translation depend vitally on data in the form of large bilingual corpora, bilingual dictionaries are also a source of information. We show how to model at least a part of the information contained in a bilingual dictionary so that we can treat a bilingual dictionary and a bilingual corpus as two facets of a unified collection of data from which to extract values for the parameters of a probabilistic machine translation system. We give an algorithm for obtaining maximum likelihood estimates of the parameters of a probabilistic model from this combined data and we show how these parameters are affected by inclusion of the dictionary for some sample words.

There is a sharp dichotomy today between rationalist and empiricist approaches to machine translation: rationalist systems are based on information cajoled fact by reluctant fact from the minds of human experts; empiricist systems are based on information gathered wholesale from data. The data most readily digested by our translation system is from bilingual corpora, but bilingual dictionaries are data too, and in this paper we show how to weave information from them into the fabric of our statistical model of the translation process.

When a lexicographer creates an entry in a bilingual dictionary, he describes in one language the meaning and use of a word from another language. Often, he includes a list of simple translations. For example, the entry for *disingenuousness* in the Harper-Collins Robert French Dictionary [1] lists the translations *déloyauté*, *manque de sincérité*, and *fourberie*. In constructing such a list, the lexicographer gathers, either through introspection or extrospection, instances in which *disingenuousness* has been used in various ways and records those of the different translations that he deems of sufficient importance. Although a dictionary is more than just a collection of lists, we will concentrate here on that portion of it that is made up of lists.

We formalize an intuitive account of lexicographic behavior as follows. We imagine that a lexicographer, when constructing an entry for the English word or phrase $\mathbf{e}$, first chooses a random size s, and then selects at random a sample of s instances of the use of $\mathbf{e}$, each with its French translation. We imagine, further, that he includes in his entry for $\mathbf{e}$ a list consisting of all of the translations that occur at least once in his random sample. The probability that he will, in this way, obtain the list $\mathbf{f}_1, \ldots, \mathbf{f}_m$, is

$$\Pr(\mathbf{f}_1, \ldots, \mathbf{f}_m|\mathbf{e}) = \sum_{s} \sum_{s_1>0} \cdots \sum_{s_m>0} \binom{s}{s_1 \cdots s_m} \Pr(s|\mathbf{e}) \textstyle\prod_{i=1}^{m} \Pr(\mathbf{f}_i|\mathbf{e})^{s_i}, \quad (1)$$

where $\Pr(\mathbf{f}_i|\mathbf{e})$ is the probability from our statistical model that the phrase $\mathbf{f}_i$ occurs as a translation of $\mathbf{e}$, and $\Pr(s|\mathbf{e})$ is the probability that the lexicographer chooses to sample s instances of $\mathbf{e}$. The multinomial coefficient is defined by

$$\binom{s}{s_1 \cdots s_k} = \frac{s!}{s_1! \cdots s_k!}, \quad (2)$$

and satisfies the recursion

$$\binom{s}{s_1 \cdots s_k} = \binom{s}{s_k} \binom{s - s_k}{s_1 \cdots s_{k-1}} \quad (3)$$

where $\binom{s}{s_k}$ is the usual binomial coefficient.

In general, the sum in Equation (1) cannot be evaluated in closed form, but we can organize an efficient calculation of it as follows. Let

$$\alpha(\sigma,\mu) = \sum_{s_1>0} \cdots \sum_{s_\mu>0} \binom{\sigma}{s_1 \cdots s_\mu} \prod_{i=1}^{\mu} p(\mathbf{f}_i|\mathbf{e})^{s_i}. \quad (4)$$

Clearly,

$$p(\mathbf{f}_1,\cdots,\mathbf{f}_m|\mathbf{e}) = \sum_s p(s|\mathbf{e})\alpha(s,m). \quad (5)$$

Using Equation (3), it is easy to show that

$$\alpha(\sigma,\mu) = \sum_{\kappa=1}^{\sigma-\mu+1} \binom{\sigma}{\kappa} p(\mathbf{f}_\mu|\mathbf{e})^\kappa \alpha(\sigma-\kappa,\mu-1), \quad (6)$$

and therefore, we can compute $p(\mathbf{f}_1,\cdots,\mathbf{f}_m|\mathbf{e})$ in time proportional to s^2m. By judicious use of thresholds, even this can be substantially reduced.

In the special case that $\Pr(s|\mathbf{e})$ is a Poisson distribution with mean $\lambda(\mathbf{e})$, *i.e.*, that

$$\Pr(s|\mathbf{e}) = \frac{\lambda(\mathbf{e})^s e^{-\lambda(\mathbf{e})}}{s!}, \quad (7)$$

we can carry out the sum in Equation (1) explicitly,

$$\Pr(\mathbf{f}_1,\cdots,\mathbf{f}_m|\mathbf{e}) = e^{-\lambda(\mathbf{e})} \prod_{i=1}^{m} (e^{\lambda(\mathbf{e})p(\mathbf{f}_i|\mathbf{e})} - 1). \quad (8)$$

This is the form that we will assume throughout the remainder of the paper because of its simplicity. Notice that in this case, the probability of an entry is a product of factors, one for each of the translations that it contains.

The series $\mathbf{f}_1, \ldots, \mathbf{f}_m$ represents the translations of $\mathbf{e}$ that are included in the dictionary. We call this set of translations $D_\mathbf{e}$. Because we ignore everything about the dictionary except for these lists, a complete dictionary is just a collection of $D_\mathbf{e}$'s, one for each of the English phrases that has an entry. We treat each of these entries as independent and write the probability of the entire dictionary as

$$\Pr(D) \equiv \prod_{\mathbf{e}\in D} \Pr(D_\mathbf{e}|\mathbf{e}), \quad (9)$$

the product here running over all entries.

Equation (9) gives the probability of the dictionary in terms of the probabilities of the entries that make it up. The probabilities of these entries in turn are given by Equation (8) in terms of the probabilities, $p(\mathbf{f}|\mathbf{e})$, of individual French phrases given individual English phrases. Combining these two equations, we can write

$$\Pr(D) = \prod_{(\mathbf{e},\mathbf{f})\in D} (e^{\lambda(\mathbf{e})p(\mathbf{f}|\mathbf{e})} - 1) \prod_{\mathbf{e}\in D} e^{-\lambda(\mathbf{e})}. \quad (10)$$

We take $p(\mathbf{f}|\mathbf{e})$ to be given by the statistical model described in detail by Brown *et al.* [2]. Their model has a set of *translation probabilities*, $t(f|e)$, giving for each French word f and each English word e the probability that f will appear as (part of) a translation of e; a set of *fertility probabilities*, $n(\phi|e)$, giving for each integer ϕ and each English word e the probability that e will be translated as a phrase containing ϕ French words; and a set of distortion probabilities governing the placement of French words in the translation of an English phrase. They show how to estimate these parameters so as to maximize the probability,

$$\Pr(H) = \prod_{(\mathbf{e},\mathbf{f})\in H} p(\mathbf{f}|\mathbf{e}), \quad (11)$$

of a collection of pairs of aligned translations, $(\mathbf{e},\mathbf{f}) \in H$.

Let Θ represent the complete set of parameters of the model of Brown *et al.* [2], and let θ represent any one of the parameters. We extend the method of Brown *et al.* to develop a scheme for estimating Θ so as to maximize the joint probability of the corpus and the dictionary, $\Pr_\Theta(H,D)$. We assume that $\Pr_\Theta(H,D) = \Pr_\Theta(H)\Pr_\Theta(D)$. In general, it is possible only to find local maxima of $\Pr_\Theta(H,D)$ as a function of Θ, which we can do by applying the EM algorithm [3, 4]. The EM algorithm adjusts an initial estimate of Θ in a series of iterations. Each iteration consists of an estimation step in which a *count* is determined for each parameter, followed by a maximization step in which each parameter is replaced by a value proportional to its count. The count c_θ for a parameter θ is defined by

$$c_\theta = \theta \frac{\partial}{\partial\theta} \log \Pr_\Theta(H,D). \quad (12)$$

Because we assume that H and D are independent, we can write c_θ as the sum of a count for H and a count for D:

$$c_\theta = c_\theta(H) + c_\theta(D). \quad (13)$$

The corpus count is a sum of counts, one for each translation in the corpus. The dictionary count is also a sum of counts, but with each count weighted by a factor $\mu(\mathbf{e},\mathbf{f})$ which we call the *effective multiplicity* of the translation. Thus,

$$c_\theta(H) = \sum_{(\mathbf{e},\mathbf{f})\in H} c_\theta(\mathbf{e},\mathbf{f}) \quad (14)$$

and

$$c_\theta(D) = \sum_{(\mathbf{e},\mathbf{f})\in D} \mu(\mathbf{e},\mathbf{f}) c_\theta(\mathbf{e},\mathbf{f}) \quad (15)$$

with

$$c_\theta(\mathbf{e},\mathbf{f}) = \theta \frac{\partial}{\partial\theta} \log p_\Theta(\mathbf{f}|\mathbf{e}). \quad (16)$$

The effective multiplicity is just the expected number of times that our lexicographer observed the translation $(\mathbf{e},\mathbf{f})$ given the dictionary and the corpus. In terms of the *a priori multiplicity*, $\mu_0(\mathbf{e},\mathbf{f}) = \lambda(\mathbf{e})p(\mathbf{f}|\mathbf{e})$, it is given by

$$\mu(\mathbf{e},\mathbf{f}) = \frac{\mu_0(\mathbf{e},\mathbf{f})}{1 - e^{-\mu_0(\mathbf{e},\mathbf{f})}}. \quad (17)$$

Figure 1 shows the effective multiplicity as a function of the *a priori* multiplicity. For small values of $\mu_0(\mathbf{e},\mathbf{f})$, $\mu(\mathbf{e},\mathbf{f})$ is approximately equal to $1 + \mu_0(\mathbf{e},\mathbf{f})/2$. For very large values, $\mu_0(\mathbf{e},\mathbf{f})$ and $\mu(\mathbf{e},\mathbf{f})$ are approximately equal. Thus, if we expect *a priori* that the lexicographer will see the translation $(\mathbf{e},\mathbf{f})$ very many times, then the effective multiplicity will be nearly equal to this number, but even if we expect *a priori* that he will scarcely ever see a translation, the effective multiplicity for it cannot fall below 1. This is reasonable because in our model for the dictionary construction process, we assume that nothing can get into the dictionary unless it is seen at least once by the lexicographer.

RESULTS

We have used the algorithm described above to estimate translation probabilities and fertilities for our statistical model in two different ways. First, we estimated them from the corpus alone, then we estimated them from the corpus and the dictionary together. The corpus that we used is the proceedings of the Canadian Parliament described elsewhere [2]. The dictionary is a machine readable version of the HarperCollins Robert French Dictionary [1].

We do not expect that including information from the dictionary will have much effect on words that occur frequently in the corpus, and this is borne out by the data. But for words that are rare, we expect that there will be an effect.

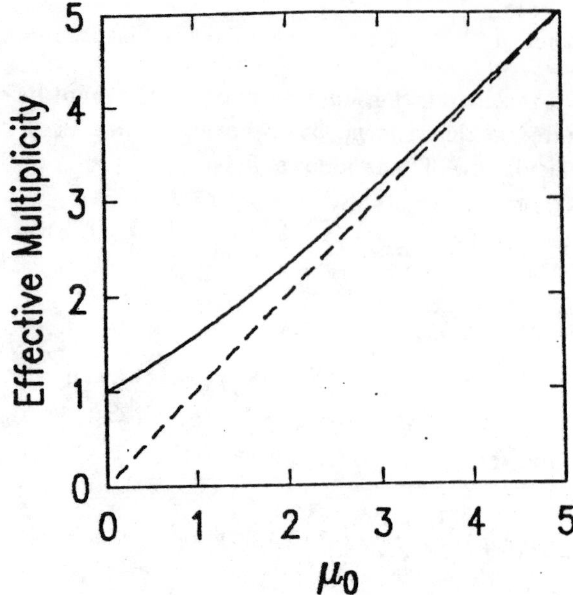

Figure 1: Effective multiplicity *vs* μ_0

f	$t(f\|e)$	ϕ	$n(\phi\|e)$
toundra	.233	3	.644
dans	.097	9	.160
autre	.048	1	.144
poser	.048	2	.021
ceux	.048	0	.029

Table 1: Parameters for *tundra*, corpus only

f	$t(f\|e)$	ϕ	$n(\phi\|e)$
toundra	.665	1	.855
dans	.040	3	.089
autre	.020	0	.029
poser	.020	9	.022
ceux	.020		

Table 2: Parameters for *tundra*, corpus and dictionary

Tables 1 and 2 show the two results for the English word *tundra*. The entry for *tundra* in the HarperCollins Robert French Dictionary [1] is simply the word *toundra*. We interpret this as a list with only one entry. We don't know how many times the lexicography ran across *tundra* translated as *toundra*, but we know that it was at least once, and we know that he never ran across it translated as anything else.

Even without the dictionary, *toundra* appears as the most probable translation, but with the dictionary, its probability is greatly improved. A more significant fact is the change in the fertility probabilities. Rare words have a tendency to act as garbage collectors in our system. This is why *tundra*, in the absence of guidance from the dictionary has, 3 as its most probable fertility and has a significant probability of fertility 9. With the dictionary, fertility 1 becomes the overwhelming favorite, and fertility 9 dwindles to insignificance.

Tables 3 and 4 show the trained parameters for *jungle*. The entry for *jungle* in the HarperCollins Robert French Dictionary is simply the word *jungle*. As with *tundra* using the dictionary enhances the probability of the dictionary translation of *jungle* and also improves the fertility substantially,

f	$t(f\|e)$	ϕ	$n(\phi\|e)$
jungle	.277	2	.401
dans	.072	1	.354
fouillis	.045	5	.120
domaine	.017	3	.080
devenir	.017	4	.020
imbroglio	.017	6	.019

Table 3: Parameters for *jungle*, corpus only

f	$t(f\|e)$	ϕ	$n(\phi\|e)$
jungle	.442	1	.598
dans	.057	5	.074
fouillis	.036	3	.049
domaine	.014	2	.024
devenir	.014	4	.012
imbroglio	.014	6	.012

Table 4: Parameters for *jungle*, corpus and dictionary

REFERENCES

[1] B. T. Atkins, A. Duval, R. C. Milne, P.-H. Cousin, H. M. A. Lewis, L. A. Sinclair, R. O. Birks, and M.-N. Lamy, *HarperCollins Robert French Dictionary*. New York: Harper & Row, 1990.

[2] P. F. Brown, S. A. DellaPietra, V. J. DellaPietra, and R. L. Mercer, "The mathematics of machine translation: Parameter estimation." Submitted to Computational Linguistics, 1992.

[3] L. Baum, "An inequality and associated maximization technique in statistical estimation of probabilistic functions of a Markov process," *Inequalities*, vol. 3, pp. 1-8, 1972.

[4] A. Dempster, N. Laird, and D. Rubin, "Maximum likelihood from incomplete data via the EM algorithm," *Journal of the Royal Statistical Society*, vol. 39, no. B, pp. 1-38, 1977.

EVALUATION OF MACHINE TRANSLATION

John S. White, Theresa A. O'Connell

PRC Inc.
McLean, VA 22102

and

Lynn M. Carlson

DoD

ABSTRACT

This paper reports results of the 1992 Evaluation of machine translation (MT) systems in the DARPA MT initiative and results of a Pre-test to the 1993 Evaluation. The DARPA initiative is unique in that the evaluated systems differ radically in languages translated, theoretical approach to system design, and intended end-user application. In the 1992 suite, a Comprehension Test compared the accuracy and interpretability of system and control outputs; a Quality Panel for each language pair judged the fidelity of translations from each source version. The 1993 suite evaluated adequacy and fluency and investigated three scoring methods.

1. INTRODUCTION

Despite the long history of machine translation projects, and the well-known effects that evaluations such as the ALPAC Report (Pierce et al., 1966) have had on that history, optimal MT evaluation methodologies remain elusive. This is perhaps due in part to the subjectivity inherent in judging the quality of any translation output (human or machine). The difficulty also lies in the heterogeneity of MT language pairs, computational approaches, and intended end-use.

The DARPA machine translation initiative is faced with all of these issues in evaluation, and so requires a suite of evaluation methodologies which minimize subjectivity and transcend the heterogeneity problems. At the same time, the initiative seeks to formulate this suite in such a way that it is economical to administer and portable to other MT development initiatives. This paper describes an evaluation of three research MT systems along with benchmark human and external MT outputs. Two sets of evaluations were performed, one using a relatively complex suite of methodologies, and the other using a simpler set on the same data. The test procedure is described, along with a comparison of the results of the different methodologies.

The authors would like to express their gratitude to Michael Naber for his assistance in compiling, expressing and interpreting data.

2. SYSTEMS

In a test conducted in July, 1992, three DARPA-sponsored research systems were evaluated in comparison with each other, with external MT systems, and with human-only translations. Each system translated 12 common Master Passages and six unique Original Passages, retrieved from commercial databases in the domain of business mergers and acquisitions. Master Passages were Wall Street Journal articles, translated into French, Spanish and Japanese for cross-comparison among the MT systems and languages. Original Passages were retrieved in French, Spanish, and Japanese, for translation into English.

The 1992 Evaluation tested three research MT systems:

CANDIDE (IBM, French - English) uses a statistical language modeling technique based on speech recognition algorithms (see Brown et al., 1990). It employs alignments generated between French strings and English strings by training on a very large corpus of Canadian parliamentary proceedings represented in parallel French and English. The CANDIDE system was tested in both Fully Automatic (FAMT) and Human-assisted (HAMT) modes.

PANGLOSS (Carnegie Mellon University, New Mexico State University, and University of Southern California) uses lexical, syntactic, semantic, and knowledge-based techniques for analysis and generation (Nirenburg, et al. 1991). The Spanish-English system is essentially an "interlingua" type. Pangloss operates in human-assisted mode, with system-initiated interactions with the user for disambiguation during the MT process.

LINGSTAT (Dragon Systems Inc.) is a computer-aided translation environment in which a knowledgeable non-expert can compose English translations of Japanese by using a variety of contextual cues with word parsing and character interpretation aids (Bamberg 1992).

Three organizations external to the DARPA initiative provided benchmark output. These systems ran all the test input that was submitted to the research systems. While these systems are not all at the same state of commercial robustness, they nevertheless provided external perspective on the state of FAMT outside the DARPA initiative.

The Pan American Health Organization provided output from the SPANAM Spanish-English system, a production system used daily by the organization.

SYSTRAN Translation Systems Inc. provided output from a French - English production system and a Spanish - English pilot prototype.

The Foreign Broadcast Information Service provided output from a Japanese-English SYSTRAN system. Though it is used operationally, SYSTRAN Japanese-English is not trained for the test domain.

3. MT EVALUATION METHODOLOGIES

The 1992 Evaluation introduced two methods to meet the challenge of developing a black-box evaluation that would minimize judgment subjectivity while allowing a measure of comparison among three disparate systems. A Comprehension Test measured the adequacy or intelligibility of translated outputs, while a Quality Panel was established to measure translation fidelity.

The 1992 Evaluation provided meaningful measures of performance and progress of the research systems, while providing quantitative measures of comparability of diverse systems. By these measures, the methodologies served their purpose. However, developing and evaluating materials was difficult and labor-intensive, involving special personnel categories.

In order to assess whether alternative metrics could provide comparable or better evaluation results at reduced costs, a Pre-test to the 1993 Evaluation was conducted. The Pre-test was also divided into two parts: an evaluation of adequacy according to a methodology suggested by Tom Crystal of DARPA; and an evaluation of fluency. The new methodologies were applied to the 1992 MT test output to compare translations of a small number of Original Passages by the DARPA and benchmark systems against human-alone translations produced by human translators. These persons were nonprofessional level 2 translators as defined by the Interagency Language Roundtable and adopted government-wide by the Office of Personnel Management in 1985.

In the second suite, three numerical scoring scales were investigated: yes/no, 1-3 and 1-5. Two determinations arise from the comparison: whether the new methodology is in fact better in terms of cost, sensitivity (how accurately the variation between systems is represented) and portability, and which scoring variant of the evaluation is the best by the same terms.

The methodologies used in the 1992 Evaluation and 1993 Pre-test are described briefly below.

3.1. Comprehension Test Methodology

In the 1992 Evaluation, a set of Master Passage versions formed the basis of a multiple-choice Comprehension Test, similar to the comprehension section of the verbal Scholastic Aptitude Test (SAT). These versions consisted of the "master passages" originally in English, professionally translated into the test source languages, and translated back into English by the systems, benchmarks and human translators.

Twelve test takers unfamiliar with the source languages answered the same multiple choice questions over different translation versions of the passages. They each read the same 12 passages, but rendered variously into the 12 outputs represented in the test (CANDIDE FAMT, CANDIDE HAMT, PANGLOSS HAMT, LINGSTAT HAMT, SPANAM FAMT, SYSTRAN FAMT for all three language pairs, human-only for all three pairs, and the Master Passages themselves.) The passages were ordered so that no person saw any passage, nor any output version twice.

3.2. Quality Panel Methodology

In the second part of the 1992 Evaluation, for each source language, a Quality Panel of three professional translators assigned numerical scores rating the fidelity of translated versions of six Original and six Master Passages against sources or back-translations. Within a given version of a passage, sentences were judged for syntactic, lexical, stylistic and orthographic errors.

3.3. Pre-test Adequacy Methodology

As part of the 1993 Pre-test, nine monolinguals judged the extent to which the semantic content of six baseline texts from each source language was present in translations produced for the 1992 Evaluation by the test systems and the benchmark systems. The 1992 Evaluation level 2 translations were used as baselines. In the 18 baselines, scorable units were bracketed fragments that corresponded to a variety of grammatical constituents. Each monolingual saw 16 machine or human-assisted translations. Each evaluator saw two passages from each system. The passages were ordered so that no person saw the same passage twice.

3.4. Pre-test Fluency Methodology

In Part Two of the Pre-test, the nine monolinguals evaluated the fluency (well-formedness) of each sentence in the same distribution of the same 16 versions that they had seen in Part One. In Part Two, these sentences appeared in paragraph form, without brackets.

4. RESULTS

In both the 1992 Evaluation and the 1993 Pre-test, the quality of output and time taken to produce that output were compared across:

- human-alone translations
- output from benchmark MT systems
- output from the research systems in FAMT and/or HAMT modes.

The results of the Comprehension Test (in which all systems used what were originally the same passages) are similar to the results of the Quality Panel, with some minor exceptions (see White, 1992). Thus for the purpose of the discussion that follows, we compare the results of the second, adequacy-fluency suite against the comparable subset of the Quality Panel test from the first suite.

The Pre-test evaluation results are arrayed in a manner that emphasizes both the adequacy or fluency of the human-assisted and machine translations and the human effort involved to produce translations, expressed in (normalized) time. For each part of the Pre-test, scores were tabulated, entered into a spreadsheet table according to scoring method and relevant unit, and represented in two dimensional arrays. The relevant unit for Part 1 is the adequacy score for each fragment in each version evaluated. For Part 2, the relevant unit is the score for fluency of each sentence in each version evaluated.

Performance for each of the systems scored was computed by averaging the fragment (or sentence) score over all fragments (or sentences), passages, and test subjects. The method for normalizing these average scores was to divide them by the maximum score per fragment (or sentence); for example, 5 for the 1-5 tests. Thus, a perfect averaged normalized system score is 1, regardless of the test.

Three evaluators each saw two passages per system; thus there was a total of six normalized average scores per system. The mean for each system is based on the six scores for that system. The eight system means were used to calculate the global variance. The F-ratio was calculated by dividing the global variance, i.e. the variance of the mean per system, by the local variance, i.e. the mean variance of each system. The F-ratio is used as a measure of sensitivity.

The Quality Panel scores were arrayed in a like manner. The quality score per passage was divided by the number of sentences in that passage. The six Original Passages were each evaluated by 3 translators producing a total of 18 scores per system. Adding the 18 scores per system together and dividing by 18 produced the mean of the normalized quality score per system. The means, variances and F-ratios were calculated as described above for adequacy and fluency.

4.1. Quality Panel Evaluation Results

Figure 1 is a representation of the Quality Panel evaluation, from the first evaluation suite, using the comparable subset of the 1992 data (i.e., the original passages). The quality scores range from .570 for Candide HAMT to .100 for Systran Japanese FAMT. The scores for time in HAMT mode, represented as the ratio of HAMT time to Human-Only translation time, range from .689 for Candide HAMT to 1.499 for Pangloss Spanish HAMT. The normalized time for FAMT systems is set at 0.

4.2. Adequacy Test Results

Figure 2 represents the results of the adequacy evaluation from the second suite. Using the 1-5 variation of the evaluation, the adequacy (vertical axis) scores range from .863 for Candide HAMT to .250 for Systran Japanese FAMT. The time axis reflects the same ratio as is indicated in Figure 1.

4.3. Fluency Test Results

Figure 3 represents the results of the fluency evaluation from the second suite. Using the 1-5 variant, fluency scores range from .853 for Candide HAMT to .214 for Systran Japanese FAMT. The time axis reflects the same ratio as is indicated in Figure 1.

5. COMPARISON OF METHODOLOGIES

The measures of adequacy and fluency used in the second suite are equated with the measure of quality used by the 1992 Evaluation Quality Panel. The methodologies were compared on the bases of sensitivity, efficiency, and expenditures of human time and effort involved in constructing, administering and performing the evaluation.

Cursory comparison of MT system performance in the three results shown in Figures 1 through 3 shows similarity in behavior. All three methodologies demonstrate higher adequacy, fluency and quality scores for

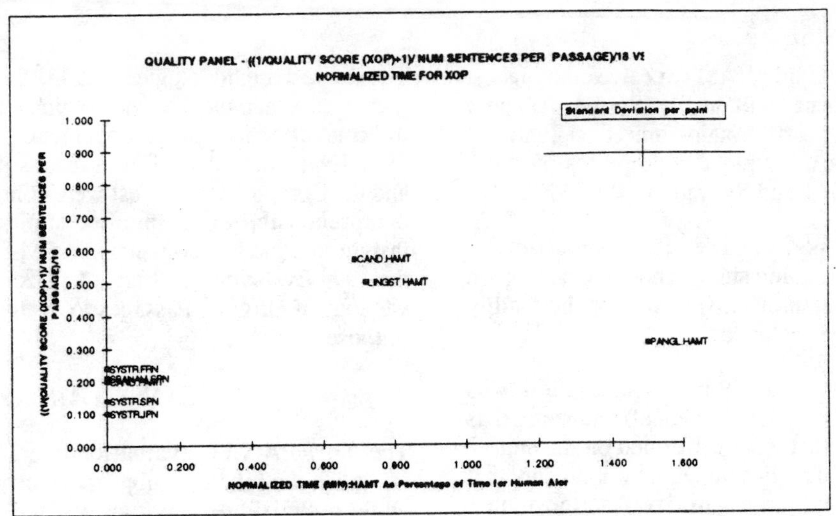

Figure 1: Quality Panel Results

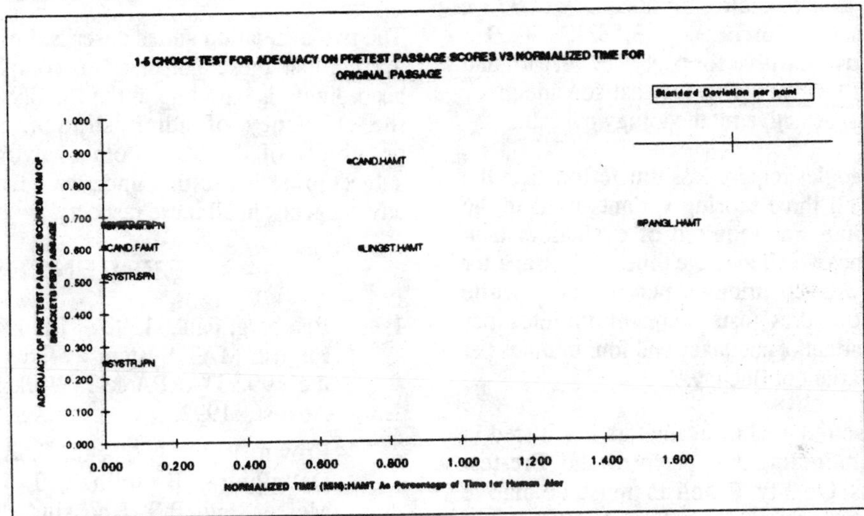

Figure 2: Adequacy Evaluation Results

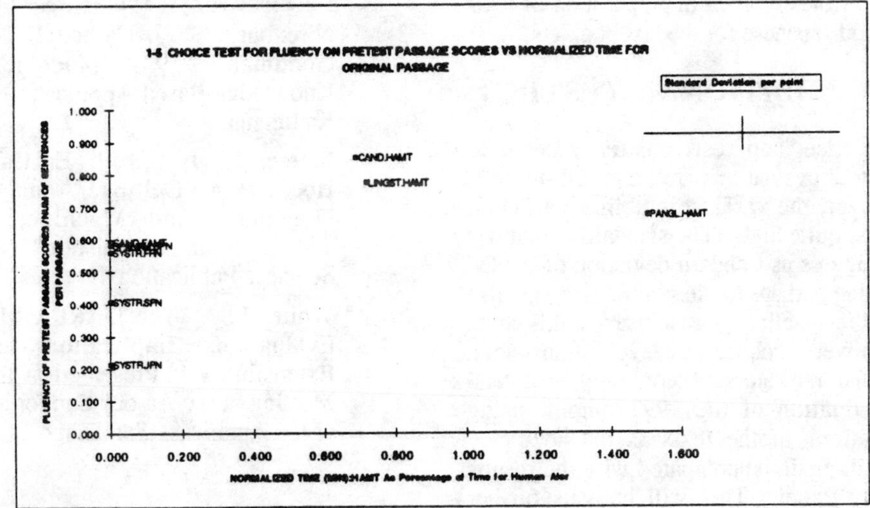

Figure 3: Fluency Evaluation Results

HAMT than FAMT. Candide HAMT receives the highest scores for adequacy, fluency and quality; Systran Japanese FAMT receives the lowest. Bounds are consistent, but occasionally Lingstat and Pangloss trade places on the y axis as do SpanAm FAMT and Systran French FAMT.

Given a similarity in performance, the comparison of evaluation suite 1 to evaluation suite 2 should depend upon the sensitivity of the measurements, as well as the facility of implementation of the evaluation.

To determine sensitivity, an F-ratio calculation was performed. For the suite 1 (Quality Panel) and suite 2, as well as for the variants that were performed on the suite 2 set (yes/no, 1-3, 1-5). The F-ratio statistic indicates that the second suite is indeed more sensitive than the suite 1 tests. (The Quality Panel test shows an F-ratio of 2.153.) The 1-3 and 1-5 versions both have certain sensitivity advantages: the 1-3 scale is central for adequacy (1.329.), but proves most sensitive for fluency (3.583). The 1-5 scale is by far the most sensitive for adequacy (4.136) and central for fluency (3.301). The 1-5 test for adequacy appears to be the most sensitive methodology overall.

The suite 2 methodologies require less time/effort than the Quality Panel. For all three scoring variants used in the second suite, less time was required of evaluators than Quality Panelists. The overall average time per passage for the Quality Panel was 26 minutes per passage, while average times for the Pre- tests were 11 minutes per passage for the 1-5 variant of adequacy and four minutes per passage for the 1-5 variant of fluency.

The level of expertise required of evaluators is reduced in the second suite; monolinguals perform the Pre-test evaluation, whereas Quality Panelists must be native speakers of English who are expert in French, Japanese or Spanish. The second suite eliminates a considerable amount of time and effort involved in preparation of texts in French, Spanish and Japanese for the test booklets.

6. NEED FOR ADDITIONAL TESTING

Human effort, expertise, and test sensitivity seem to indicate that the suite 2 evaluations are preferred over the suite 1 sets. However, the variance within a particular system result remains quite high. The standard deviations (represented in the figures as standard deviation of pooled variance) are large, due perhaps to the sample size, but also due to the fact that the baseline English used in this Suite 2 Pre-test evaluation were produced by level 2 translators, and not by professional translators. Accordingly, we intend to re-apply the evaluation of the 1992 output, using professional translations of the texts as the adequacy baseline. Results will again be compared with the results of the 1992 Quality Panel. This will help us further determine the usefulness, portability, and sensitivity of the evaluation methodologies.

The Pre-test methodologies measure the well-formedness of a translation and the degree to which a translation expresses the content of the source document. While results of the 1992 Evaluation showed that results of the Quality Panel and the Comprehension Test were comparable, a test of the comprehensibility of the translation provides unique insight into the performance of an MT system. Therefore, the 1993 Evaluation will include a Comprehension Test on versions of Original Passages to evaluate the intelligibility of those versions.

7. CONCLUSIONS

The DARPA MT evaluation methodology strives to minimize the inherent subjectivity of judging translations, while optimizing the portability and replicability of test results and accommodating the variety of approaches, languages, and end-user applications.

The two evaluation suites described in this paper sought to accomplish these goals. The comparison among them accordingly is based upon the fidelity of the measurement, the efficiency of administration, and ultimately the portability of the test to other environments. We find, subject to further testing underway, that the second suite is advantageous in all these respects.

REFERENCES

1. Bamberg, Paul. 1992. "The LINGSTAT Japanese-English MAT System" Status Report presented at the 1992 DARPA MT Workshop, Newton, MA August, 1992.
2. Brown, P. F., J. Cocke, S. A. DellaPietra, V. J. DellaPietra, F. Jelinek, J. D. Lafferty, R. L. Mercer, and P.S. Roossin. 1990. "A Statistical Approach to Machine Translation." Computational Linguistics, vol. 16, pp. 79-85.
3. Nirenburg, S., J. Carbonell, M. Tomita, and K. Goodman. 1991. Machine Translation: A Knowledge-Based Approach. New York: Morgan Kaufmann.
4. Pierce, J., J. Caroll, E. Hamp, D. Hays, C. Hockett, A. Oettinger, and A. Perlis. 1966. "Language and Machines: Computers in Translation and Linguistics." National Academy of Sciences Publication 416.
5. White, J.S. "The DARPA Machine Translation Evaluation: Implications for Methodological Extensibility." Presented at the November 1992 Meeting of the Association for Machine Translation of the Americas. San Diego.

RECENT ADVANCES IN JANUS: A SPEECH TRANSLATION SYSTEM

M.Woszczyna, N.Coccaro, A.Eisele, A.Lavie, A.McNair, T.Polzin, I.Rogina, C.P.Rose, T.Sloboda, M.Tomita, J.Tsutsumi, N.Aoki-Waibel, A.Waibel, W. Ward

Carnegie Mellon University
University of Karlsruhe

ABSTRACT

We present recent advances from our efforts in increasing coverage, robustness, generality and speed of JANUS, CMU's speech-to-speech translation system. JANUS is a speaker-independent system translating spoken utterances in English and also in German into one of German, English or Japanese. The system has been designed around the task of conference registration (CR). It has initially been built based on a speech database of 12 read dialogs, encompassing a vocabulary of around 500 words. We have since been expanding the system along several dimensions to improve speed, robustness and coverage and to move toward spontaneous input.

1. INTRODUCTION

In this paper we describe recent improvements of JANUS, a speech to speech translation system. Improvements have been made mainly along the following dimensions: 1.) better context-dependent modeling improves performance in the speech recognition module, 2.) improved language models, smoothing, and word equivalence classes improve coverage and robustness of the sentence that the system accepts, 3.) an improved N-best search reduces run-time from several minutes to now real time, 4.) trigram and parser rescoring improves selection of suitable hypotheses from the N-best list for subsequent translation. On the machine translation side, 5.) a cleaner interlingua was designed and syntactic and domain-specific analysis were separated for greater reusability of components and greater quality of translation, 6.) a semantic parser was developed to achieve semantic analysis, should more careful analysis fail.

The JANUS [1, 2] framework as it is presented here also allows us to experiment with components of a speech translation system, in an effort to achieve both robustness and high-quality translation. In the following we describe these efforts and system components that have been developed to date. At present, JANUS consists conceptually out of three major components: speech recognition, machine translation and speech synthesis. Since we have not made any significant attempts at improving performance on the synthesis end (DEC-talk and synthesizers produced by NEC and AEG-Daimler are used for English, Japanese and German output, respectively), our discussion will focus on the recognition and translation parts.

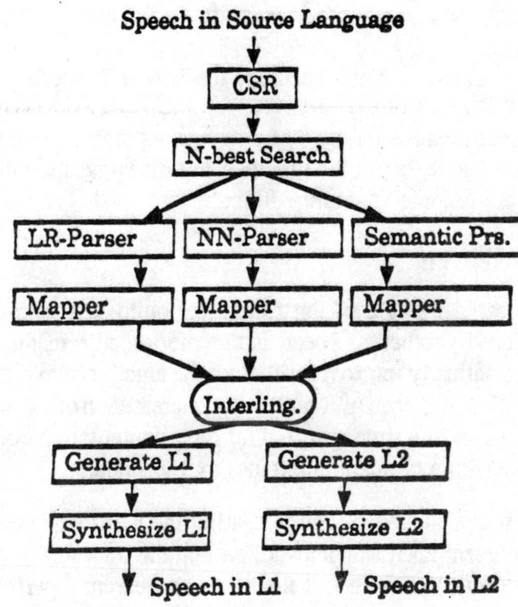

Figure 1: Overview of the System

2. RECOGNITION ENGINE

Our recognition engine uses several techniques to optimize the overall system performance. Speech input is preprocessed into time frames of spectral coefficients. Acoustic models are trained to give a score for each phoneme, representing the phoneme probability at the given frame. These scores are used by an N-best search algorithm to produce a list of sentence hypotheses. Based on this list, more computationally expensive language models are then applied to achieve further improvement of recognition accuracy.

2.1. Acoustic modeling

For acoustic modeling, several alternative algorithms are being evaluated including TDNN, MS-TDNN, MLP and LVQ [6, 5]. In the main JANUS system, an LVQ algorithm with context-dependent phonemes is now used for speaker independent recognition. For each phoneme, there is a context independent set of prototypical vectors. The output scores for each phoneme segment are computed from the euclidian distance using context dependent segment weights.

Error rates using context dependent phonemes are lower by a factor 2 to 3 for English (1.5 to 2 for German) than using context independent phonemes. Results are shown in table 1.

	English		German	
language model	PP	WA	PP	WA
none	400.0	58.2	425.0	63.0
word-pairs	28.9	83.4	20.8	89.1
bigrams	16.2	92.6	18.3	93.7
smoothed bigrams	18.1	91.5	28.90	84.7
after resorting	—	98.8		

Table 1: Word Accuracy for First Hypothesis

The performance on the RM-task at comparable perplexities is significantly better than for the CR-task, suggesting that the CR-task is somewhat more difficult.

2.2. Search

The search module of the recognizer builds a sorted list of sentence hypotheses. Speed and memory requirements could be dramatically improved: Though the amount of hypotheses computed for each utterance was increased from 6 to 100 hypotheses, the time required for their computation could be reduced from typically 3 minutes to 3 seconds.

This was achieved by implementing the word dependent N-best algorithm[3] as backward pass in the forward backward algorithm[4]: First a fast firstbest only search is performed, saving the scores at each possible word ending. In a second pass, this information is used for aggressive pruning to reduce the search effort for the N-best search. Further speedup was achieved by dynamically adapting the beam width to keep number of active states constant, and by carefully avoiding the evaluation of states in large inactive regions of words. Important for total system performance is the fact that the firstbest hypothesis can already be analyzed by the MT modules while the N-best list is computed.

All language models (word-pairs, bigrams or smoothed bigrams, and trigrams for resorting) are now trained on more than 1000 CR-sentences, using word class specific equivalence classes (digits, names, towns, languages etc.)

2.3. Resorting

The resulting N-best list is resorted using trigrams to further improve results. Resorting improves the word accuracy for the best scoring hypothesis (created using smoothed bigrams) from 91.5% to 98%, and the average rank of the correct hypothesis within the list from 5.7 to 1.1;

Much longer N-best lists have been used for experiments (500-1000). However it is very unlikely that a rescoring algorithm moves a hypothesis from the very bottom of such a long list to the 1st position. For practical application, a number of 100 hypotheses was found to be best.

3. THE MACHINE TRANSLATION (MT) ENGINE

The MT-component that we have previously used has now been replaced by a new module that can run several alternate processing strategies in parallel. To translate spoken language from one language to another, the analysis of spoken sentences, that suffer from ill-formed input and recognition errors is most certainly the hardest part. Based on the list of N-best hypotheses delivered by the recognition engine, we can now attempt to select and analyze the most plausible sentence hypothesis in view of producing and accurate and meaningful translation. Two goals are central in this attempt: *high fidelity* and *accurate translation* wherever possible, and *robustness* or *graceful degradation*, should attempts for high fidelity translation fail in face of ill-formed or misrecognized input. At present, three parallel modules attempt to address these goals: 1) an LR-parser based syntactic approach, 2) a semantic pattern based approach and 3) a connectionist approach. The most useful analysis from these modules is mapped onto a common Interlingua, a language independent, but domain-specific representation of meaning. The analysis stage attempts to derive a high precision analysis first, using a strict syntax and domain specific semantics. Connectionist and/or semantic parsers are currently applied as back-up, if the higher precision analysis fails. The Interlingua ensures that alternate modules can be applied in a modular fashion and that different output languages can be added without redesign of the analysis stage.

3.1. Generalized LR Parser

The first step of the translation process is syntactic parsing with the Generalized LR Parser/Compiler [16]. The Generalized LR parsing algorithm is an extension of LR parsing with the special device called "Graph-Structured Stack" [14], and it can handle arbitrary context-free grammars while most of the LR efficiency is preserved. A grammar with about 455 rules for general colloquial English is written in a Pseudo Unification formalism [15], that is similar to Unification Grammar and LFG formalisms. Figure2 shows the result of syntactic parsing of the sentence "Hello is this the conference office".

Robust GLR Parsing: Modifications have been made to make the Generalized LR Parser more robust against ill-formed input sentences [18]. In case the standard parsing procedure fails to parse an input sentence, the parser nondeterministically skips some word(s) in the sentence, and returns the parse with fewest skipped words. In this mode, the parser will return some parse(s) with any input sentence, unless no part of the sentence can be recognized at all.

```
(HELLO IS THIS THE CONFERENCE OFFICE $)

;++++ GLR Parser running to produce English structure ++++

 (1) ambiguities found and took 1.164878 seconds of real time

(((PREV-SENTENCES ((COUNTER 1) (MOOD *OPENING)
                               (ROOT *HELLO)))
   (COUNTER 2)
   (MOOD *INTERROGATIVE)
   (SUBJECT ((AGR *3-SING) (ROOT *THIS)
                           (CASE (*OR* *NOM *OBL))))
   (FORM *FINITE)
   (PREDICATE
     ((DET ((ROOT *THE) (DEF *DEF))) (AGR *3-SING)
                                     (ANIM *-)
                                     (A-AN *A)
                                     (ROOT *CONFERENCE-OFFICE)))
   (AGR *3-SING)
   (SUBCAT *SUBJ-PRED)
   (ROOT *COPULA)
   (TENSE *PRESENT)))
```

Figure 2: Example F-Structure

In the example in figure 3, the input sentence "Hello is this is this the office for the AI conference which will be held soon" is parsed as "Hello is this the office for the conference" by skipping 8 words. Because the analysis grammar or the interligua does not handle the relative clause "which will be held soon", 8 is the fewest possible words to skip to obtain a grammatical sentence which can be represented in the interligua. In the Generalized LR parsing, an extra procedure is applied every time a word is shifted onto the Graph Structured Stack. A heuristic similar to beam search makes the algorithm computationally tractable.

When the standard GLR parser fails on all of the 20 best sentence candidates, this robust GLR parser is applied to the best sentence candidate.

3.2. The Interlingua

This result, called "syntactic f-structure", is then fed into a mapper to produce an Interlingua representation. For the mapper, we use a software tool called Transformation Kit [17]. A mapping grammar with about 300 rules is written for the Conference Registration domain of English.

Figure 4 is an example of Interlingua representation produced from the sentence "Hello is this the conference office". In the example, "Hello" is represented as speech-act *ACKNOWLEDGEMENT, and the rest as speech-act *IDENTFY-OTHER.

```
Input sentence :
(hello is this is this the AI conference office which will be held soon $))

Parse of input sentence :
  (HELLO IS THIS THE CONFERENCE OFFICE $)

Words skipped : ((IS 2) (THIS 3) (AI 7) (WHICH 10) (WILL 11)
                 (BE 12) (HELD 13) (SOON 14))
```

Figure 3: Example for robust parsing

```
((PREV-UTTERANCES ((SPEECH-ACT *ACKNOWLEDGEMENT) (VALUE *HELLO)))
  (TIME *PRESENT)
  (PARTY
    ((DEFINITE +) (NUMBER *SG)
                  (ANIM -)
                  (TYPE *CONFERENCE)
                  (CONCEPT *OFFICE)))
  (SPEECH-ACT *IDENTIFY-OTHER))
```

Figure 4: Example: Interlingua Output

The JANUS interlingua is tailored to dialog translation. Each utterance is represented as one or more speech acts. A speech act can be thought of as what effect the speaker is intending a particular utterance to have on the listener. Our interlingua currently has eleven speech acts such as request direction, inform, and command. For purposes of this task, each sentence utterance corresponds to exactly one speech act. So the first task in the mapping process is to match each sentence with its corresponding speech act. In the current system, this is done on a sentence by sentence basis. Rules in the mapping grammar look for cues in the syntactic f-structure such as mood, combinations of auxilliary verbs, and person of the subject and object where it applies. In the future we plan to use more information from context in determining which speech act to assign to each sentence.

Once the speech act is determined, the rule for a particular speech act is fired. Each speech act has a top level semantic slot where the semantic representation for a particular instance of the speech act is stored during translation. This semantic structure is represented as a hierarchical concept list which resembles the argument structure of the sentence. Each speech act rule contains information about where in the syntactic structure to look for constituents to fill thematic roles such as agent, recipient, and patient in the semantic structure. Specific lexical rules map nouns and verbs onto concepts. In addition to the top level semantic slot, there are slots where information about tone and mood are stored. Each speech act rule contains information about what to look for in the syntactic structure in order to know how to fill this slot. For instance the auxiliary verb which is used in a command determines how imperative the command is. For example, 'You must register for the conference within a week' is much more imperative than 'You should register for the conference within a week'. The second example leaves some room for negotiation where the first does not.

3.3. The Generator

The generation of target language from an Interlingua representation involves two steps. Figure 5 shows sample traces of German and Japanese, from the Interlingua in figure 4.

First, with the same Transformation Kit used in the analysis phase, Interlingua representation is mapped into syntactic f-structure of the target language.

```
;++ TransKit rules being applied to produce G structure ++

((PREV-SENTENCES ((VALUE HALLO) (ROOT LITERAL)))
         (ROOT SEIN) (CAT V) (PERSON 3)
         (SUBJECT
           ((CAT N) (CAS N) (DIST +) (LOC +) (PERSON 3)
            (NUMBER SG) (ROOT D-PRONOUN)))
         (NUMBER SG) (FORM FIN) (MOD IND) (TENSE PRES)
         (MOOD INTERROG)
         (PRED
           ((DET ((CAS N) (GENDER NEU)
                          (NUMBER SG)
                          (CAT DET)
                          (ROOT DER)))
             (CLASS SW) (NUMBER SG) (PERSON 3) (CAT N)
             (COMPOUND
               ((CAT N) (PL-CLASS PL3)
                        (SG-CLASS SG0)
                        (GENDER FEM)
                        (ROOT KONFERENZ)))
             (ROOT SEKRETARIAT) (PL-CLASS PL5) (SG-CLASS SG3)
             (GENDER NEU) (CAS N) (ANIM -))))

;++ GenKit rules being applied to produce German text ++

"HALLO , IST DORT DAS KONFERENZSEKRETARIAT  ?"

;++ TransKit rules being applied to produce J structure ++

((PREV-UTTERANCES
   ((FOR-REMOVE-DESU *IDENTIFY-OTHER) (VALUE MOSHIMOSHI)
                                       (ROOT *LITERAL)))
  (VTYPE MEISHI)
  (SUFF (*MULTIPLE* KA DESU))
  (PRED ((ROOT GAKKAIJIMUKYOKU)  (CAT N)
                                 (DEFINITE +)
                                 (NUMBER *SG)
                                 (ANIM -)))
  (ROOT COPULA))

;++ GenKit rules being applied to produce Japanese text ++

"MOSHIMOSHI GAKKAI JIMUKYOKU DESUKA"
```

Figure 5: Output language F-structure

There are about 300 rules in the generation mapping grammar for German, and 230 rules for Japanese. The f-structure is then fed into sentence generation software called "GENKIT" [17] to produce a sentence in the target language. A grammar for GENKIT is written in the same formalism as the Generalized LR Parser: phrase structure rules augmented with pseudo unification equations. The GENKIT grammar for general colloquial German has about 90 rules, and Japanese about 60 rules. Software called MORPHE is also used for morphlogical generation for German.

3.4. Semantic Pattern Based Parsing

A human-human translation task is even harder than human-machine communication, in that the dialog structure in human-human communication is more complicated and the range of topics is usually less restricted. These factors point to the requirement for robust strategies in speech translation systems.

Our robust semantic parser combines frame based semantics with semantic phrase grammars. We use a frame based parser similar to the DYPAR parser used by Carbonell, et al. to process ill-formed text,[9] and the MINDS system previously developed at CMU.[10] Semantic information is represented in a set of frames. Each frame contains a set of slots representing pieces of information. In order to fill the slots in the frames, we use semantic fragment grammars. Each slot type is represented by a separate Recursive Transition Network, which specifies all ways of saying the meaning represented by the slot. The grammar is a semantic grammar, non-terminals are semantic concepts instead of parts of speech. The grammar is also written so that information carrying fragments (semantic fragments) can stand alone (be recognized by a net) as well as being embedded in a sentence. Fragments which do not form a grammatical English sentence are still parsed by the system. Here there is not one large network representing all sentence level patterns, but many small nets representing information carrying chunks. Networks can "call" other networks, thereby significantly reducing the overall size of the system. These networks are used to perform pattern matches against input word strings. This general approach has been described in earlier papers. [7, 8]

The operation of the parser can be viewed as "phrase spotting". A beam of possible interpretations are pursued simultaneously. An interpretation is a frame with some of its slots filled. The RTNs perform pattern matches against the input string. When a phrase is recognized, it attempts to extend all current interpretations. That is, it is assigned to slots in active interpretations that it can fill. Phrases assigned to slots in the same interpretation are not allowed to overlap. In case of overlap, multiple interpretations are produced. When two interpretations for the same frame end with the same phrase, the lower scoring one is pruned. This amounts to dynamic programming on series of phrases. The score for an interpretation is the number of input words that it accounts for. At the end of the utterance, the best scoring interpretation is picked.

Our strategy is to apply grammatical constraints at the phrase level and to associate phrases in frames. Phrases represent word strings that can fill slots in frames. The slots represent information which, taken together, the frame is able to act on. We also use semantic rather than lexical grammars. Semantics provide more constraint than parts of speech and must ultimately be delt with in order to take actions. We believe that this approach offers a good compromise of constraint and robustness for the phenomena of spontaneous speech. Restarts and repeats are most often between phases, so individual phrases can still be recognized correctly. Poorly constructed grammar often consists of well-formed phrases, and is often semantically well-formed. It is only syntactically incorrect.

The parsing grammar was designed so that each frame has exactly one corresponding speech act. Each top level slot corresponds to some thematic role or other major semantic concept such as action. Subnets correspond to more specific semantic classes of constituents. In this way, the interpretation returned by the parser can be easily mapped onto the interlingua and missing information can be filled by meaningful default values with minimal effort.

Once an utterance is parsed in this way, it must then be mapped onto the interlingua discussed earlier in this paper. The mapping grammar contains rules for each slot and subnet in the parsing gramar which correspond to either concepts or speech acts in the interlingua. These rules specify the relationship between a subnet and the subnets it calls which will be represented in the interlingua structure it will produce. Each rule potentially contains four parts. It need not contain all of them. The first part contains a default interlingua structure for the concept represented by a particular rule. If all else fails, this default representation will be returned. The next part contains a skeletal interlingua representation for that rule. This is used in cases where a net calls multiple subnets which fill particular slots within the structure corresponding to the rule. A third part is used if the slot is filled by a terminal string of words. This part of the rule contains a context which can be placed around that string of words so that it can be attempted to be parsed and mapped by the LR system. It also contains informaiton about where in the structure returned from the LR system to find the constituent corresponding to this rule. The final part contains rules for where in the skeletal structure to place interlingua structures returned from the subnets called by this net.

3.5. Connectionist Parsing

The connectionist parsing system PARSEC [12] is used as a fall-back module if the symbolic high precision one fails to analyze the input. The important aspect of the PARSEC system is that it learns to parse sentences from a corpus of training examples. A connectionist approach to parse spontaneous speech offers the following advantages:

1. Because PARSEC learns and generalizes from the examples given in the training set no explicit grammar rules have to be specified by hand. In particular, this is of importance when the system has to cope with spontaneous utterances which frequently are "corrupted" with disfluencies, restarts, repairs or ungrammatical constructions. To specify symbolic grammars capturing these phenomena has been proven to be very difficult. On the other side there is a "build-in" robustness against these phenomena in a connectionist system.

2. The connectionist parsing process is able to combine symbolic information (e.g. syntactic features of words) with non-symbolic information (e.g. statistical likelihood of sentence types). Moreover, the system can easily integrate different knowledge sources. For example, instead of just training on the symbolic input string we trained PARSEC on both the symbolic input string and the pitch contour. After training was completed the system was able to use the additional information to determine the sentence mood in cases where syntactic clues were not sufficient. We think of extending the idea of integrating prosodic information into the parsing process in order to increase the performance of the system when it is confronted with corrupted input. We hope that prosodic information will help to indicate restarts and repairs.

The current PARSEC system comprises six hierarchically ordered (back-propagation) connectionist modules. Each module is responsible for a specific task. For example, there are two modules which determine phrase and clause boundaries. Other modules are responsible for assigning to phrases or clauses labels which indicate their function and/or relationship to other constituents. The top module determines the mood of the sentence.

Recent Extensions: We applied a slightly modified PARSEC system to the domain of air travel information (ATIS). We could show that the system was able to analyze utterance like "show me flights from boston to denver on us air" and that the system's output representation could be mapped to a Semantic Query Language (SQL). In order to do this we included semantic information (represented as binary features) in the lexicon. By doing the same for the CR-task we hope to increase the overall parsing performance.
We have also changed PARSEC to handle syntactic structures of arbitrary depth (both left and right branching) [13].

the main idea of the modified PARSEC system is to make it auto recursive, i.e. in a recursion step n it will take its output of the previous step n-1 as its input. This offers the following advantages:

1. **Increased Expressive Power:** The enhanced expressive power allows a much more natural mapping of linguistic intuitions to the specification of the training set.

2. **Ease of learning:** Learning difficulties can be reduced. Because PARSEC is now allowed to make more abstraction steps each individual step can be smaller and, hence, is easier to learn.

3. **Compatibility:** Because PARSEC is now capable of producing arbitrary tree structures as its output it can be more easily used as a submodule in NLP-systems (e.g. the JANUS system). For example, it is conceivable to produce as the parsing output f-structures which then can be mapped directly to the generation component [11].

4. SYSTEM INTEGRATION

The system accepts continuous speech speaker-independently in either input language, and produces synthetic speech output in near real-time. Our system can be linked to different language versions of the system or corresponding partner systems via ethernet or via telephone modem lines. This possibility has recently been tested between sites in the US, Japan and Germany to illustrate the possibility of international telephone speech translation.

The minimal equipment for this system is a Gradient Desklab 14 A/D-converter, an HP 9000/730 (64 Meg RAM) workstation for each input laguage, and a DECtalk speech synthesizer.

Included in the processing are A/D conversion, signal processing, continuous speech recognition, language analysis and parsing (both syntactic and semantic) into a language independent interlingua, text generation from that interlingua, and speech synthesis.

The amount of time needed for the processing of an utterance, depends on its length and acoustic quality, but also on the perplexity of the language model, on whether or not the first hypothesis is parsable and on the grammatical complexity and ambiguity of the sentence. While it can take the parser several seconds to process a long list of hypotheses for a complex utterance with many relative clauses (extremely rare in spoken language), the time consumed for parsing is usually negligible (0.1 second).

For our current system, we have eliminated considerable amounts of communication delays by introducing socket communication between pipelined parts of the system. Thus the search can start before the preprocessing program is done, and the parser starts working on the first hypothesis while the N-best list is computed.

5. CONCLUSION

In this paper, we have discussed recent extensions to the JANUS system a speaker independent multi-lingual speech-to-speech translation system under development at Carnegie Mellon and Karlsruhe University. The components include an speech recognition using an N-best sentence search, to derive alternate hypotheses for later processing during the translation. The MT component attempts to produce a high-accuracy translation using precise syntactic and semantic analysis. Should this analysis fail due to ill-formed input or misrecognitions, a connectionist parser, PARSEC, and a semantic parser produce alternative minimalist analyses, to at least establish the basic meaning of an input utterance. Human-to-human dialogs appear to generate a larger and more varied breadth of expression than human-machine dialogs. Further research is in progress to quantify this observation and to increase robustness and coverage of the system in this environment.

References

1. A. Waibel, A. Jain, A. McNair, H. Saito, A. Hauptmann, and J. Tebelskis, *JANUS: A Speech-to-Speech Translation System Using Connectionist and Symbolic Processing Strategies*, volume 2, pp 793–796. ICASSP 1991.
2. L. Osterholtz, A. McNair, I. Rogina, H. Saito, T. Sloboda, J. Tebelskis, A. Waibel, and M. Woszczyna. *Testing Generality in JANUS: A Multi-Lingual Speech to Speech Translation System*, volume 1, pp 209–212. ICASSP 1992.
3. Austin S., Schwartz R. *A Comparison of Several Approximate Algorithms for Finding N-best Hypotheses*, ICASSP 1991, volume 1, pp 701–704.
4. Schwartz R., Austin S. *The Forward-Backward Search Algorithm*, ICASSP 1990, volume 1, pp 81–84.
5. O. Schmidbauer and J. Tebelskis. *An LVQ based Reference Model for Speaker-Adaptive Speech Recognition.* ICASSP 1992, volume 1, pages 441–444.
6. J. Tebelskis and A. Waibel. *Performance through consistency: MS-TDNNs for large vocabulary continuous speech recognition*, Advances in Neural Information Processing Systems, Morgan Kaufmann.
7. W. Ward, *Understanding Spontaneous Speech*, DARPA Speech and Natural Language Workshop 1989, pp 137–141.
8. W. Ward, *The CMU Air Travel Information Service: Understanding Spontaneous Speech*, DARPA Speech and Natural Language Workshop 1990.
9. J.G. Carbonell and P.J. Hayes, *Recovery Strategies for Parsing Extragrammatical Language*, Carnegie-Mellon University Computer Science Technical Report 1984, (CMU-CS-84-107)
10. S.R. Young, A.G. Hauptmann, W.H. Ward, E.T. Smith, and P. Werner, *High Level Knowledge Sources in Usable Speech Recognition Systems*, in Communications of the ACM 1989, Volume 32, Number 2, pp 183–194
11. F. D. Buø, *A learnable connectionist parser that outputs f-structures (working title)*, PhD-Thesis proposal, University of Karlsruhe, in preparation.
12. A.J. Jain, A. Waibel, D. Touretzky, *PARSEC: A Structured Connectionist Parsing System for Spoken Language*, ICASSP 1992, volume 1, pp 205–208.
13. T.S. Polzin, *Pronoun Resolution. Interaction of Syntactic and Semantic Information in Connectionist Parsing*, Master Thesis, Carnegie Mellon University, Department of Philosophy, Computational Linguistics, in preparation.
14. Tomita, M. (ed.), *Generalized LR Parsing*, Kluwer Academic Publishers, Boston MA, 1991.
15. Tomita, M., *The Generalized LR Parser/Compiler* in 13th International Conference on Computational Linguistics (COLING90), Helsinki, 1990
16. Tomita, M., Mitamura, T., Musha, H. and Kee, M.; *The Generalized LR Parser/Compiler Version 8.1: User's Guide*, Technical Memo, Center for Machine Translation, Carnegie Mellon University, CMU-CMT-88-MEMO, 1988.
17. Tomita, M. and Nyberg, E.; *The Generation Kit and The Transformation Kit: User's Guide* Technical Memo, Center for Machine Translation, Carnegie Mellon University, CMU-CMT-88-MEMO, 1988
18. Lavie, A and Tomita, M.; *An Efficient Word-Skipping Parsing Algorithm for Context-Free Grammars* submitted to 3rd International Workshop on Parsing Technologies (IWPT93) Belguim, 1993.

A SPEECH TO SPEECH TRANSLATION SYSTEM BUILT FROM STANDARD COMPONENTS

Manny Rayner[1], Hiyan Alshawi[1], Ivan Bretan[3], David Carter[1], Vassilios Digalakis[2], Björn Gambäck[3], Jaan Kaja[4], Jussi Karlgren[3], Bertil Lyberg[4], Steve Pulman[1], Patti Price[2] and Christer Samuelsson[3]

(1) SRI International, Cambridge, UK (2) SRI International, Menlo Park, CA
(3) SICS, Stockholm, Sweden (4) Telia Research AB, Haninge, Sweden

ABSTRACT

This paper[1] describes a speech to speech translation system using standard components and a suite of generalizable customization techniques. The system currently translates air travel planning queries from English to Swedish. The modular architecture is designed to be easy to port to new domains and languages, and consists of a pipelined series of processing phases. The output of each phase consists of multiple hypotheses; statistical preference mechanisms, the data for which is derived from automatic processing of domain corpora, are used between each pair of phases to filter hypotheses. Linguistic knowledge is represented throughout the system in declarative form. We summarize the architectures of the component systems and the interfaces between them, and present initial performance results.

1. INTRODUCTION

From standard components and a suite of generalizable customization techniques, we have developed an English to Swedish speech translation system in the air travel planning (ATIS) domain. The modular architecture consists of a pipelined series of processing phases that each output multiple hypotheses filtered by statistical preference mechanisms.[2] The statistical information used in the system is derived from automatic processing of domain corpora. The architecture provides greater robustness than a 1-best approach, and yet is more computationally tractable and more portable to new languages and domains than a tight integration, because of the modularity of the components: speech recognition, source language processing, source to target language transfer, target language processing, and speech synthesis.

Some aspects of adaptation to the domain task were fairly simple: addition of new lexical entries was facilitated by existing tools, and grammar coverage required adding only a few very domain-specific phrase structure rules, as described in Section 3.1. Much of the effort in the project, however, has focussed on the development of well-specified methods for adapting and customizing other aspects of the existing modules, and on tools for guiding the process. In addition to the initial results (Section 5), the reported work makes several contributions to speech translation in particular and to language processing in general:

- A general method for training statistical preferences to filter multiple hypotheses, for use in ranking both analysis and translation hypotheses (Section 3.2);
- A method for rapid creation of a grammar for the target language by exploiting overlapping syntactic structures in the source and target languages (Section 3.3);
- An Explanation Based Learning (EBL) technique for automatically chunking the grammar into commonly occurring phrase-types, which has proven valuable in maximizing return on effort expended on coverage extension, and a set of procedures for automatic testing and reporting that helps to ensure smooth integration across aspects of the effort performed at the various sites involved (Section 4).

2. COMPONENTS AND INTERFACES

The speech translation process begins with SRI's DECIPHER(TM) system, based on hidden Markov modeling and a progressive search [12, 13]. It outputs to the source language processor a small lattice of word hypotheses generated using acoustic and language model scores. The language processor, for both English and Swedish, is the SRI Core Language Engine (CLE) [1], a unification-based, broad coverage natural language system for analysis and generation. Transfer occurs at the level of quasi logical form (QLF); transfer rules are defined in a simple declarative formalism [2]. Speech synthesis is performed by the Swedish Telecom PROPHON

[1] The research reported in this paper was sponsored by Swedish Telecom (Televerket Nät). Several people not listed as co-authors have also made contributions to the project: among these we would particularly like to mention Marie-Susanne Agnäs, George Chen, Dick Crouch, Barbro Ekholm, Arnold Smith, Tomas Svensson and Torbjörn Åhs.

[2] The preference mechanism between target language text output and speech synthesis has not yet been implemented.

system [8], based on stored polyphones. This section describes in more detail these components and their interfaces.

2.1. Speech Recognition

The first component is a fast version of SRI's DECIPHER(TM) speaker-independent continuous speech recognition system [12]. It uses context-dependent phonetic-based hidden Markov models with discrete observation distributions for 4 features: cepstrum, delta-cepstrum, energy and delta-energy. The models are gender-independent and the system is trained on 19,000 sentences and has a 1381-word vocabulary. The progressive recognition search [13] is a three-pass scheme that produces a word lattice and an N-best list for use by the language analysis component. Two recognition passes are used to create a word lattice. During the forward pass, the probabilities of all words that can end at each frame are recorded, and this information is used to prune the word lattice generated in the backward pass. The word lattice is then used as a grammar to constrain the search space of a third recognition pass, which produces an N-best list using an exact algorithm.

2.2. Language Analysis and Generation

Language analysis and generation are performed by the SRI Core Language Engine (CLE), a general natural-language processing system developed at SRI Cambridge [1]; two copies of the CLE are used, equipped with English and Swedish grammars respectively. The English grammar is a large, domain-independent unification-based phrase-structure grammar, augmented by a small number of domain-specific rules (Section 3.1). The Swedish grammar is a fairly direct adaptation of the English one (Section 3.3).

The system's linguistic information is in declarative form, compiled in different ways for the two tasks. In analysis mode, the grammar is compiled into tables that drive a left-corner parser; input is supplied in the form of a word hypothesis lattice, and output is a set of possible semantic analyses expressed in Quasi Logical Form (QLF). QLF includes predicate-argument structure and some surface features, but also allows a semantic analysis to be only partially specified [3].

The set of QLF analyses is then ranked in order of *a priori* plausibility using a set of heuristic preferences, which are partially trainable from example corpus data (Section 3.2). In generation mode, the linguistic information is compiled into another set of tables, which control a version of the Semantic Head-Driven Generation algorithm [16]. Here, the input is a QLF form, and the output is the set of possible surface strings which realize the form. Early forms of the analysis and generation algorithms used are described in [1].

2.3. Speech/Language Interface

The interface between speech recognition and source language analysis can be either a 1-best or an N-best interface. In 1-best mode, the recognizer simply passes the CLE a string representing the single best hypothesis. In N-best mode, the string is replaced by a list containing all hypotheses that are active at the end of the third recognition pass. Since the word lattice generated during the first two recognition passes significantly constrains the search space of the third pass, we can have a large number of hypotheses without a significant increase in computation.

As the CLE is capable of using lattice input directly [6], the N-best hypotheses are combined into a new lattice before being passed to linguistic processing; in cases where divergences occur near the end of the utterance, this yields a substantial speed improvement. The different analyses produced are scored using a weighted sum of the acoustic score received from DECIPHER and the linguistic preference score produced by the CLE. When at least one linguistically valid analysis exists, this implicitly results in a selection of one of the N-best hypotheses. Our experimental findings to date indicate that N=5 gives a good tradeoff between speed and accuracy, performance surprisingly being fairly insensitive to the setting of the relative weights given to acoustic and linguistic scoring information. Some performance results are presented in Section 5.

2.4. Transfer

Unification-based QLF transfer [2], compositionally translates a QLF of the source language to a QLF of the target language. QLF is the transfer level of choice in the system, since it is a contextually unresolved semantic representation reflecting both predicate-argument relations and linguistic features such as tense, aspect, and modality. The translation process uses declarative transfer rules containing cross-linguistic data, i.e., it specifies only the differences between the two languages. The monolingual knowledge of grammars, lexica, and preferences is used for ranking alternative target QLFs, filtering out ungrammatical QLFs, and finally generating the source language utterance.

A transfer rule specifies a pair of QLF patterns; the left hand side matches a fragment of the source language QLF and the right hand side the corresponding target QLF. Table 1 breaks down transfer rules by type. As can been seen, over 90% map atomic constants to atomic constants; of the remainder, about half relate to spe-

Table 1: Transfer rule statistics		
Atom to atom	649	91%
Complex (lexical)	27	4%
Complex (non-lexical)	34	5%
Total	710	100%

cific lexical items, and half are general structural transfer rules. For example, the following rule expresses a mapping of English NPs postnominally modified by a progressive VP (*"Flights going to Boston"*) to Swedish NPs modified by a relative clause (*"Flygningar som går till Boston"*):

```
[and,tr(head),
 form(verb(tense=n,perf=P,prog=y),
     tr(mod))]
>=
[and,tr(head),
 [island,form(verb(tense=pres,perf=P,prog=n),
     tr(mod))]]
```

Transfer variables, of the form tr(*atom*), show how subexpressions in the source QLF correspond to subexpressions in the target QLF. Note how the transition from a tenseless, progressive VP to a present tense, non-progressive VP can be specified directly through changing the values of the slots of the "verb" term. This fairly simple transfer rule formalism seems to allow most important restructuring phenomena (e.g., change of aspect, object raising, argument switching, and to some extent also head switching) to be specified succinctly. The degree of compositionality in the rule set currently employed is high; normally no special transfer rules are needed to specify combinations of complex transfer. In addition, the vast majority of the rules are reversible, providing for future Swedish to English translation.

2.5. Speech Synthesis

The Prophon speech synthesis system, developed at Swedish Telecom, is an interactive environment for developing applications and conducting research in multilingual text-to-speech conversion. The system includes a large lexicon, a speech synthesizer and rule modules for text formatting, syntactic analysis, phonetic transcription, parameter generation and prosody. Two synthesis strategies are included in the system, formant synthesis and polyphone synthesis, i.e., concatenation of speech units of arbitrary size. In the latter case, the synthesizer accesses the database of polyphone speech waveforms according to the allophonic specification derived from the lexicon and/or phonetic transcription rules. The polyphones are concatenated and the prosody of the utterance is imposed via the PSOLA (pitch synchronous overlap add) signal processing technique [11]. The Prophon system has access to information other than the text string, in particular the parse tree, which can be used to provide a better, more natural prosodic structure than normally is possible.

3. ADAPTATION

In this section, we describe the methods used for adapting the various processing components to the English-Swedish ATIS translation task. Section 3.1 describes the domain customization of the language component, and section 3.2 the semi-automatic method developed to customize the linguistic preference filter. Finally, section 3.3 summarizes the work carried out in adapting the English-language grammar and lexicon to Swedish.

3.1. CLE Domain Adaptation

We begin by describing the customizations performed to adapt the general CLE English grammar and lexicon to the ATIS domain. First, about 500 lexical entries needed to be added. Of these, about 450 were regular content words (*airfare*, *Boston*, *seven forty seven*, etc.), all of which were added by a graduate student[3] using the interactive VEX lexicon acquisition tool [7]. About 55 other entries, not of a regular form, were also added. Of these, 26 corresponded to the letters of the alphabet, which were treated as a new syntactic class, 15 or so were interjections (*Sure*, *OK*, etc.), and seven were entries for the days of the week, which turned out to have slightly different syntactic properties in American and British English. The only genuinely new entries were for *available*, *round trip*, *first class*, *nonstop* and *one way*, all of which failed to fit syntactic patterns previously implemented within the grammar, (e.g. *"Flights available from United"*, *"Flights to Boston first class"*).

Sixteen domain-specific phrase-structure rules were also added, most of them by the graduate student. Of these, six covered 'code' expressions (e.g. *"Q X"*), and eight covered 'double utterances' (e.g. *"Flights to Boston show me the fares"*). The remaining two rules covered ordinal expressions without determiners (*"Next flight to Boston"*), and PP expressions of the form '*Name* to *Name*' (e.g. *"Atlanta to Boston Friday"*). Finally, the preference metrics were augmented by a preference for attaching 'from-to' PP pairs to the same constituent, (this is a domain-independent heuristic, but is particularly important in the context of the ATIS task), and the semantic collocation preference metrics (Section 3.2)

[3] Marie-Susanne Agnäs, the graduate student in question, was a competent linguist but had no previous experience with the CLE or other large computational grammars.

were retrained with ATIS data. The grammar and lexicon customization effort has so far consumed about three person-months of specialist time, and about two and a half person-months of the graduate student. The current level of coverage is indicated in Section 5.

3.2. Training Preference Heuristics

Grammars with thorough coverage of a non-trivial sublanguage tend to yield large numbers of analyses for many sentences, and rules for accurately selecting the correct analysis are difficult if not impossible to state explicitly. We therefore use a set of about twenty preference metrics to rank QLFs in order of *a priori* plausibility. Some metrics count occurrences of phenomena such as adjuncts, ellipsis, particular attachment configurations, or balanced conjunctions. Others, which are trained automatically, reflect the strengths of semantic collocations between triples of logical constants occurring in relevant configurations in QLFs.

The overall plausibility score for a QLF under this scheme is a weighted (scaled) sum of the scores returned by the individual metrics. Initially, we chose scaling factors by hand, but this became an increasingly skilled and difficult task as more metrics were added, and it was clear that the choice would have to be repeated for other domains. The following semi-automatic optimization procedure [4] was therefore developed.

QLFs were derived for about 4600 context-independent and context-dependent ATIS sentences of 1 to 15 words. It is easy to derive from a QLF the set of segments of the input sentence which it analyses as being either predications or arguments. These segments, taken together, effectively define a tree of roughly the form used by the Treebank project [5]. A user presented with all strings derived ¿from any QLF for a sentence selected the correct tree (if present). A skilled judge was then able to assign trees to hundreds of sentences per hour.

The "goodness" of a QLF Q with respect to an approved tree T was defined as $I(Q,T) - 10 * A(Q,T)$, where $I(Q,T)$ is the number of string segments induced by Q and present in T, and $A(Q,T)$ is the number induced by Q but absent from T. This choice of goodness function was found, by trial and error, to lead to a good correlation with the metrics. Optimization then consisted of minimizing, with respect to scaling factors c_j for each preference metric m_j, the value of

$$\sum_i (g_i - \sum_j c_j s_{ij})^2$$

where g_i is the goodness of QLF i and s_{ij} is the score assigned to QLF i by metric f_j; to remove some "noise" from the data, all values were relativized by subtracting the (average of the) corresponding scores for the best-scoring QLF(s) for the sentence.

The kth simultaneous equation, derived by setting the derivative of the above expression with respect to c_k to zero for the minimum, is

$$\sum_i s_{ik}(g_i - \sum_j c_j s_{ij}) = 0$$

These equations can be solved by Gaussian elimination.

The optimized and hand-selected scaling factors each resulted in a correct QLF being selected for about 75% of the 157 sentences from an unseen test set that were within coverage, showing that automatic scaling can produce results as good as those derived by labour- and skill-intensive hand-tuning. The value of Kendall's ranking correlation coefficient between the relativized "goodness" values and the scaled sum (reflecting the degree of agreement between the orderings induced by the two criteria) was also almost identical for the two sets of factors. However, the optimized factors achieved much better correlation (0.80 versus 0.58) under the more usual product-moment definition of correlation, $\sigma_{xy}/\sigma_x\sigma_y$, which the least-squares optimization used here is defined to maximize. This suggests that optimization with respect to a (non-linear) criterion that reflects ranking rather than linear agreement could lead to a still better set of scaling factors that might outperform both the hand-selected and the least-squares-optimal ones. A hill-climbing algorithm to determine such factors is therefore being developed.

The training process allows optimization of scaling factors, and also provides data for several metrics assessing semantic collocations. In our case, we use semantic collocations extracted from QLF expressions in the form of $(H1, R, H2)$ triples where $H1$ and $H2$ are the head predicates of phrases in a sentence and R indicates the semantic relationship (e.g. a preposition or an argument position) between the two phrases in the proposed analysis. We have found that a simple metric, original to us, that scores triples according to the average treebank score of QLFs in which they occur, performs about as well as a chi-squared metric, and better than one based on mutual information (cf [9]).

3.3. CLE Language Adaptation

The Swedish-language customization of the CLE (S-CLE) has been developed at SICS from the English-language version by replacing English-specific modules with corresponding Swedish-language versions.[4] Swedish is a Germanic language, linguistically about as "far" from English as German is. Our experience sug-

[4] The S-CLE and the adaptation process is described in detail in [10].

gests that adapting the English system to close languages is fairly easy and straight-forward. The total effort spent on the Swedish adaptation was about 14 person-months (compared with about 20 person-years for the original CLE), resulting in coverage only slightly less than that of the English version.

The amount of work needed to adapt the various CLE modules to Swedish declined steadily as a function of their "distance" from surface structure. Thus the morphology rules had to be nearly completely rewritten; Swedish morphology is considerably more complex than English. In contrast, only 33 of the 401 Swedish function word entries were not derived from English counterparts, the differences being confined to variance in surface form and regular changes to the values of a small number of features. At the level of syntax, 97 (81%) of a set of 120 Swedish syntax rules were derived from exact or very similar English rules. The most common difference is some small change in the features; for example, Swedish marks for definiteness, which means that this feature often needs to be added. 11 rules (9%) originated in English rules, but had undergone major changes, e.g., some permutation or deletion of the daughters; thus Swedish time rules demand a word-order which in English would be "o'clock five", and there is a rule that makes an NP out of a bare definite NBAR. This last rule corresponds to the English NP → DET NBAR rule, with the DET deleted but the other features instantiated as if it were present. Only 12 (10%) Swedish syntax rules were completely new. The percentage of changed semantic rules was even smaller.

The most immediately apparent surface divergences between Swedish and English word-order stem from the strongly verb-second nature of Swedish. Formation of both YN- and WH-questions is by simple inversion of the subject and verb without the introduction of an auxiliary, thus for example *"Did he fly with Delta?"* is *"Flög han med Delta?"*, lit. *"Flew he with Delta?"*. It is worth noting that these changes can all be captured by doing no more than adjusting features. The main rules that had to be written "from scratch" are those that cover adverbials, negation, conditionals, and the common *vad ... för* construction, e.g., *"Vad finns det för flygningar till Atlanta"* (lit. *"What are there for flights to Atlanta"*, i.e., *"What flights are there to Atlanta?"*).

4. RATIONAL DEVELOPMENT METHODOLOGY

In a project like this one, where software development is taking place simultaneously at several sites, regular testing is important to ensure that changes retain inter-component compatibility. Our approach is to maintain a set of test corpora to be run through the system (from text analysis to text generation) whenever a significant change is made to the code or data. Changes in the status of a sentence – the translation it receives, or the stage at which it fails if it receives no translation – are notified to developers, which facilitates bug detection and documentation of progress.

The most difficult part of the exercise is the construction of the test corpora. The original training/development corpus is a 4600-sentence subset of the ATIS corpus consisting of sentences of length not more than 15 words. For routine system testing, this corpus is too large to be convenient; if a randomly chosen subset is used instead, it is often difficult to tell whether processing failures are important or not, in the sense of representing problems that occur in a large number of corpus sentences. What is needed is a sub-corpus that contains all the commonly occurring types of construction, together with an indication of how many sentences each example in the sub-corpus represents.

We have developed a systematic method for constructing representative sub-corpora, using "Explanation Based Learning" (EBL) [15]. The original corpus is parsed, and the resulting analysis trees are grouped into equivalence classes; then one member is chosen from each class, and stored with the number of examples it represents. In the simplest version, trees are equivalent if their leaves are of the same lexical types. The criterion for equivalence can be varied easily: we have experimented with schemes where all sub-trees representing NPs are deemed to be equivalent. When generalization is performed over non-lexical classes like NPs and PPs, the method is used recursively to extract representative examples of each generalized class.

At present, three main EBL-derived sub-corpora are used for system testing. Corpus 1, used most frequently, was constructed by generalizing at the level of lexical items, and contains one sentence for each class with at least three members. This yields a corpus of 281 sentences, which together represent 1743 sentences from the original corpus. Corpus 2, the "lexical" test corpus, is a set with one analyzable phrase for each lexical item occuring at least four times in the original corpus, comprising a total of 460 phrases. Corpus 3 generalizes over NPs and PPs, and analyzes NPs by generalizing over non-recursive NP and PP constituents; one to five examples are included for each class that occurs ten or more times (depending on the size of the class), giving 244 examples. This corpus is useful for finding problems linked with constructions specific to either the NP or the sentence level, but not to a combination. The time needed to process each corpus through the system is on the order of an hour.

5. RESULTS OF SYSTEM EVALUATION

In this final section we present evaluation results for the current version of the system running on data previously unseen by the developers. There is so far little consensus on how to evaluate spoken language translation systems; for instance, no evaluation figures on unseen material are cited for the systems described in [17] and [14]. We present the results below partly in an attempt to stimulate discussion on this topic.

The sentences of lengths 1 to 12 words from the Fall 1992 test set (633 sentences from 1000) were processed through the system from speech signal to target language text output, and the translations produced were evaluated by a panel fluent in both languages. Points were awarded for meaning preservation, grammaticality of the output, naturalness of the output, and preservation of the style of the original, and a translation had to be classified as acceptable on all four counts to be regarded as acceptable in general. Judgements were also elicited for intermediate results, in particular whether a speech hypothesis could be judged as a valid variant of the reference sentence in the context of the translation task, and whether the semantic analysis sent to the transfer stage was correct. The criteria used to determine whether a speech hypothesis was a valid variant of the reference were strict, typical differences being substitution of *all the* for plural *the*, *what's* for *what is*, or *I want* for *I'd like*.

The results were as follows. For 1-best recognition, 62.4% of the hypotheses were equal to or valid variants of the reference, and 55.3% were valid and also within grammatical coverage. For 5-best recognition, the corresponding figures were 78.2% and 69.0%. Selecting the acoustically highest-ranked hypothesis that was inside grammatical coverage yielded an acceptable choice in 61.1% of the examples; a scoring scheme that chose the best hypothesis using a weighted combination of the acoustic and linguistic scores did slightly better, increasing the proportion to 63.0%. 54% of the examples received a most preferred semantic analysis that was judged correct, 45.3% received a translation, and 41.8% received an acceptable translation. The corresponding error rates for each component are shown in table 2.

Table 2: Component error rates

(1-best recognition)	(37.4%)
5-best recognition	21.8%
Speech/language interface	8.7%
Source linguistic analysis	11.8%
Source analysis preferences	13.4%
Transfer and generation	22.7%

References

1. Alshawi, H. (ed.), *The Core Language Engine*, MIT Press, 1992.
2. Alshawi, H., Carter, D., Rayner, M. and Gambäck, B., "Transfer through Quasi Logical Form", *Proc. 29th ACL*, Berkeley, 1991.
3. Alshawi, H. and Crouch, R., "Monotonic Semantic Interpretation", *Proc. 30th ACL*, Newark, 1992.
4. Alshawi, H., and Carter, D., "Optimal Scaling of Preference Metrics", SRI Cambridge Research Report, 1992.
5. Black, E., *et al.*, "A Procedure for Quantitatively Comparing the Syntactic Coverage of English Grammars," *Proc. Third DARPA Speech and Language Workshop*, P. Price (ed.), Morgan Kaufmann, June 1991.
6. Carter, D.M., "Lattice-based Word Identification in CLARE", *Proc 30th ACL*, Newark, 1992.
7. Carter, D.M., "Lexical Acquisition in the Core Language Engine", *Proc. 4th European ACL*, Manchester, 1989.
8. Ceder, K. and Lyberg, B., "Yet Another Rule Compiler for Text-to-Speech Conversion?", *Proc. ICSLP*, Banff, 1993.
9. Church, K.W. and Hanks, P., "Word Association Norms, Mutual Information, and Lexicography", *Computational Linguistics* 16:22–30, 1990.
10. Gambäck, B. and Rayner, M., "The Swedish Core Language Engine", *Proc. 3rd NOTEX*, Linköping, 1992.
11. Moulines, E. and Charpentier, F., "Pitch-Synchronous Waveform Processing Techniques for Text-to-Speech Synthesis Using Diphones", *Speech Communication* Vol. 9, 1990.
12. Murveit, H., Butzberger, J. and Weintraub, M., "Speech Recognition in SRI's Resource Management and ATIS Systems", *Proc. DARPA Workshop on Speech and Natural Language*, 1991.
13. Murveit, H., et al., "Large Vocabulary Dictation using SRI's DECIPHER(TM) Speech Recognition System: Progressive Search Techniques", *Proc. ICASSP*, 1993.
14. Roe, D.B., Pereira, F.C.N., Sproat, R.W., Riley, M.D. and Moreno, P.J., "Towards a Spoken-Language Translator for Restricted-Domain Context-Free Languages", *Proc. Eurospeech*, 1991.
15. Samuelsson, C. and Rayner, M., "Quantitative Evaluation of Explanation-Based Learning as an Optimization Tool for a Large-Scale Natural Language System", *Proc. 12th IJCAI*, Sydney, 1991.
16. Shieber, S. M., van Noord, G., Pereira, F.C.N and Moore, R.C., "Semantic-Head-Driven Generation", *Computational Linguistics*, 16:30–43, 1990.
17. Woszczyna, M. et al., "Recent advances in JANUS: A Speech Translation System", ARPA Workshop on Human Language Technology, Plainsboro, NJ, 1993.

SESSION 7: DEMONSTRATIONS

Hy Murveit, Chair

SRI International
Menlo Park, California 94025

Papers were optional in this session.

1. **PLUM: A System for Processing Text Robustly**
   Ralph Weischedel; BBN Systems & Technologies

2. **ATIS Air Traffic Information System**
   BBN Systems & Technologies

3. **Gisting Conversational Speech in Real-Time**
   Larry Denenberg, Robin Rohlicek, Will Sadkin, Man-Hung Siu; BBN Systems & Technologies

4. **CSR/WSJ (20,000 words) Real-Time Demonstration of the BBN Large Vocabulary Continuous Speech Recognition System on the WSJ Corpus**
   L. Nguyen, R. Schwartz, F. Kubala, P. Placeway; BBN Systems & Technologies

5. **ATIS Air Travel Information System**
   Carnegie Mellon University

6. **JANUS: Speech-to-Speech Translation System Demonstration**
   A.McNair and A.Waibel; Carnegie Mellon University

7. **Demonstration of Corpus and Answer-key Based Development Environment for Text Extraction**
   Lisa F. Rau; GE R&D Center

8. **Demonstration of the MIT On-Line ATIS System**
   J. Glass, D. Goddeau, D. Goodine, L. Hirschman, C. Pao, M. Phillips, J. Polifroni, S. Sakai, S. Seneff, and V. Zue; MIT

9. **Demonstration of the MIT Bilingual VOYAGER System**
   J. Glass, D. Goddeau, D. Goodine, L. Hirschman, C. Pao, M. Phillips, J. Polifroni, S. Sakai, S. Seneff, and V. Zue; MIT

10. **NORM - A System for Translators**
    Bill Ogden & Margarita Gonzalez; New Mexico State University

11. **SRI Spoken Language Demonstrations: Telephone Banking On-line Atis Demo**
    SRI International

12. **The FASTUS System**
    Jerry R. Hobbs, Douglas Appelt, Mabry Tyson, and Megumi Kameyama; SRI International

Session 8: Statistical Language Modeling

Mitchell Marcus, Chair

Department of Computer and Information Science
University of Pennsylvania
Philadelphia, PA 19104-6389

1. Introduction

Over the past several years, the successful application of statistical techniques in natural language processing has penetrated further and further into written language technology, proceding with time from the periphery of written language processing into deeper and deeper aspects of language processing. At the periphery of natural language understanding, Hidden Markov Models were first applied over ten years ago to the problem of determining part of speech (POS). HMM POS taggers have yielded quite good results for many tasks (96%+ correct, on a per word basis), and have been widely used in written language systems for the last several years. A little closer in from the periphery, extensions to probabilistic context free parsing (PCFG) methods have greatly increased the accuracy of probabilistic parsing methods within the last several years; these methods condition the probabilities of standard CFG rules on aspects of extended lingustic context. Just within the last year or two, we have begun to see the first applications of statistical methods to the problem of word sense determination and lexical semantics. It is worthy of note that the first presentation of a majority of these techniques has been within this series of Workshops sponsored by ARPA.

It is a measure of how fast this field is progressing that a majority of papers in this session, six, are on lexical semantics, an area where the effective application of statistical techniques would have been unthinkable only a few years ago. One other paper addresses the question of how a POS tagger can be built using very limited amounts of training data, another presents a method for finding word associations and two others address various aspects of statistical parsing.

2. Part of Speech Tagging

The first paper in this session, by Matsukawa, Miller and Weischedel, describes a cascade of several components, sandwiching a novel algorithm between the output of an existing black-box segmentation and POS labelling system for Japanese, JUMAN, and the POST HMM POS tagger. The middle algorithm uses what the authors call example-based correction to change some of JUMAN's initial word segmentation and to add alternative POS tags from which POST can then make a final selection. (Japanese text is printed without spaces; determining where one word stops and another starts is a crucial problem in Japanese text processing.) The example-based correction method, closely related to a method presented by Brill at this workshop last year, uses a very small amount of training data to learn a set of symbolic transformation rules which augment or change the output of JUMAN in particular deterministic contexts.

3. Grammar Induction and Probabilistic Parsing

Most current methods for probabilistic parsing either estimate grammar rule probabilities directly from an annotated corpus or else use Baker's Inside/Outside algorithm (often in combination with some annotation) to estimate the parameters from an unannotated corpus. The I/O algorithm, however, maximizes the wrong objective function for purposes of recovering the expected grammatical structure for a given sentence; the I/O algorithm finds the model that maximizes the likelihood of the observed sentence *strings* without reference to the grammatical structure assigned to that string by the estimated grammar. Often, however, probabilistic parsing is used to derive a tree structure for use with a semantic analysis component based upon syntax directed translation; for this translation to work effectively, the details of the parse tree must be appropriate for tree-based semantic composition techniques. Current techniques are also inapplicable to the recently developed class of chunk parsers, parsers which use finite-state techniques to parse the non-recursive structures of the language, and then use another technique, usually related to dependency parsing, to connect these chunks together. Two papers in this session can be viewed as addressing one or both of these issues. The paper by Abney presents a new measure for evaluating parser performance tied directly to grammatical structure, and suggests ways in which such a measure can be used for chunk parsing. Brill presents a new technique for parsing which extends the symbolic POS tagger he presented last year. Surprisingly, this simple technique performs as well as the best recent results using the I/O algorithm, using a very simple technique to learn less than two hundred purely symbolic rules which deterministically parse new input.

4. Lexical semantics: Sense class determination

The remaining papers in this session address three separate areas of lexical semantics. The first is sense class determination, determining, for example, whether a particular use of the word "newspaper" refers to the physical entity that sits by your front door in the morning, or the corporate entity that publishes it; whether a particular use of "line" means a product line, a queue, a line of text, a fishing line, etc. Several papers in this session address the question of how well automatic statistical techniques can discriminate between alternative word senses, and how much information such techniques must use. The paper by Leacock, Miller and Voorhees tests three different techniques for sense class determination: Bayesian decision theory, neural networks, and content vectors. These experiments show that the three techniques are statistically indistinguishable, each resolving between three different uses of "line" with an accuracy of about 76%, and between six different uses with an accuracy of about 73%. These techniques use an extended context of about 100 words around the target word; Yarowsky's paper presents a new technique which uses only five words on either side of the target word, but can provide roughly comparable results by itself. This new method might well be combined with one of these earlier techniques to provide improved performance over either technique individually.

5. Lexical semantics: adjectival scales

A second area of lexical semantics focuses on the semantics of adjectives that determine linguistic scales. For example, one set of adjectives lie on the linguistic scale from *hot* through *warm* and *cool* to *cold*, while another set lies on the scale that goes from *huge* through *big* to *little* to *tiny*. Many adjectives can be characterizing as picking out a point or range on some such scale. These scales play a role in human language understanding because of a phenomenon called *scalar implicature*, which underlies the fact that if someone asks if Tokyo is a big city, much better than replying "yes" is to say, "Well, no; it's actually quite huge". By the law of scalar implicature, one cannot felicitously assent to an assertion about a midpoint on a scale even if it is logically true, if an assertion about an extremum is also logically true. McKeown and Hatzivassiloglou take a first step toward using statistical techniques to automatically determine where adjectives fall along such scales by presenting a method which automatically clusters adjectives into groups which are closely related to such scales.

6. Lexical semantics: Selectional Restrictions

Another key aspect of lexical semantics is the determination of the selectional constraints of verbs; determining for each sense of any given verb what kinds of entities can serve as the subject for a given verb sense, and what kinds of entities can serve as objects. For example, for one meaning of *open*, the thing opened is most likely to be an entrance; for another meaning, a mouth; for another, a container; for another, a discourse. One key barrier to determining such selectional constraints automatically is a serious problem with sparse data; in a large corpus, a given verb is likely to occur with any particular noun as object in only a handful of instances. Two papers in this session automatically derive selectional restrictions, each with a different solution to this particular form of the sparse data problem. The paper by Resnik utilizes an information theoretic technique to automatically determine such selectional restrictions; this information is then used to resolve a number of syntactic ambiguities that any parser must deal with. Resnik uses the noun *is-a* network within Miller's WordNet to provide sufficiently large classes to obtain reliable results. Grishman and Sterling attack the problem of sparse data by using co-occurance smoothing on a set of fully automatically generated selectional constraints.

In one last paper in lexical semantics, Matsukawa presents a new method of determining word associations in Japanese text. Such word associations are useful in dealing with parsing ambiguities and should also prove useful for Japanese word segmentation.

EXAMPLE-BASED CORRECTION OF WORD SEGMENTATION AND PART OF SPEECH LABELLING

Tomoyoshi Matsukawa , Scott Miller, and Ralph Weischedel

BBN Systems and Technologies
70 Fawcett St.
Cambridge, MA 02138

ABSTRACT

This paper describes an example-based correction component for Japanese word segmentation and part of speech labelling (AMED), and a way of combining it with a pre-existing rule-based Japanese morphological analyzer and a probabilistic part of speech tagger.

Statistical algorithms rely on frequency of phenomena or events in corpora; however, low frequency events are often inadequately represented. Here we report on an example-based technique used in finding word segments and their part of speech in Japanese text. Rather than using hand-crafted rules, the algorithm employs example data, drawing generalizations during training.

1. INTRODUCTION

Probabilistic part of speech taggers have proven to be successful in English part of speech labelling [Church 1988; DeRose, 1988; de Marcken, 1990; Meteer, et. al. 1991, etc.]. Such stochastic models perform very well given adequate amounts of training data representative of operational data. Instead of merely stating what is possible, as a non-stochastic rule-based model does, probabilistic models predict the likelihood of an event. In determining the part of speech of a highly ambiguous word in context or in determining the part of speech of an unknown word, they have proven quite effective for English.

By contrast, rule-based morphological analyzers employing a hand-crafted lexicon and a hand-crafted connectivity matrix are the traditional approach to Japanese word segmentation and part of speech labelling [Aizawa and Ebara 1973]. Such algorithms have already achieved 90-95% accuracy in word segmentation and 90-95% accuracy in part-of-speech labelling (given correct word segmentation). The potential advantage of a rule-based approach is the ability of a human coding rules that cover events that are rare, and therefore may be inadequately represented in most training sets. Furthermore, it is commonly assumed that large training sets are not required.

A third approach combines a rule-based part of speech tagger with a set of correction templates automatically derived from a training corpus [Brill 1992].

We faced the challenge of processing Japanese text, where neither spaces nor any other delimiters mark the beginning and end of words. We had at our disposal the following:

- A rule-based Japanese morphological processor (JUMAN) from Kyoto University.

- A context-free grammar of Japanese based on part of speech labels distinct from those produced by JUMAN.

- A probabilistic part-of-speech tagger (POST) [Meteer, et al., 1991] which assumed a single sequence of words as input.

- Limited human resources for creating training data.

This presented us with four issues:

1) how to reduce the cost of modifying the rule-based morphological analyzer to produce the parts of speech needed by the grammar,

2) how to apply probabilistic modeling to Japanese, e.g., to improve accuracy to ~97%, which is typical of results in English,

3) how to deal with unknown words, where JUMAN typically makes no prediction regarding part of speech, and

4) how to estimate probabilities for low frequency phenomena.

Here we report on an example-based technique for correcting systemmatic errors in word segmentation and part of speech labelling in Japanese text. Rather than using handcrafted rules, the algorithm employs example data, drawing generalizations during training. In motivation, it is similar to one of the goals of Brill (1992).

2. ARCHITECTURE

The architecture in Figure 1 was chosen to minimize labor and to maximize use of existing software. It employs JUMAN first to provide initial word segmentation of the text, an annotation-based algorithm second to correct both segmentation errors and part of speech errors in JUMAN output, and POST third both to select among ambiguous alternative segmentations/part-of-speech assignments and also to predict the part of speech of unknown words.

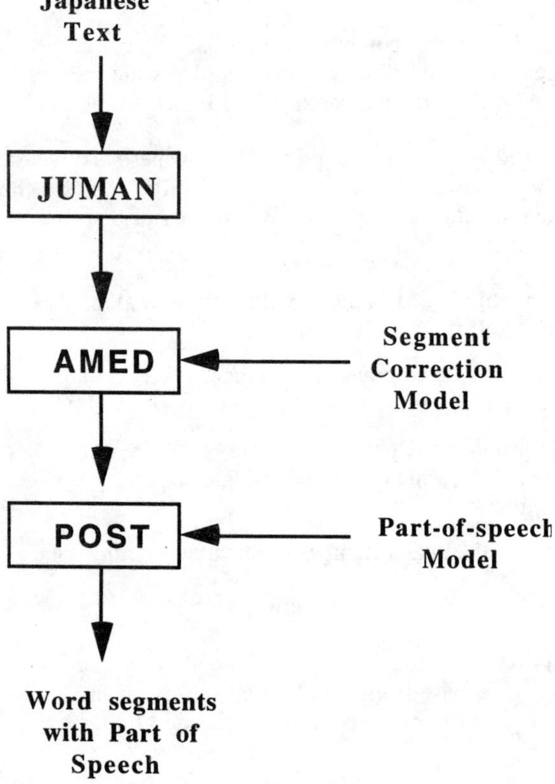

Figure 1: *Architecture*

Let us briefly review each component. JUMAN, available from Kyoto University makes segmentation decisions and part of speech assignments to Japanese text. To do this, it employs a lexicon of roughly 40,000 words, including their parts of speech. Where alternative segmentations are possible, the connectivity matrix eliminates some possibilities, since it states what parts of speech may follow a given part of speech. Where the connectivity matrix does not dictate a single segmentation and part of speech, generally longer words are preferred over shorter segmentations.

An example JUMAN output is provided in Figure 2. The Japanese segment is given first, followed by a slash and the part of speech. JUMAN employs approximately 45 parts of speech. [1]

海外旅行も楽しめる新型の旅行サービスを二月中旬から売り出す。

FIGURE 2a: *A Short Example Sentence*

海外/CN 旅行/SN も/TTM 楽/SN し/VB め/??? る/???
旅行/SN サービス/SN を/CM 二月中旬/??? から/PT
売り出す/VB 。/KT

FIGURE 2b: *JUMAN output for example 2a above*

The correction algorithm (AMED) is trained with two parallel annotations of the same text. One of the annotations is JUMAN's output. The second is manually annotated corresponding to correct segmentation and correct part-of-speech assignments for each word. During training, AMED aligns the parallel annotations, identifies deviations as "corrections", and automatically generalizes these into correction rules. An example of automatic alignment appears in Figure 3.

AMED performs the following functions:

- Corrects some segmentation errors made by JUMAN.
- Corrects some part-of-speech assignment errors made by JUMAN. Some of these "corrections" actually introduce ambiguity which POST later resolves.
- Transforms the tag set produced by JUMAN into the tag set required by the grammar.

Note that all of these functions are the result of the learning algorithm, no rules for correction nor for translating JUMAN parts of speech into those for the grammar were written by hand.

The third component is POST, which assigns parts of speech stochastically via a Hidden Markov model, has been described elsewhere [Meteer, et al., 1991]. POST performs two vital functions in the case of our Japanese processing:

1 CN = common noun; SN = sa-inflection noun (nominalized verb); VB = verb; VSUF = verb suffix; CM = case marker; etc.

- POST decides among ambiguous part-of-speech labellings and segmentations, particularly in those cases where AMED's training data includes cases where JUMAN is prone to error.

- POST predicts the most likely part of speech for an unknown word segment in context.

3. HOW THE ARCHITECTURE ADDRESSES THE ISSUES

In principle, a Hidden Markov Model implementation, such as POST, can make both part-of-speech decisions and segment text quite reliably. Therefore, why not just use POST; why use three components instead?

The clear reason was to save human effort. We did not have access to segmented and labelled Japanese text. Labelling tens of thousands (or even hundreds of thousands of words of text) for supervised training would have taken more effort and more time in a project with tight schedules and limited resources. JUMAN existed and functioned above 90% accuracy in segmentation.

A secondary reason was the opportunity to investigate an algorithm that learned correction rules from examples. A third reason was that we did not have an extensive lexicon using the parts of speech required by the grammar.

The architecture addressed the four issues raised in the introduction as follows:

1) AMED learned rules to transform JUMAN's parts of speech to those required by the grammar.

2) Accuracy was improved both by AMED's correction rules and by POST's Hidden Markov Model.

3) POST hypothesizes the most likely part of speech in context for unknown words, words not in the JUMAN lexicon.

4) The sample inspection method in AMED estimates probabilities for low frequency phenomena.

4. THE CORRECTION MODEL

The only training data for our algorithm is manually annotated word segmentation and part of speech labels. Examples of corrections of JUMAN's output are extracted by a procedure that automatically aligns the annotated data with JUMAN's output and collects pairs of differences between sequences of pairs of word segment and part of speech. Each pair of differing strings represents a correction rule; the procedure also generalizes the examples to create more broadly applicable correction rules.

JUMAN OUTPUT	DESIRED OUTPUT
海外/SN	海外/CN
旅行/SN	旅行/CN
も/TTM	も/TTM
楽/SN	楽し/VB
し/VB	
め/???	める/VSUF
る/???	
旅行/SN	旅行/CN
サービス/SN	サービス/CN
を/CM	を/CM
二月中旬/???	二月/CN
	中旬/CN
から/PT	から/PT
売り出す/VB	売り出す/VB
。/KT	。/KT

Figure 3a: *Alignment of JUMAN output with manually annotated correction data.*

楽/SN	楽し/VB
し/VB	
め/???	める/VSUF
る/???	
二月中旬/???	二月/CN
	中旬/CN

Figure 3b: *Pairs of differences collected from alignment in Figure 3a. above.*

We estimate probabilities for the correction rules via the sample inspection method. (see the Appendix.) Here, significance level is a parameter, from a low of 0.1 for ambitious correction through a high of 0.9 for conservative correction. The setting gives us some trade-off between accuracy and the degree of ambiguity in the results. One selects an appropriate value by empirically testing performance over a range of parameter settings. Correction rules are ordered and applied based on probability estimates.

When a rule matches, 1) AMED corrects JUMAN's output if the probability estimate exceeds a user-specified threshold, 2) AMED introduces an alternative if the probability falls below that threshold but exceeds a second user-supplied threshold, or 3) AMED makes no change if the probability estimate falls below both thresholds.

As a result, a chart representing word segmentation and part of speech possibilities is passed to POST, which was easily modified to handle a chart as input, since the underlying Viterbi algorithm applies equally well to a chart. POST then selects the most likely combination of word segmentation and part of speech labels according to a bi-gram probability model.

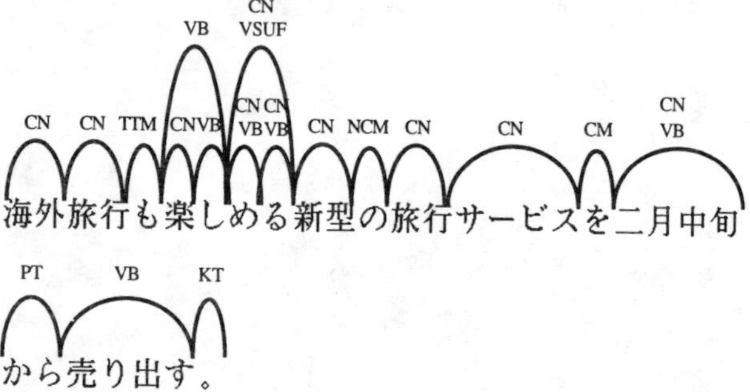

Figure 4: *Chart of alternatives produced by AMED.*

海外/CN 旅行/CN も/TTM 楽し/VB める/VSUF 新型/CN の/NCM 旅行/CN サービス/CN を/CM 二月中旬/CN から/PT 売り出す/VB 。/KT

Figure 5: *Final segmentation and labelling after POST.*

5. EXPERIENCE

The motivation for this study was the need to port our PLUM data extraction system [Weischedel, et al., 1992] to process Japanese text. The architecture was successful enough that it is part of (the Japanese version of) PLUM now, and has been used in Government-sponsored evaluations of data extraction systems in two domains: extracting data pertinent to joint ventures and extracting data pertinent to advances in microelectronics fabrication technology. It has therefore been run over corpora of over 300,000 words.

There are two ways we can illustrate the effect of this architecture: a small quanitative experiment and examples of generalizations made by AMED.

5.1 A Small Experiment

We ran a small experiment to measure the effect of the architecture (JUMAN + AMED + POST), contrasted with JUMAN alone. Japanese linguistics students corrected JUMAN's output; the annotation rate of an experienced annotator is roughly 750 words per hour, using the TREEBANK annotation tools (which we had ported to Japanese). In the first experiment, we used 14,000 words of training data and 1,400 words of test data. In a second experiment, we used 81,993 words of training data and a test set of 4,819 words.

Remarkably the results for the two cases were almost identical in error rate. In the smaller test (of 1,400 words), the error rate on part-of-speech labelling (given correct segmentation) was 3.6%, compared to 8.5%; word segmentation error was reduced from 9.4% to 8.3% using the algorithm. In the larger test (of 4,819 words), the error rate on part-of-speech labelling (given correct segmentation) was 3.4%, compared to 8.2%; word segmentation error was reduced from 9.4% to 8.3% using the algorithm.

Therefore, using the AMED correction algorithm plus POST's hidden Markov model reduced the error rate in part of speech by more than a factor of two. Reduction in word segmentation was more modest, a 12% improvement.

Error rate in part-of-speech labelling was therefore reduced to roughly the error rate in English, one of our original goals.

Both segmentation error and part of speech error could be reduced further by increasing the size of JUMAN's lexicon and/or by incorporating additional generalization patterns in AMED's learning alogrithm. However, in terms of improving PLUM's overall performance in extracting data from Japanese text, reducing word segmentation error or part-of-speech error are not the highest priority.

5.2 Examples of Rules Learned

One restriction we imposed on generalizations considered by the algorithm is that rules must be based on the first or last morpheme of the pattern. This is based on the observation in skimming the result of alignment that the first or last morpheme is quite informative. Rules which depend critically on a central element in the difference between aligned JUMAN output and supervised training were not considered. A second limitation that we imposed on the algorithm was that the right hand side of any correction rule could only contain one element, instead of the general case. Three kinds of correction rules can be inferred.

- A specific sequence of parts of speech in JUMAN's output can be replaced by a single morpheme with one part of speech.
- A specific sequence of parts of speech plus a specific word at the left edge can be replaced by a single morpheme with one part of speech.

- A specific sequence of parts of speech plus a specific word at the right edge can be replaced by a single morpheme with one part of speech.

The critical statistic in selecting among the interpretations is the fraction of times a candidate rule correctly applies in the training data versus the number of times it applies in the training. In spite of these self-imposed limitations in this initial implementation, the rules that are learned improved both segmentation and labelling by part of speech, as detailed in Section 5.1. Here we illustrate some useful generalizations made by the algorithm and used in our Japanese version of the PLUM data extraction system.

In example (1) below, the hyptohesized rule essentially recognizes proper names arising from an unknown, a punctuation mark, and a proper noun; the rule hypothesizes that the three together are a proper noun. This pattern only arises in the case of person names (an initial, a period, and a last name) in the training corpus.

1. */??? */KG */PN ===> PN

E/???	E・マークラッド/PN
・/KG	
マークラッド/PN	

Example (2) is a case where an ambiguous word ("nerai", meaning a"aim" or "purpose") is rarely used as a verb, but JUMAN's symbolic rules are predicting it as a verb. The rule corrects the rare tag to the more frequent one, common noun.

2. 狙い/VB ===> CN

狙い/VB	狙い/CN

Example (3) represents the equivalent of learning a lexical entry from annotation; if JUMAN had had it in its lexicon, no correction of segmentation (and part of speech) would have been necessary. There are many similar, multi-character, idiomatic particles in Japanese. Parallel cases arise in English, such as "in spite of" and "in regard to".

3. と/NCM */PT */CN */PT===> PT

と/NCM	との間で/PT
の/PT	
間/CN	
で/PT	

Example (4) is interesting since the rule learned corresponds to a general morphological phenomenon in Japanese. "Shita" converts an adverb to an adjective.

4. */ADV した/VB ===> ADJ

こう/ADV	こうした/ADJ
した/VB	

Example (5) represents a lexical omission where an inflected form, corresponding to the modal "can", is learned.

5. */??? る/??? ===> VSUF

め/???	める/VSUF
る/???	

6. CONCLUSION

The most interesting aspect of this work is the implementation and testing of a simple algorithm to learn correction rules from examples. Except for the annotation of text as to the correct data, the process is fully automatic. Even with as little data as we had initially (under 15,000 words), the learned correction rules improved the performance of morphological processing compared to the baseline system. Furthermore, though the original error rate of JUMAN was more than double the rate typically reported for stochastic part-of-speech labellers in English, the result of the correction algorithm plus our hidden Markov model (POST) reduced the error rate to a level comparable with that experienced in English. On the other hand, increasing the training data by a factor of five did not reduce the error rate substantially.

The architecture proposed is the morhpological component of the Japanese version of the PLUM data extraction system, and has been tested on more than 300,000 words of text in both a financial domain and a technical domain.

Hidden Markov Models, as implementd in POST, were applied to Japanese with relative ease. When additional data becomes available, we would like to test the performance of POST for both word segmentation and labelling part of speech in Japanese.

ACKNOWLEDGEMENTS

We wish to thank Professors Matsumoto and Nagao of Kyoto University who graciously made the JUMAN system available to us.

REFERENCES

1. Aizawa, T. and Ebara, T. (1973) "Mechanical Translation System of `Kana' Representations to `Kanji-kana' Mixed Representations," *NHK Thechnical Journal* 138 Vol.25 No.5, 1973.
2. Brill, E. (1992) "A Simple Rule-Based Part of Speech Tagger," *Proceedings of the Fifth DARPA Workshop on Speech and Natural Language*, Morgan Kaufmann Publishers, San Mateo, CA. February 1992, pp. 112-116.
3. Church, K. A (1988), "Stochastic Parts Program and Noun Phrase Parser for Unrestricted Text," *Proceedings of the Second Conference on Applied Natural Language Processing, ACL*, 1988, 136-143.
4. de Marcken, C.G. (1990) "Parsing the LOB Corpus," *Proceedings of the 28th Annual Meeting of the Association for Computational Linguistics* 1990, 243-251.
5. DeRose, S.J. (1988) "Grammatical Category Disambiguation by Statistical Optimization," *Computational Linguistics* 14: 31-39, 1988.
6. Meteer, M., Schwartz, R., and Weischedel, R. (1991) "Empirical Studies in Part of Speech Labelling," *Proceedings of the Fourth DARPA Workshop on Speech and Natural Language,* Morgan Kaufmann Publishers, San Mateo, CA. February 1991, pp. 331-336.
7. Weischedel, R. (1991) "A New Approach to Text Understanding," *Proceedings of the Fourth DARPA Workshop on Speech and Natural Language,* Morgan Kaufmann Publishers, San Mateo, CA. February 1991, pp. 316-322.

APPENDIX

To estimate the reliability of hypothesized correction rules, we used the sample inspection method. If the sample size is small, high frequency cases may tend to receive a higher probability estimate than if the sample were larger.

The sample inspection method provides an objective measure of how likely estimation error may be, given small samples. Suppose we have:

- a total of N elements in a population,
- R elements in a desired class,
- n sample elements in total, and
- r sample elements in the desired class

The conditional probaiblity of R > R1, given r = r1 will be:

$$p(R>R_1 \mid r=r_1) = \frac{p(R>R_1,\ r=r_1)}{p(r=r_1)}$$

Since we assume the elements of R occur independently, we have

$$= \frac{\sum_{R>R_1} p(R)\, p(r=r_1 \mid R)}{\sum_{R>0} p(R)\, p(r=r_1 \mid R)}$$

Assuming p(R) is approximately constant, we have

$$= \sum_{R>R_1} p(r=r_1 \mid R) \qquad (1)$$

Here p(r = r1 | R), the conditional probability of r desired elements given R desired elements in the population, is given by a hypergeometric distribution. The distribution will approach a binomial distribution as N gets larger.

$$p(r=r1 \mid R) = \frac{\binom{R}{r}\binom{N-R}{n-r}}{\binom{N}{n}} \xrightarrow{N \to \infty} \binom{n}{r} q^r (1-q)^{n-r} \qquad (2)$$

Therefore, substituting (2) to (1), given a significance level k (the probability that the conclusion is correct; for eacmple 0.9), we search for the largest q' which satisfies:

$$p(q>q' \mid r=r_1) = \int_{q'}^{1} \binom{n}{r} q^r (1-q)^{n-r} > k$$

MEASURES AND MODELS FOR PHRASE RECOGNITION

Steven Abney

Bell Communications Research
445 South Street
Morristown, NJ 07960

ABSTRACT

I present an entropy measure for evaluating parser performance. The measure is fine-grained, and permits us to evaluate performance at the level of individual phrases. The parsing problem is characterized as statistically approximating the Penn Treebank annotations. I consider a series of models to "calibrate" the measure by determining what scores can be achieved using the most obvious kinds of information. I also relate the entropy measure to measures of recall/precision and grammar coverage.

1. INTRODUCTION

Entropy measures of parser performance have focussed on the parser's contribution to word prediction. This is appropriate for evaluating a parser as a language model for speech recognition, but it is less appropriate for evaluating how well a parser does at *parsing*. I would like to present an entropy measure for phrase recognition, along with closely-related measures of precision and recall. I consider a series of models, in order to establish a baseline for performance, and to give some sense of what parts of the problem are hardest, and what kinds of information contribute most to a solution.

Specifically, I consider the problem of recognizing *chunks* (Abney 1991)—non-recursive pieces of major-category phrases, omitting post-head complements and modifiers. Chunks correspond to prosodic phrases (Abney 1992) and can be assembled into complete parse trees by adding head-head *dependencies.*

2. THE PARSING PROBLEM

Parsing is usually characterized as the problem of recovering parse trees for sentences, *given a grammar* that defines the mapping of sentences to parse-trees. However, I wish to characterize the problem without assuming a grammar, for two reasons. First, we cannot assume a grammar for unrestricted English. For unrestricted English, failure of coverage will be a significant problem for any grammar, and we would like a measure of performance that treats failure of coverage and failures within the grammar uniformly.

Second, I am particularly interested in parsers like Fidditch (Hindle 1983) and Cass (Abney 1990) that avoid search by relying on highly reliable patterns for recognizing individual phrases. Such parsers may need to consider competing patterns when scoring a given pattern—for example, Cass relies heavily on a preference for the pattern that matches the longest prefix of the input. Such cross-pattern dependencies cannot be expressed within, for example, a stochastic context-free grammar (SCFG). Hence I am interested in a more general evaluation framework, one that subsumes both Fidditch/Cass-style parsers and SCFG parsing.

Instead of assuming a grammar, I take the Penn Treebank (Marcus & Santorini 1991) to provide a representative sample of English, viewed as a function from sentences to parse trees. A parser's task is to statistically approximate that function. We can measure the (in)accuracy of the parser by the amount of additional information we must provide in order to specify the correct (Treebank) parse for a sentence, given the output of the parser. This is the entropy of the corpus given the parser, and approaches zero as the parser approaches perfect emulation of Treebank annotation.

We can characterize the parser's task at two levels of granularity. At the level of the sentence, the task is to assign a probability distribution over the set of possible parse-trees for the sentence. At the phrase level, the problem is to give, for each candidate phrase c, the probability that c belongs to the correct parse. I will focus on the latter characterization, for several reasons: (1) as mentioned, I am interested in developing reliable patterns for recognizing individual phrases, in order to reduce the necessity for search and to increase parsing speed, (2) evaluating at the phrase level allows us to assign blame for error at a finer grain, (3) there are applications such as data extraction where we may have good models for certain phrase types, but not for entire sentences, and (4) a phrase model can easily be embedded in a sentence model, so evaluating at the finer grain does not exclude evaluation at the coarser grain.

3. MEASURES

Given a sentence, the chunk *candidates* are all tuples $c = (x,i,j)$, for x a syntactic category, and i and j the start and end positions of the chunk. For each candidate, there are two possible events in the Treebank: the candidate is indeed a phrase in the Treebank parse (T), or it is not a true phrase (~T). For each candidate, the parsing model provides $P(T|c)$, the probability of the candidate being a true phrase, and $P(\sim T|c) = 1 - P(T|c)$.

Given the probabilities provided by the parsing model, the information that must be provided to specify that T occurs (that the candidate is a true phrase) is $-\lg P(T|c)$; and to specify that ~T occurs, $-\lg P(\sim T|c)$. The entropy of the corpus given the model is the average $-\lg P(E_c|c)$, for E_c being T or ~T according as candidate c does or does not appear in the Treebank parse. That is,

$$H = -(1/N) \sum_{c} \lg P(E_c|c) \qquad \text{for N the number of candidates}$$

A perfect model would have $P(E_c|c) = 1$ for all c, hence $H = 0$. At the other extreme, a 'random-guess' model would have $P(E_c|c) = 1/2$ for all c, hence H = 1 bit/candidate (b/c). This provides an upper bound on H, in the sense that any model that has H > 1 b/c can be changed into a model with H < 1 by systematically interchanging $P(T|c)$ and $P(\sim T|c)$. Hence, for all models, $0 \leq H \leq 1$ b/c.

There are some related measures of interest. We can translate entropy into an equivalent number of equally-likely parses (perplexity) by the relation:

$$PP = 2^{\alpha H}$$

for H in bits/candidate and α the number of candidates per sentence. In the test corpus I used, $\alpha = 8880$, so PP ranges from 1 to $2^{8880} = 10^{2670}$.

We can also measure expected precision and recall, by considering $P(T|c)$ as a probabilistic 'Yes' to candidate c. For example, if the model says $P(T|c) = 3/4$, that counts as 3/4 of a 'Yes'. Then the expected number of Yes's is the sum of $P(T|c)$ over all candidates, and the expected number of correct Yes's is the sum of $P(T|c)$ over candidates that are true chunks. From that and the number of true chunks, which can simply be counted, we can compute precision and recall:

$$E(\#Y) = \sum_{c} P(T|c)$$

$$E(\#TY) = \sum_{\text{true } c} P(T|c)$$

$$EP = E(\#TY) / E(\#Y)$$
$$ER = E(\#TY) / \#T$$

4. MODELS

To establish a baseline for performance, and to determine how much can be accomplished with 'obvious', easily-acquired information, I consider a series of models. Model 0 is a zero-parameter, random-guess model; it establishes a lower bound on performance. Model 1 estimates one parameter, the proportion of true chunks among candidates. Model XK takes the category and length of candidates into account. Model G induces a simple grammar from the training corpus. Model C considers a small amount of context. And model S is a sentence-level model based on G.

4.1. Models 0 and 1

Models 0 and 1 take $P(T|c)$ to be constant. Model 0 (the random-guess model) takes $P(T) = 1/2$, and provides a lower bound on performance. Model 1 (the one-parameter model) estimates P(T) as the proportion of true chunks among candidates in a training corpus. The training corpus I used consists of 1706 sentences, containing 19,025 true chunks (11.2 per sentence), and 14,442,484 candidates (8470 per sentence). The test corpus consisted of 1549 sentences, 17,676 true chunks (11.4 per sentence), and 13,753,628 candidates (8880 per sentence). The performance of the random-guess and one-parameter models is as follows:

	b/c	prs/sent	EP	ER
0	1	10^{2670}	.129%	(50%)
1	.014 2	10^{38}	.129%	(.132%)

For these two models (in fact, for any model with $P(T|c)$ constant), precision is at a minimum, and equals the proportion of true chunks in the test corpus. Recall is uninformative, being equal to $P(T|c)$.

4.2. Model XK

Model XK is motivated by the observation that very long chunks are highly unlikely. It takes $P(T|c) = P(T|x,k)$, for x the category of c and k its length. It estimates $P(T|x,k)$ as the proportion of true chunks among candidates of category x and length k in the training corpus. As expected, this model does better than the previous ones:

	b/c	prs/sent	EP	ER
XK	.007 95	10^{21}	5.5%	5.6%

4.3. Models G and C

For model G, I induced a simple grammar from the training corpus. I used Ken Church's tagger (Church 1988) to assign part-of-speech probabilities to words. The grammar contains a rule $x \rightarrow \gamma$ for every Treebank chunk $[_x \gamma]$ in the training corpus. (x is the syntactic category of the chunk, and γ is the part-of-speech sequence assigned to the words of the chunk.) $[_x \gamma]$ is counted as being observed $P(\gamma)$ times, for $P(\gamma)$ the probability of assigning the part-of-speech sequence γ to the words of the chunk. I used a second corpus to estimate $P(T|x,\gamma)$ for each rule in the grammar, by counting the proportion of true phrases among candidates of form $[_x \gamma]$. For candidates that matched no rule, I estimated the probabilities $P(T|x,k)$ as in the XK model.

Model C is a variant of model G, in which a small amount of context, namely, the following part of speech, is also taken into account.

The results on the test corpus are as follows:

	b/c	prs/sent	EP	ER
G	.003 81	10^{10}	47.3%	48.2%
C	.003 36	10^{9}	54.5%	58.7%

The improvement in expected precision and recall is dramatic.

4.4 Assigning Blame

We can make some observations about the sources of entropy. For example, we can break out entropy by category:

	%H	–E(%H)
NP	39.0	+18.7
PP	21.1	+7.2
VP	19.0	+4.4
Null	7.5	–8.4
AdjP	3.9	+1.4
other (23)	9.5	–23.4

The first column represents the percentage of total entropy accounted for by candidates of the given category. In the second column, I have subtracted the amount we would have expected if entropy were divided among candidates without regard to category. The results clearly confirm our intuitions that, for example, noun phrases are more difficult to recognize than verb clusters, and that the Null category, consisting mostly of punctuation and connectives, is easy to recognize.

We can also break out entropy among candidates covered by the grammar, and those not covered by the grammar. The usual measure of grammar coverage is simply the proportion of true chunks covered, but we can more accurately determine how much of a problem coverage is by measuring how much we stand to gain by improving coverage, versus how much we stand to gain by improving our model of covered candidates. On our test corpus, only 4% of the candidates are uncovered by the grammar, but 19% of the information cost (entropy) is due to uncovered candidates.

4.5. Model S

None of the models discussed so far take into account the constraint that the set of true chunks must partition the sentence. Now, if a perfect sentence model exists—if an algorithm exists that assigns to each sentence its Treebank parse—then a perfect phrase model also exists. And to the extent that a model uses highly reliably local patterns (as I would like), little information is lost by not evaluating at the sentence level. But for other phrase-level models, such as those considered here, embedding them in a sentence-level model can significantly improve performance.

Model S is designed to gauge how much information is lost in model G by not evaluating parses as a whole. It uses model G's assignments of probabilities $P(T|c)$ for individual candidates as the basis for assigning probabilities $P(s)$ to entire parses, that is, to chunk-sequences s that cover the entire sentence.

To choose a sequence of chunks stochastically, we begin with s = the null sequence at position $i = 0$. We choose from among the candidates at position i, taking the probability $P(c)$ of choosing candidate c to be proportional to $P(T|c)$. The chosen chunk c is appended to s, and the current position i is advanced to the end position of c. We iterate to the end of the sentence. In brief:

$$P(c) = P(T|c) \Big/ \sum_{c' \text{ at } i} P(T|c') \qquad \text{for } i \text{ the start position of } c$$

$$P(s) = \prod_{c \text{ in } s} P(c)$$

The entropy of a sentence given the model is $-\lg P(s)$, for s the true sequence of chunks. We can also compute actual (not expected) precision and recall by counting the true chunks in the most-likely parse according to the model. The results on the test corpus are:

M	b/s	prs/sent	Precision	Recall
S	14.1	10^4	74.1%	75.6%

(By way of comparison, the bits/sentence numbers for the other models are as follows:)

0	1	XK	G	C	S
8880	126	70.6	33.8	29.8	14.1

For model S, the number of parses per sentence is still rather high, but the precision and recall are surprisingly good, given the rudimentary information that the model takes into account. I think there is cause for optimism that the chunk recognition problem can be solved in the near term, using models that take better account of context and word-level information.

4. CONCLUSION

To summarize, I have approached the problem of parsing English as a problem of statistically approximating the Penn Treebank. For the purposes of parsing, English is a function from sentences to parse-trees, and the Treebank provides a (sufficiently representative) sample from the extension of that function. A parsing model approximates Treebank annotation. Our basic measure of the goodness of the approximation is the amount of additional information we must provide in order to specify the Treebank parse, given the probabilities assigned by the parser. I have presented a series of models to "calibrate" the measure, showing what kind of performance is achievable using obvious kinds of information.

An impetus for this work is the success of parsers like Fidditch and Cass, which are able to greatly reduce search, and increase parsing speed, by using highly reliable patterns for recognizing phrases. The limitation of such work is the impracticality of constructing reliable patterns by hand, past a certain point. One hindrance to automatic acquisition of reliable patterns has been the lack of a framework for evaluating such parsers at a fine grain, and exploring which kinds of information contribute most to parsing accuracy.

In the current work, I have presented a framework for fine-grained evaluation of parsing models. It does not assume stochastic context-free grammars, and it quantifies parsers' performance at parsing, rather than at a more indirectly related task like word prediction.

REFERENCES

1. Steven Abney (1990). Rapid Incremental Parsing with Repair. Proceedings of the 6th New OED Conference. University of Waterloo, Waterloo, Ontario.

2. Steven Abney (1991). Parsing by Chunks. In Berwick, Abney & Tenny, eds. Principle-Based Parsing, pp.257-278. Kluwer Academic Publishers, Dordrecht.

3. Steven Abney (1992). Prosodic Structure, Performance Structure and Phrase Structure. Proc. 5th DARPA Workshop on Speech and Natural Language (Harriman, NY). Morgan Kaufmann.

4. E. Black, S. Abney, D. Flickenger, R. Grishman, P. Harrison, D. Hindle, R. Ingria, F. Jelinek, J. Klavans, M. Liberman, M. Marcus, S. Roukos, B. Santorini, and T. Strzalkowski (1991). A procedure for quantitatively comparing the syntactic coverage of English grammars. DARPA Speech and Natural Language Workshop, pp.306-311. Morgan Kaufmann.

5. Peter L. Brown, Stephen A. Della Pietra, Vincent J. Della Pietra, Jennifer C. Lai, and Robert L Mercer (1992). An Estimate of an Upper Bound for the Entropy of English. Computational Linguistics 18.1, pp.31-40.

6. Kenneth Church (1988). A Stochastic Part of Speech Tagger and Noun Phrase Parser for English. Proceedings of the 2nd Conference on Applied Natural Language Processing. Austin, Texas.

7. T. Fujisaki, F. Jelinek, J. Cocke, E. Black, T. Nishino (1989). A Probabilistic Parsing Method for Sentence Disambiguation. International Workshop on Parsing Technologies 1989, pp.85-94.

8. Donald Hindle (1983). User manual for Fidditch. Naval Reserach Laboratory Technical Memorandum #7590-142.

9. F. Jelinek. Self-Organized Language Modeling for Speech Recognition. IBM report.

10. F. Jelinek, J.D. Lafferty, and R.L. Mercer. Basic Methods of Probabilistic Context-Free Grammars. IBM report.

11. Mitchell Marcus and Beatrice Santorini (1991). Building very large natural language corpora: the Penn Treebank. Ms., University of Pennsylvania.

12. Fernando Pereira and Yves Schabes (1992). Inside-Outside Reestimation from Partially Bracketed Corpora. ACL 92, pp.128-135.

Automatic Grammar Induction and Parsing Free Text: A Transformation-Based Approach

Eric Brill *

Department of Computer and Information Science
University of Pennsylvania
brill@unagi.cis.upenn.edu

ABSTRACT

In this paper we describe a new technique for parsing free text: a transformational grammar[1] is automatically learned that is capable of accurately parsing text into binary-branching syntactic trees with nonterminals unlabelled. The algorithm works by beginning in a very naive state of knowledge about phrase structure. By repeatedly comparing the results of bracketing in the current state to proper bracketing provided in the training corpus, the system learns a set of simple structural transformations that can be applied to reduce error. After describing the algorithm, we present results and compare these results to other recent results in automatic grammar induction.

1. INTRODUCTION

There has been a great deal of interest of late in the automatic induction of natural language grammar. Given the difficulty inherent in manually building a robust parser, along with the availability of large amounts of training material, automatic grammar induction seems like a path worth pursuing. A number of systems have been built which can be trained automatically to bracket text into syntactic constituents. In [10] mutual information statistics are extracted from a corpus of text and this information is then used to parse new text. [13] defines a function to score the quality of parse trees, and then uses simulated annealing to heuristically explore the entire space of possible parses for a given sentence. In [3], distributional analysis techniques are applied to a large corpus to learn a context-free grammar.

The most promising results to date have been based on the inside-outside algorithm (i-o algorithm), which can be used to train stochastic context-free grammars. The i-o algorithm is an extension of the finite-state based Hidden Markov Model (by [1]), which has been applied successfully in many areas, including speech recognition and part of speech tagging. A number of recent papers have explored the potential of using the i-o algorithm to automatically learn a grammar [9, 15, 12, 6, 7, 14].

Below, we describe a new technique for grammar induction.[2] The algorithm works by beginning in a very naive state of knowledge about phrase structure. By repeatedly comparing the results of parsing in the current state to the proper phrase structure for each sentence in the training corpus, the system learns a set of ordered transformations which can be applied to reduce parsing error. We believe this technique has advantages over other methods of phrase structure induction. Some of the advantages include: the system is very simple, it requires only a very small set of transformations, learning proceeds quickly and achieves a high degree of accuracy, and only a very small training corpus is necessary. In addition, since some tokens in a sentence are not even considered in parsing, the method could prove to be considerably more resistant to noise than a CFG-based approach. After describing the algorithm, we present results and compare these results to other recent results in automatic phrase structure induction.

2. THE ALGORITHM

The learning algorithm is trained on a small corpus of partially bracketed text which is also annotated with part of speech information. All of the experiments presented below were done using the Penn Treebank annotated corpus[11]. The learner begins in a naive initial state, knowing very little about the phrase structure of the target corpus. In particular, all that is initially known is that English tends to be right branching and that final punctuation is final punctuation. Transformations are then learned automatically which transform the output of the naive parser into output which better resembles the phrase structure found in the training corpus. Once a set of transformations has been learned, the system is capable of taking sentences tagged with parts of speech and returning a binary-branching structure with nonterminals unlabelled[3].

2.1. The Initial State Of The Parser

Initially, the parser operates by assigning a right-linear structure to all sentences. The only exception is that final punctuation is attached high. So, the sentence "*The dog and old cat ate* ." would be incorrectly bracketed as:

((The (dog (and (old (cat ate))))) .)

*The author would like to thank Mark Liberman, Meiting Lu, David Magerman, Mitch Marcus, Rich Pito, Giorgio Satta, Yves Schabes and Tom Veatch. This work was supported by DARPA and AFOSR jointly under grant No. AFOSR-90-0066, and by ARO grant No. DAAL 03-89-C0031 PRI.

[1] Not in the traditional sense of the term.

[2] A similar method has been applied effectively in part of speech tagging; see [5, 4].

[3] This is the same output given by systems described in [10, 3, 12, 14]

The parser in its initial state will obviously not bracket sentences with great accuracy. In some experiments below, we begin with an even more naive initial state of knowledge: sentences are parsed by assigning them a random binary-branching structure with final punctuation always attached high.

2.2. Structural Transformations

The next stage involves learning a set of transformations that can be applied to the output of the naive parser to make these sentences better conform to the proper structure specified in the training corpus. The list of possible transformation types is prespecified. Transformations involve making a simple change triggered by a simple environment. In the current implementation, there are twelve allowable transformation types:

- (1-8) $(Add|delete)$ a $(left|right)$ parenthesis to the $(left|right)$ of part of speech tag X.
- (9-12) $(Add|delete)$ a $(left|right)$ parenthesis between tags X and Y.

To carry out a transformation by adding or deleting a parenthesis, a number of additional simple changes must take place to preserve balanced parentheses and binary branching. To give an example, to delete a left paren in a particular environment, the following operations take place (assuming, of course, that there is a left paren to delete):

1. Delete the left paren.
2. Delete the right paren that matches the just deleted paren.
3. Add a left paren to the left of the constituent immediately to the left of the deleted left paren.
4. Add a right paren to the right of the constituent immediately to the right of the deleted paren.
5. If there is no constituent immediately to the right, or none immediately to the left, then the transformation fails to apply.

Structurally, the transformation can be seen as follows. If we wish to delete a left paren to the right of constituent X[4], where X appears in a subtree of the form:

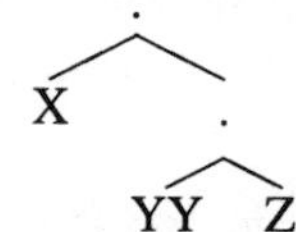

[4]To the right of the rightmost terminal dominated by X if X is a nonterminal.

carrying out these operations will transform this subtree into[5]:

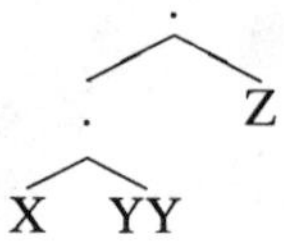

Given the sentence[6]:

The dog barked .

this would initially be bracketed by the naive parser as:

((The (dog barked)) .)

If the transformation *delete a left paren to the right of a determiner* is applied, the structure would be transformed to the correct bracketing:

(((The dog) barked) .)

To add a right parenthesis to the right of YY, YY must once again be in a subtree of the form:

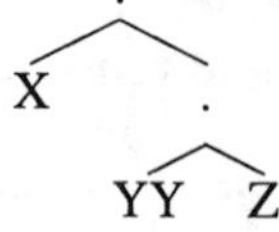

If it is, the following steps are carried out to add the right paren:

1. Add the right paren.
2. Delete the left paren that now matches the newly added paren.
3. Find the right paren that used to match the just deleted paren and delete it.
4. Add a left paren to match the added right paren.

[5]The twelve transformations can be decomposed into two structural transformations, that shown here and its converse, along with six triggering environments.

[6]Input sentences are also labelled with parts of speech.

This results in the same structural change as deleting a left paren to the right of X in this particular structure.

Applying the transformation *add a right paren to the right of a noun* to the bracketing:

((The (dog barked)) .)

will once again result in the correct bracketing:

(((The dog) barked) .)

2.3. Learning Transformations

Learning proceeds as follows. Sentences in the training set are first parsed using the naive parser which assigns right linear structure to all sentences, attaching final punctuation high. Next, for each possible instantiation of the twelve transformation templates, that particular transformation is applied to the naively parsed sentences. The resulting structures are then scored using some measure of success which compares these parses to the correct structural descriptions for the sentences provided in the training corpus. The transformation which results in the best scoring structures then becomes the first transformation of the ordered set of transformations that are to be learned. That transformation is applied to the right-linear structures, and then learning proceeds on the corpus of improved sentence bracketings. The following procedure is carried out repeatedly on the training corpus until no more transformations can be found whose application reduces the error in parsing the training corpus:

1. The best transformation is found for the structures output by the parser in its current state.[7]
2. The transformation is applied to the output resulting from bracketing the corpus using the parser in its current state.
3. This transformation is added to the end of the ordered list of transformations.
4. Go to 1.

After a set of transformations has been learned, it can be used to effectively parse fresh text. To parse fresh text, the text is first naively parsed and then every transformation is applied, in order, to the naively parsed text.

One nice feature of this method is that different measures of bracketing success can be used: learning can proceed in such a way as to try to optimize any specified measure of success. The measure we have chosen for our experiments is the same measure described in [12], which is one of the measures that arose out of a parser evaluation workshop [2]. The measure is the percentage of constituents (strings of words between matching parentheses) from sentences output by our system which do not cross any constituents in the Penn Treebank structural description of the sentence. For example, if our system outputs:

(((The big) (dog ate)) .)

and the Penn Treebank bracketing for this sentence was:

(((The big dog) ate) .)

then the constituent *the big* would be judged correct whereas the constituent *dog ate* would not.

Below are the first seven transformations found from one run of training on the Wall Street Journal corpus, which was initially bracketed using the right-linear initial-state parser.

1. Delete a left paren to the left of a singular noun.
2. Delete a left paren to the left of a plural noun.
3. Delete a left paren between two proper nouns.
4. Delet a left paren to the right of a determiner.
5. Add a right paren to the left of a comma.
6. Add a right paren to the left of a period.
7. Delete a right paren to the left of a plural noun.

The first four transformations all extract noun phrases from the right linear initial structure. The sentence "The cat meowed ." would initially be bracketed as:[8]

((The (cat meowed)) .)

Applying the first transformation to this bracketing would result in:

(((The cat) meowed) .)

[7] The *state* of the parser is defined as naive initial-state knowledge plus all transformations that currently have been learned.

[8] These examples are not actual sentences in the corpus. We have chosen simple sentences for clarity.

Applying the fifth transformation to the bracketing:

((We (ran (, (and (they walked))))) .)

would result in

(((We ran) (, (and (they walked)))) .)

3. RESULTS

In the first experiment we ran, training and testing were done on the Texas Instruments Air Travel Information System (ATIS) corpus[8].[9] In table 1, we compare results we obtained to results cited in [12] using the inside-outside algorithm on the same corpus. Accuracy is measured in terms of the percentage of noncrossing constituents in the test corpus, as described above. Our system was tested by using the training set to learn a set of transformations, and then applying these transformations to the test set and scoring the resulting output. In this experiment, 64 transformations were learned (compared with 4096 context-free rules and probabilities used in the i-o experiment). It is significant that we obtained comparable performance using a training corpus only 21% as large as that used to train the inside-outside algorithm.

Method	# of Training Corpus Sentences	Accuracy
Inside-Outside	700	90.36%
Transformation-Learner	150	91.12%

Table 1: Comparing two learning methods on the ATIS corpus.

After applying all learned transformations to the test corpus, 60% of the sentences had no crossing constituents, 74% had fewer than two crossing constituents, and 85% had fewer than three. The mean sentence length of the test corpus was 11.3. In figure 1, we have graphed percentage correct as a function of the number of transformations that have been applied to the test corpus. As the transformation number increases, overtraining sometimes occurs. In the current implementation of the learner, a transformation is added to the list if it results in *any* positive net change in the training set. Toward the end of the learning procedure, transformations are found that only affect a very small percentage of training sentences. Since small counts are less reliable than large counts, we cannot reliably assume that these transformations will also improve performance in the test corpus. One way around this overtraining would be to set a threshold: specify a minimum level of improvement that must result for a transformation to be learned. Another possibility is to use additional training material to prune the set of learned transformations.

[9] In all experiments described in this paper, results are calculated on a test corpus which was not used in any way in either training the learning algorithm or in developing the system.

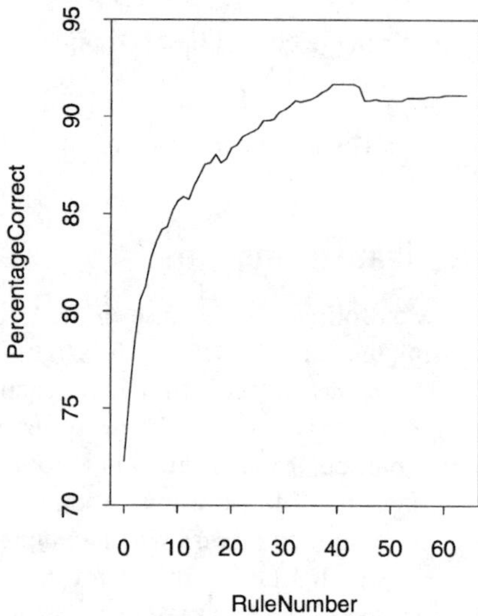

Figure 1: Results From the ATIS Corpus, Starting With Right-Linear Structure

We next ran an experiment to determine what performance could be achieved if we dropped the initial right-linear assumption. Using the same training and test sets as above, sentences were initially assigned a random binary-branching structure, with final punctuation always attached high. Since there was less regular structure in this case than in the right-linear case, many more transformations were found, 147 transformations in total. When these transformations were applied to the test set, a bracketing accuracy of 87.13% resulted.

The ATIS corpus is structurally fairly regular. To determine how well our algorithm performs on a more complex corpus, we ran experiments on the Wall Street Journal. Results from this experiment can be found in table 2.[10] Accuracy is again measured as the percentage of constituents in the test set which do not cross any Penn Treebank constituents.[11] As a point of comparison, in [14] an experiment was done using the i-o algorithm on a corpus of WSJ sentences of length 1-15. Training was carried out on 1,095 sentences, and an accuracy of 90.2% was obtained in bracketing a test set.

[10] For sentences of length 2-15, the initial right-linear parser achieves 69% accuracy. For sentences of length 2-20, 63% accuracy is achieved and for sentences of length 2-25, accuracy is 59%.

[11] In all of our experiments carried out on the Wall Street Journal, the test set was a randomly selected set of 500 sentences.

Sent. Length	# Training Corpus Sents	# of Transformations	% Accuracy
2-15	250	83	88.1
2-15	500	163	89.3
2-15	1000	221	91.6
2-20	250	145	86.2
2-25	250	160	83.8

Table 2: WSJ Sentences

In the corpus used for the experiments of sentence length 2-15, the mean sentence length was 10.80. In the corpus used for the experiment of sentence length 2-25, the mean length was 16.82. As would be expected, performance degrades somewhat as sentence length increases. In table 3, we show the percentage of sentences in the test corpus which have no crossing constituents, and the percentage that have only a very small number of crossing constituents[12].

Sent. Length	# Training Corpus Sents	% of 0-error sents	% of $\leq$1-error sents	% of $\leq$2-error sents
2-15	500	53.7	72.3	84.6
2-15	1000	62.4	77.2	87.8
2-25	250	29.2	44.9	59.9

Table 3: WSJ Sentences

In table 4, we show the standard deviation measured from three different randomly chosen training sets of each sample size and randomly chosen test sets of 500 sentences each, as well as the accuracy as a function of training corpus size.

Sent. Length	# Training Corpus Sents	% Correct	Std. Dev.
2-20	0	63.0	0.69
2-20	10	75.8	2.95
2-20	50	82.1	1.94
2-20	100	84.7	0.56
2-20	250	86.2	0.46
2-20	750	87.3	0.61

Table 4: More WSJ Results

We also ran an experiment on WSJ sentences of length 2-15 starting with random binary-branching structures with final punctuation attached high. In this experiment, 325 transformations were found using a 250-sentence training corpus, and the accuracy resulting from applying these transformations to a test set was 84.72%.

Finally, in figure 2 we show the sentence length distribution in the Wall Street Journal corpus.

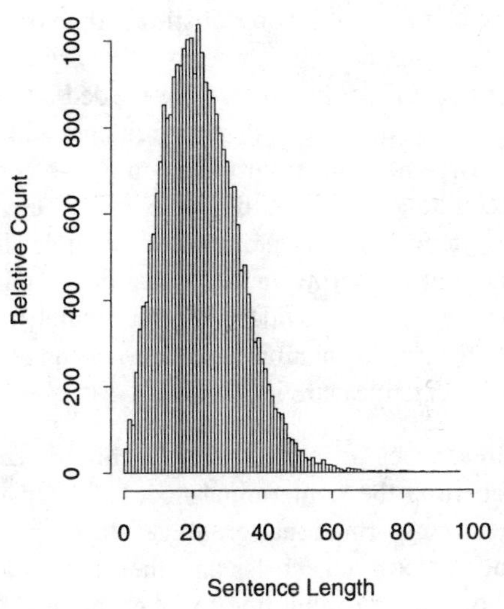

Figure 2: The Distribution of Sentence Lengths in the WSJ Corpus.

While the numbers presented above allow us to compare the transformation learner with systems trained and tested on comparable corpora, these results are all based upon the assumption that the test data is tagged fairly reliably (manually tagged text was used in all of these experiments, as well in the experiments of [12, 14].) When parsing free text, we cannot assume that the text will be tagged with the accuracy of a human annotator. Instead, an automatic tagger would have to be used to first tag the text before parsing. To address this issue, we ran one experiment where we randomly induced a 5% tagging error rate beyond the error rate of the human annotator. Errors were induced in such a way as to preserve the unigram part of speech tag probability distribution in the corpus. The experiment was run for sentences of length 2-15, with a training set of 1000 sentences and a test set of 500 sentences. The resulting bracketing accuracy was 90.1%, compared to 91.6% accuracy when using an unadulterated corpus. Accuracy only degraded by a small amount when using the corpus with adulterated part of speech tags, suggesting that high parsing accuracy rates could be achieved if tagging of the input was done automatically by a tagger.

[12]For sentences of length 2-15, the initial right linear parser parses 17% of sentences with no crossing errors, 35% with one or fewer errors and 50% with two or fewer. For sentences of length 2-25, 7% of sentences are parsed with no crossing errors, 16% with one or fewer, and 24% with two or fewer.

4. CONCLUSIONS

In this paper, we have described a new approach for learning a grammar to automatically parse free text. The method can be used to obtain good parsing accuracy with a very small training set. Instead of learning a traditional grammar, an ordered set of structural transformations is learned which can be applied to the output of a very naive parser to obtain binary-branching trees with unlabelled nonterminals. Experiments have shown that these parses conform with high accuracy to the structural descriptions specified in a manually annotated corpus. Unlike other recent attempts at automatic grammar induction which rely heavily on statistics both in training and in the resulting grammar, our learner is only very weakly statistical. For training, only integers are needed and the only mathematical operations carried out are integer addition and integer comparison. The resulting grammar is completely symbolic. Unlike learners based on the inside-outside algorithm which attempt to find a grammar to maximize the probability of the training corpus in hopes that this grammar will match the grammar that provides the most accurate structural descriptions, the transformation-based learner can readily use any desired success measure in learning.

We have already begun the next step in this project: automatically labelling the nonterminal nodes. The parser will first use the "transformational grammar" to output a parse tree without nonterminal labels, and then a separate algorithm will be applied to that tree to label the nonterminals. The nonterminal-node labelling algorithm makes use of ideas suggested in [3], where nonterminals are labelled as a function of the labels of their daughters. In addition, we plan to experiment with other types of transformations. Currently, each transformation in the learned list is only applied once in each appropriate environment. For a transformation to be applied more than once in one environment, it must appear in the transformation list more than once. One possible extension to the set of transformation types would be to allow for transformations of the form: add/delete a paren as many times as is possible in a particular environment. We also plan to experiment with other scoring functions and control strategies for finding transformations and to use this system as a postprocessor to other grammar induction systems, learning transformations to improve their performance. We hope these future paths will lead to a trainable and very accurate parser of free text.

References

1. Baker, J. (1979) Trainable grammars for speech recognition. In Jared J. Wolf and Dennis H. Klatt, eds. *Speech communication papers presented at the 97th Meeting of the Acoustical Society of America*, MIT.
2. Black, E., Abney, S., Flickenger, D., Gdaniec, C., Grishman, R., Harrison, P., Hindle, D., Ingria, R., Jelinek, F., Klavans, J., Liberman, M., Marcus, M., Roukos, S., Santorini, B. and Strzalkowski, T. (1991) A Procedure for Quantitatively Comparing the Syntactic Coverage of English Grammars. Proceedings of the DARPA Workshop on Speech and Natural Language.
3. Brill, E. and Marcus, M. (1992) Automatically acquiring phrase structure using distributional analysis. Proceedings of the 5th DARPA Workshop on Speech and Natural Language. Harriman, N.Y.
4. Brill, E. and Marcus, M. (1992) Tagging an Unfamiliar Text With Minimal Human Supervision. American Association for Artificial Intelligence (AAAI) Fall Symposium on Probabilistic Approaches to Natural Language, Cambridge, Ma. AAAI Technical Report.
5. Brill, E. (1992) A Simple Rule-Based Part of Speech Tagger. Proceedings of the Third Conference on Applied Computational Linguistics (ACL). Trento, Italy.
6. Briscoe, T and Waegner, N. (1992) Robust Stochastic Parsing Using the Inside-Outside Algorithm. In Workshop notes from the AAAI Statistically-Based NLP Techniques Workshop.
7. Carroll, G. and Charniak, E. (1992) Learning Probabilistic Dependency Grammars from Labelled Text. In: Working Notes of the AAAI Fall Symposium on Probabilistic Approaches to Natural Language. Cambridge, Ma.
8. Hemphill, C., Godfrey, J. and Doddington, G. (1990). The ATIS spoken language systems pilot corpus. In 1990 DARPA Speech and Natural Language Workshop.
9. Lari, K. and Young, S. (1990) The estimation of stochastic context-free grammars using the inside-outside algorithm. Computer Speech and Language.
10. Magerman, D. and Marcus, M. (1990) Parsing a natural language using mutual information statistics, *Proceedings, Eighth National Conference on Artificial Intelligence (AAAI 90).*
11. Marcus, M., Santorini, B., and Marcinkiewicz, M. (1993) Building a large annotated corpus of English: the Penn Treebank. To appear in Computational Linguistics.
12. Pereira, F. and Schabes, Y. (1992) Inside-outside reestimation from partially bracketed corpora. Proceedings of the 20th Meeting of the Association for Computational Linguistics. Newark, De.
13. Sampson, G. (1986) A stochastic approach to parsing. In *Proceedings of COLING 1986*, Bonn.
14. Schabes, Y., Roth, M. and Osborne, R. (1993) Parsing the Wall Street Journal with the Inside-Outside algorithm. 1993 European ACL.
15. Sharman, R., Jelinek, F. and Mercer, R. (1990) Generating a grammar for statistical training. Proceedings of the 1990 Darpa Speech and Natural Language Workshop.

Prediction of Lexicalized Tree Fragments in Text

Donald Hindle

AT&T Bell Laboratories
600 Mountain Avenue
Murray Hill, NJ 07974

ABSTRACT

There is a mismatch between the distribution of information in text, and a variety of grammatical formalisms for describing it, including ngrams, context-free grammars, and dependency grammars. Rather than adding probabilities to existing grammars, it is proposed to collect the distributions of flexibly sized partial trees. These can be used to enhance an ngram model, and in analogical parsing.

1. THE PROBLEM WITH PROBABILIZED GRAMMARS

For a variety of language processing tasks, it is useful to have a predictive language model, a fact which has recently led to the development probabilistic versions of diverse grammars, including ngram models, context free grammars, various dependency grammars, and lexicalized tree grammars. These enterprises share a common problem: there is a mismatch between the distribution of information in text and the grammar model.

The problem arises because each grammar formalism is natural for the expression of only some linguistic relationships, but predictive relationships in text are not so restricted. For example, context-free grammars naturally express relations among sisters in a tree, but are less natural for expressing relations between elements deeper the tree. In this paper, first we discuss the distribution of information in text, and its relationship to various grammars. Then we show how a more flexible grammatical description of text can be extracted from a corpus, and how such description can enhance a language model.

Ngram Models The problem can be seen most simply in ngram models, where the basic operation is to guess the probability of a word given $n - 1$ previous words. Obviously, there is a deeper structure in text than an n-gram model admits, though thus far, efforts to exploit this information have been only marginally successful. Yet even on its own terms, ngram models typically fail to take into account predictive information.

One way that ngram models ignore predictive information is in their strategy for backing off. Consider, for example, a trigram model where the basic function is to predict a word (w_0) given the two previous words (w_{-1} and w_{-2}). In our Wall Street Journal test corpus, the three word sequence *give kittens to* appears once, but not at all in the training corpus. Thus, a trigram model will have have difficulty predicting *to* given the words *give kittens.*

In this case, the standard move of backing off to a bigram model is not very informative. It is more useful to predict *to* using the word *give* than the word *kittens*, because we know little about what can follow *kittens*, but much about what typically follows *give*. We would expect for cases where the bigram (w_{-1},w_0) does not exist, the alternative bigram (w_{-2},w_0) will be a better predictor (if it exists) than the simple unigram.

Obviously, in this example, the fact that complementation in English is not expressed purely by adjacency explains some of the power of the w_{-1} predictor.

A second problem with ngram models arises because different word sequences call for a greater or smaller n. For example, while many 6-grams are unique and uninformative, some are powerful predictors.

Table 1 shows the frequencies of the top few words following the words *New York Stock Exchange* in the 60 million word Wall Street Journal corpus. More than half the time, the word that follows *New York Stock Exchange* is *composite*. However, in the 355 cases where *New York Stock Exchange* is preceded by the word *composite* (Table 1), *composite* never occurs as the following word, and the overwhelming probable choice for the following word is *trading*.

If we had settled for a 5-gram model here, we would have failed miserably compared with a 6-gram model. But of course, this raises the sparse data problem; predicting the parameters of a 6-gram model is daunting.

Context Free Grammars It is easy to see that a simple-minded probabilizing of a CFG – that is, taking an existing CFG and assigning probabilities to the rules – is not a very good predictor. There several problems. First, CFG's typically don't include enough lexical information. Indeed, the natural use of non-terminal categories is to abstract away from

New York Stock Exchange	*composite*	6597
	,	1556
	yesterday	862
	.	824
	trading	480
	..	
	TOTAL	12305
composite New York Stock Exchange	*trading*	349
	yesterday	4
	Trading	2
	composite	0
	..	
	TOTAL	355

Table 1: Ngrams with *New York Stock Exchange*

lexical considerations. Lexical associations are however critical to guessing word probabilities, not only for verb subcategorization and selection, but across the vocabulary (see e.g. Church et al. 1991). A context free grammar with a rule $N2- > ADJ * N$ is not able to naturally express selectional restrictions between adjectives and nouns, e.g. the fact that *strong tea* is probable but *powerful tea* is not.

A second problem is that CFG's naturally abstract away from syntactic function: for example, in a CFG, a noun phrase is described by the same set of rules whether it occurs as subject, object, object of preposition or whatever. While this ability to generalize across contexts is a strength of CFG's, it is disastrous for guessing whether a noun phrase will be a pronoun or not. Table 2 shows the probabilities of a noun phrase being realized as a pronoun in various contexts, in a sample of spoken and written texts produced by college students and matched for content (Hindle 1978). Clearly, ignoring whether a noun phrase is subject or not reduces the effectiveness of a predictive model. (Note too that the differences between spoken and written English are not to be ignored.

There are of course ways to admit lexical and functional information into a CFG. But except for carefully restricted domains (e.g semantic grammars), these typically lead to an explosion of nonterminals and rules, making parameter estimation difficult.

	function	p(PRO)
spoken	subject	.71 (N=2077)
	non-subject	.16 (N=1477)
written	subject	.44 (N=1195)
	non-subject	.09 (N=1088)

Table 2: Subject and non-subject noun phrases

Dependency Grammars Dependency grammars naturally address part of the mismatch between CFG's and predictive associations, since they are expressed in terms of relations between words (Melcuk 1988). Nevertheless, in dependency grammars as well, certain syntactic relationships are problematic.

In dependency grammar, there are two competing analyses both for noun phrases and for verb phrases. For noun phrases, the head may be taken to be either 1) the head noun (e.g. *man* in *the men*) or 2) the determiner (e.g *the* in *the men*); analogously, for verb phrases, the head may be taken to be either 1) the mail verb (e.g. *see* in *had seen*) or 2) the tensed verb of the verb group (e.g *have* in *had seen*). Each analysis has its virtues, and different dependency theorists have preferred one analysis or the other. It is not our purpose here to choose a dependency analysis, but to point out that whatever the choice, there are consequences for our predictive language models. The two models imply different natural generalizations for estimating probabilities, and thus will lead to different predictions about the language probabilities. If the determiner is taken to be the head of the noun phrase, then in guessing the probability of a *verb-det-noun* structure, the association between the verb and the determiner will predominate, since when we don't have enough information about a *verb-det-noun* triple, we can back off to pairs. Conversely, if the noun is taken to be the head of the noun phrase, then the predominant association will be between verb and noun. (Of course, a more complex relationship between the grammar and the associated predictive language model may be defined, overriding the natural interpretation.)

A ten million word sample of *Wall Street Journal* text was parsed, and a set of *verb-det-noun* triples extracted. Specifically, object noun phrases consisting of a noun preceded by a single determiner preceded by a verb were tabulated. That is, we consider only verbs with an object, where the object consists of a determiner and a noun. The five most common such triples (preceded by their counts) were:

213	*have*	*a*	*loss*
176	*be*		
165	*be*	*the*	*first*
140	*raise*	*its*	*stake*
127	*reach*	*an*	*agreement*

Three different probability models for predicting the specific verb, determiner, and noun were investigated, and their entropies calculated. Model 0 is the baseline trigram model, assuming no independence among the three terms. Model 1, the natural model for the determiner=head dependency model, predicts the determiner from the verb and the noun from the determiner (and thus is equivalent to an adjacent word bigram model). Model 2 is the converse, the natural model for the noun=head dependency model. Both Model 1 and Model 2

	Model for $[_{VP}\ v\ [_{N}P\ d\ n\ ]]$	Entropy
0	$Pr(vdn) = Pr(v)Pr(dn\|v)$	15.08
1	$Pr(vdn) = Pr(v)Pr(d\|v)Pr(n\|d)$	20.48
2	$Pr(vdn) = Pr(v)Pr(n\|v)Pr(d\|n)$	17.62

Table 3: Three predictive models for verb-det-noun triples in Wall Street Journal text

ignore predictive information, assuming in the first case that the choice of noun is independent of the verb, and in the second case, that the choice of determiner is independent of the verb. Neither assumption is warranted, as Table 3 shows (both have higher entropy than the trigram model), but Model 1, the determiner=head model, is considerably inferior. Model 1 is for this case like a bigram model, and Table 3 makes it clear that this is not a particularly good way to model dependencies between verb and object: the dominant dependency is between verb and noun.

In terms of using the distributional information available in text, neither choice is correct, since the answer is lexically specific. For example, in predicting the object of verbs, *answer* is a better predictor of its object noun (*call, question*), while *alter* is better a predicting its determiner (*the, its*).

In contrast to dependency grammars and context free grammars, lexicalized tree adjoining grammars have considerable flexibility in what relations are represented, since the tree is an arbitrary-sized unit (Shabes 1988). In practice however, lexicalized TAGs have typically been written to reduce the number of rules, and thus to assume independence like other grammars. In general, for any grammar that is written without regard to the distribution of forms in text, simply attaching probabilities to the grammar will always ignore useful information. This does not imply any claim about the descriptive power of various grammar formalisms; with sufficient ingenuity, just about any recurrent relation that appears in a corpus can be encoded in any formalism. However, different grammar formalisms do differ in what they can *naturally* express.

There is a clear linguistic reason for the mismatch between received grammars and the distribution of structures in text: language provides several cross cutting ways of organizing information (including various kinds of dependencies, parallel structures, listing, name-making templates, etc.), and no single model is good for all of these.

2. USING PARTIAL STRUCTURES

The preceding section has given evidence that adding probabilities to existing grammars in several formalisms is less than optimal since significant predictive relationships are necessarily ignored. The obvious solution is to enrich the grammars to include more information. To do this, we need variable sized units in our database, with varying terms of description, including adjacency relationships and dependency relationships. That is, given the unpredictable distribution of information in text, we would like to have a more flexible approach to representing the recurrent relations in a corpus. To address this need, we have been collecting a database of partial structures extracted from the Wall Street Journal corpus, in a way designed to record recurrent information over a wide range of size and terms of the description.

Extracting Partial Structures The database of partial structures is built up from the words in the corpus, by successively adding larger structures, after augmenting the corpus with the analysis provided by an unsupervised parser. The larger structures found in this way are then entered into the permanent database of structures only if a relation recurs with a frequency above a given threshold. When a structure does not meet the frequency threshold, it is generalized until it does.

The descriptive relationships admitted include:

- basic lexical features
  - spelling
  - part-of-speech
  - lemma
  - major category (maximal projection)
- dependency relations - depends on
- adjacency relations - precedes

Consider an example from the following sentence from the a training corpus of 20 million words of the Wall Street Journal.

(1) *Reserve board rules have put banks between a rock and a hard place*

The first order description of a word consists of its basic lexical features, i.e. the word spelling, its part of speech, its lemma, and its major category. Looking at the word *banks*, we have as description

TERMINAL
banks,NN,bank/N,NP

At the first level we add adjacency and dependency information, specifically

ADDED STRUCTURE
(precedes (put,VB,put/V,VG) (banks,NN,bank/N,NG))
(precedes (banks,NN,bank/N,NG) (between,IN,between/I,PG))
(depends (put,VB,put/V,VG) (banks,NN,bank/N,NG))

Assuming that we require at least two instances for a partial description to be entered into the database, none of these three descriptions qualify for the database. Therefore we must abstract away, using an arbitrarily defined abstraction path. First we abstract from the spelling to the lemma. This move admits two relations (since they are now frequent enough)

PRUNED STRUCTURES
(precedes (put,VB,put/V,VG) (,NN,bank/N,NG))
(depends (put,VB,put/V,VG) (,NN,bank/N,NG))

The third relation is still too infrequent, so we further generalize to

(precedes (,NN,,NG) (between,IN,between/I,PG))

a relation which is amply represented (3802 occurrences).

The process is iterated, using the current abstracted description of each word, adding a level of description, then generalizing when below the frequency threshold. Since each level in elaborating the description adds information to each word, it can only reduce the counts, but never increase them. This process finds a number of recurrent partial structures, including *between a rock and a hard place* (3 occurrences in 20 million words), and $[_{VP}put[_{NP}distance][_{PP}between]]$ (4 occurrences).

General Caveats There is of course considerable noise introduced by the errors in analysis that the parser makes.

There are several arbitrary decisions made in collecting the database. The level of the threshold is arbitrarily set at 3 for all structures. The sequence of generalization is arbitrarily determined before the training. And the predicates in the description are arbitrarily selected. We would like to have better motivation for all these decisions.

It should be emphasized that while the set of descriptive terms used in the collection of the partial structure database allows a more flexible description of the corpus than simple ngrams, CFG's or some dependency descriptions, it nevertheless is also restrictive. There are many predictive relationships that can not be described. For example, parallelism, reference, topic-based or speaker-based variation, and so on.

Motivation The underlying reason for developing a database of partial trees is not primarily for the language modeling task of predicting the next word. Rather the partial-tree database is motivated by the intuition that partial trees are are the locus of other sorts of linguistic information, for example, semantic or usage information. Our use of language seems to involve the composition of variably sized partially described units expressed in terms of a variety of predicates (only some of which are included in our database). Which units are selected in using language depends on a variety of factors, including meaning, subject matter, speaking situation, style, interlocutor and so on. Of course, demonstrating that this intuition is valid remains for future work.

The set of partial trees can be used directly in an analogical parser, as described in Hindle 1992. In the parser, we are not concerned with estimating probabilities, but rather with finding the structure which best matches the current parser state, where a match is better the more specific its description is.

3. ENHANCING A TRIGRAM MODEL

The partial structure database provides more information than an ngram description, and thus can be used to enhance an ngram model. To explore how to use the best available information in a language model, we turn to a trigram model of Wall Street Journal text. The problem is put into relief by focusing on those cases where the trigram model fails, that is, where the observed trigram condition (w_{-2}, w_{-1}) does not occur in the training corpus.

In the current test, we randomly assigned each sentence from a 2 million word sample of WSJ text to either the test or training set. This unrealistically minimizes the rate of unseen conditions, since typically the training and test are selected from disjoint documents (see Church and Gale 1991). On the other hand, since the training is only a million words, the trigrams are undertrained. In general, the rate of unseen conditions will vary with the domain to be modeled and the size of training corpus, but it will not (in realistic languages) be eliminated. In this test, 26% (258665/997811) of the bigrams did not appear in the test, and thus it is necessary to backoff from the trigram model.

We will assume that a trigram model is sufficiently effective at prediction in those cases where the conditioning bigram has been observed in training, and will focus on the problem of what to do when the conditioning bigram has not appeared in the training. In a standard backoff model, we would look to estimate $Pr(w_0|w_{-1})$. Here we want to consider a second predictor derived from our database of partial structures. The particular predictor we use is the lemma of the word that w_{-1} depends on, which we will call $G(w_{-1})$. In the example discussed above, the first (standard) predictor for the word *between* is the preceding word *banks* and the second predictor for the word *between* is $G(banks)$, which in this case is put/V.

We want to choose among two predictors, w_{-1} and $G(w_{-1})$. In general, if we have two conditions, C_a and C_b and we want to find the probability of the next word given these conditions. Intuitively, we would like to choose the predictor C_i for which the predicted distribution of w differs most from the unigram distribution. Various measures are possible; here we con-

model	logprob
unigram	9.55
backoff w_{-1}	8.06
backoff $G(w_{-1})$	8.20
backoff w_{-1} then $G(w_{-1})$	7.97
backoff (MAX IS of w_{-1} and $G(w_{-1})$)	7.99

Table 4: Backoff for unknown trigrams in WSJ text.

sider one, which Resnik (1993) calls *selectional preference*, namely the relative entropy between the posterior distribution $Pr(w|C)$ and the prior distribution $Pr(w)$. We'll label this measure *IS*, where

$$IS(w;C) = \sum_{w} Pr(w|C) log \frac{Pr(w|C)}{Pr(w)}$$

In the course of processing sentence (1), we need an estimate of $Pr(between|put\ banks)$. Our training corpus does not include the collocation *put banks*, so no help is available from trigrams, therefore we backoff to a bigram model, choosing the bigram predictor with maximum IS. The maximum IS is for *put/V* ($G(w_{-1})$) rather than for w_{-1} (*banks*) itself, so $G(w_{-1})$ is used as predictor, giving a logprob estimate of -10.2 rather than -13.1.

The choice of $G(w_{-1})$ as predictor here seems to make sense, since we are willing to believe that there is a complementation relation between *put/V* and its second complement *between*. Of course, the choice is not always so intuitively appealing. When we go on to predict the next word, we need an estimate of $Pr(a|banks\ between)$. Again, our training corpus does not include the collocation *banks between*, so no help is available from trigrams. In this case, the maximum IS is for *banks* rather than *between*, so we use *banks* to predict *a* rather than *between*, giving a logprob estimate of -5.6 rather than -7.10.

Overall, however, the two predictors can be combined to improve the language model, by always choosing the predictor with higher IS score.

As shown in Table 4, this slightly improves the logprob for our test set over either predictor independently. However, Table 4 also shows that a simple strategy of chosing the raw bigram first and the $G(w_{-1})$ bigram when there is no information available is slightly better. In a more general situation, where we have a set of different descriptions of the same condition, the IS score provides a way to choose the best predictor.

4. CONCLUSION

Recurrent structures in text vary widely both in size and in the terms in which they are described. Existing grammars are too restrictive both in the size of structure they admit and in their terms of description to adequately capture the variation in text. A method has been described for collecting a database of partial structures from text. Methods of fully exploiting the database for language modeling are currently being explored.

5. REFERENCES

1. Church, Kenneth W., William A. Gale, Patrick Hanks, and Donald Hindle. 1991. "Using statistics in lexical analysis." in Uri Zernik (ed.) *Lexical acquisition: using on-line resources to build a lexicon*, Lawrence Erlbaum, 115-164.
2. Church, Kenneth W. and William A. Gale. 1991. "A comparison of the enhanced Good-Turing and deleted estimation methods for estimating probabilities of English bigrams," *Computer Speech and Language*, 5, 19-54.
3. Hindle, Donald. 1992. "An analogical parser for restricted domains," In *Proceedings of the Fifth DARPA Workshop on Speech & Natural Language*, -.
4. Hindle, Donald. 1981. "A probabilistic grammar of noun phrases in spoken and written English," In David Sankoff and Henrietta Cedergren (eds.) *Variation Omnibus*, Linguistic Research, Inc. Edmonton, Alberta.
5. Melchuk, Igor A. 1988. *DependencySyntax: Theory and Practice*, State University of New York Press, Albany.
6. Resnik, Philip. 1993. "Semantic Classes and Syntactic Ambiguity," This volume.
7. Schabes, Yves. 1988. "Parsing strategies with 'lexicalized' grammars: application to tree adjoining grammars", in Proceedings fo the 12th International Conference on Computational Linguistics, COLING88, Budapest, Hungary.

HYPOTHESIZING WORD ASSOCIATION FROM UNTAGGED TEXT

Tomoyoshi Matsukawa

BBN Systems and Technologies
70 Fawcett St.
Cambridge, MA 02138

ABSTRACT

This paper reports a new method for suggesting word associations, based on a greedy algorithm that employs Chi-square statistics on joint frequencies of pairs of word groups compared against chance co-occurrence. The benefits of this new approach are: 1) we can consider even low frequency words and word pairs, and 2) word groups and word associations can be automatically generated. The method provided 87% accuracy in hypothesizing word associations for unobserved combinations of words in Japanese text.

1. INTRODUCTION

Using mutual information for measuring word association has become popular since [Church and Hanks, 1990] defined word association ratio as mutual information between two words. Word association ratios are a promising tool for lexicography, but there seem to be at least two limitations to the method: 1) much data with low frequency words or word pairs cannot be used and 2) generalization of word usage still depends totally on lexicographers.

In this paper, we propose an alternative (or extended) method for suggesting word associations using Chi-square statistics, which can be viewed as an approximation to mutual information. Rather than considering significance of joint frequencies of word pairs as [Church and Hanks, 1990] did, our algorithm uses joint frequencies of pairs of word **groups** instead. The algorithm employs a hill-climbing search for a pair of word groups that occur significantly frequently.

The benefits of this new approach are:

1) that we can consider even low frequency words and word pairs, and

2) that word groups or word associations can be automatically generated, namely automatic hypothesis of word associations, which can later be reviewed by a lexicographer.

3) word associations can be used in parsing and understanding natural language, as well as in natural language generation [Smadja and McKeown, 1990].

Our method proved to be 87% accurate in hypothesizing word associations for unobserved combinations of words in Japanese text, where accuracy was tested by human verification of a random sample of hypothesized word pairs. We extracted 14,407 observations of word co-occurrences, involving 3,195 nouns and 4,365 verb/argument pairs. Out of this we hypothesized 7,050 word associations. The corpus size was 280,000 words. We would like to apply the same approach to English.

2. RELATED WORK

Some previous work (e.g., [Weischedel, et al., 1990]) found verb-argument associations from bracketed text, such as that in TREEBANK; however, this paper, and related work has hypothesized word associations from untagged text.

[Hindle 1990] confirmed that word association ratios can be used for measuring similarity between nouns. For example, “ship”, “plane”, “bus”, etc., were automatically ranked as similar to “boat”. [Resnik 1992] reported a word association ratio for identifying noun classes from a pre-existing hierarchy as selectional constraints on the object of a verb.

[Brown et.al. 1992] proves that, under the assumption of a bi-gram class model, the perplexity of a corpus is minimized when the average mutual information between word classes is maximized. Based on that fact, they cluster words via a greedy search algorithm which finds a local maximum in average mutual information.

Our algorithm considers joint frequencies of pairs of word groups (as [Brown et. al. 1992] does) in contrast to joint frequencies of word pairs as in [Church and Hanks, 1990] and [Hindle 1990]. Here a word group means any subset of the whole set of words. For example, "ship," "plane," "boat" and "car" may be a word group. The algorithm will find pairs of such word groups. Another similarity to [Brown et. al. 1992]'s clustering algorithm is the use of greedy search for a pair of word groups that occur significantly frequently, using an evaluation function based on mutual information between classes.

On the other hand, unlike [Brown et. al. 1992], we assume some automatic syntactic analysis of the corpus, namely part-of-speech analysis and at least finite-state approximations to syntactic dependencies. Moreover, the clustering is done depth first, not breadth first as [Brown et.

al. 1992], i.e., clusters are hypothesized one by one, not in parallel.

3. OVERVIEW OF THE METHOD

The method consists of three phases:

1) **Automatic part of speech tagging of text.** First, texts are labeled by our probabilistic part of speech tagger (POST) which has been extended for Japanese morphological processing [Matsukawa et. al. 1993]. This is fully automatic; human review is not necessary under the assumption that the tagger has previously been trained on appropriate text [Meteer et. al. 1991][1]

2) **Finite state pattern matching.** Second, a finite-state pattern matcher with patterns representing possible grammatical relations, such as verb/argument pairs, nominal compounds, etc. is run over the sample text to suggest word pairs which will be considered candidates for word associations. As a result, we get a word co-occurrence matrix. Again, no human review of the pattern matching is assumed.

3) **Filtering/Generalization of word associations via Chi-square.** Third, given the word co-occurrence matrix, the program starts from an initial pair of word groups (or a submatrix in the matrix), incrementally adding into the submatrix a word which locally gives the highest Chi-square score to the submatrix. Finally, words are removed which give a higher Chi-square score by their removal. By adding and removing words until reaching an appropriate significance level, we get a submatrix as a hypothesis of word associations between the cluster of words represented as rows in the submatrix and the cluster of words represented as columns in the submatrix.

4 WORD SEGMENTATION AND PART OF SPEECH LABELING

Since in Japanese word separators such as spaces are not present, words must be segmented before we assign part of speech to words. To do this, we use JUMAN from Kyoto University to segment Japanese text into words, AMED, an example-based segmentation corrector, and a Hidden Markov Model (POST) [Matsukawa, et. al. 1993]. For example, POST processes an input text such as the following:

一方、国際協会は住友銀行系の独占状態を崩し、資金量の豊富な他の上位都市銀行の系列カード会社と提携することで、日本でのマスターカードとの取扱高逆転を狙っている。

and produces tagged text such as: [2]

一方/CONJ 、/TT 国際/CN 協会/CN は/TM
住友銀行系/PN の/NCM 独占/SN 状態/CN を/CM
崩し/ADV 、/TT 資金/CN 量/CN の/NCM 豊富な/ADJ
他/CN の/NCM 上位/CN 都市/CN 銀行/CN の/NCM
系列/CN カード/CN 会社/CN と/PT 提携/SN する/VB
こと/FN で/PT 、/TT 日本/PN で/PT の/NCM
マスター/CN カード/CN と/PT の/NCM 取扱高逆転/CN
を/CM 狙って/VB いる/VSUF 。/KT

5. FINITE STATE PATTERN MATCHING

We use the following finite state patterns for extracting possible Japanese verb/argument word co-occurrences from automatically segmented and tagged Japanese text. Completely different patterns would be used for English.

$$\begin{Bmatrix} CN \\ PN \\ SN \end{Bmatrix} \begin{Bmatrix} CM \\ PT \end{Bmatrix} \cdots \begin{Bmatrix} VB \\ SN \end{Bmatrix}$$

where CN = common noun
PN = proper name
SN = Sa-inflection noun (nominal verb)
CM = case marker (-nom/-acc argument)
PT = particle (other arguments)
VB = verb

Here, the first part (CN, PN or SN) represents a noun. Since in Japanese the head noun of a noun phrase is always at the right end of the phrase, this part should always match a head noun. The second part (CM or PT) represents a postposition which identifies an argument of a verb. The final pattern element (VB or SN) represents a verb. Sa-inflection nouns (SN) are nominalized verbs which form a verb phrase with the morpheme "suru."

---

[1] In our experience thus far in three domains and in both Japanese and English, while retraining POST on domain-specific data would reduce the error rate, the effect on overall performance of the system in data extraction from text has been small enough to make retraining unnecessary. The effect of domain-specific lexical entries (e.g., DRAM is a noun in microelectronics) often mitigates the need to retrain.

[2] CONJ = conjunction; TT = Japanese comma; CN = common noun; TM = Topic marker; PN - proper noun; etc.

Distance	Matched Text
0	系列/CN カード/CN 会社/CN と/PT 提携/SN する/VBこと/FN で/PT 、...
1	フランス/PN の/NCM 会社/CN と/PT 技術/CN 提携/SNを/CM して/VB ...
2	証券/ADJ 会社/CN と/PT デパート/CN が/CM 提携/SNして/VB ...
4	大手/CN 証券/CN 会社/CN と/PT 銀行/CN 系/NNSUカード/CN の/NCM 提携/SN の/NCM 動き/CN

Figure 1: *Examples of Pattern Matches with Skipping over Words.*

Since argument structure in Japanese is marked by postpositions, i.e., case markers (i.e., "o," "ga") and particles (e.g., "ni," "kara," . . .), word combinations matched with the patterns will represent associations between a noun filling a particular argument type (e.g., "o") and a verb. Note that topic markers (TM; i.e., "wa") and toritate markers (TTM; e.g."mo", "sae", ...) are not included in the pattern since these do not uniquely identify the case of the argument.

Just as in English, the arguments of a verb in Japanese may be quite distant from the verb; adverbial phrases and scrambling are two cases that may separate a verb from its argument(s). We approximate this in a finite state machine by allowing words to be skipped. In our experiment, up to four words could be skipped. As shown in Figure 1, matching an argument structure varies from distance 0 to 4.

By limiting the algorithm to a maximum of four word gaps, and by not considering the ambiguous cases of topic markers and taritate markers, we have chosen to limit the cases considered in favor of high accuracy in automatically hypothesizing word associations. [Brent, 1991] similarly limited what his algorithm could learn in favor of high accuracy.

6. FILTERING AND GENERALIZATION VIA CHI-SQUARE

Word combinations found via the finite state patterns include a noun, postposition, and a verb. A two dimensional matrix (a word co-occurrence matrix) is formed, where the columns are nouns, and the rows are pairs of a verb plus postposition. The cells of the matrix are the frequency of the noun (column element) co-occurring in the given case with that verb (row element).

Starting from a submatrix, the algorithm successively adds to the submatrix the word with the largest Chi-square score among all words outside the submatrix. Words are added until a local maximum is reached. Finally, the appropriateness of the submatrix as a hypothesis of word associations is checked with heuristic criteria based on the sizes of the row and the column of the submatrix. Currently, we use the following criteria for appropriateness of a submatrix:

LET l : size of row of submatrix
m : size of column of submatrix
C1, C2, C3 : parameters
IF l > C1, and
m > C1, and
l > C2 or m/l < C3, and
m > C2 or l/m < C3
THEN the submatrix is appropriate.

For any submatrix found, the co-occurrence observations for the clustered words are removed from the word co-occurrence matrix and treated as a single column of clustered nouns and a single row of clustered verb plus case pairs. Currently, we use the following values for the parameters: C1=2, C2=10, and C3=10.

Table 1. shows an example of clustering starting from the initial submatrix shown in Figure 2. The words in Figure 2 were manually selected as words meaning "organization." In Table 1, the first (leftmost) column indicates the word which was added to the submatrix at each step. The second column gives an English gloss of the word. The third column reports f(x,Y), the frequency of the co-occurrences between the word and the words that co-occur with it. For example, the first line of the table shows that the word "を／設立" (establish/-acc) co-occurred with the "organization" words 26 times. The rightmost column specifies I(X,Y), the scaled mutual information between the rows and columns of the submatrix. As the clustering proceeds, I(X,Y) gets larger.

会社(company), 本社(head quarter), 機関(organization), 企業(coorporation), 両社(both companies), 学校(school), 同社(the company), 子会社(child company), 銀行(bank), 百貨店(department store), 代理店(agency), 生協(coop.), 商社(business company), 都銀(city bank), 売店(stand), 信託銀行(trust bank), 支店(branch), 信金(credit association), 本店(head store), 大学(university), 各社(each company), デパート(department store), 農協(agriculture cooperative), メーカー(maker), 書店(book store), テレビ局(TV station), プロダクション(agency), スーパー(supermarket), 株式会社(joint-stock corporation), 医院(doctor's office), 全店(all stores)

Figure 2: *The initial word group (submatrix) for the clustering shown in Table 1.*

Word added	Gloss	Freq	I
を／設立	establish/-acc	26	0.11
と／提携	tie-up/with	25	0.19
が／提携	tie-up/-nom	18	0.25
と／組む	unite/with	11	0.29
が／協力	cooperate/-nom	7	0.32
が／持つ	possess/-nom	8	0.35
が／組む	unite/-nom	7	0.38
が／進出	advance/-nom	6	0.40
と／相次ぐ	in succession	5	0.43
が／進める	proceed/-nom	4	0.44
を／買収	purchase/-acc	5	0.46
に／委託	entrust/-acc	6	0.47
が／生産	produce/-nom	6	0.49
が／開発	develop/-nom	7	0.51
が／出資	invest/-nom	6	0.52
と／拡大	expand/with	3	0.54
が／共同開発	develop/-nom	3	0.55
が／発行	publish/-nom	4	0.56
が／合意	agree/-nom	3	0.58
に／求める	demand/from	3	0.59
に／出資	invest/in	5	0.60
が／販売	sell/-nom	7	0.61
が／買収	purchase/-nom	3	0.63
を／開設	open/-acc	4	0.64
から／導入	introduce/from	3	0.65
が／つくる	create/-nom	3	0.66
で／使う	utilize/at	3	0.67
に／限る	limit/to	3	0.68
が／扱う	treat/-nom	3	0.69
が／結ぶ	connect/-nom	3	0.69
が／する	do/-nom	5	0.70
を／除く	exclude/-acc	3	0.71
に／対抗	oppose/to	3	0.71
で／調印	sign/-copula	3	0.72
に／販売	sell/to	4	0.72
に／参加	participate/in	4	0.72
法人	corporation	9	0.74
大手	major	5	0.75
ジャパン	Japan	5	0.77
日商岩井	Nisho-Iwai	4	0.78
三者	three parties	3	0.79
製薬	Drug Company	4	0.80
ソニー	Sony	5	0.81
業者	dealer	5	0.81
研究所	Institution	5	0.82
本田	Honda	4	0.83
三菱重工	Mitsubishi	3	0.83
ＡＴＴ	AT&T	3	0.84
航	Air Line	4	0.84
それぞれ	respectively	3	0.85
本田技研	Honda	3	0.85
銀	Bank	7	0.85
航空	Air Line	6	0.85
信託	Trust Company	. 4	0.85
鉄	Steel Company	4	0.85

Table 1: *Example of Clustering*

7. EVALUATION

Using 280,000 words of Japanese source text from the TIPSTER joint ventures domain, we tried several variations of the initial submatrices (word groups) from which the search in step three of the method starts:

a) complete bipartite subgraphs,
b) pre-classified noun groups and
c) significantly frequent word pairs.

Based on the results of the experiments, we concluded that alternative (b) gives both the most accurate word associations and the highest coverage of word associations. This technique is practical because classification of nouns is generally much simpler than that of verbs. We don't propose any automatic algorithm to accomplish noun classification, but instead note that we were able to manually classify nouns in less than ten categories at about 500 words/hour. That productivity was achieved using our new tool for manual word classification, which is partially inspired by EDR's way of classifying their semantic lexical data [Matsukawa and Yokota, 1991].

Based on a corpus of 280,000 words in the TIPSTER joint ventures domain, the most frequently occurring Japanese nouns, proper nouns, and verbs were automatically identified. Then, a student classified the frequently occurring nouns into one of the twelve categories in (1) below, and each frequently occurring proper noun into one of the four categories in (2) below, using a menu-based tool, we were able to categorize 3,195 lexical entries in 12 person-hours.[3] These categories were then used as input to the word co-occurrence algorithm.

1. Common noun categories
1a. Organization
    CORPORATION
    GOVERNMENT
    UNDETERMINED-CORPORATION
    OTHER-ORGANIZATION
1b. Location
    CITY
    COUNTRY
    PROVINCE

---

3 We divided the process of classifying common nouns into two phases; classification into the four categories 1a, 1b, 1c and 1d, and further classification into the twelve categories. As a result, each word was checked twice. We found that using two phases generally improves both overall productivity and consistency.

OTHER-LOCATION

1c. Person

ENTITY-OFFICER

TITLE

OTHER-PERSON

1d. Other

2. Proper noun categories

ORGANIZATION

LOCATION

PERSON

OTHER

Using the 280,000 word joint venture corpus, we collected 14,407 word co-occurrences, involving 3,195 nouns and 4,365 verb/argument pairs, by the finite state pattern given in Section 5. 16 submatrices were clustered, grouping 810 observed word co-occurrences and 6,240 unobserved (or hypothesized) word co-occurrences. We evaluated the accuracy of the system by manual review of a random sample of 500 hypothesized word co-occurrences. Of these, 435, or 87% were judged reasonable. This ratio is fine compared with a random sample of 500 arbitrary word co-occurrences between the 3,195 nouns and the 4,365 verb/argument pairs, of which only 153 (44%) were judged reasonable. Table 2 below shows some examples judged reasonable; questionable examples are marked by "?"; unreasonable hypotheses are marked with an asterisk.

With a small corpus (280,000 words) such as ours, considering small frequency co-occurrences is critical. Looking at Table 3 below, if we had to ignore co-occurrences with frequency less than five (as [Church and Hanks 1990] did), there would be very little data. With our method, as long as the frequency of co-occurrence of the word being considered with the set is greater than two, the statistic is stable.

Frequency	Number of Word Pairs
0	6240
1	631
2	113
3	36
4	18
5	4
6	2
7	3
9	1
10	1
16	1

Table 3: *Pair Frequencies*

8. CONCLUSION

Our method achieved fully automatic hypothesis of word associations, starting from untagged text and generalizing to unobserved word associations. As a result of human review 87% of the hypotheses were judged to be reasonable. Because the technique considers low frequency cases, most of the data was used in making generalizations.

It remains to be determined how well this method will work for English, but with appropriate finite state patterns, similar results may be achieved.

	Noun	Verb/argument
	オーナー (owner)	に／就任 (take office/as)
	ＡＴＴ (AT&T)	から／導入 (introduce/from)
	首都圏 (metropolitan)	に／建設 (build/at)
	要員 (personnel)	を／派遣 (dispatch/-acc)
	委員会 (Commitee)	と／組む (unite/with)
	図書館 (library)	が／販売 (sell/-nom)
	商会 (Company)	を／結成 (organize/-acc)
	代理店 (agency)	が／発行 (publish/-nom)
	郵便局 (post office)	と／提携 (tie-up/with)
	州 (State)	に／展開 (develop/to)
	キャノン (Cannon)	に／入る (enter/-acc)
	医院 (doctor's office)	に／限る (limit/to)
	諸国 (nations)	に／持つ (have/in)
?	野村 (Nomura)	が／生産 (produce/-nom)
?	駅員 (station employee)	が／就任 (take office/-nom)
*	ＤＲＡＭ (DRAM)	が／結ぶ (unite/-nom)
*	スイス (Switzerland)	が／みる (see/-nom)
*	取締役 (director)	に／発表 (announce/to)

Table 2: *Examples of reasonable hypothesized co-occurrences*

ACKNOWLEDGMENTS

The author wishes to thank Madeleine Bates, Ralph Weischedel and Sean Boisen for significant contributions to this paper.

REFERENCES

1. Brent, M.R., (1991) "Automatic Acquisition of Subcategorization Frames from Untagged Text," *Proceedings of the 29th annual Meeting of the ACL,* pp. 209-214.
2. Brown, P.F., et. al., (1992) "Class-based N-gram Models of Natural Language," *Computational Linguistics* Vol. 18 (4), pp. 467-479.
3. Church, K. and Hanks, P., (1990) "Word Association Norms, Mutual Information, and Lexicography," *Computational Linguistics* Vol. 16 (1), pp.22-29.
4. Hindle, D., (1990) "Noun Classification from Predicate-Argument Structures," *Proceedings of the 28th Annual Meeting of the ACL,* pp. 268-275.
5. Hoel P. G., (1971): *Introduction to Mathematical Statistics,* Chapter 9. 2.
6. Resnik, P., (1992) "A Class-based Approach to Lexical Discovery," *Proceedings of the 30th Annual Meeting of the ACL,* pp. 327-329.
7. Smadja F.A. and McKeown, K.R., (1990) "Automatically Extracting and Representing Collocations for Language Generation," *Proceedings of the 28th Annual Meeting of the ACL,* pp. 252-259.
8. Matsukawa T., Miller S. and Weischedel R. (1993) "Example-based Correction of Word Segmentation and Part of Speech Labelling," *Proceedings of DARPA Human Language Technologies Workshop.*
9. Matsukawa , T. and Yokota, E. (1991) "Development of the Concept Dictionary - Implementation of Lexical Knowledge," *Proc. of pre-conference workshop sponsored by the special Interest Group on the Lexicon (SIGLEX) of the Association for Computational Linguistics,* 1991.
10. Weischedel, R. et al. (1991) "Partial Parsing: A Report on Work in Progress," *Proceedings of the Workshop on Speech and Natural Language,* pp. 204-210.

APPENDIX: JUSTIFICATION OF CHI SQUARE

Chi-square score is given by the following formula :

$$I(X, Y) = \sum \mathrm{I(X, Y)}$$

$$= \sum \mathrm{p(X, Y)} \log \frac{\mathrm{p(X, Y)}}{\mathrm{p(X)\,p(Y)}} \qquad (0)$$

where *X*, *Y* = columns and rows of a word co-occurrence matrix

X, Y = subsets of *X*, *Y*, respectively

(i.e. word classes at the columns and the rows)

This can be justified as follows.

According to [Hoel 1971], the likelihood ratio *LAMBDA* for a test of the hypothesis: p(i) = po(i) (i = 1, 2, . . ., k), where p(i) is the probability of case i and po(i) is a hypothesized probability of it, when observations are independent of each other, is given as:

$$-2 \log LAMBDA = 2 \sum_{i=1}^{k} n(i) \log \frac{n(i)}{e(i)} \qquad (1)$$

where n(i) is the number of observations of case i, and e(i) is its expectation, i.e., e(i) = n p(i), where n is the total number of observations.

The distribution is chi-square when n is large. If we assume two word classes, ci and cj, occur independently, then the expected value of the probability of their co-occurrence will be,

$$e(c_i, c_j) = n\, p(c_i)\, p(c_j) \qquad (2)$$

where p(ci) and p(cj) are estimations of the probability of occurrence of ci and cj. The maximum likelihood estimate of p(ci) and p(cj) is f(ci)/n and f(cj)/n, where f(cj) and f(cj) are the number of observations of words classified in ci and cj. The maximum likelihood estimate of p(ci, cj), the probability of the co-occurrences of words in ci and cj, is f(ci, cj)/n, where f(ci, cj) is the number of observations of the co-occurrences. Then the number of the co-occurrences n(ci, cj) (which is the same as f(ci, cj)) can be represented as,

$$n(c_i, c_j) = n\, p(c_i, c_j) \qquad (3)$$

Therefore, given k classes, c1, c2, ..., ck, substituting (2) and (3) into (1).

$$2 \sum_{i=0}^{k} \sum_{j=0}^{i} n\, p(c_i, c_j) \log \frac{p(c_i, c_j)}{p(c_i)\, p(c_j)} \qquad (4)$$

If n is large, this will have a chi-square distribution; therefore, we can estimate how unlikely our assumption of independence among word classes is. Since formula (4) gives a scaled average mutual information among the word classes, searching for a partition of words that provides maximum average mutual information among word classes is equivalent to seeking classes where independence among word classes is minimally likely. The algorithm reported in this paper searches for pairs of word classes which provide a local maximum I(X, Y), a term in the summation of formula (0).

SMOOTHING OF AUTOMATICALLY GENERATED SELECTIONAL CONSTRAINTS

Ralph Grishman and John Sterling

Department of Computer Science
New York University
New York, NY 10003

ABSTRACT

Frequency information on co-occurrence patterns can be automatically collected from a syntactically analyzed corpus; this information can then serve as the basis for selectional constraints when analyzing new text from the same domain. Better coverage of the domain can be obtained by appropriate generalization of the specific word patterns which are collected. We report here on an approach to automatically make suitable generalizations: using the co-occurrence data to compute a confusion matrix relating individual words, and then using the confusion matrix to smooth the original frequency data.

1. INTRODUCTION

Semantic (selectional) constraints are necessary for the accurate analysis of natural language text. Accordingly, the acquisition of these constraints is an essential yet time-consuming part of porting a natural language system to a new domain. Several research groups have attempted to automate this process by collecting co-occurrence patterns (e.g., subject-verb-object patterns) from a large training corpus. These patterns are then used as the source of selectional constraints in analyzing new text.

However, the patterns collected in this way involve specific word combinations from the training corpus. Unless the training corpus is very large, this will provide only limited coverage of the range of acceptable semantic combinations, even within a restricted domain. In order to obtain better coverage, it will be necessary to generalize from the patterns collected so that patterns with semantically related words will also be considered acceptable. In most cases this has been done by manually assigning words to semantic classes and then generalizing from specific words to their classes. This approach still implies a substantial manual burden in moving to a new domain, since at least some of the semantic word classes will be domain-specific.

In order to fully automate the process of semantic constraint acquisition, we would like to be able to automatically identify semantically related words. This can be done using the co-occurrence data, by identifying words which occur in the same contexts (for example, verbs which occur with the same subjects and objects). From the co-occurrence data one can compute a similarity relation between words, and then cluster words of high similarity. This approach was taken by Sekine et al. at UMIST, who then used these clusters to generalize semantic patterns [6]. A similar approach to word clustering was reported by Hirschman et al. in 1975 [5].

For our current experiments, we have adopted a slightly different approach. We compute from the co-occurrence data a confusion matrix, which also measures the interchangeability of words in particular contexts. We then use the confusion matrix directly to generalize the semantic patterns.

2. THE NATURE OF THE CONSTRAINTS

The constraints we wish to acquire are local semantic constraints; more specifically, constraints on which words can occur together in specific syntactic relations. These include head-argument relations (e.g., subject-verb-object) and head-modifier relations. Some constraints may be general (domain independent), but others will be specific to a particular domain. Because it is not practical to state all the allowable word combinations, we normally place words into (semantic) word classes and then state the constraints in terms of allowable combinations of these classes.

When these constraints were encoded by hand, they were normally stated as absolute constraints—a particular combination of words was or was not acceptable. With corpus-derived constraints, on the other hand, it becomes possible to think in terms of a probabilistic model. For example, based on a training corpus, we would estimate the probability that a particular verb occurs with a particular subject and object (or with subject and object from particular classes), or that a verb occurs with a particular modifier. Then, using the (obviously crude) assumption of independent probabilities, we would estimate the probability of a particular sentence derivation as the product of the probabilities of all the operations (adding arguments to heads, adding modifiers to heads) required to produce the sentence, and the probability of a sentence as the sum of the probabilities of its derivations.

3. ACQUIRING SEMANTIC PATTERNS

Based on a series of experiments over the past year (as reported at COLING-92) we have developed the following procedure for acquiring semantic patterns from a text corpus:

1. Using unsupervised training methods, create a stochastic grammar from a (non-stochastic) augmented context-free grammar. Use this stochastic grammar to parse the training corpus, taking only the most probable parse(s) of each sentence.
2. Regularize the parses to produce something akin to an LFG f-structure, with explicitly labeled syntactic relations such as SUBJECT and OBJECT.[1]
3. Extract from the regularized parse a series of triples of the form

   head syntactic-relation arg

   where *arg* is the head of the argument or modifier. We will use the notation $< w_i \; r \; w_j >$ for such a triple, and $< r \; w_j >$ for a relation-argument pair.
4. Compute the frequency F of each head and each triple in the corpus. If a sentence produces N parses, a triple generated from a single parse has weight 1/N in the total.

For example, the sentence

Mary likes young linguists from Limerick.

would produce the regularized syntactic structure

```
(s like (subject (np Mary))
    (object (np linguist (a-pos young)
                (from (np Limerick)))))
```

from which the following four triples are generated:

like	subject	Mary
like	object	linguist
linguist	a-pos	young
linguist	from	Limerick

Given the frequency information F, we can then estimate the probability that a particular head w_i appears with a particular argument or modifier $< r \; w_j >$:[2]

$$\frac{F(< w_i \; r \; w_j >)}{F(w_i \text{ appears as a head in a parse tree})}$$

This probability information would then be used in scoring alternative parse trees. For the evaluation below, however, we will use the frequency data F directly.

[1]But with somewhat more regularization than is done in LFG; in particular, passive structures are converted to corresponding active forms.

[2]Note that $F(w_i$ appears as a head in a parse tree$)$ is different from $F(w_i$ appears as a head in a triple$)$ since a single head in a parse tree may produce several such triples, one for each argument or modifier of that head.

Step 3 (the triples extraction) includes a number of special cases:

(a) if a verb has a separable particle (e.g., "out" in "carry out"), this is attached to the head (to create the head *carry-out*) and not treated as a separate relation. Different particles often correspond to very different senses of a verb, so this avoids conflating the subject and object distributions of these different senses.

(b) if the verb is "be", we generate a relation *be-complement* between the subject and the predicate complement.

(c) triples in which either the head or the argument is a pronoun are discarded

(d) triples in which the argument is a subordinate clause are discarded (this includes subordinate conjunctions and verbs taking clausal arguments)

(e) triples indicating negation (with an argument of "not" or "never") are ignored

4. GENERALIZING SEMANTIC PATTERNS

The procedure described above produces a set of frequencies and probability estimates based on specific words. The "traditional" approach to generalizing this information has been to assign the words to a set of semantic classes, and then to collect the frequency information on combinations of semantic classes [7,3].

Since at least some of these classes will be domain specific, there has been interest in automating the acquisition of these classes as well. This can be done by clustering together words which appear in the same context. Starting from the file of triples, this involves:

1. collecting for each word the frequency with which it occurs in each possible context; for example, for a noun we would collect the frequency with which it occurs as the subject and the object of each verb
2. defining a similarity measure between words, which reflects the number of common contexts in which they appear
3. forming clusters based on this similarity measure

Such a procedure was performed by Sekine et al. at UMIST [6]; these clusters were then manually reviewed and the resulting clusters were used to generalize selectional patterns.

A similar approach to word cluster formation was described by Hirschman et al. in 1975 [5].

Cluster creation has the advantage that the clusters are amenable to manual review and correction. On the other hand, our experience indicates that successful cluster generation depends on rather delicate adjustment of the clustering criteria. We have therefore elected to try an approach which directly uses a form of similarity measure to smooth (generalize) the probabilities.

Co-occurrence smoothing is a method which has been recently proposed for smoothing n-gram models [4].[3] The core of this method involves the computation of a co-occurrence matrix (a matrix of confusion probabilities) $P_C(w_j|w_i)$, which indicates the probability of word w_j occurring in contexts in which word w_i occurs, averaged over these contexts.

$$\begin{aligned} P_C(w_j|w_i) &= \sum_s P(w_j|s)P(s|w_i) \\ &= \frac{\sum_s P(w_j|s)P(w_i|s)P(s)}{P(w_i)} \end{aligned}$$

where the sum is over the set of all possible contexts s. For an n-gram model, for example, the context might be the set of $n-1$ prior words. This matrix can be used to take a basic trigram model $P_B(w_n|w_{n-2}, w_{n-1})$ and produce a smoothed model

$$P_S(w_n|w_{n-2}, w_{n-1}) = \sum_{w'_n} P_C(w_n|w'_n)P_B(w'_n|w_{n-2}, w_{n-1})$$

We have used this method in a precisely analogous way to compute smoothed semantic triples frequencies, F_S. In triples of the form *word1 relation word2* we have initially chosen to smooth over *word1*, treating *relation* and *word2* as the context.

$$\begin{aligned} P_C(w_i|w'_i) &= \sum_{r,w_j} P(w_i| < r\ w_j >) \cdot P(< r\ w_j > |w'_i) \\ &= \sum_{r,w_j} \frac{F(< w_i\ r\ w_j >)}{F(< r\ w_j >)} \\ &\cdot \frac{F(< w'_i\ r\ w_j >)}{F(w'_i \text{ appears as a head of a triple})} \end{aligned}$$

$$F_S(< w_i\ r\ w_j >) = \sum_{w'_i} P_C(w_i|w'_i) \cdot F(< w'_i\ r\ w_j >)$$

In order to avoid the generation of confusion table entries from a single shared context (which quite often is the result of an incorrect parse), we apply a filter in generating P_C: for $i \neq j$, we generate a non-zero $P_C(w_j|w_i)$ only if the w_i and w_j appear in at least two common contexts, and there is some common context in which both words occur at least twice. Furthermore, if the value computed by the formula for P_C is less than some threshold τ_C, the value is taken to be zero; we have used $\tau_C = 0.001$ in the experiments reported below. (These filters are not applied for the case $i = j$; the diagonal elements of the confusion matrix are always computed exactly.) Because these filters may yeild an un-normalized confusion matrix (i.e., $\sum_{w_j} P_C(w_j|w_i) < 1$), we renormalize the matrix so that $\sum_{w_j} P_C(w_j|w_i) = 1$.

[3]We wish to thank Richard Schwartz of BBN for referring us to this method and article.

5. EVALUATION

5.1. Evaluation Metric

We have previously (at COLING-92) described two methods for the evaluation of semantic constraints. For the current experiments, we have used one of these methods, where the constraints are evaluated against a set of manually classified semantic triples.

For this evaluation, we select a small test corpus separate from the training corpus. We parse the corpus, regularize the parses, and extract triples just as we did for the semantic acquisition phase (with the exception that we use the non-stochastic grammar in order to generate all grammatically valid parses of each sentence). We then manually classify each triple as semantically valid or invalid (a triple is counted as valid if we believe that this pair of words could meaningfully occur in this relationship, even if this was not the intended relationship in this particular text).

We then establish a threshold T for the weighted triples counts in our training set, and define

v_+	number of triples in test set which were classified as valid and which appeared in training set with count $> T$
v_-	number of triples in test set which were classified as valid and which appeared in training set with count $\leq T$
i_+	number of triples in test set which were classified as invalid and which appeared in training set with count $> T$
i_-	number of triples in test set which were classified as invalid and which appeared in training set with count $\leq T$

and then define

$$\begin{aligned} \text{recall} &= \frac{v_+}{v_+ + v_-} \\ \text{error rate} &= \frac{i_+}{i_+ + i_-} \end{aligned}$$

w	$P_C(attack\|w)$
harden	0.252
attack	0.251
assault	0.178
dislodge	0.131
torture	0.123
harass	0.114
machinegun	0.096
massacre	0.094
reinforce	0.093
board	0.091
abduct	0.086
specialize	0.076
occupy	0.072
engage	0.068
blow-up	0.064
blow	0.063

w	$P_C(terrorist\|w)$
terrorist	0.309
ally	0.137
job	0.119
world	0.091
ceasefire	0.069
commando	0.058
guerrilla	0.045
urban commando	0.043
coup	0.043
assassin	0.041
individual	0.035
journalist	0.029
offensive	0.029
history	0.026
rebel	0.025
fighter	0.023

Figure 1: Verbs closely related to the verb "attack" and nouns closely related to the noun "terrorist", ranked by P_C. ("harden" appears at the top of the list for "attack" because both appear with the object "position".)

At a given threshold T, our smoothing process should increase recall but in practice will also increase the error rate. How can we tell if our smoothing is doing any good? We can view the smoothing process as moving some triples from v_- to v_+ and from i_- to i_+.[4] Is it doing so better than some random process? I.e., is it preferentially raising valid items above the threshold? To assess this, we compute (for a fixed threshold) the quality measure

$$Q = \frac{\frac{v_+^S - v_+}{v_-}}{\frac{i_+^S - i_+}{i_-}}$$

where the values with superscript S represent the values with smoothing, and those without superscripts represent the values without smoothing. If $Q > 1$, then smoothing is doing better than a random process in identifying valid triples.

5.2. Test Data

The training corpus was the set of 1300 messages (with a total of 18,838 sentences) which constituted the development corpus for Message Understanding Conferences - 3 and 4 [1,2]. These messages are news reports from the Foreign Broadcast Information Service concerning terrorist activity in Central and South America. The average sentence length is about 24 words. In order to get higher-quality parses of these sentences, we disabled several of the recovery mechanisms normally used in parsing, such as longest-substring parsing; with these mechanisms disabled, we obtained parses for 9,903 of the 18,838 sentences. These parses were then regularized and reduced to triples. We generated a total of 46,659 distinct triples from this test corpus.

The test corpus—used to generate the triples which were manually classified—consisted of 10 messages of similar style, taken from one of the test corpora for Message Understanding Conference - 3. These messages produced a test set containing a total of 636 distinct triples, of which 456 were valid and 180 were invalid.

5.3. Results

In testing our smoothing procedure, we first generated the confusion matrix P_C and examined some of the entries. Figure 1 shows the largest entries in P_C for the verb "attack" and the noun "terrorist", two very common words in the terrorist domain. It is clear that (with some odd exceptions) most of the words with high P_C values are semantically related to the original word.

To evaluate the effectiveness of smoothing, we have compared three sets of triples frequency data:

1. the original (unsmoothed) data
2. the data as smoothed using P_C
3. the data as generalized using a manually-prepared classification hierarchy for a subset of the words of the domain

[4] In fact, some triples will move above the threshold and other will move below the threshold, but in the regions we are considering, the net movement will be above the threshold.

generalization strategy	T	v_+	v_-	i_+	i_-	recall	error rate	Q
1. no smoothing	0	139	317	13	167	30%	7%	
2. confusion matrix	0	237	219	50	130	52%	28%	1.39
3. classification hierarchy	0	154	302	18	162	34%	10%	1.58
4. confusion matrix	0.29	154	302	17	163	34%	9%	1.90

Table 1: A comparison of the effect of different generalization strategies.

For the third method, we employed a classification hierarchy which had previously been prepared as part of the information extraction system used for Message Understanding Conference-4. This hierarchy included only the subset of the vocabulary thought relevant to the information extraction task (not counting proper names, roughly 10% of the words in the vocabulary). From this hierarchy we identified the 13 classes which were most frequently referred to in the lexico-semantic models used by the extraction system. If the head (first element) of a semantic triple was a member of one of these classes, the generalization process replaced that word by the most specific class to which it belongs (since we have a hierarchy with nested classes, a word will typically belong to several classes); to make the results comparable to those with confusion-matrix smoothing, we did not generalize the argument (last element) of the triple.

The basic results are shown in rows 1, 2, and 3 of Table 1. For all of these we used a threshold (T) of 0, so a triple with any frequency > 0 would go into the v_+ or i_+ category. In each case the quality measure Q is relative to the run without smoothing, entry 1 in the table. Both the confusion matrix and the classification hierarchy yield Qs substantially above 1, indicating that both methods are performing substantially better than random. The Q is higher with the classification hierarchy, as might be expected since it has been manually checked; on the other hand, the improvement in recall is substantially smaller, since the hierarchy covers only a small portion of the total vocabulary. As the table shows, the confusion matrix method produces a large increase in recall (about 73% over the base run).

These comparisons all use a T (frequency threshold) of 0, which yields the highest recall and error rate. Different recall/error-rate trade-offs can be obtained by varying T. For example, entry 4 of the table shows the result for T=0.29, the point at which the recall using the confusion matrix and the classification hierarchy is the same (the values without smoothing and the values using the classification hierarchy are essentially unchanged at T=0.29). We observe that, for the same recall, the automatic smoothing does as well as the manually generated hierarchy with regard to error rate. (In fact, the Q value with smoothing (line 4) is much higher than with the classification hierarchy (line 3), but this reflects a difference of only 1 in i_+ and should not be seen as significant.)

6. DISCUSSION

We have demonstrated that automated smoothing methods can be of some benefit in increasing the coverage of automatically acquired selectional constraints. This is potentially important as a step in developing tools for porting natural language systems to new domains. It is still too early to assess the relative merits of different approaches to generalizing these selectional constraints, given our limited testing and the different evaluation metrics of the few others groups experimenting with such acquisition procedures.

Our experimental results are not uniformly positive. We did achieve substantially higher recall levels with smoothing. On the other hand, over the range of recalls obtainable without smoothing, smoothing did not consistently improve the error rate. Therefore at present the principal benefit of the smoothing technique is to raise the recall beyond that possible using unsmoothed data.

In addition, preliminary experiments with smoothing applied to the *argument* position in a triple indicate that the comparison between automated smoothing and manual classification hierarchies is not so favorable. This is not too surprising because when the classification hierarchy was initially created, its primary use was to specify the allowable values of arguments and modifiers in semantic case frames; as a result, while the hierarchy is of benefit in generalizing heads (as described above), it is more effective in generalizing the argument position.

We recognize that the size of the corpus we have used is quite minimal for the task of computing similarities, since to get a fully populated similarity matrix we would require each pair of semantically related words to occur in several common contexts. We hope therefore to repeat these experiments with a substantially larger corpus in the near future. A larger corpus will also allow us to use larger patterns, including in particular subject-verb-object patterns, and thus reduce the confusion due to treating different words senses as common contexts.

7. Acknowledgement

This material is based upon work supported by the Advanced Research Projects Agency through the Office of Naval Research under Grant No. N00014-90-J-1851.

References

1. *Proceedings of the Third Message Understanding Conference (MUC-3)*. Morgan Kaufmann, May 1991.
2. *Proceedings of the Fourth Message Understanding Conference (MUC-4)*. Morgan Kaufmann, June 1992.
3. Jing-Shin Chang, Yih-Fen Luo, and Keh-Yih Su. GPSM: A generalized probabilistic semantic model for ambiguity resolution. In *Proceedings of the 30th Annual Meeting of the Assn. for Computational Linguistics*, pages 177–184, Newark, DE, June 1992.
4. U. Essen and V. Steinbiss. Cooccurrence smoothing for stochastic language modeling. In *ICASSP92*, pages I--161 – I–164, San Francisco, CA, May 1992.
5. Lynette Hirschman, Ralph Grishman, and Naomi Sager. Grammatically-based automatic word class formation. *Information Processing and Management*, 11(1/2):39–57, 1975.
6. Satoshi Sekine, Sofia Ananiadou, Jeremy Carroll, and Jun'ichi Tsujii. Linguistic knowledge generator. In *Proc. 14th Int'l Conf. Computational Linguistics (COLING 92)*, pages 560–566, Nantes, France, July 1992.
7. Paola Velardi, Maria Teresa Pazienza, and Michela Fasolo. How to encode semantic knowledge: A method for meaning representation and computer-aided acquisition. *Computational Linguistics*, 17(2):153–170, 1991.

CORPUS-BASED STATISTICAL SENSE RESOLUTION

Claudia Leacock,[1] *Geoffrey Towell,*[2] *Ellen Voorhees*[2]

[1]Princeton University, Cognitive Science Laboratory, Princeton, New Jersey 08542
[2]Siemens Corporate Research, Inc., Princeton, New Jersey 08540

ABSTRACT

The three corpus-based statistical sense resolution methods studied here attempt to infer the correct sense of a polysemous word by using knowledge about patterns of word co-occurrences. The techniques were based on Bayesian decision theory, neural networks, and content vectors as used in information retrieval. To understand these methods better, we posed a very specific problem: given a set of contexts, each containing the noun *line* in a known sense, construct a classifier that selects the correct sense of *line* for new contexts. To see how the degree of polysemy affects performance, results from three- and six-sense tasks are compared.

The results demonstrate that each of the techniques is able to distinguish six senses of *line* with an accuracy greater than 70%. Furthermore, the response patterns of the classifiers are, for the most part, statistically indistinguishable from one another. Comparison of the two tasks suggests that the degree of difficulty involved in resolving individual senses is a greater performance factor than the degree of polysemy.

1. INTRODUCTION

The goal of this study is to systematically explore the effects of such variables as the number of senses per word and the number of training examples per sense on corpus-based statistical sense resolution methods. To enable us to study the effects of the number of word senses, we selected the highly polysemous noun *line*, which has 25 senses in WordNet.[1]

Automatic sense resolution systems need to resolve highly polysemous words. As Zipf [2] pointed out in 1945, frequently occurring words tend to be polysemous. The words encountered in a given text will have far greater polysemy than one would assume by simply taking the overall percentage of polysemous words in the language. Even though 86% of the nouns in WordNet have a single sense, the mean number of WordNet senses per word for the one hundred most frequently occurring nouns in the Brown Corpus is 5.15, with only eight words having a single sense.

[1] WordNet is a lexical database developed by George Miller and his colleagues at Princeton University.[1]

2. PREVIOUS WORK

Yarowsky [3] compared the Bayesian statistical method with the published results of other corpus-based statistical models. Although direct comparison was not possible due to the differences in corpora and evaluation criteria, he minimizes these differences by using the same words, with the same definition of sense. He argues, convincingly, that the Bayesian model is as good as or better than the costlier methods.

As a pilot for the present study, a two-sense distinction task for *line* was run using the content vector and neural network classifiers, achieving greater than 90% accuracy. A three-sense distinction task was then run, which is reported in Voorhees, *et. al.* [4], and discussed in Section 5.

3. METHODOLOGY

The training and testing contexts were taken from the 1987-89 *Wall Street Journal* corpus and from the APHB corpus.[2] Sentences containing '[Ll]ine(s)' were extracted and manually assigned a single sense from WordNet. Sentences containing proper names such as 'Japan Air Lines' were removed from the set of sentences. Sentences containing collocations that have a single sense in WordNet, such as *product line* and *line of products*, were also excluded since the collocations are not ambiguous.

Typically, experiments have used a fixed number of words or characters on either side of the target as the context. In this experiment, we used linguistic units – sentences – instead. Since the target word is often used anaphorically to refer back to the previous sentence, we chose to use two-sentence contexts: the sentence containing *line* and the preceding sentence. However, if the sentence containing *line* is the first sentence in the article, then the context consists of one sentence. If the preceding sentence also contains *line* in the same sense, then an additional preceding sentence is added to the context, creating contexts three or more sentences long.

[2]The 25 million word corpus, obtained from the American Printing House for the Blind, is archived at IBM's T.J. Watson Research Center; it consists of stories and articles from books and general circulation magazines.

The average size of the training and testing contexts is 44.5 words.

The sense resolution task used the following six senses of the noun *line*:

1. a *product*: 'a new line of workstations'
2. a *formation* of people or things: 'stand in line'
3. spoken or written *text*: 'a line from Shakespeare'
4. a thin, flexible object; *cord*: 'a nylon line'
5. an abstract *division*: 'a line between good and evil'
6. a telephone *connection*: 'the line went dead'

The classifiers were run three times each on randomly selected training sets. The set of contexts for each sense was randomly permuted, with each permutation corresponding to one *trial*. For each trial, the first 200 contexts of each sense were selected as training contexts. The next 149 contexts were selected as test contexts. The remaining contexts were not used in that trial. The 200 training contexts for each sense were combined to form a final training set (called the 200 training set) of size 1200. The final test set contained the 149 test contexts from each sense, for a total of 894 contexts.

To test the effect that the number of training examples has on classifier performance, smaller training sets were extracted from the 200 training set. The first 50 and 100 contexts for each sense were used to build the new training sets. The same set of 894 test contexts were used with each of the training sets in a given trial. Each of the classifiers used the same training and test contexts within the same trial, but processed the text differently according to the needs of the method.

4. THE CLASSIFIERS

The only information used by the three classifiers is co-occurrence of character strings in the contexts. They use no other cues, such as syntactic tags or word order. Nor do they require any augmentation of the training contexts that is not fully automatic.

4.1. A Bayesian Approach

The Bayesian classifier, developed by Gale, Church and Yarowsky [5], uses Bayes' decision theory for weighting tokens that co-occur with each sense of a polysemous target. Their work is inspired by Mosteller and Wallace [6], who applied Bayes' theorem to the problem of author discrimination. The main component of the model, a *token*, was defined as any character string: a word, number, symbol, punctuation or any combination. The entire token is significant, so inflected forms of a base word (*wait* vs. *waiting*) and mixed case strings (*Bush* vs. *bush*) are distinct tokens. Associated with each token is a set of *saliences*, one for each sense, calculated from the training data. The salience of a token for a given sense is $\Pr(token|sense)/\Pr(token)$. The *weight* of a token for a given sense is the log of its salience.

To select the sense of the target word in a (test) context, the classifier computes the sum of the tokens' *weights* over all tokens in the context for each sense, and selects the sense with the largest sum. In the case of author identification, Mosteller and Wallace built their models using high frequency function words. With sense resolution, the salient tokens include content words, which have much lower frequencies of occurrence. Gale, *et. al.* devised a method for estimating the required probabilities using sparse training data, since the maximum likelihood estimate (MLE) of a probability – the number of times a token appears in a set of contexts divided by the total number of tokens in the set of contexts – is a poor estimate of the true probability. In particular, many tokens in the test contexts do not appear in any training context, or appear only once or twice. In the former case, the MLE is zero, obviously smaller than the true probability; in the latter case, the MLE is much larger than the true probability. Gale, *et. al.* adjust their estimates for new or infrequent words by interpolating between local and global estimates of the probability.

The Bayesian classifier experiments were performed by Kenneth Church of AT&T Bell Laboratories. In these experiments, two-sentence contexts are used in place of a fixed-sized window of ± 50 tokens surrounding the target word that Gale, *et. al.* find optimal,[3] resulting in a smaller amount of context used to estimate the probabilities.

4.2. Content Vectors

The content vector approach to sense resolution is motivated by the vector-space model of information retrieval systems [8], where each *concept* in a corpus defines an axis of the vector space, and a text in the corpus is represented as a point in this space. The concepts in a corpus are usually defined as the set of word stems that appear in the corpus (e.g., the strings *computer(s), computing, computation(al)*, etc. are conflated to the concept *comput*) minus *stopwords*, a set of about 570 very high frequency words that includes function words (e.g., *the*, *by*, *you*, *that*, *who*, etc.) and content words (e.g., *be*, *say*, etc.). The similarity between two texts is computed as a function of the vectors representing the two texts.

[3] Whereas current research tends to confirm the hypothesis that humans need a narrow window of ± 2 words for sense resolution [7], Gale, *et. al.* have found much larger window sizes are better for the Bayesian classifier, presumably because so much information (e.g., word order and syntax) is thrown away.

Product			Formation			Text		
Bayesian	Vector	Network	Bayesian	Vector	Network	Bayesian	Vector	Network
Chrysler	comput	comput	night	wait	wait	Biden	speech	familiar
workstations	ibm	sell	checkout	long	long	ad	writ	writ
Digital	produc	minicomput	wait	checkout	stand	Bush	mr	ad
introduced	corp	model	gasoline	park	checkout	opening	bush	rememb
models	sale	introduc	outside	mr	park	famous	ad	deliv
IBM	model	extend	waiting	airport	hour	Dole	speak	fame
Compaq	sell	acquir	food	shop	form	speech	read	speak
sell	introduc	launch	hours	count	short	Dukakis	dukak	funny
agreement	brand	continu	long	peopl	custom	funny	biden	movie
computers	mainframe	quak	driver	canad	shop	speeches	poem	read
Cord			**Division**			**Phone**		
Bayesian	Vector	Network	Bayesian	Vector	Network	Bayesian	Vector	Network
fish	fish	hap	blurred	draw	draw	phones	telephon	telephon
fishing	boat	fish	walking	fine	priv	toll	phon	phon
bow	wat	wash	crossed	blur	hug	porn	call	dead
deck	hook	pull	ethics	cross	blur	Bellsouth	access	cheer
sea	wash	boat	narrow	walk	cross	gab	dial	hear
boat	float	rope	fine	narrow	fine	telephone	gab	henderson
water	men	break	class	mr	thin	Bell	bell	minut
clothes	dive	hook	between	tread	funct	billion	servic	call
fastened	cage	exercis	walk	faction	genius	Pacific	toll	bill
ship	rod	cry	draw	thin	narrow	calls	porn	silent

Table 1: The ten most heavily weighted tokens for each sense of *line* for the Bayesian, content vector and neural network classifiers.

For the sense resolution problem, each sense is represented by a single vector constructed from the training contexts for that sense. A vector in the space defined by the training contexts is also constructed for each test context. To select a sense for a test context, the inner product between its vector and each of the sense vectors is computed, and the sense whose inner product is the largest is chosen.

The components of the vectors are weighted to reflect the relative importance of the concepts in the text. The weighting method was designed to favor concepts that occur frequently in exactly one sense. The weight of a concept c is computed as follows:

$$\begin{aligned} \text{Let } n_s &= \text{number of times } c \text{ occurs in sense } s \\ p &= n_s / \textstyle\sum_{\text{senses}} n_s \\ d &= \text{difference between the two largest } n_s \\ &\quad \text{(if difference is 0, } d \text{ is set to 1)} \\ \text{then } w_s &= p * \min(n_s, d) \end{aligned}$$

For example, if a concept occurs 6 times in the training contexts of sense 1, and zero times in the other five sets of contexts, then its weights in the six vectors are (6, 0, 0, 0, 0, 0). However, a concept that appears 10, 4, 7, 0, 1, and 2 times in the respective senses, has weights of (1.25, .5, .88, 0, .04, .17), reflecting the fact that it is not as good an indicator for any sense. This weighting method is the most effective among several variants that were tried.

We also experimented with keeping all words in the content vectors, but performance degraded, probably because the weighting function does not handle very high frequency words well. This is evident in Table 1, where 'mr' is highly weighted for three different senses.

4.3. Neural Network

The neural network approach [9] casts sense resolution as a supervised learning paradigm. Pairs of [input features, desired response] are presented to a learning program. The program's task is to devise some method for using the input features to partition the training contexts into non-overlapping sets corresponding to the desired responses. This is achieved by adjusting link weights so that the output unit representing the desired response has a larger activation than any other output unit.

Each context is translated into a bit-vector. As with the content vector approach, suffixes are removed to conflate related word forms to a common stem, and *stopwords* and punctuation are removed. Each concept that appears at least twice in the entire training set is assigned to a bit-vector position. The resulting vector has ones in positions corresponding to concepts in the context and zeros otherwise. This procedure creates vectors with more than 4000 positions. The vectors are, however, extremely sparse; on average they contain slightly more than 17 concepts.

Networks are trained until the output of the unit corresponding to the desired response is greater than the output of any other unit for every training example. For testing, the classification determined by the network is given by the unit with the largest output. Weights in a neural network link vector may be either positive or negative, thereby allowing it to accumulate evidence both for and against a sense.

The result of training a network until all examples are classified correctly is that infrequent tokens can acquire disproportionate importance. For example, the context *'Fine,' Henderson said, aimiably* [sic]. *'Can you get him on the line?'* clearly uses *line* in the *phone* sense. However, the only non-stopwords that are infrequent in other senses are 'henderson' and 'aimiably'; and, due to its misspelling, the latter is conflated to 'aim'. The network must raise the weight of 'henderson' so that it is sufficient to give *phone* the largest output. As a result, 'henderson' appears in Table 1, in spite of its infrequency in the training corpus.

To determine a good topology for the network, various network topologies were explored: networks with from 0 to 100 hidden units arranged in a single hidden layer; networks with multiple layers of hidden units; and networks with a single layer of hidden units in which the output units were connected to both the hidden and input units. In all cases, the network configuration with no hidden units was either superior or statistically indistinguishable from the more complex networks. As no network topology was significantly better than one with no hidden units, all data reported here are derived from such networks.

5. RESULTS AND DISCUSSION

All of the classifiers performed best with the largest number (200) of training contexts. The percent correct results reported below are averaged over the three trials with 200 training contexts. The Bayesian classifier averaged 71% correct answers, the content vector classifier averaged 72%, and the neural network classifier averaged 76%. None of these differences are statistically significant due to the limited sample size of three trials.

The results reported below are taken from trial A with 200 training contexts. Confusion matrices of this trial are given in Tables 2 – 4.[4] The diagonals show the number of correct classifications for each sense, and the off-diagonal elements show classification errors. For example, the entry containing 5 in the bottom row of Table 2 means that 5 contexts whose correct sense is the *product* sense were classified as the *phone* sense.

Ten heavily weighted tokens for each sense for each classifier appear in Table 1. The words on the list seem, for the most part, indicative of the target sense. However, there are some consistent differences among the methods. For example, whereas the Bayesian method is sensitive to proper nouns, the neural network appears to have no such preference.

To test the hypothesis that the methods have different response patterns, we performed the χ^2 test for correlated proportions. This test measures how consistently the methods treat individual test contexts by determining whether the classifiers are making the same classification errors in each of the senses. For each sense, the test compares the off-diagonal elements of a matrix whose columns contain the responses of one classifier and the rows show a second classifier's responses in the same test set. This process constructs a square matrix whose diagonal elements contain the number of test contexts on which the two methods agree.

The results of the χ^2 test for a three-sense resolution task (*product*, *formation* and *text*),[5] indicate that the response pattern of the content vector classifier is very significantly different from the patterns of both the Bayesian and neural network classifiers, but the Bayesian response pattern is significantly different from the neural network pattern for only the *product* sense. In the six-sense disambiguation task, the χ^2 results indicate that the Bayesian and neural network classifiers' response patterns are not significantly different for any sense. The neural network and Bayesian classifiers' response patterns are significantly different from the content vector classifier only in the *formation* and *text* senses. Therefore, with the addition of three senses, the classifiers' response patterns appear to be converging.

The pilot two-sense distinction task (between *product* and *formation*) yielded over 90% correct answers. In the three-sense distinction task, the three classifiers had a

[4] The numbers in the confusion matrix in Table 4 are averages over ten runs with randomly initialized networks.

[5] Training and test sets for these senses are identical to those in the six-sense resolution task.

Correct Sense

		Product	Formation	Text	Cord	Division	Phone
Classified Sense	Product	120	7	4	2	4	5
	Formation	9	97	19	6	14	11
	Text	5	26	93	6	20	11
	Cord	2	10	11	129	5	10
	Division	8	8	21	5	103	3
	Phone	5	1	1	1	3	109

Table 2: Confusion matrix for Bayesian classifier (columns show the correct sense, rows the selected sense).

Correct Sense

		Product	Formation	Text	Cord	Division	Phone
Classified Sense	Product	139	33	32	5	17	14
	Formation	2	88	15	12	8	5
	Text	3	7	71	3	8	6
	Cord	0	7	7	120	2	5
	Division	0	9	12	4	108	0
	Phone	5	5	12	5	6	119

Table 3: Confusion matrix for content vector classifier (columns show the correct sense, rows the selected sense).

Correct Sense

		Product	Formation	Text	Cord	Division	Phone
Classified Sense	Product	122	11	4	1	3	6
	Formation	4	90	17	9	8	2
	Text	9	14	83	4	10	7
	Cord	2	11	13	125	3	3
	Division	4	13	16	4	121	1
	Phone	8	10	16	6	4	130

Table 4: Confusion matrix for neural network classifier (columns show the correct sense, rows the selected sense).

mean of 76% correct,[6] yielding a sharp degradation with the addition of a third sense. Therefore, we hypothesized degree of polysemy to be a major factor for performance. We were surprised to find that in the six-sense task, all three classifiers degraded only slightly from the three-sense task, with a mean of 73% correct. Although the addition of three new senses to the task caused consistent degradation, the degradation is relatively slight. Hence, we conclude that some senses are harder to resolve than others, and it appears that overall accuracy is a function of the difficulty of the sense rather than being strictly a function of the number of senses. The hardest sense to learn, for all three classifiers, was *text*, followed by *formation*. To test the validity of this conclusion, further tests need to be run.

If statistical classifiers are to be part of higher-level NLP tasks, characteristics other than overall accuracy are important. Collecting training contexts is by far the most time-consuming part of the entire process. Until training-context acquisition is fully automated, classifiers requiring smaller training sets are preferred. Figure 1 shows that the content vector classifier has a flatter learning curve between 50 and 200 training contexts than the neural network and Bayesian classifiers, suggesting that the latter two require more (or larger) training contexts. Ease and efficiency of use is also a factor. The three classifiers are roughly comparable in this regard, although the neural network classifier is the most expensive to train.

[6] The Bayesian classifier averaged 76% correct answers, the content vector classifier averaged 73%, and the neural networks 79%.

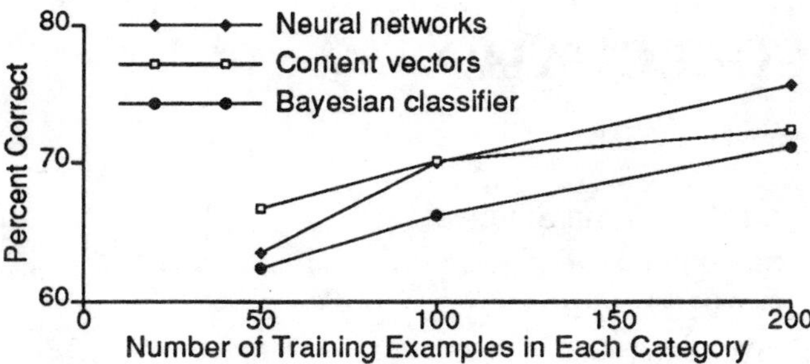

Figure 1: Learning curves.

6. CONCLUSION

The convergence of the response patterns for the three methods suggests that each of the classifiers is extracting as much data as is available in word counts from training contexts. If this is the case, any technique that uses only word counts will not be significantly more accurate than the techniques tested here.

Although the degree of polysemy does affect the difficulty of the sense resolution task, a greater factor of performance is the difficulty of resolving individual senses. Using hindsight, it is obvious that the *text* sense is hard for these statistical methods to learn because one can talk or write about anything. In effect, all words between a pair of quotation marks are noise (unless *line* is within the quotes). In the three-sense task, the Bayesian classifier did best on the *text* sense, perhaps because it had open and closed quotes as important tokens. This advantage was lost in the six-sense task because quotation marks also appear in the contexts of the *phone* sense. It is not immediately obvious why the *formation* sense should be hard. From inspection of the contexts, it appears that the crucial information is close to the word, and context that is more than a few words away is noise.

These corpus-based statistical techniques use an impoverished representation of the training contexts: simple counts of tokens appearing within two sentences. We believe significant increases in resolution accuracy will not be possible unless other information, such as word order or syntactic information, is incorporated into the techniques.

ACKNOWLEDGMENTS

This work was supported in part by Grant No. N00014-91-1634 from the Defense Advanced Research Projects Agency, Information and Technology Office, by the Office of Naval Research, and by the James S. McDonnell Foundation. We thank Kenneth Church of AT&T Bell Laboratories for running the Bayesian classifier experiment, and Slava Katz of IBM's T.J. Watson Research Center for generously supplying *line* contexts from the APHB corpus. We are indebted to George A. Miller for suggesting this line of research.

References

1. Miller, G. A. (ed.), WordNet: An on-line lexical database. *International Journal of Lexicography* (special issue), 3(4):235-312, 1990.
2. Zipf, G. K., The meaning-frequency relationship of words. *Journal of General Psychology*, 3:251-256, 1945.
3. Yarowsky, D., Word-sense disambiguation using statistical models of Roget's categories trained on large corpora, *COLING-92*, 1992.
4. Voorhees, E. M., Leacock C., and Towell, G., Learning context to disambiguate word senses. *Proceedings of the 3rd Computational Learning Theory and Natural Learning Systems Conference, 1992*, MIT Press (to appear). Also available as a Siemens technical report.
5. Gale, W., Church, K. W., and Yarowsky, D., A method for disambiguating word senses in a large corpus. Statistical Research Report 104, AT&T Bell Laboratories, 1992.
6. Mosteller F. and Wallace, D., *Inference and Disputed Authorship: The Federalist.* Addison-Wessley, Reading, MA, 1964.
7. Choueka Y. and Lusignan, S., Disambiguation by short contexts. *Computers and the Humanities*, 19:147-157, 1985.
8. Salton, G., Wong, A., and Yang, C. S., A vector space model for automatic indexing. *Communications of the ACM*, 18(11):613-620, 1975.
9. Rumelhart, D. E., Hinton, G. E., and Williams, R J., Learning internal representations by error propagation. in Rumelhart, D. E. and McClelland, J. L. (eds.), *Parallel Distributed Processing: Explorations in the Microstructure of Cognition, Volume 1: Foundations.* MIT Press, Cambridge, MA, 1986, pp. 318-363.

ONE SENSE PER COLLOCATION

*David Yarowsky**

Department of Computer and Information Science
University of Pennsylvania
Philadelphia, PA 19104
yarowsky@unagi.cis.upenn.edu

ABSTRACT

Previous work [Gale, Church and Yarowsky, 1992] showed that with high probability a polysemous word has one sense per discourse. In this paper we show that for certain definitions of collocation, a polysemous word exhibits essentially only one sense per collocation. We test this empirical hypothesis for several definitions of sense and collocation, and discover that it holds with 90-99% accuracy for binary ambiguities. We utilize this property in a disambiguation algorithm that achieves precision of 92% using combined models of very local context.

1. INTRODUCTION

The use of collocations to resolve lexical ambiguities is certainly not a new idea. The first approaches to sense disambiguation, such as [Kelly and Stone 1975], were based on simple hand-built decision tables consisting almost exclusively of questions about observed word associations in specific positions. Later work from the AI community relied heavily upon selectional restrictions for verbs, although primarily in terms of features exhibited by their arguments (such as +DRINKABLE) rather than in terms of individual words or word classes. More recent work [Brown et al. 1991][Hearst 1991] has utilized a set of discrete local questions (such as *word-to-the-right*) in the development of statistical decision procedures. However, a strong trend in recent years is to treat a reasonably wide context window as an unordered bag of independent evidence points. This technique from information retrieval has been used in neural networks, Bayesian discriminators, and dictionary definition matching. In a comparative paper in this volume [Leacock et al. 1993], all three methods under investigation used words in wide context as a pool of evidence independent of relative position. It is perhaps not a coincidence that this work has focused almost exclusively on nouns, as will be shown in Section 6.2. In this study we will return again to extremely local sources of evidence, and show that models of discrete syntactic relationships have considerable advantages.

*This research was supported by an NDSEG Fellowship and by DARPA grant N00014-90-J-1863. The author is also affiliated with the Linguistics Research Department of AT&T Bell Laboratories, and greatly appreciates the use of its resources in support of this work. He would also like to thank Eric Brill, Bill Gale, Libby Levison, Mitch Marcus and Philip Resnik for their valuable feedback.

2. DEFINITIONS OF SENSE

The traditional definition of word sense is "One of several meanings assigned to the same orthographic string". As meanings can always be partitioned into multiple refinements, senses are typically organized in a tree such as one finds in a dictionary. In the extreme case, one could continue making refinements until a word has a slightly different sense every time it is used. If so, the title of this paper is a tautology. However, the studies in this paper are focused on the sense distinctions at the top of the tree. A good working definition of the distinctions considered are those meanings which are not typically translated to the same word in a foreign language.

Therefore, one natural type of sense distinction to consider are those words in English which indeed have multiple translations in a language such as French. As is now standard in the field, we use the Canadian Hansards, a parallel bilingual corpus, to provide sense tags in the form of French translations. Unfortunately, the Hansards are highly skewed in their sense distributions, and it is difficult to find words for which there are adequate numbers of a second sense. More diverse large bilingual corpora are not yet readily available.

We also use data sets which have been hand-tagged by native English speakers. To make the selection of sense distinctions more objective, we use words such as *bass* where the sense distinctions (*fish* and *musical instrument*) correspond to pronunciation differences ([bæs] and [beIs]). Such data is often problematic, as the tagging is potentially subjective and error-filled, and sufficient quantities are difficult to obtain.

As a solution to the data shortages for the above methods, [Gale, Church and Yarowsky 1992b] proposed the use of "pseudo-words," artificial sense ambiguities created by taking two English words with the same part of speech (such as *guerilla* and *reptile*), and replacing each instance of both in a corpus with a new polysemous word *guerrilla/reptile*. As it is entirely possible that the concepts guerrilla and reptile are represented by the same orthographic string in some foreign language, choosing between these two meanings based on context is a problem a word sense disambiguation algorithm could easily face. "Pseudo-words" are very useful for developing and testing disambiguation methods because of their nearly unlimited availability and the known, fully reliable ground truth they provide when grading performance.

Finally, we consider sense disambiguation for mediums other than clean English text. For example, we look at word pairs such as *terse/tense* and *cookie/rookie* which may be plausibly confused in optical character recognition (OCR). Homophones, such as *aid/aide*, and *censor/sensor*, are ideal candidates for such a study because large data sets with known ground truth are available in written text, yet they are true ambiguities which must be resolved routinely in oral communication.

We discover that the central claims of this paper hold for all of these potential definitions of sense. This corroborating evidence makes us much more confident in our results than if they were derived solely from a relatively small hand-tagged data set.

- **Hand Tagged (homographs):** bass, axes, chi, bow, colon, lead, IV, sake, tear, ...
- **French Translation Distinctions:** sentence, duty, drug, language, position, paper, single, ...
- **Homophones:** aid/aide, cellar/seller, censor/sensor, cue/queue, pedal/petal, ...
- **OCR Ambiguities:** terse/tense, gum/gym, deaf/dear, cookie/rookie, beverage/leverage, ...
- **Pseudo-Words:** covered/waved, kissed/slapped, abused/escorted, cute/compatible, ...

Table 1: A sample of the words used in the experiments

3. DEFINITIONS OF COLLOCATION

Collocation means the co-occurrence of two words in some defined relationship. We look at several such relationships, including direct adjacency and first word to the left or right having a certain part-of-speech. We also consider certain direct syntactic relationships, such as verb/object, subject/verb, and adjective/noun pairs. It appears that *content words* (nouns, verbs, adjectives, and adverbs) behave quite differently from *function words* (other parts of speech); we make use of this distinction in several definitions of collocation.

We will attempt to quantify the validity of the one-sense-per-collocation hypothesis for these different collocation types.

4. EXPERIMENTS

In the experiments, we ask two central, related questions: For each definition of sense and collocation,

- What is the mean entropy of the distribution $Pr(Sense|Collocation)$?
- What is the performance of a disambiguation algorithm which uses only that collocation type as evidence?

We examine several permutations for each, and are interested in how the results of these questions differ when applied to polysemous nouns, verbs, and adjectives.

To limit the already very large number of parameters considered, we study only binary sense distinctions. In all cases the senses being compared have the same part of speech. The selection between different possible parts of speech has been heavily studied and is not replicated here.

4.1. Sample Collection

All samples were extracted from a 380 million word corpus collection consisting of newswire text (AP Newswire and Wall Street Journal), scientific abstracts (from NSF and the Department of Energy), the Canadian Hansards parliamentary debate records, Grolier's Encyclopedia, a medical encyclopedia, over 100 Harper & Row books, and several smaller corpora including the Brown Corpus, and ATIS and TIMIT sentences.[1]

The homophone pairs used were randomly selected from a list of words having the same pronunciation or which differed in only one phoneme. The OCR and pseudo-word pairs were randomly selected from corpus wordlists, with the former restricted to pairs which could plausibly be confused in a noisy FAX, typically words differing in only one character. Due to the difficulty of obtaining new data, the hand-tagged and French translation examples were borrowed from those used in our previous studies in sense disambiguation.

4.2. Measuring Entropies

When computing the entropy of $Pr(Sense|Collocation)$, we enumerate all collocations of a given type observed for the word or word pair being disambiguated. Table 2 shows the example of the homophone ambiguity *aid/aide* for the collocation type *content-word-to-the-left*. We list all words[2] appearing in such a collocation with either of these two "senses" of the homograph, and calculate the raw distributional count for each.

Note that the vast majority of the entries in Table 2 have zero as one of the frequency counts. It is not acceptable, however,

[1] Training and test samples were not only extracted from different articles or discourses but also from entirely different blocks of the corpus. This was done to minimize long range discourse effects such as one finds in the AP or Hansards.

[2] Note: the entries in this table are *lemmas* (uninflected root forms), rather than raw words. By treating the verbal inflections *squander, squanders, squandering, and squandered* as the same word, one can improve statistics and coverage at a slight cost of lost subtlety. Although we will refer to "words in collocation" throughout this paper for simplicity, this should always be interpreted as "lemmas in collocation."

Collocation	Frequency as **Aid**	Frequency as **Aide**
foreign	718	1
federal	297	0
western	146	0
provide	88	0
covert	26	0
oppose	13	0
future	9	0
similar	6	0
presidential	0	63
chief	0	40
longtime	0	26
aids-infected	0	2
sleepy	0	1
disaffected	0	1
indispensable	2	1
practical	2	0
squander	1	0

Table 2: A typical collocational distribution for the homophone ambiguity *aid/aide*.

to treat these as having zero probability and hence a zero entropy for the distribution. It is quite possible, especially for the lower frequency distributions, that we would see a contrary example in a larger sample. By cross-validation, we discover for the *aid/aide* example that for collocations with an observed 1/0 distribution, we would actually expect the minor sense to occur 6% of the time in an independent sample, on average. Thus a fairer distribution would be .94/.06, giving a cross-validated entropy of .33 bits rather than 0 bits. For a more unbalanced observed distribution, such as 10/0, the probability of seeing the minor sense decreases to 2%, giving a cross-validated entropy of H(.98,.02) = .14 bits. Repeating this process and taking the weighted mean yields the entropy of the full distribution, in this case .09 bits for the *aid/aide* ambiguity.

For each type of collocation, we also compute how well an observed probability distribution predicts the correct classification for novel examples. In general, this is a more useful measure for most of the comparison purposes we will address. Not only does it reflect the underlying entropy of the distribution, but it also has the practical advantage of showing how a working system would perform given this data.

5. ALGORITHM

The sense disambiguation algorithm used is quite straightforward. When based on a single collocation type, such as the object of the verb or word immediately to the left, the procedure is very simple. One identifies if this collocation type exists for the novel context and if the specific words found are listed in the table of probability distributions (as computed above). If so, we return the sense which was most frequent for that collocation in the training data. If not, we return the sense which is most frequent overall.

When we consider more than one collocation type and combine evidence, the process is more complicated. The algorithm used is based on decision lists [Rivest, 1987], and was discussed in [Sproat, Hirschberg, and Yarowsky 1992]. The goal is to base the decision on the single best piece of evidence available. Cross-validated probabilities are computed as in Section 4.2, and the different types of evidence are sorted by the absolute value of the log of these probability ratios: $Abs(Log(\frac{Pr(Sense_1|Collocation_i)}{Pr(Sense_2|Collocation_i)}))$. When a novel context is encountered, one steps through the decision list until the evidence at that point in the list (such as *word-to-left*="presidential") matches the current context under consideration. The sense with the greatest listed probability is returned, and this cross-validated probability represents the confidence in the answer.

This approach is well-suited for the combination of multiple evidence types which are clearly not independent (such as those found in this study) as probabilities are never combined. Therefore this method offers advantages over Bayesian classifier techniques which assume independence of the features used. It also offers advantages over decision tree based techniques because the training pools are not split at each question. The interesting problems are how one should re-estimate probabilities conditional on questions asked earlier in the list, or how one should prune lower evidence which is categorically subsumed by higher evidence or is entirely conditional on higher evidence. [Bahl et al. 1989] have discussed some of these issues at length, and there is not space to consider them here. For simplicity, in this experiment no secondary smoothing or pruning is done. This does not appear to be problematic when small numbers of independent evidence types are used, but performance should increase if this extra step is taken.

6. RESULTS AND DISCUSSION

6.1. One Sense Per Collocation

For the collocations studied, it appears that the hypothesis of one sense per collocation holds with high probability for binary ambiguities. The experimental results in the *precision* column of Table 3 quantify the validity of this claim. Accuracy varies from 90% to 99% for different types of collocation and part of speech, with a mean of 95%. The significance of these differences will be discussed in Section 6.2.

These precision values have several interpretations. First, they reflect the underlying probability distributions of sense

Collocation Type	Part of Sp.	Ent	Prec	Rec	No Coll	No Data
Content	ALL	.18	.97	.29	.57	.14
word to	Noun		.98	.25	.66	.09
immediate	Verb		.95	.14	.71	.15
right [A]	Adj		.97	.51	.27	.22
Content	ALL	.24	.96	.26	.58	.16
word to	Noun		.99	.33	.56	.11
immediate	Verb		.91	.23	.47	.30
left [B]	Adj		.96	.15	.75	.10
First	ALL	.33	.94	.51	.09	.40
Content	Noun		.94	.49	.13	.38
Word to	Verb		.91	.44	.05	.51
Right	Adj		.96	.58	.04	.38
First	ALL	.40	.92	.50	.06	.44
Content	Noun		.96	.58	.06	.36
Word to	Verb		.87	.37	.05	.58
Left	Adj		.90	.45	.06	.49
Subject ↔	Noun	.33	.94	.13	.87	.06
Verb Pairs	Verb	.43	.91	.28	.33	.38
Verb ↔	Noun	.46	.90	.07	.81	.07
Object Pairs	Verb	.29	.95	.36	.32	.32
Adj ↔ Noun	Adj	.14	.98	.54	.20	.26
A&B Above	ALL	–	.97	.47	.31	.21
All Above	ALL	–	.92	.98	.00	.02

Table 3: Includes the entropy of the $Pr(Sense|Collocation)$ distribution for several types of collocation, and the performance achieved when basing sense disambiguation solely on that evidence. Results are itemized by the part of speech of the ambiguous word (*not* of the collocate). Precision (Prec.) indicates percent correct and Recall (Rec.) refers to the percentage of samples for which an answer is returned. Precision is measured on this subset. No collocation (No Coll) indicates the failure to provide an answer because no collocation of that type was present in the test context, and "No Data" indicates the failure to return an answer because no data for the observed collocation was present in the model. See Section 7.3 for a discussion of the "All Above" result. The results stated above are based on the average of the different types of sense considered, and have a mean prior probability of .69 and a mean sample size of 3944.

conditional on collocation. For example, for the collocation type *content-word-to-the-right*, the value of .97 indicates that on average, given a specific collocation we will expect to see the same sense 97% of the time. This mean distribution is also reflected in the *entropy* column.

However, these numbers have much more practical interpretations. If we actually build a disambiguation procedure using exclusively the content word to the right as information, such a system performs with 97% precision on new data where a content word appears to the right and for which there is information in the model.[3] This is considerably higher than the

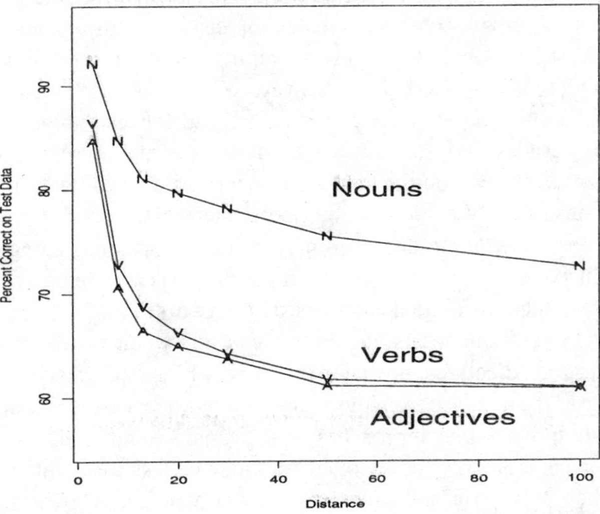

Figure 1: Comparison of the performance of nouns, verbs and adjectives based strictly on a 5 word window centered at the distance shown on the horizontal axis.

performance of 69% one would expect simply by chance due to the unbalanced prior probability of the two senses.

It should be noted that such precision is achieved at only partial recall. The three rightmost columns of Table 3 give the breakdown of the recall. On average, the model *content-word-to-right* could only be applied in 29% of the test samples. In 57% of the cases, no content word appeared to the right, so this collocational model did not hold. In 14% of the cases, a content word did appear to the right, but no instances of that word appeared in the training data, so the model had no information on which to base a decision. There are several solutions to both these deficiencies, and they are discussed in Section 7.

6.2. Part of Speech Differences

It is interesting to note the difference in behavior between different parts of speech. Verbs, for example, derive more disambiguating information from their objects (.95) than from their subjects (.90). Adjectives derive almost all of their disambiguating information from the nouns they modify (.98). Nouns are best disambiguated by directly adjacent adjectives or nouns, with the content word to the left indicating a single sense with 99% precision. Verbs appear to be less useful for noun sense disambiguation, although they are relatively better indicators when the noun is their object rather than their subject.

[3]The correlation between these numbers is not a coincidence. Because the probability distributions are based on cross-validated tests on independent data and weighted by collocation frequency, if on average we find that 97% of samples of a given collocation exhibit the same sense, this is the expected precision of a disambiguation algorithm which assumes one sense per collocation, when applied to new samples of these collocations.

Figure 1 shows that nouns, verbs and adjectives also differ in their ability to be disambiguated by wider context. [Gale et al. 1993] previously showed that nouns can be disambiguated based strictly on distant context, and that useful information was present up to 10,000 words away. We replicated an experiment in which performance was calculated for disambiguations based strictly on 5 word windows centered at various distances (shown on the horizontal axis). Gale's observation was tested only on nouns; our experiment also shows that reasonably accurate decisions may be made for nouns using exclusively remote context. Our results in this case are based on test sets with equal numbers of the two senses. Hence chance performance is at 50%. However, when tested on verbs and adjectives, precision drops off with a much steeper slope as the distance from the ambiguous word increases. This would indicate that approaches giving equal weight to all positions in a broad window of context may be less well-suited for handling verbs and adjectives. Models which give greater weight to immediate context would seem more appropriate in these circumstances.

A similar experiment was applied to function words, and the dropoff beyond strictly immediate context was precipitous, converging at near chance performance for distances greater than 5. However, function words did appear to have predictive power of roughly 5% greater than chance in directly adjacent positions. The effect was greatest for verbs, where the function word to the right (typically a preposition or particle) served to disambiguate at a precision of 13% above chance. This would indicate that methods which exclude function words from models to minimize noise should consider their inclusion, but only for restricted local positions.

6.3. Comparison of Sense Definitions

Results for the 5 different definitions of sense ambiguity studied here are similar. However they tend to fluctuate relative to each other across experiments, and there appears to be no consistent ordering of the mean entropy of the different types of sense distributions. Because of the very large number of permutations considered, it is not possible to give a full breakdown of the differences, and such a breakdown does not appear to be terribly informative. The important observation, however, is that the basic conclusions drawn from this paper hold for *each* of the sense definitions considered, and hence corroborate and strengthen the conclusions which can be drawn from any one.

6.4. Performance Given Little Evidence

One of the most striking conclusions to emerge from this study is that for the local collocations considered, decisions based on a single data point are highly reliable. Normally one would consider a 1/0 sense distribution in a 3944 sample training set to be noise, with performance based on this information not

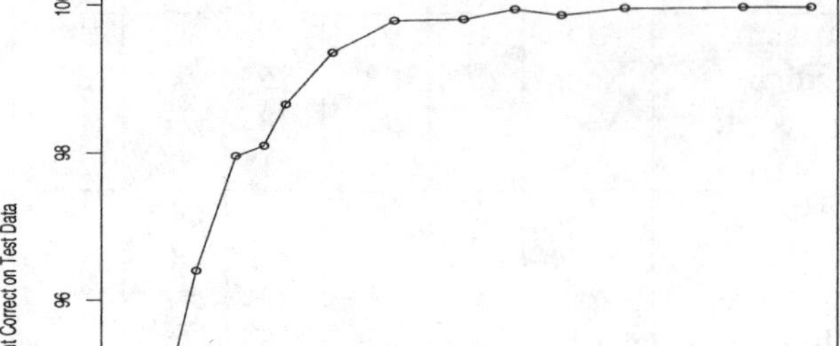

Figure 2: Percentage correct for disambiguations based solely on a single *content-word-to-the-right* collocation seen *f* times in the training data without counter-examples.

likely to much exceed the 69% prior probability expected by chance. But this is not what we observe. For example, when tested on the *word-to-the-right* collocation, disambiguations based solely on a single data point exceed 92% accuracy, and performance on 2/0 and 3/0 distributions climb rapidly from there, and reach nearly perfect accuracy for training samples as small as 15/0, as shown in Figure 2. In contrast, a collocation 30 words away which also exhibits a 1/0 sense distribution has a predictive value of only 3% greater than chance. This difference in the reliability of low frequency data from local and wide context will have implications for algorithm design.

7. APPLICATIONS

7.1. Training Set Creation and Verification

This last observation has relevance for new data set creation and correction. Collocations with an ambiguous content word which have frequency greater than 10-15 and which do not belong exclusively to one sense should be flagged for human reinspection, as they are most likely in error. One can speed the sense tagging process by computing the most frequent collocates, and for each one assigning all examples to the same sense. For the data in Table 2, this will apparently fail for the *foreign Aid/Aide* example in 1 out of 719 instances (still 99.9% correct). However, in this example the model's classification was actually correct; the given usage was a misspelling in the 1992 AP Newswire: "Bush accelerated foreign *aide* and weapons sales to Iraq.". It is quite likely that if were indeed a foreign assistant being discussed, this example would also have another collocation (with the verb, for example), which would indicate the correct sense. Such inconsistencies should also be flagged for human supervision. Working from the most to least frequent collocates in this manner, one can use previously tagged collocates to automatically suggest the classification of other words appearing in different collocation types for those tagged examples. The one sense per discourse constraint can be used to refine this process further. We are working on a similar use of these two constraints for unsupervised sense clustering.

7.2. Algorithm Design

Our results also have implications for algorithm design. For the large number of current approaches which treat wide context as an unordered bag of words, it may be beneficial to model certain local collocations separately. We have shown that reliability of collocational evidence differs considerably between local and distant context, especially for verbs and adjectives. If one one is interested in providing a probability with an answer, modeling local collocations separately will improve the probability estimates and reduce cross entropy.

Another reason for modeling local collocations separately is that this will allow the reliable inclusion of evidence with very low frequency counts. Evidence with observed frequency distributions of 1/0 typically constitute on the order of 50% of all available evidence types, yet in a wide context window this low frequency evidence is effectively noise, with predictive power little better than chance. However, in very local collocations, single data points carry considerable information, and when used alone can achieve precision in excess of 92%. Their inclusion should improve system recall, with a much-reduced danger of overmodeling the data.

7.3. Building a Full Disambiguation System

Finally, one may ask to what extent can local collocational evidence alone support a practical sense disambiguation algorithm. As shown in Table 3, our models of single collocation types achieve high precision, but individually their applicability is limited. However, if we combine these models as described in Section 5, and use an additional function word collocation model when no other evidence is available, we achieve full coverage at a precision of 92%. This result is comparable to those previously reported in the literature using wider context of up to 50 words away [5,6,7,12]. Due to the large number of variables involved, we shall not attempt to compare these directly. Our results are encouraging, however, and and we plan to conduct a more formal comparison of the "bag of words" approaches relative to our separate modeling of local collocation types. We will also consider additional collocation types covering a wider range of syntactic relationships. In addition, we hope to incorporate class-based techniques, such as the modeling of verb-argument selectional preferences [Resnik, 1992], as a mechanism for achieving improved performance on unfamiliar collocations.

8. CONCLUSION

This paper has examined some of the basic distributional properties of lexical ambiguity in the English language. Our experiments have shown that for several definitions of sense and collocation, an ambiguous word has only one sense in a given collocation with a probability of 90-99%. We showed how this claim is influenced by part-of-speech, distance, and sample frequency. We discussed the implications of these results for data set creation and algorithm design, identifying potential weaknesses in the common "bag of words" approach to disambiguation. Finally, we showed that models of local collocation can be combined in a disambiguation algorithm that achieves overall precision of 92%.

References

1. Bahl, L., P. Brown, P. de Souza, R. Mercer, "A Tree-Based Statistical Language Model for Natural Language Speech Recognition," in *IEEE Transactions on Acoustics, Speech, and Signal Processing*, 37, 1989.
2. Brown, Peter, Stephen Della Pietra, Vincent Della Pietra, and Robert Mercer, "Word Sense Disambiguation using Statistical Methods," *Proceedings of the 29th Annual Meeting of the Association for Computational Linguistics*, 1991, pp 264-270.
3. Gale, W., K. Church, and D. Yarowsky, "One Sense Per Discourse," *Proceedings of the 4th DARPA Speech and Natural Language Workshop*, 1992.
4. Gale, W., K. Church, and D. Yarowsky, "On Evaluation of Word-Sense Disambiguation Systems," in *Proceedings, 30th Annual Meeting of the Association for Computational Linguistics*, 1992b.
5. Gale, W., K. Church, and D. Yarowsky, "A Method for Disambiguating Word Senses in a Large Corpus," in *Computers and the Humanities*, 1993.
6. Hearst, Marti, "Noun Homograph Disambiguation Using Local Context in Large Text Corpora," in *Using Corpora*, University of Waterloo, Waterloo, Ontario, 1991.
7. Leacock, Claudia, Geoffrey Towell and Ellen Voorhees "Corpus-Based Statistical Sense Resolution," in *Proceedings, ARPA Human Language Technology Workshop*, 1993.
8. Kelly, Edward, and Phillip Stone, *Computer Recognition of English Word Senses*, North-Holland, Amsterdam, 1975.
9. Resnik, Philip, "A Class-based Approach to Lexical Discovery," in *Proceedings of 30th Annual Meeting of the Association for Computational Linguistics*, 1992.
10. Rivest, R. L., "Learning Decision Lists," in *Machine Learning*, 2, 1987, pp 229-246.
11. Sproat, R., J. Hirschberg and D. Yarowsky "A Corpus-based Synthesizer," in *Proceedings, International Conference on Spoken Language Processing*, Banff, Alberta. October 1992.
12. Yarowsky, David "Word-Sense Disambiguation Using Statistical Models of Roget's Categories Trained on Large Corpora," in *Proceedings, COLING-92*, Nantes, France, 1992.

Augmenting Lexicons Automatically: Clustering Semantically Related Adjectives

Kathleen McKeown
Vasileios Hatzivassiloglou

Department of Computer Science
450 Computer Science Building
Columbia University
New York, N.Y. 10027

ABSTRACT

Our work focuses on identifying various types of lexical data in large corpora through statistical analysis. In this paper, we present a method for grouping adjectives according to their meaning, as a step towards the automatic identification of adjectival scales. We describe how our system exploits two sources of linguistic knowledge in a corpus to compute a measure of similarity between two adjectives, using statistical techniques and a clustering algorithm for grouping. We evaluate the significance of the results produced by our system for a sample set of adjectives.

1. INTRODUCTION

A linguistic scale is a set of words, of the same grammatical category, which can be ordered by their semantic strength or degree of informativeness [1]. For example, "lukewarm," "warm", "hot" fall along a single adjectival scale since they indicate a variation in the intensity of temperature of the modified noun. Linguistic properties of scales derive both from conventional logical entailment on the linear ordering of their elements and from Gricean scalar implicature [1]. Despite these properties and their potential usefulness in both understanding and generating natural language text, dictionary entries are largely incomplete for adjectives in this regard. Yet, if systems are to use the information encoded in adjectival scales for generation or interpretation (e.g. for selecting an adjective with a particular degree of semantic strength, or for handling negation), they must have access to the sets of words comprising a scale.

While linguists have presented various tests for accepting or rejecting a particular scalar relationship between any two adjectives (e.g., [2], [3]), the common problem with these methods is that they are designed to be applied by a human who incorporates the two adjectives in specific sentential frames (e.g. "X is *warm*, even *hot*") and assesses the semantic validity of the resulting sentences. Such tests cannot be used computationally to identify scales in a domain, since the specific sentences do not occur frequently enough in a corpus to produce an adequate description of the adjectival scales in the domain [4]. As scales vary across domains, the task of compiling such information is compounded.

In this paper we describe a technique for automatically grouping adjectives according to their meaning based on a given text corpus, so that all adjectives placed in one group describe different values of the same property. Our method is based on statistical techniques, augmented with linguistic information derived from the corpus, and is completely domain independent. It demonstrates how high-level semantic knowledge can be computed from large amounts of low-level knowledge (essentially plain text, part-of-speech rules, and optionally syntactic relations). While our current system does not distinguish between scalar and non-scalar adjectives, it is a first step in the automatic identification of adjectival scales, since the scales can be subsequently ordered and the non-scalar adjectives filtered on the basis of independent tests, done in part automatically and in part by hand in a post-editing phase. The result is a semi-automated system for the compilation of adjectival scales.

In the following sections, we first describe our algorithm in detail, present the results obtained, and finally provide a formal evaluation of the results.

2. ALGORITHM

Our algorithm is based on two sources of linguistic data: data that help establish that two adjectives are related, and data that indicate that two adjectives are unrelated. We extract adjective-noun pairs that occur in a modification relation in order to identify the distribution of nouns an adjective modifies and, ultimately, determine which adjectives it is related to. This is based on the expectation that adjectives describing the same property tend to modify the same set of nouns. For example, temperature is normally defined for physical objects and we can expect to find that adjectives conveying different values of temperature will all modify physical objects. Therefore, our algorithm finds the distribution of nouns that each adjective modifies and categorizes adjectives as similar if they have similar distributions.

Second, we use adjective-adjective pairs occurring as premodifiers within the same NP as a strong indication that the two adjectives do not belong in the same group. There are three cases:

1. If both adjectives modify the head noun and the two adjectives are antithetical, the NP

would be self-contradictory, as in the scalar sequence *hot cold* or the non-scalar *red black*.

2. For non-antithetical scalar adjectives which both modify the head noun, the NP would violate the Gricean maxim of Manner [1] since the same information is conveyed by the strongest of the two adjectives (e.g. *hot warm*).

3. Finally, if one adjective modifies the other, the modifying adjective has to qualify the modified one in a different dimension. For example, in *light blue shirt*, *blue* is a value of the property color, while *light* indicates the shade*.

The use of linguistic data, in addition to statistical measures, is a unique property of our work and significantly improves the accuracy of our results. One other published model for grouping semantically related words [5], is based on a statistical model of bigrams and trigrams and produces word groups using no linguistic knowledge, but no evaluation of the results is performed.

Our method works in three stages. First, we extract linguistic data from the parsed corpus in the form of syntactically related word pairs; in the second stage, we compute a measure of similarity between any two adjectives based on the information gathered in stage one; and in the last stage, we cluster the adjectives into groups according to the similarity measure, so that adjectives with a high degree of similarity fall in the same cluster (and, consequently, adjectives with a low degree of similarity fall in different clusters).

2.1. Stage One: Extracting Word Pairs

During the first stage, the system extracts adjective-noun and adjective-adjective pairs from the corpus. To determine the syntactic category of each word, and identify the NP boundaries and the syntactic relations between each word, we used the Fidditch parser [6]**. For each NP, we then determine its **minimal NP**, that part of an NP consisting of the head noun and its adjectival pre-modifiers. We match a set of regular expressions, consisting of syntactic categories and representing the different forms a minimal NP can take, against the NPs. From the minimal NP, we produce the different pairs of adjectives and nouns.

The resulting adjective-adjective and adjective-noun pairs are filtered by a morphology component, which removes pairs that contain erroneous information (such as mistyped words, proper names, and closed-class words which may be mistakenly classified as adjectives (e.g. possessive pronouns)). This component also reduces the number of different pairs without losing information by transforming words to an equivalent, base form (e.g. plural nouns are converted to singular) so that the expected and actual frequencies of each pair are higher. Stage one then produces as output a simple list of adjective-adjective pairs that occurred within the same minimal NP and a table with the observed frequencies of every adjective-noun combination. Each row in the table contains the frequencies of modified nouns for a given adjective.

2.2. Stage Two: Computing Similarities Between Adjectives

This stage processes the output of stage one, producing a measure of similarity for each possible pair of adjectives. The adjective-noun frequency table is processed first; for each possible pair in the table we compare the two distributions of nouns.

We use a robust non-parametric method to compute the similarity between the modified noun distributions for any two adjectives, namely Kendall's τ coefficient [7] for two random variables with paired observations. In our case, the two random variables are the two adjectives we are comparing, and each paired observation is their frequency of co-occurrence with a given noun. Kendall's τ coefficient compares the two variables by repeatedly comparing two pairs of their corresponding observations. Formally, if (X_i,Y_i) and (X_j,Y_j) are two pairs of observations for the adjectives X and Y on the nouns i and j respectively, we call these pairs **concordant** if $X_i>X_j$ and $Y_i>Y_j$ or if $X_i<X_j$ and $Y_i<Y_j$; otherwise these pairs are **discordant*****. If the distributions for the two adjectives are similar, we expect a large number of concordances, and a small number of discordances.

Kendall's τ is defined as

$$\tau = p_c - p_d$$

where p_c and p_d are the probabilities of observing a concordance or discordance respectively. τ ranges from -1 to +1, with +1 indicating complete concordance, -1 complete discordance, and 0 no correlation between X and Y.

An unbiased estimator of τ is the statistic

$$T = \frac{C-Q}{\binom{n}{2}}$$

where n is the number of paired observations in the sample and C and Q are the numbers of observed concordances and discordances respectively [8]. We compute T for each pair of adjectives, adjusting for possible ties in the values

*Note that sequences such as *blue-green* are usually hyphenated and thus better considered as a compound.

**We thank Diane Litman and Donald Hindle for providing us with access to the parser at AT&T Bell Labs.

***We discard pairs of observations where $X_i=X_j$ or $Y_i=Y_j$.

of each variable. We determine concordances and discordances by sorting the pairs of observations (noun frequencies) on one of the variables (adjectives), and computing how many of the $\binom{n}{2}$ pairs of paired observations agree or disagree with the expected order on the other adjective. We normalize the result to the range 0 to 1 using a simple linear transformation.

After the similarities have been computed for any pair of adjectives, we utilize the knowledge offered by the observed adjective-adjective pairs; we know that the adjectives which appear in any such pair cannot be part of the same group, so we set their similarity to 0, overriding the similarity produced by τ.

2.3. Stage Three: Clustering The Adjectives

In stage three we first convert the similarities to dissimilarities and then apply a non-hierarchical clustering algorithm. Such algorithms are in general stronger than hierarchical methods [9]. The number of clusters produced is an input parameter. We define dissimilarity as (1 - similarity), with the additional provision that pairs of adjectives with similarity 0 are given a higher dissimilarity value than 1. This ensures that these adjectives will never be placed in the same cluster; recall that they were determined to be definitively dissimilar based on linguistic data.

The algorithm uses the exchange method [10] since the more commonly used K-means method [9] is not applicable; the K-means method, like all centroid methods, requires the measure d between the clustered objects to be a distance; this means, among other conditions, that for any three objects x, y, and z the triangle inequality applies. However, this inequality does not necessarily hold for our dissimilarity measure. If the adjectives x and y were observed in the same minimal NP, their dissimilarity is quite large. If neither z and x nor z and y were found in the same minimal NP, then it is quite possible that the sum of their dissimilarities could be less than the dissimilarity between x and y.

The algorithm tries to produce a partition of the set of adjectives in such a way that adjectives with high dissimilarities are placed in different clusters. This is accomplished by minimizing an **objective function** Φ which scores a partition $\mathcal{P}$. The objective function we use is

$$\Phi(\mathcal{P}) = \sum_{C \in \mathcal{P}} \left[\frac{1}{|C|} \sum_{x,y \in C} d(x,y) \right]$$

The algorithm starts by producing a random partition of the adjectives, computing its Φ value and then computing for each adjective the improvement in Φ for every cluster where it can be moved; if there is at least one move for an adjective that leads to an overall improvement of Φ, then the adjective is moved to the cluster that yields the best improvement and the next adjective is considered. This procedure is repeated until no more moves lead to an improvement of Φ.

This is a hill-climbing method and therefore is guaranteed to converge, but it may lead to a local minimum of Φ, inferior to the global minimum that corresponds to the optimal solution. To alleviate this problem, the partitioning algorithm is called repeatedly with different random starting partitions and the best solution in these runs is kept. It should be noted that the problem of computing the optimal solution is NP-complete, as a generalization of the basic NP-complete clustering problem [11].

antitrust	new
big	old
economic	political
financial	potential
foreign	real
global	serious
international	severe
legal	staggering
little	technical
major	unexpected
mechanical	

Figure 1: Adjectives to be grouped.

3. RESULTS

We tested our system on a 8.2 million word corpus of stock market reports from the AP news wire[****]. A subset of 21 of the adjectives in the corpus (Figure 1) was selected for practical reasons (mainly for keeping the evaluation task tractable). We selected adjectives that have one modified noun in common (*problem*) to ensure some semantic relatedness, and we included only adjectives that occurred frequently so that our similarity measure would be meaningful.

The partition produced by the system for 9 clusters appears in Figure 2. Since the number of clusters is not determined by the system, we present the partition with a similar number of clusters as humans used for the same set of adjectives (the average number of clusters in the human-made models was 8.56).

Before presenting a formal evaluation of the results, we note that this partition contains interesting data. First, the results contain two clusters of gradable adjectives which fall in the same scale. Groups 5 and 8 contain adjectives that indicate the size, or scope, of a problem; by augmenting the system with tests to identify when an adjective is gradable, we could separate out these two groups from other potential scales, and perhaps consider combining them. Second, groups 1 and 6 clearly identify separate sets of non-gradable, non-scalar adjectives; the former group contains adjectives that describe the geographical scope of the problem, while the latter contains adjectives that

[****]We thank Karen Kukich and Frank Smadja for providing us access to the corpus.

	Answer should be Yes	Answer should be No
The system says Yes	a	b
The system says No	c	d

Table 1: Contingency table model for evaluation.

1. foreign global international
2. old
3. potential
4. new real unexpected
5. little staggering
6. economic financial mechanical political technical
7. antitrust
8. big major serious severe
9. legal

Figure 2: Partition found for 9 clusters.

specify the nature of the problem. It is interesting to note here that the expected number of adjectives per cluster is $\frac{21}{9} \approx 2.33$, and the clustering algorithm employed discourages long groups; nevertheless, the evidence for the adjectives in group 6 is strong enough to allow the creation of a group with more than twice the expected number of members. Finally, note that even in group 4 which is the weakest group produced, there is a positive semantic correlation between the adjectives *new* and *unexpected.* To summarize, the system seems to be able to identify many of the existent semantic relationships among the adjectives, while its mistakes are limited to creating singleton groups containing adjectives that are related to other adjectives in the test set (e.g., missing the semantic associations between *new-old* and *potential-real*) and ''recognizing'' a non-significant relationship between *real* and *new-unexpected* in group 4.

We produced good results with relatively little data; the accuracy of the results can be improved if a larger, homogeneous corpus is used to provide the raw data. Furthermore, some of the associations between adjectives that the system reports appear to be more stable than others, e.g. when we vary the number of clusters in the partition. We have noticed that adjectives with a higher degree of semantic content (e.g. *international* or *severe*) appear to form more stable associations than relatively semantically empty adjectives (e.g. *little* or *real*). This observation can be used to actually filter out the adjectives which are too general to be meaningfully clustered in groups.

4. EVALUATION

To evaluate the performance of our system we compared its output to a model solution for the problem designed by humans. Nine human judges were presented with the set of adjectives to be partitioned, a description of the domain, and a simple example. They were told that clusters should not overlap but they could select any number of clusters.

For our scoring mechanism, we converted the comparison of two partitions to a series of yes-no questions, each of which has a correct answer (as dictated by the model) and an answer assigned by the system. For each pair of adjectives, we asked if they fell in the same cluster (''yes'') or not (''no''). Since human judges did not always agree, we used fractional values for the correctness of each answer instead of 0 (''incorrect'') and 1 (''correct''). We used multiple human models for the same set of adjectives and defined the correctness of each answer as the relative frequency of the association between the two adjectives among the human models. We then sum these correctness values; in the case of perfect agreement between the models, or of only one model, the measures reduce to their original definition.

Then, the contingency table model [12], widely used in Information Retrieval, is applicable. Referring to the classification of the yes-no answers in Table 1, the following measures are defined :

- Recall $= \frac{a}{a+c} \cdot 100\%$
- Precision $= \frac{a}{a+b} \cdot 100\%$
- Fallout $= \frac{b}{b+d} \cdot 100\%$

In other words, recall is the percentage of correct ''yes'' answers that the system found among the model ''yes'' answers, precision is the percentage of correct ''yes'' answers among the total of ''yes'' answers that the system reported, and fallout is the percentage of incorrect ''yes'' answers relative to the total number of ''no'' answers[*****]. We also compute a combined measure for recall and precision, the F-measure [13], which always takes a value between the values of recall and precision, and is higher when recall and precision are closer; it is defined as

[*****] Another measure used in information retrieval, **overgeneration**, is in our case always equal to (100 - precision)%.

	Recall	Precision	Fallout	F-measure (β=1)
7 clusters	50.78%	43.56%	7.48%	46.89%
8 clusters	37.31%	38.10%	6.89%	37.70%
9 clusters	49.74%	46.38%	6.54%	48.00%
10 clusters	35.23%	41.98%	5.54%	38.31%

Table 2: Evaluation results.

$$F = \frac{(\beta^2+1) \times \text{Precision} \times \text{Recall}}{\beta^2 \times \text{Precision} + \text{Recall}}$$

where β is the weight of recall relative to precision; we use β=1.0, which corresponds to equal weighting of the two measures.

The results of applying our evaluation method to the system output (Figure 2) are shown in Table 2, which also includes the scores obtained for several other sub-optimal choices of the number of clusters. We have made these observations related to the evaluation mechanism :

1. Recall is inversely related to fallout and precision. Decreasing the number of clusters generally increases the recall and fallout and simultaneously decreases precision.
2. We have found fallout to be a better measure overall than precision, since, in addition to its decision-theoretic advantages [12], it appears to be more consistent across evaluations of partitions with different numbers of clusters. This has also been reported by other researchers in different evaluation problems [14].
3. For comparison, we evaluated each human model against all the other models, using the above evaluation method; the results ranged from 38 to 72% for recall, 1 to 12% for fallout, 38 to 81% for precision, and, covering a remarkably short range, 49 to 59% for the F-measure, indicating that the performance of the system is not far behind human performance.

Finally, before interpreting the scores produced by our evaluation module, we need to understand how they vary as the partition gets better or worse, and what are the limits of their values. Because of the multiple models used, perfect scores are not attainable. Also, because each pair of adjectives in a cluster is considered an observed association, the relationship between the number of associations produced by a cluster and the number of adjectives in the cluster is not linear (a cluster with k adjectives will produce $\binom{k}{2} = O(k^2)$ associations). This leads to lower values of recall, since moving a single adjective out of a cluster with k elements in the model will cause the system to miss k-1 associations. In general, defining a scoring mechanism that compares one partition to another is a hard problem.

To quantify these observations, we performed a Monte Carlo analysis [15] for the evaluation metrics, by repeatedly creating random partitions of the sample adjectives and evaluating the results. Then we estimated a (smoothed) probability density function for each metric from the resulting histograms; part of the results obtained are shown in Figure 3 for F-measure and fallout using 9 clusters. We observed that the system's performance (indicated by a square in the diagrams) was significantly better than what we would expect under the null hypothesis of random performance; the probability of getting a better partition than the system's is extremely small for all metrics (no occurrence in 20,000 trials) except for fallout, for which a random system may be better 4.9% of the time. The estimated density functions also show that the metrics are severely constrained by the structure imposed by the clustering as they tend to peak at some point and then fall rapidly.

5. CONCLUSIONS AND FUTURE WORK

We have described a system for extracting groups of semantically related adjectives from large text corpora. Our evaluation reveals that it has significantly high performance levels, comparable to human models. Its results can be filtered to produce scalar adjectives that are applicable in any given domain.

Eventually, we plan to use the system output to augment adjective entries in a lexicon and test the augmented lexicon in an application such as language generation. In addition, we have identified many directions for improving the quality of our output:

- Investigating non-linear methods for converting similarities to dissimilarities.
- Experimenting with different evaluation models, preferably ones based on the goodness of each cluster and not of each association.
- Developing methods for automatically selecting the desired number of clusters for the produced partition. Although this is a particularly hard problem, a steepest-descent method based on the tangent of the objective function may offer a solution.
- Investigating additional sources of linguistic

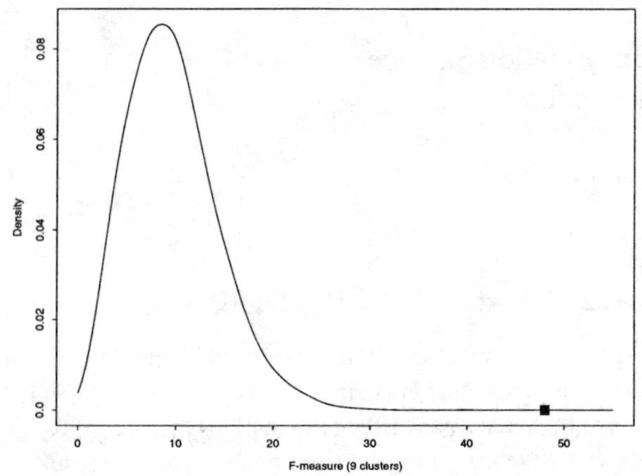

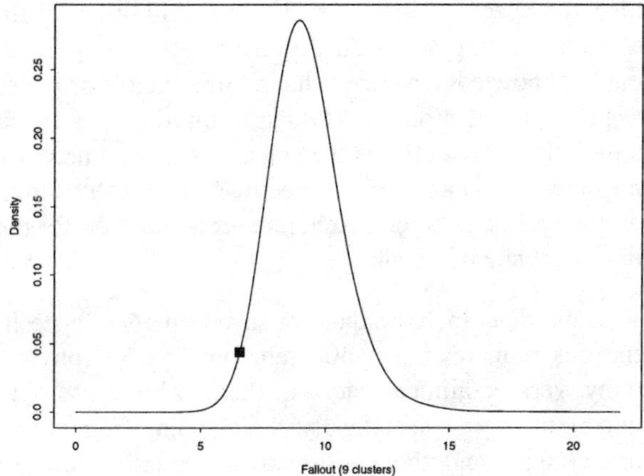

Figure 3: Estimated probability densities for F-measure and fallout with 9 clusters.

knowledge, such as the use of conjunctions and adverb-adjective pairs.

- Augmenting the system with tests particular to scalar adjectives; for example, exploiting gradability, checking whether two adjectives are antonymous (essentially developing tests in the opposite direction of the work by Justeson and Katz [16]), or comparing the relative semantic strength of two adjectives.

ACKNOWLEDGEMENTS

This work was supported jointly by DARPA and ONR under contract N00014-89-J-1782, by NSF GER-90-24069, and by New York State Center for Advanced Technology Contract NYSSTF-CAT(91)-053.

REFERENCES

1. Levinson, S.C., *Pragmatics,* Cambridge University Press, Cambridge, England, 1983.

2. Horn, L., ''A Presuppositional Analysis of *Only* and *Even*'', *Papers from the Fifth Regional Meeting*, Chicago Linguistics Society, 1969, pp. 98-107.

3. Bolinger, D., *Neutrality, Norm, and Bias,* Indiana University Linguistics Club, Bloomington, IN, 1977.

4. Smadja, F., *Retrieving Collocational Knowledge from Textual Corpora. An Application: Language Generation,* PhD dissertation, Department of Computer Science, Columbia University, 1991.

5. Brown P., Della Pietra V., deSouza P., Lai J., and Mercer R., ''Class-based n-gram Models of Natural Language'', *Computational Linguistics*, Vol. 18:4, 1992, pp. 467-479.

6. Hindle, D. M., ''Acquiring Disambiguation Rules from Text'', *Proceedings of the 27th meeting of the Association for Computational Linguistics*, Vancouver, B.C., 1989, pp. 118-125.

7. Kendall, M.G., ''A New Measure of Rank Correlation'', *Biometrika*, Vol. 30, 1938, pp. 81-93.

8. Wayne, D.W., *Applied Nonparametric Statistics (2nd edition),* PWS-KENT Publishing Company, Boston, The Duxbury Advanced Series in Statistics and Decision Sciences, 1990.

9. Kaufman, L. and Rousseeuw, P.J., *Finding Groups in Data: An Introduction to Cluster Analysis,* Wiley, New York, Wiley Series in Probability and Mathematical Statistics, 1990.

10. Spath, Helmuth, *Cluster Dissection and Analysis : Theory, FORTRAN Programs, Examples,* Ellis Horwood, Chichester, West Sussex, England, Ellis Horwood Series in Computers and their Applications, 1985.

11. Brucker, P., ''On the complexity of clustering problems'', in *Optimierung und Operations Research,* Henn, R., Korte, B., and Oletti, W., eds., Springer, Berlin, Lecture Notes in Economics and Mathematical Systems, 1978.

12. Swets, J.A., ''Effectiveness of Information Retrieval Methods'', *American Documentation*, Vol. 20, January 1969, pp. 72-89.

13. Van Rijsbergen, C.J., *Information Retrieval (2nd edition),* Butterwoths, London, 1979.

14. Lewis, D. and Tong, R., ''Text Filtering in MUC-3 and MUC-4'', *Proceedings of the Fourth Message Understanding Conference (MUC-4)*, DARPA Software and Intelligent Systems Technology Office, 1992, pp. 51-66.

15. Rubinstein, R.Y., *Simulation and the Monte Carlo method,* Wiley, New York, Wiley Series in Probability and Mathematical Statistics, 1981.

16. Justeson, J.S. and Katz, S.M., ''Co-occurences of Antonymous Adjectives and Their Contexts'', *Computational Linguistics*, Vol. 17:1, 1991, pp. 1-19.

SEMANTIC CLASSES AND SYNTACTIC AMBIGUITY

*Philip Resnik**

Department of Computer and Information Science
University of Pennsylvania
Philadelphia, PA 19104
resnik@linc.cis.upenn.edu

ABSTRACT

In this paper we propose to define selectional preference and semantic similarity as information-theoretic relationships involving conceptual classes, and we demonstrate the applicability of these definitions to the resolution of syntactic ambiguity. The space of classes is defined using WordNet [8], and conceptual relationships are determined by means of statistical analysis using parsed text in the Penn Treebank.

1. INTRODUCTION

The problem of syntactic ambiguity is a pervasive one. As Church and Patil [2] point out, the class of "every way ambiguous" constructions — those for which the number of analyses is the number of binary trees over the terminal elements — includes such frequent constructions as prepositional phrases, coordination, and nominal compounds. They suggest that until it has more useful constraints for resolving ambiguities, a parser can do little better than to efficiently record all the possible attachments and move on.

In general, it may be that such constraints can only be supplied by analysis of the context, domain-dependent knowledge, or other complex inferential processes. However, we will suggest that in many cases, syntactic ambiguity can be resolved with the help of an extremely limited form of semantic knowledge, closely tied to the lexical items in the sentence.

We focus on two relationships: selectional preference and semantic similarity. From one perspective, the proposals here can be viewed as an attempt to provide new formalizations for familiar but seldom carefully defined linguistic notions; elsewhere we demonstrate the utility of this approach in linguistic explanation [11]. From another perspective, the work reported here can be viewed as an attempt to generalize statistical natural language techniques based on lexical associations, using knowledge-based rather than distributionally derived word classes.

*This research has been supported by an IBM graduate fellowship and by DARPA grant N00014-90-J-1863. The comments of Eric Brill, Marti Hearst, Jamie Henderson, Aravind Joshi, Mark Liberman, Mitch Marcus, Michael Niv, and David Yarowsky are gratefully acknowledged.

2. CLASS-BASED STATISTICS

A number of researchers have explored using lexical co-occurrences in text corpora to induce word classes [1, 5, 9, 12], with results that are generally evaluated by inspecting the semantic cohesiveness of the distributional classes that result. In this work, we are investigating the alternative of using WordNet, an explicitly semantic, broad coverage lexical database, to define the space of semantic classes. Although WordNet is subject to the attendant disadvantages of any hand-constructed knowledge base, we have found that it provides an acceptable foundation upon which to build corpus-based techniques [10]. This affords us a clear distinction between domain-independent and corpus-specific sources of information, and a well-understood taxonomic representation for the domain-independent knowledge.

Although WordNet includes data for several parts of speech, and encodes numerous semantic relationships (meronymy, antonymy, verb entailment, etc.), in this work we use only the noun taxonomy — specifically, the mapping from words to word classes, and the traditional IS-A relationship between classes. For example, the word *newspaper* belongs to the classes ⟨newsprint⟩ and ⟨paper⟩, among others, and these are immediate subclasses of ⟨material⟩ and ⟨publisher⟩, respectively.[1]

Class frequencies are estimated on the basis of lexical frequencies in text corpora. The frequency of a class c is estimated using the lexical frequencies of its members, as follows:

$$\text{freq}(c) = \sum_{\{n \mid n \text{ is subsumed by } c\}} \text{freq}(n) \qquad (1)$$

The class probabilities used in the section that follows can then be estimated by simply normalizing (MLE) or by other methods such as Good-Turing [3].[2]

[1]For expository convenience we identify WordNet noun classes using a single descriptive word in angle brackets. However, the internal representation assigns each class a unique identifier.

[2]We use Good-Turing. Note, however, that WordNet classes are not necessarily disjoint; space limitations preclude further discussion of this complication here.

3. CONCEPTUAL RELATIONSHIPS

3.1. Selectional Preference

The term "selectional preference" has been used by linguists to characterize the source of anomaly in sentences such as (1b), and more generally to describe a class of restrictions on co-occurrence that is orthogonal to syntactic constraints.

(1) a. John admires sincerity.
    b. Sincerity admires John.

(2) a. Mary drank some wine.
    b. Mary drank some gasoline.
    c. Mary drank some pencils.
    d. Mary drank some sadness.

Although selectional preference is traditionally formalized in terms of feature agreement using notations like [+Animate], such formalizations often fail to specify the set of allowable features, or to capture the gradedness of qualitative differences such as those in (2).

As an alternative, we have proposed the following formalization of selectional preference [11]:

Definition. The *selectional preference* of w for C is the relative entropy (Kullback-Leibler distance) between the prior distribution Pr(C) and the posterior distribution Pr(C | w).

$$\mathrm{D}(\Pr(C|w)\ ||\ \Pr(C)) = \sum_c \Pr(c|w)\log\frac{\Pr(c|w)}{\Pr(c)} \quad (2)$$

$$= \sum_c \Pr(c|w)\,\mathrm{I}(c;w) \quad (3)$$

Here w is a word with selectional properties, C ranges over semantic classes, and co-occurrences are counted with respect to a particular argument — e.g. verbs and direct objects, nominal modifiers and the head noun they modify, and so forth. Intuitively, this definition works by comparing the distribution of argument classes *without* knowing what the word is (e.g., the *a priori* likelihood of classes in direct object position), to the distribution *with respect to* the word. If these distributions are very different, as measured by relative entropy, then the word has a strong influence on what can or cannot appear in that argument position, and we say that it has a strong selectional preference for that argument.

The "goodness of fit" between a word and a particular class of arguments is captured by the following definition:

Definition. The *selectional association* of w with c is the contribution c makes to the selectional preference of w.

$$A(w,c) = \frac{\Pr(c|w)\log\frac{\Pr(c|w)}{\Pr(c)}}{\mathrm{D}(\Pr(C|w)\ ||\ \Pr(C))} \quad (4)$$

The selectional association $A(w_1, w_2)$ of two words is taken to be the maximum of $A(w_1, c)$ over all classes c to which w_2 belongs.

VERB, ARGUMENT	"BEST" ARGUMENT CLASS	A
drink wine	⟨beverage⟩	0.088
drink gasoline	⟨substance⟩	0.075
drink pencil	⟨object⟩	0.030
drink sadness	⟨psychological_feature⟩	-0.001

The above table illustrates how this definition captures the qualitative differences in example (2). The "best" class for an argument is the class that maximizes selectional association. Notice that finding that class represents a form of sense disambiguation using local context (cf. [15]): of all the classes to which the noun *wine* belongs — including ⟨alcohol⟩, ⟨substance⟩, ⟨red⟩, and ⟨color⟩, among others — the class ⟨beverage⟩ is the sense of *wine* most appropriate as a direct object for *drink*.

3.2. Semantic Similarity

Any number of factors influence judgements of semantic similarity between two nouns. Here we propose to use only one source of information: the relationship between classes in the WordNet IS-A taxonomy. Intuitively, two noun classes can be considered similar when there is a single, specific class that subsumes them both — if you have to travel very high in the taxonomy to find a class that subsumes both classes, in the extreme case all the way to the top, then they cannot have all that much in common. For example, ⟨nickel⟩and ⟨dime⟩ are both immediately subsumed by ⟨coin⟩, whereas the most specific superclass that ⟨nickel⟩ and ⟨mortgage⟩ share is ⟨possession⟩.

The difficulty, of course, is how to determine which superclass is "most specific." Simply counting IS-A links in the taxonomy can be misleading, since a single link can represent a fine-grained distinction in one part of the taxonomy (e.g. ⟨zebra⟩ IS-A ⟨equine⟩) and a very large distinction elsewhere (e.g. ⟨carcinogen⟩ IS-A ⟨substance⟩).

Rather than counting links, we use the *information content* of a class to measure its specificity (i.e., $-\log \Pr(c)$); this permits us to define noun similarity as follows:

Definition. The *semantic similarity* of n_1 and n_2 is

$$\mathrm{sim}(n_1, n_2) = \sum_i \alpha_i[-\log \Pr(c_i)], \quad (5)$$

where $\{c_i\}$ is the set of classes dominating both n_1 and n_2. The α_i, which sum to 1, are used to weight the contribution of each class — for example, in accordance with word sense probabilities. In the absence of word sense constraints we can compute the "globally" most specific class simply by setting α_i to 1 for the class maximizing $[-\log \Pr(c)]$, and 0 otherwise. For example, according to that "global" measure, sim(*nickel,dime*) = 12.71 (= – log Pr($\langle coin \rangle$)) and sim(*nickel,mortgage*) = 7.61 (= – log Pr($\langle possession \rangle$)).

4. SYNTACTIC AMBIGUITY

4.1. Coordination and Nominal Compounds

Having proposed formalizations of selectional preference and semantic similarity as information-theoretic relationships involving conceptual classes, we now turn to the application of these ideas to the resolution of syntactic ambiguity.

Ambiguous coordination is a common source of parsing difficulty. In this study, we investigated the application of class-based statistical methods to a particular subset of coordinations, noun phrase conjunctions of the form *noun1 and noun2 noun3*, as in (3):

(3) a. a (bank and warehouse) guard
b. a (policeman) and (park guard)

Such structures admit two analyses, one in which *noun1* and *noun2* are the two heads being conjoined (3a) and one in which the conjoined heads are *noun1* and *noun3* (3b).

As pointed out by Kurohashi and Nagao [7], similarity of form and similarity of meaning are important cues to conjoinability. In English, similarity of form is to a great extent captured by agreement in number:

(4) a. several *business* and *university* groups
b. several *businesses* and university *groups*

Semantic similarity of the conjoined heads also appears to play an important role:

(5) a. a *television* and *radio* personality
b. a *psychologist* and sex *researcher*

In addition, for this particular construction, the appropriateness of noun-noun modification for *noun1* and *noun3* is relevant:

(6) a. *mail* and securities *fraud*
b. *corn* and peanut *butter*

We investigated the roles of these cues by conducting a disambiguation experiment using the definitions in the previous section. Two sets of 100 noun phrases of the form [NP *noun1 and noun2 noun3*] were extracted from the *Wall Street Journal* (WSJ) corpus in the Penn Treebank and disambiguated by hand, with one set to be used for development and the other for testing.[3] A set of simple transformations were applied to all WSJ data, including the mapping of all proper names to the token *someone*, the expansion of month abbreviations, and the reduction of all nouns to their root forms.

Similarity of form, defined as agreement of number, was determined using a simple analysis of suffixes in combination with WordNet's database of nouns and noun exceptions. Similarity of meaning was determined "globally" as in equation (5) and the example that followed; noun class probabilities were estimated using a sample of approximately 800,000 noun occurrences in Associated Press newswire stories.[4] For the purpose of determining semantic similarity, nouns not in WordNet were treated as instances of the class ⟨thing⟩. Appropriateness of noun-noun modification was determined using selectional association as defined in equation (4), with co-occurrence frequencies calculated using a sample of approximately 15,000 noun-noun compounds extracted from the WSJ corpus. (This sample did not include the test data.) Both selection of the modifier for the head and selection of the head for the modifier were considered.

Each of the three sources of information — form similarity, meaning similarity, and modification relationships — was used alone as a disambiguation strategy, as follows:

- Form:
  - If noun1 and noun2 match in number and noun1 and noun3 do not then conjoin noun1 and noun2;
  - if noun1 and noun3 match in number and noun1 and noun2 do not then conjoin noun1 and noun3;
  - otherwise remain undecided.
- Meaning:
  - If sim(noun1,noun2) > sim(noun1,noun3) then conjoin noun1 and noun2;
  - if sim(noun1,noun3) > sim(noun1,noun2) then conjoin noun1 and noun3;
  - otherwise remain undecided.
- Modification:
  - If A(noun1,noun3) > τ, a threshold, *or* if A(noun3,noun1) > τ, then conjoin noun1 and noun3;
  - If A(noun1,noun3) < σ *and* A(noun3,noun1) < σ then conjoin noun1 and noun2;
  - otherwise remain undecided.[5]

In addition, we investigated several methods for combining the three sources of information. These included: (a) "backing off" (i.e., given the form, modification, and meaning

[3] Hand disambiguation was necessary because the Penn Treebank does not encode NP-internal structure. These phrases were disambiguated using the full sentence in which they occurred, plus the previous and following sentence, as context.

[4] I am grateful to Donald Hindle for making these data available.

[5] Thresholds τ and σ were fixed before evaluating the test data.

strategies in that order, use the first strategy that isn't undecided); (b) taking a "vote" among the three strategies and choosing the majority; (c) classifying using the results of a linear regression; and (d) constructing a decision tree classifier.

The training set contained a bias in favor of conjoining *noun1* and *noun2*, so a "default" strategy — always choosing that bracketing — was used as a baseline. The results are as follows:

STRATEGY	ANSWERED (%)	PRECISION (%)
Default	100.0	66.0
Form	53.0	90.6
Modification	75.0	69.3
Meaning	66.0	71.2
Backing off	95.0	81.1
Voting	89.0	78.7
Regression	100.0	79.0
ID3 Tree	100.0	80.0

Not surprisingly, the individual strategies perform reasonably well on the instances they can classify, but recall is poor; the strategy based on similarity of form is highly accurate, but arrives at an answer only half the time. Of the combined strategies, the "backing off" approach succeeds in answering 95% of the time and achieving 81.1% precision — a reduction of 44.4% in the baseline error rate.

We have recently begun to investigate the disambiguation of more complex coordinations of the form [NP *noun1 noun2 and noun3 noun4*], which permit five possible bracketings:

(7) a. freshman ((business and marketing) major)
b. (food (handling and storage)) procedures
c. ((mail fraud) and bribery) charges

d. Clorets (gum and (breath mints))
e. (baby food) and (puppy chow)

These bracketings comprise two groups, those that conjoin *noun2* and *noun3* (a–c) and those that conjoin *noun2* and *noun4* (d–e). Rather than tackling the five-way disambiguation problem immediately, we began with an experimental task of classifying a noun phrase as belonging to one of these two groups.

We examined three classification strategies. First, we used the form-based strategy described above. Second, as before, we used a strategy based on semantic similarity; this time, however, selectional association was used to determine the α_i in equation (5), incorporating modifier-head relationships into the semantic similarity strategy. Third, we used "backing off" (from form similarity to semantic similarity) to combine the two individual strategies. As before, one set of items was used for development, and another set (89 items) was set aside for testing. As a baseline, results were evaluated against a simple default strategy of always choosing the group that was more common in the development set.

STRATEGY	ANSWERED (%)	PRECISION (%)
Default	100.0	44.9
Form	40.4	80.6
Meaning	69.7	77.4
Backing off	85.4	81.6

In this case, the default strategy defined using the development set was misleading, leading to worse than chance precision. However, even if default choices were made using the bias found in the test set, precision would be only 55.1%. The results in the above table make it clear that the strategies using form and meaning are far more accurate, and that combining them leads to good coverage and precision.

The pattern of results in these two experiments demonstrates a significant reduction in syntactic misanalyses for this construction as compared to the simple baseline, and it confirms that form, meaning, and modification relationships all play a role in disambiguation. In addition, these results confirm the effectiveness of the proposed definitions of selectional preference and semantic similarity.

4.2. Prepositional Phrase Attachment[6]

Prepositional phrase attachment represents another important form of parsing ambiguity. Empirical investigation [14] suggests that lexical preferences play an important role in disambiguation, and Hindle and Rooth [5] have demonstrated that these preferences can be acquired and utilized using lexical co-occurrence statistics.

(8) a. They foresee little progress in exports.
b. [VP foresee [NP little progress [PP in exports]]]
c. [VP foresee [NP little progress] [PP in exports]]

Given an example such as (8a), Hindle and Rooth's "lexical association" strategy chooses between bracketings (8b) and (8c) by comparing $\Pr(in|foresee)$ with $\Pr(in|progress)$ and evaluating the direction and significance of the difference between the two conditional probabilities. The object of the preposition is ignored, presumably because the data would be far too sparse if it were included.

As Hearst and Church [4] observe, however, the object of the preposition can provide crucial information for determining attachment, as illustrated in (9):

(9) a. Britain reopened its embassy in December.
b. Britain reopened its embassy in Teheran.

[6]This section reports work done in collaboration with Marti A. Hearst.

Hoping to overcome the sparseness problem and use this information, we formulated a strategy of "conceptual association," according to which the objects of the verb and preposition are treated as members of semantic classes and the two potential attachment sites are evaluated using class-based rather than lexical statistics.

The alternative attachment sites — verb-attachment and noun-attachment — were evaluated according to the following criteria:

$$\text{vscore} = \text{freq(v,PP) I(v;PP)} \quad (6)$$

$$\text{nscore} = \text{freq(class1,PP) I(class1;PP)} \quad (7)$$

where PP is an abbreviation for (preposition,class2), and class1 and class2 are classes to which the object of the verb and object of the preposition belong, respectively. These scores were used rather than conditional probabilities Pr(PP | v) and Pr(PP | class1) because, given a set of possible classes to use as class2 (e.g. *export* is a member of ⟨export⟩, ⟨commerce⟩, ⟨group_action⟩, and ⟨human_action⟩), conditional probability will always favor the most general class. In contrast, comparing equations (6) and (7) with equation (4), the verb- and noun-attachment scores resemble the selectional association of the verb and noun with the prepositional phrase.

Because nouns belong to many classes, we required some way to combine scores obtained under different classifications. Rather than considering the entire cross-product of classifications for the object of the verb and the object of the preposition, we chose to first consider all possible classifications of the object of the preposition, and then to classify the object of the verb by choosing class1 so as to maximize I(class1;PP). For example, sentence (8a) yields the following classifications:

CLASS1	PP	NSCORE	VSCORE
⟨situation⟩	in ⟨export⟩	67.4	39.8
⟨rise⟩	in ⟨commerce⟩	178.3	23.8
⟨advance⟩	in ⟨group_action⟩	104.9	19.9
⟨advance⟩	in ⟨act⟩	149.5	40.6

The "conceptual association" strategy merges evidence from alternative classifications in an extremely simple way: by performing a paired samples t-test on the nscores and vscores, and preferring attachment to the noun if t is positive, and to the verb if negative. A combined strategy uses this preference if t is significant at $p < .1$, and otherwise uses the lexical association preference. For example (8a), $t(3) = 3.57, p < .05$, with (8b) being the resulting choice of bracketing.

We evaluated this technique using the Penn Treebank *Wall Street Journal* corpus, comparing the performance of lexical association alone (LA), conceptual association alone (CA), and the combined strategy (COMBINED) on a held-out set of 174 ambiguous cases. The results were as follows:

	LA	CA	COMBINED
% Correct	81.6	77.6	82.2

When the individual strategies were constrained to answer only when confident ($|t| > 2.1$ for lexical association, $p < .1$ for conceptual association), they performed as follows:

STRATEGY	Answered (%)	Precision (%)
LA	44.3	92.8
CA	67.2	84.6

Despite the fact that this experiment used an order of magnitude less training data than Hindle and Rooth's, their lexical association strategy performed quite a bit better than in the experiments reported in [5], presumably because this experiment used hand-disambiguated rather than heuristically disambiguated training data.

In this experiment, the bottom-line performance of the conceptual association strategy is worse than that of lexical association, and the combined strategy yields at best a marginal improvement. However, several observations are in order. First, the coverage and precision achieved by conceptual association demonstrate some utility of class information, since the lexical data are impossibly sparse when the object of the preposition is included. Second, a qualitative evaluation of what conceptual association actually did shows that it is capturing relevant relationships for disambiguation.

(10) To keep his schedule on track, he flies two personal secretaries in from Little Rock to *augment his staff in Dallas.*

For example, *augment* and *in* never co-occur in the training corpus, and neither do *staff* and *in*; as a result, the lexical association strategy makes an incorrect choice for the ambiguous verb phrase in (10). However, the conceptual association strategy makes the correct choice on the basis of the following classifications:

CLASS1	PP	NSCORE	VSCORE
⟨gathering⟩	in ⟨dallas⟩	38.18	45.54
⟨people⟩	in ⟨urban_area⟩	1200.21	28.46
⟨personnel⟩	in ⟨region⟩	314.62	23.38
⟨personnel⟩	in ⟨geographical_area⟩	106.05	26.80
⟨people⟩	in ⟨city⟩	1161.22	28.61
⟨personnel⟩	in ⟨location⟩	320.85	22.83

Third, mutual information appears to be a successful way to select appropriate classifications for the direct object, given a classification of the object of the preposition. For example, despite the fact that *staff* belongs to 25 classes in WordNet — including ⟨musical_notation⟩ and ⟨rod⟩, for instance — the classes to which it is assigned in the above table seem contextually appropriate. Finally, it is clear that in many instances the paired t-test, which effectively takes an unweighted average over multiple classifications, is a poor way to combine sources of evidence.

In two additional experiments, we examined the effect of semantic classes on robustness, since presumably a domain-independent source of noun classes should be able to mitigate the effects of a mismatch between training data and test data. In the first of these experiments, we used the WSJ training material, and tested on 173 instances from Associated Press newswire, with the following results:

	LA	CA	COMBINED
% Correct	69.9	72.3	72.8

STRATEGY	ANSWERED (%)	PRECISION (%)
LA	31.8	80.0
CA	49.7	77.9

In the second experiment, we retained the *test* material from the WSJ corpus, but trained on the Brown corpus material in the Penn Treebank. The results were as follows:

	LA	CA	COMBINED
% Correct	77.6	73.6	79.3

STRATEGY	ANSWERED (%)	PRECISION (%)
LA	35.6	85.5
CA	59.2	81.6

These additional experiments demonstrate large increases in coverage when confident (55–65%) with only moderate decreases in precision (< 5%). Overall, the results of the three experiments seem promising, and suggest that further work on conceptual association will yield improvements to disambiguation strategies using lexical association alone.

5. Conclusions

In this paper, we have used a knowledge-based conceptual taxonomy, together with corpus-based lexical statistics, to provide new formalizations of selectional preference and semantic similarity. Although a complete characterization of these and other semantic notions may ultimately turn out to require a full-fledged theory of meaning, lexical-conceptual representation, and inference, we hope to have shown that a great deal can be accomplished using a simple semantic representation combined with appropriate information-theoretic ideas. Conversely, we also hope to have shown the utility of knowledge-based semantic classes in arriving at a statistical characterization of linguistic phenomena, as compared to purely distributional methods. A detailed comparison of knowledge-based and distributionally-derived word classes is needed in order to assess the advantages and disadvantages of each approach.

"Every way ambiguous" constructions form a natural class of practical problems to investigate using class-based statistical techniques. The present results are promising, and we are exploring improvements to the particular algorithms and results illustrated here. In future work we hope to investigate other ambiguous constructions, and to explore the implications of selectional preference for word-sense disambiguation.

References

1. Brown, P., V. Della Pietra, P. deSouza, J. Lai, and R. Mercer, "Class-based N-gram Models of Natural Language," Computational Linguistics 18(4), December, 1992.
2. Church, K. W. and R. Patil, "Coping with Syntactic Ambiguity or How to Put the Block in the Box on the Table," American Journal of Computational Linguistics, 8(3-4), 1982.
3. Good, I.J., "The Population Frequencies of Species and the Estimation of Population Parameters," Biometrika 40(3 and 4), pp. 237-264, (1953).
4. Hearst, M. A. and K. W. Church, "An Investigation of the Use of Lexical Associations for Prepositional Phrase Attachment," in preparation.
5. Hindle, D., "Noun Classification from Predicate-Argument Structures," *Proceedings of the 28th Annual Meeting of the Assocation of Computational Linguistics*, 1990.
6. Hindle, D. and M. Rooth, "Structural Ambiguity and Lexical Relations," *Proceedings of the 29th Annual Meeting of the Association for Computational Linguistics*, 1991.
7. Kurohashi, S. and M. Nagao, "Dynamic Programming Method for Analyzing Conjunctive Structures in Japanese," Proceedings of COLING–92, Nantes, France, August, 1992.
8. Miller, G. A., "WordNet: An On-Line Lexical Database," International Journal of Lexicography 3(4), 1990.
9. Pereira, Fernando and Naftali Tishby, "Distributional Similarity, Phase Transitions and Hierarchical Clustering," presented at the AAAI Fall Symposium on Probabilistic Approaches to Natural Language, Cambridge, Massachusetts, October, 1992.
10. Resnik, Philip, "WordNet and Distributional Analysis: A Class-based Approach to Lexical Discovery," AAAI Workshop on Statistically-based NLP Techniques, San Jose, California, July, 1992.
11. Resnik, Philip, "Selectional Preference and Implicit Objects," CUNY Sentence Processing Conference, Amherst, Massachusetts, March, 1993.
12. Schuetze, Hinrich, "Word Space," in Hanson, S. J., J. D. Cowan, and C. L. Giles (eds.) *Advances in Neural Information Processing Systems 5*, Morgan Kaufmann, to appear.
13. Weischedel, R., M. Meteer, R. Schwartz, and J. Palmucci, "Coping with Ambiguity and Unknown Words through Probabilistic Models," DARPA workshop, 1989.
14. Whittemore, G., K. Ferrara,and H. Bruner, "Empirical Study of Predictive Powers of Simple AttachmentSchemes for Post-modifier Prepositional Phrases," *Proceedings of the 28th Annual Meeting of the Assocation of Computational Linguistics*, 1990.
15. Yarowsky, David, "One Sense Per Collocation," this volume.
16. Zernik, Uri, ed., *Lexical Acquisition: Using On-line Resources to Build a Lexicon*, Lawrence Erlbaum, 1991.

SESSION 9: GOVERNMENT PANEL

Carol J. Van Ess-Dykema, Chair

U.S. Department of Defense
Fort Meade, Maryland

1. ABSTRACT

The purpose of the Government Panel session is to inform the research community about Human Language Technology research sponsored by the individual Government agencies that the panelists represent. The researchers gain a better understanding of the potential market beyond ARPA, for their research skills and product. Government agencies who may need what the researchers can offer benefit when the informed researchers contact the agencies. In the climate of declining Government funding for the Defense Department, the Session Chair noted that the contracts will be fewer and go to the contractors who are most knowledgable about the research that is going on Government-wide and to those who are knowledgeable about how their skills and products can meet Government user needs. The Government Panel session was moved closer to the middle of the agenda this year to facilitate continued discussion among the panelists and other Government representatives present, with the research community, before the Workshop ended.

2. PANEL STATEMENTS

Dr. Helen Gigley, Head of the Human-Computer Interaction Laboratory at the Naval Research Laboratory, Washington, D.C., described Government-wide Human Language Technology needs and the role of researchers in meeting them. She specifically addressed Government Human Language Technology in terms of business uses and needs, military uses, and education/training needs. She pointed out that introducing technology does not necessarily increase effectiveness, arguing that we need to consider the impact of adopting technology before rather than after it is put in place. She cited the military need of real time and accurate speech processing performance and the lack of military commanders' trust of technology that might contain or produce errors. Lastly, she argued that researchers need to consider their contribution not only as a basic scientific result but as a result within society having social and moral implications.

Dr. Joseph Kielman, Chief Scientist at the Federal Bureau of Investigation (FBI), Washington, D.C., indicated that in the past the FBI had focussed significant resources on the intercept of spoken language and written text, with the first priority being to increase the efficiency or effectiveness of collection and distribution of data. He reported, however, that the situation was changing, identifying the following Human Language Technology capabilities to be of current interest to the FBI: 1) speech detection, 2) speaker and language recognition, 3) speech understanding, 4) text understanding and 5) machine translation. He reported that these technologies would be used to process language data in the domains of counter intelligence, terrorism and white collar crime, by FBI's personnel at headquarters, four regional data centers, 56 field offices, 400 resident agencies, permanent monitoring plants and temporary lookouts.

Dr. Susan Chipman, a Program Manager at the Office of Naval Research (ONR) in Arlington, Virginia, described the Cognitive Science Program research sponsored by ONR. She defined the ONR mission as one of improving naval training for its personnel. Two clusters of language-related research currently underway include tutorial discourse and improving the readability of instructional texts and documentation. She attributed the interest in emulating the effectiveness of human tutors with artificially intelligent computerized instructional systems, to the reported effectiveness of one-on-one tutorial instruction by human tutors. The need to improve text readability stems from the fact that the military services and their contractors produce enormous amounts of text, system documentation and training materials for the personnel who will operate and maintain those systems, and which must be readable and comprehensible by ONR personnel.

Dr. Jesse Fussell, Chief of the Communications Sciences Division, at the Department of Defense, Fort Meade, Maryland, identified both technical and nontechnical problems in technology transfer as well as making recommendations to the research community about how to stimulate the technology transfer process. He believes that insufficient study of the process of converting an algorithm from one domain, that is supported by a well defined and documented corpus, to a different operational domain, which may have little or no pre-marked training or testing data, is a technical problem that researchers still need to overcome. Nontechnical problems he believes still need to be overcome to achieve technology transfer include the researcher's lack of understanding of the customer's needs and operating procedures. He challenged the researchers to broaden their research efforts by producing prototype systems for extended evaluation in an operational setting.

Dr. Y. T. Chien, Director of the Information, Robotics and Intelligent Systems Division, at the National Science Foundation (NSF), Washington, D.C., defined NSF's mission as that of maintaining the health of the U.S. science and technology base. He contrasted NSF with ARPA, saying that NSF supports more and smaller projects, resulting in NSF being more broad-based than ARPA. He discussed the Clinton administration's technology policies, particularly the creation of a national information infrastructure which he noted will create societal needs in knowledge intensive activities. He encouraged researchers to add value to this national information infrastructure. He also encouraged them to act like researchers in the larger sciences and to define an aggressive research agenda for Human Language Technology.

3. AUDIENCE REACTIONS

The first question was if any of the panelists knew whether the Clinton administration planned to invest as much money in advanced technologies as has been invested by large companies in the past. Jess Fussell responded that only 7% of DoD's research and development budget was for research, in contrast to 93% for development. He said it was necessary for researchers to convince the developers that research is worthwhile. Joe Kielman stated that the FBI's budget had little research and development money but that he felt that by cooperation and collaboration among Government agencies, a worthwhile Government research effort could be continued. A Government representative in the audience from the National Institute of Standards and Technology (NIST) stated that the Department of Commerce may receive funding for high risk-high payoff "opportunistic" research.

One of the foreign visitors responded by stating she believed it was a government's responsibility to market technological research results. A discussion then ensued regarding the cost of deploying technology in the form of a product in the workplace. One researcher stated that technology could be sold more successfully to the Government if it were presented in the form of a visionary idea. Another researcher defined the customer as the person that can convince someone to take a risk and can provide the researchers access to real problems. In response to this latter comment, Joe Kielman responded that management is often loathe to take a risk without seeing a demonstration capability first.

The discussion then turned to an inquiry about collaboration between U.S. and foreign researchers in performing Human Language Technology research with a pedagogical emphasis. Y.T. Chien responded that based on his experience at NSF, there were many occasions when researchers declined to participate in an international exchange because they did not want to take a year off from their present endeavors.

The discussion period ended with a researcher's observation that the research community did not have access to real problems, and thus he called for better communication between researchers and users. Another researcher responded by citing the "dual use" principle advocated by the Clinton administration, as a way for researchers to lower the cost of technology transfer and to open the door for better researcher - user communication.

PROJECTED GOVERNMENT NEEDS IN HUMAN LANGUAGE TECHNOLOGY AND THE ROLE OF RESEARCHERS IN MEETING THEM

Helen M. Gigley, Ph.D.

Head, Human Computer Interaction Laboratory
Naval Research Laboratory
CODE 5530
Washington, D.C. 20375-5337

ABSTRACT[1]

After a brief discussion of current government uses and needs for human language technology, this paper will discuss the uses which will probably survive in the future as well as attempt to define some anticipated ones. Business uses, military uses, and education/training receive the most focus today. Current state of the art technologies are providing initial resources to enable better management of the above. Suggested critical efforts to make the technologies more appropriate for the tasks at hand in the government will be discussed. A tentative view of the role of researchers, in providing the basis to obtain adequate critical natural language technologies, will be presented.

1. CURRENT GOVERNMENT NEEDS IN HUMAN LANGUAGE TECHNOLOGY

The functions of government fall into three general classes:

1. business, both external and internal;
2. military, beyond the business uses; and
3. educational/training responsibilities.

One very important question related to determining current human language technology needs is to look at these three broad areas and to assess what technology exists today and how effectively it can be applied. Another equally important question which must be considered is, "Does technology help or hinder the functionality of the government?"

1.1 Human Language Technology and Current Government Business Needs

Government business needs are coextensive with operational business needs of the United States. Access to information, interpersonal communication, and joint work environments within government operations are all critical functional needs. Inter- and intra-agency coordination and information dissemination are critical to efficient and proper functioning of our government. When is natural language technology a suitable solution to maximize the effectiveness in these efforts? Some examples will shed light on the nature of our current human language technology capabilities and provide guidance on what still is needed even within our current government operations.

Information Management Functions of the Government:

- Access to personnel.
- Dissemination of information.
- Acquisition of information.
- Protection of access to information.

Communication Functions of the Government:

- External Communication Functions -- need to communicate with the general public and provide suitable responses not only in content but in presentation style.
- Internal Communication Functions -- communication of protocols, procedural modifications, relevant day to day operational changes.

  * Multi-language interaction facility where the interaction may be in any of several languages as well as translation capabilities.

  * Joint work environments where multiple decision making is enhanced via multi-tasking environments at distributed locations.

[1] The opinions and assertions in this paper are those of the author and are not to be construed as official or reflecting the views of the Department of the Navy.

Education/Training Functions of the Government:

- Required to maintain up-to-date knowledge of system operations and procedures.

- New personnel must be brought up to speed on how to function.

The bottom line for government-needed human language technology is that it should provide alternative resources for communication which increase the functional precision and response to enhance productivity.

1.2 Human Language Technology and Current Military Needs

Military human language technology needs include many of the logistical and business-type needs just mentioned. In addition, military needs include factors of real-time performance and secure access which are not absolute within business ones. The functions of military systems assume a different purpose. Presently, they also insist on a role for humans which many business functions attempt to minimize; these systems are Human-in-the-Loop Systems. Military systems enhance decision making, include dissemination of information having various forms, and often must work in real-time response arenas, under secure conditions. How to maximize the information capacity within Human-in-the-Loop decision support systems is a critical need. Human language technology has a vital part to play in providing this capability. Language capabilities need to function precisely, correctly, and efficiently in multiple modalities.

Military Decisions require real-time language facilities. Military decisions require integration of many types of information which exist in disparate forms. Language technologies provide a possible addition to current methods to increase the information available in stressful, short-response-time decision situations. A primary concern is to determine what language technologies to employ and under what conditions.

Security implications for human language technology appear chiefly as constraints on its use. Speech is available to all within range of its audible production. Its internal form may also be accessible. What language technologies maintain security and how might language technologies provide added secure access constraints? Voice recognition can be a key, but is it sufficient?

1.3 Human Language Technology and Education / Training Needs

Education and training needs in government function do not appear to be diminishing. Even though the work force might shrink, its demography is constantly changing. Meeting the challenge of developing suitably capable individuals from the current and future work force will greatly depend on how education needs for the entire U.S. are met.

Currently, demands on the government work force beyond physical plant maintenance and related in-house infrastructure function, minimally require language fluency in English. All positions require literacy in English. Second language fluency and literacy also have become a staffing criteria for some positions. All of these facts present problems for many individual's qualifications to work for the government.

Lack of language fluency and literacy will create a possible problem in the near future as older workers retire. Many of the tasks government workers perform are language based, whether accessing information, providing it, or collecting it. An issue is can we use technology to replace them? Do we want to? And if not, how will we guarantee that they can do the job? Training systems for language skills can be one viable solution. These systems will be multimodal and require all aspects of language function.

As an additional need for training and education, we will need to continually update the skills and facility of personnel on the job. This is a critical need in the military. Having language technology available to develop the training methodologies is critical. What will documents be like? How will one use the available language tools? Answers to these questions are unknown but are hinted at in the current multimode capabilities which can now be integrated on our workstations.

When considering education and training for the government, it should be the case that developed technology is also relevant and available to education systems throughout the country.

2. CURRENT TECHNOLOGIES--ARE THEY HELPING OR HINDERING?

As previously mentioned, successful application of technology can only be measured by its efficiency and precision in use. Otherwise we are in a state of technology only for technology's sake. Let's look at some currently available technologies which have been introduced into government. What can we learn from their introduction?

Immediately, one is struck by the fact that more often than not a technology is introduced and deployed publicly without any study as to its impact. We need to consider the impact of such adoptions before rather than after they get put into place. One only has to keep in mind the work of Gray, John, and Atwood (1) which demonstrated through analysis and data evaluation that introducing technology does not necessarily increase effectiveness. We are in that situation now with our language technologies. Caution is advised and careful scrutiny of the effects should be considered when adopting any new technological invention. A case in point is voice mail. My personal opinion is that it is one of the greatest cogs in U.S. competitiveness today.

Imagine yourself as a foreign business person calling a U.S. top company to place an order and having to sit for two minutes or more to reach the appropriate ordering department while menu options are read sequentially Often, in voice mail, one is not even sure the menu item selected is the appropriate one. The language technology relies on hardware selection which is sequential and numeric, but is this necessary?

We need to develop methods for studying the impact of potential technologies and their effect on function. We need to consider the problem from two viewpoints, the function being served within the government and equally important, the functional demands it places on non-government or citizen users of the technology even without their consent. Language technology more than other types of technology subtly conveys an institution's attitude toward its clientele. This interaction for many government functions is vital.

Functional transaction speed is an important factor of any technology that should always be considered. We need to minimize the impact of the technology on the efficiency of human functioning, and still be able to get necessary things done.

3. ROLE OF RESEARCHERS IN MEETING LANGUAGE TECHNOLOGY NEEDS

Researchers' primary focus continues to be studying basic scientific principles and using them to expand the capabilities of language technology regardless of modality. Evaluation and determination of constraints on applicability of the technology also need to be developed. Furthermore, researchers need not only to consider their contribution as a basic scientific result but must be aware of the potential use of the result within our society, both favorably and adversely.

Suppose many access functions are completely assigned to machines and that as a user, you need to obtain some vital information. When the machine responds that you are not permitted access even though you know you are, how will you be able to get to a responsible agent to correct the problem if you are talking to a machine? Will the responsible agent also be a machine? How will you find out it is a machine if all interactions are via language technology? Ultimately, with automatic language processes in place, how would you determine how to correct the situation? This is bordering on the question of reality and virtual environments and their detectability if and when we really produce language technologies that are indeterminable from real speakers. Is this possible?

Even now we can produce speech that sounds like a given individual based on sampling of the person's actual speech. Where will we draw the limits of such use? Where will be draw the limits of appropriateness for language technology usage in general? There are vital research issues to be addressed regarding these concerns.

4. CONCLUSION

Government needs for language technology encompass those of general business as well as more demanding military constraints. The technologies we currently have in place have not always been introduced expeditiously and beneficially. This does not mean that we should abandon all efforts to develop language, but instead points to a more cautionary view of accepting language technology as a solution. The basic efforts now underway will advance the role of language technology and will enhance functionality of government. We as researchers need to accept some of the responsibility for making sure the contributions to government function in the future remain as positive enhancements rather than harmful ones.

5. REFERENCES

1. Gray, Wayne D.; John, Bonnie E.; and Atwood, Michael E.; "The Precis of Project Ernestine or An Overview of a Validation of GOMS," *CHI 92 Conference Proceedings*, Monterey, CA, pp. 307-312, 1992.

LANGUAGE RESEARCH SPONSORED BY ONR

Susan Chipman

Program Manager, Cognitive Science
Office of Naval Research
Arlington, VA 22217-5660

In contrast to DARPA, ONR has not had a defined program that is focused exclusively on language research. However, there have been some clusters of projects concerned with language that have been supported within the Cognitive Science Program and its prior incarnation, the Personnel and Training Research Program. The ONR program is a basic research program, but a mission-oriented one which seeks to generate results that will prove applicable to significant Navy applications. Traditionally, as the earlier name indicates, those applications were sought primarily in training; more recently, the targets have been broadened to include human factors applications, especially in human-system interaction. Originally, the program was a psychological research program, but it evolved into a cognitive science program, the first government research program to be so labeled. The ONR Cognitive Science Program emphasizes the use of AI techniques to model human cognitive performance, and it has also emphasized the special sub-field of AI concerned with artificially intelligent computerized instruction or tutoring systems (ICAI or ITS). Thus, the ONR Cognitive Science Program also contrasts with the DARPA Human Language Technology Program in being concerned with understanding how human language actually is produced and processed by humans. (There is also an AI program within the Computer Science Division of ONR.) The management style of the program might be best described as <u>dynamic coherence</u>. That is, a degree of coherence or focus is necessary in order to enhance the likelihood of identifiable impact on application areas, but the focal clusters do evolve over time, partially in response to promising proposals that are received. New proposals are judged partially by the extent to which they cohere with and enhance the current portfolio of projects, not merely on isolated merit and inclusion in the broad area of cognitive science. Two salient clusters of language-related research that emerged have been the currently active emphasis on tutorial discourse and an earlier interest in improving the readability of instructional texts and documentation. Both have had significant natural language AI aspects, but not all projects have involved computation.

TUTORIAL DISCOURSE

This cluster of projects follows earlier major investments in artificially intelligent tutoring systems. The striking effectiveness of one-on-one tutorial instruction by human tutors (estimated to be a 2 standard deviation improvement over conventional classroom instruction) has sparked great interest in efforts to emulate that effectiveness with artificially intelligent computerized instructional systems. Despite enough success in that endeavor to make the production of intelligent tutoring systems a more applied research or development activity, present intelligent tutoring systems circumvent, evade, and finesse the problem of natural language interaction in various ways because the demands of tutorial interaction are really beyond the state of the art in computerized natural language. In the ONR Cognitive Science Program, human tutorial interaction is being studied from the perspectives of linguists, psychologists, and computational linguists who aim to emulate it in artificial systems. Among the issues that arise in these studies are the size or scope of the discourse organization imparted by the tutor, the balance between the tutor's agenda and immediate responsiveness to the student, the extent to which tutors revise their plans dynamically, the nature and breadth of knowledge required to support these interactions, the relationship between tutorial interaction and normal conversational patterns, and the nature of repair and correction processes, including the use of positive, neutral and negative feedback. The ease or feasibility of emulating these features of human tutorial discourse certainly varies, but it is also true that the introduction of a computer as a conversational participant is a significant change: what is the perceived social status or role of a computer? Similarly, it is possible that ideal computerized tutorial discourse might differ from what is observed among humans. The diverse research perspectives required to address these issues typify the interdisciplinary character of cognitive science.

Apart from some informal studies conducted within larger projects concerned with building early intelligent tutoring systems, the first of these recent studies of tutorial discourse was conducted by Barbara Fox, a linguist at the University of Colorado. Her primary data were four hour-long sessions of math/science tutoring which were video-taped and transcribed in a very detailed way that records pauses and non-verbal behavior (according to the methods of Sacks, Schegloff and Jefferson). She focused on correction and repair processes in tutorial discourse. She concluded that tutors structure correction activity so as to enable students to correct their own errors, whenever possible. Tutoring, in spite of its emphasis on learning, and therefore on making and correcting mistakes, is organized by the same principle of correction that organizes everyday conversation -- the preference for self correction. She found that tutors make heavy use of pre-correction strategies and of silence, in order to accomplish this preference for self correction (on the part of the students). Pre-correction strategies signal an upcoming correction from the tutor; they serve to alert the student to the possibility of that she has made an error. The student can then engage in trying to figure out what the error might be, and then can try to correct it him/herself. Throughout this process, the tutor provides further feedback to the student to indicate whether or not the student is on the right track. Tutors also give students a considerable amount of time in answering questions before they step in to redirect or correct (depending on the context, the silence can be from 1 to 5 seconds or so). That is, tutors often wait to see if the student will self correct. And tutors do not force an immediate answer; they give the student time to address the question. If the student is displaying obvious signs of being lost or stuck, however, the tutor provides immediate guidance. Fox also studied some tutorial sessions conducted by teletype in which the tutees were led to believe that the tutor was a computer. These sessions revealed some interesting differences in interaction. Students expect tutoring computers to be capable of complex numerical computations, and they feel free to leave dead time and to make off-the-wall remarks. These students appeared to believe that they actually were interacting with a computer.

A project by Arthur Graesser at Memphis State that is still on-going includes much larger samples of interacting students and tutors. One sample was of school children being tutored in arithmetic. Another analyzed interaction patterns in 44 one-hour tutoring sessions involving college students. Undergraduate students were tutored by graduate students on troublesome topics in a research methods course in psychology (e.g., variables, statistics, factorial designs, hypothesis testing). Similar to Fox, the primary focus was on collaborative exchanges and feedback mechanisms during question asking and question answering. Graesser has identified substantial problems in knowledge tracking and feedback mechanisms between student and tutor; the pragmatic principles of politeness and cooperativity during conversation often seemed to present a barrier to effective pedagogy during tutoring. The relationship between student question asking and level of achievement has been analyzed, as well as the way tutors handled student errors. A model of tutorial interaction is being developed which specifies dialogue patterns, pragmatic assumptions, goal structures, and pedagogical strategies during question asking and answering. Although the present project does not include artificial production of tutoring dialogue, Graesser, a psychologist with a joint appointment in computer science, has previously done computer simulations of question asking and answering. He regards these studies of naturalistic tutoring as a necessary preliminary to the design of effective dialogue facilities in intelligent tutoring systems, although he believes that there might be ways in which artificial tutorial dialogue could improve upon the natural.

Two other current projects do involve artificial production of tutorial dialogue. Martha Evens, a computational linguist at IIT, has been working to develop an intelligent tutoring system with genuine natural language interaction capacity. She and her collaborators are building an intelligent tutoring system that can carry out a tutorial dialogue with first year medical students, helping them to understand the negative feedback system that controls blood pressure, guiding them in building a qualitative, causal mental model of the system. With the goal of understanding how human tutors generate tutorial dialogues in this situation, they have captured seven face-to-face and thirty-seven keyboard-to-keyboard tutoring sessions, each lasting an hour or more. The tutors are professors of physiology at Rush Medical College; the students are first year medical students from their classes. The study of human tutoring sessions reveals many examples where the expert tutors produce large-scale discourse structures: multi-turn discourse structures, multi-stage hints, series of Socratic questions, directed chains of reasoning. Investigating tutors' responses to student initiatives, Evens and her associates found that tutors always respond to student initiatives to some extent. Revelations of serious misconceptions change the tutor's agenda to elimination of the misconception. An initiative from the student that is relevant to the tutor's current agenda results in a modification of the plan to incorporate the issue raised by the students. Other student initiatives evoke a brief response, followed by a return to the tutor's agenda. Unlike Fox, they found direct negative feedback in their tutorial dialogs 25% of the time as well as direct contradictions of what the student has just said 10% of the time. Keyboard-to-keyboard communication resulted in more elaborate positive and negative feedback responses from the tutors, fewer turns, and slower initiation of student responses. The current version of the tutor, Circsim-Tutor Version 2, generates lesson plans and tactics on both large and small scales, but in the process of executing a given plan, it generates the actual dialogue a turn at a time. The next version will attempt to emulate the larger structures of the human tutors. Evens judges that the tutorial repair processes described by Fox seem extremely difficult to emulate. Therefore, she is attempting to avoid repair by studying the source of repair situations and avoiding them: the most common source of conversational misunderstanding is vague "how" questions from the tutor. Evens and her collaborators are trying to generate more specific questions. Another source of misunderstanding is the tutor's misinterpretation of very terse and ill-formed input from the student; Evens' tutor is checking those interpretations with the student. Although Evens studied tutorial interaction over a computer link (as well as face-to-face tutoring) in order to approximate the conditions of computer tutoring, although she has devoted considerable effort to dealing with the error-ridden, abbreviated, and elliptical input from the students, this tutor may interest DARPA grantees as a potential testbed for the integration of speech recognition with natural language. Speech interaction would be a highly desirable feature for computerized training systems. Given the limited resources of the ONR program, however, we are relying upon DARPA to solve the speech recognition problem.

The project in this cluster that has begun most recently is that of Johanna Moore, a computer scientist at Pittsburgh. Although the aim of her project is the artificial generation of tutorial explanations, she also has begun by studying human tutors in order to identify the properties that make them effective. She replaced the natural language component of an existing ITS with a human tutor, and gathered protocols of students interacting with the human tutor. (The existing tutor is the Sherlock tutor of skill in diagnosing problems with an avionics test station, an Air Force project. The existing tutor has been evaluated in workplace training and found highly effective; it is the first of a large number of maintenance training tutors which the Air Force plans to develop for actual, practical training use.) She then systematically compared the human's responses to those that would have been produced by the ITS, identifying two critical features that distinguish human tutorial explanations from those of their computational counterparts. First, human explainers freely exploit the previous discourse in their subsequent explanations. This facilitates understanding and learning by relating new information effectively to recently conveyed material, and avoiding repetition of old material that could distract the student from what is new. Second, human tutors make extensive use of discourse markers to express relationships among individual units of information. These markers provide cues to the structure of the explanation and the information being conveyed, and thus make the explanations easier to understand. Moore is now constructing a computational explanation planner capable of assigning appropriate discourse markers and of generating explanations that make use of prior discourse in ways done by human tutors.

TEXT READABILITY

A second cluster of language research projects has focused on improving text readability. The military services and their contractors produce enormous amounts of text, system documentation and training materials for the personnel who will operate and maintain those systems. Consequently, there has been interest in research aiming to make these materials readable and comprehensible for their users. A few years ago, the ONR program supported a cluster of projects concerned with the design of readable and comprehensible procedural instructions, a special genre that has been neglected in general educational research on reading and text design. Among these projects was an effort by David Kieras, now at the University of Michigan. In a basic research project, Kieras demonstrated an automated system that could provide rather sophisticated comments on text structure and quality, such as, "This paragraph does not seem to have a main idea." This was done without any true comprehension of the text. The text was parsed and a propositional representation of the text was constructed. Propositions were linked by repeated mentions of the same term. Comments on text coherence could then be derived.

In conjunction with a project to develop a system to aid the authors of Navy training materials (AIM), the Navy Personnel Research and Development Center provided somewhat more applied funding (6.2) for further work by Kieras on the development of a text critiquing system that might enhance the capabilities of AIM. Kieras reviewed the psycholinguistic research literature on the determinants of text readability and comprehensibility. (Current standards for readability are based on crude formulas that measure sentence length and the frequency/familiarity of words used in the text. Yet, it is known that conversions to shorter sentences can sometimes make texts less comprehensible by obscuring the connections among ideas in the text.) As a first step, Kieras put considerable effort into building a parser that could handle actual Navy training documents in production. These do have some unusual structural format features that are not found in the texts for which most existing parsers were designed. In addition, many of these texts are written by senior enlisted personnel with subject matter expertise, personnel who are not trained or talented as writers. They can present severe parsing challenges even to highly skilled human readers. Experts in computational linguistics will not be surprised to hear that the "finished" version of Kieras' parser cannot parse many of the sentences or so-called sentences in these training documents, although failure to parse might sometimes be appropriate grounds for criticizing the writing. (Kieras's parser is written in Common Lisp and is available for those who might want to use it, along with a documenting manual that explains how to add additional capabilities to it.) Kieras did go on to build a text critiquing system based on his earlier work and the broader psycholinguistic research literature. Experimentation with this system revealed some interesting problem areas: for example, the system makes too many spurious complaints about the introduction of "new referents". This happens because it does not know about semantic relations among the words in the text, such as synonymy and part-whole relations. If the F-14 has been discussed, it will respond to "the wing" as a new referent. In its present state, the critiquing system does not have a practical, reasonably friendly user interface. In addition to making errors, it does not prune or prioritize comments but outputs an overwhelming barrage. Design of an effective user interface has not yet been supported.

(NPRDC has also been interested in related work by Bruce Britton, a psychologist at the University of Georgia, who was initially supported by the Air Force. Britton has shown that revisions guided by the same principles implemented in Kieras' system do improve text comprehension. Britton has developed some simple computer programs that aid human users in doing the same kinds of analyses done by the Kieras program, relying upon the human users to do parsing and supply semantic knowledge.)

In addition to the Kieras project, several others have been supported with a view to potential applications in a system like AIM. Navy support of George Miller's WordNet project began with this rationale, although it was obvious that WordNet would be a very general lexical resource with diverse potential applications in natural language computing. WordNet might be used to aid authors in finding more frequent and familiar words to substitute for rare words in their initial drafts. Specialists in natural language computing might note an interesting irony here: very frequent words tend to be very ambiguous semantically. Thus, to make a text readable to human readers of limited ability, one is advised to substitute very ambiguous words for less ambiguous ones. Semantic ambiguity does not seem to be problematic for human readers. In addition, of course, WordNet seemed to have promise as a way of eliminating some of the erroneous comments generated by the text critiquing system.

Another project has been a system of automated text formatting developed by Thomas Bever, a psycholinguist at Rutgers. Bever's system inserts slightly larger spaces at phrase boundaries (roughly speaking) in the text. Perhaps surprisingly, this has significant effects on reading speed and comprehension performance, especially for less skilled readers, although the text retains a normal appearance. (All of the services have many personnel with rather poor reading skills. Remedial reading instruction is a major training expense.) Formatted texts have even been shown to improve performance in an entire training course. Preliminary results suggest that the effects of text formatting are much larger for texts presented on computer screens -- the expected future format of military documentation. Bever's system does not parse the text in order to insert these spaces; he has developed a set of surface rules for doing it. However, he has also shown that a neural net can be trained to do space insertion very quickly when trained by a few texts that have been marked by a human. In this way, formatting could be applied to languages other than English with a very small expenditure of effort. It might be a very useful feature for the translators' work stations that have been a target application for DARPA work in machine translation and machine-added translation. At this time, the psychological mechanism by which this formatting aids readers is unknown; presumably it relieves some of the processing burden of parsing the text. Because of its demonstrated effectiveness and unobtrusiveness, Bever's text formatting is likely to move into practical application in major Navy training manuals soon.

At one time, we had hoped that the AIM system would remain an on-going applied project with periodic upgrades that would provide a conduit for the ready application of research advances. However, a managerial decision was made that all such projects would be limited to a 3-year span. The AIM system, which is implemented on Sun computers, was declared finished and fielded as little more than a fancy word processing system that helps to meet the special formatting requirements of Navy training documents, supplemented by a MacDraw-like capability for scanning in and manipulating illustrative diagrams. It is very popular with its users. Obviously, efforts may be made to initiate a new project that would incorporate more sophisticated language processing capabilities.

Although psychological research on text design has a long history, advances in linguistic understanding change the nature of the questions that can be asked in such research and the nature of the phenomena that are noticed. In particular, as in the research on tutorial discourse, much is being discovered about larger-scale discourse structures. Related issues, such as the effective design and use of diagrams, are much less well understood. At present, these are not high priority topics in the basic research Cognitive Science Program at ONR, but they may receive attention in the future, and some projects may receive support through the 6.2 Manpower, Personnel and Training R&D Committee at ONR.

TECHNOLOGY TRANSFER: PROBLEMS AND PROSPECTS

Jesse W. Fussell

Department of Defense
9800 Savage Road
Fort Meade, MD 20755

1. INTRODUCTION

For at least the last twenty years, DARPA and other government organizations have been sponsoring language processing research. The goal of this research is to develop processes to automate or semi-automate manual speech or text operations and to create new, capabilities to make it easier for humans to work with speech and textual data. During that time, a substantial amount of money has been provided to the nation's best organizations which have employed the most innovative and intelligent individuals. However, while there is a large body of objective evidence which demonstrates continuous progress toward the various technical goals of the programs, the fact remains there has been virtually no success to date in transferring any of the research effort into day-to-day operational use by any of the government sponsors. The purpose of this paper is to explore the reasons for the dearth of technology transfer in this technical area in the past, to forecast prospects for technology transfer in the future, and to suggest some ideas for stimulating the process.

2. TECHNOLOGY TRANSFER PROBLEMS

Many reasons can be cited for lack of technology transfer successes in the past. The one which typically is of greatest interest to the research community is that the algorithms developed in the past were not considered adequate for operational use. In the speech recognition area, word recognition error rates were intolerably high unless the speech source was limited vocabulary, isolated word, wide bandwidth and free of background noise. In addition, applications were limited to the simplest uses because there was little understanding of how to apply language processing results to speech. In the text processing area, problems being addressed were often severely constrained in terms of vocabulary, grammar and application. But it was virtually impossible to find real-world problems that were constrained enough to allow application of the newly developed techniques. The substantial progress that has been made by the research community has changed this situation. The current state-of-the-art, while clearly inadequate for very general problems, has great prospects for certain moderately specialized applications.

An additional problem that has impeded technology transfer has been the high cost and limited capability of the data and signal processing equipment needed to implement the algorithms researchers developed. In the speech processing area, researchers used to be restricted to general-purpose hardware which was tens or hundreds of time slower than real time, or of using special, fixed-point signal processors with very limited memory and dynamic range which were programmed in assembly language. Use of more modern computer languages such as LISP allowed faster design and implementation of experiments, but even with machines specially designed for that environment, processing was very slow. In addition, the graphics needed for a good user interface was limited in display speed and resolution. The net result of these limitations was that, except for the simplest algorithms, it was impractical to transfer research successes into operational use. However, while the thirst of researchers for ever greater computing, storage, networking and display capability still exists, it is greatly slackened. The explosive progress of computing over the past decade, led by the development of modern, high-performance, low-cost, graphics workstations, now allows real-time or faster operation of fairly computational and memory intensive algorithms on floating point processors programmed in high-level languages.

Another fundamental problem has been that the customer processing environment did not contain the infrastucture needed for the introduction of the techniques being developed. New digital speech processing systems could not be easily introduced into systems in which speech signals were being processed as analog signals and stored on analog tape. Text processing systems could not be made to operate in an environment in which textual information was still being handled on paper and data bases were on file cards. Again, thanks to major advances in data networks, low-cost terminals, optical character recognition, data base software, A/D and D/A conversion, and other technologies, many offices now contain the backbone of the system needed to make use of new text or speech processing techniques. In addition, the adoption of standards for programming languages, operating systems, windowing systems and network protocols often is resulting in the users obtaining computing systems which are compatible or which can easily be made compatible with the systems on which the processes are being developed. Thus, standardization will result in technology transfer being an easier job.

The problems described so far may be classed as technical problems. And, as stated above, these technical problems are rapidly decreasing in importance. However there is one technical problem that still must be overcome before technology transfer can occur on a widespread basis. And unfortunately this remaining major technical problem has received little attention to date, probably because of the way in which the research problem has been structured. That is, the problems reported on by most researchers at this conference are primarily defined by two things: the selected (or created) and marked training and test data, or corpus, and a criterion or criteria for testing the researchers system against that corpus. This standardization of problem domain, goals and test criteria has been a powerful tool of the research managers. It has focussed researchers' attention onto relatively specific goals and objectives and, since the performance of the algorithms produced by different researchers can be directly compared, it has simultaneously created an environment of constructive competition. However this narrow focus has resulted in the neglect of one critical area of work: the study of the process of converting an algorithm or process from one domain, that is supported by a well defined and documented corpus, to a different, operational domain, which may have little marked training or testing data. The result is there has been little work to even formally define the process necessary to convert from one domain to another and from one objective function to another one, much less to automate or semi-automate that process. In other words, there has been insufficient emphasis on or efforts to achieve technology transfer.

There are also a number of political, managerial or psychological problems which need to be addressed if the transfer of language processing techniques into operational use is to be successful. All of these nontechnical problems are associated with the potential customers of the research. And, it is important to recognize that in general, the customers are not the sponsors of the research. The sponsors are usually other researchers or research managers who are supposed to represent the customers. The true customers are the people or organizations that will be the end user of any new product or capability that results from the research effort.

The first problem involving the potential customer is that the customer usually not directly involved in the research efforts of the human language technology program. Or to put the shoe on the other foot, most researchers are not sufficiently familiar with the customers' needs and operating procedures to know whether a test corpus is truly representative of "real" data and whether the research goals will solve any "real" problem.

Government customers also tend to be relatively conservative and sometimes even suspicious of new ideas and new technology. They frequently have developed a well understood routine and procedure for doing their jobs and are reluctant to change. In other words, there is often a lot of inertia which may only be overcome through the use of force. In this context, one such force which comes from demonstrated success. But since the voice and text processing technology is (and probably always will be) imperfect, "success", like "beauty" will be defined in the eye of the beholder. Since customers will be the ultimate judge of our products, we need to ensure that those products are demonstrated in the best possible manner. Another force for change results from budget reductions. The conflicting pressures of less resources and desire to maintain capability tends to make some customers much more open to accepting new, imperfect technology.

3. RECOMMENDATIONS

First and foremost, the current program of research must be continued. Over the last few years, there has been substantial progress in understanding the fundamental problems of language processing and in developing ever better techniques for addressing those problems. This progress must continue if we are to have any hope of success against the less constrained problems.

However, the goal of this research program should be broadened to explicitly include technology transfer. The task of adapting speech and text understanding processes from one domain to another needs to be specified as one of the program goals. Algorithms need to be developed which can be easily converted from one task to another without requiring years of additional work by highly trained scientists. Techniques need to be developed which will allow supervised adaptation to new situations.

One implication of broadening the program to extend across domains is the need to increase the dimensionality of the research corpora so they also extend across domains. Instead of having data for a single situation which is segmented into portions for training, test and validation, this single set should be considered as the training portion for one domain, with another similar set for a different, but related domain which could be used to test how well the algorithm performs on the new domain, and possibly a third set of data from yet a third domain to validate the results of the domain transfer test.

There also needs to be additional efforts by researchers and research managers to find potential customers in the government, to educate them on the goals and results of the program and to solicit their inputs into those goals. In addition, researchers need to spend more time working with customers to better understand the manual processes currently being used so they can better understand what is needed in order to produce a "successful" language processing capability.

Finally, the overall goal of the program should be broadened, and funding provided to produce pilot or prototype systems which have been designed to be moved into operational situations and used for extended periods of time. Experimental operational prototypes are an absolutely necessary step in any long-term research effort. The trick is to determine the time for that step. The time is now.

Session 10: THE LEXICON

Ralph Grishman

Department of Computer Science
New York University
New York, NY 10003

Work in natural language processing has been moving rapidly towards the creation of large-scale systems addressed to real tasks. One aspect of this has been a rapid increase in the vocabulary size of these systems. "Toy" lexicons of 500 or 1000 words are no longer adequate; several tens of thousands lexical entries will be required, at a minimum. Developers of machine translation systems — who have confronted the problems of "real," largely unrestricted, text much longer than most other natural language researchers — have long recognized the central role of large, high quality lexicons.

Such broad-coverage lexical resources are of course costly and time-consuming to develop. Fortunately, however, there seems a reasonable prospect that they can be developed as shared resources. Current lexicons record for the most part relatively shallow (simply structured) information about the pronunciation, syntax, and semantics of words. There appears to be a general agreement between different system developers on at least some of the features to be captured in the lexicon, even though these features may be represented very differently in the various systems. The agreement seems to be clearest regarding syntactic information, but there is reason to believe that at least a partial consensus can be reached regarding pronunciation and possibly for semantic information as well.

All of the presentations in this session addressed the need for broad-coverage lexical resources. In addition to the papers included in this volume, there were presentations by Prof. Mark Liberman of the Univ. of Pennsylvania and Prof. Makoto Nagao of Kyoto Univ.

Prof. Liberman discussed some of the plans of the Linguistic Data Consortium. The Linguistic Data Consortium was created in 1992 with a combination of government and private funds in order to create a rich repository of resources for research and development of natural language systems. As part of its mandate, the Consortium intends to assemble a range of lexical resources including pronunciation, syntactic, and semantic information, under the general heading of COMLEX (a COMmon LEXicon). Among these efforts, the work on a syntactic lexicon — COMLEX Syntax — is furthest advanced; the paper by the group at New York University describes the status of this project.

These works are small in scale when compared to the dictionary efforts in Japan, which were summarized in Prof. Nagao's presentation. The largest of these efforts is the EDR Project of the Japan Electronic Dictionary Research Institute. This project is producing a collection of interrelated dictionaries, including a Japanese dictionary and an English dictionary (each of about 300,000 entries) whose entries are both linked to a "concept dictionary".

Prof. George Miller and his associates at Princeton University have for the past several years been constructing a lexical knowledge base called WordNet. In WordNet, English nouns, verbs, and adjectives are organized into synonym sets ("synsets"), each representing one underlying lexical concept; these synsets are connected by various semantic relations, such as antonymy, hyponymy, and meronymy. A word may have several meanings and so be assigned to several synsets; a word with its synset can thus be used to identify a particular sense of a word. The paper "A Semantic Concordance" describes an ongoing effort to "tag" a corpus by identifying, for each content word (noun, verb, adjective, and adverb), the synset to which it belongs in that context.

Corpus tagging can be even more valuable if the same corpus is tagged for several different lexical characteristics. For example, the COMLEX Syntax group is considering the possibility of tagging the verbs in a corpus according to the subcategorization frame used in each context. Although the COMLEX Syntax Lexicon will initially not be sense distinguished, correlating the subcategorization tags with WordNet sense tags would give some indication of the correspondence between subcategorizations and word senses.

Identifying the general vocabulary — nouns, verbs, adjectives, ... — is only part of the battle in lexical analysis. Many texts are replete with proper nouns (names). Although we can include the most frequent of these in our lexicon, the list can never be complete. A good lexicon must therefore be complemented by effective strategies for identifying and classifying proper nouns, which typically involve some combination of pattern matching with information from the lexicon. The final paper in this session, from Syracuse University, describes an approach to proper noun identification and and evaluation of this approach on a sample from the Tipster corpus.

The COMLEX Syntax Project

Ralph Grishman and Catherine Macleod and Susanne Wolff

Department of Computer Science
New York University
New York, NY 10003

Developing more shareable resources to support natural language analysis will make it easier and cheaper to create new language processing applications and to support research in computational linguistics. One natural candidate for such a resource is a broad-coverage dictionary, since the work required to create such a dictionary is large but there is general agreement on at least some of the information to be recorded for each word. The Linguistic Data Consortium has begun an effort to create several such lexical resources, under the rubric "COMLEX" (COMmon LEXicon); one of these projects is the COMLEX Syntax Project.

The goal of the COMLEX Syntax Project is to create a moderately-broad-coverage shareable dictionary containing the syntactic features of English words, intended for automatic language analysis. We are initially aiming for a dictionary of 35,000 to 40,000 base forms, although this of course may be enlarged if the initial effort is positively received. The dictionary should include detailed syntactic specifications, particularly for subcategorization; our intent is to provide sufficient detail so that the information required by a number of major English analyzers can be automatically derived from the information we provide. As with other Linguistic Data Consortium resources, our intent is to provide a lexicon available without license constraint to all Consortium members. Finally, our goal is to provide an initial lexicon relatively quickly — within about a year, funding permitting. This implies a certain flexibility, where some of the features will probably be changed and refined as the coding is taking place.

1. Some COMLEX History

There is a long history of trying to design shareable or "polytheoretic" lexicons and interchange formats for lexicons. There has also been substantial work on adapting machine-readable versions of conventional dictionaries for automated language analysis using a number of systems. It is not our intent to review this work here, but only to indicate how our particular project — COMLEX Syntax — got started.

The initial impetus was provided by Charles Wayne, the DARPA/SISTO program manager, in discussions at a meeting held at New Mexico State University in January 1992 to inaugurate the Consortium for Lexical Research. These discussions were further developed at a session at the February, 1992 DARPA Speech and Natural Language Workshop at Arden House; a number of proposals were offered there for both interchange standards and shareable dictionaries and grammars. At a subsequent DARPA meeting in July 1992 these ideas crystallized into a proposal by James Pustejovsky and Ralph Grishman to the Linguistic Data Consortium to fund a COMLEX effort.

Starting from this general proposal, a detailed and formal specification of the syntactic features to be encoded in the lexicon was developed at New York University in the fall of 1992. These specifications were presented at several meetings, at NYU, at the Univ. of Pennsylvania, and at New Mexico State University, and form the basis for the project described here.

2. Structure of the Entries

Each entry is organized as a nested set of feature-value lists, using a Lisp-style notation. Each list consists of a type symbol followed by zero or more keyword-value pairs. Each value may in turn be an atom, a string, a list of strings, feature-value list, or a list of feature-value lists. This is similar in appearance to the typed feature structures which have been used in some other computer lexicons, although we have not yet made any significant use of the inheritance potential of these structures.

Sample dictionary entries are shown in Figure 1. The first symbol gives the part of speech; a word with several parts of speech will have several dictionary entries, one for each part of speech. Each entry has an :orth feature, giving the base form of the word. Nouns, verbs, and adjectives with irregular morphology will have features for the irregular forms :plural, :past, :pastpart, etc. Words which take complements will have a subcategorization (:subc) feature. For example, the verb "abandon" can occur with a noun phrase followed by a prepositional phrase with the preposition "to" (e.g., "I abandoned him to the linguists.") or with just a noun phrase complement ("I abandoned the ship."). Other syntactic features are recorded under :features. For example, the noun "abandon" is marked as (countable :pval ("with")), indicating that it must appear in the singular with a determiner unless

```
(verb        :orth "abandon" :subc ((np-pp :pval ("to")) (np)))
(noun        :orth "abandon" :features ((countable :pval ("with"))))
(prep        :orth "above")
(adverb      :orth "above")
(adjective   :orth "above" :features ((ainrn) (apreq)))
(verb        :orth "abstain" :subc ((intrans)
                                    (pp :pval ("from"))
                                    (p-ing-sc :pval ("from"))))
(verb        :orth "accept" :subc ((np) (that-s) (np-as-np)))
(noun        :orth "acceptance")
```

Figure 1: Sample COMLEX Syntax dictionary entries.

it is preceded by the preposition "with".

Other formats have been suggested for dictionary sharing, notably those developed under the Text Encoding Initiative using SGML (Standard Generalized Markup Language). We do not expect that it would be difficult to map the completed lexicon into one of these formats if desired. In addition, some dictionary standards require an entry for each inflected form, whereas COMLEX will have an entry for each base form (lemma). COMLEX has taken this approach in order to avoid having duplicate and possibly inconsistent information for different inflected forms (e.g., for subcategorization). It is straightforward, however, to "expand" the dictionary to have one entry for each inflected form.

In addition to the information shown, each entry will have revision control information: information on by whom and when it was created, and by whom and when it was revised. We are also intending to include frequency information, initially just at the part-of-speech level, but eventually at the subcategorization frame level as well.

3. Subcategorization

We have paid particular attention to providing detailed subcategorization information (information about complement structure), both for verbs and for those nouns and adjectives which do take complements. The names for the different complement types are based on the conventions used in the Brandeis verb lexicon, where each complement is designated by the names of its constituents, together with a few tags to indicate things such as control phenomena. Each complement type is formally defined by a frame (see Figure 2). The frame includes the constituent structure, :cs, the grammatical structure, :gs, one or more :features, and one or more examples, :ex.[1] The constituent structure lists the constituents in sequence; the grammatical structure indicates the functional role played by each constituent. The elements of the constituent structure are indexed, and these indices are referenced in the grammatical structure field (in vp-frames, the index "1" in the grammatical structures refers to the subject of the verb).

Three verb frames are shown in Figure 2. The first, s, is for full sentential complements with an optional "that" complementizer. The second and third frames both represent infinitival complements, and differ only in their functional structure. The to-inf-sc frame is for subject-control verbs — verbs for which the surface subject is the functional subject of both the matrix and embedded clauses. The notation :subject 1 in the :cs field indicates that surface subject is the subject of the embedded clause, while the :subject 1 in the :gs field indicates that it is the subject of the matrix clause. The indication :features (:control subject) provides this information redundantly; we include both indications in case one is more convenient for particular dictionary users. The to-inf-rs frame is for raising-to-subject verbs — verbs for which the surface subject is the functional subject only of the embedded clause. The functional subject position in the matrix clause is unfilled, as indicated by the notation :gs (:subject () :comp 2).

We have compared our subcategorization codes to those used by a number of other major lexicon projects in order to insure that our codes are reasonably complete and that it would not be too difficult to map our codes into those of other systems. Among the projects we have studied are the Brandeis Verb Lexicon[2], the ACQUILEX Project [3], the NYU Linguistic String Project [2], and the Oxford Advanced Learner's Dictionary [1].

[1] The general format used for constituent structures was suggested by Bob Ingria for the DARPA Common Lexicon.

[2] Developed by J. Grimshaw and R. Jackendoff.

```
(vp-frame s          :cs ((s 2 :that-comp optional))
                     :gs (:subject 1 :comp 2)
                     :ex "they thought (that) he was always late")

(vp-frame to-inf-sc :cs ((vp 2 :mood to-infinitive :subject 1))
                     :features (:control subject)
                     :gs (:subject 1 :comp 2)
                     :ex "I wanted to come.")

(vp-frame to-inf-rs :cs ((vp 2 :mood to-infinitive :subject 1))
                     :features (:raising subject)
                     :gs (:subject () :comp 2)
                     :ex "I seemed to wilt.")
```

Figure 2: Sample COMLEX Syntax subcategorization frames.

4. Creation and Verification

We are deriving the word and part-of-speech lists for COMLEX from two sources: (1) the dictionary file prepared by Prof. Roger Mitton, which was derived from the Oxford Advanced Learner's Dictionary; (2) word lists (with frequency information) obtained from corpora and tagged corpora. We are already using the "joint ventures" corpus prepared for the Tipster information extraction task (and for MUC-5); we expect to employ other and larger corpora in the future.

Using these word lists, a number of part-time staff members will manually assign syntactic features to each word. These staff members will have access to several conventional dictionaries as well as a large on-line text concordance.

We intend to use a variety of techniques to verify the dictionary information. A portion of the dictionary will be coded twice; a comparison of the resulting entries will give us some estimate of the error rate. We will compare the subcategorization information produced by our codes with the codes derived from the Oxford Advanced Learner's Dictionary, and review discrepancies.[3] For the less frequent features, we will list all the words assigned a particular feature; this often will point up inconsistencies in coders' judgements. Finally, we hope in the near future to couple the assignment of subcategorization features with the tagging of a corpus.

5. Status

As of April 1993,

- the formal specifications have been further revised and are now largely complete
- a manual has been prepared with more extensive narrative descriptions of the classes to assist coders in preparing dictionary entries
- a menu-based program has been developed for rapid preparation of dictionary entries; this program is coded in Lisp using the Garnet graphical user interface package
- an initial dictionary of all closed-class words (those with parts of speech other than noun, verb, adjective, and adverb) has been prepared

Creation of dictionary entries for the open-class words is just beginning. We hope that corpus tagging of word instances with respect to their subcategorization pattern can begin in the summer and proceed in parallel with the dictionary preparation effort.

6. Acknowledgement

This material is based upon work supported by the Advanced Research Projects Agency through the Office of Naval Research under Award No. MDA972-92-J-1016 and The Trustees of the University of Pennsylvania.

References

1. A. S. Hornby, ed. *Oxford Advanced Learner's Dictionary of Current English*, 1980.
2. Naomi Sager. *Natural Language Information Processing*, Addison-Wesley, 1981.
3. Antonio Sanfilippo. LKB Encoding of Lexical Knowledge. In *Default Inheritance in Unification-Based Approaches to the Lexicon*, T. Briscoe, A. Copestake, and V. de Pavia, eds., Cambridge University Press, 1992.

[3]We would hope to obtain permission to compare our dictionary with other broad-coverage dictionaries, and use the result to further improve our dictionary.

A SEMANTIC CONCORDANCE

George A. Miller, Claudia Leacock, Randee Tengi, Ross T. Bunker

Cognitive Science Laboratory
Princeton University
Princeton, NJ 08542

ABSTRACT

A semantic concordance is a textual corpus and a lexicon so combined that every substantive word in the text is linked to its appropriate sense in the lexicon. Thus it can be viewed either as a corpus in which words have been tagged syntactically and semantically, or as a lexicon in which example sentences can be found for many definitions. A semantic concordance is being constructed to use in studies of sense resolution in context (semantic disambiguation). The Brown Corpus is the text and WordNet is the lexicon. Semantic tags (pointers to WordNet synsets) are inserted in the text manually using an interface, ConText, that was designed to facilitate the task. Another interface supports searches of the tagged text. Some practical uses for semantic concordances are proposed.

1. INTRODUCTION

We wish to propose a new version of an old idea. Lexicographers have traditionally based their work on a corpus of examples taken from approved usage, but considerations of cost usually limit published dictionaries to lexical entries having only a scattering of phrases to illustrate the usages from which definitions were derived. As a consequence of this economic pressure, most dictionaries are relatively weak in providing contextual information: someone learning English as a second language will find in an English dictionary many alternative meanings for a common word, but little or no help in determining the linguistic contexts in which the word can be used to express those different meanings. Today, however, large computer memories are affordable enough that this limitation can be removed; it would now be feasible to publish a dictionary electronically along with all of the citation sentences on which it was based. The resulting combination would be more than a lexicon and more than a corpus; we propose to call it a *semantic concordance*. If the corpus is some specific text, it is a *specific semantic concordance*; if the corpus includes many different texts, it is a *universal semantic concordance*.

We have begun constructing a universal semantic concordance in conjunction with our work on a lexical database. The result can be viewed either as a collection of passages in which words have been tagged syntactically and semantically, or as a lexicon in which illustrative sentences can be found for many definitions. At the present time, the correlation of a lexical meaning with examples in which a word is used to express that meaning must be done by hand. Manual semantic tagging is tedious; it should be done automatically as soon as it is possible to resolve word senses in context automatically. It is hoped that the manual creation of a semantic concordance will provide an appropriate environment for developing and testing those automatic procedures.

2. WORDNET: A LEXICAL DATABASE

The lexical component of the universal semantic concordance that we are constructing is WordNet, an on-line lexical resource inspired by current psycholinguistic theories of human lexical memory [1, 2]. A standard, handheld dictionary is organized alphabetically; it puts together words that are spelled alike and scatters words with related meanings. Although on-line versions of such standard dictionaries can relieve a user of alphabetical searches, it is clearly inefficient to use a computer merely as a rapid page-turner. WordNet is an example of a more efficient combination of traditional lexicography and modern computer science.

The most ambitious feature of WordNet is the attempt to organize lexical information in terms of word meanings, rather than word forms. WordNet is organized by semantic relations (rather than by semantic components) within the open-class categories of noun, verb, adjective, and adverb; closed-class categories of words (pronouns, prepositions, conjunctions, etc.) are not included in WordNet. The semantic relations among open-class words include: synonymy and antonymy (which are semantic relations between words and which are found in all four syntactic categories); hyponymy and hypernymy (which are semantic relations between concepts and which organize nouns into a categorical hierarchy); meronymy and holonymy (which represent part-whole relations among noun concepts); and troponymy (manner relations) and entailment relations between verb concepts. These semantic relations were chosen to be intuitively obvious to nonlinguists and to have broad applicability throughout the lexicon.

The basic elements of WordNet are sets of synonyms (or synsets), which are taken to represent lexicalized concepts. A synset is a group of words that are synonymous, in the sense that there are contexts in which they can be interchanged without changing the meaning of the statement. For example, WordNet distinguishes between the synsets:

{board, plank, (a stout length of sawn timber)}

{board, committee, (a group with supervisory powers)}

In the context, "He nailed a board across the entrance," the word "plank" can be substituted for "board." In the context, "The board announced last quarter's dividend," the word "committee" can be substituted for "board."

WordNet also provides sentence frames for each sense of every verb, indicating the kinds of simple constructions into which the verb can enter.

WordNet contains only uninflected (or base) forms of words, so the interface to WordNet includes `morphy`, a morphological analyzer that is applied to input strings to generate the base forms. For example, given "went" as the input string, `morphy` returns "go"; given "children," it returns "child," etc. `morphy` first checks an exception list; if the input string is not found, it then uses standard rules of detachment.

Words (like "fountain pen") that are composed of two or more simpler words with spaces between them are called collocations. Since collocations are less polysemous than are individual words, their inclusion in WordNet promises to simplify the task of sense resolution. However, the morphology of collocations poses certain problems. Special algorithms are required for inflected forms of some collocations: for example, "standing astride of" will return the phrasal verb, "stand astride of."

As of the time this is written, WordNet contains more than 83,800 entries (unique character strings, words and collocations) and more than 63,300 lexicalized concepts (synsets, plus defining glosses); altogether there are more than 118,600 entry-concept pairs. The semantic relations are represented by more than 87,600 pointers between concepts. Approximately 43% of the entries are collocations. Approximately 63% of the synsets include definitional glosses. And approximately 14% of the nouns and 25% of the verbs are polysemous.

WordNet continues to grow at a rate of almost 1,000 concepts a month. The task of semantic tagging has provided a useful stimulus to improve both coverage and precision.

3. THE BROWN CORPUS

The textual component of our universal semantic concordance is taken from the Brown Corpus [3, 4]. The corpus was assembled at Brown University in 1963-64 under the direction of W. Nelson Francis with the intent of making it broadly representative of American English writing. It contains 500 samples, each approximately 2,000 words long, for a total of approximately 1,014,000 running words of text, where a "word" is defined graphically as a string of contiguous alphanumeric characters with a space at either end. The genres of writing range from newspaper reporting to technical writing, and from fiction to philosophical essays.

The computer-readable form of the Brown Corpus has been used in a wide variety of research studies, and many laboratories have obtained permission to use it. It was initially used for studies of word frequencies, and subsequently was made available with syntactic tags for each word. Since it is well known in a variety of contexts, and widely available, the Brown Corpus seemed a good place to begin.

4. SEMANTIC TAGGING

Two contrasting strategies for connecting a lexicon and a corpus emerge depending on where the process starts. The targeted approach starts with the lexicon: target a polysemous word, extract all sentences from the corpus in which that word occurs, categorize the instances and write definitions for each sense, and create a pointer between each instance of the word and its appropriate sense in the lexicon; then target another word and repeat the process. The targeted approach has the advantage that concentrating on a single word should produce better definitions—it is, after all, the procedure that lexicographers regard as ideal. And it also makes immediately available a classification of sentences that can be used to test alternative methods of automatic sense resolution.

The alternative strategy starts with the corpus and proceeds through it word by word: the sequential approach. This procedure has the advantage of immediately revealing deficiencies in the lexicon: not only missing words (which could be found more directly), but also missing senses and indistinguishable definitions—deficiencies that would not surface so quickly with the targeted approach. Since the promise of improvements in WordNet was a major motive for pursuing this research, we initially adopted the sequential approach for the bulk of our semantic tagging.

A second advantage of the sequential approach emerged as the work proceeded. One objective test of the adequacy of a lexicon is to use it to tag a sample of text, and to record the number of times it fails to have a word, or fails to have the appropriate sense for a word. We have found that such records for WordNet show considerable variability depending on the particular passage that is tagged, but over several months the averaged estimates of its coverage have been slowly improving: coverage it is currently averaging a little better than 96%.

5. ConText: A TAGGING INTERFACE

The task of semantically tagging a text by hand is notoriously tedious, but the tedium can be reduced with an appropriate user interface. ConText is an X-windows interface designed specifically for annotating written texts with WordNet sense tags [5]. Since WordNet contains only open-class words, ConText is used to tag only nouns, verbs, adjectives, and adverbs; that is to say, only about 50% of the running words in the Brown Corpus are semantically tagged.

Manual tagging with ConText requires a user to examine each word of the text in its context of use and to decide which WordNet sense was intended. In order to facilitate this task, ConText displays the word to be tagged in its context, along with the WordNet synsets for all of the senses of that word (in the appropriate part of speech). For example, when the person doing the tagging reaches "horse" in the sentence:

The **horse** and men were saved, but the oxen drowned.

ConText displays WordNet synsets for five meanings of noun "horse":

1. sawhorse, horse, sawbuck, buck (a framework used by carpenters)
2. knight, horse (a chess piece)
3. horse (a gymnastic apparatus)
4. heroin, diacetyl morphine, H, horse, junk, scag, smack (a morphine derivative)
5. horse, Equus caballus (herbivorous quadruped)

The tagger uses the cursor to indicate the appropriate sense (5, in this example), at which point ConText attaches a label, or semantic tag, to that word in the text. ConText then moves on to "men," the next content word, and the process repeats. If the word is missing, or if the appropriate sense is missing, the tagger can insert comments calling for the necessary revisions of WordNet.

5.1. Input to ConText

In the current version of ConText, text to be tagged semantically must be preprocessed to indicate collocations and proper nouns (by concatenating them with underscores) and to provide syntactic tags. Since different corpora come in different formats and so require slightly different preprocessing, we have not tried to incorporate the preprocessor into ConText itself.

A tokenizer searches the input text for collocations that WordNet knows about and when one is found it is made into a unit by connecting its parts with underscores. For example, if a text contains the collocation "took place," the tokenizer will convert it to "took_place." ConText can then display the synset for "take place" rather than successive synsets for "take" and "place."

Syntactic tags indicate the part of speech of each word in the input text. We have used an automatic syntactic tagger developed by Eric Brill [6] which he generously adapted to our needs. For example, "store" can be a noun or a verb; when the syntactic tagger encounters an instance of "store" it tries to decide from the context whether it is being used as a noun or a verb. ConText then uses this syntactic tag to determine which part of speech to display to the user. ConText also uses syntactic tags in order to skip over closed-class words. Since the automatic syntactic tagger sometimes makes mistakes, ConText allows the user to change the part of speech that is being displayed, or to tag words that should not have been skipped.

After the text has been syntactically tagged, all contiguous strings of proper nouns are joined with an underscore. For example, the string "Mr. Charles C. Carpenter" is output as "Mr._Charles_C._Carpenter." Here, too, the user can manually correct any mistaken concatenations.

An example may clarify what is involved in preprocessing. The 109th sentence in passage k13 of the Brown Corpus is:

He went down the hall to Eugene's bathroom, to turn on the hot-water heater, and on the side of the tub he saw a pair of blue wool swimming trunks.

After preprocessing, this sentence is passed to ConText in the following form:

br-k13:109: He/PP went_down/VB the/DT hall/NN to/TO Eugene/NP '/POS s/NN bathroom/NN ,/, to/TO turn_on/VB the/DT hot-water/NN heater/NN ,/, and/CC on/IN the/DT side/NN of/IN the/DT tub/NN he/PP saw/VBD a/DT pair/NN of/IN blue/JJ wool/NN swimming_trunks/NN ./.

The version displayed to the tagger, however, looks like the Brown Corpus, except that collocations are indicated by underscores. Note, incidentally, that the processor has made a mistake in this example: "went_down" (as in "the ship went down") is not the sense intended here.

5.2. Output of ConText

The output of ConText is a file containing the original text annotated with WordNet semantic tags; semantic tags are given in square brackets, and denote the particular WordNet synset that is appropriate. For example, when "hall" is tagged with [noun.artifact.1] it means that the word is being used to express the concept defined by the synset containing "hall1" in the noun.artifact file. (Since WordNet is constantly growing and changing, references to the lexicographers' files have been retained; if the lexical component were frozen, some more general identifier could be used instead.) In cases where the appropriate sense of a word is not in WordNet, the user annotates that word with a comment that is later sent to the appropriate lexicographer. After the lexicographer has edited WordNet, the text must be retagged. In the retag mode, ConText skips from one commented word to the next.

In addition to the syntactic and semantic tags, ConText adds SGML markers and reformats the text one word to a line. The SGML markers delimit sentences <s>, sentence numbers <stn>, words in the text <wd>, base forms of text words <mwd>, comments <cmt>, proper nouns <pn>, part-of-speech tags <tag> and semantic tags <sn> or <msn>. The sentence preprocessed above might come out of ConText looking like this:

<stn>109</stn>

```
<wd>He</wd><tag>PP</tag>
<wd>went</wd><mwd>go</mwd><msn>[verb.motion.6]
  </msn><tag>VB</tag>
<wd>down</wd>
<wd>the</wd><tag>DT</tag>
<wd>hall</wd><sn>[noun.artifact.1]</sn><tag>NN</tag>
<wd>to</wd><tag>TO</tag>
<wd>Eugene</wd><pn>person</pn><sn>[noun.Tops.0]
  </sn><tag>NP</tag>
<wd>'</wd><tag>POS</tag>
<wd>s</wd><tag>NN</tag>
<wd>bathroom</wd><sn>[noun.artifact.0]</sn>
  <tag>NN</tag>
<wd>,</wd><tag>,</tag>
<wd>to</wd><tag>TO</tag>
<wd>turn_on</wd><sn>[verb.contact.0]</sn>
  <tag>VB</tag>
<wd>the</wd><tag>DT</tag>
<wd>hot-water_heater</wd><cmt>WORD_MISSING
  </cmt><tag>NN</tag>
<wd>,</wd><tag>,</tag>
<wd>and</wd><tag>CC</tag>
<wd>on</wd><tag>IN</tag>
<wd>the</wd><tag>DT</tag>
<wd>side</wd><sn>[noun.location.0]</sn><tag>NN</tag>
<wd>of</wd><tag>IN</tag>
<wd>the</wd><tag>DT</tag>
<wd>tub</wd><sn>[noun.artifact.1]</sn><tag>NN</tag>
<wd>he</wd><tag>PP</tag>
<wd>saw</wd><mwd>see</mwd><msn>[verb.perception.0]
  </msn><tag>VBD</tag>
<wd>a</wd><tag>DT</tag>
<wd>pair</wd><sn>[noun.quantity.0]</sn><tag>NN</tag>
<wd>of</wd><tag>IN</tag>
<wd>blue</wd><sn>[adj.all.0.col.3]</sn><tag>JJ</tag>
<wd>wool</wd><sn>[noun.artifact.0]</sn><tag>NN</tag>
<wd>swimming_trunks</wd><sn>[noun.artifact.0]</sn>
  <tag>NN</tag>
<wd>.</wd><tag>.</tag>
</s>
```

Note that the tokenizer's mistaken linking of "went_down" has now been corrected by the tagger. Also note "<cmt>WORD_MISSING</cmt>" on line 16 of the output: that comment indicates that the tagger has connected "hot-water" and "heater" to form the collocation "hot-water_heater," which was not in WordNet. This illustrates the kind of comments that are passed on to the lexicographers, who use them to edit or add to WordNet.

The WordNet database is constantly growing and changing. Consequently, previously tagged texts must be updated periodically. In the update mode, ConText searches the tagged files for pointers to WordNet senses that have subsequently been revised. A new semantic tag must then be inserted by the tagger.

5.3 Tracking

As the number of semantically tagged files increased, the difficulty of keeping track of which files had been preprocessed, which had been tagged, which were ready to be retagged, which had been retagged, and which were complete and cleared for use made it necessary to create a master tracking system that would handle the record keeping automatically. Scripts were written that allowed an administrator to preprocess files and add them to the tracking system. Once files are in the tracking system, other scripts keep a log of all the tagging activities pertaining to each file, and insure that taggers will not try to perform operations that are invalid for files with a given status. The administrator can easily generate simple reports on the status of all files in the tracking system.

6. QUERYING THE TAGGED TEXT

A program to query the semantically tagged database has also been written: `prsent` (print sentences) allows a user to retrieve sentences by entering the base form of a word and its semantic tag. It was developed as a simple interface to the semantic concordance, and puts the burden of knowing the word's semantic tag on the user. This program is useful to the lexicographers, who are intimately familiar with WordNet semantic tags and who use it to find sample sentences. A more robust interface is needed, however.

Presently under development is a comprehensive querying tool that will allow a user the flexibility of specifying various retrieval criteria and display options. Envisioned is an X-Windows application with two main windows: one area for entering searching information and another for displaying the retrieved sentences. A primary search key is the only required component. Additional search keys can be specified to find words that co-occur in sentences. This alone is a powerful improvement over `prsent`. Other options will restrict or expand the retrieval, as listed here:

1. Search only given part(s) of speech.
2. Search only for a specific sense.
3. Expand search to include sentences for synonyms of search key.
4. Expand search to include sentences for hyponyms of search key.
5. Use primary key and all secondary keys, or primary key and any secondary key.
6. Search for a secondary key that is within *n* words of the primary key.

As important as specifying searching criteria is how the retrieved information is displayed. An option will be provided to display retrieved sentences in a concordance format (all the target words vertically aligned and surrounded by context to the window's borders) or left justified. Search keys will be highlighted in the retrieved sentences.

Implementation of this program requires the creation of a "master list" of semantically tagged words. Each line in the alphabetized list contains the target word, its semantic tag, and for each sentence containing the word, a list of all the co-occurring nouns, verbs, adjectives, and adverbs with numbers indicating their position in the sentence. For example, the sentence already dissected provides a context for "hall" that might look like this:

hall/5 [noun.artifact.1]:

{bathroom/10 [noun.artifact.0]; hot-water_heater/15 [noun.artifact.0]; side/19 [noun.location.0]; tub/22 [noun.artifact.1]; pair/25 [noun.quantity.0]; wool/28 [noun.artifact.0]; swimming_trunks/29 [noun.artifact.0]}

{go/2 [verb.motion.6]; turn_on/13 [verb.contact.0]; see/23 [verb.perception.0]}

{blue/27 [adj.all.col.3]}

{ }

Collecting entries for this sense of "hall" provides valuable information about the contexts in which it can occur.

7. APPLICATIONS

Our reasons for building this universal semantic concordance were to test and improve the coverage of WordNet and to develop resources for developing and testing procedures for the automatic sense resolution in context. It should be pointed out, however, that semantic concordances can have other uses.

7.1. Instruction

Dictionaries are said to have evolved from the interlinear notations that medieval scholars added for difficult Latin words [7]. Such notations were found to be useful in teaching students; as the number of such notations grew, collections of them were extracted and arranged in lists. When the lists took on a life of their own their educational origins were largely forgotten. A semantic concordance brings this story back to its origins: lexical "footnotes" indicating the meaning that is appropriate to the context are immediately available electronically.

One obvious educational use of a semantic concordance would be for people trying to learn English as a second language. By providing them with the appropriate sense of an unfamiliar word, they are spared the task of selecting a sense from the several alternatives listed in a standard dictionary. Moreover, they can retrieve other sentences that illustrate the same usage of the word, and from such sentences they can acquire both local and topical information about the use of a word: (1) local information about the grammatical constructions in which that word can express the given concept, and (2) topical information about other words that are likely to be used when that concept is discussed.

A use for specific semantic concordances would be in science education: much of the new learning demanded of beginning students in any field of science is terminological.

7.2. Sense Frequencies

Much attention has been paid to word frequencies, but relatively little to the frequencies of occurrence of different meanings. Some lexicographers have atempted to order the senses of polysemous words from the most to the least frequent, but the more general question has not been asked because the data for answering it have not been available. We have enough tagged text now, however, to get an idea what such data would look like. For example, here are preliminary data for the 10 most frequent concepts expressed by nouns, based on some 80 selections from the Brown Corpus:

172 {year, (time_period)}
144 {person, individual, someone, man, mortal, human, soul, (a human being)}
139 {man, adult_male, (a grown man)}
105 {consequence, effect, outcome, result, upshot, (a phenomenon that follows and is caused by some previous phenomenon)}
104 {night, night_time, dark, (time after sunset and before sunrise while it is dark outside)}
102 {kind, sort, type, form, ("sculpture is a form of art" or "what kind of man is this?")}
94 {eye, eyeball, oculus, optic, peeper, (organ of sight)}
89 {day, daytime, daylight, (time after sunrise and before sunset while it is light outside)}
88 {set, class, category, type, family, (a collection of things sharing a common attribute)}
87 {number, count, complement, (a definite quantity)}

Our limited experience suggests, however, that such statistics depend critically on the subject matter of the corpus that is used.

7.4. Sense Co-occurrences

One shortcoming of WordNet that several users have pointed out to us is its lack of topical organization. Peter Mark Roget's original conception of his thesaurus relied heavily on his list of topics, which enabled him to pull together in one place all of the words used to talk about a given topic. This tradition of topical organization has survived in many modern thesauri, even though it requires a double look-up by the reader. For example, under "baseball" a topically organized thesaurus would pull together words like "batter," "team," "lineup," "diamond," "homer," "hit," and so on. Topical organization obviously facilitates sense resolution: if the topic is baseball, the meaning of "ball" will differ from its meaning when the topic is, say, dancing. In WordNet, those same words are scattered about: a baseball is an artifact, batters are people, a team is a group, a lineup is a list, a diamond is a location, a homer is an act, to hit is a verb, and so on. By itself, WordNet does not provide topical groupings of words that can be used for sense resolution.

One solution would be to draw up a list of topics and index all of the WordNet synsets to the topics in which they are likely to occur. Chapman [8], for example, uses 1,073 such classes and categories. But such lists are necessarily arbitrary. A universal semantic concordance should be able to accomplish the same result in a more natural way. That is to say, a passage discussing baseball would use words together in their baseball senses; a passage discussing the drug trade would use words together with senses appropriate to that topic, and so on. Instead of a long list of topics, the corpus should include a large variety of passages.

In order to take advantage of this aspect of universal semantic concordances, it is necessary to be able to query the textual component for associated concepts. Data on sense co-occurrences build up slowly, of course, but they will be a valuable by-product of this line of work.

7.4. Testing

We are developing a version of the ConText interface that can be used for psychometric testing. The tagger's task in using ConText resembles an extended multiple-choice examination, and we believe that that feature can be adapted to test reading comprehension. Given a text that has already been tagged, readers' comprehension can be tested by seeing whether they are able to choose correct senses on the basis of the contexts of use.

No doubt there are other, even better uses for semantic concordances. As the variety of potential applications grows, however, the need to automate the process of semantic tagging will become ever more pressing. But we must begin with what we have. We are now finishing a first installment of semantically tagged text consisting of 100 passages from the Brown Corpus; as soon as that much has been completed and satisfactorily cleaned up, we plan to make it, and the corresponding WordNet database, available to other laboratories that also have permission to use the Brown Corpus. We expect that such distribution will stimulate further uses for semantic concordances, uses that we have not yet imagined.

8. CONCLUSION

The fact that we have control of the lexical component of our semantic concordance enables us to shape the lexicon to fit the corpus. It would be possible, of course, to create a specific semantic concordance with a lexicon limited strictly to the words occurring in the accompanying corpus. That constraint would have certain size advantages, but would miss the opportunity to build a single general lexicon onto which a wide variety of corpora could be mapped.

The universal semantic concordance described here has enabled us to improve WordNet and has given us a tool for our studies of sense resolution in context. In the course of this exercise, however, it has become apparent to us that cross-referencing a lexicon and a textual corpus produces a hybrid resource that will be useful in a variety of practical and scientific applications. It has occurred to us that semantic concordances might be even more useful if a richer syntactic component could be incorporated, but how best to accomplish that is presently a question for the future.

ACKNOWLEDGMENTS

This work has been supported in part by Grant No. N00014-91-J-1634 from the Defense Advanced Research Projects Agency, Information and Technology Office, and the Office of Naval Research, and in part by grants from the James S. McDonnell Foundation and from the Pew Charitable Trusts. We are indebted to Henry Kučera and W. Nelson Francis for permission to use the Brown Corpus in our research. And we are indebted for assistance and advice to Anthony Adler, Christiane Fellbaum, Kathy Garuba, Dawn Golding, Brian Gustafson, Benjamin Johnson-Laird, Philip N. Johnson-Laird, Shari Landes, Elyse Michaels, Katherine Miller, Jeff Tokazewski, and Pamela Wakefield. The designation, "semantic concordance," was suggested to us by Susan Chipman.

REFERENCES

1. Miller, G. A. (ed.), WordNet: An on-line lexical database. *International Journal of Lexicography* (special issue), 3(4):235-312, 1990.
2. Miller, G. A. and Fellbaum, C. Semantic networks of English. *Cognition* (special issue), 41(1-3):197-229, 1991.
3. Kučera, H. and Francis, W. N. *Computational analysis of present-day American English.* Providence, RI: Brown University Press, 1967.
4. Francis, W. N. and Kučera, H. *Frequency analysis of English Usage: Lexicon and Grammar*. Boston, MA: Houghton Mifflin, 1982.
5. Leacock, C. ConText: A tool for semantic tagging of text: User's guide. Cognitive Science Laboratory, Princeton University: CSL Report No. 54, February 1993.
6. Brill, E. A simple rule-based part of speech tagger. In *Proceedings of Speech and Natural Language Workshop*, 112-116, February 1992. San Mateo, CA: Morgan Kaufman.
7. Landauer, S. I. *Dictionaries: The art and craft of lexicography*. New York: Scribner's, 1984.
8. Chapman, R. L. (ed.) *Roget's International Thesaurus*, (5th edition). New York: HarperCollins, 1992.

INTERPRETATION OF PROPER NOUNS FOR INFORMATION RETRIEVAL

Woojin Paik [1], *Elizabeth D. Liddy* [1], *Edmund Yu* [2], *Mary McKenna* [1]

[1] School of Information Studies
Syracuse University
Syracuse, NY 13244

[2] College of Engineering and Computer Science
Syracuse University
Syracuse, NY 13244

1. INTRODUCTION

Most of the unknown words in texts which degrade the performance of natural language processing systems are proper nouns. On the other hand, proper nouns are recognized as a crucial source of information for identifying a topic in a text, extracting contents from a text, or detecting relevant documents in information retrieval (Rau, 1991).

In information retrieval, proper nouns in queries frequently serve as the most important key terms for identifying relevant documents in a database. Furthermore, common nouns (e.g. 'developing countries') or group proper nouns (e.g. 'U.S. government') in queries sometimes need to be expanded to their constituent set of proper nouns in order to serve as useful retrieval terms. We have implemented two solutions to this problem: one approach is to expand a term in a query such as 'U.S. government' to all possible names and variants of United States government entities. Another approach assigns categories from a proper noun classification scheme to every proper noun in both documents and queries to permit proper noun matching at the category level. Category matching is more efficient than keyword matching if the request is for an entity of a particular type. For example, queries about government regulations of use of agrochemicals on produce from abroad, require presence of the following proper noun categories: government agency, chemical and foreign country.

Our proper noun classification scheme, which was developed through corpus analysis of newspaper texts, is organized as a hierarchy which consists of 9 branching nodes and 30 terminal nodes. Currently, we use only the terminal nodes to assign categories to proper nouns in texts. Based on an analysis of 588 proper nouns from a set of randomly selected documents from Wall Street Journal, we found that our 29 meaningful categories correctly accounted for 89% of all proper nouns in texts. We reserve the last category as a miscellaneous category. Figure 1 shows a hierarchical view of our proper noun categorization scheme.

2. BOUNDARY IDENTIFICATION

The proper noun processor herein described is a module in the DR-LINK System (Liddy et al, in press) for document detection being developed under the auspices of DARPA's TIPSTER Program. In our implementation, documents are first processed using a probabilistic part of speech tagger (Meeter et al, 1991) and general-purpose noun phrase bracketter which identifies proper nouns and proper noun phrases in texts. We have developed a special purpose proper noun phrase boundary identification module which extends the proper noun bracketting to include proper noun phrases with embedded conjunctions and prepositions. The module utilizes heuristics developed through corpus analysis. The success ratio is approximately 95%. Incorrectly identified proper noun phrases are due mainly to two reasons: 1) the part of speech tagger identifies common words as proper nouns; and, 2) conflicts between the general-purpose noun phrase bracketter and the special-purpose proper noun boundary identifier. While the first source of error is difficult to fix, we are currently experimenting with applying the special purpose proper noun boundary identifier before the general-purpose noun phrase bracketter. Our preliminary results show that this would result in a 97% correct ratio for identifying boundaries of proper nouns.

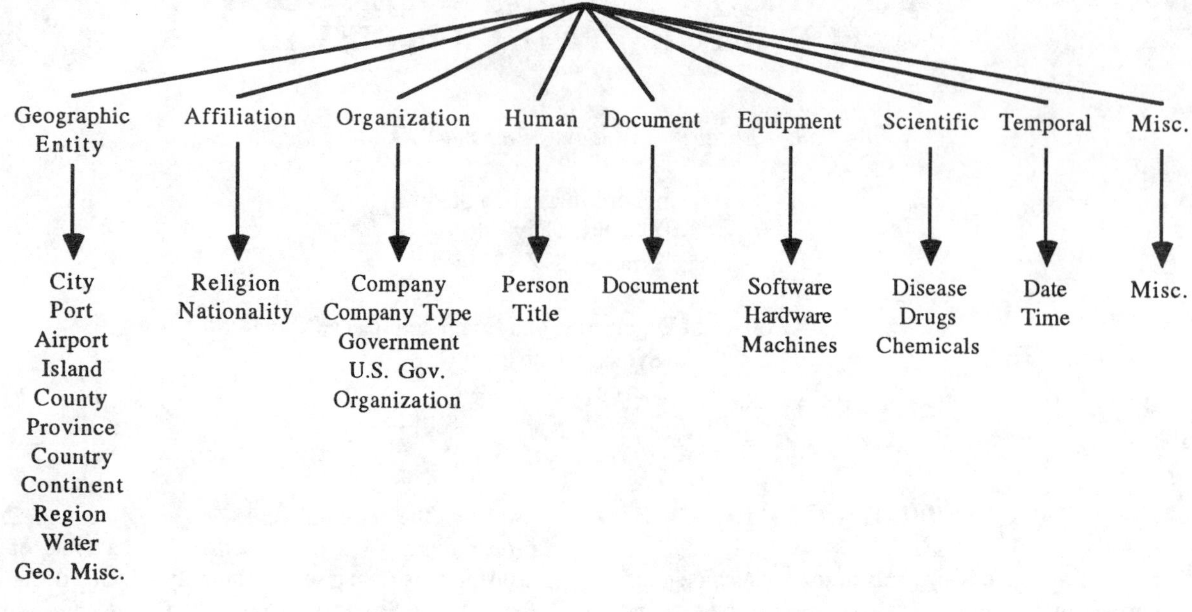

Figure 1: Proper Noun Categorization Scheme

3. CATEGORIZATION

Next, the system categorizes all the identified proper nouns using several methods:

1) comparison to lists of known prefixes, infixes and suffixes for each category of proper noun;
2) consulting an alias database consisting of alternate names for some proper nouns;
3) look-up in a proper noun knowledge-base of proper nouns and their categories extracted from online lexical resources (e.g., World Factbase, Gazetteer), and finally;
4) applying context heuristics developed from corpus analysis of the contexts which suggest certain categories of proper nouns.

While being categorized, the proper nouns are standardized in three ways:

1) prefixes, infixes, and suffixes of proper nouns are standardized;
2) proper nouns in alias forms are translated into their official form, and;
3) the partial string of a proper noun which was mentioned in full earlier in the document is co-indexed for reference resolution.

A new field containing the list of each standardized proper noun and its category code is added to the document for later use in several stages of matching and representation. The first two techniques improve retrieval performance, while the co-indexing of references produces a full representation of a proper noun entity and all its accompanying information. Figure 2 shows a schematic view of DR-LINK's proper noun categorizer.

4. USE OF PROPER NOUN IN MATCHING

When matching documents to queries, either the lexical entry for the proper noun can be matched or the match can be at the category level, as each proper noun occurring in a document is recorded in the proper noun field of the document along with its appropriate category code. For example, if a query is about a business merger, we can limit the potentially relevant documents to those documents which contain at least two different company names, flagged by two company category codes in the proper noun field. For many queries, using the standardized form of a proper noun reduces the number of possible variants which the system would otherwise need to search for. For example, 'MCI Communications Corp.', 'MCI Communications', and 'MCI', are all standardized as 'MCI Communications CORP' by our proper noun categorizer. This process is similar in purpose to the common practice in standard retrieval matching of reducing variants by stemming. However, stemming is not a viable means for standardizing proper names.

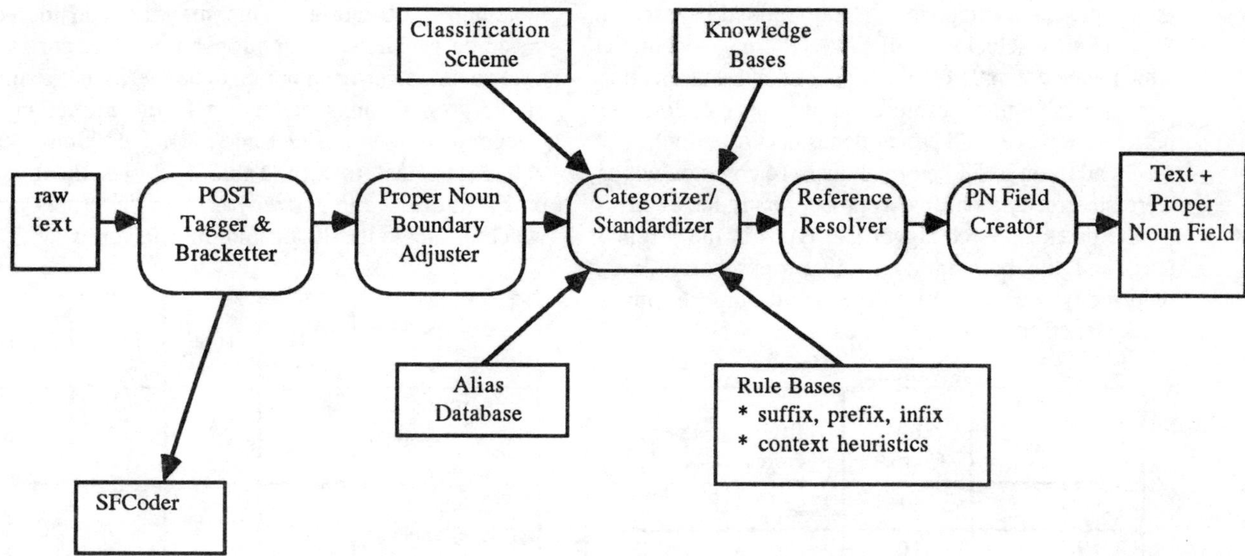

Figure 2: DR-LINK Proper Noun Categorizer

While the category matching strategy is useful in many cases, an expansion of a group proper noun such as 'European Community', which occurs in a query, to member country names is also beneficial. Relevant documents to a query about sanctions against Japan by European Community countries are likely to mention actions against Japan by member countries by name rather than the term in the query, European Community. We are currently using a proper noun expansion database with 168 expandable entries for query processing. In addition, certain common nouns or noun phrases in queries such as 'socialist countries' need to be expanded to the names of the countries which satisfy the definition of the term to improve performance in detecting relevant documents. The system consults a list of common nouns and noun phrases which can be expanded into proper nouns and actively searches for these terms during the query processing stage. Currently, the common noun expansion database has 37 entries.

The creation and use of proper noun information is first utilized in DR-LINK system as an addition to the subject-content based filtering module which uses a scheme of 122 subject field codes (SFCs) from a machine readable dictionary rather than keywords to represent documents. Although SFC representation and matching provides a very good first level of document filtering, not all proper nouns reveal subject information, so the proper noun concepts in texts are not actually represented in the SFC vectors.

For processing the queries for their proper noun requirements, we have developed a Boolean criteria script which determines which proper nouns or combinations of proper nouns are needed by each query. This requirement is then run against the proper noun field of each document to rank documents according to the extent to which they match this requirement. In the recent testing of our system, these values were used to rerank the ranked list of documents received from the SFC module. The results of this reranking placed all the relevant documents within the top 28% of the database. It should also be noted that the precision figures on the output of the SFC module plus the proper noun matching module produced very reasonable precision results (.22 for the 11-point precision average), even though the combination of these two modules was not intended to function as a stand-alone retrieval system.

Also, the categorization information of proper nouns is currently used in the system's later module which extract concepts and relations from text to produce a more refined representation. For example, proper nouns reveal the location of a company or the nationality of an individual. The proper noun extraction and categorization module, although developed as part of the DR-LINK System, could be used to provide improved document representation for any information retrieval system, because it permits queries and documents to be matched with greater precision and the expansion functions improve recall.

5. PERFORMANCE EVALUATION

While we have processed more than one gigabyte of text using the current version of the proper noun categorizer for the TIPSTER 18 month testing, the evaluation of the proper noun categorizer herein reported is based on 25 randomly selected Wall Street Journal documents which were compared to the proper noun categorization done by a human. Table 1 shows the categorizer's performance over 588 proper nouns occurring in the test set. In addition to 588 proper nouns, 14 common words were incorrectly identified as proper nouns due to errors by the part of speech tagger and typos in the original text; and the boundaries of 17 proper nouns were incorrectly recognized by the general-purpose phrase bracketter error.

	Total Correct	Total Incorrect	Precision *
City	11	33	0.25
Port	10	2	0.83
Province	23	1	0.96
Country	66	1	0.99
Continent	1	0	1.00
Region	1	7	0.13
Religion	2	0	1.00
Nationality	32	2	0.94
Company	87	13	0.87
Government	5	1	0.83
U.S. Gov.	20	8	0.71
Organization	9	1	0.90
Person	48	57	0.46
Title	42	4	0.91
Document	1	2	0.33
Machine	0	1	0.00
Date	27	0	1.00
Misc.	65	0	1.00
TOTAL	450	133	0.77
TOTAL-Misc.	385	133	0.74

$$* \text{Precision} = \frac{\text{Total \# Correct}}{\text{Total \# Correct + Total \# Incorrect}}$$

Table 1: DR-LINK Proper Noun Categorizer Performance

65 proper nouns were correctly categorized as miscellaneous as they did not belong to any of our 29 meaningful categories. This may be considered a coverage problem in our proper noun categorization scheme, not an error in our categorizer. Some examples of the proper nouns belonging to the miscellaneous category are: 'Promised Land', 'Mickey Mouse', and 'IUD'. The last row of Table 1 shows the overall precision of our categorizer based on the proper nouns which belong to the 29 meaningful categories.

	Total Correct	Total Incorrect	Total Missing	Recall *
With Miscellaneous Category	450	133	17	0.75
Without Miscellaneous Category	385	133	17	0.72

$$* \text{Recall} = \frac{\text{Total \# Correct}}{\text{Total \# Actual}}$$

Total # Actual =
Total # Correct + Total # Incorrect + Total # Missing

Table 2: DR-LINK Categorizer Overall Recall

Most of the wrongly categorized proper nouns are assigned to the miscellaneous category, not mis-categorized to another meaningful category. The only notable case where a proper noun was mis-categorized as another meaningful category, occurred between the city and the province categories. Our categorizer assigned the province category (IDA's Gazetteer calls states provinces) to 'New York' when the proper noun was actually referring to the name of the city.

Errors in the categorization of person and city names account for 68% of the total errors. To correct the categorization errors in person names, we are currently experimenting with a list of common first names as a special lexicon to consult when there is no match in prefix and suffix lists nor any context clues to other meaningful categories. The main reason for mis-categorizing city names as miscellaneous proper nouns was due to a special convention of newspaper text. The locational source of the news, when mentioned at the beginning of the document, is usually capitalized. For example, if the story is about a company in Dallas then the text will start as below:

DALLAS: American Medical Insurance Inc. said that ...

This problem will be solved in the new version of our proper noun categorizer by incorporating a capitalization normalizer, which converts words in all upper case to lower case except the first character of a word, before the part of speech tagging. We are also in the process of incorporating context information for identifying city names in our categorizer based on the observation that city names are usually followed by a country name or a province name from the United States and Canada.

Low precision in categorizing region names such as 'Pacific Northwest' is due to incomplete coverage of possible region names in the proper noun database. We are currently developing a strategy based on context clues using locational prepositions.

Table 2 shows the overall recall figure of our categorizer which is affected by the proper noun phrase boundary identification errors caused by the general-purpose phrase bracketter.

6. CONCLUSION

In comparing our proper noun categorization result to others in the literature, Coates-Stephens' (1992) result on acquiring genus information of proper nouns was contrasted to our overall precision. While his approach is to acquire information about unknown proper nouns' detailed genus and differentia description, we consider our approach of assigning a category from a classification scheme of 30 classes to an unknown proper noun generally similar in purpose to his acquisition of genus information.

Based on 100 unseen documents which had 535 unknown proper nouns, FUNES (Coates-Stephens, 1992) successfully acquired genus information of 340 proper nouns. Of the 195 proper nouns not acquired, 92 were due to the system's parse failure. Thus, the success ratio based on only the proper nouns which were analyzed by the system, was 77%. DR-LINK proper noun categorizer's overall precision, which is computed with the same formula, was 75%, including proper nouns which were correctly categorized as miscellaneous.

Katoh's (1991) evaluation of his machine translation system, which was based on translating the 1,000 most frequent names in the AP news corpus, 94% of the 1,000 names were analyzed successfully. Our precision figure of categorizing person names was 46%. However, Katoh's system kept a list of 3,000 entries as a system lexicon before the testing. Thus, a considerable number of the 1,000 most frequent names would have been already known, while DR-LINK system's proper noun categorizer had only 47 entries of person names in the proper noun knowledge base before the testing. Therefore, we believe that the performance of our person name categorization will improve significantly by the addition of a list of common first names in our knowledge base.

Finally, the evaluation result from Rau's (1991) company name extractor is compared to the precision figure of our company name categorization. Both system relied heavily on company name suffixes. Rau's result showed 97.5% success ratio of the program's extraction of company names that had company name suffixes. Our system's precision figure was 87%. However, it should be noted that our results are based on all company names, even those which did not have any clear suffixes or prefixes.

REFERENCES

Coates-Stephens, S. (1992). The Analysis and Acquisition of Proper Names for Robust Text Understanding. Unpublished doctoral dissertation, City University, London.

Katoh, N., Uratani, N., & Aizawa, T. (1991). Processing Proper Nouns in Machine Translation for English News. Proceedings of the Conference on 'Current Issues in Computational Linguistics', Penang, Malaysia.

Liddy, E.D., Paik, W., Yu, E.S., & McVearry, K.: (In press). An overview of DR-LINK and its approach to document filtering. Proceedings of the Human Language Technology Workshop. Princeton, NJ: March 1993.

Meteer, M., Schwartz, R. & Weischedel, R. (1991). POST: Using probabilities in language processing. Proceedings of the Twelfth International Conference on Artificial Intelligence. Sydney, Australia.

Rau L. (1991). Extracting Company Names from Text. Proceedings of the Seventh Conference on Artificial Intelligence Applications. Miami Beach, Florida.

SESSION 11: PROSODY

M. Ostendorf

Electrical, Computer and Systems Engineering
Boston University, Boston, MA 02215

ABSTRACT

This paper provides a brief introduction to prosody research in the context of human-computer communication and an overview of the contributions of the papers in the session.

1. WHAT IS PROSODY?

In large part, prosody is "the relative temporal groupings of words and the relative prominence of certain syllables within these groupings" (Price and Hirschberg [1]). This organization of the words, as Silverman points out [2], "annotates the information structure and discourse role of the text, and indicates to the listener how the speaker believes the content relates to the ...prior knowledge within the discourse context." For example, the relative groupings of words can provide cues to syntactic structure as well as discourse segmentation, and the relative prominence of words can provide cues to semantically important or focused items. Segmentation and focus represent two of the major uses of prosody, but other information may also be cued by intonation patterns, e.g. indication of continuation, finality or a yes-no question with phrase final "boundary tones".

Prosody is typically also defined with a reference to its suprasegmental nature: "Prosody comprises all the sound attributes of a spoken utterance that are not a property of the individual phones" (Collier) [2]. In addition, prosody can operate at multiple levels (e.g., word, phrase, sentence, paragraph), making computational modeling of prosody particularly challenging. The acoustic correlates of prosody, which include duration of segments and pauses, fundamental frequency (F0), amplitude and vowel quality, may be influenced by prosodic patterns at more than one level, as well as inherent segmental properties. Modeling the interactions among the different factors is an important and difficult problem.

Most current linguistic theories of prosody include an abstract or phonological representation of prosody to characterize aspects of phrasing, prominence, and intonation or melody. However, here we also see that abstract representations are of interest for computational modeling. Since it is generally agreed that prosody is not directly related to standard representations of syntactic structure, it is useful to have an intermediate representation to facilitate automatic learning and to simplify model structure. Thus, the form of an abstract representation is an important issue. Ideally, it should include all three main aspects of prosody, and address the needs of theory and computational models. Many different schemes have been proposed, and variations of two different prosodic transcription systems are used in the papers presented in this session. The TOBI (Tones and Break Indices) system for American English [3] is a prosodic transcription system that has evolved from a series of workshops where researchers met with the goal of defining a common core of transcription labels. The TOBI system is used to varying degrees in the papers by Silverman, Veilleux and Ostendorf, and Nakatani and Hirschberg. The IPO taxonomy of intonation for Dutch [4], which is used in the work of Collier, de Pijper and Sanderman, was developed from a long tradition of research in intonation that has recently been applied to several languages.

2. PROSODY & HUMAN-COMPUTER COMMUNICATION

The theme of this workshop is on technology for automated language processing, and thus the emphasis in this overview is on representations and computational models of prosody for spoken language processing applications. There are two classes of problems in speech processing for human-computer interactions: speech synthesis and speech understanding. Prosody plays a role in both problems, as is clearly seen in the different papers covered in this session. Prosodic patterns are determined by the information structure of language and realized in the speech waveform in terms of F0, duration and energy patterns. As illustrated in Figure 1, the overall problem in computational modeling of prosody is to move from one domain to the other, optionally via an intermediate abstract representation.

Until recently, almost all research in computational modeling of prosody has been in speech synthesis applications, where it has been claimed that good prosody models are among the most important advances needed for

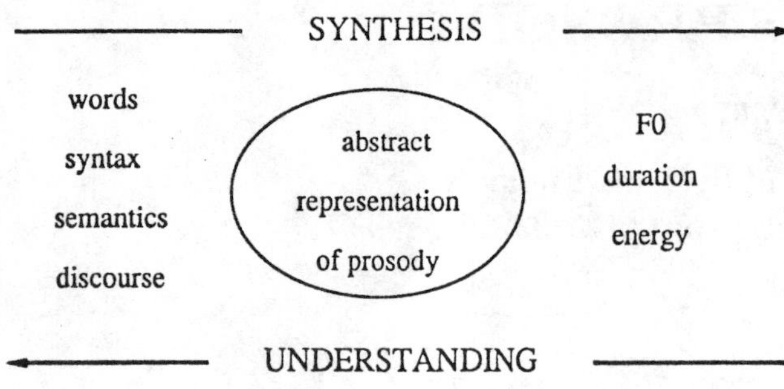

Figure 1: Problems in computational modeling of prosody for human-machine communication.

high quality synthesis. The papers by Silverman, van Santen, and Collier *et al.* each address different problems related to prosody synthesis. Silverman attacks the problem of predicting abstract prosodic labels, while van Santen presents a model for predicting duration from text (and optionally abstract labels). Collier *et al.*, on the other hand, analyzes the relation between automatically predicted boundary levels and perceived level in natural speech. Both Silverman and van Santen make the point that good prosody models can improve naturalness, but Silverman also shows that *intelligibility* can be improved.

Speech understanding is a relatively recent area of research for prosody, although researchers have long cited anecdotal evidence for its usefulness. Within the speech understanding domain, the papers in this session are directed mainly at contributions of prosody to natural language processing. An example is the use of prosody in combination with other "knowledge sources" to choose among the different possible interpretations of an utterance, investigated by Veilleux and Ostendorf. Some utterances from the ATIS domain that illustrate the potential role of prosody in interpretation include:

Does flight US six oh four leave San Francisco on Friday or Thursday?

where both intonation and phrase structure can be used to distinguish between the yes-no question and the "Thursday vs. Friday" alternative, and

Show me the itineraries for Delta flights eighty two one three one two seven five and one seven nine.

where knowledge of phrasing can help determine the specific flights referred to. Prosody can also serve speech understanding systems in an entirely different way, as discussed in the paper by Nakatani and Hirschberg, which is to cue the presence of a disfluency and the interval of replacement. As an example, consider another sentence from the ATIS domain, where prosody would be useful in automatically distinguishing a disfluency from a speech recognition error:

What is the <light> latest flight on Wednesday going from Atlanta to Washington DC?

Of course, the presence of disfluencies complicates the design of prosodic models, e.g. since fluent and disfluent pauses may cue different types of syntactic constituents.

An important question in current approaches to computational modeling of prosody is the specification of (or even use of) an intermediate phonological representation. Although all papers use some sort of discrete prosody labels, the paper by Collier *et al.* specifically investigates the perceptual relevance of one type of prosodic label – an integer representation of relative phrase breaks – and its acoustic correlates.

3. IMPORTANT THEMES

Several important and common themes, indicative of recent research trends, cut across subsets of these papers. First, it is significant that both synthesis and understanding applications of prosody are represented in this session, and useful since the developments in one field can benefit the other. Second, we see corpus-based analysis and automatic training methods being introduced into many aspects of prosody modeling. Third, Silverman's results argue the case for developing models in constrained domains, but this approach is also supported by the development of automatic training methods and probably used to advantage in the papers focussed on the ATIS domain. Fourth, all of the papers use an intermediate prosodic representation at some level, which raises the issue of representation as an important research question in its own right. Perhaps the most important contribution of this session is the collection of experimental results demonstrating the benefits of prosody in actual synthesis and understanding applications, providing concrete and not just anecdotal evidence that prosody is a useful component of a spoken language system. Since these themes represent relatively new directions in computational modeling of prosody, the applications and modeling possibilities are only beginning to open up and we can expect many more gains in the future.

References

1. P. Price and J. Hirschberg, "Session 13: Prosody," *Proc. of the DARPA Workshop on Speech and Natural Language*, pp. 415–418, 1992.
2. Prosody definitions, personal communication.
3. K. Silverman *et al.*, "TOBI: A Standard Scheme for Labeling Prosody," *Proc. of the Inter. Conf. on Spoken Language Processing*, pp. 867–870, 1992.
4. J. 't Hart, R. Collier and A. Cohen, *A Perceptual Study of Intonation*, Cambridge University Press, 1990.

ON CUSTOMIZING PROSODY IN SPEECH SYNTHESIS: NAMES AND ADDRESSES AS A CASE IN POINT

Kim E. A. Silverman

Artificial Intelligence Laboratory
NYNEX Science and Technology, Inc.
500 Westchester Avenue
White Plains, New York 10604

1. ABSTRACT

This work assesses the contribution of domain-specific prosodic modelling to synthetic speech quality in a name-and-address information service. A prosodic processor analyzes the textual structure of labelled input strings, and inserts markers which specify the intended prosody for the DECtalk text-to-speech synthesizer. These markers impose discourse-level prosodic organization, annotate the information structure, and adapt the speaking rate to listeners in real time. In a quantitative comparison of this domain-specific modelling with the default rules in DECtalk, the domain-specific prosody was found to reduce the transcription error rate from 14.6% to 6.4%, reduce the number of repeats requested by listeners from 2.6 to 1.1, and to sound significantly easier to understand and more natural. This result demonstrates the importance of prosodic modelling in synthesis, and implies an even more important role for prosody in more complicated domains and discourse structures.

2. INTRODUCTION

Text-to-speech synthesis could profitably be used to automate or create many information services, if only it were of better quality. Unfortunately it remains too unnatural and machine-like for all but the simplest and shortest texts. It has been described as sounding monotonous, boring, mechanical, harsh, disdainful, peremptory, fuzzy, muffled, choppy, and unclear. Synthesized isolated words are relatively easy to recognize, but when these are strung together into longer passages of connected speech (phrases or sentences) then it is much more difficult to follow the meaning: the task is unpleasant and the effort is fatiguing [1].

This less-than-ideal quality seems paradoxical, because published evaluations of synthetic speech yield intelligibility scores that are very close to natural speech. For example, Greene, Logan and Pisoni [2] found the best synthetic speech could be transcribed with 96% accuracy; the several studies that have used human speech tokens typically report intelligibility scores of 96% to 99% for natural speech. (For a review see [1]).

However, segmental intelligibility does not always predict comprehension. A series of experiments [3] compared two high-end commercially-available text-to-speech systems on application-like material such as news items, medical benefits information, and names and addresses. The result was that the one with the significantly *higher* segmental intelligibility had the *lower* comprehension scores.

Although there may be several possible reasons for segmental intelligibility failing to predict comprehension, the current work focuses on the single most likely cause: synthesis of prosody. Prosody is the organization imposed onto a string of words when they are uttered as connected speech. It includes pitch, duration, pauses, tempo, rhythm, and every known aspect of articulation. When the prosody is incorrect then at best the speech will be difficult or impossible to understand [4], at worst listeners will be *mis*-understand it with being aware that they have done so.

Arguments for the importance of prosody in language abound in the literature. However, the cited examples of prosodic resolution of ambiguity usually are either anecdotal citations or are illustrated by small sets of carefully-constructed cited sentences. It is not clear how important prosody is in more normal everyday texts. This brings us to the first question addressed in the current study: how much will prosody contribute to perception of synthetic speech for non-contrived, real-world textual material?

2.1. Current Approaches to Prosody in Speech Synthesis

Text-to-speech systems are typically designed to cope with "unrestricted text" [5]. Each sentence in the input text is analyzed independently, and the prosody that is applied is a trade-off to avoid one the one hand not sounding too monotonous, and on the other hand implementing the prosodic features so saliently that egregious errors occur when the wrong prosodic features are applied. The approach taken in these systems to generating the prosody has been to derive it from an impoverished syntactic analysis of the text to be spoken. Usually content words receive pitch-related prominence, function words do not. Small prosodic boundaries, marked with pitch falls and some lengthening of the syllables on the left, are inserted wherever there is a content word on the left and a function word on the right. Larger boundaries are placed at punctuation marks, accompanied by a short pause and preceded by either a falling-then-rising pitch shape to cue nonfinality in the case of a comma, or finality in the case of a period. Declination of pitch is imposed over the duration of each sentence.

There are several ways in which deviations from the above principles can be implemented to add variety and interest to an intonation contour. For example the declination may be partially reset at commas within a sentence. Or the extent of prominence-lending pitch excursions on content words may be varied according to their lexical class (higher pitch peaks on nouns or adjectives, lower on verbs) or their position in the phrase (alternating higher and lower peaks). These variations may be based on stochastically trained models.

One problem with the above approach is that prosody is not a lexical property of English words — English is not a tone language. Neither is prosody completely predictable from English syntax — prosody is not a redundant encoding of already-inferable information.

Rather, prosody annotates the information structure of the accompanying text string. It depends on the prior mutual knowledge of the speaker and listener, and on the role a particular utterance takes within its particular discourse. It marks which concepts are considered by the speaker to be new in the dialogue, which ones are topics, and which ones are comments. It encodes the speaker's expectations about how the current utterance relates to that the listener's current knowledge, it indicates focussed versus background information. This realm of information is very difficult to derive in an unrestricted text-to-speech system, and it is correspondingly difficult to generate correct discourse-relevant prosody. This is a primary reason why long passages of synthetic speech sound so unnatural.

2.2. Application-specific discourse constraints on prosody

There are many different applications for synthetic speech, but what they tend to share in common is that usually within each application (i) the text is *not* unrestricted, but rather is a constrained topic and a limited subset of the language, and (ii) the speech is spoken within a known discourse context. Therefore within the constraints of a particular application it is possible to make assumptions about the type of text structures to expect, the reasons the text is being spoken, and the expectations of the listener. These are just the types of information that are necessary to constraint the prosody. This brings us to the second aim of the current research: is it possible to create application-specific rules to improve the prosody in a real text-to-speech synthesis application?

Prior work has shown that discourse characteristics of simulated applications can be used to constrain prosody. Young and Fallside [6] built a system that enabled remote access to status information about East Anglia's water supply system. This system answered queries by generating text around numerical data and then synthesizing the resulting sentences. The desired prosody was generated along with the text, rather than being left to the default rules of an unrestricted text-to-speech system. Silverman developed paragraph-level rules to vary pitch range and place accents based on a model of recently-activated concepts. Hirschberg and Pierrehumbert [7] generated the prosody in synthetic speech according to a block structure model of discourse in an automated tutor for the `vi` text editor. Davis [8] built a system that generated travel directions within the Boston metropolitan area. In one version of the system, elements of the discourse structure (such as given-versus-new, repetition, and grouping of sentences into larger units) were used to manipulate accent placement, boundary placement, and pitch range.

Each of these pieces of research consists of a carefully-elaborated set of rules to improve synthetic speech quality. However the evidence that the speech did indeed sound better was more intuitive than based on formal perceptual assessments. Yet systematic and controlled evaluation is crucial in order to test whether hypothesized rules are correct, and whether they have a measurable effect on how the speech is perceived.

The current work builds on the progress made in the above systems by evaluating prosodic modelling in the context of an existing information-provision service.

3. PROSODY FOR A NAME AND ADDRESS INFORMATION RETRIEVAL SERVICE

The text domain for the current work is synthesis of names and addresses. The associated pronunciation rules and text processing are well understood, and there are many applications that require this type of information. At the same time this represents a particularly stringent test for the contribution of prosody to synthesis quality because names and addresses have such a simple linear structure. There is little structural ambiguity, no center-embedding, no relative clauses. There are no indirect speech acts. There are no digressions. Utterances are usually very short. In general, names and addresses contain few of the features common in cited examples of the centrality of prosody in spoken language. This class of text seems to offer little opportunity for prosody to aid perception.

On the other hand, if prosody can be shown to influence synthetic speech quality even on such simple material as names and addresses, then it is all the more likely to be important in spoken language systems where the structure of the material is more complex and the discourse is richer.

3.1. The application dialogue

This work took place within the context of a field trial of speech synthesis to automate NYNEX's reverse-directory service [9]. Callers are real users of the information service. They know the nature of the information provision service, before they call. They have 10-digit telephone numbers, for which they want the associated listing information. At random, their call may arrive at the automated position. The dialogue with the automated system consists of two phases: information gathering and information provision. The information-gathering phase used standard Voice Response Unit technology: they hear recorded prompts and answer questions by pressing DTMF keys on their telephones. This phases establishes features of the discourse that are important for generating the prosody: callers are aware of the topic and purpose of the discourse and the information they will be asked to supply by the interlocutor (in this case the automated voice). It also establishes that the interlocutor can and will use the telephone numbers as a key to indicate how the to-be-spoken information (the listings) relates to what the caller already knows (thus "*555 1234 is listed to Kim Silverman, 555 2345 is listed to Sara Basson*").

The second phase is information provision: the listing information for each telephone number is spoken by a speech synthesizer. Specifically, the number and its associated name and town are embedded in carrier phrases, as in:

<number> is listed to <name> in <town>

The resultant sentence is spoken by the synthesizer, after which a recorded human voice offers to repeat the listing, spell the name, or continue to the next listing.

These features may seem too obvious to be worthy of comment, but they very much constrain likely interpretations of what is to be spoken, and similarly define what the appropriate prosody should be in order for the to-be-synthesized information to be spoken in a compliant way.

3.2. Rules for Prosody in Names and Addresses

In the field trial, text fields from NYNEX's Customer Name and Address database (approximately 20 million entries) are sent to a text processor [10] which identifies and labels logical fields, corrects many errors, and expands abbreviations. For the current research, a further processor was written which takes the cleaned-up text which is output from that text processor, analyzes its information structure, and inserts prosodic markers into it before passing it on to a speech synthesizer. The prosodic markers control such things as accent type, accent location, overall pitch range, boundary tones, pause durations, and speaking rate. These are recognized by the synthesizer and will override that synthesizer's own inbuilt prosody rules.

The prosodic choices were based on analyses of 371 interactions between real operators and customers. The operators use a careful, clear, deliberately-helpful style when saying this information. The principles that underlie their choice of prosody, however, are general and apply to all of language. The tunes they use appear to be instances of tunes in the repertoire shared by all native speakers, their use of pitch range is consistent with observational descriptions in the Ethnomethodology literature, their pauses are neither unrepresentatively long nor rushed. What makes their prosody different from normal everyday speech is merely which tunes and categories they select from the repertoire, rather than the contents of the repertoire itself. This reflects the demand characteristics of the discourse.

The synthesizer which was chosen for this prosodic preprocessor was DECtalk, within the DECvoice platform. This synthesizer has a reputation for very high segmental intelligibility [2]. It is widely used in applications and research laboratories, and has an international reputation.

There are three categories of processing performed by the prosodic rules: (i) discourse-level shaping of the overall prosody; (ii) field-specific accent and boundary placement, and (iii) interactive adaptation of the speaking rate.

(i) Discourse-level shaping of the prosody within a turn. That turn might be one short sentence, as in **914 555 2145 shows no listing**, or several sentences long, as in **The number 914 555 2609 is an auxiliary line. The main number is 914 555 2000. That number is handled by US Communications of Westchester doing business as Southern New York Holdings Incorporated in White Plains NY 10604**. The general principle here is that prosodic organization can span multiple intonational phrases, and therefore multiple sentences. These turns are all prosodically grouped together by systematic variation of the overall pitch range, lowering the final endpoint, deaccenting items in compounds (e.g. "*auxiliary* line"), and placing accents correctly to indicate backward references (e.g. "*That* number..."). The phone number which is being echoed back to the listener, which the listener only keyed in a few seconds prior, is spoken rather quickly (the 914 555 2145, in this example). The one which is new is spoken more slowly, with larger prosodic boundaries after the area code and local exchange, and an extra boundary between the eighth and ninth digits. This is the way native speakers say this type of information when it is new and important in the discourse.

Another characteristic of this level of prosodic control is the type and duration of pauses within and between some of the sentences. Some pauses are inserted within intonational phrases, immediately prior to information-bearing words. These pauses are NOT preceded by boundary-related pitch tones, and only by a small amount of lengthening of the preceding material. They serve to alert the listener that something important is about to be spoken, thereby focussing the listener's attention. In the TOBI transcription system, these would be transcribed as a 2 or 2p boundary. Example locations of these pauses include: **"The main number is... 914 555 2000."** and **"In... White Plains, NY 10604.**"

The duration of the sentence-final pause between names and their associated addresses is varied according to the length and complexity of the name. This allows listeners more time to finish processing the acoustic signal for the name (to perform any necessary backtracking, ambiguity resolution, or lexical access) before their auditory buffer is overwritten by the address.

(ii) Signalling the internal structure of labelled fields. The most complicated and extensive set of rules is for name fields. Rules for this field first of all identify word strings which are inferable markers of information structure, rather than being information-bearing in themselves, such as "... doing business as...". The relative pitch range is reduced, the relative speaking rate is increased, and the stress is lowered. These features jointly signal to the listener the role that these words play. In addition, the reduced range allows the synthesizer to use its normal and boosted range to mark the start of information-bearing units on either side of these markers. These units themselves are either residential or business names, which are then analyzed for a number of structural features. Prefixed titles (Mr, Dr, etc.) are cliticized (assigned less salience so that they prosodically merge with the next word), unless they are head words in their own right (e.g. "Misses Incorporated"). Accentable suffixes (incorporated, the second, etc.) are separated from their preceding head and placed in an intermediate-level phrase of their own. After these are stripped off, the right hand edge of the head itself is searched for suffixes that indicate a complex nominal. If one of these is found is has its pitch accent removed, to yield for example Building Company, Plumbing Supply, Health Services, and Savings Bank. However if the preceding word is a function word then they are NOT deaccented, to allow for constructs such as "John's Hardware and Supply", or "The Limited". The rest of the head is then searched for a prefix on the right, in the form of "<word> and <word>". If found, then this is put into its own intermediate phrase, which separates it from the following material for the listener. This causes constructs like "A and P Tea Company" to NOT sound like "A, and P T Company" (prosodically analogous to "A, and P T Barnum").

Within a head, words are prosodically separated from each other very slightly, to make the word boundaries clearer. The pitch contour at these separations is chosen to signal to the listener that although slight disjuncture is present, these words cohere together as a larger unit.

Similar principles are applied within the other address fields. In address fields, for example, a longer address starts with a higher pitch than a shorter one, deaccenting is performed to distinguish "Johnson Avenue" from "Johnson Street", ambiguities like "120 3rd Street" versus "100 23rd Street" versus "123rd Street" are detected and resolved with boundaries and pauses, and so on. In city fields, items like "Warren Air Force Base" have the accents removed from the right hand two words.

An important component of signalling the internal structure of fields is to mark their boundaries. Rules concerning inter-field boundaries prevent listings like "Sylvia Rose in Baume Forest" from being misheard as "Sylvia Rosenbaum Forest".

(iii) Adapting the speaking rate. Speaking rate is a powerful contributor to synthesizer intelligibility: it is possible to understand even an extremely poor synthesizer if it speaks slowly enough. But the slower it speaks, the more pathological it sounds. Moreover as listeners become more familiar with a synthesizer, they understand it better and become less tolerant of unnecessarily-slow speech. Consequently it is unclear what the appropriate speaking rate should be for a particular synthesizer, since this depends on the characteristics of both the synthesizer and the application.

To address this problem, a module modifies the speaking rate from listing to listing on the basis of whether customers request repeats. Briefly, repeats of listings are presented faster than the first presentation, because listeners typically ask for a repeat in order to hear only one particular part of a listing. However if listener consistently requests repeats for several consecutive listings, then the starting rate for new listings within that call is slowed down. If this happens over sufficient consecutive calls, then the default starting rate for a new call is slowed down. Similarly, if over successive listings or calls there are no repeats, then the speaking rate will be increased again. By modelling three different levels of speaking rate in this way (within-listing, within-call, and across-calls), this module attempts to distinguish between a particularly difficult listing, a particularly confused listener, and an altogether-too-fast (or too slow) synthesizer.

In addition to the above prosodic controls, there is a specific module to control the way items are spelled when listeners request spelling This works in two ways. Firstly, using the same prosodic principles and features as above, it employs variation in pitch range, boundary tones, and pause durations to define the end of the spelling of one item from the start of the next (to avoid "Terrance C McKay Sr." from being spelled "T-E-R-R-A-N-C-E-C, M-C-K-A Why Senior"), and it breaks long strings of letters into groups, so that "Silverman" is spelled "S-I-L, V-E-R, M-A-N". Secondly, it spells by analogy letters that are ambiguous over the telephone, such as "F for Frank", using context-sensitive rules to decide when to do this, so that it is not done when the letter is predictable by the listener. Thus N is spelled "N for Nancy" in a name like "Nike", but not in a name like "Chang". The choice of analogy itself also depends on the word, so that "David" is NOT spelled "D for David, A,...."

4. PRELIMINARY EVALUATION

A transcription experiment was carried out to evaluate the impact of the prosodic rules on the synthetic speech quality in terms of both objective transcription accuracy and of subjective ratings.

4.1. Test material

A set of twenty-three names and addresses had been already been developed by Sara Basson (unpublished ms, 1992) for assessing the accuracy with which listeners can transcribe such material. This set had been constructed to represent the variation in internal structure and length that occurred in NYNEX's database. Although it did contain some material that would be ambiguous if synthesized with incorrect prosody, it was not intended to focus exclusively on prosodic variability and was developed before the prosodic processor was finished. It contained phonemic diversity;, a variety of personal names, cities and states; short and long name fields, and digit strings. There were roughly equal proportions of easy, moderate, and difficult listings, as measured by how well listeners could transcribe the material when spoken by a human. Henceforth each of these names and addresses shall be referred to as *items*.

4.2. Procedure

The 23 items were divided into two sets. Listeners were all native speakers of English with no known hearing loss, and all employees of NYNEX Science and Technology. On the basis of our previous experience with synthetic speech perception experiments, we expect these listeners will perform better on the transcription task than general members of the public. Thus the results of this transcription test represent a "best case" in terms of how well we can expect real users to understand the utterances.

Listeners called the computer over the public telephone network from their office telephones: their task was to transcribe each of the 23 items. Each listener heard and transcribed the items in two blocks: one of the sets of items spoken by DECtalk's default prosody rules, and the other spoken with application-specific prosody. The design was counter-balanced with roughly half of the listeners hearing each version in the first block, and roughly half hearing each item set in the first block. For each item, listeners could request as many repeats as they wanted in order to transcribe the material as accurately as they felt was reasonably possible. Listeners were only allowed to request spelling in two of the items, which were constructed to sound like pronounceable names and contain every letter in the alphabet.

4.3. Dependent variables

Transcription scores per item. Each word in each item could score up to 3 points. One point would be deducted if the right-hand word boundary was misplaced, one point if one phoneme was wrong, and two points of more than one phoneme was wrong.

Number of repeats requested per item. For items that were spelled, this was the number of times after the first spelling.

Perceived intelligibility. Each version of the synthesis was rated by each listener on a five-point scale labelled: "How easy was it to understand this voice?" (where 1 = "Consistently failed to understand much of the speech" and 5 = "Consistently effortless to understand").

Perceived naturalness. Each version was similarly rated, on a five-point scale labelled "How natural (i.e. like a human voice) did this voice sound? (where 1 = extremely unnatural and 5 = extremely natural).

Preferences. Since each listener heard each voice, they were asked for which voice they preferred: voice 1, voice 2, or no preference.

4.4. Results

So far results have been analyzed for 17 listeners. Summing over all transcriptions, the maximum possible transcription score for each synthesizer was 5032. The per-word error rate for items spoken with the synthesizer's default prosody was 14.6%. With the domain-specific prosody this was only 6.4%. Thus listeners could transcribe the vowels and consonants significantly more accurately even though the vowels and consonants are pronounced by exactly the same segmental rules in both cases. The only difference is the prosody.

Transcription scores do not reflect how much effort listeners expended to achieve their transcription accuracy. One measure of that effort is the number of repeats they requested. Listeners needed on average 2.6 repeats per listing for the default prosody, but only 1.1 repeats per listing with the domain-specific prosody. Interestingly, in a prior transcription test with a *human* voice saying a superset of the listings used in this experiment, listeners needed 1.2 repeats per listing (Sara Basson, personal communication).

On the "ease of understanding" scale, the default prosody scored 1.8 (standard deviation = 0.8), while domain-specific prosody scored 3.3 (standard deviation = 0.8). Thus listeners' subjective perceptions matched their objective transcription results: they were aware that the version with domain-specific prosody was easier to understand, though clearly it was not effortless.

On the "naturalness" scale, the default prosody scored 1.9 (standard deviation = 0.9) and domain-specific prosody scored 2.9 (standard deviation = 0.8). Though statistically significant, this difference is smaller than on the previous scale. Alteration of the just the pitch and duration made the speech made the speech sound somewhat more natural, but it is still is a long way from sounding "extremely natural".

One the preference ratings, so far all of the listeners preferred the speech versions with domain-specific prosody.

5. CONCLUSION

Although this evaluation is preliminary, it suggests that even in such simple material as names and addresses domain-specific prosody can make a clear improvement to synthetic speech quality. The transcription error rate was more than halved, the number of repetitions was more than halved, the speech was rated as more natural and easier to understand, and it was preferred by listeners. This result encourages further research on methods for capitalizing on application constraints to improve prosody. The principles in the literature for customizing the prosody will generalize to other domains where the structure of the material and discourse purpose can be inferred.

The second conclusion is that at least in this domain, although domain-specific rules can improve synthetic prosody over that in domain-independent rules, the domain-specific customization can be severely limited if the synthesizer does not make the right prosodic controls available. In an ideal world, the markers that are embedded in the text would specify exactly how the text is to be spoken. In reality, however, they specify at best an approximation. This exercise is constrained by the controls made available by that synthesizer. Some manipulations that are needed for this type of customization are not available, and some of the controls that are available interact in mutually-detrimental ways. Consequently to the extent that the application-specific prosody did indeed improve synthesis quality, this is all the more supporting evidence for both the importance of generating domain-relevant prosody on the one hand, and for NOT doing it with such an improper prosodic model on the other.

The immediate next steps in this work are to more systematically evaluate the perceptual impact of the above rules, both in transcription tests and with the quantitative measures of acceptance by real users that are already being used in the field trial. In addition, we are currently developing a set of rules to customize the prosody in a spoken language system for remote financial transactions, combining text-specific rules of the type evaluated in this work, with rules that will use the discourse history to dynamically derive information about topics, discourse functions of replies, and given versus new information.

The development and evaluation of this work furthers our understanding of (i) how to use prosody to clarify names and addresses in particular, and other texts in general; (ii) prosody's importance in a real application context, rather than in laboratory-generated unrepresentative sentences; (iii) one way to incorporate user-modelling of speaking rate into speech synthesis (speakers should not ignore their listeners); and (iv) what prosodic controls a synthesizer should make available.

6. ACKNOWLEDGEMENTS

This work could not have proceeded without the context and focus of the ACNA trial in general, and in particular the efforts and insights of Dina Yashchin, Ashok Kalyanswamy, Sara Basson, John Pitrelli, and Judy Spitz. Shortcomings of course remain my own responsibility.

REFERENCES

1. Silverman, K.E.A. *The Structure and Processing of Fundamental Frequency Contours*. Ph.D. Dissertation, Cambridge University, 1987.

2. Greene, B.G.; Logan, J.S. and Pisoni, D.B. "Perception of synthetic speech produced automatically by rule: Intelligibility of eight text-to-speech systems", *Behavior Research Methods, Instruments, and Computers*, Vol. **18**, 1986, pp 100-107

3. Silverman, K.E.A., Basson, S. and Levas, S. Evaluating Synthesizer Performance: Is Segmental Intelligibility Enough? Proc. ICSLP-90, Vol. **1**, 1990.

4. Huggins, A.W.F. "Speech Timing and Intelligibility. In J. Requin (Ed): *Attention and Performance VII*. Erlbaum, Hillsdale. 1978.

5. Allen, J, Hunnicutt, M.S., Klatt, D., Armstrong, R.C. and Pisoni, D.B. *From Text to Speech: The MITalk System*. Cambridge University Press, Cambridge, 1987

6. Young, S.J. and Fallside, F. "Synthesis by rule of prosodic features in word concatenation synthesis", *Int. J. Man-Machine Studies*, Vol. **12**, 1980, pp 241-258.

7. Hirschberg, J. and Pierrehumbert, J.B. "The Intonational Structuring of Discourse", *Proc. 24th ACL Meeting*, 1986, pp 136-144.

8. Davis, J.R. "Generating intonational support for discourse", *J. Acoust. Soc. Am. Suppl. 1*, Vol. **82**, 1987, p S17.

9. Yashchin, D, Basson, S., Kalyanswamy, A., Silverman, K.E.A. "Results from automating a name and address service with speech synthesis". *Proc AVIOS-92*, 1992.

10. Kalyanswamy, A. and Silverman, K.E.A. "Processing information in preparation for text-to-speech synthesis". *Proc AVIOS-92*, 1992.

QUANTITATIVE MODELING OF SEGMENTAL DURATION

Jan P. H. van Santen

AT&T Bell Laboratories
600 Mountain Avenue
Murray Hill, NJ 07974-0636, U.S.A.

ABSTRACT

In natural speech, durations of phonetic segments are strongly dependent on contextual factors. Quantitative descriptions of these contextual effects have applications in text-to-speech synthesis and in automatic speech recognition. In this paper, we describe a speaker-dependent system for predicting segmental duration from text, with emphasis on the statistical methods used for its construction. We also report results of a subjective listening experiment evaluating an implementation of this system for text-to-speech synthesis purposes.

1. INTRODUCTION

This paper describes a system for prediction of segmental duration from text. In most text-to-speech synthesizer architectures, a duration prediction system is embedded in a sequence of modules, where it is preceded by modules that compute various linguistic features[1] from text. For example, the word "unit" might be represented as a sequence of five feature vectors: (< */u/, word - initial, monosyllabic,* $\cdots$, >) $\cdots$ (< $/t/_{burst}$, *word - final, monosyllabic,* $\cdots$, >). In automatic speech recognition, a (hypothesized) phone is usually annotated only in terms of the preceding and following phones. If some form of lexical access is performed, more complete contextual feature vectors can be computed.

Broadly speaking, construction of duration prediction systems has been approached in two ways. One is to use general-purpose statistical methods such as CART[2] or neural nets. In CART, for example, a tree is constructed by making binary splits on factors that minimize the variance of the durations in the two subsets defined by the split [2]. These methods are called "general purpose" because they can be used across a variety of substantive domains.

There also exists an older tradition exemplified by Klatt [3, 4, 5] and others [6, 7, 8, 9] where duration is computed with duration models, i.e., simple arithmetic models specifically designed for segmental duration. For example, in Klatt's model the duration for feature vector $\mathbf{f} \in \mathbf{F}$ is given by

$$\mathrm{DUR}(\mathbf{f}) = s_{1,1}(f_1) \times \cdots \times s_{1,n+1}(f_{n+1}) + s_{2,n+1}(f_{n+1}). \quad (1)$$

Here, f_j is the j-th component[3] of the vector **f**, the second subscript (j) in $s_{i,j}$ likewise refers to this component, and the first subscript (i) refers to the fact that the model consists of two *product terms* numbered 1 and 2. The parameters $s_{i,j}$ are called *factor scales.* For example, $s_{1,1}$ $(stressed) = 1.40$. All current duration models have in common that they (1) use factor scales, and (2) combine the effects of multiple factors using only the addition and multiplication operations. The general class of models defined by these two characteristics, *sums-of-products models,* has been found to have useful mathematical and statistical properties [10].

Briefly, here is how these two standard approaches compare with ours. We share with general-purpose statistical methods the emphasis on formal data analysis methods, and with the older tradition the usage of sums-of-products models. Our approach differs in the following respects. First, although we concur with the modeling tradition that segmental duration data – and in particular the types of interactions one often finds in these data – can be accurately described by sums-of-products models, this class of models is extremely large so that one has to put considerable effort in searching for the most appropriate model.[4] The few models that this tradition has generated make up a vanishingly small portion of a vast space of possibilities, and because they have not been systematically tested against these other possibilities [11] we should consider the search for better models completely open. Second, in contrast with the general-purpose methods approach, the process by which we construct our prediction system is not a one-step procedure but is a multi-step process with an important role being played by various forms of exploratory data analysis.

[1] We define a *factor,* F_j, to be a partition of mutually exclusive and exhaustive possibilities such as {*1-stressed, 2-stressed, unstressed*}. A feature is a "level" on a factor such as *1-stressed.* The *feature space* **F** is the product space of all factors: $F_1 \times \cdots \times F_n$. Because of phonotactic and other constraints, only a small fraction of this space can actually occur in a language; we call this the *linguistic space.*

[2] Classification and Regression Trees [1].

[3] In its original form, the Klatt model uses p for the phonetic segment factor where we use f_{n+1}.

[4] For example, for two factors there are already five models: $s_{1,1} \times s_{1,2}$, $s_{1,1} + s_{2,2}$, $s_{1,1} \times s_{1,2} + s_{2,1}$, $s_{1,1} \times s_{1,2} + s_{2,2}$, and $s_{1,1} \times s_{1,2} + s_{2,1} + s_{3,2}$ (note the use of subscripts).

2. PROPERTIES OF SEGMENTAL DURATION DATA

In this section, we first discuss properties of segmental duration data that pose serious obstacles for prediction, and next properties that may help in overcoming these obstacles.

2.1. Interactions between contextual factors

A first reason for duration prediction being difficult is that segmental duration is affected by many interacting factors. In a recent study, we found eight factors to have large effects on vowel duration [12], and if one were to search the literature for all factors that at least one study found to have statistically significant effects the result would be a list of two dozen or more factors [13, 14, 15].

Segment	Unstressed/ Stressed	Stressed/ Unstressed	Differ- ence	Percent
/s/	149	112	37	33
/f/	126	101	26	25
$/t/_{burst}$	71	9	62	716
$/p/_{burst}$	61	18	43	238
$/d/_{burst}$	12	7	5	67
$/b/_{burst}$	9	8	1	12
$/t/_{closure}$	75	20	55	274
$/p/_{closure}$	90	68	22	33
/n/	63	39	24	62
/m/	75	62	14	22

Table 1: Durations (in ms) of intervocalic consonants in two stress conditions: *unstressed/stressed* and *stressed/unstressed.*

These factors interact in the quantitative sense that the magnitude of an effect (in ms or in percent) is affected by other factors. Table 1 shows durations of intervocalic consonants in two contexts defined by syllabic stress: *preceding vowel unstressed / following vowel stressed* (/f/ in "before"); and: *preceding vowel stressed / following vowel unstressed* (/f/ in "buffer"; /t/ is usually flapped in this context). The Table shows that the effects of stress are much larger for some consonants than for others: a *consonant* × *stress* interaction. Other examples of interactions include *postvocalic consonant* × *phrasal position* and *syllabic stress* × *pitch accent* [12].

These interactions imply that segmental duration can be described neither by the additive model [9] (because the differences vary) nor by the multiplicative model [7] (because the percentages vary).[5] In contrast, the Klatt model was specifically constructed to describe certain interactions, in particular the *postvocalic consonant* × *phrasal position* interaction. However, in an effort to use the Klatt model for text-to-speech synthesis it became clear that this model needed significant modifications to describe interactions involving other factors [5]. Recent tests further confirmed systematic violations of the model [11].

Thus, the existence of large interactions is undeniable, but current sums-of-products models have not succeeded in capturing these interactions. General-purpose prediction systems such as CART, of course, can handle arbitrarily intricate interactions [16].

2.2. Lopsided sparsity

Because there are many factors – several of which have more than two values – the feature space is quite large. The statistical distribution of the feature vectors exhibits an unpleasant property that we shall call "lopsided sparsity". We mean by lopsided sparsity that *the number of very rare vectors is so large that even in small text samples one is assured to encounter at least one of them.*

Sample Size	Type Count	Lowest Type Frequency
20	18	13
320	254	≈ 1
5,120	1,767	< 1
81,920	5,707	< 1
1,310,720	11,576	< 1
22,249,882	17,547	< 1

Table 2: Type counts and lowest type frequencies (per million) of contextual vectors for various sample sizes.

Table 2 illustrates the concept. We analyzed 797,524 sentences, names, and addresses (total word token count: 5,868,172; total segment count 22,249,882) by computing for each segment the feature vector characterizing those aspects of the context that we found to be relevant for segmental duration. This characterization is relatively coarse and leaves out many distinctions (such as – for vowel duration – the place of articulation of post-vocalic consonants). Nevertheless, the total feature vector type count was 17,547. Of these 17,547 types, about 10 percent occurred only once in the entire data base and 40 percent occurred less than once in a million.

Two aspects of the table are of interest. The second column shows that once sample size exceeds 5,000 the type count increases linearly with the logarithm of the sample size, with no signs of deceleration. In other words, although the linguistic space is certainly much smaller than the feature space, it is unknown whether its size is 20,000, 30,000, or significantly

[5] In the additive model $\mathrm{DUR}(\mathbf{f}) = s_{1,1}(f_1) + \cdots + s_{n,n}(f_n)$; in the multiplicative model $\mathrm{DUR}(\mathbf{f}) = s_{1,1}(f_1) \times \cdots \times s_{1,n}(f_n)$.

larger than that. The third column shows that even in samples as small as 320 segments (the equivalent of a small paragraph) one can be certain to encounter feature vectors that occur only once in a million segment tokens.

It is often suspected that general-purpose prediction systems can have serious problems with frequency imbalance in the training set, in particular when many feature vectors are outright missing. Experiments performed with CART confirmed this suspicion. In a three-factor, 36-element feature space, with artificial durations generated by the Klatt model, we found that removing 66 percent of the feature vectors from the training set produced a CART tree that performed quite poorly on test data. Similarly, neural nets can have the property that decision boundaries are sensitive to relative frequencies of feature vectors in the training sample (e.g., [17]), thereby leading to poor performance on infrequent vectors.

The key reason for these difficulties is that the ability to accurately predict durations for feature vectors for which the training set provides few or no data points is a form of *interpolation*, which in turn requires assumptions about the general form of the mapping from the feature space onto durations (the *response surface*). Precisely because they are general-purpose, these methods make minimal assumptions about the response surface, which in practice often means that the duration assigned to a missing feature vector is left to chance. For example, in CART an infinitesimal disturbance can have a major impact on the tree branching pattern. Even when this has little effect on the fit of the tree to the training data, it can have large effects on which duration is assigned to a missing feature vector. In subsection 2.4, we will argue that the response surface for segmental duration can be described particularly well by sums-of-products models, so that these models are able to generate accurate durations for (near-) missing feature vectors.

It should be noted that for certain applications, in particular automatic speech recognition, poor performance on infrequent feature vectors need not be critical because lexical access can make up for errors. Current implementations of text-to-speech synthesis systems, however, do not have error correction mechanisms. Having a seriously flawed segmental duration every few sentences is not acceptable.

2.3. Text-independent variability

A final complicating aspect of segmental duration is that, given the same input text, the same speaker (speaking at the same speed, and with the same speaking instructions) produces durations that are quite variable. For example, we found that vowel duration had a residual standard deviation of 21.4 ms, representing about 15 percent of average duration. This means that one needs either multiple observations for each feature vector so that statistically stable mean values can be computed, or data analysis techniques that are relatively insensitive to statistical noise.

In large linguistic spaces, text-independent variability implies that training data may require tens of thousands of sentences, even if one uses text selection techniques that maximize coverage such as greedy algorithms[20]. And even such texts will still contain serious frequency imbalances.

2.4. Ordinal patterns in data

A closer look at the interactions in Table 1 reveals that they are, in fact, quite well-behaved, as is shown by the following patterns:

Pattern 1. The durations in the first column are always larger than those in the second column.
Pattern 2. The effects of stress – whether measured as differences or as percentages – are always larger for alveolars than for labials in the same consonant class (i.e., having the same manner of production and voicing feature).
Pattern 3. Within alveolars and labials, the effects of stress (measured as differences) have the same order[6] over consonant classes (voiceless stop bursts largest, voiced stop bursts smallest).
Pattern 4. However, the order of the durations of the consonants is not the same in the two stress conditions. For example, /t/ is longer than /n/ in the first column, but much shorter in the second column.

This pattern of *reversals* and *non-reversals*, or *ordinal pattern*, can be captured by the following sums-of-product model:

$$DUR(C, P, S) =$$

$$s_{1,1}(C) \times s_{1,2}(P) \times s_{1,3}(S) + s_{2,1}(C) \times s_{2,2}(P) \qquad (2)$$

Here, C is consonant class, P place of articulation, and S stress condition; it is assumed that factor scales have positive values only. It is easy to show that this model implies Patterns 1–3 (for differences). Pattern 4 is not in any way *implied* by the model, but can be *accommodated* by appropriate selection of factor scale values. This accommodation would not be possible if the second term had been absent.

There are many other factors that exhibit similarly regular ordinal patterns [11, 12, 18]. In general, factors often interact, but the interactions tend to be well-behaved so that the response surface can be described by simple sums-of-products models.

Now, showing that an ordinal pattern can be captured by a sums-of-products model does not imply that there aren't many other types of models that can accomplish the same.

[6]Except for one minor reversal: 22 ms vs. 26 ms for $/p/_{closure}$ vs. $/f/$.

Intuitively, it would appear that ordinal patterns are not terribly constraining. However, there exist powerful mathematical results that show this intuition to be wrong [19]. For example, there are results showing that if data exhibit a certain ordinal pattern then we can be *assured* that the additive model will fit. Similar results have been shown for certain classes of sums-of-products models (see [19], Ch. 7). Taken together these results make it quite plausible that when data exhibit the types of ordinal patterns often observed in segmental duration, some sums-of-products model will fit the data.

To really make the case for the importance of ordinal patterns, we must make the further key assumption that the ordinal patterns of the response surface discovered in the training data base can be found in the language in general (restricted to the same speaker and speaking mode). This is based on the belief that the structure discovered in the data is the result of stable properties of the speech production apparatus. For example, the non-reversal of the syllabic stress factor can be linked to the supposition that stressed syllables are pronounced with more subglottal pressure, increased tension of the vocal chords, and larger articulatory excursions than unstressed syllables. A systematic by-product of these differences would be a difference in timing.

3. SYSTEM CONSTRUCTION

We now describe construction of a duration prediction system based on sums-of-products models.

3.1. Training data

The data base is described in detail elsewhere [12]. A male American English speaker read 2,162 isolated, short, meaningful sentences. The utterances contained 41,588 segments covering 5,073 feature vector types. Utterances were screened for disfluencies and re-recorded until none were observed. The database was segmented manually aided by software which displays the speech wave, spectrogram, and other acoustic representations. Manual segmentation was highly reliable, as shown by an average error of only 3 ms (this was obtained by having four segmentors independently segment a set of 38 utterances).

3.2. Category structure

First, we have to realize that modeling segmental duration for the entire linguistic space with a single sums-of-products model is a lost cause because of the tremendous heterogeneity of this space in terms of articulatory properties and phonetic and prosodic environments. For example, the factor "stress of the surrounding vowels" was shown to be a major factor affecting durations of intervocalic consonants; however, this factor is largely irrelevant for the – barely existing – class of intervocalic vowels. Thus, we have to construct a *category structure*, or *tree*, that divides the linguistic space into categories and develop separate sums-of-products models for these categories. In our system, we first distinguish between vowels and consonants. Next, for consonants, we distinguish between intervocalic and non-intervocalic consonants. Non-intervocalic consonants are further divided into consonants occurring in syllable onsets vs. non-phrase-final syllable codas vs. phrase-final syllable codas. Finally, all of these are split up by consonant class. Note that construction of this category structure is not based on statistical analysis but on standard phonetic and phonological distinctions.

3.3. Factor relevance and distinctions

For each category (e.g., non-intervocalic voiceless stop bursts in syllable onsets), we perform a preliminary statistical analysis to decide which factors are relevant and which distinctions to make on these factors (see [12] for details).

3.4. Model selection

We already hinted that the number of distinct sums-of-products models increases sharply with the number of factors; for example, for five factors there are more than 2 billion sums-of-products models, and for the eight factors we used for modeling vowel duration there are more than 10^{76} models.[7] Thus, in cases with more than three or four factors it is computationally unattractive to fit all possible models and select the one that fits best. Fortunately, there are methods that allow one to find the best model with far less computational effort [10, 11] – requiring only 31 analyses (each the computational equivalent of an analysis of variance) for five factors. These methods are "diagnostic" because they can detect trends in the data that eliminate entire classes of sums-of-products models from consideration.

3.5. Parameter estimation

Once a sums-of-products is selected, parameters are estimated with a weighted least-squares method using a simple parameter-wise gradient technique.

4. RESULTS

4.1. Statistical fit

Forty-two sums-of-products models were constructed – one for each "leaf" of the category tree. Overall, 619 parameters were estimated (32 for vowels, 196 for intervocalic consonants, and 391 for non-intervocalic consonants). On average, each parameter was based on eight data points.

The overall correlation (over all 41,588 segments) between observed and predicted durations was 0.93 (0.90, 0.90, and 0.87, when computed separately for vowels, intervocalic con-

[7] The number of distinct models converges to $2^{2^n-1} - 1$, where n is the number of factors.

sonants, and non-intervocalic consonants, respectively).

When we computed average durations for each feature vector in two equal-sized subsets of the data base, and estimated parameters for the sums-of-products model for vowels separately on each subset, the durations predicted from the two parameter sets correlated 0.987. Similarly, when we estimated parameters from data obtained on a second (female) speaker, male durations (feature vector means) were predicted with a correlation of 0.96.

In addition to these correlational findings, we also found that the key interactions were mimicked closely by the predicted durations (e.g., see Figs. 14–16 in [12]).

4.2. Text-to-speech synthesizer evaluation

A new duration module for the AT&T Bell Laboratories text-to-speech synthesizer was written based on the 42 sums-of-products models and their parameter estimates. We then compared the durations generated by the new module with those generated by the old module in a subjective listening experiment using naive listeners (see [20] for details). The old module consists of a list of several hundred duration rules similar to, but somewhat simpler than, the Klatt rules [5]. In the experiment, a listener heard two versions of the same sentence, selected the preferred version, and indicated strength of choice on a 1–6 scale (where 1 denotes complete indifference and 6 the strongest possible preference). All listeners preferred the new version. Across listeners, the new version was preferred on 73 percent of the presentations (80 percent for strength ratings of three or more). On only one of the 200 sentences was there a statistically significant majority of listeners preferring the old version; on 81 percent of the sentences listeners preferred the new version – on 60 percent with a statistically significant majority.

5. DISCUSSION

The approach taken in the paper raises some general issues that we want to briefly touch upon here.

5.1. "With Enough Data"

A general theme in our approach to modeling segmental duration is that this domain has properties distinguishing it from other domains and that this requires special-purpose methods. However, the ever-increasing amount of data that can be collected, processed, and stored, may lead one to believe that in the near future general-purpose prediction systems will be able to outperform any special-purpose system – the "With Enough Data" argument. We submit that this may rest on a misappreciation of the magnitude of sparsity encountered in certain linguistic spaces. When a training set does not provide a good number of data points for every feature vector in the linguistic space, it is unclear how general-purpose methods can be called upon to fill in the holes in the response surface without making explicit assumptions about the phenomena being modeled, or, in other words, without de facto being a special-purpose system.

5.2. Manually vs. automatically generated segment boundaries

Although manually generated phoneme boundaries have some degree of arbitrariness, there is enough overlap between various conventions to produce a remarkable degree of consensus between durational findings obtained in different studies. However, automatic speech recognition systems often produce phoneme boundaries that do not correspond to those produced manually, which may lead to very different durational behavior. For example, we found in a sub-word unit based system that vowels followed by /z/ were quite short, whereas in manually segmented data such vowels tend to be long [12]. Apparently, the training algorithm achieved higher likelihoods by putting the boundary well into the vowel. Mismatches such as these make duration models based on manually segmented data irrelevant for speech recognition. Thus, either one has to develop models for these automatically generated segment durations, or one has to constrain training algorithms to produce boundaries that correspond more closely to those generated manually.

5.3. Segments vs. other units

The final issue concerns the use of segments vs. larger units, in particular syllables. It has been suggested that not segments but syllables should play a central role in duration prediction [21, 22], the hypothesis being that speakers control durations of syllables more carefully than the durations of the segments that make up a syllable. However, the following three considerations make this proposal somewhat less appealing. First, in our factorial characterization of context, the role of the syllable is as important as that of the segment or the word. To illustrate, we define within-word position in terms of syllables (and segments, but only to distinguish between open vs. closed syllables), and within-phrase position in terms of words, syllables, and segments.

Second, there are implications from research on sub-segmental timing effects [23, 24, 25]. An example of such an effect is that the steady-state part of /a^y/ expands much more than the glide part (comparing "bite" with "bide"); in other diphthongs or in vowels, primarily the final part is stretched. Timing of some of these phenomena appears to be quite precise: Gay [23] found near-identical formant velocities across three different speaking rates. These findings urge close scrutiny of the claim that larger units are timed with more precision than smaller units. They also imply that whatever unit one selects for the lead role, timing must be specified on a fine, sub-segmental scale.

Third, it is not clear how to explain the well-documented fact that phrasal position amplifies the effects of post-vocalic voicing on vowel duration. In Campbell's [21] approach, each segment is characterized by a mean duration and an "elasticity" (variance) parameter to allow for some segments to be stretched more than others when a syllable is stretched by extra-syllabic factors. Because elasticity is assumed to be a context-independent segmental parameter, it cannot explain the amplification effect of phrasal position. Although syllable-based conceptualizations other than Campbell's might be able to address this problem, the challenge of how to specify sub-syllabic timing within a syllabic framework is clearly a serious one.

A possible resolution of the unit issue is that it may not need to be resolved. The timing pattern of speech might be viewed as the resultant of multiple constraints – some computable locally and others, say, at the paragraph level; some being inescapable consequences of the physiology of the vocal tract and others under voluntary control. These constraints could be embedded in a multi-level model where no unit or level is more central than others, but where timing is computed on a sub-segmental scale.

It should also be understood that the very concept of unit tacitly makes the concatenative assumption. This assumption is not shared by approaches based on asynchronous entities such as feature bundles [26] or formant control parameters [27]. In these systems, at any point in time more than one entity can be "on" and their on- and offsets need not coincide.

References

1. Breiman, L., Friedman, J. H., Olshen, R. A., and Stone, C. J., *Classification and regression trees*. Wadsworth & Brooks, Monterey, CA, 1984.
2. Riley, M. D., "Tree-based modeling for speech synthesis", In G. Bailly, C. Benoit, and T.R. Sawallis, editors, *Talking Machines: Theories, Models, and Designs*, pp. 265–273, Elsevier, Amsterdam, 1992.
3. Klatt, D. H., "Linguistic uses of segmental duration in English: Acoustic and perceptual evidence", *Journal of the Acoustical Society of America*, Vol. 59, 1976, pp. 1209–1221.
4. Klatt, D. H., "Review of text-to-speech conversion for English", *Journal of the Acoustical Society of America*, Vol. 82(3), 1987, pp. 737–793.
5. Allen, J., Hunnicut, S., and Klatt, D. H., *From Text to Speech: The MITalk System*. Cambridge University press, Cambridge, U.K., 1987.
6. Coker, C. H., Umeda, N., and Browman, C. P., "Automatic synthesis from ordinary English text", *IEEE Transactions on Audio and Electroacoustics*, AU-21(3), 1973, pp. 293–298.
7. Lindblom, D., and Rapp, K., "Some temporal properties of spoken Swedish", *PILUS*, Vol. 21, 1973, pp. 1–59.
8. Carlson, R., "Duration models in use", In *Proceedings of the XIIth Meeting*, Aix-en-Provence, France. International Congress of Phonetic Sciences, 1991.
9. Kaiki, N., Takeda, K., and Sagisaka, Y., "Statistical analysis for segmental duration rules in Japanese speech synthesis", In *Proceedings ICSLP '90*, 1990, pp. 17–20.
10. van Santen, J. P. H., "Analyzing n-way tables with sums-of-products models", *Journal of Mathematical Psychology*, Vol. 37, 1993 (In press).
11. van Santen, J. P. H., and Olive, J. P., "The analysis of contextual effects on segmental duration", *Computer Speech and Language*, Vol. 4, 1990, pp. 359–391.
12. van Santen, J. P. H., "Contextual effects on vowel duration", *Speech Communication*, Vol. 11, 1992, pp. 513–546.
13. Crystal, T. H., and House, A. S., "Segmental durations in connected-speech signals: Current results", *Journal of the Acoustical Society of America*, Vol. 83, 1988a, pp. 1553–1573.
14. Crystal, T. H., and House, A. S., "Segmental durations in connected-speech signals: Syllabic stress", *Journal of the Acoustical Society of America*, Vol. 83, 1988b, pp. 1574–1585.
15. Crystal, T. H., and House, A. S., 1990. "Articulation rate and the duration of syllables and stress groups in connected speech", *Journal of the Acoustical Society of America*, Vol. 88, 1990, pp. 101–112.
16. Hastie, T. J., and Tibshirani, R. J., *Generalized Additive Models*. Chapman and Hall, London, 1990.
17. Sabourin, M., and Mitiche, A., "Optical character recognition by a neural network", *Neural Networks*, Vol. 5, 1992, pp. 843–852.
18. van Santen, J. P. H., "Deriving text-to-speech durations from natural speech", In G. Bailly and C. Benoit, editors, *Talking Machines: Theories, Models, and Designs*, pp. 275-285, Elsevier, Amsterdam, 1992.
19. Krantz, D. H., Luce, R. D., Suppes, P., and Tversky, A., *Foundations of Measurement, Vol. I*, Wiley, New York, 1971.
20. van Santen, J. P. H., "Perceptual experiments for diagnostic testing of text-to-speech systems", *Computer Speech and Language*, Vol. 7, 1993 (In press).
21. Campbell, W. N., "Syllable-based segmental duration", In G. Bailly, C. Benoit, and T.R. Sawallis, editors, *Talking Machines: Theories, Models, and Designs*, pp. 211–224, Elsevier, Amsterdam, 1992.
22. Collier, R., "A comment on the prediction of prosody", In G. Bailly, C. Benoit, and T.R. Sawallis, editors, *Talking Machines: Theories, Models, and Designs*, pp. 205–207, Elsevier, Amsterdam, 1992.
23. Gay, Th., "Effect of speaking rate on diphthong formant movements", *Journal of the Acoustical Society of America*, Vol. 44, 1968, pp. 1570–1573.
24. Hertz, S. R., "Streams, phones and transitions: toward a new phonological and phonetic model of formant timing", *Journal of Phonetics*, Vol. 19, 1991, pp. 91–109.
25. van Santen, J. P. H., Coleman, J. C., and Randolph, M. A., "Effects of postvocalic voicing on the time course of vowels and diphthongs", *J. Acoust. Soc. Am.*, Vol. 92(4, Pt. 2), 1992, pp. 2444.
26. Coleman, J.S., "Synthesis-by-rule" without segments of rewrite-rules", In G. Bailly, C. Benoit, and T.R. Sawallis, editors, *Talking Machines: Theories, Models, and Designs*, pp. 43–60, Elsevier, Amsterdam, 1992.
27. Stevens, K. N., and Bickley, C. A., "Constraints among parameters simplify control of Klatt formant synthesizer", *Journal of Phonetics*, Vol. 19, 1991, pp. 161–174.

A SPEECH-FIRST MODEL FOR REPAIR DETECTION AND CORRECTION

Christine Nakatani
Division of Applied Sciences
Harvard University
Cambridge MA 02138

Julia Hirschberg
2D-450, AT&T Bell Laboratories
600 Mountain Avenue
Murray Hill NJ 07974-0636

ABSTRACT

Interpreting fully natural speech is an important goal for spoken language understanding systems. However, while corpus studies have shown that about 10% of spontaneous utterances contain self-corrections, or REPAIRS, little is known about the extent to which cues in the speech signal may facilitate repair processing. We identify several cues based on acoustic and prosodic analysis of repairs in the DARPA Air Travel Information System database, and propose methods for exploiting these cues to detect and correct repairs.

1. INTRODUCTION

Disfluencies in spontaneous speech pose serious problems for spoken language systems. First, a speaker may produce a partial word or FRAGMENT, a string of phonemes that does not form the complete word intended by the speaker. Some fragments may coincidentally match words actually in the lexicon, as in (1); others will be identified with the acoustically closest lexicon item(s), as in (2).[1]

(1) What is the earliest **fli–** flight from Washington to Atlanta leaving on Wednesday September fourth?

(2) *Actual string*: What is the fare **fro–** on American Airlines fourteen forty three
Recognized string: With fare **four** American Airlines fourteen forty three

Even if all words in a disfluent segment are correctly recognized, failure to detect the location of a disfluency may lead to interpretation errors during subsequent processing, as in (3):

(3) ...Delta leaving Boston seventeen twenty one arriving Fort Worth **twenty two** twenty one forty and flight number ...

Here, '*twenty two twenty one forty*' must somehow be interpreted as a flight arrival time; the system must choose on some basis among '21:40', '22:21', and '22:40'.

[1] We indicate the presence of a word fragment in examples by the diacritic '–'. Self-corrected portions of the utterance, or REPARANDA, appear in boldface. Unless otherwise noted, all repair examples in this paper are drawn from the corpus described in Section 4. Recognizer output shown is from the recognition system described in [1] on the ATIS June 1990 test.

Although studies of large speech corpora have found that approximately 10% of spontaneous utterances contain disfluencies involving self-correction, or REPAIRS [2, 3], little is known about how to integrate repair processing with real-time speech recognition and with incremental syntactic and semantic analysis of partial utterances in spoken language systems. In particular, the speech signal itself has been relatively unexplored as a source of processing cues that may facilitate the detection and correction of repairs. In this paper, we present results from a pilot study examining the acoustic and prosodic characteristics of all repairs (146) occurring in 1,453 utterances from the DARPA Air Travel Information System (ATIS) database. Our results are interpreted within a new "speech-first" framework for investigating repairs, the REPAIR INTERVAL MODEL, which builds upon Labov 1966 [4] and Hindle 1983 [2].

2. PREVIOUS COMPUTATIONAL APPROACHES

While self-correction has long been a topic of psycholinguistic study, computational work in this area has been sparse. Early work in computational linguistics included repairs as one type of ill-formed input and proposed solutions based upon extensions to existing text parsing techniques such as augmented transition networks (ATNs), network-based semantic grammars, case frame grammars, pattern matching and deterministic parsing [5, 6, 2, 7, 8]. Recently, Shriberg et al. 1992 and Bear et al.1992 [3, 9] have proposed a two-stage method for processing repairs that integrates lexical, syntactic, semantic, and acoustic information. In the first stage, lexical pattern matching rules are used to retrieve candidate repair utterances. In the second stage, syntactic, semantic, and acoustic information is used to filter the true repairs from the false positives. By these methods, [9] report identifying 309 repairs in the 406 utterances in their 10,718 utterance corpus which contained 'nontrivial' repairs and incorrectly hypothesizing repairs in 191 fluent utterances, which represents recall of 76% with precision of 62%. Of the 62% containing self-repairs, [9] report finding the appropriate correction for 57%.

While Shriberg et al. promote the important idea that automatic repair handling requires integration of knowledge from multiple sources, we argue that such "text-first" pattern-matching approaches suffer from several limitations. First, the assumption that correct text transcriptions will be available from existing speech recognizers is problematic, since current systems rely primarily upon language models and lexicons derived from fluent speech to decide among competing acoustic hypotheses. These systems usually treat disfluencies in training and recognition as noise; moreover, they have no way of modeling word fragments, even though these occur in the majority of repairs. Second, detection and correction strategies are defined in terms of ad hoc patterns; it is not clear how one repair type is related to another or how the set of existing patterns should be augmented to improve performance. Third, from a computational point of view, it seems preferable that spoken language systems detect a repair as early as possible, to permit early pruning of the hypothesis space, rather than carrying along competing hypotheses, as in "text-first" approaches. Fourth, utterances containing overlapping repairs such as (4) (noted in [2, p. 123]) cannot be handled by simple surface structure manipulations.

(4) I think that **it you get–** it's more strict in Catholic schools.

Finally, on a cognitive level, there is recent psycholinguistic evidence that humans detect repairs in the vicinity of the interruption point, well before the end of the repair utterance [10, 11, 12].

An exception to "text-first" approaches is Hindle 1983 [2]. Hindle decouples repair detection from repair correction. His correction strategies rely upon an inventory of three repair types that are defined in relation to independently formulated linguistic principles. Importantly, Hindle allows non-surface-based transformations as correction strategies. A related property is that the correction of a single repair may be achieved by sequential application of several correction rules.

Hindle classifies repairs as 1) full sentence restarts, in which an entire utterance is re-initiated; 2) constituent repairs, in which one syntactic constituent is replaced by another;[2] and 3) surface level repairs, in which identical strings appear adjacent to each other. Correction strategies for each repair type are defined in terms of extensions to a deterministic parser. The application of a correction routine is triggered by an hypothesized acoustic/phonetic EDIT SIGNAL, "a markedly abrupt cut-off of the speech signal" (Hindle 1983 [2, p. 123], cf. Labov 1966 [4]), which is assumed to mark the interruption of fluent speech.

Hindle's methods achieved a success rate of 97% on a transcribed corpus of 1,500 sentences in which the edit signal was orthographically represented. This rate of success suggests that identification of the edit signal site is crucial for repair correction.

3. THE REPAIR INTERVAL MODEL

In contrast to "text-first" approaches, we introduce an alternative, "speech-first" model for repair detection/correction, the REPAIR INTERVAL MODEL (RIM). RIM provides a framework for testing the extent to which cues from the speech signal itself can contribute to the identification and correction of repair utterances. RIM incorporates two main assumptions of Hindle 1983 [2]: 1) correction strategies are linguistically rule-governed, and 2) linguistic cues must be available to signal when a disfluency has occurred and to 'trigger' correction strategies. As Hindle [2] noted, if the processing of disfluencies were not rule-governed, it would be difficult to reconcile the infrequent intrusion of disfluencies on human speech comprehension, especially for language learners, with their frequent rate of occurrence in spontaneous speech. We view Hindle's results as evidence supporting the first assumption. Our study tests the second assumption by exploring the acoustic and prosodic features of repairs that might serve as some kind of edit signal for rule-governed correction strategies. While text-first strategies rely upon 'triggers' of a lexical nature, we will argue that our speech-first model is consistent with psycholinguistic evidence concerning the human detection of repairs, and is therefore cognitively plausible as well as linguistically principled.

RIM divides the repair event into three consecutive temporal intervals and identifies time points within those intervals which are computationally critical. A full repair comprises three intervals, the REPARANDUM INTERVAL, the DISFLUENCY INTERVAL, and the REPAIR INTERVAL. Following Levelt [13], we identify the REPARANDUM as the lexical material which is to be repaired. The end of the reparandum coincides with the termination of the fluent portion of the utterance and corresponds to the locus of the edit signal. We term this point the INTERRUPTION SITE (IS). The DISFLUENCY INTERVAL extends from the IS to the resumption of fluent speech, and may contain any combination of silence, pause fillers ('*uh*'), or CUE PHRASES ('*Oops*' or '*I mean*'), which indicate the speaker's recognition of his/her performance error. RIM extends the edit signal hypothesis that repairs are phonetically signaled at the point of interruption to include acoustic-prosodic phenomena across the disfluency interval. The REPAIR INTERVAL corresponds to the uttering of the correcting material, which is intended to 'replace' the reparandum. It extends from the offset of the disfluency interval to the resumption of non-repair speech. In (5), for example, the reparandum occurs from 1 to 2, the disfluency interval from 2 to 3, and the repair interval from 3 to 4.

(5) Give me airlines **1** [**flying to Sa–**] **2** [SILENCE uh

[2] This is consistent with Levelt 1983's [13] observation that the material to be replaced and the correcting material in a repair often share structural properties akin to those shared by coordinated constituents.

SILENCE] **3** [flying to Boston] **4** from San Francisco next summer that have business class.

4. ACOUSTIC-PROSODIC CHARACTERISTICS OF REPAIRS

We report results from a pilot study on the acoustic and prosodic correlates of repair events as defined in the RIM framework. Our corpus consisted of 1,453 utterances by 64 speakers from the DARPA Airline Travel and Information System (ATIS) database [14, 15]. The utterances were collected at Texas Instruments and at SRI and will be referred to as the "TI set" and "SRI set," respectively. 132 (9.1%) of these utterances contained at least one repair, and 48 (75%) of the 64 speakers produced at least one repair. We defined repairs for our study as the self-correction of one or more phonemes (up to and including sequences of words) in an utterance.

Orthographic transcriptions of the utterances were prepared by DARPA contractors according to standardized conventions. The utterances were labeled at Bell Laboratories for word boundaries and intonational prominences and phrasing following Pierrehumbert's description of English intonation [16, 17]. Disfluencies were categorized as REPAIR (self-correction of lexical material), HESITATION ("unnatural" interruption of speech flow without any following correction of lexical material), or OTHER DISFLUENCY. For RIM analysis, each of the three repair intervals was labeled. All speech analysis was carried out using Entropics WAVES software [18].

4.1. Identifying the Reparandum Interval

From the point of view of repair detection and correction, acoustic-prosodic cues to the onset of the reparandum would clearly be useful in the choice of appropriate correction strategy. However, perceptual experiments by Lickley and several co-authors [10, 11, 12] show that humans do *not* detect an oncoming disfluency as early as the onset of the reparandum. Subjects *were* able to detect disfluencies in the vicinity of the disfluency interval — and sometimes before the last word of the reparandum. Reparanda ending in word fragments were among those few repairs subjects detected at the interruption site (i.e. the RIM IS), but only a small number of the test stimuli contained such fragments [11]. In our corpus, about two-thirds of reparanda end in word fragments.[3]

Based on these experimental results, the reparandum offset is the earliest time point where we would expect to find evidence of Labov's and Hindle's hypothesized edit signal. In RIM, the notion of the edit signal is extended conceptually to include any phenomenon which may contribute to the perception of an "abrupt cut-off" of the speech signal — including phonetic cues such as coarticulation phenomena, word fragments, interruption glottalization, pause, and prosodic cues which occur from the reparandum offset through the disfluency interval. Our acoustic and prosodic analysis of the reparandum interval focuses on identifying acoustic-phonetic properties of word fragments, as well as additional phonetic cues marking the reparandum offset.

[3] Shriberg et al. found that 60.2% of repairs in their corpus contained fragments.

Syllables	Tokens (N=117)	%
0	44	37.6%
1	60	51.3%
2	11	9.4%
3	1	0.9%
4	1	0.8%

Table 1: Length of Reparandum Offset Word Fragments

To build a model of word fragmentation for eventual use in fragment identification, we first analyzed the length and initial phoneme classes of fragment repairs. Almost 90% of fragments in our corpus are one syllable or less in length (Table 1). Table 2 shows the distribution of initial phonemes for all fragments, for single syllable fragments, and for single consonant fragments. From Table 2 we see that single consonant fragments occur six times more often as fricatives than as the next most common phoneme class, stop consonants. However, fricatives and stops occur almost equally as the initial consonant in single syllable fragments. So (regardless of the underlying distribution of lexical items in the corpus), we find a difference in the distribution of phonemic characteristics of fragments based on fragment length, which can be modeled in fragment identification.

We also analyzed the broad word class of the speaker's intended word for each fragment, where the intended word was recoverable. Table 3 shows that there is a clear tendency for fragmentation at the reparandum offset to occur on content words rather than function words. Therefore, systems that rely primarily on lexical, semantic or pragmatic processing to detect and correct repairs will be faced with the problem of reconstructing content words from very short fragments, a

Phoneme Class	% of All Fragments (N=117)	% of Single Syllable Fragments (N=60)	% of Single Consonant Fragments (N=44)
stop	21%	28%	11%
vowel	15%	18%	7%
fricative	44%	25%	73%
nasal/glide/liquid	15%	22%	9%
h	3%	7%	0%

Table 2: Feature Class of Initial Phoneme in Fragments by Fragment Length

Lexical Class	Tokens	%
Content	61	52.1%
Function	13	11.1%
Unknown	43	36.8%

Table 3: Lexical Class of Word Fragments at Reparandum Offset (N=117)

task that even human transcribers find difficult.[4]

One acoustic cue marking the IS which Bear et al. [9] noted is the presence of INTERRUPTION GLOTTALIZATION, irregular glottal pulses, at the reparandum offset. This form of glottalization is acoustically distinct from laryngealization (creaky voice), which often occurs at the end of prosodic phrases; glottal stops, which often precede vowel-initial words; and epenthetic glottalization. In our corpus, 29.5% of reparanda offsets are marked by interruption glottalization.[5] Although interruption glottalization is usually associated with fragments, it is not the case that fragments are usually glottalized. In our database, 61.7% of fragments are not glottalized and 16.3% of glottalized reparanda offsets are not fragments.

Finally, sonorant endings of fragments in our corpus sometimes exhibited coarticulatory effects of an unrealized subsequent phoneme. When these effects occur with a following pause (see Section 4.2), they could be used to distinguish fragments from full phrase-final words — such as *'fli–'* from *'fly'* in Example (1).

To summarize, our corpus shows that most reparanda offsets end in word fragments. These fragments are usually intended (where that intention is recoverable) to be content words, are almost always short (one syllable or less) and show different distributions of initial phoneme class depending on their length. Also, fragments are sometimes glottalized and sometimes exhibit coarticulatory effects of missing subsequent phonemes. These properties of the reparandum offset might be used in direct modeling of word fragmentation in speech recognition systems, enabling repair detection for a majority of repairs using primarily acoustic-phonetic cues. Besides noting the potential of utilizing distributional regularities and other acoustic-phonetic cues in a speech-first approach to repair processing, we conclude that the difficulty of recovering intended words from generally short fragments makes a text-first approach inapplicable for the majority class of fragment repairs.

4.2. Identifying the Disfluency Interval

In the RIM model, the disfluency interval (DI) includes all cue phrases, filled pauses, and silence from the offset of the reparandum to the onset of the repair. While the literature contains a number of hypotheses about this interval (cf. [19, 3]), our pilot study supports a new hypothesis associating fragment repairs and the duration of pauses following the IS.

Table 4 shows the average duration of DIs in repair utterances compared to the average length of utterance-internal silent pauses for all fluent utterances in the ATIS TI set. Although, over all, DIs in repair utterances are shorter than utterance-internal pauses in fluent utterances, the difference is only weakly significant ($p<.05$, tstat=1.98, df=1325). If we break down the repair utterances based on fragmentation, we find that the DI duration for fragments is significantly shorter than for nonfragments ($p<.01$, tstat=2.81, df=139). The fragment DI duration is also significantly shorter than fluent pause intervals ($p<.001$, tstat=3.39, df=1268), while there is no significant difference for nonfragment DIs and fluent utterances. So, while DIs in general appear to be distinct from fluent pauses, our data indicate that the duration of DIs in fragment repairs could be exploited to identify these cases as repairs as well as to distinguish them from nonfragment repairs. While Shriberg et al. claim that pauses can be used to distinguish false positives from true repairs for two of their patterns, they do not investigate the use of pausal duration as a primary cue for repair detection.

4.3. Identifying the Repair

Several influential studies of acoustic-prosodic repair cues have relied upon lexical, semantic, and pragmatic definitions of repair types [20, 13]. Levelt & Cutler 1983 [20] claim that repairs of erroneous information (ERROR REPAIRS) are marked by increased intonational prominence on the correcting information, while other kinds of repairs such as additions to descriptions (APPROPRIATENESS REPAIRS) generally are not. We investigated whether the repair interval is marked by special intonational prominence relative to the reparandum for repairs in our corpus.

To obtain objective measures of relative prominence, we compared absolute f0 and energy in the sonorant center of the last accented lexical item in the reparandum with that of the first accented item in the repair interval.[6] We found a small but reliable increase in f0 from the end of the reparandum to the beginning of the repair (mean=5.2 Hz, $p<.001$, tstat=3.16, df=131). There was also a small but reliable increase in amplitude across the DI (mean=+2 db, $p<.001$, tstat=4.83, df=131). We analyzed the same phenomena across utterance-internal fluent pauses for the ATIS TI set and found no similarly reliable changes in either f0 or intensity — perhaps because the variation in the fluent population was much greater than the observed changes for the repair population. And when

[4] Transcribers were unable to identify intended words for over one-third of the fragments in our corpus.

[5] Shriberg et al. report glottalization on 24 out of 25 vowel-final fragments.

[6] We performed the same analysis for the last and first syllables in the reparandum and repair respectively; results did not substantially differ from those reported here for accented values.

Utterance Type	Mean	Std Dev	N
Fluent pauses	513 msec	15 msec	1186
All repairs	389 msec	57 msec	146
a) Fragment repairs	252 msec	32 msec	94
b) Nonfragment repairs	637 msec	143 msec	52

Table 4: Duration of Disfluency Intervals vs. Utterance-Internal Fluent Pauses

we compared the f0 and amplitude changes from reparandum to repair with those observed for fluent pauses, we found no significant differences between the two populations.

So, while small but reliable differences in f0 and amplitude exist between the reparandum offset and the repair onset, we conclude that these differences do not help to distinguish repairs from fluent speech. Although it is not entirely straightforward to compare our objective measures of intonational prominence with Levelt and Cutler's perceptual findings, our results provide only weak support for theirs. While we find small but significant changes in two correlates of intonational prominence from the reparandum to the repair, the distributions of change in f0 and energy for our data are unimodal; when we separate repairs in our corpus into Levelt and Cutler's error repairs and appropriateness repairs, statistical analysis does *not* support Levelt and Cutler's claim that only the former group is intonationally 'marked'.

Previous studies of disfluency have paid considerable attention to the vicinity of the IS but little to the repair offset. Yet, locating the repair offset (the end of the correcting material) is crucial for the delimitation of segments over which correction strategies operate. One simple hypothesis we tested is that repair interval offsets are intonationally marked by minor or major prosodic phrase boundaries. We found that the repair offset co-occurs with minor phrase boundaries for 49% of TI set repairs. To see whether these boundaries were distinct from those in fluent speech, we compared the phrasing of repair utterances with phrasing predicted for the corresponding 'correct' version of the utterance. To predict phrasing, we used a procedure reported by Wang & Hirschberg 1992 [21] that uses statistical modeling techniques to predict phrasing from a large corpus of labeled ATIS speech; we used a prediction tree that achieves 88.4% accuracy on the ATIS TI corpus. For the TI set, we found that, for 40% of all repairs, an actual boundary occurs at the repair offset where one is predicted; and for 33% of all repairs, no actual boundary occurs where none is predicted. For the remaining 27% of repairs for which predicted phrasing diverged from actual phrasing, for 10% a boundary occurred where none was predicted; for 17%, no boundary occurred when one was predicted.

In addition to these difference observed at the repair offset, we also found more general differences from predicted phrasing over the entire repair interval, which we hypothesize may be partly understood as follows: Two strong predictors of prosodic phrasing in fluent speech are syntactic constituency [22, 23, 24], especially the relative inviolability of noun phrases [21], and the length of prosodic phrases [23, 25]. On the one hand, we found occurrences of phrase boundaries at repair offsets which occurred within larger NPs, as in (6), where it is precisely the noun modifier — not the entire noun phrase — which is corrected.[7]

(6) Show me all **n–** round-trip | flights | from Pittsburgh | to Atlanta.

We speculate that, by marking off the modifier intonationally, a speaker may signal that operations relating just this phrase to earlier portions of the utterance can achieve the proper correction of the disfluency. We also found cases of 'lengthened' intonational phrases in repair intervals, as illustrated in the single-phrase reparandum in (7), where the corresponding fluent version of the reparandum is predicted to contain four phrases.

(7) **What airport is it | is located** | what is the name of the airport located in San Francisco

Again, we hypothesize that the role played by this unusually long phrase is the same as that of early phrase boundaries in NPs discussed above. In both cases, the phrase boundary delimits a meaningful unit for subsequent correction strategies. For example, we might understand the multiple repairs in (7) as follows: First the speaker attempts a VP repair, with the repair phrase delimited by a single prosodic phrase '*is located*'. Then the initially repaired utterance '*What airport is located*' is itself repaired, with the reparadum again delimited by a single prosodic phrase, '*What is the name of the airport located in San Francisco*'.

While a larger corpus must be examined in order to fully characterize the relationship between prosodic boundaries at repair offsets and those in fluent speech, we believe that the differences we have observed are promising. A general speech-first cue such as intonational phrasing could prove useful both for lexical pattern matching strategies as well as syntactic

[7] Prosodic boundaries are indicated by '|'.

constituent-based strategies, by delimiting the region in which these correction strategies must seek the repairing material.

5. DISCUSSION

In this paper, we propose a "speech-first" model, the Repair Interval Model, for studying repairs in spontaneous speech. This model divides the repair event into a reparandum interval, a disfluency interval, and a repair interval. We present empirical results from acoustic-phonetic and prosodic analysis of a corpus of spontaneous speech. In this study, we found that most reparanda offsets ended in word fragments, usually of (intended) content words, and that these fragments tended to be quite short and to exhibit particular acoustic-phonetic characteristics. We found that the disfluency interval could be distinguished from intonational phrase boundaries in fluent speech in terms of duration of pause, and that fragment and nonfragment repairs could also be distinguished from one another in terms of the duration of the disfluency interval. For our corpus, repair onsets could be distinguished from reparandum offsets by small but reliable differences in f0 and amplitude, and repair intervals differed from fluent speech in their characteristic prosodic phrasing. We are currently analyzing a larger sample of the ATIS corpus to test our initial results and to evaluate other possible predictors of repair phenomena.

REFERENCES

1. Lee, C.-H., Rabiner, L. R., Pieraccini, R., and Wilpon, J. Acoustic modeling for large vocabulary speech recognition. *Computer Speech and Language*, 4:127–165, April 1990.
2. Hindle, D. Deterministic parsing of syntactic non-fluencies. In *Proceedings of the 21st Annual Meeting*, pages 123–128, Cambridge MA, 1983. Association for Computational Linguistics.
3. Shriberg, E., Bear, J., and Dowding, J. Automatic detection and correction of repairs in human-computer dialog. In *Proceedings of the Speech and Natural Language Workshop*, pages 419–424, Harriman NY, 1992. DARPA, Morgan Kaufmann.
4. Labov, W. On the grammaticality of everyday speech. Paper Presented at the Linguistic Society of America Annual Meeting, 1966.
5. Weischedel, R. M. and Black, J. Responding to potentially unparseable sentences. *American Journal of Computational Linguistics*, 6:97–109, 1980.
6. Carbonell, J. and Hayes, P. Recovery strategies of parsing extragrammatical language. *American Journal of Computational Linguistics*, 9(3-4):123–146, 1983.
7. Weischedel, R. M. and Sondheimer, N. K. Meta-rules as a basis for processing ill-formed input. *American Journal of Computational Linguistics*, 9(3-4):161–177, 1983.
8. Fink, P. E. and Biermann, A. W. The correction of ill-formed input using history-based expectation with applications to speech understanding. *Computational Linguistics*, 12(1):13–36, 1986.
9. Bear, J., Dowding, J., and Shriberg, E. Integrating multiple knowledge sources for detection and correction of repairs in human-computer dialog. In *Proceedings of the 30th Annual Meeting*, pages 56–63, Newark DE, 1992. Association for Computational Linguistics.
10. Lickley, R. J., Bard, E. G., and Shillcock, R. C. Understanding disfluent speech: Is there an editing signal? In *Proceedings of the International Congress of Phonetic Sciences*, pages 98–101, Aix-en-Provence, 1991. ICPhS.
11. Lickley, R. J., Shillcock, R. C., and Bard, E. G. Processing disfluent speech: How and when are disfluencies found? In *Proceedings of the Second European Conference on Speech Communication and Technology, Vol. III*, pages 1499–1502, Genova, September 1991. Eurospeech-91.
12. Lickley, R. J. and Bard, E. G. Processing disfluent speech: Recognising disfluency before lexical access. In *Proceedings of the International Conference on Spoken Language Processing*, pages 935–938, Banff, October 1992. ICSLP.
13. Levelt, W. Monitoring and self-repair in speech. *Cognition*, 14:41–104, 1983.
14. Hemphill, C. T., Godfrey, J. J., and Doddington, G. R. The atis spoken language systems pilot corpus. In *Proceedings of the Speech and Natural Language Workshop*, pages 96–101, Hidden Valley PA, June 1990. DARPA.
15. MADCOW. Multi-site data collection for a spoken language corpus. In *Proceedings of the Speech and Natural Language Workshop*, pages 7–14, Harriman NY, February 1992. DARPA, Morgan Kaufmann.
16. Pierrehumbert, J. B. *The Phonology and Phonetics of English Intonation*. PhD thesis, Massachusetts Institute of Technology, September 1980. Distributed by the Indiana University Linguistics Club.
17. Pierrehumbert, J. B. and Beckman, M. E. *Japanese Tone Structure*. MIT Press, Cambridge MA, 1988.
18. Talkin, D. Looking at speech. *Speech Technology*, 4:74–77, April-May 1989.
19. Blackmer, E. R. and Mitton, J. L. Theories of monitoring and the timing of repairs in spontaneous speech. *Cognition*, 39:173–194, 1991.
20. Levelt, W. and Cutler, A. Prosodic marking in speech repair. *Journal of Semantics*, 2:205–217, 1983.
21. Wang, M. Q. and Hirschberg, J. Automatic classification of intonational phrase boundaries. *Computer Speech and Language*, 6:175–196, 1992.
22. Cooper, W. E. and Sorenson, J. M. Fundamental frequency contours at syntactic boundaries. *Journal of the Acoustical Society of America*, 62(3):683–692, September 1977.
23. Gee, J. P. and Grosjean, F. Performance structure: A psycholinguistic and linguistic apprasial. *Cognitive Psychology*, 15:411–458, 1983.
24. Selkirk, E. O. Phonology and syntax: The relation between sound and structure. In Freyjeim, T., editor, *Nordic Prosody II: Proceedings of the Second Symposium on Prosody in the Nordic language*, pages 111–140, Trondheim, 1984. TAPIR.
25. Bachenko, J. and Fitzpatrick, E. A computational grammar of discourse-neutral prosodic phrasing in English. *Computational Linguistics*, 16(3):155–170, 1990.

PROSODY/PARSE SCORING AND ITS APPLICATION IN ATIS

N. M. Veilleux *M. Ostendorf*

Electrical, Computer and Systems Engineering
Boston University, Boston, MA 02215

ABSTRACT

Prosodic patterns provide important cues for resolving syntactic ambiguity, and might be used to improve the accuracy of automatic speech understanding. With this goal, we propose a method of scoring syntactic parses in terms of observed prosodic cues, which can be used in ranking sentence hypotheses and associated parses. Specifically, the score is the probability of acoustic features of a hypothesized word sequence given an associated syntactic parse, based on acoustic and "language" (prosody/syntax) models that represent probabilities in terms of abstract prosodic labels. This work reports initial efforts aimed at extending the algorithm to spontaneous speech, specifically the ATIS task, where the prosody/parse score is shown to improve the average rank of the correct sentence hypothesis.

1. INTRODUCTION

Human listeners bring several sources of information to bear in interpreting an utterance, including syntax, semantics, discourse, pragmatics and prosodic cues. Prosody, in particular, provides information about syntactic structure (via prosodic constituent structure) and information focus (via phrasal prominence), and is encoded in the acoustic signal in terms of timing, energy and intonation patterns. Since computer knowledge representations are not as sophisticated as human knowledge, utterances that are straightforward for a human to interpret may be "ambiguous" to an automatic speech understanding system. For this reason, it is useful to include as many knowledge sources as possible in automatic speech understanding, and prosody is currently an untapped resource. In fact, some syntactic ambiguities can be resolved by listeners from prosody alone [1].

One way to incorporate prosody in speech understanding is to score the expected prosodic structure for each candidate sentence hypothesis and syntactic parse in relation to the observed prosodic structure. In a speech understanding system where multiple sentence hypotheses are passed from recognition to natural language processing, the prosody/parse score could be used to rank hypotheses and associated parses, directly or in combination with other scores. The parse scoring approach was proposed in previous work [2], where automatically detected prosodic phrase breaks were scored either in terms of their correlation with prosodic structure predicted from parse information or in terms of their likelihood according to a probabilistic prosody/syntax model. Recently, the parse scoring approach was reformulated [3] to avoid explicit recognition of prosodic patterns, which is a sub-optimal intermediate decision. Specifically, the new score is the probability of a hypothesized word sequence and associated syntactic parse given acoustic features, where both an acoustic model and a "language" (prosody/syntax) model are used to represent the probability of utterance, analogous to speech recognition techniques. The parse scoring formalism was also extended to incorporate phrasal prominence information, in addition to phrase breaks. In previous work, we demonstrated the feasibility of using parse scoring to find the correct interpretation in a corpus of professionally read ambiguous sentences. In this work, we use the parse scoring approach to rerank a speech understanding system's N-best output, specifically in the ATIS task domain, in order to improve sentence understanding accuracy.

In the following section, we describe the parse scoring system and the probabilistic acoustic and prosody/syntax models. Next, we discuss issues that arose in extending the parse scoring algorithm to the ATIS task, including several modifications needed to handle new problems associated with spontaneous speech and the new parser and recognizer. We then present experimental results for the task of reranking the top N recognizer hypotheses and associated parses using prosody/parse scores. Finally, we discuss the implications of the results for future work.

2. PARSE SCORING

2.1. General Formalism

The goal of this work is to reorder the set of N-best recognizer hypotheses by ranking each hypothesis and associated parse in terms of a prosody score. More specifically, the prosody-parse score is the probability of a sequence of acoustic observations $\mathbf{x} = \{x_1, \ldots, x_n\}$ given the hypothesized parse, p(**x**|parse), where **x** is a sequence of duration and f0 measurements associated with the recognizer output. We compute this probability using an intermediate phonological representation of a sequence of abstract prosodic labels $\mathbf{a} = \{a_1, \ldots, a_n\}$:

$$\mathrm{p}(\mathbf{x}|\mathrm{parse}) = \sum_{\mathbf{a}} \mathrm{p}(\mathbf{x}|\mathbf{a})\mathrm{p}(\mathbf{a}|\mathrm{parse}). \quad (1)$$

This representation implies the development of two probabilistic models: an acoustic model of prosodic patterns, $\mathrm{p}(\mathbf{x}|\mathbf{a})$, and a model of the relationship between prosody and syntax $\mathrm{p}(\mathbf{a}|\mathrm{parse})$, analogous to a language model in speech recognition.

The general formalism can accommodate many types of abstract labels in the prosodic pattern sequence **a**. Here, the prosodic labeling scheme is an extension of that proposed in [1] and includes integer break indices, one for each word to indicate prosodic constituent structure, and a binary indicator of presence vs. absence of prominence on every syllable. Thus, the prosodic label sequence is given by $\mathbf{a} = (\mathbf{b}, \mathbf{p})$, where **b** represents the break sequence and **p** represents the prominence sequence. To simplify the current implementation, we assume **b** and **p** are independent. This assumption implies the use of two acoustic models, $\mathrm{p}(\mathbf{x}|\mathbf{b})$ and $\mathrm{p}(\mathbf{x}|\mathbf{p})$, and two prosody/syntax models, $\mathrm{p}(\mathbf{b}|\mathrm{parse})$ and $\mathrm{p}(\mathbf{p}|\mathrm{parse})$. (Relaxation of the independence assumption is discussed in Section 5.)

Both the acoustic and prosody/syntax models make use of (different) binary decision trees. A binary decision tree [4] is an ordered sequence of binary questions that successively split the data, ultimately into sets associated with the tree's terminal nodes or leaves. Decision trees are particularly useful for prosody applications because they can easily model feature sets with both categorical and continuous variables without requiring independence assumptions. During training, the sequence of questions is selected from a specified set to minimize some impurity criterion on the sample distribution of classes in the training data. For typical classification problems, a leaf would then be associated with a class label. In this work, however, leaves are associated with the posterior distribution of the classes given the leaf node, and the tree can be thought of as "quantizing" the feature vectors. Here, the classes are either the different levels of breaks, one after each word, or the binary prominence labels, one for each syllable.

2.2. Acoustic Model

The acoustic models, one for breaks and one for prominences, are based on decision trees originally developed for automatic prosodic labeling [5, 6]. The form of the two models is essentially the same. The break model, for example, represents the probability distribution of the different breaks at a word boundary $\mathrm{p}(b|T_{Ab}(x))$, where $T_{Ab}(x)$ is the terminal node of the acoustic break tree corresponding to observation x. Assuming the observations are conditionally independent given the breaks, the probability of the observation sequence is given by

$$\mathrm{p}(\mathbf{x}|\mathbf{b}) = \prod_{i=1}^{n} \mathrm{p}(x_i|b_i) = \prod_{i=1}^{n} \frac{\mathrm{p}(b_i|T_{Ab}(x_i))\mathrm{p}(x_i)}{\mathrm{p}(b_i)}$$

using the decision tree acoustic model. The probability $\mathrm{p}(\mathbf{x}|\mathbf{p})$ is computed using a similar formula with a separate acoustic tree $T_{Ap}(x)$ trained to model prominence.

The key differences between the two acoustic models are in the labels represented and the acoustic features used. The break model represents several different levels of breaks, while the prominence model represents $\pm$ prominence. Breaks are associated with words and prominence markers are associated with syllables, so the observation sequences for the two models are at the word level and syllable level, respectively. Both models rely on features computed from speech annotated with phone and word boundary markers found during speech recognition. Phonetic segmentations facilitate the use of timing cues, that in this work are based on segment duration normalized according to phone-dependent means and variances adapted for estimated speaking rate. The observation vectors used in the break model T_{Ab} [5] include features associated with normalized phone duration and pause duration. The observation vectors used to model prominence T_{Ap} [6] include similar features, as well as F0 and energy measurements.

2.3. Prosody/Syntax Model

The break and prominence prosody/syntax models are also based on decision trees, in this case originally designed for synthesis applications. Hirschberg and colleagues have proposed the use of decision trees to predict presence vs. absence of prosodic breaks [7] and of pitch accents [8], with very good results. Our use of trees for prosody/syntax models differs from this work, in the number of prosodic labels represented, in the use of trees to provide probability distributions rather than classification labels, and in the use of trees for parse scoring rather than prediction. Again, the break and prominence models share the same basic form. The leaves of the prosody/syntax break tree T_{Sb}, for example, are associated with a probability distribution of the breaks given the syntactic feature vector z_i, $\mathrm{p}(b|T_{Sb}(z_i))$. These probabilities are used directly in computing $\mathrm{p}(\mathbf{b}|\mathrm{parse})$, assuming the breaks are conditionally independent given the quantized features $T_{Sb}(z_i)$:

$$\mathrm{p}(\mathbf{b}|\mathrm{parse}) = \prod_{i=1}^{n} \mathrm{p}(b_i|T_{Sb}(z_i)).$$

Again, the probability p(**p**|parse) can be computed using the same approach but with a separate prosody/syntax prominence tree T_{Sp}.

For all prosody/syntax models, the feature vectors used in the tree are based on part-of-speech tags and syntactic bracketing associated with the hypothesized word sequence. For the break model T_{Sb}, the feature vectors (one for each word) include content/function word labels, syntactic constituent labels at different levels of bracketing, measures of distance in branches from the top and the bottom of the syntactic tree, and location in the sentence in terms of numbers of words. For the prominence model T_{Sp} [9], the feature vectors (one for each syllable) include part-of-speech labels, lexical stress assignment and syllable position within the word.

2.4. Joint Probability Score

Using the acoustic and prosody/syntax models and the independence assumptions described above, the probability of the acoustic observations $\mathbf{x} = (\mathbf{x}^{(b)}, \mathbf{x}^{(p)})$ given an hypothesized parse is:

$$\mathrm{p}(\mathbf{x}|\mathrm{parse}) = \mathrm{p}(\mathbf{x}^{(b)}|\mathrm{parse})\mathrm{p}(\mathbf{x}^{(p)}|\mathrm{parse})$$

where the break models contribute to the term

$$\mathrm{p}(\mathbf{x}^{(b)}|\mathrm{parse}) = \prod_{i=1}^{n_w} \mathrm{p}(x_i) \sum_b \frac{\mathrm{p}(b|T_{Ab}(x_i))\mathrm{p}(b|T_{Sb}(z_i))}{\mathrm{p}(b)}$$

and the prominence models contribute a similar term. If the problem is to rank different hypothesized parses for the same word sequence, i.e., the same observation sequence **x**, then the term $\prod_i \mathrm{p}(x_i)$ can be neglected. However, if different observation sequences are being compared, as is the case for different recognition hypotheses, then an explicit model of the observations is needed. Since the acoustic model readily available to this effort does not provide the $\mathrm{p}(x_i)$ information, we simply normalize for differences in the length of the word sequence (n_w) and of the syllable sequence (n_s):

$$\begin{aligned} S_J &= \frac{1}{n_w}\sum_{i=1}^{n_w} \log \sum_b \frac{\mathrm{p}(b|T_{Ab}(x_i))\mathrm{p}(b|T_{Sb}(z_i))}{\mathrm{p}(b)} \\ &+ \frac{1}{n_s}\sum_{i=1}^{n_s} \log \sum_p \frac{\mathrm{p}(p|T_{Ap}(x_i))\mathrm{p}(p|T_{Sp}(z_i))}{\mathrm{p}(p)}. \quad (2) \end{aligned}$$

The score given by Equation 2 differs from the probabilistic score reported in previous work [2] primarily in that it uses the probability of breaks at each word boundary rather than a single detected break, but also in that it incorporates information about phrasal prominence.

3. APPLICATION TO ATIS

The speech corpus is spontaneous speech from the ATIS (Air Travel Information Service) domain, collected by several different sites whose efforts were coordinated by the MADCOW group [10]. The ATIS corpus includes speech from human subjects who were given a set of air travel planning "scenarios" to solve via spoken language communication with a computer. Queries made by the subjects are classified differently according to whether they are evaluable in isolation (class A), require contextual information (class D) or having no canonical database answer (class X), but these distinctions are ignored in our work. In the ATIS task domain, speech understanding performance is measured in terms of response accuracy with a penalty for incorrect responses, as described in [11]. Our experiments will not assess understanding accuracy, which is a function of the complete speech understanding system, but rather the rank of the correct answer after prosody/parse scoring.

A subset of the ATIS corpus was hand-labeled with prosodic breaks and prominences for training the acoustic and prosody/syntax models. Since the spoken language systems at the various data collection sites differ in their degree of automation, mode of communication, and display, the training subset was selected to represent a balanced sample from each of four sites (BBN, CMU, MIT and SRI) and from males and females. The October 1991 test set is used in the experiments reported in Section 4.

The prosody/parse scoring mechanism was evaluated in the context of the MIT ATIS system [12], which communicates the top N recognition hypotheses to the natural language component for further processing. The speech recognition component, the SUMMIT system, was used to provide phone alignments for the acoustic model. The SUMMIT system uses segment-based acoustic phone models, a bigram stochastic language model and a probabilistic left-right parser to provide further linguistic constraints [12]. TINA, MIT's natural language component [13], interleaves syntactic and task-specific semantic constraints to parse an utterance. As a result, the parse structure captures both syntactic and semantic constituents. For example, parse tree nodes may be labeled as *CITY-NAME* or *FLIGHT-EVENT* rather than with general syntactic labels. In addition, TINA falls back on a robust parsing mechanism when a complete parse is not found, using a combination of the basic parser and discourse processing mechanism applied within the utterance [14]. The robust parser enables TINA to handle many more queries, which may be difficult to parse because they contain complex and/or incomplete syntactic structures, disfluencies, or simply recognition errors. The robust parser assigns constituent structure to as much of the utterance as possible and leaves the unassigned terminals in the word string, and therefore generates bracketings with a flatter syntactic structure than that for a complete parse.

In order to port our models and scoring algorithm to the ATIS task, the first change needed was a revision to the prosodic labeling system to handle spontaneous speech phenomena. The changes included the addition of two markers introduced in the TOBI prosodic labeling system [15]. First, the diacritic "p" was added to break indices where needed to indicate that an exceptionally long pause or lengthening occurs due to hesitation [15]. As in our previous work, we used a seven level break index system to represent levels in a constituent hierarchy, a superset of the TOBI breaks. (The binary accent labels represent a simplification or core subset of the TOBI system.) The "p" diacritic is used fairly often: on 5% of the total breaks, on 14% of the breaks at levels 2 and 3, and somewhat more often in utterances that required a robust parse. In addition, a new intonational marker, %r, was added to indicate the beginning of an intonational phrase when the previous phrase did not have a well-formed terminus, e.g. in the case of repairs and restarts. The %r marker was rarely used and therefore not incorporated in the models. Two other prosodic "break" labels were added to handle problems that arose in the ATIS corpus: "L" for linking was added for marking the boundaries within a lexical item (e.g. *San L Francisco*) and "X" for cases where the labelers did not want to mark a word boundary between items (e.g. after an interrupted word such as *fli-*). The different break markers were grouped in the following classes for robust probability estimates in acoustic modeling: (0,1,L), 2, 3, 4-5, 6, (2p,3p), and (4p,5p). In these experiments, the relatively few sentences with an "X" break were simply left out of the training set.

Another new problem introduced by the ATIS task was the definition of a "word", an important issue because prosodic break indices are labeled at each word boundary. The human labelers, the SUMMIT recognition system and the TINA natural language processing system all used different lexicons, differing on the definition of a "compound word" (e.g. *air-fare, what-is-the*). These differences were handled in training by: defining word boundaries according to the smallest unit marked in any of the three systems, using the MIT lexicons to associate the parse and recognition word boundaries, and assigning any hand-labeled "L" breaks to "1" where the recognizer or parser indicated a word boundary. In testing, only the mapping between the recognition and natural language components is needed, and again the smallest word units are chosen.

The main changes to the acoustic model in moving to the ATIS task were associated with the particular phone inventory used by the SUMMIT system. The differences in the phone inventory resulted in some minor changes to the syllabification algorithm (syllable boundaries are needed for acoustic feature extraction). In addition, the phone label set was grouped into classes for estimating robust duration means and variances. We also revised the pause duration feature to measure the total duration of all interword symbols.

The changes to the prosody/syntax model simply involved defining new questions for the decision tree design. The first change involved introducing new categories of parse tree bracketing labels, in part to handle the different naming conventions used in TINA and in part to take advantage of the semantic information provided by TINA. In addition, new types of questions were added to handle cases that included non-branching non-terminals, specifically, questions about the full level of bracketing and the bracketing defined only by binary branching non-terminals (i.e., using two definitions of the "bottom" of the syntactic tree) and questions about the non-terminal labels at multiple levels. Because of the differences in syntactic structure for word strings associated with a robust parse as opposed to a complete parse, we chose to model the prosody of breaks given a robust parse separately, which is equivalent to forcing the first branch of the tree to test for the use of the robust parser.

In summary, many changes were necessary in porting the algorithm to ATIS, some of which were required by the task of understanding spontaneous speech while others were specific to the particular recognizer and parser used here.

4. EXPERIMENTS

In the experimental evaluation of the prosody/parse scoring algorithm on ATIS, the acoustic and prosody/syntax models were trained on the subset of ATIS utterances that were hand-labeled with prosodic markers. The acoustic model was trained from phonetic alignments provided by the MIT recognizer, where the recognizer output was constrained to match the transcribed word sequence. The prosody/syntax model was trained from TINA parses of the transcribed word sequence.

For the parse scoring experiments, MIT provided the N

best recognition hypotheses and one parse per hypothesis for each utterance in the October 1991 test set. The sentence accuracy rate of the top recognition hypothesis, before any prosodic or natural language processing, was 32%. We rescored the top 10 hypotheses, choosing the same number used by the current version of the MIT ATIS system. 185 of 383 utterances (48%) included the correct word string in the top 10. Excluding a few other sentences because of processing difficulties, a total of 179 utterances were used in evaluating improvements in rank due to prosody. For each sentence hypothesis, we extracted a sequence of acoustic features from the phone alignments and F0 contours and a sequence of syntactic features from the associated parse. Thus, every utterance yielded ten sequences of acoustic observation vectors and ten associated sequences of parse features, one pair for each of the ten-best hypothesized word sequences. Each observation sequence was then scored according to the syntactic structure of the corresponding parse, yielding $p(\mathbf{x}_i|\text{parse}_i)$, $i = 1, \ldots, 10$ for each utterance.

The prosody/parse score was used as one component in a linear combination of scores, also including the MIT SUMMIT acoustic score and language model score, which was used to rerank the sentence hypotheses. We investigated the use of a combined prosody score and separate break and prominence scores, and separating the scores gave slightly better performance. The weights in the linear combination are estimated on the October 1991 data, using the method reported in [16]. (Although this is not a fair test in the sense that we are training the three weights on the test set, our experiments in recognition indicate that performance improvements obtained typically translate to improvements on independent test sets.) The acoustic scores were normalized by utterance length in frames, and the other scores by utterance length in words. We compared the rankings of the correct word string for the score combination using only the MIT acoustic and language scores with the rankings according to the score combination that also used the prosody/parse probability. The average rank of the correct utterance, for those in the top 10 to begin with, moved from 1.87 without the prosody score to 1.67 with the prosody score, a gain of about 23% given that the best rank is 1.0. A paired difference test indicates that the difference in performance is significant ($t_\alpha = 2.47$, $\alpha/2 < .005$). In addition, we noticed that incorporation of the prosody score rarely dropped the rank of the correct sentence by more than one, whereas it often improved the rank by more than one.

5. DISCUSSION

In summary, we have described a prosody/parse scoring criterion based on the probability of acoustic observations given a candidate parse. The model is general enough to handle a variety of prosodic labels, though we have focused here on prosodic breaks and prominences. Motivated by the good results in previous experiments with this algorithm on professionally read speech, the goal of this work was to extend the model to spontaneous speech and evaluate its usefulness in the context of an actual speech understanding system, i.e. the MIT ATIS system. Experimental results indicate that prosody can be used to improve the ranking of the correct sentence among the top N. We expect the improved ranking will translate to improved understanding accuracy, though clearly this needs to be confirmed in experiments with a spoken language system.

There are several alternatives for improving both the acoustic and prosody/syntax models. In particular, the current score uses a heuristic to account for differences in observation sequences, which could be better handled by explicitly representing $p(x|a)$ rather than the posterior probability $p(a|x)$ in the acoustic model. Other possible extensions include relaxation of independence assumptions, in particular the independence of breaks and prominences, since other work [9] has shown that breaks are useful for predicting prominence. Of course, this would require increased amounts of training data and somewhat more complex algorithms for computing the parse score. Finally, these experiments represent initial efforts in working with the MIT recognizer and parser, and new acoustic and syntactic features might take better advantage of the MIT system.

The parse scoring algorithm is trained automatically and is in principal easily extensible to other tasks and other speech understanding systems. However, our effort to evaluate the algorithm in the ATIS domain raised some issues associated with portability. New prosodic labels were added to accommodate hesitation and disfluency phenomena observed in spontaneous speech, a problem that we expect will diminish as prosodic labeling conventions converge. Problems arose due to the differences in the definition of a "word" among component modules in the system, which might be addressed by standardization of lexical representation and/or by additional changes to prosodic labeling conventions. Finally, the specific choice of questions used in the decision trees was determined in part by hand to accommodate the output "vocabulary" of the particular recognizer and parser used. Though this aspect could be completely automated by creating standards for parse trees and recognizer "phone" labels, the use of some hand-tuning of questions allows us to optimize performance by taking advantage of the features of different systems and knowledge of the task domain.

Clearly, performance in different spoken language systems will be affected by several factors, including the reliability and level of detail of the parser, the accuracy of the recognizer, the types of ambiguities in the task domain and the sophistication of other knowledge sources (e.g. semantic, discourse) in the system. We plan to explore these issues further by assessing performance of the algorithm in the SRI ATIS system. (Of course, it may be that the constrained semantics of the ATIS task make it difficult to assess the potential benefits of prosodic information.) Implementation and evaluation of prosody/parse scoring in the two systems should have implications for spoken language system design, and our initial work already raises some issues. In particular, there are cases where prosody could benefit speech understanding, but is not useful unless the natural language component provides more than one parse for a hypothesized word string, e.g. for lists of numbers and for utterances with possible disfluencies. In addition, it might be useful to have explicit filled pause models used in recognition (a capability available in some versions of the MIT system that was not used in this experiment), to help distinguish hesitations (marked by the "p" diacritic) from well-formed prosodic boundaries.

In conclusion, we emphasize that these experiments represent initial efforts at integrating prosody in speech understanding and there is clearly much more work to be done in this area. In addition to improving the basic components of the model and evaluating more parse hypotheses, there are many other possible architectures that might be investigated for integrating prosody in speech understanding.

ACKNOWLEDGMENTS

The authors gratefully acknowledge: C. Wightman for the use of his acoustic models; K. Ross for his prominence prediction model; E. Shriberg, K. Hunicke-Smith, C. Fong and M. Hendrix for help with prosodic labeling; and L. Hirschman, M. Phillips and S. Seneff for providing the MIT recognizer and parser outputs as well as many helpful discussions about the features/format of the MIT SUMMIT and TINA systems. This research was jointly funded by NSF and DARPA under NSF grant no. IRI-8905249.

References

1. P. Price, M. Ostendorf, S. Shattuck-Hufnagel, & C. Fong, "The Use of Prosody in Syntactic Disambiguation" *J. of the Acoust. Society of America 90*, 6, pp. 2956–2970, 1991.
2. M. Ostendorf, C. Wightman, and N. Veilleux, "Parse Scoring with Prosodic Information: An Analysis/Synthesis Approach," *Computer Speech and Language*, to appear 1993.
3. N. Veilleux and M. Ostendorf, "Probabilistic Parse Scoring with Prosodic Information," *Proc. of the Inter. Conf. on Acoustics, Speech and Signal Processing*, pp. II51–54, 1993.
4. L. Breiman, J. Friedman, R. Olshen, and C. Stone, *Classification and Regression Trees*, Wadsworth and Brooks/Cole Advanced Books and Software, Monterey, CA, 1984.
5. C. Wightman and M. Ostendorf, "Automatic Recognition of Prosodic Phrases," *Proc. of the Inter. Conf. on Acoustics, Speech and Signal Processing*, pp. 321–324, 1991.
6. C. Wightman and M. Ostendorf, "Automatic Recognition of Intonation Features," *Proc. of the Inter. Conf. on Acoustics, Speech and Signal Processing*, pp. 221–224, 1992.
7. M. Wang and J. Hirschberg, "Automatic classification of intonational phrase boundaries," *Computer Speech and Language*, 6-2, pp. 175–196, 1992.
8. J. Hirschberg, "Pitch Accent in Context: Predicting Prominence from Text," *Artificial Intelligence*, to appear.
9. K. Ross, M. Ostendorf and S. Shattuck-Hufnagel, "Factors Affecting Pitch Accent Placement," *Proc. of the Inter. Conf. on Spoken Language Processing*, pp. 365–368, 1992.
10. L. Hirschman *et al.*, "Multi-Site Data Collection for a Spoken Language Corpus," *Proc. of the DARPA Workshop on Speech and Natural Language*, pp. 7–14, 1992.
11. D. Pallett *et al.*, "DARPA February 1992 ATIS Benchmark Test Results," *Proc. of the DARPA Workshop on Speech and Natural Language*, pp. 15–27, 1992.
12. V. Zue *et al.*, "The MIT ATIS System: February 1992 Progress Report," *Proc. of the DARPA Workshop on Speech and Natural Language*, pp. 84–88, 1992.
13. S. Seneff, "TINA: A Natural Language System for Spoken Language Applications," *J. Association for Computational Linguistics*, pp. 61–86, March 1992.
14. S. Seneff, "A Relaxation Method for Understanding Spontaneous Speech Utterances," *Proc. of the DARPA Workshop on Speech and Natural Language*, pp. 299–304, February 1992.
15. K. Silverman, M. Beckman, J. Pitrelli, M. Ostendorf, C. Wightman, P. Price, J. Pierrehumbert, and J. Hirschberg, "TOBI: A Standard Scheme for Labeling Prosody," *Proc. of the Inter. Conf. on Spoken Language Processing*, pp. 867–870, Banff, October 1992.
16. M. Ostendorf, A. Kannan, S. Austin, O. Kimball, R. Schwartz and J. R. Rohlicek, "Integration of Diverse Recognition Methodologies Through Reevaluation of N-Best Sentence Hypotheses," *Proc. of the DARPA Workshop on Speech and Natural Language*, February 1991, pp. 83–87.

PERCEIVED PROSODIC BOUNDARIES AND THEIR PHONETIC CORRELATES

René Collier, Jan Roelof de Pijper and Angelien Sanderman
Institute for Perception Research / IPO
P.O. Box 513, 5600 MB Eindhoven, The Netherlands

ABSTRACT

This paper addresses two main questions: (a) Can listeners assign values of perceived boundary strength to the juncture between any two words? (b) If so, what is the relationship between these values and various (combinations of) suprasegmental features. Three speakers read a set of twenty utterances of varying length and complexity. A panel of nineteen listeners assigned boundary strength values to each of the 175 word boundaries in the material. Then the correlation was established between the variable strength of the perceived boundaries and three prosodic variables: melodic discontinuity, declination reset and pause. The results show that speakers may differ in their strategies of prosodic boundary marking and listeners agree in the perceptual weight they attribute to the prosodic cues.

1. INTRODUCTION

Any two successive words may vary as to their syntactic or semantic cohesiveness. The latter is likely to be stronger if the two words are part of the same linguistic constituent; conversely, the occurrence of a constituent boundary between words decreases their degree of cohesiveness. For example, in the sentence "(the man) (is sitting) (in the chair)", any two words separated by round brackets are structurally farther apart than those within a pair of brackets. Speakers are capable of making the juncture between constituents audible by prosodic means: they may produce appropriate cues in terms of pause, pitch and duration parameters. Listeners, on the other hand, can make use of these cues to segment the incoming flow of speech into word sequences that may be treated as a whole, which facilitates the comprehension process. In certain cases, prosodic demarcation may help in resolving structural ambiguity, for instance in utterances of the type "The girl saw the man with the telescope", in which the prepositional phrase specifies either the verb or its direct object [1, 2]. But in utterances containing no surface syntactic homonymy, too, prosodic boundaries may delineate coherent word groups and lend support to the listener's hypotheses about syntactic-semantic structure as, for instance, in "the beautiful girl / with brown eyes / told her story / to the psychiatrist" [3].

This paper presents results of research that, starting from the observation that listeners do provide prosodic boundary cues, addresses two main questions:

(a) Can listeners assign a value of Perceived Boundary Strength (PBS) to word boundaries?

(b) If so, what is the relationship between PBS and different (combinations of) suprasegmental features?

The answer to these questions may lead to a better model of what prosodic resources a speaker can draw on to highlight the syntactic-semantic structure of an utterance. Such insight may, in turn, contribute to improved prosody in speech synthesis, by making it sound more natural and –more importantly– by making it linguistically more transparent and therefore easier to comprehend. This research may also shed light on how a listener makes use of the demarcative information encoded in prosodic features. In that respect, it has relevance for (knowledge-based) automatic speech recognition, where the inclusion of prosodic information may support the syntactic-semantic parse of the input, especially if the latter contains structural ambiguities.

This line of research is in agreement with the growing interest in the communicative function of prosody, which may contain information not only about utterance-internal phrasing, as already suggested above [4], but also about the topical organization of discourse in monologues and dialogues [5] or about speaker-dependent features such as emotional state [6].

2. EXPERIMENTAL APPROACH

In this section we present part of the results obtained in an experiment that aimed at answering the two questions mentioned in the introduction. To this effect we have collected appropriate speech material, in which we asked listeners to score the PBS of each word boundary. Subsequently, the material was subjected to various phonetic analyses, the results of which were then correlated with the PBS's. Finally, the predictions of an algorithm that assigns prosodic structure to unmarked text were verified against the PBS's.

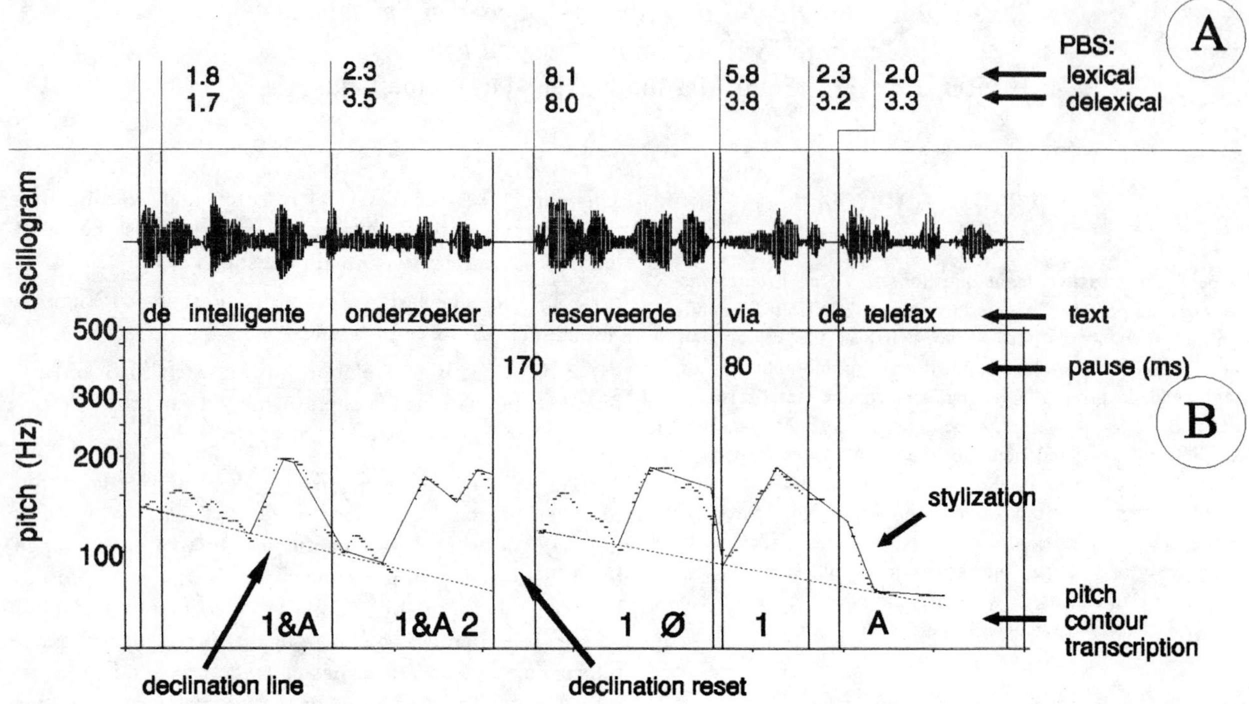

Figure 1: (A) PBS values and (B) results of the phonetic analyses for one of the test utterances of the professional speaker.

2.1. Speech Material

A set of twenty Dutch sentences was constructed, which differed sufficiently in length and complexity to warrant the occurrence of prosodic boundaries of varying strengths. These sentences contained a total of 175 word boundaries. This set was read out by three native speakers: two males, of whom one was a professional speaker, and one female. To evaluate the possible influence of syntactic and semantic information, all 20 utterances spoken by the professional speaker and 3 of the utterances spoken by the other two were processed in such a way that the contents of the utterances was rendered unintelligible, while the prosodic features were kept intact. In this way, a so-called 'delexicalized' version of the test material was created in addition to the 'normal' version.

2.2. PBS Assignment

In a number of successive sessions, nineteen listeners were confronted with the 3 x 20 = 60 utterances in the normal version and the (1 x 20) + (2 x 3) = 26 in the delexicalized version. They were asked to indicate, on a 10-point scale, how strong they felt the juncture at each word boundary to be. The mean of the nineteen scores per word boundary was taken as a measure of the perceptual boundary strength (PBS) of that word boundary. Thus, the PBS was obtained for each word boundary as produced by each of the speakers in each test version.

An example of the PBS values obtained for one of the test utterances is shown in Figure 1a. As can be seen, listeners appear to be quite capable of distinguishing a diversity of PBS values, both in the lexical and delexical conditions.

2.3 Phonetic Analysis

The acoustic / phonetic analysis of the material concentrated on the speakers' use of pauses and intonation to highlight word boundaries. It was determined for each word boundary in the 60 utterances 1) whether there was a pause and, if so, of what length; 2) whether there was melodic discontinuity across the boundary and, if so, of what type; and 3) whether the boundary was associated with a declination reset.

The location and length of pauses were determined by straightforward inspection of the waveforms. Melodic transcriptions of the 60 utterances were obtained by a combination of pitch measurement, pitch stylization and independent perceptual evaluation by experts. Following the typology outlined in 't Hart et al. ([7], p.81), four types of melodic discontinuity were distinguished in the way the speakers marked the word boundaries: '1Ø, 1E, 12, 1A2'.

Figure 1b presents a survey of the results of the phonetic analyses for one of the test utterances.

3. RESULTS

For all three speakers, a high correlation was found between the PBS's obtained in the normal and delexicalized test versions (r_s = .78, p < .01). This warrants the conclusion that, in this experiment, syntactic and semantic factors did not affect the listeners' judgments. The delexicalized test version is ignored in the rest of this paper.

3.1. Perceptual Boundary Strength And Phonetic Cues

	Prof	Nonprof-1	Nonprof-2
melodic discontinuities	43	37	31
pauses	28	14	11
declination resets	14	2	0

Table 1: Frequency of occurrence of the three phonetic cues across the three speakers.

The three speakers appear to make different use of phonetic cues to mark prosodic boundaries, as shown in Table 1. The table shows that the professional speaker made more extensive use of all three phonetic cues than the other two speakers and was the only one to employ declination resets in a systematic fashion. Not shown in the table is the fact that there were also clear differences between the speakers in preferred type of melodic discontinuity.

Combinations of the three cues can be considered as possible phonetic strategies of the speakers to mark prosodic boundaries. Figure 2 shows the relation of these strategies to PBS. Generally speaking, PBS values are higher as more phonetic cues are associated with a given word boundary. While the speakers differ in their preferences for certain strategies, the impact of strategy on PBS is roughly the same across speakers.

Additional trends not shown in Figure 2 are the following. First, there was a trend for longer pauses to be associated with greater PBS's for all speakers. As for the four types of melodic discontinuity, the main tendency is that melodic discontinuity involving a continuation rise '2' (a steep pitch rise very late in the pre-boundary syll-

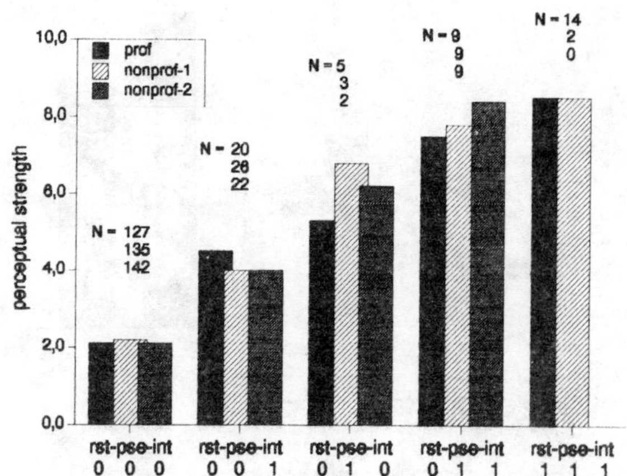

Figure 2: PBS per phonetic cue combination: *rst* = declination reset, *pse* = pause, *int* = melodic cue, *0* and *1* = absence or presence of a cue.

able) is associated with greater PBS's than other types.

The data show strong interactions between the three phonetic cues. The main observations are that 1) the presence of a declination reset implies the presence of a pause in all cases, 2) the presence of a pause implies the presence of a melodic discontinuity in about 80% of the cases, for all speakers, 3) pauses not accompanied by a melodic cue are usually shorter than 100 ms, and 4) it is quite common for word boundaries to be marked only by a melodic cue.

3.2. Perceptual Boundary Strength And Prosodic Boundaries

The prosodic analysis of the test material consisted of the application of the latest version of the so-called Pros-3 algorithm [8]. This is a program currently under development at IPO to automatically determine accent and prosodic phrase structure of sentences on the basis of syntactic and metrical analysis. In this way, each word boundary was assigned to one of three predicted prosodic boundary categories: no boundary, Phi-boundary or I-boundary.

As can be seen in figure 3, word boundaries that were designated as I-boundaries by the Pros-3 algorithm have greater PBS's than Phi-boundaries, while these in turn are perceived as stronger than unlabelled boundaries. This effect is apparent for all speakers, but is clearest in the professional speaker.

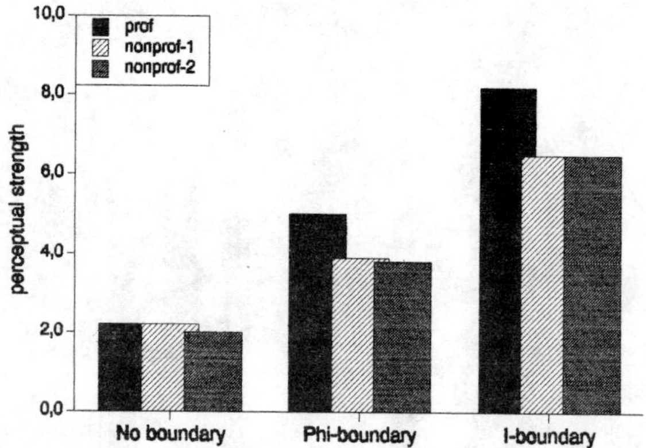

Figure 3: PBS per prosodic boundary.

4. CONCLUSIONS

Our experimental investigation has brought to light that speakers and listeners alike are aware of the role pitch and pause can play in utterance-internal phrasing. These prosodic parameters can effectively highlight how the utterance is to be chunked into coherent word groups. As is often the case with prosody, there is no obligation on the speaker's side to actually use pitch or pause for a communicative purpose, such as boundary marking. In fact, we have seen (in Table 1) that our professional speaker produces more numerous prosodic cues and that all three speakers differ in the relative frequency of use of pitch or pause devices. But, whenever listeners are offered particular (combinations of) prosodic cues, they agree well on how to interpret them in terms of PBS (see Figure 2). Thus, there seems to be prosodic freedom on the speaker's side, while the listener cannot help but pay attention to melodic or temporal cues whenever they are present.

Apparently, a certain amount of gradience is involved in the marking of constituent boundaries: the strength of a prosodic boundary reflects to some extent the depth of the syntactic-semantic juncture at a given point in the utterance. It is not unlikely that the inclusion of additional prosodic parameters, such as local variations in speech rhythm (in particular preboundary lengthening), will add detail to the emerging picture of syntax-to-prosody correspondence. But pitch and pause alone already show sufficiently clear relations to the linguistic structure of the utterance, that their capacity to reveal this structure can be exploited tentatively in text-to-speech conversion and in automatic speech recognition.

Finally, the gradience that can be observed in the PBS values of Figure 2, shows that listeners can do better than merely distinguishing between presence or absence of a boundary. On the basis of our limited set of data, it is not possible to determine exactly how many categories listeners can discriminate reliably. This will be partly determined by the number and the nature of the phonetic cues, and need not be limited to a maximum of three (no boundary, minor boundary, major boundary). Indeed, Figure 2 suggests that it is not unreasonable to assume that listeners can handle five PBS categories. Interestingly, such a five-level distinction is used in the TOBI labelling scheme [9]. However, an important difference between the two approaches is that the TOBI scheme obliges labelers to explicitly assess the nature of the phonetic cues, while PBS values are the result of a purely intuitive judgment.

References

1. Price, P., Ostendorf, M., and Wightman, C. "Prosody and parsing", In: *Proc. of the Second DARPA Workshop on Speech and Natural Language*, 1989, Morgan-Kaufman, San Mateo, CA, pp. 5–11.

2. Price, P., Ostendorf, M., Shattuck-Hufnagel, S. and Fong, C. "The use of prosody in syntactic disambiguation", *J. Acoust. Soc. Amer.*, Vol. 90, 1991, pp. 2956–2970.

3. Terken, J. and Collier, R. "Syntactic influences on prosody", In: *Speech perception, production and linguistic structure*, Y. Tohkura, E. Vatikiotis-Bateson and Y. Sagisaka (eds.), Ohmsa Press, Tokyo, 1991, pp. 427–438.

4. Ladd, D.R. "Declination 'reset' and the hierarchical organization of utterances", *J. Acoust. Soc. Amer.*, Vol. 84, 1988, pp. 530–544.

5. Pierrehumbert, J., and Hirschberg, J. "The meaning of intonational contours in the interpretation of discourse", In: *Intentions in communication*, P. Cohen, S. Morgan and M. Pollock (Eds), MIT Press, Cambridge MA, 1990, pp. 271–311.

6. Carlson, R., Granstrom, B., and Nord, L. "Experiments with emotive speech-acted utterances and synthesized replicas", In: *Proceedings Int. Conf. on Spoken Languague Processing, Banff*, 1992, pp. 671-674.

7. 't Hart, J., Collier, R. and Cohen, A. *A perceptual study of intonation*, Cambridge University Press, 1990.

8. Dirksen, A. "Accenting and deaccenting: a declarative approach", In: *Proc. 15th Int. Conf. on Computational Linguis-*

tics, COLING, Association for Computational Linguistics, 1992, pp. 865–869.

9. Silverman, K., Beckman, M., Pitrelli, J., Ostendorf, M., Wightman, C., Price, P., Pierrehumbert, J. and Hirschberg, J. (1992). "TOBI: A standard for labeling English prosody", In: *Proc. Int. Conf. on Spoken Language Processing*, 1992, pp. 867–870.

Document retrieval and text retrieval

Karen Sparck Jones

Computer Laboratory, University of Cambridge
New Museums Site, Pembroke Street, Cambridge CB2 3QG, UK

1. Essentials of document retrieval

Document retrieval (DR) is for the user who wants to find out about something by reading about it.

DR systems illustrate every variety of indexing language, request and document description, and search mechanism. Controlled languages (CLs) have been commonly used, across the range from only slightly restricted natural language (NL) to a carefully designed artificial language. With CLs professional indexing is required and professional searching is the norm. However automatic DR systems have also encouraged the use of NL through searching on titles and abstracts. This naturally makes end-user searching practicable, though not necessarily easy; and end-users often lack the experience to search effectively when strict word matching fails to identify appropriate documents. The essential requirement in retrieval is that a match between request and document descriptions should reflect the underlying relation between user need and document content.

Indexing, providing for matches, thus aims to promote precision and/or recall. It often has to do this under the external constraints of large files with small relevance sets. It always has to do it under the internal constraints on indexing itself. These are, for both requests and documents, *variability* of language, whether this stems from ambiguity or differences of perspective; for requests, *underspecification*, whether through vagueness or incompleteness; and for documents, information *reduction*, whether through generalisation or selection. Reduction is essential for DR, for both efficiency in scanning and effectiveness in concentrating on key content.

The implications of these constraints for index language design and use are conflicting, and suggest many alternative possibilities within the CL/NL space for the treatment of terms and term relations, of implicit and explicit relations, and of syntagmatic and paradigmatic relations. Mixes and tradeoffs are possible, and the necessary flexibility is achieved, because descriptions are manipulated in searching.

However though the conventional preference is for CLs, extensive tests have shown that very competitive performance can be obtained through cheap and simple indexing using coordinated single NL terms along with statistical selection and weighting, ranked output, and relevance feedback. The gains from this approach come from allowing for *late binding* and *redundancy*, along with *derivation* from source documents, in topic characterisation. The findings have been supported by many tests investigating different DR system factors, and the approach has been implemented commercially. But the test evidence is not always strong, and the tests have been on a limited scale; further, the strategy depends on request quality and probably also on working with document surrogates, like abstracts, which concentrate information. Even so, the puzzle is that linguistic sophistication, even with human LP, does not provide clear performance gains, and routine performance typically falls within an undistinguished 30-60% R-P tradeoff area.

2. Text retrieval

However a new situation has arisen with the availability of machine-readable full text. For text retrieval (TR), NLP to provide more sophisticated indexing may be needed because more discrimination within large files of long texts is required, or may be desired because more focusing is possible. This suggests the more NLP the better, but whether for better-motivated simple indexing or for more complex representation has to be determined.

Given past experience, and the need for flexibility in the face of uncertainty, a sound approach appears to be to maintain overall simplicity but to allow for more complex indexing descriptors than single terms, derived through NLP and NL-flavoured, e.g. simple phrases or predications. These would be just coordinated for descriptions but, more importantly, statistically selected and weighted. To obtain the reduced descriptions still needed to emphasise important text content, text-locational or statistical information could be exploited. To support indexing, and, more critically, searching a terminological apparatus again of a simple NL-oriented kind providing term substitutes or collocates, and again statistically controlled, could be valuable. Searching should allow the substitution or relaxation of elements and relations in complex terms, again with weighting, especially via feedback. This whole approach would emphasise the NL of the texts while recognising the statistical properties of large files and long documents. The crux is thus to demonstrate that linguistically-constrained terms are superior to e.g. co-locational ones.

Heavy testing is needed to establish performance for the suggested approach, given the many factors affecting retrieval systems, both environment variables e.g. document type, subject domain, user category, and system parameters e.g. description exhaustivity, language specificity, weighting formula. There are also different evaluation criteria, performance measures, and application methods to consider. Proper testing is hard (and costly) since it requires large collections, of requests as much as documents, with relevance assessments, and implies fine-grained comparisons within a grid of system contexts and design options.

Various approaches along the lines suggested, as well as simpler DR-derived ones, are being investigated within ARPA TREC. The TREC experiments are important as the largest retrieval tests to date, with an earnest evaluation design, as well as being TR tests on the grand scale. But any conclusions drawn from them must be treated with caution since the TREC queries are highly honed, and are for standing interests (matching a document against many requests not vice versa), with tightly specified response needs. TREC is not typical of many retrieval situations, notably the 'wants to read about' one, so any results obtained, especially good ones relying on collection tailoring, may not be generally applicable and other tests are mandatory.

3. HLT issues

In the present state of TR research, and the HLT context, the issues are as follows:

1. With respect to the *objects* manipulated in retrieval, i.e. index descriptions, given that indexing is making predictions for future searching:

   What kind of sophistication is in order: what concepts should be selected and how should they be represented? How should linguistic and statistical facts be related? For example, how should weights for compounds be derived, by wholes or from constituents, and how should matching, by wholes or constituents, be handled?

2. Wrt the *process* of retrieval, given that searching is fundamentally interactive:

   What way of developing requests is best: should the system be proactive or reactive? How can the user be involved? For example, how can the user cope with CLs that are incomprehensible (through notation) or misleading (through pseudo-English); or with statistical numbers?

3. Wrt the *implementation* of retrieval systems, given their asymmetry with requests demanding notice but many documents never wanted:

   What distribution of effort is rational: should effort be at file time or search time? How can flexibility be maintained? For instance, when should compounds be formed, or their weights computed?

4. Wrt the *model* adopted to underpin systems, given the lumpiness inherent in system operation in the mass and average but user interest in the individual and distinctive:

   What strength of assumptions is rational: should the system work with the vector, or probabilistic, or some other model? How can an abstract formal model supply specific instructions for action? For instance, can the model say precisely how matches should be scored?

5. Wrt retrieval using *full text*, given that with more detail there is also more noise:

   What functions should TR serve: should it help to refine indexing or offer passage retrieval? How might indexing and searching on two levels operate? For instance, how can a dispersed concept, spread over text, be identified?

6. Wrt system *testing*, given the enormous variety of environment factors and system possibilities:

   What degree of reality and representativeness is required for validity: can collections be picked up or must they be designed? How can control be imposed to isolate factor effects? For instance, how should non-repeatable user search data be treated?

These issues reflect the conflict between the fact of interdependencies within systems and the aim of decomposition for understanding and design. Thus the key points for DR and TR as potential NLP tasks, as opposed to e.g. database query or translation, is that *scale phenomena* count; thus the value of index descriptions is in file discrimination, not document definition; and retrieval output is contingent on the lifetime file, not the local situation. At the same time, information retrieval experience has shown that *any* approach can seem plausible, as also that whatever one does comes out grey in the wash.

The Importance of Proper Weighting Methods

Chris Buckley

Department of Computer Science
Cornell University
Ithaca, NY 14853

ABSTRACT

The importance of good weighting methods in information retrieval — methods that stress the most useful features of a document or query representative — is examined. Evidence is presented that good weighting methods are more important than the feature selection process and it is suggested that the two need to go hand-in-hand in order to be effective. The paper concludes with a method for learning a good weight for a term based upon the characteristics of that term.

1. INTRODUCTION

Other than experimental results, the first part of this paper contains little new material. Instead, it's an attempt to demonstrate the relative importance and difficulties involved in the common information retrieval task of forming documents and query representatives and weighting features. This is the sort of thing that tends to get passed by word of mouth if at all, and never gets published. However, there is a tremendous revival of interest in information retrieval; thus this attempt to help all those new people just starting in experimental information retrieval.

A common approach in many areas of natural language processing is to

1. Find "features" of a natural language excerpt
2. Determine the relative importance of those features within the excerpt
3. Submit the weighted features to some task-appropriate decision procedure

This presentation focuses on the second sub-task above: the process of weighting features of a natural language representation. Features here could be things like single word occurrences, phrase occurrences, other relationships between words, occurrence of a word in a title, part-of-speech of a word, automatically or manually assigned categories of a document, citations of a document, and so on. The particular overall task addressed here is that of information retrieval – finding textual documents (from a large set of documents) that are relevant to a user's information need. Weighting features is something that many information retrieval systems seem to regard as being of minor importance as compared to finding the features in the first place; but the experiments described here suggest that weighting is considerably more important than additional feature selection.

This is not an argument that feature selection is unimportant, but that development of feature selection and methods of weighting those features need to proceed hand-in-hand if there is to be hope of improving performance. There have been many papers (and innumerable unpublished negative result experiments) where authors have devoted tremendous resources and intellectual insights into finding good features to help represent a document, but then weighted those features in a haphazard fashion and ended up with little or no improvement. This makes it extremely difficult for a reader to judge the worthiness of a feature approach, especially since the weighting methods are very often not described in detail.

Long term, the best weighting methods will obviously be those that can adapt weights as more information becomes available. Unfortunately, in information retrieval it is very difficult to learn anything useful from one query that will be applicable to the next. In the routing or relevance feedback environments, weights can be learned for a query and then applied to that same query. But in general there is not enough overlap in vocabulary (and uses of vocabulary) between queries to learn much about the usefulness of particular words. The second half of this paper discusses an approach that learns the important characteristics of a good term. Those characteristics can then be used to properly weight all terms.

Several sets of experiments are described, with each set using different types of information to determine the weights of features. All experiments were done with the SMART information retrieval system, most using the TREC/TIPSTER collections of documents, queries, and relevance judgements. Each run is evaluated using the "11-point recall-precision average" evaluation method that was standard at the TREC 1 conference.

The basic SMART approach is a completely automatic indexing of the full text of both queries and documents. Common meaningless words (like 'the' or 'about') are removed, and all remaining words are stemmed to a root form. Term weights are assigned to each unique word (or other feature) in a vector by the statistical/learning processes described below. The final form of a representative for a document (or query) is a vector

$$D_i = (w_{i,1}, w_{i,2}, \ldots, w_{i,n})$$

where D_i represents a document (or query) text and $w_{i,k}$ is a term weight of term T_k attached to document D_i. The similarity between a query and document is set to the inner-product of the query vector and document vector; the information retrieval system as a whole will return those documents with the highest similarity to the query.

2. AD-HOC WEIGHTS

Document or query weights can be based on any number of factors; two would be statistical occurrence information and a history of how well this feature (or other similar features) have performed in the past. In many situations, it's impossible to obtain history information and thus initial weights are often based purely on statistical information. A major class of statistical weighting schemes is examined below, showing that there is an enormous performance range within the class. Then the process of adding additional features to a document or query representative is examined in the context of these weighting schemes. These are issues that are somewhat subtle and are often overlooked.

2.1. Tf * Idf Weights

Over the past 25 years, one class of term weights has proven itself to be useful over a wide variety of collections. This is the class of tf*idf (term frequency times inverse document frequency) weights [1, 6, 7], that assigns weight w_{ik} to term T_k in document D_i in proportion to the frequency of occurrence of the term in D_i, and in inverse proportion to the number of documents to which the term is assigned. The weights in the document are then normalized by the length of the document, so that long documents are not automatically favored over short documents. While there have been some post-facto theoretical justifications for some of the tf*idf weight variants, the fact remains that they are used because they work well, rather than any theoretical reason.

Table 1 presents the evaluation results of running a number of tf*idf variants for query weighting against a number of variants for document weighting (the runs presented here are only a small subset of the variants actually run). All of these runs use the same set of features (single terms), the only differences are in the term weights. The exact variants used aren't important; what is important is the range of results. Disregarding one extremely poor document weighting, the range of results is from 0.1057 to 0.2249. Thus a good choice of weights may gain a system over 100%. As points of comparison, the best official TREC run was 0.2171 (a system incorporating a very large amount of user knowledge to determine features) and the median TREC run in this category was 0.1595. The best run (DOCWT = lnc, QWT = ltc), is about 24% better than the most generally used tf*idf run (DOCWT = QWT = ntc).

24%is a substantial difference in performance, in a field where historically an improvement of 10% is considered quite good. The magnitude of performance improvement due to considering additional features such as syntactic phrases, titles and parts of speech is generally quite small (0 – 10%). Adding features and using good weights can of course be done at the same time; but the fact that somewhat subtle differences in weighting strategy can overwhelm the effect due to additional features is worrisome. This means the experimenter must be very careful when adding features that they do not change the appropriateness of the weighting strategy.

2.2. Adding New Features

Suppose an experimenter has determined a good weighting strategy for a basic set of features used to describe a query or document and now wishes to extend the set of features. In the standard tf*idf, cosine-normalized class of weights, it is not as simple as it may first appear. The obvious first step, making sure the weights before normalization of the new set of features and the old set are commensurate, is normally straightforward. But then problems occur because of the cosine normalization. For example, suppose there were two documents in a collection, one of them much longer then the other:

- $D_1 = (w_{1,1}, w_{1,2}, w_{1,3})$
- $D_2 = (w_{2,1}, w_{2,2}, \ldots w_{2,100})$

Now suppose the new approach adds a reasonably constant five features onto each document representative. (Examples of such features might be title words, or categories the document is in.) If the new features are just added on to the list of old features, and then the weights of the features are normalized by the total length of the document, then there are definite problems. Not only does the weight of the added features vary according to the length of the document (that could very well be what is wanted), but the weight of the old features have changed. A query that does not take advantage of the new features will suddenly find it much more difficult to retrieve short documents like D_1. D_1 is now much longer than it was, and therefore the values of $w_{1,k}$ have all decreased because of normalization.

Similarly, if the number of new added features tends to be much more for longer documents than short (for example, a very loose definition of phrase), a query composed of only old features will tend to favor short documents more than long (at least, more than it did originally). Since the original weighting scheme was a supposedly good one, these added features will hurt performance on the original feature portion of the similarity. The similarity on the added feature portion might help, but it will be difficult to judge how much.

These normalization effects can be very major effects. Using a loose definition of phrase on CACM (a small test collection), adding phrases in the natural fashion above will hurt performance by 12%. However, if the phrases are added in such a way that the weights of the original single terms are not affected by normalization, then the addition of phrases improves performance by 9%.

One standard approach when investigating the usefulness of adding features is to ensure that the weights of the old features remain unchanged throughout the investigation. In this way, the contribution of the new features can be isolated and studied separately at the similarity level. [Note that if this is done, the addition of new features may mean the re-addition of old features, if the weights of some old features are supposed to be modified.] This is the approach we've taken, for instance with the weighting of phrases in TREC. The single term information and the phrase information are kept separate within a document vector. Each of the separate sub-vectors is normalized by the length of the single term sub-vector. In this way, the weights of all terms are kept commensurate with each other, and the similarity due to the original single terms is kept unchanged.

The investigation of weighting strategies for additional features is not a simple task, even if separation of old features and new features is done. For example, Joel Fagan in his excellent study of syntactic and statistical phrases[2], spent over 8 months looking at weighting strategies. But if it's not designed into the experiment from the beginning, it will be almost impossible.

2.3. Relevance Feedback

One opportunity for good term weighting occurs in the routing environment. Here, a query is assumed to represent a continuing information need, and there have been a number of documents already seen for each query, some subset of which has been judged relevant. With this wealth of document features and information available, the official TREC routing run that proved to be the most effective was one that took the original query terms and assigned weights based on probability of occurrence in relevant and non-relevant documents[3, 5]. Once again, weighting, rather than feature selection, worked very well. (However, in this case the feature selection process did not directly adversely affect the weighting process. Instead, it was mostly the case that the additional features from relevant documents were simply not chosen or weighted optimally.)

In this run, using the RPI feedback model developed by Fuhr[3], relevance feedback information was used for computing the feedback query term weight q_i of a term as $p_i(1-r_i)/[r_i(1-p_i)]-1$ Here p_i is the average document term weight for relevant documents, and r_i is the corresponding factor for nonrelevant items. Only the terms occurring in the query were considered here, so no query expansion took place. Having derived these query term weights, the query was run against the document set. Let d_i denote the document term weight, then the similarity of a query to a document is computed by $S(q,d) = \sum(\log(q_i * d_i + 1))$

3. LEARNING WEIGHTS BY TERM FEATURES

The ad-hoc tf*idf weights above use only collection statistics to determine weights. However, if previous queries have been run on this collection, the results from those queries can be used to determine what term weighting factors are important for this collection. The final term weight is set to a linear combination of term weight factors, where the coefficient of each factor is set to minimize the squared error for the previous queries[4, 5]. The official TREC runs using this approach were nearly the top results; which was somewhat surprising given the very limited and inaccurate training information which was available.

This approach to learning solves the major problem of learning in an ad-hoc environment: the fact that there is insufficient information about individual terms to learn reasonable weights. Most document terms have not occurred in previous queries, and therefore there is no evidence that can be directly applied. Instead, the known relevance information determines the importance of features of each term. The particular features used in TREC 1 were combinations of the following term factors:

tf: within-document frequency of the term

logidf: log ((N+1)/n), where N is the number of documents in the collection and n is the number of documents containing the term

lognumterms: log (number of different terms of the document)

imaxtf: 1 / (maximum within-document frequency of a term in the document)

After using the relevance information, the final weight for a term in a TREC 1 document was

$$\begin{aligned} W(t_i) &= 0.00042293 + \\ & 0.00150083 * \text{tf} * \text{logidf} * \text{imaxtf} + \\ & -0.00150665 * \text{tf} * \text{imaxtf} + \\ & 0.00010465 * \text{logidf} + \\ & -0.00122627 * \text{lognumterms} * \text{imaxtf}. \end{aligned}$$

There is no reason why the choice of factors used in TREC 1 is optimal; slight variations had been used for an earlier experiment. Experimentation is progressing on the choice of factors, especially when dealing with both single terms and phrases. However, even so, the TREC 1 evaluation results were very good. If the minimal learning information used by this approach is available, the results suggest it should be preferred to the ad-hoc weighting schemes discussed earlier.

4. CONCLUSION

The sets of experiments described above focus on feature weighting and emphasize that feature weighting seems to be more important than feature selection. This is not to say that good feature selection is not needed for optimal performance, but these experiments suggest that good weighting is of equal importance. Feature selection is sexy, and weighting isn't, but optimal performance seems to demand that weighting schemes and feature selection need to be developed simultaneously.

References

1. Buckley, C. and Salton, G. and Allan, J., "Automatic Retrieval With Locality Information Using SMART." Proceedings of the First TREC Conference, 1993.
2. Fagan, J., *Experiments in Automatic Phrase Indexing for Document Retrieval: A Comparison of Syntactic and Nonsyntactic Methods*, Doctoral Dissertation, Cornell University, Report TR 87-868, Department of Computer Science, Ithaca, NY, 1987.
3. Fuhr, N., "Models for Retrieval with Probabilistic Indexing." Information Processing and Management 25(1), 1989, pp. 55-72.
4. Fuhr, N. and Buckley, C., "A Probabilistic Learning Approach for Document Indexing." ACM Transactions on Information Systems 9(3), 1991, pages 223–248.
5. Fuhr, N. and Buckley, C., "Optimizing Document Indexing and Search Term Weighting Based on Probabilistic Models" Proceedings of the First TREC Conference, 1993.
6. Salton, G. and Buckley, C., "Term Weighting Approaches in Automatic Text Retrieval." Information Processing and Management 24(5), 1988, pages 513–523.
7. Salton, G. and Yang, C.S., "On the Specification of Term Values in Automatic Indexing." Journal of Documentation 29(4), 1973, pages 351-372.

Query Doc	ntc	nnc	atc	btc	ltc	lnc
ntc	1813	1594	1834	1540	1908	1738
nnc	1818	1453	1916	1595	1993	1607
atc	1558	1473	1682	1437	1757	1499
anc	1892	1467	1908	1645	2000	1396
btc	1241	1179	1454	1231	1493	1237
bnc	1569	1130	1577	1421	1689	1057
ltc	1909	1815	1986	1726	2061	1843
lnc	2221	1857	2126	1887	2249	1716
nnn	0062	0051	0059	0067	0061	0050

Table 1: Comparison of tf * idf variants.
All weights expressed as triplets:
{tf contribution} {idf contribution} {normalization}

- tf:
  - n : Normal tf (ie, number of times term occurs in vector)
  - l : Log. 1.0 + ln (tf).
  - a : Augmented. normalized between 0.5 and 1.0 in each vector. 0.5+0.5*tf/MaxTfInVector
  - b : Binary (ie, always 1)
- idf:
  - n : None (ie, always 1)
  - t : Traditional (log ((N+1)/n)) where N is number of documents in collection and n is number of documents
- normalization:
  - n : None
  - c : Cosine.

QUERY PROCESSING FOR RETRIEVAL FROM LARGE TEXT BASES

John Broglio and W. Bruce Croft

Computer Science Department
University of Massachusetts
Amherst, MA 01003

ABSTRACT

Natural language experiments in information retrieval have often been inconclusive due to the lack of large text bases with associated queries and relevance judgments. This paper describes experiments in incremental query processing and indexing with the INQUERY information retrieval system on the TIPSTER queries and document collection. The results measure the value of processing tailored for different query styles, use of syntactic tags to produce search phrases, recognition and application of generic concepts, and automatic concept extraction based on interword associations in a large text base.

1. INTRODUCTION: TIPSTER AND INQUERY

Previous research has suggested that retrieval effectiveness might be enhanced by the use of multiple representations and by automated language processing techniques. Techniques include automatic or interactive introduction of synonyms [Har88], forms-based interfaces [CD90], automatic recognition of phrases [CTL91], and relevance feedback [SB90]. The recent development of the TIPSTER corpus with associated queries and relevance judgments has provided new opportunities for judging the effectiveness of these techniques on large heterogenous document collections.

1.1. TIPSTER Text Base and Query Topics

The TIPSTER documents comprise two volumes of text, of approximately one gigabyte each, from sources such as newspaper and magazine articles and government publications (Federal Register). Accompanying the collections are two sets of fifty *topics*. Each topic is a full text description, in a specific format, of an information need. (Figure 1).

Each TIPSTER topic offers several representations of the same information need. The *Topic* and *Description* fields are similar to what might be entered as a query in a traditional information retrieval system. The *Narrative* field expands on the information need, giving an overview of the classes of documents which would or would not be considered satisfactory, and describes facts that must be present in relevant documents, for example, *the location of the company*. The *Concepts* field lists words and phrases which are pertinent to the query. The *Factors* field lists constraints on the geographic and/or time frame of the query. All of these fields offer opportunities for different kinds of natural language processing.

<top>
<dom> Domain: International Economics
<Title> Topic: Satellite Launch Contracts
<desc> Description:
Document will cite the signing of a contract or preliminary agreement, or the making of a tentative reservation, to launch a commercial satellite.

<narr> Narrative:
A relevant document will mention the signing of a contract or preliminary agreement, or the making of a tentative reservation, to launch a commercial satellite.

<con> Concept(s):
1. contract, agreement
2. launch vehicle, rocket, payload, satellite
3. launch services, commercial space industry, commercial launch industry
4. Arianespace, Martin Marietta, General Dynamics, McDonnell Douglas
5. Titan, Delta II, Atlas, Ariane, Proton

</top>

Figure 1: A TIPSTER topic.

1.2. The INQUERY Information Retrieval System

INQUERY is a probabilistic information retrieval system based upon a Bayesian inference network model [TC91, Tur91]. The object network consists of object nodes (documents) (o_j's) and concept representation nodes (r_m's). In a typical network information retrieval system, the text representation nodes will correspond to words extracted from the text [SM83], although representations based on more sophisticated language analysis are possible. The estimation of the probabilities $P(r_m|o_j)$ is based on the occurrence frequencies of concepts in both individual objects and large collections of objects. In the INQUERY system, representation nodes are the word stems and numbers that occur in the text, after stopwords are discarded.

2. QUERY PROCESSING EXPERIMENTS

Our current set of natural language techniques for query enhancement are:

- deletion of potentially misleading text;
- grouping of proper names and interrelated noun phrase concepts;
- automatic concept expansion;
- simple rule-based interactive query modification.

Future experiments will use more extensive automatic noun phrase processing and paragraph level retrieval.

In addition to the traditional recall/precision table, we show tables of the precision for the top n documents retrieved, for 5 values of n. The recall/precision table measures the ability of the system to retrieve all of the documents known to be relevant. The precision for the top n documents gives a better measure of what a person would experience in using the system.

2.1. Deletion processes.

Table 1 illustrates an incremental query treatment. The (**Words**) column shows results from the unprocessed words of the query alone. (Formatting information, such as field markers, has been removed.) The first active processing (**Del1**) removes words and phrases which refer to the information retrieval processes rather than the information need, for example, *A relevant document will describe ....* We further remove words and phrases which are discursive, like *point of view*, *sort of*, *discuss*, *mention* as well as expressions which would require deep inference to process, such as *effects of* or *purpose of* (Figure 2). Some of these expressions would be useful in other retrieval contexts and different lists would be appropriate in different domains. An interactive user is given feedback regarding deletions and could have the capability of selectively preventing deletion.

In the experiment in the fourth column (**-NARR**) the Narrative field has been deleted from each query. Since the Narrative field is usually a very abstract discussion of the criteria for document relevance, it is not well-suited to a system like INQUERY, which relies on matching words from the query to words in the document. New terms introduced by the Narrative field are rarely useful as retrieval terms (but note the small loss in precision at the very lowest level of recall).

2.2. Grouping Noun Phrases and Recognizing Concepts

The simplest phrasing or grouping techniques are recognition of proper noun groups (**Caps** in Table 1) and recognition of multiple spellings for common concepts such as *United States*.

Proximity and phrase operators for noun phrases. Simple noun phrase processing is done in two ways. Sequences of proper nouns are recognized as names and grouped as arguments to a proximity operator. The proximity operator requires that its arguments appear in strict order in a document, but allows an interword distance of three or less. Thus a query such as *George Bush* matches *George Herbert Walker Bush* in a document.

Secondly, the query is passed through a syntactic part of speech tagger [Chu88], and rules are used rules to identify noun phrases (Figure 2). Experiments showed that very simple noun phrase rules work better than longer, more complex, noun phrases. We believe this is because the semantic relationships expressed in associated groups of noun phrases in a query may be expressed in a document as a compound noun group, a noun phrase with prepositional phrase arguments, a complex sentence, or a sequence of sentences linked by anaphora. This hypothesis is supported by the success of the unordered text window operator used in the interactive query modification experiments (Table 4).

On the other hand, there are verbal "red herrings" in some query noun phrases due to overprecise expression. For example, the phrase *U.S. House of Representatives* would be more effective for retrieval without the *U.S.* component (*Congress* might be even nicer).

2.3. Concept Recognition

Controlled vocabulary. The INQUERY system has been designed so that it is easy to add optional object types to implement a controlled indexing vocabulary [CCH92]. For example, when a document refers to a company by name, the document is indexed both by the the company name (words in the text) and the object type (*#company*). The standard INQUERY document parsers recognize the names of companies [Rau91], coun-

Table 1: Precision and recall tables for experiments starting with *words-only* queries (**Words**) through phrase (**Del1**) and word (**Del2**) deletion to proper noun (*Caps*) and noun phrase (**NP**) grouping. The queries were evaluated on Volume 1 of the TIPSTER document collection, using relevance judgements from the 1992 Text Retrieval and Evaluation Conference (TREC).

	Precision (% change) – 50 queries										
Recall	Words	Del1		Del2		-Narr		Caps		NP	
0	71.6	73.5	(+ 2.7)	76.2	(+ 6.4)	83.2	(+16.2)	81.9	(+14.4)	83.5	(+16.6)
10	49.2	52.7	(+ 7.0)	54.7	(+11.0)	59.6	(+21.1)	60.0	(+21.9)	62.9	(+27.8)
20	41.2	44.2	(+ 7.5)	46.1	(+12.1)	50.6	(+22.9)	51.3	(+24.6)	54.5	(+32.4)
30	35.3	38.9	(+10.4)	40.5	(+14.8)	45.2	(+28.2)	45.9	(+30.1)	48.8	(+38.5)
40	30.7	34.6	(+12.6)	35.9	(+17.1)	39.9	(+30.0)	40.5	(+32.1)	43.6	(+42.1)
50	26.2	30.3	(+15.6)	31.7	(+21.1)	35.9	(+37.1)	35.6	(+36.0)	37.8	(+44.1)
60	22.1	25.5	(+15.5)	26.9	(+21.8)	31.0	(+40.4)	30.9	(+40.3)	32.6	(+47.9)
70	18.7	21.1	(+12.9)	22.0	(+17.9)	26.1	(+40.0)	25.8	(+38.2)	27.2	(+46.1)
80	15.0	17.0	(+13.4)	17.8	(+18.4)	20.5	(+36.6)	19.9	(+32.8)	21.4	(+42.6)
90	9.2	10.5	(+13.7)	11.1	(+20.0)	12.7	(+37.3)	12.3	(+33.4)	12.9	(+39.8)
100	2.4	2.8	(+19.9)	3.2	(+33.8)	2.6	(+10.2)	2.5	(+ 5.2)	2.9	(+23.2)
avg	29.2	31.9	(+ 9.2)	33.3	(+13.9)	37.0	(+26.7)	37.0	(+26.5)	38.9	(+33.2)

	Precision (% change) – 50 queries										
Recall	Words	Del1		Del2		-Narr		Caps		NP	
5	54.4	57.2	(+ 5.1)	58.4	(+ 7.4)	66.4	(+22.1)	65.6	(+20.6)	66.8	(+22.8)
15	46.4	49.7	(+ 7.1)	50.9	(+ 9.7)	57.1	(+23.1)	57.5	(+23.9)	62.8	(+35.3)
30	44.2	47.2	(+ 6.8)	49.3	(+11.5)	53.6	(+21.3)	53.3	(+20.6)	56.3	(+27.4)
100	33.9	37.0	(+ 9.1)	38.7	(+14.2)	43.0	(+26.8)	43.2	(+27.4)	45.0	(+32.7)
200	27.5	30.1	(+ 9.5)	31.5	(+14.5)	35.4	(+28.7)	35.2	(+28.0)	37.2	(+35.3)

tries, and cities in the United States.

With wide-ranging queries like the TIPSTER topics, we have had some success with adding *#city* (and *#foreign-country*) concepts to queries that request information on the *location* of an event (Table 2). But the terms *#company* and *#usa* have not yet proved consistently useful. The *#company* concept may be used to good effect to restrict other operators. For example, looking for the terms *machine, translation*, and *#company* in an *n*-word text window would give good results with respect to companies working on or marketing machine translation products. But, the current implementation of the *#company* concept recognizer has some shortcomings which are exposed by this set of queries. Our next version of the recognizer will be more precise and complete[1], and we expect significant improvement from these it.

The *#usa* term tends to have unexpected effects, because a large part of the collection consists of articles from U.S. publications. In these documents U.S. nationality is often taken for granted (term frequency of *#usa*=294408, *#foreigncountry*=472021), and it is likely that it may be mentioned explicitly only when that presupposition is violated, or when both U.S. and non-U.S. issues are being discussed together in the same document. Therefore, because focussing on the *#usa* concept will bring in otherwise irrelevant documents, it is more effective to put negative weight on the *#foreign-country* concept where the query interest is restricted to U.S. matters. For the same reason, in a query focussed only on non-U.S. interests, we would expect the opposite: using *#foreigncountry* should give better performance than *#NOT(#usa)*.

Research continues on the 'right' mix of concept recognizers for a document collection. In situations where text and queries are more predictable, such as commercial customer support environments, an expanded set of special terms and recognizers is appropriate. Names of products and typical operations and objects can be recognized and treated specially both at indexing and at query time. Our work in this area reveals a significant improvement due to domain-specific concept recognizers, however, standardized queries and relevance judgments are still being developed.

[1] Ralph Weischedel's group at BBN have been generous in sharing their company database for this purpose.

Original:
Document will cite the signing of a contract or preliminary agreement, or the making of a tentative reservation, to launch a commercial satellite.

Discourse phrase and word deletion:
the signing of a contract or preliminary agreement, or the making of a tentative reservation, to launch a commercial satellite.

Proper noun group recognition (Concept field):
#3(Martin Marietta) #3(General Dynamics)
#3(McDonnell Douglas) #3(Delta II)

Noun phrase grouping (and stopword deletion):
#PHRASE (signing contract)
#PHRASE (preliminary agreement)
#PHRASE (making tentative reservation)
#PHRASE (commercial satellite)

Figure 2: Progressive changes in the *Description* field of the Topic.

Automatic concept expansion. We have promising preliminary results for experiments in automatic concept expansion. The **Expand** results in Table 3 were produced by adding five additional concepts to each query. The concepts were selected based on their preponderant association with the query terms in text of the 1987 Wall Street Journal articles from Volume 1 of the TIPSTER corpus. The improvement is modest, and we anticipate better results from refinements in the selection techniques and a larger and more heterogenous sample of the corpus.

2.4. Semi-Automatic query processing.

In the following experiments in interactive query processing, human intervention was used to modify the output of the best automatic query processing. The person making the modifications was permitted to

1. Add words from the Narrative field;
2. Delete words or phrases from the query;
3. Specify a text window size for the occurrence of words or phrases in the query.

The third restriction simulates a paragraph-based retrieval.

Table 4 summarizes the results of the interactive query modification techniques compared with the best automatic query processing **Q-1** (similar to **NP** in the other tables). The **Q-M** query-set was created with rules (1) and (2) only. The **Q-O** query-set used all three rules.

Table 2: The effect of replacing the query word *location* with the concepts *#us-city* and *#foreigncountry*. (We do not yet have a *#foreigncity* recognizer).

	Precision (8 queries)				
Recall	NoCity	— City —		– City+FC –	
25	45.8	46.7	(+2.0)	46.8	(+2.3)
50	30.3	30.4	(+0.2)	30.7	(+1.2)
75	15.0	14.9	(−1.2)	15.2	(+1.4)
avg	30.4	30.6	(+0.9)	30.9	(+1.8)

The improvement over the results from automatically generated queries demonstrates the effectiveness of simple user modifications after automatic query processing has been performed. The most dramatic improvement comes at the top end of the recall scale, which is a highly desirable behavior in an interactive system. The results also suggest that, based on the text window simulation, paragraph-based retrieval can significantly improve effectiveness.

3. CONCLUSION

The availability of the large TIPSTER text base and query sets has enabled us to undertake a series of experiments in natural language processing of documents and queries for information retrieval. We have seen steady improvements due to lexical and phrase-level processing of natural language queries. Our experiments with interactive modification of the resulting queries indicate how much potential gain there is in this area, provided we can refine our phrasing and selection criteria, and provided actual paragraph retrieval is at least as good as our text window simulation of it. Refinement of our recognition and use of controlled indexing vocabulary is already showing benefits in more predictable domains, and we expect to see improvement in the results in the TIPSTER queries as well.

The experiments in automatic concept expansion based on cooccurrence behavior in large corpora are extremely interesting. Although the effects shown here are very preliminary, it is reassuring that they are positive even at this early stage.

It is clear that incremental application of local (word and phrase-level) natural language processing is beneficial in information retrieval. At this stage, the only expected limits to this approach are represented by the improvement achieved with the experiments in interactive query modification.

Table 3: Automatic concept expansion (**Expand**) compared with the automatic query baseline (**NP**).

	Precision (50 queries)		
Recall	NP	– Expand –	
0	77.1	75.2	(–2.4)
10	55.2	56.1	(+1.7)
20	48.3	49.0	(+1.4)
30	41.5	43.0	(+3.4)
40	36.7	37.7	(+2.8)
50	32.0	32.9	(+3.0)
60	27.9	27.9	(+0.3)
70	22.1	22.9	(+3.5)
80	17.5	18.0	(+2.8)
90	12.5	12.8	(+2.7)
100	2.4	2.7	(+12.1)
avg	33.9	34.4	(+1.4)

	Precision (50 queries)		
Recall (#Docs)	NP	– Expand –	
5	58.4	58.0	(–0.7)
15	51.5	53.5	(+3.9)
30	48.7	50.1	(+2.9)
100	34.6	35.5	(+2.6)
200	26.3	26.9	(+2.3)

References

[CCH92] James P. Callan, W. Bruce Croft, and Stephen M. Harding. The INQUERY retrieval system. In *Proceedings of the Third International Conference on Database and Expert Systems Applications*, pages 78–83. Springer-Verlag, 1992.

[Chu88] Kenneth Church. A stochastic parts program and noun phrase parser for unrestricted text. In *Proceedings of the 2nd Conference on Applied Natural Language Processing*, pages 136–143, 1988.

[CD90] W. B. Croft and R. Das. Experiments with query acquisition and use in document retrieval systems. In *Proceedings of the ACM SIGIR Conference on Research and Development in Information Retrieval*, pages 349–368, 1990.

[CTL91] W. B. Croft, H.R. Turtle, and D.D. Lewis. The use of phrases and structured queries in information retrieval. In *Proceedings of the ACM SIGIR Conference on Research and Development in Information Retrieval*, pages 32–45, 1991.

[Har88] D. Harman. Towards interactive query expansion. In Y. Chiaramella, editor, *Proceedings of the 11th International Conference on Research and Development in Information Retrieval*, pages 321–332. ACM, June 1988.

[Rau91] Lisa F. Rau. Extracting company names from text. In *Proceedings of the Sixth IEEE Conference on Artificial Intelligence Applications*, 1991.

[SM83] Gerard Salton and Michael J. McGill. *Introduction to Modern Information Retrieval.* McGraw-Hill, 1983.

Table 4: A comparison of two semi-automatic methods of constructing adhoc queries. The methods were evaluated on Volume 1 of the TIPSTER document collection, using relevance judgements from the 1992 Text Retrieval and Evaluation Conference (TREC).

	Precision (50 queries)				
Recall	Q-1	– – Q-M – –		– – Q-O – –	
0	83.9	83.8	(–0.2)	93.0	(+10.8)
10	60.5	64.1	(+6.0)	71.6	(+18.3)
20	52.7	55.4	(+5.1)	63.4	(+20.3)
30	46.6	48.6	(+4.3)	54.2	(+16.3)
40	40.5	42.1	(+3.9)	46.8	(+15.5)
50	35.0	36.4	(+4.1)	40.4	(+15.6)
60	30.5	30.9	(+1.5)	34.1	(+11.8)
70	25.4	25.0	(–1.4)	28.4	(+11.6)
80	19.9	18.3	(–7.8)	21.7	(+ 9.1)
90	12.1	11.8	(–3.0)	13.4	(+10.3)
100	2.5	2.3	(–6.5)	2.4	(– 2.5)
avg	37.2	38.1	(+2.3)	42.7	(+14.6)

	Precision (50 queries)				
Recall (#Docs)	Q-1	– – Q-M – –		– – Q-O – –	
5	64.8	67.2	(+3.7)	76.4	(+17.9)
15	59.2	63.9	(+7.9)	72.4	(+11.7)
30	54.1	57.5	(+6.3)	64.9	(+20.0)
100	42.4	45.5	(+7.3)	49.4	(+16.5)
200	35.6	36.7	(+3.1)	39.2	(+10.1)

[SB90] Gerard Salton and Chris Buckley. Improving retrieval performance by relevance feedback. *JASIS*, 41:288–297, 1990.

[TC91] Howard Turtle and W. Bruce Croft. Evaluation of an inference network-based retrieval model. *ACM Transactions on Information Systems*, 9(3), July 1991.

[Tur91] Howard Robert Turtle. *Inference networks for document retrieval.* PhD thesis, Department of Computer and Information Science, University of Massachusetts, Amherst, 1991.

AN OVERVIEW OF DR-LINK AND ITS APPROACH TO DOCUMENT FILTERING

Elizabeth D. Liddy [1], *Woojin Paik* [1], *Edmund S. Yu* [2], *Kenneth A. McVearry* [3]

[1] School of Information Studies
Syracuse University
Syracuse, NY 13244

[2] College of Engineering and Computer Science
Syracuse University
Syracuse, NY 13244

[3] Coherent Research, Inc.
1 Adler Drive
East Syracuse, NY 13057

1. MOTIVATION

DR-LINK is an information retrieval system, complex in design and processing, with the potential for providing significant advances in retrieval results due to the range and richness of semantic representation done by the various modules in the system. By using a full continuum of linguistic-conceptual processing, DR-LINK has the capability of producing documents which precisely match users' needs. Each of DR-LINK's six processing modules add to the conceptual enhancement of the document and query representation by means of continual semantic enrichments to the text. Rich representations are essential to meet the retrieval requirements of complex information needs and to reduce the ambiguities associated with keyword-based retrieval. To produce this enriched representation, the system uses lexical, syntactic, semantic, and discourse linguistic processing techniques for distilling from documents and topic statements all the rich layers of knowledge incorporated in their deceptively simple textual surface and for producing a textual representation which has been shaped by all these levels of linguistic processing.

A vital aspect of our approach which is evidenced in the various semantic enrichments (e.g. Subject Field Codes, proper noun categories, discourse components, concept-relation-concept triples, Conceptual Graphs) added to the basic text, is the real attention paid to representation at a deeper than surface level. That is, DR-LINK deals with lexical entities via conceptually-based linguistic processing. For example, complex nominals are interpreted as meaningful multi-word constituents because the combination of individual terms in complex nominals conveys quite different meanings than if the individual constituents were interpreted separately. In addition, verbs are represented by case-frames so that other lexical entities in the sentence which perform particular semantic roles in relation to the verb are represented according to these semantic roles. Also, the rich semantic data (e.g. location, purpose, nationality) that are conveyed in the appositional phrases typically accompanying proper nouns, are represented in such a way that the semantic relations implicitly conveyed in the appositions are explicitly available for more refined representation and matching.

2. OVERVIEW

DR-LINK's system architecture is modular in design, with six processing modules, each of which enhance the document and query representation in terms of continual semantic enrichments to the text. Briefly overviewed, the system's six modules function as follows:

1. <u>The Subject Field Coder</u> uses semantic word knowledge to produce a summary-level topical vector representation of a document's contents that is matched to a vector representation of a topic statement in order to rank all documents for subject-based similarity to a query. All of the documents with their Subject Field Code vectors are passed to:

2. The Proper Noun Interpreter, which uses a variety of knowledge bases and context heuristics to categorize every proper noun in the text. The similarity between a query's proper noun requirements and each document's Proper Noun Field is evaluated and combined with the similarity value from the Subject Field Coder for a reranking of all documents in response to the query. Those documents with a mathematically determined potential for being relevant to the query are then passed to:

3. The Text Structurer, which sub-divides a text into its discourse-level segments in order to focus query matching to the appropriate discourse component in response to particular types of information needs. All of the structured texts, with the appropriate components weighted, are passed to:

4. The Relation-Concept Detector, whose purpose is to raise the level at which we do matching from a key-word or key-phrase level to a more conceptual level by expanding terms in the topic statement to all terms which have been shown to be 'substitutable' for them. Then, semantic relations between concepts are recognized in both documents and topic statements using separate handlers for the various parts of speech. This module produces concept-relation-concept triples which are passed to:

5. The Conceptual Graph Generator which converts these triples into the CG formalism (Sowa, 1984), a variant of semantic networks in which arcs between nodes are coded for relations. The resultant CGs are passed to:

6. The Conceptual Graph Matcher, which measures the degree to which a particular topic statement CG and candidate document CGs share a common structure, and does a final ranking of the documents.

In combination, these six stages of processing produce textual representations that capture breadth and variety of semantic knowledge. However, since the Conceptual Graph generation and matching are so computationally expensive, we also take care to eliminate from further processing for each query, those documents which have no likelihood of being relevant to a well-specified query or query-profile.

3. DOCUMENT FILTERING WITHIN DR-LINK

The fact that information-intense government organizations receive thousands of documents daily with only a relatively small subset of them being of potential interest to any individual user suggests that the routing application of information retrieval can be approached as a filtering process, with the types and optimal number of filterings dependent on the desired granularity of filtering. Our research demonstrates how a first, rough-cut, purely content-based document filter can be used to produce its appropriate preliminary ranking of an incoming flow of documents for each user. Using the similarity values produced by the SFC Filter, later system modules further refine the ranking and perform finer levels of analysis and matching.

The success of our filtering approach is attributable to the representation scheme we use for all texts, both documents and queries. The Subject Field Codes (SFCs) are based on a culturally validated semantic coding scheme developed for use in Longman's Dictionary of Contemporary English (LDOCE), a general purpose dictionary. Operationally, our system tags each word in a document with the appropriate SFC from the dictionary. The within-document SFC frequencies are normalized and each document is represented as a frequency-weighted, fixed-length vector of the SFCs occurring in that document (see Figure 1). For routing, queries are likewise represented as SFC vectors. The system matches each query SFC vector to the SFC vector of all incoming documents, which are then ranked on the basis of their vectors' similarity to the query. Those documents whose SFC vectors exceed a predetermined criterion of similarity to the query SFC vector can be displayed to the user immediately or passed on to the Proper Noun Interpreter for further processing and a second-level re-ranking.

The real merit of the SFC vectors is that they represent texts at a more abstract, conceptual level than the individual words in the natural language texts themselves, thereby addressing the dual problems of synonymy and polysemy. On the one hand, the use of SFCs takes care of the "synonymous phrasing" problem by representing text at a level above the word-level by the assignment of one SFC from amongst 124 possible codes to each word in the document. This means that if four synonymous terms were used within a text, our system would assign each of them the same SFC since they share a common domain which would be reflected by their sharing a common SFC. For example, several documents that discuss the effects of recent political movements on legislation regarding civil rights would have similar SFC vector representations even though the vocabulary choices of the individual authors might be quite varied. Even more importantly, if a user who is seeking documents on this same topic expresses her

A U. S. magistrate in Florida ordered Carlos Lehder Rivas, described as among the world's leading cocaine traffickers, held without bond on 11 drug-smuggling counts. Lehder, who was captured last week in Colombia and immediately extradited to the U.S., pleaded innocent to the charges in federal court in Jacksonville.

LAW	.2667	SOCIOLOGY	.1333
BUSINESS	.1333	ECONOMICS	.0667
DRUGS	.1333	MILITARY	.0667
POLITICAL SCIENCE	.1333	OCCUPATIONS	.0667

Fig. 1: Sample Wall Street Journal document and its SFC representation

information need in terms which do not match the vocabulary of any of the documents, her query will still show high similarity to these documents' representations because both the query's representation and the documents' representations are at the more abstract, semantic-field level and the distribution of SFCs on the vectors of the query and the relevant documents would be proportionately similar across the SFCs.

The other problem with natural language as a representation alternative that has plagued its use in information retrieval is polysemy, the ability of a single word to have multiple senses or meanings. Our SFCoder uses psycholinguistically-justified sense disambiguation procedures (Liddy & Paik, 1992) to select a single sense for each word. Ambiguity is a serious problem, particularly in regard to the most frequently used lexical items. According to Gentner (1981) the twenty most frequent nouns in English have an average of 7.3 senses each, while the twenty most frequent verbs have an average of 12.4 senses each. Since a particular word may function as more than one part of speech and each word may also have more than one sense, each of these entries and/or senses may be assigned different SFCs. This is a slight variant of the standard disambiguation problem, which has shown itself to be nearly intractable for most NLP applications, but which is successfully handled in DR-LINK, thereby allowing the system to produce semantically accurate SFC vectors.

We based our computational approach to successful disambiguation on current psycholinguistic research literature which we interpret as suggesting that there are three potential sources of influence on the human disambiguation process: 1) local context, 2) domain knowledge, and 3) frequency data. We have computationally approximated these three knowledge sources in our disambiguator. The disambiguation procedures were tested by having the system select a single SFC for each word. These SFCs were compared to the sense-selections made by an independent judge. The disambiguation implementation selected the correct SFC 89% of the time. This means that a word such as 'drugs', which might refer to either medically prescribed remedies or illegal intoxicants that are traded on the street would be represented by different SFCs based on the context in which it occurred.

4. PROCESSING IN THE SUBJECT FIELD CODER

In the Subject Field Coder, the following stages of processing are done:

In **Stage 1** processing, we run the documents and query through a probabilistic part of speech tagger (Meteer et al, 1991) in order to restrict candidate SFCs of a word to those of the appropriate syntactic category.

Stage 2 processing retrieves SFCs of each word's correct part of speech from the lexical database and assigns the SFCs.

Stage 3 then uses an ordered set of sentence-level context-heuristics to determine a word's correct SFC if multiple SFCs have been assigned to a word's different senses. First, the SFCs attached to all words in a sentence are evaluated to determine at the sentence level whether any words have only one SFC assigned to all their senses in LDOCE (unique-SFC), and; secondly, the SFCs which are assigned to more than three words in the sentence (frequent-SFC).

Stage 4 scans the SFCs of each remaining word to determine whether the unique-SFCs or frequent-SFCs discovered in Stage 3 occur amongst the multiple SFCs assigned by LDOCE to the ambiguous word. Those ambiguous words which have no SFC in common with the unique-SFCs or frequent-SFCs for that sentence are passed on to the next stage.

Stage 5 incorporates two global knowledge sources to complete the sense disambiguation task. The primary source is a correlation matrix which reflects stable estimates of SFC co-occurrences within documents. The second source is the order in which the senses of a word are listed in LDOCE which is based on frequency of use in the English language. In Stage 5, each of the remaining ambiguous words is resolved a word at a time, accessing the matrix via the unique and most frequent-SFCs of the sentence. The system evaluates the correlation coefficients between the unique and most frequent-SFCs of the sentence and the multiple SFCs assigned to the word being disambiguated to determine which of the multiple SFCs has the highest correlation with a unique-SFC or frequent-SFC. The system then selects that SFC as the unambiguous representation of the sense of the word.

Stage 6 processing produces a vector of SFCs and their frequencies for each document and for the query.

Stage 7 normalizes the vectors of each text, and at:

Stage 8, the document vectors are compared to the query vector using a similarity measure. A ranked listing of the documents in decreasing order of similarity is produced.

The assignment of SFCs is fully automatic and does not require any human intervention. In addition, this level of semantic representation of texts is efficient and has been empirically tested as a reasonable approach for ranking documents from a very large incoming flux of documents. For the 18th month TIPSTER evaluation, the use of this representation allowed the system to quickly rank 60 megabytes of text in the routing situation that was tested. All the later-determined relevant documents were within the top 37% of the ranked documents produced by the SFC Module.

A second level of lexical-semantic processing further improves the performance of DR-LINK as a reasonable document filter. That is, the Proper Noun Interpreter (Paik et al; this volume) computes the similarity between a query's proper noun requirements and each document's Proper Noun Field and combines this value with the similarity value produced by the SFCoder for a reranking in relation to the query. In the 18th month testing of our system, the results of this reranking based on the SFC values and the Proper Noun values placed <u>all</u> the relevant documents within the top 28% of the database.

5. DOCUMENT CLUSTERING USING SUBJECT FIELD CODES

These summary-level semantic vector representations of each text's contents produced by the SFCoder have also proven useful as a means for dividing a database into clusters of documents pertaining to the same subject area. The SFC vectors are clustered using Ward's agglomerative clustering algorithm (Ward, 1963) to form classes in the document database. Ad hoc queries are represented as SFC vectors and matched to the centroid SFC vector of each cluster in the database. Clusters whose centroid SFC vector exhibit high similarity to the query SFC vector can then be browsed by users who do not have a fully specified query, but who prefer to browse groups of documents whose optimum content they can only loosely define to the system (Liddy, Paik, & Woelfel, 1992).

A qualitative analysis revealed that clustering SFC vectors using Ward's clustering algorithm resulted in meaningful groupings of documents that were similar across concepts not directly encoded in SFCs. Two examples: all of the documents about AIDS clustered together, although AIDS is not in LDOCE. Secondly, all of the documents about the hostages in Iran clustered together even though proper nouns are not included in LDOCE and the word 'hostage' is tagged with the same SFC as hundreds of other terms. What the SFC representation of documents accomplishes, is that documents about the same or very similar topics have relatively equal distributions of words with the same SFCs and will therefore cluster together in meaningful groups.

6. CONCLUSION

Our implementation and testings of the SFCoder as a means for semantically representing the content of texts, either for the purpose of ranking a document set according to likelihood of being relevant to an individual query or for producing conceptually related clusters of documents for browsing are very promising. Particularly worthy of note is the observation that in a large operational system, the ability to filter out an average of 72% of the incoming flux of millions of documents will have a significant impact on any document detection system's performance with which this semantic-based document filter is combined.

REFERENCES

Gentner, D. (1981). Some interesting differences

between verbs and nouns. Cognition and brain theory. 4(2), 161-178.

Liddy, E.D., McVearry, K.A., Paik, W., Yu, E.S. & McKenna, M; (In press). Development, implementation & testing of a discourse model for newspaper texts. Proceedings of the Human Language Technology Workshop. Princeton, NJ: March, 1993.

Liddy, E.D. & Paik, W. (1992). Statistically-guided word sense disambiguation. In Proceedings of AAAI Fall Symposium Series: Probabilistic approaches to natural language. Menlo Park, CA: AAAI.

Liddy, E.D., Paik, W. & Woelfel, J.K. (1992). Use of subject field codes from a machine-readable dictionary for automatic classification of documents. Advances in Classification Research: Proceedings of the 3rd ASIS SIG/CR Classification Research Workshop. Medford, NJ: Learned Information, Inc.

Meteer, M., Schwartz, R. & Weischedel, R. (1991). POST: Using probabilities in language processing. Proceedings of the Twelfth International Conference on Artificial Intelligence. Sydney, Australia.

Paik, W., Liddy, E.D., Yu, E.S. & McKenna, M. (In press). Interpretation of Proper Nouns for Information Retrieval. Proceedings of the Human Language Technology Workshop. Princeton, NJ: March, 1993.

Sowa, J. (1984). Conceptual structures: Information processing in mind and machine. Reading, MA: Addison-Wesley.

Ward, J. (1963). Hierarchical grouping to optimize an objection function. Journal of the American Statistical Association. 58, p. 237-254.

SESSION 13: NEW DIRECTIONS

Ralph Weischedel

BBN Systems and Technologies
70 Fawcett Street
Cambridge, MA 02138

The three papers of Session 13 address issues differing from those in the remainder of the workshop. Two employ a methodology to discover preferences for speech input in a multi-modal interface. The third raises issues of processing human language without any assumption that the speech or text has been converted to an online sequence of ASCII characters (or other character codes).

As an introduction to the first two papers, consider Wizard of Oz experiments such as used in collecting ATIS data. In such an experiment, the subject is asked to use a system to solve one or more problems. The "system" could be a person who simulates a proposed capability, for instance to determine language and interface properties for a proposed computer capability. Alternatively, the system might be an existing capability.

Perhaps the first such experiment was performed by Ashok Malhotra (1975) to collect data that would suggest how varied (and challenging) textual queries would be in an interactive query application. Malhotra simulated the whole system, a very labor-intensive task.

The first paper ("Mode Preference in a Simple Data-Retrieval Task") employs fully implemented components to measure user preference for spoken input, versus filling a form, versus employing a scroll bar to look up telephone numbers in an online telephone book. The paper immediately got my attention with the following statement in the introduction, "For activities in a workstation environment, formal comparisons of speech with other input modes have failed to demonstrate a clear advantage for speech on conventional aggregate measures of performance, such as time-to-completion . . . ". The author's experiments demonstrate a flaw in the analysis of previous results and go on to measure a marked preference for speech input, even when speech may not give the best time-to-completion results.

The second paper, "A Simulation-Based Research Strategy for Designing Complex NL Systems," involves a person behind the scenes (the wizard) simulating the system, though much is automated. The resulting environment being simulated for the user is quite rich, allowing both speech and handwriting input. Careful preparation of the experimental environment enabled automated support so that response to the user is streamlined, thereby allowing the user to move at his/her own pace. To illustrate the kind of studies the methodology supports, the authors show some results suggesting that syntactic ambiguity is less when filling out a form (rather than when producing unconstrained input) and is also less in handwriting than in speech.

The third paper, "Speech and Text-Image Processing in Documents," assumes minimal signal processing. For instance, they describe editing and indexing of audio forms rather than the text file resulting from continuous speech recognition. Similarly "text-image" processing, is the editing of the bitmap representation resulting from scanning a document in, rather than editing a sequence of bytes in some character code such as ASCII. One of the tools described is therefore aptly named "Image Emacs". A third effort described in this paper is document image decoding, a framework for processing scanned-in documents.

REFERENCES

Malhotra, A. "Design Criteria for a Knowledge-Based English Language System for Management: An Experimental Analysis", Massachusetts Institute of Technology, Cambridge, Ma., MAC TR, No. 146, February, 1975.

Mode preference in a simple data-retrieval task

Alexander I. Rudnicky
School of Computer Science, Carnegie Mellon University
Pittsburgh, PA 15213 USA

ABSTRACT

This paper describes some recent experiments that assess user behavior in a multi-modal environment in which actions can be performed with equivalent effect in speech, keyboard or scroller modes. Results indicate that users freely choose speech over other modalities, even when it is less efficient in objective terms, such as time-to-completion or input error.

INTRODUCTION

Multi-modal systems allow users to both tailor their input style to the task at hand and to use input strategies that combine several modes in a single transaction. As yet no consistent body of knowledge is available for predicting user behavior in multi-modal environments or to guide the design of multi-modal systems. This is particularly true when interfaces incorporate new technologies such as speech recognition.

For activities in a workstation environment, formal comparisons of speech with other input modes have failed to demonstrate a clear advantage for speech on conventional aggregate measures of performance such as time-to-completion [1, 8, 4], despite a consistent advantage displayed by speech at the level of single input operations. The difference can actually be attributed to the additional incurred costs of non-real-time recognition and error correction. While real-time performance can be achieved, it is unlikely that error-free recognition will be available in the near future. Given these shortcomings, we might ask if speech can provide advantages to the user along dimensions other than task speed, for example by reducing the effort needed to generate an input.

There is reason to believe that users are quite good at estimating the response characteristics of an interface and can choose an input strategy that optimizes salient aspects of performance, for example decreasing time-to-completion or minimizing task error [5, 9]. By observing the behavior of users in a situation in which they can freely choose between different strategies, we can gain insight into the factors that govern their preference for different input styles.

A simple data retrieval task was chosen for this study, as the task was one amenable to execution in each of the three modalities that were examined: speech, keyboard and scroller. The database contained information about individuals, such as address, telephone, etc selected from a list of conference attendees. The task consisted of retrieving the record for an individual and recording the last group of digits in their work telephone number (typically of length four). The database contained 225 names for the first experiment and was expanded to 240 names for the second experiment.

SYSTEM IMPLEMENTATION

The Personal Information Database (PID) component of the OM system [3, 7] served as the database system in this study. Given a search request specified in some combination of first name, last name and affiliation, PID displays a window with the requested information (in this study, the information consisted of name, affiliation and all known telephone numbers). If an unknown name was entered, an error panel came up. If a query was underspecified, a choice panel containing all entries satisfying the query was shown; for example asking for "Smith" produced a panel showing all Smiths in the database. The existing PID was altered to incorporate a scroll window in addition to the already available keyboard and speech interfaces. The remainder of this section provides detailed descriptions for each input mode.

Speech Input

The OM system uses a hidden Markov model (HMM) recognizer based on Sphinx [2] and is capable of speaker-independent continuous speech recognition. The subject interacted with the system through a

NeXT computer which provided attention management [3] as well as application-specific displays. To offload computation, the recognition engine ran on a separate NeXT computer and communicated through an ethernet connection. For the 731-word vocabulary and perplexity 33 grammar used in the first experiment, the system responded in 2.1 times real-time (xRT). Database retrieval was by a command phrase such as **SHOW ME ALEX RUDNICKY**. While subjects were instructed to use this specific phrase, the system also understood several variants, such as **SHOW**, **GIVE (ME)**, **LIST**, etc. The input protocol was "Push and Hold", meaning that the user had to depress the mouse button before beginning to speak and release it after the utterance was complete. Subjects were instructed to keep repeating a spoken command in case of recognition error, until it was processed correctly and the desired information appeared in the result window.

Keyboard
Subjects were required to click a field in a window then type a name into it, followed by a carriage return (which would drop them to the next field or would initial the retrieval). Three fields were provided: First name, Last Name and Organization. Subjects were provided with some shortcuts: last names were often unique and might be sufficient for a retrieval. They were also informed about the use of a wildcard character which would allow then to minimize the number of keystrokes need for a retrieval. Ambiguous search patterns produced a panel of choices; the subject could click on the desired one.

Scroller
The scroller window displayed the names in the database sorted alphabetically by last name. Eleven names were visible in the window at any one time, providing approximately 4–5% exposure of the 225 name list. The NeXT scroller provides a handle and two arrow buttons for navigation. Clicks on the scrollbar move the window to the corresponding position in the text and the arrow buttons can be amplified to jump by page when a control key is simultaneously depressed. Each navigation technique was demonstrated to the subject.

Session controller
The experiment was controlled by a separate process visible to the subject as a window displaying a name to look up, a field in which to enter the retrieved information and a field containing special instructions such as **Please use KEYBOARD only** or **Use any mode**. The subject progressed through the experiment by clicking a button in this window labeled **Next**; this would display the next name to retrieve. Equidistant from the the **Next** button were three windows corresponding to the three input modes used in the experiment: voice, keyboard and scroller. All modes required a mouse action to initiate input, either a click on the speech input button, a click on a text input field or button in the keyboard window or the (direct) initiation of activity in the scroller.

Figure 1: *Trial time line, showing events logged by the control program.*

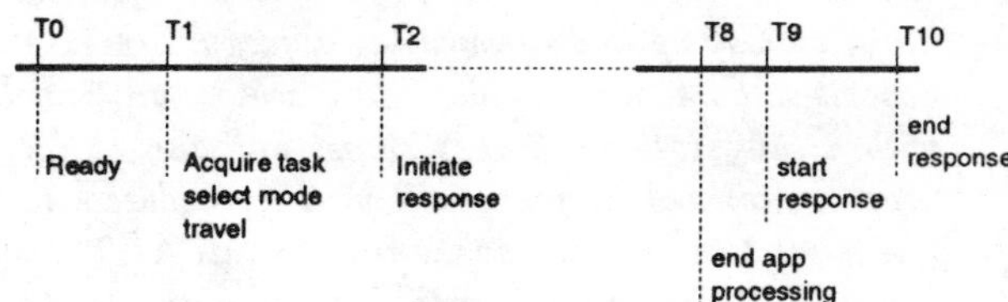

Instrumentation
All applications were instrumented to generate a stream of time-stamped events corresponding to user and system actions. Figure 1 shows the time line for a single trial. In addition to the overall time-line, each mode was also instrumented to generate logging events corresponding to significant internal events. All logged events were time-stamped using absolute system time, then merged in analysis to produce a composite timeline corresponding to the entire experimental session.

The merged event stream was processed using a hierarchical set of finite-state machines (FSMs). Figure 2 shows the FSM for a single transaction with the database retrieval program. Figures 3 show the FSM for the voice mode. During the analysis process, the latter FSM (as well as FSMs for keyboard and scroller) would be invoked within state 1 of the transaction FSM (Figure 2). An intermediate level of analysis (corresponding to conditions) is also used to simplify analysis. Arcs in the FSMs correspond to observable events, either system outputs or user inputs. The products of the analysis include transition frequencies for all arcs in an FSM as well as transition times. The analysis can be treated in terms of Markov chains [6] to compactly describe recognition error, user mode preferences and other system characteristics.

USER MODE PREFERENCE IN DATA RETRIEVAL

The purpose of the first experiment was to establish what mode-preference patterns users would display when using the PID system. To ensure that subjects

Figure 2: *FSM for a single transaction. From the initial state (*0*) the subject can click the* **Next** *button to move to state* 1 *at which point the subject has a name to look up and can initiate a query. Queries are described by mode-specific FSMs which are invoked within this state. Figure 3 shows one such FSM. If properly formed, a query will produce a database retrieval and move the transaction to state* 4. *The subject can opt to enter a response, moving the transaction to state* 2 *or to repeat queries (by re-entering state* 1*). At this point, the subject is ready to begin a new trial by transitioning to state* 0.

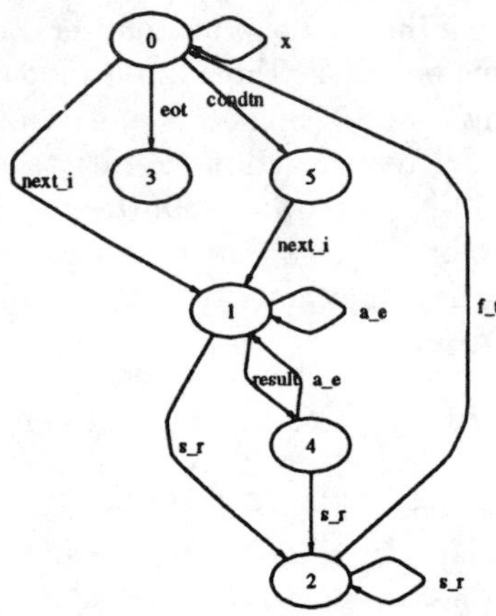

Figure 3: *FSM used for the analysis of voice input.*

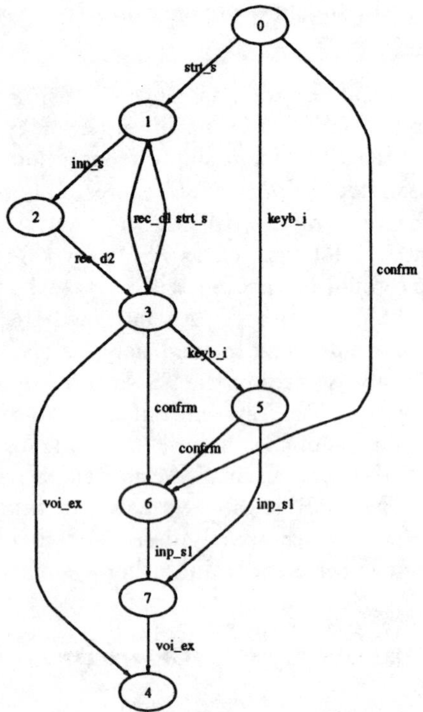

were equally familiar with each of the input modes, the experiment was divided into two parts (although it was run as a single session, without breaks). In the first part, subjects were asked to perform 20 retrievals using each mode. Initial testing determined that this was sufficient to acquaint the subjects with the operation of each mode. In the second part, they were instructed to use "any mode", with the expectation that they would choose on the basis of their assessment of the suitability of each mode. A total of 55 entries were presented in the second part.

The same sequence of 60 entries was used for the familiarization stage for all subjects. However, the order in which the subject was exposed to the different modes was counter-balanced according to a Latin square. Three different blocks of test items (each containing 55 entries) were used, for a total of nine different combinations.

Details about the operation of the different modes as well as the experiment controller were explained to the subject during a practice session prior to the experiment proper (a total of four practice retrievals were performed by the subject in this phase).

Subjects

Nine subjects participated in this study, 7 male and 2 female. All had had some previous exposure to speech systems, primarily through their participation in ongoing speech data collection efforts conducted by our research group. This prior exposure ensured that the subjects were familiar with the mechanics of using a microphone and of interacting with a computer by voice. No attempt was made to select on demographic characteristics or on computer skills. The group consisted primarily of students, none of whom however were members of our research group.

Results and Analysis

A finite state machine (FSM) description of user behavior was used to analyze session data. Separate FSMs were defined for condition, transaction, sequence and intra-modal levels and were used to tabulate metrics of interest.

Table 1 shows the durations of transactions for each of the modes during the familiarization phase. A transaction is timed from the click on the **Next** button to the carriage return terminating the entry of the retrieved telephone number. Speech input leads to the longest transaction times. Input time measures the duration between the initiation of input and system response (note that these times include recognition time, as well as the consequences of mis-recognition,

Table 1: *Times (in sec) for the familiarization blocks in the first experiment.*

Mode	Transaction	Input	Utterance duration
Scroller	13.623	4.917	—
Keyboard	14.526	5.371	—
Voice	15.041	5.593	2.464

Table 2: *User mode choices in the Free block (trials 61–115).*

Transaction Mode	Choice (%)	First Choice (%)
Scroller	14.3	14.7
Keyboard	21.8	22.4
Voice	48.3	62.8
mixed	15.5	—

Table 3: *User mode preference in the Free block of the second experiment.*

Transaction Mode	Input Choice (%)	Filtered Choice (%)
Scroller	5.8	4.4
Keyboard	14.2	11.3
Voice	74.9	79.9
mixed	5.1	4.4

Table 4: *Times (in sec) for the second experiment (using unfiltered data). The input time for voice is the utterance duration.*

Mode	Transaction	Input
Scroller	10.863	4.394
Keyboard	9.560	3.035
Voice	9.463	2.078

i.e., having to repeat an input). Here speech is also at a disadvantage (though note that the duration of a single utterance is only 2.464 sec). Transaction durations for modes are statistically different ($F(2,14) = 5.54$, $MS_{err} = 0.836$, $p < 0.05$), though in individual comparisons only voice and scroller differ ($p < 0.05$, the Neuman-Keuls procedure was used for this and all subsequent comparisons). Order of presentation was a significant factor ($F(2,14) = 8.3$, $p < 0.01$), with the first mode encountered requiring the greatest amount of time.

Table 2 shows choice of mode in the Free block. The mixed mode line refers to cases where subjects would first attempt a lookup in one mode then switch to another (for example because of misrecognition in the speech mode). The right-hand column in the table shows the first mode chosen in a mixed-mode transaction. In this case, voice is preferred 62.8% of the time as a first choice. The pattern of choices is statistically significant ($F(2,14) = 6.31, MS_{err} = 288, p < 0.01$), with speech preferred significantly more than either keyboard or scroller($p < 0.05$).

This experiment suggests that speech is the preferred mode of interaction for the task we examined. This is particularly notable since speech is the least efficient of the three modes offered to the user, as measured in traditional terms such as time-to-completion. Most previous investigations (see, e.g. the review in [4]) have concentrated on this dimension, treating it as the single most important criterion for the suitability of speech input. The present result suggests that other aspects of performance may be equally important to the user.

EXTENDED EXPERIENCE

One possible explanation of the above result is that it's due to a novelty effect. That is, users displayed a preference for speech input in this task not because of any inherent preference or benefit but simply because it was something new and interesting. Over time we might expect the novelty to wear off and users to refocus their attention on system response characteristics and perhaps shift their preference.

To test this possibility, we performed a second experiment, scaling up the amount of time spent on a task by different amounts. Since it was not possible to predict the length of a novelty effect *a priori*, three separate experience levels were examined. A total of 9 subjects participated (4 male and 5 female): 3 did 720 trials, 3 did 1440 trials and 3 did 2160. This is in contrast to the 115 trials per subject in the first experiment.

Method

Based on observations made during the first experiment, several changes were made to the system, primarily to make the speech and keyboard inputs more efficient. Recognition response was improved from 2.1 xRT to 1.5 xRT by the use of an IBM 6000/530 computer as the recognition engine. Keyboard entry was made more efficient by eliminating the need for the user to clear entry fields prior to entry. These changes resulted in improved transaction times for these two modes relative to the scroller, which was unchanged except for a slight reduction in exposure (this due to an increase of the number of entries to 240, done to facilitate details of the design).

Figure 4: *User preference over blocks (filtered data). Note that the spikes at blocks 19 and 34 are due to equipment failure.*

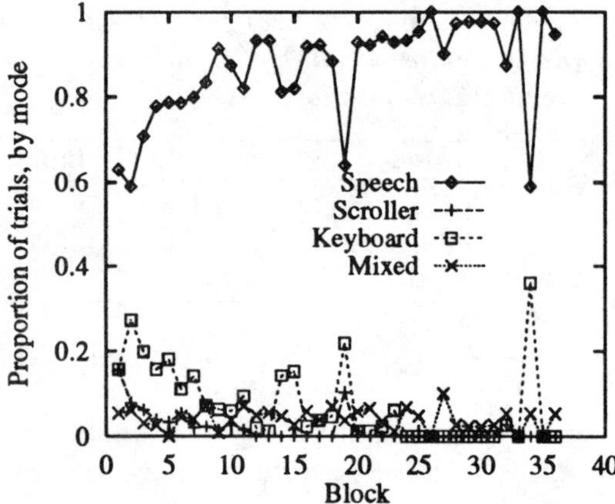

Results and Analysis

The mean preference for different modes in this experiment is shown in Table 3. Subjects display a strong bias in favor of voice input (74.9%). Preference for voice across individual subjects ranged from 28% to 91% with all but one subject (S3) showing preference levels above 70% (the median preference is 82.5%). Differences in mode preference are significant ($F(2,16) = 34.6, MS_{err} = 0.037, p < 0.01$) and the preference is greater ($p < 0.01$) for voice than for either of the other input modes.

Since some of the names in the database were difficult to pronounce, we also tabulated choice data excluding such names. Nineteen names (about 8% of the database) were excluded on the basis of ratings provided by subjects.[1] The data thus filtered are shown in Table 3; in this case (for names that subjects were reasonably comfortable about pronouncing) preference for speech rises to 79.9% (median of 86.1%).

[1]Participants in this experiment rated each name in the database prior to the experiment itself. A name was presented to the subject, who was asked to rate on a 4-point scale their lack of confidence in their ability to pronounce it. They then heard a recording of the name pronounced as expected by the recognizer and finally rated the degree to which the canonical pronunciation disagreed with their own expectation. A conservative criterion was used to place names on the exclusion list: any name for which both ratings averaged over 1.0 (on a 0–3 scale) was excluded.

Table 4 shows the mean transaction and input times for the second experiment, computed over subjects. Compared to the first experiment, these times are faster, probably reflecting the greater amount of experience with the task for the second group of subjects. Transaction times are significantly different ($F(2,16) = 16.8, MS_{err} = 0.327, p < 0.01$), with scroller times longer than keyboard or speech times ($p < 0.01$) which in turn are not different. If subjects were attending to the time necessary to carry out the task, keyboard and voice should have been chosen with about equal frequency. The subjects in this experiment nevertheless chose speech over keyboard (and scroller) input.

Figure 4 shows preference for voice input over the course of the experiment. Preference for speech increases over time, and begins to asymptote at about 10–15 blocks (representing about 250 utterances). This phenomenon suggests that speech input, while highly appealing to the user requires a certain amount of confidence building, certainly a period of extended familiarization with what is after all a novel input mode. Additional investigation would be needed, however, to establish the accuracy of this observation. In any case, this last result underlines the importance of providing sufficient training.

As can be seen in Figure 4 that preference for speech shows no sign of decreasing over time for the duration examined in this experiment. Preference for voice input appears to be robust. The 36 block version of the experiment took on the average 8–9 hours to complete, with subjects working up to 2 hours per day.

A possible explanation for this finding may be that, rather than basing their choice on overall transaction time, users focus on simple input time (in both experiments voice input is the fastest). This would imply that users are willing to disregard the cost of recognition error, at least for the error levels associated with the system under investigation. Data from followup experiments not reported here suggest that this may be the case: increasing the duration of the query utterance decreases the preference for speech.

CONCLUSION

The study reported in this paper indicates that users show a preference for speech input despite its inadequacies in terms of classic measures of performance, such as time-to-completion. Subjects in this study based their choice of mode on attributes other than transaction time (quite possibly input time) and were willing to use speech input even if this meant spending a longer time on the task. This preference appears to persist and even increase with continuing use, suggesting that preference for speech cannot be attributed to short-term novelty effects.

This paper also sketches an analysis technique based on FSM representations of human–computer interaction that permits rapid automatic processing of long event streams. The statistical properties of these event streams (as characterized by Markov chains) may provide insight into the types of information that users themselves compute in the course of developing satisfactory interaction strategies.

References

[1] BIERMANN, A. W., FINEMAN, L., AND HEIDLAGE, J. F. A voice- and touch-driven natural language editor and its performance. *International Journal of Man-Machine Studies 37* (1992), 1–21.

[2] LEE, K.-F. *Automatic Speech Recognition: The Development of the SPHINX System.* Kluwer Academic Publishers, Boston, 1989.

[3] LUNATI, J.-M., AND RUDNICKY, A. I. The design of a spoken language interface. In *Proceedings of the Third Darpa Speech and Natural Language Workshop* (Hidden Valley, June 1990), Morgan Kaufmann, San Mateo, CA, 1990, pp. 225–229.

[4] MARTIN, G. The utility of speech input in user-computer interfaces. *International Journal of Man-Machine Studies 29* (1989), 355–376.

[5] RUDNICKY, A. System response delay and user strategy selection in a spreadsheet task. CHI'90, invited poster, April 1990.

[6] RUDNICKY, A. I., AND HAUPTMANN, A. G. Models for evaluating interaction protocols in speech recognition. In *Proceedings of CHI* (New Orleans, Louisiana, April 1991), ACM, New York, 1991, pp. 285–291.

[7] RUDNICKY, A. I., LUNATI, J.-M., AND FRANZ, A. M. Spoken language recognition in an office management domain. *Proceedings of ICASSP* (May 1991), 829–832.

[8] RUDNICKY, A. I., SAKAMOTO, M. H., AND POLIFRONI, J. H. Spoken language interaction in a spreadsheet task. In *Human-Computer Interaction – INTERACT'90*, D. Diaper et al., Eds. Elsevier, 1990, pp. 767–772.

[9] TEAL, S. L., AND RUDNICKY, A. I. A performance model of system delay and user strategy selection. In *Proceedings of CHI* (Monterey, CA, May 1992), ACM, New York, 1992, pp. 295–206.

A SIMULATION-BASED RESEARCH STRATEGY FOR DESIGNING COMPLEX NL SYSTEMS*

Sharon Oviatt, Philip Cohen, Michelle Wang & Jeremy Gaston[†]

Computer Dialogue Laboratory
A.I. Center, SRI International
333 Ravenswood Avenue
Menlo Park, California, U.S.A. 94025

ABSTRACT

Basic research is critically needed to guide the development of a new generation of multimodal and multilingual NL systems. This paper summarizes the goals, capabilities, computing environment, and performance characteristics of a new semi-automatic simulation technique. This technique has been designed to support a wide spectrum of empirical studies on highly interactive speech, writing, and multimodal systems incorporating pen and voice. Initial studies using this technique have provided information on people's language, performance, and preferential use of these communication modalities, either alone or in multimodal combination. One aim of this research has been to explore how the selection of input modality and presentation format can be used to reduce difficult sources of linguistic variability in people's speech and writing, such that more robust system processing results. The development of interface techniques for channeling users' language will be important to the ability of complex NL systems to function successfully in actual field use, as well as to the overall commercialization of this technology. Future extensions of the present simulation research also are discussed.

1. INTRODUCTION

Basic research is critically needed to guide the development of a new generation of complex natural language systems that are still in the planning stages, such as ones that support multimodal, multilingual, or multiparty exchanges across a variety of intended applications. In the case of planned multimodal systems, for example, the potential exists to support more robust, productive, and flexible human-computer interaction than that afforded by current unimodal ones [3]. However, since multimodal systems are relatively complex, the problem of how to design optimal configurations is unlikely to be solved through simple intuition alone. Advance empirical work with human subjects will be needed to generate a factual basis for designing multimodal systems that can actually deliver performance superior to unimodal ones.

In particular, there is a special need for both methodological tools and research results based on high-quality simulations of proposed complex NL systems. Such simulations can reveal specific information about people's language, task performance, and preferential use of different types of systems, so that they can be designed to handle expected input. Likewise, simulation research provides a relatively affordable and nimble way to compare the specific advantages and disadvantages of alternative architectures, such that more strategic designs can be developed in support of particular applications. In the longer term, conclusions based on a series of related simulation studies also can provide a broader and more principled perspective on the best application prospects for emerging technologies such as speech, pen, and multimodal systems incoporating them.

In part for these reasons, simulation studies of spoken language systems have become common in the past few years, and have begun to contribute to our understanding of human speech to computers [1, 5, 6, 7, 8, 17]. However, spoken language simulations typically have been slow and cumbersome. There is concern that delayed responding may systematically distort the data that these simulation studies were designed to collect, especially for a modality like speech from which people expect speed [6, 10, 15]. Unlike research on spoken language systems, there currently is very little literature on handwriting and pen systems. In particular, no simulation studies have been reported on: (1) interactive handwriting[1] [6], (2) comparing interactive speech versus handwriting as alternative ways to interact with a system, or (3) examining the combined use of speech and handwriting to simulated multimodal systems of different types. Potential advantages of a combined pen/voice system have been outlined previously [4, 12]. High quality simulation

*This research was supported in part by Grant No. IRI-9213472 from the National Science Foundation to the first authors, as well as additional funding and equipment donations from ATR International, Apple Computer, USWest, and Wacom Inc. Any opinions, findings, or conclusions expressed in this paper are those of the authors, and do not necessarily reflect the views of our sponsors.

[†]Michelle Wang is affiliated with the Computer Science Department and Jeremy Gaston with the Symbolic Systems Program at Stanford University.

[1]Although we are familiar with noninteractive writing from everyday activities like personal notetaking, very little is known about *interactive* writing and pen use as a modality of human-computer interaction.

research on these topics will be especially important to the successful design of mobile computing technology, much of which will emphasize communications and be keyboardless.

The simulation technique developed for this research aims to: (1) support a very rapid exchange with simulated speech, pen, and pen/voice systems, such that response delays are less than 1 second and interactions can be subject-paced, (2) provide a tool for investigating interactive handwriting and other pen functionality, and (3) devise a technique appropriate for comparing people's use of speech and writing, such that differences between these communication modalities and their related technologies can be better understood. Toward these ends, an adaptable simulation method was designed that supports a wide range of studies investigating how people speak, write, or use both pen and voice when interacting with a system to complete qualitatively different tasks (e.g., verbal/temporal, computational/numeric, graphic/cartographic). The method also supports examination of different issues in spoken, written, and combined pen/voice interactions (e.g., typical error patterns and resolution strategies).

In developing this simulation, an emphasis was placed on providing automated support for streamlining the simulation to the extent needed to create facile, subject-paced interactions with clear feedback, and to have comparable specifications for the different modalities. Response speed was achieved in part by using scenarios with correct solutions, and by preloading information. This enabled the assistant to click on predefined fields in order to respond quickly. In addition, the simulated system was based on a conversational model that provides analogues of human backchannel and propositional confirmations. Initial tasks involving service transactions embedded propositional-level confirmations in a compact transaction "receipt," an approach that contributed to the simulation's clarity and speed. Finally, emphasis was placed on automating features to reduce attentional demand on the simulation assistant, which also contributed to the fast pace and low rate of technical errors in the present simulation.

2. SIMULATION METHOD

Basic simulation features for the studies completed to date are summarized below, and have been detailed elsewhere [16], although some adaptations to these specifications are in progress to accommodate planned research.

2.1. Procedure and Instructions

Volunteer participants coming into the Computer Dialogue Laboratory at SRI are told that the research project aims to develop and test a new pen/voice system for use on future portable devices. To date, subjects have included a broad spectrum of white-collar professionals, excluding computer scientists. All participants so far have believed that the "system" was a fully functional one. Following each session, they are debriefed about the nature and rationale for conducting a simulation.

During the study, subjects receive written instructions about how to enter information on an LCD tablet when writing, when speaking, and when free to use both modalities. When writing, they are told to handwrite information with the electronic stylus directly onto active areas on the tablet. They are free to print or write cursive. When speaking, subjects are instructed to tap and hold the stylus on active areas as they speak into the microphone. During free choice, people are completely free to use either modality in any way they wish. Participants also receive written instructions about how to use the system to complete realistic tasks, which currently focus on the broad class of service-oriented transactions (e.g., car rental reservations, personal banking, real estate selection). Then they practice several scenarios using spoken and written input until the system and the tasks are completely clear.

People are encouraged to speak and write naturally. They are asked to complete the tasks according to instructions, while working at their own pace. Other than providing motivation to complete the tasks and specifying the input modality, an effort is made not to influence the specific manner in which subjects express themselves. They are encouraged to focus on completing the tasks and are told that, if their input cannot be processed for any reason, this will be clear immediately since the system will respond with ??? to prompt them to try again. Subjects are told how to remove or replace information as needed. Otherwise, they are told that input will be confirmed by the system on a transaction receipt, which they can monitor to check that their requests are being met (see next section for details). Of course, participants' input actually is received by an informed assistant, who performs the role of interpreting and responding as the system would.

The simulation assistant is instructed to respond as accurately and rapidly as possible to any spoken or written information corresponding to predefined receipt fields. Essentially, the assistant tracks the subject's input, clicking with a mouse on predefined fields on a Sun SPARCstation to send confirmations back to the subject. Under some circumstances, the assistant is instructed to send a ??? prompt instead of a confirmation. For example, subjects receive ??? feedback when input is judged to be inaudible or illegible, when the subject forgets to supply task-critical information, or when input clearly is inappropriate, ambiguous, or underspecified. In general, however, the assistant is instructed to use ??? feedback sparingly in order to minimize intervention with people's natural tendencies to speak or write. If the subject commits a procedural error, such as forgetting to click before entering speech or attempting to enter information using the wrong modality, then the assistant is instructed not to respond until the subject recovers and correctly engages the system. The assistant's task is sufficiently automated that he or she is free to focus attention on monitoring the accuracy of incoming information, and on maintaining sufficient vigilance to respond promptly with confirmations.

2.2. Presentation Format

For studies completed to date, two different prompting techniques have been used to guide subjects' spoken and written input— one unconstrained and one forms-based. In the relatively unconstrained presentation format, subjects must take the initiative to ask questions or state needs in one general workspace area. No specific system prompts direct their input. They simply continue providing information until their transaction receipt is completed, correctly reflecting their requests. In this case, guidance is provided primarily by the task itself and the receipt. When the presentation format is a form, labeled fields are used to elicit specific task content, for example: **Car pickup location**[ ]. In this case, the interaction is more system-guided, and linguistic and layout cues are used to channel the content and order of people's language as they work.

For other studies in which people work with visual information (e.g., graphic/cartographic tasks), different graphic dimensions of presentation format are manipulated. In all studies, the goal is to examine the impact of presentation format on people's language and performance as they either speak or write to a simulated system. As a more specific aim, assessments are being conducted of the extent to which different formats naturally constrain linguistic variability, resulting in opportunities for more robust natural language processing.

2.3. Conversational Feedback

With respect to system feedback, a conversational model of human-computer interaction was adopted. As a result, analogues are provided of human backchannel and propositional-level confirmations. These confirmations function the same for different input modalities and presentation formats. With respect to backchannel signals, subjects receive *** immediately following spoken input, and an electronic ink trace following written input. These confirmations are presented in the tablet's active area or a narrow "confirmation panel" just below it. Subjects are told that this feedback indicates that their input has been legible/audible and processable by the system, and that they should continue.

In addition to this backchannel-level signal, subjects are told to verify that their requests are being met successfully by checking the content of the receipt at the bottom of the tablet. This receipt is designed to confirm all task-critical information supplied during the interaction, thereby providing propositional confirmations. It remains visible throughout the transaction, and is completed gradually as the interaction proceeds. Although the receipt varies for different tasks, its form and content remains the same for different modalities and presentation formats.

Apart from confirmation feedback, the simulation also responds to people's questions and commands by transmitting textual and tabular feedback. For example, if a subject selects the car model that he or she wants and then says, "Do you have infant seats?" or "Show me the car options," a brief table would be displayed in which available items like infant seats and car phones are listed along with their cost.

2.4. Automated Features

To simplify and speed up system responding, the correct receipt information associated with each task is preloaded for the set of tasks that a subject is to receive. A series of preprogrammed dependency relations between specified task-critical information and associated receipt fields is used to support the automation of propositional confirmations. As mentioned earlier, with this arrangement the assistant simply needs to click on certain predefined fields to send appropriate acknowledgments automatically as the subject gradually supplies relevant information. Of course, if the subject makes a performance error, the assistant must manually type and confirm the error that occurs. In such cases, however, canonical answers are maintained so that they can be confirmed quickly when people self-correct, which they tend to do over 50% of the time. The automated simulation strategy described above works well when research can take advantage of task scenarios that entail a limited set of correct answers.

An additional automated feature of the present simulation technique is a "random error generator," which is designed to ensure that subjects encounter at least a minimal level of simulated system errors, in part to support the credibility of the simulation. In this research, if subjects do not receive at least one ??? response from the system during a set of two tasks, then the simulation generates one. This results in a minimum baseline rate of one simulated error per 33 items of information supplied, or 3%, which in this research has been considered a relatively error-free environment. The simulated errors are distributed randomly across all task-critical information supplied for the set of tasks.

2.5. Performance Characteristics

The described method for organizing simulated response feedback was responsible in part for the fast pace of the present simulation. In studies conducted to date, response delays during the simulation have averaged 0.4 second between a subject's input and visible confirmation on the tablet receipt, with less than a 1-second delay in all conditions. The rate of technical errors in executing the assistant's role according to instructions has been low, averaging 0.05 such errors per task. Furthermore, any major error by the assistant would result in discarding that subject's data, which currently has been averaging 6% of subjects tested. The present simulation also appears to be adequately credible, since no participants to date have doubted that it was a fully functional system. As a result, no data has been discarded for this reason.

2.6. Simulation Environment

The computing equipment that supports this simulation technique includes two Sun workstations, one a SPARCstation 2, that are linked via ethernet. A Wacom HD-648A integral transparent digitizing tablet/LCD display is interfaced to the SPARC 2 through a Vigra S-bus VGA card. An accompanying cordless digitizing pen is used for writing, clicking to speak, pointing, or otherwise operating the tablet. A Crown PCC 160 microphone transmits spoken input from the subject to the simulation assistant, who listens through a pair of stereo speakers from a remote location. The assistant also views an image of the subject working at the tablet, along with an image of all visible input and feedback occurring on the tablet.

The user interface is based on the X-windows system, employing MIT Athena widgets. X-windows is used for its ability to display results on multiple screens, including the subject's tablet and the assistant's workstation, and because the resulting program runs on equipment from several manufacturers. Two aspects of the system architecture are designed for rapid interface adaptability. First, Widget Creation Language (WCL) enables non-programmers to alter the user interface layout. Second, a simple textual language and interpreter were created to enable declarative specification of widget behavior and interrelations. Some widget behavior also is written in the C programming language.

Various modifications to the standard X-windows operation have been deployed to ensure adequate real-time responding needed for acceptable handwriting quality and speed. To avoid objectionable lag in the system's electronic ink echo, a high-performance workstation (i.e., Sun SPARCstation 2) is used to process the subject's input.

2.7. Data Capture

With respect to data collection, all human-computer interactions are videotaped for subsequent analysis. The recording is a side-by-side split-screen image, created using a JVC KM-1200U special-effects generator. Videotaping is conducted unobtrusively with a remote genlocked Panasonic WV-D5000 videocamera filming through a one-way mirror. Data capture includes a close-up of the subject working at the LCD tablet, and a real-time record of interactions on the tablet, including the subject's input, simulated feedback, and the gradually completed receipt. This image is recorded internally from the assistant's workstation, is processed through a Lyon Lamb scan converter, and then is merged using the special-effects generator and preserved on videotape for later analysis. In addition to being transmitted to the simulation assistant, the subject's speech is recorded and stored in analog form on a timecoded videotape, and later is transcribed for data analysis. All handwritten input is recorded on-line during real-time tablet interactions, which then is preserved on videotape and available for hardcopy printout.

3. RESEARCH DESIGN

In studies conducted at SRI to date, the experimental design usually has been a completely-crossed factorial with repeated measures, or a within-subjects design. Primary factors of interest have included: (1) communication modality (speech-only, pen-only, combined pen/voice), and (2) presentation format (form-based, unconstrained). In a typical study, each subject completes a series of 12 tasks, two representing each of the six main conditions. The order of presenting conditions is counterbalanced across subjects.

This general design has been selected for its relative efficiency and power and, in particular, for its ability to control linguistic variability due to individual differences. In brief, for example, this design permits comparing how the *same* person completing the *same* tasks displays one type of language and performance while speaking, but then switches this language and performance when writing.

4. SAMPLE RESULTS

The variability inherent in people's language, whether spoken or written, poses a substantial challenge to the successful design of future NL systems. One aspect of this research has been a comprehensive assessment of the linguistic variability evident in people's speech and writing at various levels of processing, including acoustic, lexical, syntactic, and semantic. Full reports of these results are forthcoming [11, 14]. Special emphasis has been placed on identifying problematic sources of variability for system processing, as well as an explanation of the circumstances and apparent reasons for their occurrence. In connection with these analyses, one goal of this research program has been to identify specific interface techniques that may naturally channel users' language in ways that reduce or eliminate difficult sources of variability, so that more robust system processing can be achieved. In particular, the impact of selecting a particular input modality or presentation format is being examined, so that future system designers will have the option of choosing a particular modality or format because doing so will minimize expected performance failures of their planned NL systems.

To briefly illustrate the research theme of reducing linguistic variability through selection of modality and format, the results of an analysis related to syntactic ambiguity are summarized. Two indices of relative ambiguity were measured for all phrasal and sentential utterances that people spoke to an unconstrained format (SNF), wrote in an unconstrained format (WNF), spoke to a form (SF), or wrote in a form (WF). Two different estimates of parse ambiguity were computed to check for convergence of results. First, utterances produced under the different simulation conditions were parsed using DIALOGIC [9], a robust text processing system developed at SRI that employs a broad coverage grammar. Second, a summary was computed of the number of *canonical* parses produced by DIALOGIC, through a mapping of each DIALOGIC parse to an emerging national standard parse tree representation called PARSEVAL form[2] [2]. The average number of DIALOGIC and PARSEVAL parses generated per utterance for the different simulation conditions is summarized in Table 1, along with the percentage of all utterances in each condition that were phrases or sentences and therefore appropriate for parsing.

None of the subjects produced phrases or sentences when writing to a form, so none of the simple utterances from this condition were appropriate for parsing. The percentage of phrase and sentential utterances available for parsing was greater for unconstrained than form-based input, and greater for spoken than written input. Comparison of both parse metrics for unconstrained and form-based speech revealed that using a form significantly reduced the average number of parses per utterance, t (paired) = 2.50 (df = 5), $p < .03$, one-tailed (DIALOGIC), and t (paired) = 2.35 (df = 5), $p < .04$, one-tailed (PARSEVAL). When comparisons were made of the same subjects accomplishing the same tasks, the parse ambiguity of utterances in the unconstrained format averaged 232% higher for DIALOGIC and 157% higher for PARSEVAL than when communicating to a form. However, comparison of both parse metrics for speech and writing in an unconstrained format did not confirm that use of the written modality reduced the average number of parses per utterance, t (paired) = 1.18 (df = 14), $p > .10$, one-tailed (DIALOGIC), and $t < 1$ (PARSEVAL). That is, reliable reduction of parse ambiguity was obtained only through manipulation of the presentation format.

COND.	DIALOGIC	PARSEVAL	UTTERANCES PARSED
SNF	20.9	7.2	36%
WNF	10.7	4.4	18%
SF	6.3	2.8	8%
WF	—	—	0%

Table 1: Average number of DIALOGIC and PARSEVAL parses per utterance as a function of modality and format.

This pattern of results suggests that selection of presentation format can have a substantial impact on the ease of natural language processing, with direct implications for improved system robustness. In addition, post-experimental interviews indicated that participants preferred form-based interactions over unconstrained ones by a factor of 2-to-1 in the present tasks. In particular, both the guidance and assurance of completeness associated with a form were considered desirable. This indicates that the *a priori* assumption that any type of constraint will be viewed by people as unacceptable or unnatural clearly is not always valid. Furthermore, such a presumption may simply bias system development away from good prospects for shorter-term gain. The application of this kind of interface knowledge will be important to the successful performance and commercialization of future natural language technology.

[2]PARSEVAL form is designed to reflect agreement among computational linguists simply on the major constituent bracketings, so PARSEVAL identification of syntactic structures should tend to represent the commonalities among many different systems.

5. FUTURE DIRECTIONS

The long-term goal of the present research method is to support a wide spectrum of advance empirical studies on interactive speech, pen, and pen/voice systems under different circumstances of theoretical and commercial interest. Future extensions of the present simulation research are under way to examine issues relevant to multilingual and other multiparty applications [13]. In addition, a taxonomy of tasks is being developed in order to establish a more analytical basis for distinguishing when findings do or do not generalize to qualitatively different domains, such that future work need not approach each new application as an unknown entity. Efforts also are under way to define the important dimensions of system interactivity, such as feedback characteristics and error resolution strategies, as well as their impact on human-computer interaction. Finally, in addition to providing proactive guidance for system design, a further aim of this simulation research is to yield better information about the range of preferred metrics for conducting performance assessments of future NL systems, including their accuracy, efficiency, learnability, flexibility, ease of use, expressive power, and breadth of utility.

6. ACKNOWLEDGMENTS

Thanks to John Dowding, Dan Wilk, Martin Fong, and Michael Frank for invaluable programming assistance during the design and adaptation of the simulation. Special thanks also to Dan Wilk and Martin Fong for acting as the simulation assistant during experimental studies, to Zak Zaidman for general experimental assistance, and to John Bear, Jerry Hobbs, and Mabry Tyson for assisting with the preparation of DIALOGIC and PARSEVAL parses. Finally, thanks to the many volunteers who so generously offered their time to participate in this research.

References

1. F. Andry, E. Bilange, F. Charpentier, K. Choukri, M. Ponamalé, and S. Soudoplatoff. Computerised simulation tools for the design of an oral dialogue system. In *Selected Publications, 1988-1990, SUNDIAL Project (Esprit P2218)*. Commission of the European Communities, 1990.

2. E. Black, S. Abney, D. Flickinger, C. Gdaniec, R. Grishman, P. Harrison, D. Hindle, R. Ingria, F. Jelinek, J. Klavans, M. Liberman, M. Marcus, S. Roukos, B. Santorini, and T. Strzalkowski. A procedure for quantitatively comparing the syntactic coverage of English grammars. In *Proceedings of the DARPA Speech and Natural Language Workshop*, pages 306–311. Morgan Kaufmann, Inc., February 1991.

3. R. Cole, L. Hirschman, L. Atlas, M. Beckman, A. Bierman, M. Bush, J. Cohen, O. Garcia, B. Hanson, H. Hermansky, S. Levinson, K. McKeown, N. Morgan, D. Novick, M. Ostendorf, S. Oviatt, P. Price, H. Silverman, J. Spitz, A. Waibel, C. Weinstein, S. Zahorain, and V. Zue. NSF workshop on spoken language understanding. Technical Report CS/E 92-014, Oregon Graduate Institute, September 1992.

4. H. D. Crane. Writing and talking to computers. Business Intelligence Program Report D91-1557, SRI International, Menlo Park, California, July 1991.

5. N. Dahlbäck, A. Jönsson, and L. Ahrenberg. Wizard of Oz studies — why and how. In L. Ahrenberg, N. Dahlbäck, and A. Jönsson, editors, *Proceedings from the Workshop on Empirical Models and Methodology for Natural Language Dialogue Systems*, Trento, Italy, April 1992. Association for Computational Linguistics, Third Conference on Applied Natural Language Processing.

6. N. M. Fraser and G. N. Gilbert. Simulating speech systems. *Computer Speech and Language*, 5(1):81–99, 1991.

7. M. Guyomard and J. Siroux. Experimentation in the specification of an oral dialogue. In H. Niemann, M. Lang, and G. Sagerer, editors, *Recent Advances in Speech Understanding and Dialog Systems*. Springer Verlag, Berlin, B. R. D., 1988. NATO ASI Series, vol. 46.

8. C. T. Hemphill, J. J. Godfrey, and G. R. Doddington. The ATIS spoken language systems pilot corpus. In *Proceedings of the 3rd Darpa Workshop on Speech and Natural Language*, pages 96–101, San Mateo, California, 1990. Morgan Kaufmann Publishers, Inc.

9. J. R. Hobbs, D. E. Appelt, J. Bear, M. Tyson, and D. Magerman. Robust processing of real-world natural-language texts. In P. S. Jacobs, editor, *Text-Based Intelligent Systems: Current Research and Practice in Information Extraction and Retrieval*. Lawrence Erlbaum Associates, Publishers, Hillsdale, New Jersey, 1992.

10. A. F. Newell, J. L. Arnott, K. Carter, and G. Cruickshank. Listening typewriter simulation studies. *International Journal of Man-machine Studies*, 33(1):1–19, 1990.

11. S. L. Oviatt. Writing and talking to future interactive systems. manuscript in preparation.

12. S. L. Oviatt. Pen/voice: Complementary multimodal communication. In *Proceedings of Speech Tech'92*, pages 238–241, New York, February 1992.

13. S. L. Oviatt. Toward multimodal support for interpreted telephone dialogues. In M. M. Taylor, F. Néel, and D. G. Bouwhuis, editors, *Structure of Multimodal Dialogue*. Elsevier Science Publishers B. V., Amsterdam, Netherlands, in press.

14. S. L. Oviatt and P. R. Cohen. Interface techniques for enhancing robust performance of speech and handwriting systems. manuscript in preparation.

15. S. L. Oviatt and P. R. Cohen. Discourse structure and performance efficiency in interactive and noninteractive spoken modalities. *Computer Speech and Language*, 5(4):297–326, 1991a.

16. S. L. Oviatt, P. R. Cohen, M. W. Fong, and M. P. Frank. A rapid semi-automatic simulation technique for investigating interactive speech and handwriting. In *Proceedings of the 1992 International Conference on Spoken Language Processing*, Banff, Canada, October 1992.

17. E. Zoltan-Ford. How to get people to say and type what computers can understand. *International Journal of Man-Machine Studies*, 34:527–547, 1991.

Speech and Text-Image Processing in Documents

Marcia A. Bush

Xerox Palo Alto Research Center
3333 Coyote HIll Road
Palo Alto, CA 94304

ABSTRACT

Two themes have evolved in speech and text image processing work at Xerox PARC that expand and redefine the role of recognition technology in document-oriented applications. One is the development of systems that provide functionality similar to that of text processors but operate directly on audio and scanned image data. A second, related theme is the use of speech and text-image recognition to retrieve arbitrary, user-specified information from documents with signal content. This paper discusses three research initiatives at PARC that exemplify these themes: a text-image editor[1], a wordspotter for voice editing and indexing[12], and a decoding framework for scanned-document content retrieval[4]. [1] The discussion focuses on key concepts embodied in the research that enable novel signal-based document processing functionality.

1. INTRODUCTION

Research on application of spoken language processing to document creation and information retrieval has focused on the use of speech as an interface to systems that operate primarily on text-based material. Products of such work include commercially available voice transcription devices, as well as DARPA-sponsored systems developed to support speech recognition and database interaction tasks (e.g., the Resource Management[9] and Air Travel Information Systems[8] tasks, respectively). Similarly, work on text image processing has focused primarily on optical character recognition (OCR) as a means of transforming paper-based documents into manipulable (i.e., ASCII-based) electronic form. In both cases, the paradigm is one of format conversion, in which audio or image data are converted into symbolic representations that fully describe the content and structure of the associated document or query.

Over the past few years, two themes have evolved in speech and text image processing work at Xerox PARC that expand and redefine the role of recognition technology in document-oriented applications. The first of these is the development of systems that provide functionality similar to that of text processors but operate directly on audio and scanned image data. These systems represent alternatives to the traditional format conversion paradigm. They are based on a principle of *partial document modeling*, in which only enough signal analysis is performed to accomplish the user's goal. The systems are intended to facilitate authoring and editing of documents for which input and output medium are the same. Examples include authoring of voice mail and editing of facsimile-based document images.

[1] Thanks to S. Bagley, P. Chou, G. Kopec and L. Wilcox for agreeing to have their work discussed here. This work represents a sample, rather than a full survey, of relevant speech and text-image research at PARC.

A second, and related, research theme is the use of speech and text-image recognition to retrieve arbitrary, user-specified information from documents with signal content. The focus is again on partial document models that are defined in only enough detail to satisfy task requirements. Depending upon application, format conversion may or may not be a desired goal. For example, in retrieving relevant portions of a lengthy audio document via keyword spotting, a simple time index is sufficient. On the other hand, extracting numerical data from tabular images to facilitate on-line calculations requires at least partial transcription into symbolic form.

This paper discusses three research initiatives at PARC that exemplify these themes: a text-image editor[1], a wordspotter for voice editing and indexing[12], and a decoding framework for scanned-document content retrieval[4]. Overviews of the three systems are provided in Sections 2 through 4, respectively; concluding comments are contained in Section 5. The discussion focuses on key concepts embodied in the research that enable novel signal-based document processing functionality. Technical details of the individual efforts are described in the associated references.

2. TEXT IMAGE EDITING: IMAGE EMACS

Image EMACS is an editor for scanned documents in which the inputs and outputs are binary text images[1]. The primary document representation in Image EMACS is a set of image elements extracted from scanned text through simple geometrical analysis. These elements consist of groupings of connected components (i.e., connected regions of black pixels)[2] that correspond roughly to character images. Editing is performed via operations on the connected components, using editing commands patterned after the text editor EMACS[11].

Image EMACS supports two classes of editing operations.

The first class is based on viewing text as a linear sequence of characters, defined in terms of connected components. Traditional "cut and paste" functionality is enabled by a selection of insertion and deletion commands (e.g., delete-character, kill-line, yank region). As with text, editing is typically performed in the vicinity of a cursor, and operations to adjust cursor position are provided (e.g., forward-word, end-of-buffer). Characters can also be inserted by normal typing. This is accomplished by binding keyboard keys to character bitmaps from a stored font or, alternatively, to user-selected character images in a scanned document. Correlation-based matching of the character image bound to a given key against successive connected-component groupings allows for image-based character search.

The second class of operations supported by Image EMACS is based on viewing text as a two-dimensional arrangement of glyphs on an image plane[1]. These operations provide typographic functionality, such as horizontal and vertical character placement, interword spacing, vertical line spacing, indentation, centering and line justification. Placement of adjacent characters is accomplished using font metrics estimated for each character directly from the image[5]. These metrics allow for typographically acceptable character spacing, including character overlap where appropriate.

Taken together, Image EMACS commands are intended to convey the impression that the user is editing a text-based document. In actuality, the system is manipulating image components rather than character codes. Moreover, while the user is free to assign character labels to specific image components, editing, including both insertion and search, is accomplished *without* explicit knowledge of character identity. This approach enables interactive text-image editing and reproduction, independent of font or writing system.

Figures 1 and 2 show an example of a scanned multilingual document before and after editing with Image EMACS. The example demonstrates the results of image-based insertion, deletion, substitution and justification, as well as intermingling of text in several writing systems and languages (paragaphs 4 through 7).[2] Such capabilities are potentially achievable using a format-conversion paradigm; however, this would require more sophisticated OCR functionality than currently exists, as well as access to fonts and stylistic information used in rendering the original document.

3. AUDIO EDITING AND INDEXING

A second example of signal-based document processing is provided by a wordspotter developed to support editing and indexing of documents which originate and are intended to remain in audio form[12]. Examples include voice mail, dictated instructions and pre-recorded radio broadcasts or commentaries. The wordspotter can also be used to retrieve relevant portions of less structured audio, such as recorded lectures or telephone messages. In contrast with most previous wordspotting applications (e.g., [15, 10]), unconstrained keyword vocabularies are critical to such editing and indexing tasks.

[2]Syntax and semantics are not necessarily preserved in the example, thanks to the user's lack of familiarity with most of the languages involved.

The wordspotter is similar to Image Emacs in at least three ways: 1) it is based on partial modeling of signal content; 2) it requires user specification of keyword models; and 3) it makes no explicit use of linguistic knowledge during recognition, though users are free to assign interpretations to keywords. The wordspotter is also speaker or, more accurately, sound-source dependent. These constraints allow for vocabulary and language independence, as well as for the spotting of non-speech audio sounds.

The wordspotter is based on hidden Markov models (HMM's) and is trained in two stages[13]. The first is a *static* stage, in which a short segment of the user's speech (typically 1 minute or less) is used to create a background, or non-keyword, HMM. The second stage of training is *dynamic*, in that keyword models are created while the system is in use. Model specification requires only a single repetition of a keyword and, thus, to the system user, is indistinguishable from keyword spotting. Spotting is performed using a HMM network consisting of a parallel connection of the background model and the appropriate keyword model. A *forward-backward* search[13] is used to identify keyword start and end times, both of which are required to enable editing operations such as keyword insertion and deletion.

The audio editor is implemented on a Sun Microsystems Sparcstation and makes use of its standard audio hardware. A videotape demonstrating its use in several multilingual application scenarios is available from SIGGRAPH[14].

4. DOCUMENT IMAGE DECODING

Document image decoding (DID) is a framework for scanned document recognition which extends hidden Markov modeling concepts to two-dimensional image data[4]. In analogy with the HMM approach to speech recognition, the decoding framework assumes a communication theory model based on three elements: an image generator, a noisy channel and an image decoder. The image generator consists of a message source, which generates a symbol string containing the information to be communicated, and an imager, which formats or encodes the message into an ideal bitmap. The channel transforms this ideal image into a noisy observed image by introducing distortions associated with printing and scanning. The decoder estimates the message from the observed image using *maximum a posteriori* decoding and a Viterbi-like decoding algorithm[6].

A key objective being pursued within the DID framework is the automatic generation of optimized decoders from explicit models of message source, imager and channel[3]. The goal is to enable application-oriented users to specify such models without sophisticated knowledge of image analysis and recognition techniques. It is intended that both the format and type of information returned by the document decoder be under the user's control. The basic approach is to support declarative specification of a priori document infomation (e.g., page layout, font metrics) and task constraints via formal stochastic grammars.

Figures 3 through 5 illustrate the application of DID to the extraction of subject headings, listing types, business names and telephone numbers from scanned yellow pages[7]. A slightly reduced version of a sample scanned yellow page column is shown in Figure 3 and a finite-state top-level source model in Figure 4. The yellow page column includes a subject heading and examples of several different listing types. These, in turn, are associated with branches of the source model. The full model contains more than 6000 branches and 1600 nodes. Figure 5 shows the result of using a decoder generated from the model to extract the desired information from the yellow page column. Automatically generated decoders have also been used to recgnize a variety of other document types, including dictionary entries, musical notation and baseball box scores.

5. SUMMARY

The speech and text-image recognition initiatives discussed in the preceding sections illustrate two research themes at Xerox PARC which expand and redefine the role of recognition technology in document-oriented applications. These include the development of editors which operate directly on audio and scanned image data, and the use of speech and text-image recognition to retrieve arbitrary information from documents with signal content. Key concepts embodied in these research efforts include partial document models, task-oriented document recognition, user specification and intepretation of recognition models, and automatic generation of recognizers from declarative models. These concepts enable the realization of a broad range of signal-based document processing operations, including font, vocabulary and language-independent editing and retrieval .

References

1. Bagley, S. and Kopec, G. "Editing images of text". Technical Report P92-000150, Xerox PARC, Palo Alto, CA, November, 1992.
2. Horn, B. *Robot Vision*, The MIT Press, Cambridge, MA, 1986.
3. Kopec, G. and Chou, P. "Automatic generation of custom document image decoders". Submitted to ICDAR'93: Second IAPR Conference on Document Analysis and Recognition, Tsukuba Science City, Japan, October, 1993.
4. Kopec, G. and Chou, P. "Document image decoding using Markov sources". To be presented at ICASSP-93, Minneapolis, MN, April 1993.
5. Kopec, G. "Least-squares font metric estimation from images, EDL Report EDL-92-008, Xerox PARC, Palo Alto, CA, July, 1992.
6. Kopec, G. "Row-major scheduling of image decoders". Submitted to *IEEE Trans. on Image Processing*, February, 1992.
7. Pacific Bell *Smart Yellow Pages, Palo Alto, Redwood City and Menlo Park*, 1992.
8. Price P., "Evaluation of Spoken Language Systems: The ATIS Domain," *Proc. Third DARPA Speech and Language Workshop*, P. Price (ed.), Morgan Kaufmann, June 1990.
9. Price, P., Fisher, W., Bernstein, J. and Pallett, D. "The DARPA 1000-Word Resource Management Database for Continous Speech Recognition". *Proceedings of ICASSP-88*, 1988, pp 651-654.
10. Rohlicek, R., Russel, W., Roukos, S. and Gish, H. "Continuous hidden Markov modeling for speaker-independent word spotting". *Proceedings ICASSP-89*, 1989, 627-630.
11. Stallman, R. *GNU Emacs Manual*, Free Software Foundation, Cambridge, MA, 1986.
12. Wilcox, L. and Bush, M. "HMM-based wordspotting for voice editing and audio indexing". *Proceedings of Eurospeech-91*, Genova, Italy, 1991, pp 25-28.
13. Wilcox, L. and Bush, M. "Training and search algorithms for an interactive wordspotting system". *Proceedings of ICASSP-92*, 1992, pp II-97 - II-100.
14. Wilcox, L., Smith, I. and Bush, M. "Wordspotting for voice editing and indexing". *Proceedings of CHI '92*, 1992, pp 655-656. Video on SIGGRAPH Video Review 76-77.
15. Wilpon, J., Miller, L., and Modi, P. "Improvements and applications for key word recognition using hidden Markov modeling techniques". *Proceedings of ICASSP-91*, 1991, pp 309-312.

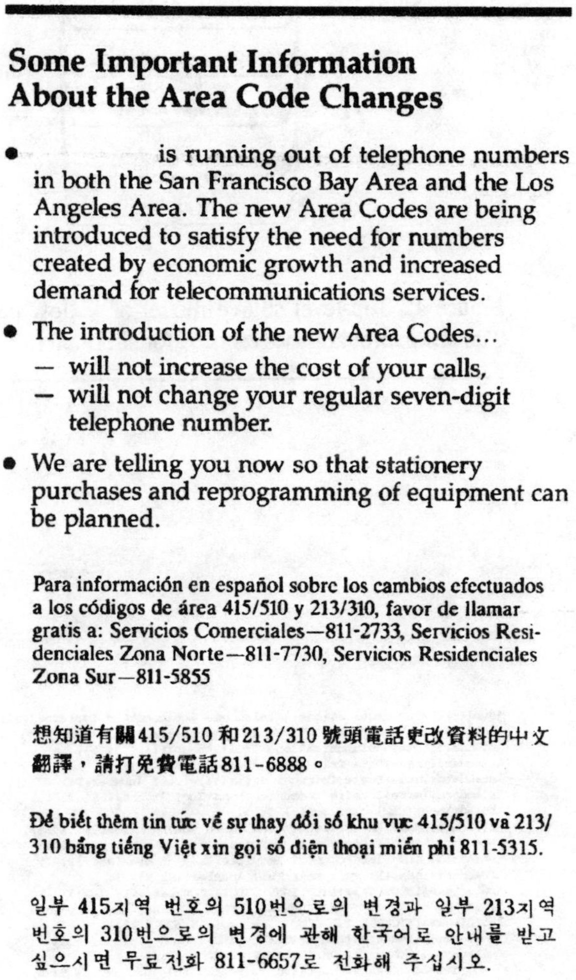

Some Important Information About the Area Code Changes

- is running out of telephone numbers in both the San Francisco Bay Area and the Los Angeles Area. The new Area Codes are being introduced to satisfy the need for numbers created by economic growth and increased demand for telecommunications services.
- The introduction of the new Area Codes...
  - will not increase the cost of your calls,
  - will not change your regular seven-digit telephone number.
- We are telling you now so that stationery purchases and reprogramming of equipment can be planned.

Para información en español sobrc los cambios cfectuados a los códigos de área 415/510 y 213/310, favor de llamar gratis a: Servicios Comerciales—811-2733, Servicios Residenciales Zona Norte—811-7730, Servicios Residenciales Zona Sur—811-5855

想知道有關415/510 和213/310 號頭電話更改資料的中文翻譯，請打免費電話811-6888。

Để biết thêm tin tức về sự thay đổi số khu vực 415/510 và 213/310 bằng tiếng Việt xin gọi số điện thoại miễn phí 811-5315.

일부 415지역 번호의 510번으로의 변경과 일부 213지역 번호의 310번으로의 변경에 관해 한국어로 안내를 받고 싶으시면 무료전화 811-6657로 전화해 주십시오.

Figure 1: Original scanned document image.

Some Important Information About the Area Code Changes

- is running out of telephone profits in both the San Francisco Bay Area and the Los Angeles Area. So, we require all telephones in these areas to be replaced to offset the decline in our economic growth and the decreased demand for our telecommunications services.
- Also, you can anticipate that we...
  - will increase the cost of your calls,
  - will change your regular seven-digit telephone number.
- We are telling you now so that new telephone purchases and replacement of equipment can be planned.

Para información en 想知道有關415 los cambios efectuados a los códigos de área 415/510 y 213/310, favor de llama testbed gratis a: Servicios Comerciales—811-2733, Servicios Residenciales Zona Norte—811-7730, Servicios Residenciales Zona Sur—811-5855

想知道有關415/510 和213/310 號頭電 tức về sự thay 號頭翻譯，請打免費電話811-6888。

Để biết thêm tin tức về sự thay đổi số khu vực 415/510 và 213/310 bằng tiếng Việt xin 일부지역번호 miễn phí 811-5315.

일부 415지역 번호의 510번으로의 변경과 일부 213지역 번호의 310번으로의 변경에 관해 한국어로 안내를 받고 싶으시면 무료선화 811-6657로 선화해 주십시오.

Figure 2: Scanned document image after Image EMACS editing.

Telecommunications-
Telephone Equipment
& Systems-Service &
Repair

APEX COMMUNICATIONS INC
254 San Geronimo
Sunnyvale 408 773 9600
Communications 2001
Voice Mail System
433 Airport Bl Burl 347 1500
Data-Tel SMto 349 6010
Davis Communication Services
683 Crane Av FosterCty 341 0214
G'raffe Communications Inc 594 9196
HBC
24 HOUR
PHONE SERVICE
REPAIR
SALES & SERVICE
JACK INST. - REWIRE
SERVICE CALLS
3628 El Camino Rl PA 493 3663
Integrated Technologies Inc 345 4484
Interconnect Services-Inc 591 3120
Interconnect Services Inc 851 9224
Mr Telephone Man 692 4128
Please See Advertisement This Page

MODERN APPLICATIONS GROUP
Telecommunications Professionals
"Quality Value Service"
.... 961 8181
NEC BUSINESS COMMUNICATION
SYSTEMS
6960 Koll Center Pkwy
Pleasanton 510 484 2010
NICKELL TEL COMM
4046 Mira Loma Wy
SanJose 408 629 1011
NORTHERN TELECOM INC
Worldwide Leader in
Telecommunications
Technology
northern telecom
• Meridian 1 and Norstar
• Business Telephone Systems
• Integrated Voice and Data Networks
• Private Communications Networks
• Telephone Industry Sales
"FOR INFORMATION CALL"
Northern Telecom Inc
685 E Middlefield Rd MtView . 969 9170
PacTel Meridian Systems
333 Lakeside Dr FosterCity ... 358 3300
PacTel Meridian Systems
2305 Mission College Bl
SantaClara 408 988 5550
Or
No Charge To Calling
Party 800 667 8437

PANASONIC AUTHORIZED
SERVICENTERS-PARTS
DISTRIBUTORS—
PARTS & SERVICE
INFORMATION SERVICES Peoriall
No Charge To Calling
Party 800 545 2672
FACTORY SERVICE CENTERS
MATSUSHITA SERVICES COMPANY
800 Dubuque Av SSF 871 6373

PRECISION PHONE 728 3823
Please See Advertisement This Page

PRECISION PHONE
BUSINESS SYSTEMS
COMPLETE SYSTEMS
PLUS
- REASONABLE REPAIRS -
- ADDITIONS OR MOVES
OF EXISTING SYSTEMS -
NEW OR REBUILT
ITT • TIE • COMDIAL
ALL BELL PRODUCTS
TOSHIBA & OTHERS
728-3623
CALL FOR FREE ESTIMATES

Figure 3: Scanned yellow page column, slightly reduced.

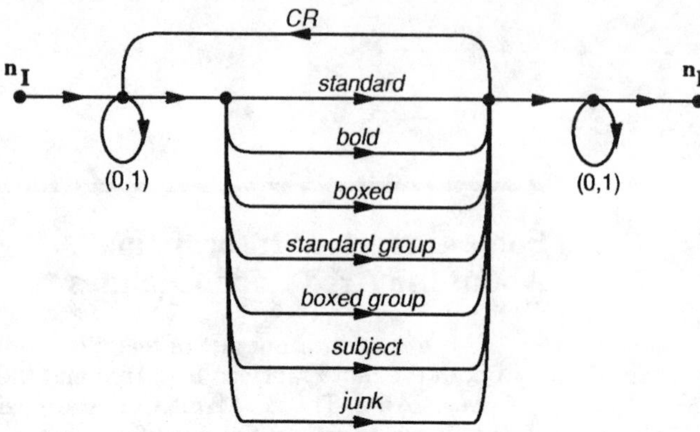

Figure 4: Top-level source model of yellow page column. Transition probabilities omitted for simplicity.

```
\subject{Telecommunications-\\Telepbone Equipment\\& Systems-Service &\\Repair}
\bold{\name{APEX COMMUNICATIONS INC} \number{408 773 9600}}
\standard{\name{Coinmuhications ZOOI} \number{347 1500}}
\standard{\name{Data-Tel 'SMto} \number{349 6010}}
\standard{\name{Davis Coinmuhication Services} \number{341 0214}}
\standard{\name{G'raffe Communicatlons Inc} \number{594 9196}}
\boxed{\name{HBC} \number{493 3663}}
\standard{\name{Integrated Tecnnologies Inc} \number{345 4484}}
\standard{\name{Interconnect Services-Inc} \number{591 3120}}
\standard{\name{Interconnect Services Inc} \number{851 9224}}
\standard{\name{Mr Telephone Man} \number{692 4128}}
\bold{\name{MOOERN APPLICATIONS GROUP} \number{961 8181}}
\bold{\name{NEC BUSINESS COMMUNICATION\\SYSTEMS} \number{510 484 2010}}
\bold{\name{NICKELL TEL COMM} \number{408 629 1011}}
\boxedgroup{\name{NORTHERN TELECOM INC}
   \subgroup{\name{''FOR INFORMATION CALL''}
      \standard{\name{Northern Telecorn Inc} \number{969 9170}}
      \standard{\name{PacTel Meridian Systems} \number{358 3300}}
      \standard{\name{PacTel Meridian Systems} \number{408 988 5550}}
      \standard{\name{' Qr} \number{0 667 8437}}}}
\standardgroup{\name{PANASONIC AUTHORIZED\\SERVICENTERS-PARTS\\DISTRIBUTDRS}
   \subgroup{\name{PARTS & SERVICE}
      \stdgrpmem{\name{INFQRMATION SERVICES 'P-J--JH} \number{545 2672}}}
   \subgroup{\name{FACTORY SERVICE CENTERS}
      \stdgrpmem{\name{MATSUSHITA SERVICES COMPANY} \number{871 6373}}}}
\bold{\name{PRECISION PHONE} \number{728 3623}}
\boxed{\name{NNNNNNNNNNNNNNNNNNNNNMNNNNNNNNNNI} \number{8888881}}
```

Figure 5: Decoder output for yellow-page column in fig 3.

SITE REPORTS

MACHINE LEARNING TECHNIQUES FOR DOCUMENT FILTERING

Richard M. Tong, Lee A. Appelbaum

Advanced Decision Systems
(a division of Booz•Allen & Hamilton, Inc.)
1500 Plymouth Street, Mountain View, CA 94043

PROJECT GOALS

Booz•Allen & Hamilton's Advanced Decision Systems Division is conducting a program of research to investigate machine learning techniques that can automatically construct probabilistic structures from a training set of documents with respect to a single target filtering concept, or a set of related concepts. These structures can then be applied to individual documents to derive a posterior probability that the document is about a particular target concept.

Our primary goal is to investigate the use of the CART (Classification and Regression Trees) algorithm as the basis of a totally automatic approach to generating document classification structures, working only with information need statements and training data supplied by users. That is, we are interested in testing the hypothesis that effective descriptions of what constitutes a "relevant document" can be constructed using just document exemplars and broad statements about document features. Such a scenario is common in organizations that monitor large volumes of real-time electronic documents.

RECENT RESULTS

Our most recent results are those from the first ARPA sponsored TREC (Text Retrieval Conference) held in November 1992.

The TREC corpus represents a significant challenge for our approach. Our previous results with a small corpus, while encouraging, did not allow us to evaluate how well the technique might do with realistically sized document collections. Our conclusion based on the results we have from TREC is that CART does exhibit some interesting behaviors on a realistic corpus, and that, despite the small size of the training sets and the restricted choice of features, for some topics it produces competitive results. So although the overall performance is moderate (relative to the better performing systems at TREC), we believe that the absolute performance (given that the system is totally automatic) is at least encouraging and definitely acceptable in several instances.

Some specific observations on the performance of the current implementation of the CART algorithm as used for TREC are:

- Relying on the re-substitution estimates for the terminal nodes is a very weak method for producing an output ranking. A scheme that makes use of surrogate split information to generate a *post hoc* ranking shows much promise as a technique for improving our scores in the TREC context.
- While our approach is totally automatic, we restricted ourselves to using as features only those words that appear in the information need statement. This is obviously a severe limitation since the use of even simple query expansion techniques (e.g., stemming and/or a synonym dictionary) is likely to provide a richer and more effective set of initial features.
- Using words as features is possibly too "low-level" to ever allow stable, robust classification trees to be produced. At a minimum, we probably need to consider working with concepts rather than individual words. Not only would this reduce the size of the feature space but would probably result in more intuitive trees.
- We need to work with much bigger and more representative training sets. Our preliminary experiment in this area shows, not surprisingly, that adding more training examples can lead to dramatic changes in the classification trees.

PLANS FOR THE COMING YEAR

The main activity planned for the coming year is to participate in TREC 2. We intend to perform a series of additional experiments designed to explore some obvious extensions suggested by the TREC 1 results. That is we will perform experiments to determine: (1) the effect of training set size on the overall performance of the learning algorithm, (2) the effectiveness of using surrogate splits information to help perform a *post hoc* ranking of the documents classified as relevant, (3) the effectiveness of knowledge-based query expansion techniques, and (4) the value of using concepts, detected using our RUBRIC text retrieval technology, as document features.

To facilitate the experimental procedure we plan to integrate the CART technology into Booz•Allen & Hamilton's distributed information integration system (MINERVA). The primary feature of MINERVA is a distributed operating environment, which is an implementation of an intelligent Ethernet token ring that uses TCP/IP and standard UNIX socket protocols. This provides a unique transport layer that allows multiple databases and information access services to communicate transparently using a common metalanguage.

Gisting Continuous Speech

J. R. Rohlicek, Principal Investigator

BBN Systems and Technologies
70 Fawcett St.
Cambridge, MA 02138

PROJECT GOALS

The objective of this work is automatic, real-time "gisting" of voice traffic for updating of information in databases, for producing timely reports, and for prompt notification of events of interest. Specifically, the goal is to build a prototype, real-time system capable of processing radio communication between air traffic controllers and pilots, identifying dialogs and extracting their "gist" (e.g., identifying flights, determining whether they are landing or taking off), and producing a continuous output stream with that information. The approach is intended to be general and applicable to other domains.

The system is built upon state-of-the-art techniques in speech recognition, speaker identification, natural language analysis, and topic statistical classification. These techniques have been extended where necessary to address specific aspects of the gisting problem. Because various sources of information must be combined, the system design features a high degree of interaction between the natural language and domain-knowledge components and the speech processing components.

RECENT RESULTS

We have made additions and modifications to our prototype system [1]. The primary goal of the effort was to achieve real-time performance. This involved both system architectural and algorithmic modifications described fully in [2].

A prototype system has been evaluated using approximately 14 hours of data recorded at Logan airport. Performance was measured on approximately four hours of data held out for final evaluation. On that data, the system achieved approximately 88% recall and 82% precision for detection of controller-pilot dialogs. Also, of the flights correctly detected, the fight identification was correctly extracted 59% of the time.

A real-time prototype system has been constructed. The system builds on a flexible software system developed as part of this effort. The system allows multiple processes to be coordinated across multiple hosts and provides facilities for efficient stream connections between modules as well as flexible message-based communication between modules.

PLANS FOR THE COMING YEAR

The remainder of the effort will focus on completion of the prototype system and on system testing. System testing includes investigation of the sensitivity of overall system performance to the performance of various component.

REFERENCES

[1] J. R. Rohlicek, *et al*, "Gisting conversational speech," Proceedings of the International Conference on Acoustics, Speech and Signal Processing, Mar 1992, pp. II-113.

[2] L. Denenberg, et. al., "Gisting conversational speech in real time," to appear in Proceedings of the International Conference on Acoustics, Speech and Signal Processing, April 1993.

ROBUST CONTINUOUS SPEECH RECOGNITION

PIs: John Makhoul and Richard Schwartz
makhoul@bbn.com, schwartz@bbn.com

BBN Systems and Technologies
70 Fawcett Street
Cambridge, MA 02138

PROJECT GOALS

The primary objective of this basic research program is to develop robust methods and models for speaker-independent acoustic recognition of spontaneously-produced, continuous speech. The work has focussed on developing accurate and detailed models of phonemes and their coarticulation for the purpose of large-vocabulary continuous speech recognition. Important goals of this work are to achieve the highest possible word recognition accuracy in continuous speech and to develop methods for the rapid adaptation of phonetic models to the voice of a new speaker.

RECENT RESULTS

- Ported the BYBLOS system to the Wall Street Journal (WSJ) corpus. We found that the techniques that we had developed for recognition of the ATIS corpus worked quite well without modification on the WSJ corpus.

- Performed several key experiments on the WSJ corpus. We verified our conjecture that a speaker-independent system trained on a small number of speakers has about the same word error rate as a system trained on a large number of speakers, assuming the same total amount of training speech. This is the first time that this result has been performed in a well-controlled way for large vocabulary speech recognition. We also verified that training the system separately on each of the speakers and averaging the resulting models results in essentially the same performance as training on all of the data at once. These results have wide ranging implications for data collection and system design.

- We have shown that, for large vocabulary recognition, a speaker-independent system will have about the same error rate as a speaker-dependent system when the speaker-independent system is trained on about 15 times as much speech as the corresponding speaker-dependent system.

- We showed that a simple blind deconvolution method for microphone independence, in which the mean cepstrum is subtracted from each cepstrum vector, is somewhat better than the RASTA method.

- Developed a new algorithm for microphone independence which uses a codebook transformation, based on selection among several known microphones. The algorithm reduced the word error rate for unknown microphones by 20% over using blind deconvolution alone.

- In the Nov. 1992 speech recognition test on the ATIS domain, our BYBLOS system continued to give the best results of all sites tested, with a 30% reduction in word error over last year. In our first test on the WSJ corpus, our system had the second lowest error rates.

- Chaired the CSR Corpus Coordinating Committee.

PLANS FOR THE COMING YEAR

For the coming year, we plan to continue our work on improving speech recognition performance both on the Wall Street Journal corpus and on the spontaneous ATIS speech corpus. We plan to explore different parameterizations of the speech signal and new models for microphone and speaker adaptation.

ROBUSTNESS, PORTABILITY, AND SCALABILITY OF NATURAL LANGUAGE SYSTEMS

Ralph Weischedel

BBN Systems and Technologies
70 Fawcett Street
Cambridge, MA 02138

1. OBJECTIVE

In the DoD, every unit, from the smallest to the largest, communicates through messages. Messages are fundamental in command and control, intelligence analysis, and in planning and replanning. Our objective is to create algorithms that will

1) robustly process open source text, identifying relevant messages, and updating a data base based on the relevant messages;

2) reduce the effort required in porting natural language (NL) message processing software to a new domain from months to weeks; and

3) be scalable to broad domains with vocabularies of tens of thousands of words.

2. APPROACH

Our approach is to apply probabilistic language models and training over large corpora in all phases of natural language processing. This new approach will enable systems to adapt to both new task domains and linguistic expressions not seen before by semi-automatically acquiring 1) a domain model, 2) facts required for semantic processing, 3) grammar rules, 4) information about new words, 5) probability models on frequency of occurrence, and 6) rules for mapping from representation to application structure.

For instance, a statistical model of categories of words will enable systems to predict the most likely category of a word never encountered by the system before and to focus on its most likely interpretation in context, rather than skipping the word or considering all possible interpretations. Markov modelling techniques will be used for this problem.

In an analogous way, statistical models of language will be developed and applied at the level of syntax (form), at the level of semantics (content), and at the contextual level (meaning and impact).

3. RECENT RESULTS

• Consistently achieved high performance in Government-sponsored evaluations (e.g., MUC-3, MUC-4, etc.) of data extraction systems with significantly less human effort to port the PLUM system to each domain, compared with the effort reported in porting other high-performing systems.

• Sped up the PLUM data extraction system by a factor of three.

• Ported PLUM to a microelectronics domain with only seven person weeks of effort. (Typically, systems are ported to a new domain in half a person year or more.)

• Developed a probabilistic model of answer correctness which requires only a set of articles and correct output (the data that should be extracted for each article) as training. This can be used as a model of confidence or certainty on each data item extracted by the system from text.

• Successfully applied a statistical text classification algorithm in MUC-4. The algorithm is trained automatically from examples of relevant and irrelevant texts. The user can specify the degree of certainty desired.

• Distributed POST, our software for statistically labelling words in text, to several other DARPA contractors (New Mexico State University, New York University, Syracuse University, and the University of Chicago).

4. PLANS FOR THE COMING YEAR

Create a probabilistic model for predicting the most likely (partial) interpretation of an input, whether well-formed, novel, complex, or ill-formed.

Develop procedures for automatically learning template fill rules from examples.

Participate in MUC-5 evaluation in all domains.

USABLE, REAL-TIME, INTERACTIVE SPOKEN LANGUAGE SYSTEMS

John Makhoul and Madeleine Bates, Principal Investigators

BBN Systems and Technologies
70 Fawcett St.
Cambridge, MA 02138

PROJECT GOALS

The primary objective of this project is develop a robust, high-performance, domain-independent spoken language system. The system, termed HARC (Hear And Respond to Continuous speech), is composed of the BYBLOS speech recognition and the DELPHI natural language understanding system. The goal is to develop systems that exhibit the following advances: high-accuracy speech understanding with vocabulary of up to 10,000 words; a highly interactive user interface capable of mixed-initiative dialogue and other types of system feedback; transparent adaptability to new users; easy portability to new applications; a system implementable in real-time on cost-effective COTS (commercial, off-the-shelf) hardware.

RECENT RESULTS

- Developed the first complete real-time spoken language system on a workstation, without the use of additional hardware. The system integrated our real-time speech recognition and NL systems through the N-best interface. The real-time system was demonstrated in the ATIS domain at the DARPA 1992 and 1993 workshops on speech and natural language processing. The system was developed on a Silicon Graphics Indigo workstation and has been ported to other Unix-based workstations.
- Built a new semantic interpretation component that enables a cleaner separation between the domain-independent knowledge stored in a general grammar of English and the domain-dependent knowledge associated with particular lexical items, thus enhancing portability and domain-independence. The new component is based on the notion of translating from grammatical relations to semantic relations.
- Developed a hybrid approach to semantic representation that combines the expressive power of logic with the reasoning power of frames. This allows the system to detect contradictions (e.g., "flights to denver ... uhh to Boston") without being forced into the simple frame-slot approach that is inadequate for many types of natural language phenomena.
- Developed the Semantic Linker, a new fallback understanding component using probabilities that reduces the understanding error rate by 30%. The Semantic Linker makes extensive use of the hybrid representation and interpretation component above to take over when DELPHI's regular parser cannot understand an input utterance.
- Laid out an initial design and developed an initial representation for a new statistical model of understanding, the Hidden Undersatanding Model. The new model will enable us to carry out studies in the alignment of corpora to semantic interpretations, with the goal of automatically deriving semantic rules.
- Participated in the November 1992 speech, NL and SLS evaluations, and in the end-to-end log-file evaluation dry-run experiment.
- Chaired the organization of the March 1993 DARPA Human Language Technology workshop.

PLANS FOR THE COMING YEAR

Our plans for the coming year center on extending the work above in several areas. In particular, we plan to:

- Integrate the Semantic Linker and the parser, to increase the capabilities of both.
- Improve our discourse understanding component, making it more domain-independent.
- Develop ways of extending our grammar for different domains. This will allow us to keep our domain-independent knowledge base, but to tailor it for domain-specific syntactic constructions.
- Continue the development of the Hidden Understanding Model and test it by deriving the semantic rules for a real domain.
- Collect additional ATIS data for the general community, using our real-time system and the new, expanded database.

Evaluating the Use of Prosodic Information in Speech Recognition and Understanding

Mari Ostendorf *Patti Price*

Boston University SRI International
Boston, MA 02215 Menlo Park, CA 94025

PROJECT GOALS

The goal of this project is to investigate the use of different levels of prosodic information in speech recognition and understanding. There are two thrusts in the current work: use of prosodic information in parsing and detection/correction of disfluencies. The research involves determining a representation of prosodic information suitable for use in a speech understanding system, developing reliable algorithms for detection of the prosodic cues in speech, investigating architectures for integrating prosodic cues in a speech understanding system, and evaluating the potential performance improvements possible through the use of prosodic information in a spoken language system (SLS). This research is sponsored jointly by DARPA and NSF, NSF grant no. IRI-8905249, and in part by a DARPA SLS grant to SRI.

RECENT RESULTS

- Evaluated the break index and prominence recognition algorithms on a larger corpus, with paragraphs (as opposed to sentences) of radio announcer speech.
- Extended the prosody-parse scoring algorithm to use a more integrated probabilistic scoring criterion and to include prominence information, making use of tree-based recognition and prediction models.
- Collaborated with a multi-site group for development of a core, standard prosody transcription method: TOBI, (TOnes and Break Indices), and labeled over 800 utterances from the ATIS corpus with prosodic break and prominence information. Analyses of consistency between labelers shows good agreement for the break and prominence labels on ATIS.
- Ported prosody-parse scoring algorithms to ATIS, which required: developing new features for the acoustic and prosody/syntax models and representing new classes of breaks to represent hesitation; currently evaluating the algorithm for reranking the N-best sentence hypotheses in the MIT and SRI SLS systems. (This work was made possible by researchers at MIT and SRI who provided the parses and recognition outputs needed for training and evaluating the prosody models.)
- Developed a new approach to duration modeling in speech recognition, involving context-conditioned parametric duration distributions and increased weighting on duration.
- Developed tools for analysis of large number of repairs and other disfluencies; analyzed the prosody of filled pauses in ATIS data and extended the work on disfluencies to data in the Switchboard corpus of conversational speech.
- Developed methods for automatic detection and correction of repairs in ATIS corpus, based on integrating information from text pattern-matching, syntactic and semantic parsing.

PLANS FOR THE COMING YEAR

- Evaluate the break index and prominence recognition algorithms on spontaneous speech, specifically the ATIS corpus, and further refine algorithms to improve performance in this domain.
- Improve the parse scoring algorithm performance in the ATIS domain by exploring new syntactic features, and asses performance on SRI vs. MIT SLS systems.
- Investigate alternative approaches to integrating prosody in speech understanding.
- Continue study of acoustic and grammatical cues to repairs and other spontaneous speech effects.
- Based on the results of the acoustic analyses, develop automatic detection algorithms for flagging repairs that are missed by the syntactic pattern matching algorithms and develop algorithms for classifying detected repairs to aid in determining the amount of traceback in the repair.

Segment-Based Acoustic Models for Continuous Speech Recognition

Mari Ostendorf *J. Robin Rohlicek*

Boston University
Boston, MA 02215

BBN Inc.
Cambridge, MA 02138

PROJECT GOALS

The goal of this project is to develop improved acoustic models for speaker-independent recognition of continuous speech, together with efficient search algorithms appropriate for use with these models. The current work on acoustic modeling is focussed on stochastic, segment-based models that capture the time correlation of a sequence of observations (feature vectors) that correspond to a phoneme, hierarchical stochastic models that capture higher level intra-utterance correlation, and multi-pass search algorithms for implementing these more complex models. This research has been jointly sponsored by DARPA and NSF under NSF grant IRI-8902124 and by DARPA and ONR under ONR grant N00014-92-J-1778.

RECENT RESULTS

- Implemented different auditory-based signal processing algorithms and evaluated their use in recognition on the TIMIT corpus, finding no performance gains relative to cepstral parameters probably due to the non-Gaussian nature of auditory features.
- Improved the score combination technique for N-Best rescoring, through normalizing scores by sentence length to obtain more robust weights that alleviate problems associated with test set mismatch.
- Further investigated agglomerative and divisive clustering methods for estimating robust context-dependent models, and introduced a new clustering criterion based on a likelihood ratio test; obtained a slight improvement in performance with an associated reduction in storage costs of a factor of two.
- Extended the classification and segmentation scoring formalism to handle context-dependent models without requiring the assumption of independence of features between phone segments (using maximum entropy methods); evaluated different segmentation scores with results suggesting more work is needed in this area.
- Evaluated a new distribution mapping, which led to an 8% reduction in error on the development test set but no improvement on other test sets.
- Investigated the use of different phone sets and probabilistic multiple-pronunciation networks; no improvements were obtained on the RM corpus, though there may be gains in another domain.
- Extended the two level segment/microsegment formalism to application in word recognition using context-dependent models; evaluated the trade-offs associated with modeling trajectories vs. (non-tied) microsegment mixtures, finding that mixtures are more useful for context-independent modeling but representation of a trajectory is more useful for context-dependent modeling.
- Investigated the use of tied mixtures at the frame level (as opposed to the microsegment level), evaluating different covariance assumptions and training conditions; developed new, faster mixture training algorithms; and achieved a 20% reduction in word error over our previous best results on the Resource Management task. Current SSM performance rates are 3.6% word error on the Oct89 test set and 7.3% word error on the Sep92 test set.

PLANS FOR THE COMING YEAR

- Continue work in the classification and segmentation scoring paradigm; demonstrate improvements associated with novel models and/or features.
- Port the BU recognition system to the Wall Street Journal (WSJ) task, 5000 word vocabulary.
- Develop a stochastic formalism for modeling intra-utterance dependencies assuming a hierarchical structure.
- Investigate unsupervised adaptation in the WSJ task domain.
- Investigate multi-pass search algorithms that use a lattice rather than N-Best representation of recognition hypotheses.

SPOKEN-LANGUAGE RESEARCH AT CARNEGIE MELLON

Raj Reddy, Principal Investigator

School of Computer Science
Carnegie Mellon University
Pittsburgh, Pennsylvania 15213

PROJECT GOALS

The goal of speech research at Carnegie Mellon continues to be the development of spoken language systems that effectively integrate speech processing into the human-computer interface in a way that facilitates the use of computers in the performance of practical tasks. Research in spoken language is currently focussed in the following areas:

- **Improved speech recognition technologies:** Extending the useful vocabulary of SPHINX-II by use of better phonetic and linguistic models and better search techniques, providing for rapid configuration for new tasks.
- **Fluent human/machine interfaces:** Developing tools that allow users to easily communicate with computers by voice and understanding the role of voice in the computer interface.
- **Understanding spontaneous spoken language:** Developing flexible recognition and parsing strategies to cope with phenomena peculiar to the lexical and grammatical structure of spontaneous spoken language. Investigate methods of integrating speech recognition and natural language understanding. Development of automatic training procedures for these grammars.
- **Acoustical and environmental robustness:** Developing procedures to enable good recognition in office environments with desktop microphones and a useful level of recognition in more severe environments.
- **Rapid integration of speech technology:** Developing an approach that will enable application developers and end users to incorporate speech recognition into their applications quickly and easily, as well as the dynamic modification of grammars and vocabularies.

RECENT RESULTS

- SPHINX-II has been extended with a multi-pass search algorithm that incorporates two passes of beam search and a final A-star pass that can apply long-distance language models as well as produce alternative hypotheses.
- Joint training of acoustic models and language models is currently being explored in the context of the Unified Stochastic Engine (USE).
- A framework for long-distance language modeling was developed, in collaboration with IBM researchers. A pilot system using this model yielded significant reduction in perplexity over the trigram model.
- Developed improved recognition, grammar coverage and context handling that reduced SLS errors for the ATIS Benchmark by 67%. We also improved the robustness and user feedback in our live ATIS demo.
- Developed and evaluated two methods for more tightly integrating speech recognition and natural language understanding, producing error reductions of 20% compared to the loosely-coupled system.
- Added automatic detection capability for out-of-vocabulary words and phrases. New words are now entered instantly into the phone dialer application given only their spelling.
- Acoustical pre-processing algorithms for environmental robustness were extended to the CSR domain and made more efficient.

PLANS FOR THE COMING YEAR

- Use our existing language modeling framework to model long-distance dependence on words and word combinations. These new models will be allow the recognizer to take advantage of improved linguistic knowledge at the earliest possible stage.
- Implement confidence measures for large-vocabulary SLS systems, for new-word detection and greater accuracy.
- Continue to explore issues associated with very large vocabulary (100,000-word) recognition systems.
- Continue to develop methods for automatically acquisition of Natural Language information used by an SLS system.
- Improve user interaction in the ATIS system, including clarification and mixed initiative dialogs, speech output and form-based displays.
- Begin to develop a new SLS application, such as a telephone-based form filling application.
- Provide grammar switching and instantaneous new word addition for the general SPHINX-II decoder.
- Develop and test a 100,000-word pronunciation lexicon that will be available in the public domain.
- Continue to improve our cepstrum-based environmental compensation procedures.
- Demonstrate more robust microphone-array techniques.
- Extend our work on environmental robustness to long-distance telephone lines.
- Continue to enhance our spoken language interfaces, by introducing speech response capabilities and facilities for user customizing. Continue to investigate the appropriate use of speech in multi-modal interfaces.

Extracting Constraints on Word Usage from Large Text Corpora

Kathleen McKeown and Rebecca Passonneau

Department of Computer Science
450 Computer Science Building
Columbia University

PROJECT GOALS

Our research focuses on the identification of word usage constraints from large text corpora. Such constraints are useful both for the problem of selecting vocabulary for language generation and for disambiguating lexical meaning in interpretation. We are developing systems that can automatically extract such constraints from corpora and empirical methods for analyzing text. Identified constraints will be represented in a lexicon that will be tested computationally as part of a natural language system. We are also identifying lexical constraints for machine translation using the aligned Hansard corpus as training data and are identifying many-to-many word alignments.

One primary class of constraints we are examining is lexical; that is, constraints on word usage arriving from collocations (word pairs or phrases that commonly appear together). We are also looking at constraints deriving from domain scales which influence use of scalar adjectives and determiners, constraints on temporal markers and tense, constraints on reference over text, and constraints on cue words and phrases that may be used to convey explicit information about discourse structure.

RECENT RESULTS

- Packaged Xtract, a collocation extraction system, with windows interface for use by other sites and have licensed to several sites.
- Implemented a prototype system to compile candidate translations for English collocations by identifying collocations in the source language using Xtract, and incrementally building the target collocation from highly correlated words in the target corpus. The system has been evaluated on a small number of collocations, yielding 80% accuracy.
- Implemented a system for retrieving semantically related adjectives from a parsed text corpus, using a similarity metric and clustering techniques. Evaluation and comparison with human judges shows that system performance is comparable to human performance.
- Experimented with a genetic programming algorithm to identify statistically significant links between cue words and other words or part of speech in a large text corpus. Early results are promising, predicting, for example, that sentence initial cue words are used in their discourse sense.
- Implemented semantic and syntactic constraints on historical information in statistical reports as revision rules in a report generation system.
- Developed 3 simple algorithms for identifying segment boundaries using features of the text, and evaluated their success at identifying the segment boundaries that humans identify. The algorithms each use different linguistic information: speech pauses, cue words, and referring expressions.
- Developed method for extracting tense sequences across adjacent sentences from corpora and evaluated behavior of semantically under-constrained past and past perfect tenses in the Brown corpus. Developed a semantic representation for past and for perfect, and an algorithm for understanding tense in discourse.

PLANS FOR THE COMING YEAR

In the area of machine translation, we are improving the implementation to prepare for large scale experimentation, including indexing the corpus to speed up testing and automating subcomponents. We will begin large scale testing within the month, beginning with 1 month's worth of data (about 100 collocations) and moving to 1 year's worth of data or 1000 collocations. We will continue to improve the accuracy of our method for retrieving scalar adjectives; we are investigating the use of other sources of linguistic data such as conjunction and negation. We will add tests that exploit gradability in order to identify scalar and non-scalar groups. We will refine methods for extracting tense sequences from corpora that fit certain criteria by adding new tenses, or adverbs, or aspectual type to the criteria and will identify additional constraints on tense understanding. We will further refine our algorithms for identifying discourse structure. We are developing a generation system to test constraints on historical information and a bidirectional semantic engine to test constraints on tense, aspect, and discourse cues.

The SMART Information Retrieval Project

C. Buckley, G. Salton, J. Allan

Department of Computer Science
Cornell University
Ithaca, NY 14853

PROJECT GOALS

The primary goal of the SMART information retrieval project at Cornell University remains, as it has for the past 30 years, investigating the effectiveness and efficiency of automatic methods of retrieval of text. In recent years this has expanded to include retrieval of parts of documents in response to both user queries (passage retrieval) and parts of other documents (automatic hypertext links). The emphasis of SMART has always been on purely automatic text retrieval — starting from an arbitrary piece of natural language text from the user and matching against automatically indexed documents — and this continues.

RECENT RESULTS

Under this rather broad goal, we've performed a number of investigations this past year. These include:

- Local/global matching: Looking at the effect of determining an overall global similarity between query and document, and then requiring that some small local portion of the document (paragraph or sentence) focuses in on the query. The overall performance level of local/global matching for the TREC 1 workshop was quite good, though it appears the local requirement only gains about 10% improvement over a pure global match.
- Phrases: Examining methods for both statistical phrase selection and phrase weighting. For TREC 1, SMART's statistical phrases gained 5 to 9% over our single term methods.
- Learned Features of Terms: In cooperation with Norbert Fuhr, we've been looking at learning good term weights based upon characteristics of a term rather than history of how that term itself behaves. This enables us to come up with good term weights based upon much less information than conventional weight learning techniques. This did very well for TREC 1: tied at the top of the automatic ad-hoc category with the local/global approach above.
- Efficiency and Effectiveness Trade-offs: A number of tradeoffs were also examined at TREC 1. Major conclusions were
  - Retrieval effectiveness can be very reasonably traded for retrieval efficiency by truncating the retrieval appropriately.
  - Massive stemming of words to their root forms has efficiency benefits and costs, but offers no significant effectiveness gains.
  - Document indexing can be sped up significantly, at a large cost in disk space.
- Evaluation: Examining evaluation measures suitable for TREC. We supplied the TREC 1 evaluation routines, and have designed several other measures that may be used for TREC 2.
- Automatic Hypertext: Local/global matching was used to automatically construct hypertext links between articles of a 29 volume encyclopedia.
- Passage Retrieval: Local/global matching was used again to retrieve appropriate scopes of encyclopedia articles in response to a query.
- SMART System: A new publicly-available release of SMART (for research purposes only) was finished in June. This release provides support for multi-gigabyte databases.

PLANS FOR THE COMING YEAR

We'll be continuing with most of the investigations above in the coming year. We'll use automatic learning techniques to help combine local and global similarities, and to help weight phrases. Local/global matching will be used heavily in the TREC routing environment to regain precision after query expansion techniques. Passage retrieval and automatic document linkage will be extended to automatically form a coherent summary reading pattern for a topic. The SMART system itself will be revamped to enable very large distributed databases to be searched effectively and efficiently.

LINGSTAT: AN INTERACTIVE, MACHINE-AIDED TRANSLATION SYSTEM*

Jonathan Yamron and James Baker

Dragon Systems, Inc., 320 Nevada Street, Newton, MA 02160

PROJECT GOALS

The goal of LINGSTAT is to produce an interactive machine translation system designed to increase the productivity of a user, with little knowledge of the source language, in translating or extracting information from foreign language documents. This system will make use of statistical information gathered from parallel and single-language corpora, and linguistic information at all levels (lexical, syntactic, and semantic). Initial efforts have been focused on the translation of Japanese to English, but work has also begun on a Spanish version of the system. As resources become available, particularly parallel corpora, the Spanish system will be further developed and work will be extended to include other European languages.

RECENT RESULTS

Productivity tests have been conducted on the rudimentary Spanish version of the workstation. This system incorporates a Spanish de-inflector, provides word for word translation to English, and has fast access to an online dictionary. On a scaled down version of the DARPA test of 7/92 (6 documents instead of 18, including 3 by hand and 3 with the aid of the system), a fluent speaker of Italian (a language very similar to Spanish) showed no productivity gain. At the other extreme, a user with no Spanish knowledge and no recent training in any European language was about 50% faster using the system's online tools than with a paper dictionary.

There are currently two programs underway to improve the translation system. The first is an effort to expand the Japanese and Spanish dictionaries, which requires not only adding words, but also glosses, pronunciations (for Japanese), and multi-word objects. Part of this task involves updating the Japanese and Spanish word frequency statistics, which will improve the performance of the tokenizer in Japanese and the de-inflector in both languages. Part of speech information is also being added, in anticipation of the use of grammatical tools.

*This work was sponsored by the Defense Advanced Research Projects Agency under contract number J-FBI-91-239

The second program is the development of a probabilistic grammar to parse the source and provide grammatical information to the user. This will supplement or replace the current rule-based finite-state parser currently implemented in the system. In the current phase, Dragon has chosen a lexicalized context-free grammar, which has the property that the probability of choosing a particular production rule in the grammar is dependent on headwords associated with each non-terminal symbol. Lexicalization is a useful tool for resolving attachment questions and in sense disambiguation. This grammar will be trained using the inside-outside algorithm on Japanese and Spanish newspaper articles.

PLANS FOR THE COMING YEAR

The grammar will be used to provide more accurate glossing of the source by making use of co-occurrence statistics among the phrase headwords. This requires developing an English word list with frequency and part of speech information, as well as constructing an English inflector-deinflector. These tools, along with an English grammar, will enable us to construct candidate translations of Japanese phrases and simple Spanish sentences.

For Japanese sentences and more sophisticated Spanish, Dragon plans to implement lexicalized tree-adjoining grammars in both source and target. Tree-adjoining grammars provide a rich framework for handling the difficult rearrangement of Japanese syntax into English. As in the case of context-free grammar, lexicalization helps keep the grammar small by resolving attachment and disambiguation questions. A translation can be constructed by transferring a parse in the source grammar into a parse in the (synchronized) target grammar.

Each of the analysis methods may produce several candidate translations of phrases or sentences in the target language. All of these candidates will then be rescored using a statistical language model in the target language, as well as translation and alignment probabilities with the source text. The maximum likelihood candidate will then be chosen for display to the user, who may then ask for more information or alternate translations.

RESEARCH IN LARGE VOCABULARY CONTINUOUS SPEECH RECOGNITION*

Janet Baker, Larry Gillick, and Robert Roth

Dragon Systems, Inc.
320 Nevada St.
Newton, MA 02160

PROJECT GOALS

The primary long term goal of speech research at Dragon Systems is to develop algorithms that are capable of achieving very high performance large vocabulary continuous speech recognition. At the same time, in the long run we are also concerned to keep the demands of those algorithms for computational power and memory as modest as possible, so that the results of our research can be incorporated into products that will run on moderately priced personal computers.

RECENT RESULTS

Much of the past year's effort has been devoted to work on speaker independent training, linear discriminant analysis, and acoustic modeling, using the Wall Street Journal corpus as our development vehicle, with the goal of attaining very high accuracy large vocabulary SI CSR. In the past, Dragon had focused primarily on speaker dependent and speaker adaptive recognition, so that speaker independent research was a new departure for us in this past year. Similarly, in the past Dragon had confined itself to recognition algorithms that were highly parsimonious in both computation and memory usage, but we have now, temporarily, dropped those constraints in the interest of seeing just what is attainable with greater computational resources.

Our research in the area of speaker independent training has focused on the use of tied mixture models with multiparameter streams in representing the effect of context on the acoustic realization of a phoneme. These models are built using Bayesian smoothing in the context of the EM algorithm. The prior distribution for a tied mixture model for a phoneme in a specific context represents our opinion about that model based on other more generic models for that phoneme that have typically been built from much more data.

An important theme of our research has been the exploration of the tradeoff between the greater ability to model the dependence among acoustic parameters when streams are high dimensional versus the greater acoustic resolution possible in streams with fewer parameters. Another important thread has been the investigation of a variety of strategies for building the basis components for the mixtures.

The use of IMELDA, a particular form of linear discriminant analysis, has played a crucial role in our development in the last year as a way of eliminating some of the interspeaker variability represented in the parameters and, perhaps as a consequence, some of the dependence among our parameters, thus reducing the need for high dimensional streams. IMELDA also was used for the purpose of eliminating some of the variability due to the microphone in the DARPA "stress test". A further beneficial effect of this method lay in the reduction of the number of signal processing parameters (from 32 to 16) and thus the size of the acoustic models.

The need to retrain our system many times during the course of our research led us to re-engineer the training so that models for different phonemes could simultaneously be built on different computers.

PLANS FOR THE COMING YEAR

Dragon plans to continue to focus on improving the overall quality of the acoustic models for large vocabulary speaker independent continuous speech recognition. We intend to enhance the set of acoustic parameters which are an input to the IMELDA transform, which is likely to continue to play a key role in our system. We will again cluster the output distributions of the states into PELs, or phonetic elements, as our earlier systems did, both for the purpose of reducing the size of the models and for the purpose of smoothing noisy estimates based on insufficient training data. Another direction for exploration will be the use of mixture models without tied basis components.

We also intend to investigate cross-word modeling more intensively, through the use of the position of the word boundary as part of the context of a triphone model, and possibly through the use of probabilistic phonological rules.

*This work was sponsored by the Defense Advanced Research Projects Agency under contract number J-FBI-92-060.

SHOGUN - MULTILINGUAL DATA EXTRACTION FOR TIPSTER

P. Jacobs, Principal Investigator

GE Research and Development Center
1 River Rd., Schenectady, NY 12301

PROJECT GOALS

The TIPSTER/SHOGUN project aims at substantive improvements in coverage and accuracy for automatic data extraction through innovative strategies in knowledge acquisition, run-time integration, and control. One of four teams in the data extraction component of the TIPSTER program, TIPSTER/SHOGUN includes GE Corporate Research and Development, Carnegie Mellon University - Center for Machine Translation, and GE Management and Data Systems.

Data extraction systems interpret the key content of natural language text, producing a structured representation of items that range from high-level business relationships to detailed knowledge coding of technologies and industry classifications. This task applies to both Japanese and English in each of two domains—joint ventures and micro-electronics. As such, TIPSTER is considerably more detailed and comprehensive than previous text interpretation experiments, including prior MUC (Message Understanding Conference) evaluations. The goals for SHOGUN are the following:

- Accuracy significantly ahead of MUC-4, with levels near those of trained human analysts at about 100 times human speed using conventional hardware and software.
- Automated knowledge acquisition and extensibility tools that support customization times of a few weeks for new applications.
- Multi-lingual performance, with comparable levels in both languages and the highest possible overlap between languages.

The project is now within a few months of completion, and is on target toward all of these goals.

RECENT RESULTS

During the early stages of the project, the team reached very good initial levels of performance on MUC-4 by successfully integrating methods used at GE and CMU, marking the first time that parsing systems of this level of coverage have been effectively combined. This provided an important testbed and also allowed for multilingual development—In recent months, Japanese performance has remained close to English performance. As the system coverage and accuracy have continued to improve, the most important recent thrust has been the incorporation of most of the knowledge and control strategies of the system into a finite-state driven analyzer, effectively replacing the traditional parsing layer with a detailed knowledge base of finite-state rules compiled from syntactic and lexical resources. While this seems close to work done in the speech community, it is an unusual approach for text, where the high perplexity and long sentence length have seemed to favor semantics-driven and high-level syntactic models.

The finite-state model allows different knowledge sources, particularly corpus-based knowledge, to have more of an impact on interpretation. Data extraction is a knowledge-intensive task, and it has been much simpler to augment the finite-state rules with corpus data than it was for the more abstract rules.

While the performance on all tasks still lags behind human analysts, closing this gap may not be as hard as we first expected. Much of the difference comes from portions of the work that are still incomplete. In addition, the ability to use automatically-acquired corpus data gives the programs a distinct advantage on certain portions of the task.

PLANS FOR THE COMING YEAR

As the project nears completion, the team is approaching the goal of near-human accuracy mostly by finishing certain key details, such as better reference resolution and word sense discrimination. At the same time, we are close to some significant advances in corpus-based training methods that will not only isolate the context required to discriminate nuances of meaning but also significantly reduce development time by acquiring domain knowledge from the corpus. This may the key to future applications of TIPSTER technology.

MatchPlus: A CONTEXT VECTOR SYSTEM FOR DOCUMENT RETRIEVAL

Stephen I. Gallant, Principal Investigator
William R. Caid, Project Manager

HNC, Inc.
5501 Oberlin Drive
San Diego, CA 92121

PROJECT GOALS

There are two primary goals for *MatchPlus*. First we want to incorporate into the system a notion of *similarity of use*. For example, if a query deals with 'autos' we want to be able to recognize as relevant a document with many mentions of 'cars'.

Second, we want to apply machine learning algorithms to improve both ad-hoc retrieval and routing performance. Several different algorithms come into play here:

- a "bootstrap" algorithm develops context vector representations for stems so that similar stems have similar vector representations
- neural network algorithms produce routing queries from initial queries and lists of relevant and non-relevant documents
- clustering algorithms help generate a word-sense disambiguation subsystem (being implemented)
- neural network algorithms interactively improve ad-hoc user queries (being implemented)
- clustering algorithms can also speed retrieval algorithms using a new "cluster tree" pruning algorithm (planned)

A *context vector representation* is central to all *MatchPlus* system capabilities. Every word (or stem), document (part), and query is represented by a fixed length vector with about 300 real-valued entries. For any two of these items, we can easily compute a similarity measure by taking a dot product of their respective vectors. This gives a build-in, generalized thesaurus capability to the system.

RECENT RESULTS

- We have built a system for 800,000 documents (2 GB of text). This system takes Tipster topics, automatically generates queries, and performs retrievals.
- Hand-entered queries may be given using a simple syntax. Terms, paragraphs, and documents can comprise a query (all optionally weighted), along with an (optional) Boolean filter. Documents are always returned in order by estimated likelihood of relevance.
- Documents may be "highlighted" to show hotspots, or areas of maximum correspondence with the query.
- We have implemented routing using neural network learning algorithms. This resulted in a 20–30% improvement compared with the automated ad-hoc system.
- Lists of stems closest to a given stem provide useful and interesting insight into the system's vector representations.

PLANS FOR THE COMING YEAR

We have been running many bootstrap learning experiments, and some variations have resulted in significant improvements to performance. We expect that this improvement will carry over to all aspects of the system, including routing.

Currently we are implementing word sense disambiguation. We hope that this will give performance improvements, possibly even eliminating the need for phrase processing. This module should also be able to serve as a stand-alone package, providing help for machine translation and speech understanding systems.

We plan to apply learning algorithms for automated interactive query improvement in a manner similar to our approach with routing. It seems likely that this will give a significant boost to ad-hoc query performance.

Finally, we are performing additional learning experiments to improve routing.

Applying Statistical Methods to Machine Translation

Peter F. Brown, Principal Investigator

IBM / T.J. Watson Research Center
P.O. Box 704
Yorktown Heights, NY 10598

PROJECT GOALS

The goal of our project is to demonstrate the effectiveness of statistical techniques in machine translation by improving the state of the art in large-vocabulary French-to-English translation.

A common paradigm in machine translation is analysis, transfer, and synthesis. In French-to-English translation, for example, a French sentence is analyzed into an intermediate structure in which various ambiguities present in the surface form have been resolved. This structure is then transferred to a similar English structure. Finally, an English sentence is synthesized from the intermediate English structure. Analysis, transfer, and synthesis each require considerable linguistic insight for their successful dispatch.

The approach taken in this project is to incorporate models of statistical transfer into the analysis-transfer-synthesis paradigm. This will be done by constructing deterministic, invertible transformations of the surface forms in the bilingual data which improve the locality of the transfer process and which reduce its variety. An example of the former is part-of-speech labeling, which is best performed by an examination of the global properties of the sentence and simplifies transfer by distinguishing, for example, between 'le' the article, and 'le' the direct object. An example of the latter is morphological analysis which exposes the fraternity of different forms of the same root and obviates the discovery of separate statistics relating these different forms in the two languages.

RECENT RESULTS

Developed Translator's Workstation.
In the spring of 1992, we wrote TransMan, a post-editor's workstation, which permits a human translator to rapidly edit translations produced automatically by a machine. TransMan allows cutting and pasting of sections of machine translations, and rapid access to an on-line dictionary. In a July of 1992 DARPA evaluation, TransMan was used by human subjects to translate 35 percent more rapidly than they could translate without machine assistance.

Speech Recognition in Machine Translation.
It has been observed that humans can translate nearly four times as quickly with little loss in accuracy simply by dictating, as opposed to typing, their translations. We considered the integration of speech recognition into a translator's workstation. In particular, we showed how to combine statistical models of speech, language, and translation into a single system that decodes a sequence of words in a target language from a sequence of words in a source language together with an utterance of the target language sequence. We obtained results which demonstrate that the difficulty of the speech recognition task can be reduced by making use of information contained in the source text being translated.

PLANS FOR THE COMING YEAR

In the July evaluation of our system we found a number of sources of errors. Some of the major problems include limited vocabularies, translation of numbers, translation of names, morphological errors, errors in syntactic transformations, and limitations in our trigram language model.

We plan to construct name and number detectors and translators. These module will detect names and numbers in French text, and replace them by name and number markers. The markers will then be translated statistically into English name and number markers. The English markers will then be translated by rule into English names and numbers. Incorporating these modules into our system will permit our language model to 'see back through' multi-word names and numbers.

We plan to increase the number of surface forms in our French vocabulary from 60,000 to 280,000 and the number of surface forms in our English vocabulary from 40,000 to 70,000. We will also completely reconstruct our morphological tables for both French and English.

A number of new rule-based syntactic transformations will be added to account for problems encountered in the July evaluation.

Finally, we plan to incorporate a decision-tree language model into our system which can make predictions based on significantly more context than our existing trigram model.

Automatic Extraction of Grammars From Annotated Text

Salim Roukos, Principal Investigator

roukos@watson.ibm.com
IBM T.J. Watson Research Center
P.O. Box 704
Yorktown Heights, NY 10598

PROJECT GOALS

The primary objective of this project is to develop a robust, high-performance parser for English by automatically extracting a grammar from an annotated corpus of bracketed sentences, called the Treebank. The project is a collaboration between the IBM Continuous Speech Recognition Group and the University of Pennsylvania Department of Computer Sciences[1]. Our initial focus is the domain of *computer manuals* with a vocabulary of 3000 words. We use a Treebank that was developed jointly by IBM and the University of Lancaster, England, during the past three years.

RECENT RESULTS

We have an initial implementation of our parsing model where we used a simple set of features to guide us in our development of the approach. We used for training a Treebank of about 28,000 sentences. The parser's accuracy on a sample of 25 new sentences of length 7 to 17 words as judged, when compared to the Treebank, by three members of the group, is 52%. This is encouraging in light of the fact that we are in the process of increasing the features that the parser can look at. We give below a brief sketch of our approach.

Traditionally, parsing relies on a grammar to determine a set of parse trees for a sentence and typically uses a scoring mechanism based on either rule preference or a probabilistic model to determine a preferred parse (or some higher level processing is expected to do further disambiguation). In this conventional approach, a linguist must specify the basic constituents, the rules for combining basic constituents into larger ones, and the detailed conditions under which these rules may be used.

Instead of using a grammar, we rely on a probabilistic model, $p(T|W)$, for the probability that a parse tree, T, is a parse for sentence W. We use data from the Treebank, with appropriate statistical modeling techniques, to capture implicitly the plethora of linguistic details necessary to correctly parse most sentences. Once we have built our model, we parse a sentence by simply determining the most probable parse, T^*, for the given sentence W from the set of all trees that span the given sentence.

[1] Co-Principal Investigators: Mark Liberman and Mitchell Marcus

In our model of parsing, we associate with any parse tree a set of bottom-up derivations; each derivation describing a particular order in which the parse tree is constructed. Our parsing model assigns a probability to a derivation, denoted by $p(d|W)$. The probability of a parse tree is the sum of the probability of all derivations leading to the parse tree.

The probability of a derivation is a product of probabilities, one for each step of the derivation. These steps are of three types:

- a tagging step: where we want the probability of tagging a word with a tag in the context of the derivation up to that point.
- a labeling step: where we want the probability of assigning a non terminal label to a node in the derivation.
- an extension step: where we want to determine the probability that a labeled node is extended, for example, to the left or right (i.e. to combine with the preceding or following constituents).

The probability of a step is determined by a decision tree appropriate to the type of the step. The three decision trees examine the derivation up to that point to determine the probability of any particular step.

PLANS FOR THE COMING YEAR

We plan to continue working with our new parser by completing the following tasks:

- implement a set of detailed questions to capture information about conjunction, prepositional attachment, etc.
- build automatically a new set of classes for the words in our vocabulary.
- tune the search strategy for the parser.

EVALUATION AND ANALYSIS OF AUDITORY MODEL FRONT ENDS FOR ROBUST SPEECH RECOGNITION PROGRAM SUMMARY*

Richard P. Lippmann, Principal Investigator

Lincoln Laboratory, M.I.T.
Lexington, MA 02173- 9108

PROGRAM GOALS

The purpose of this work is to integrate a number of auditory model front ends into a high-performance HMM recognizer, to test and evaluate these front ends on noisy speech, and to analyze the results in order to develop a more robust front end which may combine features of a number of the current auditory model-based systems.

BACKGROUND

This project was motivated by the need for improved speech recognition in noise, and by expectation that auditory model front ends could make recognition more robust to noise, microphone variation, and speaking style. The project has focussed on implementing, evaluating, and comparing three promising auditory front ends: (1) the mean-rate and synchrony outputs of S. Seneff's auditory model; (2) the ensemble interval histogram (EIH) model developed by O. Ghitza; and (3) the IMELDA model due to M. Hunt. Additional comparisons have been carried out between baseline systems using mel-cepstra derived from filterbank and LPC analysis.

RECENT ACCOMPLISHMENTS

The three auditory models (Seneff, EIH and IMELDA) have been compared extensively among themselves and with a mel-cepstrum front end for HMM isolated-word recognition on the TI-105 isolated word corpus. Conditions tested have included additive white noise, additive speech babble noise, and spectral variability due to microphone placement, channel, and acoustic recording environment. The best results from the auditory models were shown to provide small but consistent improvement over mel-cepstrum under conditions of high noise and spectral variability. These small improvements may not warrant the added complexity of the auditory models.

Additional comparisons between mel-filterbank (MFB) and LPC-based cepstrum front ends were conducted, showing significant advantages for MFB in noise; the gain in moving from LPC to MFB was greater than the gain in moving from MFB to any of the auditory models. Most recently, selected CSR experiments have been performed on resource management comparing auditory models to MFB. These results were confirmed at other sites.

As yet, no improvements have been achieved with the auditory models.

PLANS

Plans include: (1) further investigation of dimensionality reduction using principal components and linear discriminant analysis, and (2) completion of the CSR resource management tests on the auditory models.

*THIS WORK WAS SPONSORED BY THE DEFENSE ADVANCE RESEARCH PROJECTS AGENCY. THE VIEWS EXPRESSED ARE THOSE OF THE AUTHOR AND DO NOT REFLECT THE OFFICIAL POLICY OR POSITION OF THE U.S. GOVERNMENT.

ROBUST CONTINUOUS SPEECH RECOGNITION TECHNOLOGY PROGRAM SUMMARY*

Clifford J. Weinstein and Douglas B. Paul, Principal Investigators

Lincoln Laboratory, M.I.T.
Lexington, MA 02173-9108

PROGRAM GOALS

The major objective of this program is to develop and demonstrate robust, high performance continuous speech recognition (CSR) techniques focussed on applications in Spoken Language Systems (SLS). The effort focusses on developing advanced acoustic modelling, efficient search techniques, rapid enrollment, and adaptation techniques for robust large vocabulary CSR. An additional Lincoln goal is to define and develop application of robust CSR to military and civilian systems, and to expedite effective technology transfer.

BACKGROUND

The Lincoln program began with a focus on improving speaker stress robustness for the fighter aircraft environment. A robust hidden Markov model (HMM) system was developed with very high performance under stress conditions. The robust HMM techniques were then extended to yield state-of-the-art performance on the DARPA Resource Management corpus, using a tied-mixture HMM CSR approach.

Recent work has focussed on the large-vocabulary Wall Street Journal (WSJ) corpus, with vocabularies of 5K, 20K, and up to 64K words. The HMM CSR has been converted to a stack-decoder-based control strategy to operate efficiently with good performance in these tasks.

RECENT ACCOMPLISHMENTS

Recent accomplishments include: (1) development of the stack decoder and demonstration of its effectiveness on vocabularies up to 64K words; (2) development and integration of fast-match and detailed match; (3) further development of acoustic modelling techniques for the large vocabulary task; (4) a full set of evaluation tests in the November 1992 WSJ tests, including (e.g.) a 4.5% error rate on a 5K speaker-dependent test; (5) development of recognition-time speaker adaptation techniques with substantial improvements due to adaptation from both speaker-specific and speaker-independent initial models; (6) participation in and contributions to development of the WSJ corpus, including providing baseline language models to all sites; (7) survey and study of opportunities for military and government applications of spoken language technology, and organization of a workshop focussing on technology transfer; and (8) continuing leadership of the DARPA spoken Language Coordinating Committee.

PLANS

Plans for the current program include: (1) development of advanced acoustic modelling techniques; (2) development and improvement of stack-decoder-based HMM for large vocabulary tasks, via development and integration of advanced acoustic models, acoustic fast match, and efficient search techniques; (3) development of technique for integration of stack-based CSR with natural language processors; (4) extension of run-time adaptation techniques to adapt acoustic parameters of the tied-mixture HMM to speaker channel, and environment; and (5) continued investigation of applications opportunities for spoken language systems.

*THIS WORK WAS SPONSORED BY THE DEFENSE ADVANCED RESEARCH PROJECTS AGENCY. THE VIEWS EXPRESSED ARE THOSE OF THE AUTHOR AND DO NOT REFLECT THE OFFICIAL POLICY OF POSITION OF THE U.S. GOVERNMENT.

Spoken Language Recognition and Understanding

Victor Zue and Lynette Hirschman

Spoken Language Systems Group
Laboratory for Computer Science
Massachusetts Institute of Technology
Cambridge, Massachusetts 02139

1. PROJECT GOALS

The goal of this research is to demonstrate spoken language systems in support of interactive problem solving. The MIT spoken language system combines SUMMIT, a segment-based speech recognition system, and TINA, a probabilistic natural language system, to achieve speech understanding. The system accepts continuous speech input and handles multiple speakers without explicit speaker enrollment. It engages in interactive dialogue with the user, providing output in the form of tabular and graphical displays, as well as spoken and written responses. We have demonstrated the system on several applications, including travel planning and direction assistance; it has also been ported to several languages, including Japanese and French.

2. RECENT RESULTS

- **Improved recognition and understanding:** Reduced word error rate by over 30% through the use of improved phonetic modeling and more powerful N-gram language models; improved language understanding by 35% making use of stable corpus of annotated data; other improvements include the ability to generate a word lattice.
- **Real-time, software-only SLS system:** Developed near (1.5 times) real-time software only version of SUMMIT, using MFCC and fast match in the mixture Gaussian computation, running on a DEC Alpha or an HP735 workstation.
- **Evaluation of interactive dialogue:** Continued study of interactive dialogue, focusing on error detection and recovery issues; supported multi-site logfile evaluation through distribution of portable logfile evaluation software and instructions.
- **On-line ATIS:** Applied spoken language technology to access on-line dynamic air travel system via Compuserve; the demonstration system, extending the MIT ATIS system, provides an interactive language-based interface to find flights, make reservations and show seating assignments.
- **Multi-lingual VOYAGER:** Ported SUMMIT and TINA to Japanese, to create a speaker-independent bilingual VOYAGER; English and Japanese use the same semantic frame representation and the generation mechanism is modular and language-independent, supporting a system with independently toggled input and output languages.
- **Support to DARPA SLS community:** Chaired the ISAT Study Group on *Multi-Modal Language-Based Systems*; continued to chair MADCOW coordinating multi-site data collection, including introduction of experimental end-to-end evaluation; chaired first Spoken Language Technology Workshop at MIT, Jan. 20-22, 1993.

3. FUTURE PLANS

- **Large vocabulary spoken language systems:** Explore realistic large vocabulary spoken language applications, (e.g., on-line air travel planning), including issues of system portability and language-based interface design.
- **Multilingual knowledge-base access:** Use a uniform language-independent semantic frame to support extensions of VOYAGER and ATIS to other (more inflected) languages, e.g., French, German, Italian, and Spanish.
- **Interfacing speech and language:** Investigate loosely and tightly coupled integration, using word lattice and TINA-2's layered bigram model.
- **Dialogue modeling:** Incorporate dialogue state-specific language models to improve recognition in interactive dialogue, collect and study data on human-human interactive problem-solving, and explore alternative generation and partial understanding strategies.
- **Language modeling:** Investigate low-perplexity language models and the capture of higher level information, e.g., semantic class, phrase level information, and automatic grammar acquisition.

NIST-DARPA Interagency Agreement: Spoken Language Program

David S. Pallett, Principal Investigator

National Institute of Standards and Technology
Room A216, Building 225 (Technology)
Gaithersburg, MD 20899

PROJECT GOALS

1. To coordinate the design, development and distribution of speech and natural language corpora for the DARPA Spoken Language research community.

2. To design, coordinate implementation, and analyze the results of performance assessment benchmark tests for DARPA's speech recognition and spoken language understanding systems.

RECENT RESULTS

1. Acquired hardware and installed the MIT/LCS-developed "TINA" and SRI-developed "DECIPHER"(tm) ATIS systems.

2. Revised the NIST speech recognition software to incorporate phonologically-motivated string alignment procedures, and prepared an ICASSP'93 paper to document the advantages of this approach.

3. Developed a speech data quality assurance software package to measure S/N and other properties. Shared this software package with other sites, including SRI, for use in monitoring quality for the WSJ-CSR corpora.

4. Acquired and made use of recordable CD-ROM technology for preliminary, limited, distribution of speech corpora.

5. Participated, with SRI, in annotation and "bug fixes" for the ATIS MADCOW-collected corpora.

6. Prepared for, and implemented benchmark tests for: (1) the Resource Management corpus (final test set, September), (2) the WSJ-CSR corpus (November), (3) the "dry run stress test" (December), (4) the ATIS MADCOW corpus (November), and (5) the "dry run end-to-end" evaluation (January).

PLANS

1. Produce and distribute the next phase of the WSJ-CSR corpora, "WSJ-CSR Phase II, Part 1", and some portion of Part 2, on pressed CD-ROM in collaboration with the Linguistic Data Consortium.

2. Coordinate collection, screening and processing of the next portion of ATIS MADCOW data, to be collected with the 46-city OAG- derived relational database.

3. Implement benchmark tests in the WSJ-CSR and ATIS domains, as required by the DARPA Program Manager and Coordinating Committee.

INFORMATION EXTRACTION SYSTEM EVALUATION

Beth M. Sundheim

Naval Command, Control and Ocean Surveillance Center
RDT&E Division (NRaD), Code 444
San Diego, CA

PROJECT GOALS

This year, project efforts are focused on reapplying and revising existing evaluation techniques for the purpose of evaluating English and Japanese information extraction systems in the joint ventures and microelectronics domains. This year's effort will culminate in the Fifth Message Understanding Conference (MUC-5) in August, 1993.

RECENT RESULTS

MUC-4: The MUC-4 evaluation was conducted in FY92, the conference was held in June, 1992, and a proceedings was published in September. A single-value metric based on recall and precision was developed, and statistical significance tests were conducted. A blind test of 17 seventeen systems was conducted using an improved version of the Latin American terrorism information extraction task originally defined for MUC-3. Higher levels of performance by nearly all veteran systems were achieved for MUC-4, but the top scores are still only moderate. Progress in controlling the tendency to generate spurious data was obvious, but the problem still exists, along with the problem of insufficient domain coverage and general world knowledge. The push to extend the systems has brought into the focus the adverse effect that errors made in early stages of processing at the sentence and phrasal level have on suprasentential processing done in subsequent stages.

TIPSTER INTERIM EVALUATIONS: The scoring software used for MUC-4 was rewritten for the object-oriented Tipster template design. Accomodations were made for scoring Japanese. Alternative scoring procedures and new metrics were introduced. The Tipster English and Japanese systems were evaluated in September, 1992 on joint ventures, and they were evaluated in February, 1993 on both joint ventures and microelectronics. The results of these evaluations are being used to make decisions concerning the evaluation methodology to be used for the final Tipster evaluation (which will be the MUC-5 evaluation).

MUC-5: The call for participation in MUC-5 was issued in October, 1992, and participants began development in March, 1993, in preparation for the evaluation in July and the conference in August. Over 20 organizations (including Tipster-sponsored organizations) are planning to participate. Most of the non-Tipster organizations will be working only on the English joint ventures task or the English microelectronics task; however, two will be working on joint ventures in both languages, and one will be working on microelectronics in Japanese only.

PLANS FOR THE YEAR

- Improve the evaluation methodology to be used for MUC-5 based on the experiences of the Tipster interim evaluations.

- Coordinate the MUC-5 evaluation and conduct the conference.

- Foster interest in resource-sharing among evaluation participants to support future R&D on information extraction and NLP in general.

THE CONSORTIUM FOR LEXICAL RESEARCH

Y. Wilks, Principal Investigator

Computing Research Laboratory
New Mexico State University
Las Cruces, New Mexico 88003

PROJECT GOALS

The Consortium for Lexical Research (CLR), established by the Association for Computational Linguistics, with funding from DARPA, is now beginning its third year. The Consortium is sited at the Computing Research Laboratory, New Mexico, USA, under its Director, Yorick Wilks, Associate Director Louise Guthrie, and an ACL advisory committee consisting of Roy Byrd, Ralph Grishman, Mark Liberman and Don Walker.

The objective of the Consortium for Lexical Research is to act as a clearinghouse, in the US and internationally, for lexical data and software. It shares lexical data and tools used to perform research on natural language dictionaries and lexicons, as well as communicating the results of that research, thus accelerating the scale and speed of the development of natural language understanding programs via standard lexicons and software.

The task of the CLR is primarily to facilitate research, making available to the whole natural language processing community certain resources now held only by a few groups that have special relationships with companies or dictionary publishers. The CLR, as far as is practical, accepts contributions from any source, regardless of theoretical orientation, and makes them available as widely as possible for research.

RECENT RESULTS

Our focus this year has been on the acquisition of new materials and the recruiting of new members. Response to the Consortium has been enthusiastic and continuous. The repository has grown significantly and the consortium membership has quadrupled in the last year. Information about the CLR including the catalog of offerings, the membership or provider agreements or any previous newsletter can be obtained from lexical@nmsu.edu.

Our current status can be summarized as follows:

Collection A group of public domain resources has been obtained and cataloged and acquisitions of software and data from publishers and researchers is ongoing. We now offer nearly 100 items.

Contracts Together with our university lawyers, we have developed contracts for members and providers. Negotiations with dictionary publishers have been difficult, but we now have arrangements with Longman and Harper-Collins publishers which facilitate the purchase of their machine readable dictionaries by members. At present the distribution of the dictionaries is still in the hands of the publishers and is slow. We are working on ways to expedite the process.

Membership We now have 54 members of the CLR: 28 universities, 20 companies (including Apple, Microsoft and Xerox) and 4 government organizations. We have had over 2,000 ftp accesses in the last six months from more than 20 countries around the world.

Publicity The Consortium has begun a newsletter which is distributed to members and to anyone who has requested information about the CLR. The newsletter highlights a different piece of software or data each month, and informs its readers of any new items which are available.

Conferences In December 1992 the Computing Research Laboratory hosted the second workshop of the Consortium for Lexical Research: U.S./European Cooperation. The workshop was sponsored jointly by NSF and the European Commission to discuss international cooperation of lexical computation. Twenty-five researchers participated in the workshop. A report is available through the Computing Research Laboratory.

PLANS FOR THE COMING YEAR

We plan to expand membership and holdings steadily over the year, and progress toward our long term goal of establishing the Consortium as a self-supporting entity. We hope to do this by signing agreements with other dictionary publishers to make their products available through the CLR and by more actively seeking contributions of software or data from researchers. Our membership drive will focus on obtaining more international members, and members from the community of researchers and language specialists who may not have everyday access to the internet.

Diderot: TIPSTER Program, Automatic Data Extraction from Text Utilizing Semantic Analysis

Y. Wilks, J. Pustejovsky[†]*, J. Cowie*

Computing Research Laboratory, New Mexico State University, Las Cruces, NM 88003
&
Computer Science[†], Brandeis University, Waltham, MA 02254

PROJECT GOALS

The Computing Research Laboratory at New Mexico State University and the Computer Science Department at Brandeis University have been working for the past 18 months on the development of a system to perform automatic data extraction from texts on restricted subject areas (for business - joint ventures and for microelectronics - improvements in semiconductor technology) in two languages (English and Japanese).

The eventual aim is to be able to automatically populate data-bases containing information relevant to the work of government analysts.

The system, *Diderot*, is to be extendible and the techniques used not explicitly tied to the two particular languages, nor to the finance and electronics domains which are the initial targets of the Tipster project. To achieve this objective the project has as a primary goal the exploration of the usefulness of machine readable dictionaries and corpora as source for the semi-automatic creation of data extraction systems.

RECENT RESULTS

In the past year we have implemented 5 different text extraction systems three for English and two for Japanese. Experiments have been carried out on the derivation of syntactic and semantic information automatically from machine readable dictionaries and text corpora. Statistical methods have been developed for recognizing relevant texts or sections of texts. Methods have been developed which tag text using finite state automata which mark organizations, human names, places, products and dates. A parser generator has been produced which converts Generative Lexical Semantic structures into Definite Clause Grammar rules.

Japanese and English systems for a subset of the joint venture domain were evaluated on their performance against unseen texts for the Tipster 12 month evaluation. Full coverage Japanese and English systems for micro electronics were tested for the 18 month evaluation. Full coverage systems for the business domain were not completed in time for this evaluation and enhanced versions of the 12 month systems were used. The detailed results of the evaluations are reported in the Tipster 12 and 18 month session notebooks. The performance of the English systems is still very poor. The performance of the Japanese systems is significantly better, with the most recently developed micro-electronics system performing with a precision of 48% and a recall of 26%. It would appear that a combination of factors has influenced this result including more specific hand tuning and a single system developer.

Tools have been created to support human text extraction for Japanese and English for both domains. These have been used by IDA to produce all the training data (key structures extracted from over 4,000 texts) for the Tipster extraction project. Work has commenced on a tool (Tabula Rasa) which allows the creation of template extraction tools for human analysts and which also supports the definition of an extraction task.

PLANS FOR THE COMING YEAR

The principal objective for the next six months is to produce systems for English and Japanese which perform uniformly well (around 50% precision and 40% recall). Initially we plan to hand tune our English systems to provide a 'core' system of good quality. We then intend to extend the coverage of this system by automatically extending the lexicon using machine readable dictionaries and information extracted automatically from corpora. At present most parts of the Diderot system are easily configurable for new languages and/or domains. The modules which perform reference resolution were specifically written for each domain (topic) and language. We intend to modify these and separate as far as possible domain information from the general purpose reference resolution mechanism.

Subsequently, we hope to be involved in the next phase of Tipster, both in the provision of modules for information extraction and in the provision of tools to assist the design process and to support the integration of automatic and human information extraction.

Pangloss: A Knowledge-based Machine Assisted Translation Research Project – Site 2

Y. Wilks, Principal Investigator

Computing Research Laboratory
New Mexico State University, Las Cruces, New Mexico 88003

PROJECT GOALS

The Computing Research Laboratory (CRL) at New Mexico State University, jointly with the Center for Machine Translation (CMT) at Carnegie Mellon University and the Information Sciences Institute (ISI) at the University of Southern California, are developing a Translator's Workstation to assist a user in the translation of newspaper articles in the area of finance (mergers and acquisitions, followed by joint ventures) in one language (Spanish initially, followed by Japanese) into a second language (English). At its core is a multilingual, knowledge-based, interlingual, interactive, machine-assisted translation system consisting of a source language analysis component, an interactive augmentor, and a target language generation component.

During the initial phase, the CRL's objectives were to develop tools for constructing lexical items and ontological entries automatically from on-line resources, to develop the initial Spanish analysis component, and, jointly with CMT and ISI, to establish the infrastructure for the three site project, develop the formats and initial content of the interlingua, the ontology, and the knowledge base, and to prepare design documents for the second phase versions of the analysis and generation components, the augmentor, and the translator's workstation.

The second phase is a two-year program, and we are currently in the first six months of this phase. Building on the results of the initial phase, the second phase calls for the construction of a new analysis component, with a considerably broader base than the first year analysis sytem, and incorporating a wider variety of fail-soft techniques; development and incorporation of the ontology into the year-two system; use of the jointly-developed interlingua; continued emphasis on automatic acquisition of lexical and semantic information.

RECENT RESULTS

At this point, a first version of the year-two analysis system has been completed and is undergoing expansion and refinement. The initial ontology has been constructed, and a large number of sense-tokens have been incorporated. A phrasal lexicon has been extracted from on-line dictionary resources and is being prepared for incorporation into the Translator's Workstation.

The second year analysis sytem begins with a dictionary-based part-of-speech tagger, followed by a component which chunks the tagged text into small syntactic sections. These are analyzed and semantic/lexical information accessed and incorporated into the representation by a constituent parser. These smaller constituents will be grouped into predicates and arguments, which are then further grouped into clausal structures. At each level, possible readings are rated for syntactic and semantic likelihood.

With respect to automatic acquisition, several advances have occurred in the past year. We have provided the ontology with a sense-disambiguated hierarchy of nominal word senses drawn from *Longman's Dictionary of Contemporary English.* The hierarchy is derived from disambiguated genus terms and rooted in the semantic categories provided by Longman's. We have gathered from our bilingual dictionaries a large number of phrases correlated with translations for that phrase. Verb classes for Spanish verbs, used as the basis for the morphological analysis program that feeds the part-of-speech tagger, were provided by *Collin's Spanish-English/English-Spanish Dictionary.* In a final note, the CRL has contracted with EFE (Spanish newswire service) for a continuous line feed.

PLANS FOR THE COMING YEAR

By next fall we hope to extend the project to a second source language (Japanese). During the remainder of phase 2, we will deepen and broaden the coverage of the analysis system. Broadening will include further addition of domain-specific lexical items (and a new domain) and the inclusion of proper name recognizers of various types (gazetteers, company names, personal names and titles). Deepening will involve working with the ontology to sharpen the semantic coherence judgments–providing fewer but more likely analyses for each input sentence.

RESEARCH IN NATURAL LANGUAGE PROCESSING

Ralph Grishman, Principal Investigator

Department of Computer Science
New York University
New York, NY 10003

PROJECT GOALS

Our central research focus is on the automatic acquisition of knowledge about language (both syntactic and semantic) from corpora. We wish to understand how the knowledge so acquired can enhance natural language applications, including document retrieval, information extraction, and machine translation. In addition to experimenting with acquisition procedures, we are continuing to develop the infrastructure needed for these applications (grammars and dictionaries, parsers, grammar evaluation procedures, etc.).

The work on information retrieval and supporting technologies (in particular, robust, fast parsing), directed by Tomek Strzalkowski, is described in a separate page in this section.

RECENT ACCOMPLISHMENTS

- Developed techniques for computing word similarities based on the co-occurrence of words in the same (syntactic) contexts in a large corpus. Used these similarities to "smooth" automatically-acquired frequency data on verb-argument and head-modifier co-occurrence, and demonstrated that the smoothing increases coverage of the patterns found in new texts. (This work is described in a paper in this volume.)

- Participated in Message Understanding Conference - 4. Incorporated an enhanced time analysis module, an enhanced reference resolution module, and a stochastic part-of-speech tagger into our information extraction component, as well as making general improvements to the semantic models of descriptions of terrorist incidents. Demonstrated a significant improvement in performance over MUC-3.

- In order to gain a better understanding of the problems involved in porting natural language systems to new domains, "translated" our MUC-3/MUC-4 system for extracting information about terrorist incidents to process Spanish news reports. This required development of a relatively broad-coverage Spanish grammar and adaptation of the Collins Spanish-English machine-readable dictionary.

- Developed a prototype procedure for acquiring transfer rules from bilingual corpora through automatic alignment of parse trees in the source and target languages.

- Developed specifications for a common, broad-coverage syntactic dictionary of English (COMLEX).

- Continued participation in a group to define common metrics for grammar evaluation. Applied these metrics to the output of two different NYU parsers (the Proteus parser and the Tagged Text Parser) analyzing a Wall Street Journal corpus.

PLANS FOR THE COMING YEAR

- Participate in Message Understanding Conference - 5. Apply procedures for semantic pattern acquisition from corpora to speed the acquisition and broaden the coverage of the patterns for the "joint-venture" domain.

- Continue work on semantic pattern acquisition procedures. Experiment with larger corpora, with alternative measures of word similarity, and with clustering procedures to identify semantic classes.

ROBUST TEXT PROCESSING AND INFORMATION RETRIEVAL

Tomek Strzalkowski, Principal Investigator

Department of Computer Science
New York University
New York, New York, 10003

PROJECT GOALS

The general objective of this research has been the enhancement of traditional key-word based statistical methods of document retrieval with advanced natural language processing techniques. In the work to date the focus has been on obtaining a better representation of document contents by extracting representative phrases from syntactically preprocessed text. In addition, statistical clustering methods have been developed that generate domain-specific term correlations which can be used to obtain better search queries via expansion.

RECENT RESULTS

A prototype text retrieval system has been developed in which a robust natural language processing module is integrated with a traditional statistical engine (NIST's PRISE). Natural language processing is used to (1) preprocess the documents in order to extract contents-carrying terms, (2) discover inter-term dependencies and build a conceptual hierarchy specific to the database domain, and (3) process user's natural language requests into effective search queries. The statistical engine builds inverted index files from pre-processed documents, and then searches and ranks the documents in response to user queries. The feasibility of this approach has been demonstrated in various experiments with 'standard' IR collections such as CACM-3204 and Cranfield, as well as in the large-scale evaluation with TIPSTER database.

The centerpiece of the natural language processing module is the TTP parser, a fast and robust syntactic analyzer which produces 'regularized' parse structures out of running text. The parser, presently the fastest of this type, is designed to produce full analyses, but is capable of generating approximate 'best-fit' structures if under a time pressure or when faced with unexpected input.

We participated in the first Text Retrieval Conference (TREC-1), during which the total of 500 MBytes of Wall Street Journal articles have been parsed. An enhanced version of TTP parser has been developed for this purpose with the average speed ranging from 0.3 to 0.5 seconds per sentence. We also developed and improved the morphological word stemmer, syntactic dependencies extractor, and tested several clustering formulas. A close co-operation with BBN has produced a better part-of-speech tagger which is an essential pre-processor before parsing.

We also took part in the continuing parser/grammar evaluation workshop. In an informal test runs with 100 sentence sample of WSJ material, TTP has come suprisingly strong among 'regular' parsers which are hundreds times slower and far less robust. During the latest meeting the focus of evaluation effort has shifted toward 'deeper' representations, including operator-argument structures which is the standard form of output from TTP. During last year TTP licenses have been issued to several sites for research purposes.

In another effort, in co-operation with the Canadian Institute of Robotics and Intelligent Systems (IRIS), a number of qualitative methods for predicting semantic correctness of word associations are being tested. When finished, these results will be used to further improve the accuracy of document representation with compound terms.

Research on reversible grammars continued last year with some more important results including a formal evaluation system for generation algorithms, and a generalized notion of guides for controling the order of evaluation.

PLANS FOR THE COMING YEAR

The major effort in the coming months is the participation in TREC-2 evaluation. For this purpose we aquired a new version of PRISE system, which is currently being adapted to work with language processing module. New methods of document ranking are also considered, including local scores for most relevant fragments within a document. New clustering methods are tested for generating term similarities, as well as more effective filters to subcategorize similarities into semantic classes.

WORDNET: A LEXICAL DATABASE FOR ENGLISH

George A. Miller, Principal Investigator

Cognitive Science Laboratory
Princeton University
Princeton, NJ 08542

PROJECT GOALS

Work under this grant is intended to provide lexical resources for research on natural languages. The principal product is WordNet, a lexical database for English whose organization is inspired by current psycholinguistic theories of human lexical knowledge. Lexicalized concepts are organized by semantic relations for nouns, verbs, adjectives, and adverbs.

The principal goal of the project is to upgrade WordNet and make it available to interested users. A secondary goal is to explore practical applications of WordNet; its possible use in the resolution of word senses in context (semantic disambiguation) is viewed as a necessary precursor for many other applications.

RECENT RESULTS

WordNet Upgrade. The basic elements of WordNet are sets of synonyms (synsets), which are taken to represent lexicalized concepts. The database is organized by bidirectional pointers between synsets which correpond to familiar semantic relations: (synonymy, antonymy, hyponymy, meronymy, troponymy, entailment, etc.). During the past year the number of entries (words and collocations) in WordNet has grown from 62,700 to 82,600; the number of lexicalized concepts (synsets) from 50,300 to 62,700; the number of unique word-sense combinations from 98,300 to 117,300; and the number of synsets that include definitional glosses from 20,700 to 39,400. The syntactic category of adverb has been added; there are now 1,200 adverb synsets.

Software Development and Distribution. WordNet is available to the research community via anonymous ftp or on diskettes for PC users. A fourth version of the database, WordNet 1.3, was released 9 December 1992; notices were sent to 175 individuals and laboratories who had previously expressed interest. An X-windows interface that includes a program to recognize inflectional morphology is available for Sun SPARCstations; interfaces are also available for DECstations, NeXT, Microsoft Windows, and MacIntosh. Address inquiries to wordnet@princeton.edu.

Sense Resolution. A corpus of sentences using the noun "line" in different senses has been compiled and used to compare different methods of automatically determining from context which sense was intended. Preliminary efforts have been made to explore the use of WordNet to generalize the contexts that emerge from such studies.

Semantic Tagging. In support of the studies of sense resolution, a portion of the Brown Corpus has been tagged with pointers to WordNet. The result is a semantic concordance: a textual corpus and a lexicon so combined that every substantive word in the text is linked to its appropriate sense in the lexicon. To facilitate the task, an X-windows interface, ConText, has been developed that displays the text along with the WordNet entry for each content word; the user selects the appropriate sense, or inserts a comment that is used by the lexicographers to upgrade WordNet.

PLANS FOR THE COMING YEAR

WordNet will continue to be expanded and improved, and made available to interested users. There is interest in including more syntactic information, although that step would probably require formulating WordNet as a relational database. We have been considering that move for some time, but have lacked the necessary personnel. We are also considering how to incorporate more syntactic information in the output of ConText, and have secured permission from IBM to use McCord's English Slot Grammar on an experimental basis.

We plan to collect more systematic data on the adequacy of WordNet. The use of WordNet for semantic tagging provides a valuable test of its coverage and precision; the percentage of words in a text that are either missing or are used to express senses not included in WordNet fluctuates radically depending on the topic of a passage, but the average should decline steadily as the work proceeds. By summer 1993 we expect to be able to release an initial corpus of semantically tagged passages to authorized users of the Brown Corpus.

We are also developing a method to analyze the cooccurrences of concepts in the same sentences, in the expectation that such information will facilitate sense resolution. The value of such analyses will guide us in deciding how much farther to proceed with the construction of a semantic concordance based on the Brown Corpus.

Information Retrieval from Large Textbases

K.L. Kwok

Computer Science Department
Queens College, City University of New York
Flushing, NY 11367

PROJECT GOALS

Our objective is to enhance the effectiveness of retrieval and routing operations for large scale textbases. Retrieval concerns the processing of ad hoc queries against a static document collection, while routing concerns the processing of static, trained queries against a document stream. Both may be viewed as trying to rank relevant answer documents high in the output. Our text processing and retrieval system PIRCS is based on the probabilistic model and extended with the concept of document components. Components are regarded as single content-bearing terms as an approximation. Considering documents and queries as constituted of conceptual components allows one to define initial term weights naturally, to make use of nonbinary term weights, and to facilitate different types of retrieval processes. The approach is automatic, based mainly on statistical techniques, and is generally language and domain independent.

Our focus is on three areas: 1) improvements on document representation; 2) combination of retrieval algorithms; and 3) network implementation with learning capabilities. Using representation with more restricted contexts such as phrases or sub-document units help to decrease ambiguity. Combining evidences from different retrieval algorithms is known to improve results. Viewing retrieval in a network helps to implement query-focused and document-focused retrieval and feedback, as well as query expansion. It also provides a platform for using other learning techniques such as those from artificial neural networks.

RECENT RESULTS

During 1992, we participated in TREC1 and experimented with the 0.5 GByte Wall Street Journal collection of the Tipster program. Our results based on precision-recall evaluation compared very favorably with other participants in both ad hoc retrieval and routing environments. Our experimental results support the general conclusion that techniques which work for small collections also work in this large scale environment. Specifically:

• Breaking documents with unrelated stories, or long documents into more uniform length sub-documents at paragraph boundaries, together with Inverse Collection Term Frequency weighting to account for the discrimination power of content terms, is a viable initial term weighting strategy. It is also useful to augment single terms with two-word phrases for representation.

• PIRCS's combination of query-focused and document-focused retrieval works well. Combining them with a soft-boolean retrieval strategy produces additional gains. Our boolean expressions for queries are manually formed.

• Known relevant documents used for feedback learning in our network lead to improvements compared with no feedback. More performance increases are obtained by expanding queries with terms from the relevant feedback documents.

PLANS FOR THE COMING YEAR

We will enhance our system in both hardware and software in order to handle the two GByte multi-source textbase. We need to segment our network to fit available memory. In document representation, we will test a more powerful initial term weighting method based on document self-learning. We will generate two-word phrases automatically using word adjacency information captured during text processing. We plan to obtain boolean expressions from the well-structured query 'topics' automatically. Because more relevant documents are known, we will experiment with various learning schedules and different learning samples.

EXPLOITING CONCEPT SPACES FOR TEXT RETRIEVAL

Ellen M. Voorhees, Project Leader

Siemens Corporate Research, Inc.
Princeton, NJ 08540

PROJECT GOALS

The Learning Systems Department at Siemens Corporate Research is investigating the use of *concept spaces* to increase retrieval effectiveness. Similar to a semantic net, a concept space is a construct that defines the semantic relationships among ideas. The current focus of our research is to exploit the information in such a structure to ameliorate known shortcomings of statistical retrieval methods while maintaining the statistical methods' robustness. Our initial concept space is extracted from WordNet, a manually-constructed lexical database developed at Princeton University.

Our focus on statistical methods is a consequence of our goal to develop techniques that are applicable to matching texts in very large corpora. In particular, we impose two constraints on our research to meet this goal. First, we want to keep human intervention in the indexing and retrieval processes at a minimum, and so we use strictly automatic procedures. Second, since even automatic procedures need to be relatively efficient, and we believe this efficiency requirement precludes the use of deep analyses of document content for the foreseeable future, we restrict ourselves to shallow (statistical) processing of the text and concept space.

The specific problems we are addressing are the effects polysemy and synonymy have on retrieval performance. Polysemy depresses precision by causing false matches between texts, while synonymy depresses recall by causing true conceptual matches to be missed. We are investigating ways to index the content of text by the concepts of the concept space rather than the words that appear in the text, and thus avoid both polysemy and synonymy problems. With this approach, additional expense is incurred only during indexing — efficient concept-matching routines can be used for retrieval.

RECENT RESULTS

Our first experiments investigated the effectiveness of expanding a text's representation with words that are related to original text words in WordNet. The experimental evidence indicates that in the absence of a method to resolve word senses, expansion is almost always detrimental. For TREC-1, we were able to improve the performance of some queries using an expansion procedure that added only synonyms (as opposed to words related by other lexical relations) and required at least two original text words agree on the synonym (as a rudimentary check on the sense). However, this same procedure degrades the performance of other queries; overall performance is roughly comparable to the better statistical methods that do no special processing for synonyms.

Given the importance of sense resolution to workable expansion schemes, and the belief that polysemy is an important retrieval problem in its own right, we are currently studying automatic sense resolution procedures. In one approach, we use the nouns that co-occur within a text and the IS-A links within WordNet to select WordNet synonym sets as the senses for ambiguous nouns in the text. Retrieval performance degrades using this technique for two main reasons: the information inherent in the generalization/specialization hierarchy induced by the IS-A links is not sufficient to reliably select the correct sense of a noun from the set of fine distinctions in WordNet; and short query statements provide little context for disambiguation. In a separate approach, we are investigating the utility of classifiers that learn the contexts of the different senses of a given ambiguous word from training examples.

PLANS FOR THE COMING YEAR

Our research in the coming year will continue to focus on classifier-based sense resolution methods. We hope to improve the effectiveness of the classifiers by allowing them to learn syntactic templates that are indicative of a sense in addition to the more general context models they already learn. We must also integrate classifiers into the indexing phase of a retrieval system. Our intention is to annotate the synonym sets in the WordNet hierarchy with *sense vectors*, vectors that summarize the contexts in which members of the synonym set are likely to appear, and to select a sense based on the text's similarities to the sense vectors.

ANNOTATION OF ATIS DATA

Kate Hunicke-Smith, Project Leader
Jared Bernstein, Principal Investigator

SRI International
Menlo Park, California 94025

PROJECT GOALS

The performance of spoken language systems on utterances from the ATIS domain is evaluated by comparing system-produced responses with hand-crafted (and -verified) standard responses to the same utterances. The objective of SRI's annotation project is to provide SLS system developers with the range of correct responses to human utterances produced during experimental sessions with ATIS domain interactive systems. These correct responses are then used in system training and evaluation.

RECENT RESULTS

Since June 1991, SRI has produced classification and response files for about 9,000 utterances of training data (2900 of these since February, 1992). A dry run system evaluation and two official evaluations have been held since the project began in 1991. SRI has produced the standard responses for all of these evaluations; in all, about 2300 utterances.

These tests were performed according to the Common Answer Specification (CAS) protocol which is used in training. All systems are evaluated on a common set of data, with system responses measured against official reference answers produced at SRI in the same manner as the training data.

In addition to producing the classification and standard response files, SRI takes an active role in the adjudication of test and training data bug reports, initiates nearly all of the changes to the *Principles of Interpretation* document (a basic set of principles for interpreting the meaning of ATIS sentences agreed upon by the DARPA community), and continues to support NIST by modifying software and acting as a consultant regarding the annotation of data.

In 1992 the DARPA community developed a complementary evaluation method, referred to alternately as "end-to-end" or "logfile" evaluation, to better evaluate system-user interfaces. Using an interactive program developed by David Goodine at MIT, human evaluators from SRI and NIST used this end-to-end method in a dry run evaluation in December, 1992. For each query/response pair in 128 interactions, the human evaluators judged the correctness or appropriateness of system responses, and classified the type of user request and type of system response.

The use of human evaluators allowed more flexibility in scoring than an automatic, comparator-based method. This method allowed partial correctness judgements and the opportunity to score system responses which were not database retrievals, such as diagnostic messages and directives to the user. Because human evaluators saw the interaction from the point of view of the user, the results of the logfile evaluation method aided system developers by identifying dialogue and user interface problems which were not indicated by the usual CAS evaluation method.

PLANS FOR THE COMING YEAR

In the next year, SRI will continue to provide MADCOW annotation and other services to the DARPA community.

CSR CORPUS COLLECTION

Denise Danielson, Project Leader
Jared Bernstein, Principal Investigator

SRI International
Menlo Park, California 94025

PROJECT GOALS

The objective of the CSR Corpus Development is to collect and deliver a large corpus of continuous speech data to support DARPA research efforts in continuous speech recognition (CSR). SRI's current goal is the completion of Phase 2, Part 1 of the planned CSR Corpus. This consists of 86,000 sentences from 275 speakers, including 8000 spontaneous sentences from 40 journalists.

The Phase 2 Corpus collection task is a high volume data production task. SRI's major goal has been efficiency. Other goals include gathering data that is more representative of the *real world* by minimizing controls on vocabulary, microphones, background noise and speaker disfluencies, while improving data quality controls.

RECENT RESULTS

SRI began work on the current phase of CSR in September, 1992 and expects to complete delivery of this portion in June, 1993.

Data Production — As of 12 March 1993, SRI has collected the following portion of this CSR database:

Subject type	Required	Collected
Non-journalist long	25	22
Non-journalist short	210	125
Journalist	40	17

Subject Efficiency — SRI's first goal was to speed up subject interaction with the data collection software. Additional memory was added to the data collection systems, and data collection software made much faster, so that now the pace of the data collection process is directly controlled by the subject and no longer limited by the software. As a result, the average data collection pace has increased from 125 utts/hr to 200 utts/hr. For a typical short-term non-journalist subject collecting 190 read sentences, these changes and a faster paced orientation have reduced subject time from 120 minutes to 90 minutes. The shorter time requirement also makes it easier to attract and schedule subjects.

Process Efficiency — SRI has also been concerned with reducing the labor required to process speech data. A labor savings was realized by removing monitors from the data collection room. The data collection monitor now spends about 25 minutes instructing and observing while subjects collect their first few utterances, and then leaves the room. Two other changes have significanly improved labor efficiency. SRI has developed a new transcription tool that has led to a 15% to 20% reduction in transcription time and improved accuracy. We have also automated most pre-archival and archival steps.

Data Quality — SRI has incorporated NIST data quality software into its procedures. Sample files are collected at the start of each day on each data collection system. These files are run through the *wavmd* program, which runs a signal-to-noise (SNR) evaluation and other tests. Additional checks are performed on all files as they are collected to ensure that problems (e.g. dead microphone) are caught.

Labor Analysis — SRI is analyzing labor costs as we proceed with the current project to enable us to predict costs in the future, as well as to target specific tasks for efficiency improvements. A first round of labor analysis in January of this year identified transcription as one of the biggest labor costs. This has led to efforts to make the transcription task easier and more efficient. SRI continues to work with NIST and the CCCC to clarify transcription guidelines and implement changes recommended by CCCC. An analysis of recent project labor indicates that 10-15% of SRI's CSR project time has been spent on tasks in support of communication with NIST and various DARPA program committees.

PLANS FOR THE COMING YEAR

- Collect the remainder of the CSR Corpus.
- Work with NIST and CCCC to define goals and constraints for alternate microphones and environments.
- Work with NIST and the Data Quality Committee to further improve and automate quality tests of speech files.
- Work with NIST and the Data Quality Committee to define documentation requirements.
- Refine the spontaneous speech collection paradigm.

A REAL-TIME SPOKEN-LANGUAGE SYSTEM FOR INTERACTIVE PROBLEM SOLVING

Patti Price and Robert C. Moore

SRI International
Menlo Park, CA 94025

1. PROJECT GOALS

The goal of this project, to develop a spoken language interface to the Official Airline Guide (OAG) database, has been developed along two overlapping research and development lines: one focussed on an SLS kernel for database query, and the other on the interactive system.

2. RECENT RESULTS

SRI has developed a spoken language system to retrieve air travel planning information. Progress can be measured by comparing DARPA benchmark results in February 1992 and November 1992. Between February 1992 and November 1992, for all utterances tested, SRI's word error rate in the ATIS speech recognition test improved from 11.0% to 9.1%. Weighted utterance error improved from 31.1% to 23.6% in the natural-language understanding test, and from 45.4% to 33.2% in the spoken-language understanding test. Other recent results include:

- Ported ATIS system to new, 46-city database; coordinated with internally funded effort to port to the online OAG.
- Improved speech understanding by modeling spontaneous speech phenomena, including filled pauses and verbal repairs. The study included development of method for labeling and classifying repairs and tools for their analysis.
- Developed algorithms for tracking discourse structure that correctly determine discourse context with greater than 90% accuracy on the ATIS training corpus.
- Improved GEMINI system's linguistic coverage of the ATIS task to 93% syntactic coverage and 86% semantic coverage in a fair test on the evaluable utterances in the November 1992 ATIS benchmark test set.
- Integrated GEMINI system into overall ATIS system, and used it for the benchmark tests in conjunction with the Template Matcher.
- Performed pilot experiments on the use of natural language constraints to improve speech recognition; initial evidence showed an encouraging 22% reduction in word error rate.
- Analyzed human-machine problem solving using SRI's ATIS system. Analyzed user satisfaction and system performance as a function of system errors and user experience.
- Collected ATIS training and test data (speech, transcriptions, and logfiles) using SRI ATIS system, including about a thousand utterances using the new database.
- Improved user interface of SRI ATIS system, including better paraphrasing of system's understanding, easier to read displays, and improved system error messages.
- Produced one journal publication, sixteen conference talks and proceedings papers, and many invited talks; provided support and training for four graduate students.

3. PLANS

- Complete integration of GEMINI system into SRI ATIS, including tighter integration with Template Matcher.
- Explore tighter integration of speech and NL processing for better overall SLS performance, perhaps via lattices.
- Improve system robustness, portability and scalability.
- Develop complete telephone-based ATIS system.

HIGH PERFORMANCE SPEECH RECOGNITION USING CONSISTENCY MODELING

Vassilios Digalakis
Hy Murveit
Mitch Weintraub

SRI International
Speech Research and Technology Program
Menlo Park, CA, 94025

PROJECT GOALS

The primary goal of this project is to develop acoustic modeling techniques that advance the state-of-the-art in speech recognition, focusing on those techniques that relax the hidden Markov model's improper independence assumptions. Such techniques should both improve robustness to systematic variations such as microphone, channel, and speaker, by conditioning state's acoustic output distributions on long-term measurements, as well as improve general acoustic calibration by removing improper short-term (e.g. frame to frame) independence assumptions.

In order to perform this work certain infrastructure needs to be developed. This includes the development of a state-of-the-art baseline recognition system for the development task (ARPA's Wall-Street Journal Task); the development of search techniques that allow experiments with computationally expensive techniques to have reasonable turn-around times; and the development of modular software that enables rapid prototyping of new algorithms.

RECENT RESULTS

- We have built a software library that implements the components of an HMM recognition system dealing with the observation distributions. The functional interface is designed to enable fast integration of new acoustic modeling techniques
- We introduced a new search strategy, called Progressive Search, that constrains the search space of computationally expensive systems using simpler and faster systems in an iterative fashion. Using the word graphs created during the initial recognition pass as grammars in subsequent recognition passes, we have been able to reduce recognition time of systems that use more complex acoustic models and higher order language models by more than an order of magnitude.
- We developed a less-traditional, continuous output distribution system where different allophones of the same phone share the same sets of Gaussians, but different Gaussians are used for different phones. Our phonetically-tied mixture system achieved a 16% reduction in error rate over a typical tied mixture system.
- We found that the different pronunciation dictionaries and the corresponding phone sets that the various sites used in the last CSR evaluations can account for differences in performance in the order of 10 - 15%.
- We developed new algorithms for local consistency by modeling the correlation between spectral features at neighboring time frames. This acoustic correlation is used to improve the accuracy of the acoustic model by conditioning the state output probabilities on the previous frame's observations.
- We have achieved a 31% reduction in error rate over our November evaluation system on the 5K, non verbalized punctuation development set. The improvement is the combined effect of the phonetically-tied mixtures, the improved pronunciation dictionaries and replacement of RASTA filtering with cepstral-mean removal on a sentence basis.

PLANS FOR THE COMING YEAR

- Continue exploring trade-offs in parameter tying for continuous distribution acoustic models. We will sample other points beyond tied-mixture, phonetically-tied mixture, and untied Gaussian-mixture systems.
- Explore techniques for modeling the global consistencies of speaker and channel effects across the speech acoustic models.
- Continue to develop search techniques that both allow us to perform experiments using computationally burdensome techniques, as well as those that allow us to implement these systems as real-time demonstrations.

DR-LINK: Document Retrieval Using Linguistic Knowledge

Elizabeth D. Liddy, Sung H. Myaeng

School of Information Studies
Syracuse University
Syracuse, NY 13244

PROJECT GOALS

DR-LINK is a modular information retrieval system which takes a conceptual-linguistic approach to document detection by satisfying two apparently opposing task requirements: the need to handle large numbers of documents efficiently and the need to represent and retrieve on well-specified information needs. DR-LINK's approach is to enrich the semantic representation of the texts, while focusing its processing on those documents which have real potential of being relevant to a user's query. DR-LINK consists of six modules which, in combination, produce textual representations that capture great breadth and variety of semantic knowledge which will be used to improve retrieval effectiveness, in terms of both recall and precision. To produce this enriched representation, the system uses lexical, syntactic, semantic, and discourse linguistic processing techniques for distilling from documents and topic statements all the rich layers of knowledge incorporated in their deceptively simple textual surface and producing a representation which has been shaped by all these levels of linguistic processing. Specifically, these modules: 1) create summary-level content-vector representations of each text; 2) assign conceptual categories to all proper-noun entities; 3) delineate each text's discourse-level structure; 4) detect relations among concepts; 5) expand lexical representations with semantically-related terms, and; 6) represent and match concepts and relations via Conceptual Graphs.

CURRENT STATUS

The system's six modules are:

* Subject Field Coder
* Proper Noun Interpreter
* Discourse-level Text Structurer
* Relation-Concept Detector
* Conceptual Graph Generator
* Conceptual Graph Matcher

Although our system is now functional, it was run with incomplete knowledge bases, partial implementation of some modules, absence of some important functionalities, and only minimal integration of the output from early system modules by later modules.

RECENT RESULTS

At the 18th month TIPSTER evaluation meeting, the full DR-LINK System was run on 25 Topic Statements against the Wall Street Journal corpora for the ad hoc testing. In addition, the first three system modules were tested in the routing situation on a equal footing with the other systems. For the ad hoc testing, our 11-point precision was .2638. However, the cut-off criterion algorithm which will determine for each individual query how many of the top-ranked documents by the Subject Field Coder (SFC) and Proper Noun Interpreter (PNI) ranking should be processed by the remaining modules was not implemented. Therefore, the full system simply ran against the top 2,000 ranked documents for each query. Once the algorithm is in place, there will be a reasonable mathematical means for determining how many documents should be passed on to later modules so that the set will contain all the relevant documents. In addition, some of the modules were tested alone or in combination as system runs. For example, the 11-point average precision of the SFC + PNI run was a respectable .2245. And although the cut-off criterion was not implemented, by simply ranking the documents in terms of their SFC + PNI similarity to the Topic Statements, all of the relevant documents were ranked in the top 28% of the database.

PLANS FOR THE COMING YEAR

Our major thrust in the months ahead is to complete the system's unfinished knowledge bases and algorithms, and to fully integrate the rich representations which the various system modules produce. We are still analyzing results which will suggest necessary adjustments. Our goal is to accomplish the very refined level of matching which the system is capable of producing.